Lecture Notes in Computer Science 6212

Commenced Publication in 1973
Founding and Former Series Editors:
Gerhard Goos, Juris Hartmanis, and Jan van Leeuwen

Michel Abdalla   Paulo S.L.M. Barreto (Eds.)

Progress in Cryptology – LATINCRYPT 2010

First International Conference on Cryptology
and Information Security in Latin America
Puebla, Mexico, August 8-11, 2010
Proceedings

 Springer

Volume Editors

Michel Abdalla
École Normale Supérieure, Computer Science Department
45 Rue d'Ulm, 75230 Paris Cedex 05, France
E-mail: michel.abdalla@ens.fr

Paulo S.L.M. Barreto
Universidade de São Paulo
Computer Architecture and Networking Laboratory (LARC)
Av. Prof. Luciano Gualberto, trav. 3, no. 158, 05508-900 São Paulo (SP), Brazil
E-mail: pbarreto@larc.usp.br

Library of Congress Control Number: 2010931085

CR Subject Classification (1998): E.3, C.2, K.6.5, D.4.6, G.2, E.4

LNCS Sublibrary: SL 4 – Security and Cryptology

ISSN   0302-9743
ISBN-10   3-642-14711-9 Springer Berlin Heidelberg New York
ISBN-13   978-3-642-14711-1 Springer Berlin Heidelberg New York

springer.com

© Springer-Verlag Berlin Heidelberg 2010
Printed in Germany

Typesetting: Camera-ready by author, data conversion by Scientific Publishing Services, Chennai, India
Printed on acid-free paper   06/3180

Preface

LATINCRYPT 2010 was the First International Conference on Cryptology and Information Security in Latin America and took place during August 8–11, 2010 in Puebla, Mexico. LATINCRYPT 2010 was organized by the Centro de Investigación y de Estudios Avanzados del IPN (CINVESTAV-IPN) and the Benemérita Universidad Autónoma de Puebla (BUAP) in cooperation with The International Association for Cryptologic Research (IACR). The General Chair of the conference was Francisco Rodríguez Henríquez.

The conference received 62 submissions and each submission was assigned to at least three committee members. Submissions co-authored by members of the Program Committee were assigned to at least five committee members. The reviewing process was challenging due to the large number of high-quality submissions, and we are deeply grateful to the committee members and external reviewers for their outstanding work. After meticulous deliberation, the Program Committee, which was chaired by Michel Abdalla and Paulo S. L. M. Barreto, selected 19 submissions for presentation at the conference. These are the articles included in this volume. In addition to these presentations, the program also included four invited talks.

The reviewing process was run using the iChair software, written by Thomas Baignères from CryptoExperts, France and Matthieu Finiasz from EPFL, LASEC, Switzerland. We are grateful to them for letting us use their software and to Jacques Beigbeder from the École Normale Supérieure for helping with the setup of the reviewing website.

Finally, we would like to thank our sponsors CINVESTAV-IPN, BUAP, and the Intel Guadalajara Design Center for their financial support as well as all the people who contributed to the success of this conference. In particular, we are indebted to the members of the LATINCRYPT Steering Committee and the General Chair Francisco Rodríguez Henríquez for their diligent work and for making this conference possible. We would also like to thank Springer for accepting to publish the proceedings in the *Lecture Notes in Computer Science* series.

August 2010

Michel Abdalla
Paulo S. L. M. Barreto

LATINCRYPT 2010

First International Conference on
Cryptology and Information Security in Latin America

Puebla, Mexico
August 8–11, 2010

Organized by
Centro de Investigación y de Estudios Avanzados del IPN (CINVESTAV-IPN)
Benemérita Universidad Autónoma de Puebla (BUAP)

In Cooperation with
The International Association for Cryptologic Research (IACR)

General Chair

Francisco Rodríguez Henríquez CINVESTAV-IPN, Mexico

Program Chairs

Michel Abdalla	École Normale Supérieure, France
Paulo S. L. M. Barreto	Universidade de São Paulo, Brazil

Steering Committee

Paulo Barreto	Universidade de São Paulo, Brazil
Ricardo Dahab	Universidade Estadual de Campinas, Brazil
Alejandro Hevia	Universidad de Chile, Chile
Julio López	Universidade Estadual de Campinas, Brazil
Daniel Panario	Carleton University, Canada
Alfredo Viola	Universidad de la República, Uruguay

Local Organizing Committee

Debrup Chakraborty	CINVESTAV-IPN, Mexico
Nareli Cruz Cortés	CIC-IPN, Mexico
Arturo Díaz Pérez	CINVESTAV-IPN, Mexico
Luis Gerardo de la Fraga	CINVESTAV-IPN, Mexico
Miguel León Chávez	University of Puebla, Mexico
Guillermo Morales-Luna	CINVESTAV-IPN, Mexico

Program Committee

Roberto Avanzi	Ruhr Universität Bochum, Germany
Dan Bernstein	University of Illinois at Chicago, USA
Carlos Cid	Royal Holloway, University of London, UK
Ricardo Dahab	Universidade Estadual de Campinas, Brazil
Orr Dunkelman	Weizmann Institute of Science, Israel
Philippe Gaborit	Université de Limoges, France
Alejandro Hevia	Universidad de Chile, Chile
Dennis Hofheinz	Karlsruher Institut für Technologie, Germany
Antoine Joux	Université de Versailles, France
Marcelo Kaihara	EPFL, Switzerland
Aggelos Kiayias	University of Connecticut, USA
Eike Kiltz	CWI, The Netherlands
Çetin Kaya Koç	University of California in Santa Barbara, USA
Tanja Lange	Technische Universiteit Eindhoven, The Netherlands
Sven Laur	University of Tartu, Estonia
Benoît Libert	Université Catholique de Louvain, Belgium
Julio López	Universidade Estadual de Campinas, Brazil
Vadim Lyubashevsky	Tel-Aviv University, Israel
Alfred Menezes	University of Waterloo, Canada
Jorge Nakahara Jr.	EPFL, Switzerland
Anderson C.A. Nascimento	Universidade de Brasília, Brazil
Eiji Okamoto	University of Tsukuba, Japan
Adriana Palacio	Bowdoin College, USA
Daniel Panario	Carleton University, Canada
Kenny Paterson	Royal Holloway, University of London, UK
Bart Preneel	Katholieke Universiteit Leuven, Belgium
Christian Rechberger	Katholieke Universiteit Leuven, Belgium
Vincent Rijmen	Technische Universität Graz, Austria and Katholieke Universiteit Leuven, Belgium
Palash Sarkar	Indian Statistical Institute, India
Mike Scott	Dublin City University, Ireland
Willy Susilo	University of Wollongong, Australia
Nicolas Thériault	Universidad de Talca, Chile
Jeroen van de Graaf	Universidade Federal de Ouro Preto, Brazil
Frederik Vercauteren	Katholieke Universiteit Leuven, Belgium
Damien Vergnaud	École Normale Supérieure, France
Alfredo Viola	Universidad de la República, Uruguay
Bogdan Warinschi	University of Bristol, UK
Moti Yung	Google Inc., USA
Jianying Zhou	Institute for Infocomm Research, Singapore

External Reviewers

Martin Albrecht
Elena Andreeva
Diego F. Aranha
Man Ho Au
Naomi Benger
Jean-Luc Beuchat
Dan Bogdanov
Joppe Bos
Philippe Camacho
Sherman S. M. Chow
Cheng-Kang Chu
M. Prem Laxman Das
Junfeng Fan
Reza Rezaeian Farashahi
Pooya Farshim
David Galindo
Theo Garefalakis
Pierrick Gaudry
Fuchun Guo
Jens Hermans
Martin Hirt

Simon Hoerder
Xinyi Huang
Hendrik Hubrechts
Liina Kamm
Naoki Kanayama
Thorsten Kleinjung
Arjen Lenstra
Françoise Levy-dit-Vehel
Joseph K. Liu
Eduardo Moraes de Morais
Erick Nogueira do Nascimento
Onur Ozen
Olivier Pereira
Benny Pinkas
Amin Sakzad
Rosemberg A. da Silva
Deian Stefan
David Thomson
Stefan Tillich
Deniz Toz
Tsz Hon Yuen

Sponsoring Institutions

Centro de Investigación y de Estudios Avanzados del IPN (CINVESTAV-IPN)
Benemérita Universidad Autónoma de Puebla (BUAP), Mexico
Consejo de Ciencia y Tecnología del Estado de Puebla (CONCYTEP), Mexico
Vicerrectoria de Investigación y Estudios de Posgrado (VIEP-BUAP), Mexico
Dirección General de Innovación Educativa BUAP, Mexico
Facultad de Ciencias de la Computación BUAP, Mexico
Intel Guadalajara Design Center

Table of Contents

Encryption

Elliptic Curves

Implementation of Pairings

Implementation of Cryptographic Algorithms

Cryptographic Protocols and Foundations

Cryptanalysis of Symmetric Primitives

Post-Quantum Cryptography

Side-Channel Attacks

Broadcast Encryption with Multiple Trust Authorities

Kent D. Boklan[1], Alexander W. Dent[2], and Christopher A. Seaman[3]

[1] Department of Computer Science,
Queens College, City University of New York, USA
[2] Information Security Group,
Royal Holloway, University of London, UK
[3] Department of Mathematics,
Graduate Center, City University of New York, USA

Abstract. In this paper we extend the notion of hierarchical identity-based encryption with wildcards (WIBE) from the domain of a single Trusted Authority (TA) to a setting with multiple, independent Trusted Authorities each with their own WIBE. In this multi-trust-authority WIBE environment, a group of TA's may form coalitions, enabling secure communication across domains. These coalitions can be created in an *ad-hoc* fashion and membership of one coalition does not give a trust authority any advantage in decrypting a ciphertext for a different coalition. This allows the broadcast of confidential messages to large groups of users within a coalition with a single ciphertext. We provide a full syntax and security model for multi-trust-authority WIBEs, and give a constructions based on the Boneh-Boyen WIBE scheme for both passive and active attackers.

1 Introduction

Identity-based encryption [12] is a type of public-key encryption in which a user's public key is set to be equal to some bitstring which uniquely identifies them within some context. This removes the need for costly and complex public-key infrastructures. Since a user's public key can now be deduced from the user's identity, the user's private decryption key can only be produced by a trusted authority (TA) with some special "trapdoor" information. This TA will release the private key to a user in the TA's trust domain after that user has proven its identity to the TA. A hierarchical identity-based encryption (HIBE) scheme [9] is an extension of identity-based encryption in which identities are arranged in a tree structure with the trust authority at the root. Users are associated with nodes in the tree and any user that has been issued with a private key can deduce a private key for any subordinate user in the tree structure. This reduces the key management requirements for the TA in a manner similar to the use of certificate chains in a public-key infrastructure.

A WIBE scheme is a HIBE scheme that allows one-to-many communication within the domain of the trust authority [1]. In a WIBE scheme, encryption is

M. Abdalla and P.S.L.M. Barreto (Eds.): LATINCRYPT 2010, LNCS 6212, pp. 1–19, 2010.

performed with respect to a pattern of bitstrings and wildcards, and a ciphertext can only be decrypted by a user whose identity matches the pattern at every non-wildcard level. This allows broadcast encryption to large numbers of users simultaneously. However, encryption is still restricted to a single trust domain. We extend the concept of a WIBE to a situation with multiple trusted authorities. In a multiple-trust-authority WIBE (MTA-WIBE) scheme, trust authorities can communicate to form coalitions that enable broadcast encryption across multiple trust domains. This allows simple broadcast encryption to large numbers of recipients in multiple trust domains. Our scheme model has the following properties:

- Trust authorities can initially implement independent instances of the MTA-WIBE scheme (without communication with other trust authorities).
- Trust authorities form coalitions through a two-stage process in which trust authorities first exchange *public* messages and then broadcast *public* "key update" messages to users in their trust domain. These key update messages allow users to form *coalition decryption keys* (based on their existing WIBE decryption keys) and so decrypt MTA-WIBE ciphertexts.
- Encryption of a message for a specific coalition is achieved using only the public parameters of the trust authorities in the coalition and does not require the sender to obtain extra information about the coalition.
- Messages are encrypted for a given coalition and under a given pattern. The resulting ciphertext can only be decrypted by users whose identities match the pattern and whose trust authority is currently in the coalition.
- Coalitions are secure in the sense that membership of one coalition does not allow a trust authority to deduce information about a message encrypted for a coalition which does not include that trust authority.

We provide a full syntax and security model for an MTA-WIBE scheme. We give a selective-identity instantiation based on the Boneh-Boyen WIBE scheme [1,4]. We also give a generic method to transform a passively secure scheme into an actively secure scheme via a novel implementation of the Boneh-Katz transform [5]. This is the most efficient generic transform for creating IND-CCA2 secure WIBEs or MTA-WIBEs from IND-CPA WIBEs or MTA-WIBEs in the literature. (The Boneh-Katz transform's application to the construction of secure WIBEs may be of independent interest.)

Usage Scenarios. We believe that MTA-WIBEs are useful in a variety of contexts. We believe that the uses of MTA-WIBEs by organisations involved in a joint project are obvious. However, we also believe that there are number of more unusual usage scenarios. For example, suppose a number of companies produce sensors for use in an ad-hoc network (including, e.g., "IBM") and suppose that these sensors can be classified according to the function they perform (including, e.g., "climate sensor"). We assume that there is a common naming structure for these sensors (e.g. (MANUFACTURER, SENSOR TYPE, PROJECT)). If the manufacturers agree to form a coalition, then a message encrypted using the coalition parameters and the pattern (*, "climate sensor", "Project Intercept") could be decrypted by any climate sensor on Project Intercept. Alternatively, a message encrypted using the pattern ("IBM", "climate sensor", *) can only be decrypted by IBM's climate sensors. This provides a method to address all sensors within a project (for project information distribution) or to address all sensors produced by an individual manufacturer (e.g. for software patching).

Related Work. Several researchers have considered the problem of developing broadcast or multi-receiver encryption schemes based on HIBE-like encryption schemes. The idea appears to have originated in the literature with the work of Dodis and Fazio [8]; other examples were given by Abdalla et al. [2] and Chatterjee and Sarkar [7,10]. These schemes concentrate on either sending a message to a (small) named set of users or to all users except for a (small) named set of revoked users. None of these schemes support multiple trust authorities or the "pattern-based" encryption capability provided by a WIBE. Our work extends the concept of a "pattern-based" encryption system of Abdalla et al. [1] to a situation with multiple trust authorities.

Other researchers have considered the question of developing IBE systems with multiple trusted authorities. Paterson and Srinivasan [11] constructed an IBE scheme which supported multiple trust authorities in a way which makes it infeasible for an attacker to determine which trust authority's public parameters was used to form the ciphertext - i.e. the ciphertext preserves the anonymity of the trust authority. However, the Paterson and Srinivasan scheme does not allow trust authorities to form trust coalitions. A scheme of Boklan et al. [3] allows trust authorities to cooperate to form trust coalitions, in the sense that within the coalition a private key issued by TA_i for an identity ID can be translated into a private key issued by TA_j for the same identity. However, in order to achieve this functionality, the scheme requires that the coalition trust authorities setup their master private keys simultaneously. Furthermore, every trust authority can deduce the master private key of every other trust authority. This is clearly a disadvantage in any setting where the trust authorities share anything less than complete trust in each other. Unlike our scheme, no prior scheme simultaneously supports multiple trust authorities, secure ad-hoc coalitions, hierarchical identity-based encryption, and one-to-many communication.

Trivial Solutions. We note that the coalition functionality is only useful for broadcast encryption across the entire coalition (i.e. when the message is to be sent to a set of users which include members of distinct organisations). Broadcast encryption to a set of users contained within a single organisation can be achieved through the use of that organisation's existing WIBE. Since organisations must communicate before setting up a coalition, one could implement a trivial solution in which the organisations generate an independent WIBE to represent the coalition. Broadcast encryption across the coalition can then be achieved using this WIBE. This scheme would offer similar functionality to our scheme but has significant disadvantages:

- A sender (in possession of the public parameters for all members of the coalition) may not be able to deduce the public parameters for the coalition. In our scheme, knowledge of the public parameters for individual trust authorities allows cross-domain broadcast encryption.
- In the trivial scheme, all users within a trust domain must obtain new coalition keys from their TA individually. This requires a large amount of secure communication between the TA and the users. Our scheme allows users to deduce coalition decryption keys from a (short) publicly-broadcast "key update" message from the TA. This simplifies the key management architecture and massively reduces the workload of the TA.

2   Multiple-Trust-Authority WIBEs

Throughout the paper we will use standard notation for algorithms and assignment – see Appendix A.1.

2.1   Syntax

A Trusted Authority is the root of a domain of trust with responsibilities over the namespace of its organization. In general we will refer to a Trusted Authority TA as a hierarchy of identities of the form $ID = (ID_0, ID_1, \ldots, ID_k)$ with the same first identity $(ID_0 = TA)$ and maximum depth of L. Given a population of TA's $\mathcal{U} = \{TA_1, TA_2, \ldots, TA_n\}$ we define a coalition $\mathcal{C} = \{TA_a, TA_b, \ldots, TA_\ell\} \subseteq \mathcal{U}$. We define a pattern to be a vector of identities and wildcards, i.e. $P = (P_0, \ldots, P_k)$ where $P_i \in \{0,1\}^* \cup \{*\}$ for $1 \leq i \leq k$. We say that an identity $ID = (ID_0, \ldots, ID_k)$ matches a pattern $P = (P_0, \ldots, P_{k'})$, written $ID \in_* P$, if $k \leq k'$ and $P_i \in \{ID_i, *\}$ for all $0 \leq i \leq k$. For a pattern $P = (P_0, \ldots, P_k)$, we define $W(P)$ to be the set of wildcard levels $W(P) = \{0 \leq i \leq k : P_i = *\}$ and $\bar{W}(P)$ to be the set of non-wildcard levels $\bar{W}(P) = \{0 \leq i \leq k : P_i \neq *\}$.

A multi-trust-authority WIBE (MTA-WIBE) consists of a number PPT algorithms. The following algorithms may be used by a TA:

- Setup: This algorithm produces public parameters used by all trust authorities. This is written $param \xleftarrow{\$} \text{Setup}(1^k)$. These public parameters are assumed to be an implicit input to all other algorithms.
- CreateTA: This algorithm creates the master public/private keys for a trust authority with a particular name ("TA_i"). The algorithm takes as input the proposed name for the trusted authority ("TA_i") and outputs a master key-pair (pk_i, sk_i), written $(pk_i, sk_i) \xleftarrow{\$} \text{CreateTA}("TA_i")$.
- CoalitionBroadcast: Once a set of trust authorities agree to setup a coalition between them, each trust authority runs this algorithm to produce the information which allows the other trust authorities in the coalition to produce coalition keys for the members of their hierarchy. For some coalition $\mathcal{C} \subseteq \mathcal{U}$ containing TA_i, trust authority TA_i uses its secret key and the public keys of participating authorities to generate public parameters specific to

every other authority. This is written as $W_i \xleftarrow{\$} \texttt{CoalitionBroadcast}(TA_i,$ $sk_i, \mathcal{C}, PK)$, where $PK = \{pk_j : TA_j \in \mathcal{C}\}$ is the set of master public keys in the coalition and $W_i = \{w_{i,j} : TA_j \in \mathcal{C} \setminus TA_i\}$ is the set of key update elements. Each $w_{i,j}$ is sent from TA_i to TA_j through a *public* channel.

– $\texttt{CoalitionUpdate}$: After every member TA_i of the coalition has provided a message $w_{i,j}$ to TA_j, trust authority TA_j uses this algorithm to combine those messages to allow creation of coalition-specific secret keys. It outputs a message v_j to be (publicly) broadcast to every member of TA_j's hierarchy (who then run the $\texttt{CoalitionExtract}$ algorithm). This is written $v_j \xleftarrow{\$}$ $\texttt{CoalitionUpdate}(TA_j, sk_j, \mathcal{C}, PK, \hat{W}_j)$ where $PK = \{pk_i : TA_i \in \mathcal{C}\}$ and $\hat{W}_j = \{w_{i,j} : TA_i \in \mathcal{C} \setminus TA_j\}$ is the coalition parameters received by TA_j.

The security of the scheme does depend upon some user running the $\texttt{Setup}$ algorithm correctly, deleting any internally-used variables, and widely distributing the result. Everyone must trust this user has not abused its privileges. This is a common problem in situations where several users have to share common parameters. In most scenarios, simple techniques can be used to provide some measure of assurance of the security of the common parameters, e.g. independent elements may be created by hashing publicly known, random data, such as astronomical signals. These techniques are considered out of scope for this paper, although the security proofs could be trivially altered to include this phase.

We also note that our security model allows the coalition broadcast messages $w_{i,j}$ and key update message v_j to be broadcast publicly. The key update message v_j may be publicly broadcast to all users, but we require that this message is sent via an integrity protected/origin authenticated channel. The $w_{i,j}$ messages exchanged between TA's do not require integrity protection or origin authentication. We now describe the algorithms required by the individual users.

– $\texttt{Extract}$: This algorithm is used by an individual to generate private keys for their subordinates (entities on the level below them in the hierarchical structure). The keys generated are specific to the TA's WIBE, although they may later be adjusted for use in a coalition environment. For entity $ID = (ID_0, ID_1, \dots, ID_k)$ extracting a private key for subordinate $ID^\dagger = (ID_0, ID_1, \dots, ID_k, ID')$ the algorithm outputs $d_{ID^\dagger} \xleftarrow{\$} \texttt{Extract}(ID, d_{ID}, ID')$.

– $\texttt{CoalitionExtract}$: Users in a trust authority's hierarchy may use this algorithm to adapt their TA-specific WIBE private key for use within a coalition. To accomplish this their TA, TA_i, must provide an adjustment parameter v_i to be combined with the user's private key d_{ID}. A user generates its coalition key as $c_{ID} \leftarrow \texttt{CoalitionExtract}(d_{ID}, v_i)$.

– $\texttt{Encrypt}$: This algorithm can be used by an individual to encrypt a message m to any individual whose identity matches a pattern P in the coalition $\mathcal{C}$. This is computed as $C \xleftarrow{\$} \texttt{Encrypt}(\mathcal{C}, PK, P, m)$ where $PK = \{pk_i : TA_i \in \mathcal{C}\}$. We assume that if the message is encrypted for users in a single hierarchy (i.e. $P_0 \neq *$) then the coalition parameters PK used to encrypt the message will just be the parameters of the (single) trust authority P_0 (i.e. $\mathcal{C} = \{P_0\}$

when $ID_0 = P_0$). The coalition $\mathcal{C}$ should contain the identities of multiple TAs only when a message is to be sent to users in each TA's hierarchy (i.e $|\mathcal{C}| \geq 2$ if and only if $ID_0 = *$).

- Decrypt: This algorithm can be used to decrypt a ciphertext C under a coalition key c_{ID} and outputs either a message m or the error symbol $\perp$. We write this operation as $\text{Decrypt}(ID, c_{ID}, C)$. If no coalition is currently defined, then $c_{ID} \leftarrow d_{ID}$.

It is, of course, possible to extend the MTA-WIBE syntax so that coalition update values v_j are produced after a protocol interaction between trust authorities in the coalition, but we use the simpler broadcast case as it is sufficient for our instantiation. We require that the scheme is correct in the obvious sense that decryption "undoes" encryption for correctly generated trust authorities and coalitions.

2.2   Security Model

We provide a security model for an MTA-WIBE. We begin by defining a selective-identity sID-IND-CPA model. This is a game played between a PPT attacker $\mathcal{A} = (\mathcal{A}_0, \mathcal{A}_1)$ and a hypothetical challenger: (1) the attacker runs $(\mathcal{C}^*, P^*, \omega) \xleftarrow{\$} \mathcal{A}_0(1^k)$ where $\mathcal{C}^*$ is the list of TA identifiers in the challenge coalition, P^* is the challenge pattern, and ω is state information; (2) the challenger generates $param \xleftarrow{\$} \text{Setup}(1^k)$ and $(pk_i, sk_i) \xleftarrow{\$} \text{CreateTA}(TA_i)$ for all $TA_i \in \mathcal{C}^*$; (3) the attacker outputs a bit $b' \xleftarrow{\$} \mathcal{A}_1(param, PK, \omega)$ where $PK \leftarrow \{pk_i : TA_i \in \mathcal{C}^*\}$. During $\mathcal{A}_1$'s execution, it may access the following oracles:

- CreateTA(TA): The oracle computes $(pk, sk) \xleftarrow{\$} \text{CreateTA}(TA)$ and returns pk. This oracle can only be queried for values of TA that do not already have an associated public key. This TA is labelled "honest". (All TA's in $\mathcal{C}^*$ are also labelled "honest".)
- SubmitTA(TA, pk): This oracle associates the identity TA with the public key pk. It is used to model rogue TAs. This oracle can only be queried for values of TA that do not already have an associated public key. This TA is labelled "corrupt".
- CoalitionBroadcast($TA, \mathcal{C}$): This oracle computes the coalition key update set $W \xleftarrow{\$} \text{CoalitionBroadcast}(TA, sk, \mathcal{C}, PK)$ where TA is "honest", sk is the private key associated with TA, $\mathcal{C}$ is a coalition containing TA, and PK is the set of public keys for trust authorities in $\mathcal{C}$. The oracle returns the set $W = \{w_j : TA_j \in \mathcal{C} \setminus TA\}$.
- CoalitionUpdate($TA, \mathcal{C}, \hat{W}$): The oracle computes the adjustment parameter $v \xleftarrow{\$} \text{CoalitionUpdate}(TA, sk, \mathcal{C}, PK, \hat{W})$ where TA is honest, sk is the private key associated with TA, $\mathcal{C}$ is a coalition containing TA, PK is the set of public keys for $\mathcal{C}$, and $\hat{W} = \{w_i : TA_i \in \mathcal{C} \setminus TA\}$ is the set of key update messages that purport to be from TA_i. The oracle returns the value v. Note that we do not require that $\hat{W}$ corresponds to the elements returned by CoalitionBroadcast.

- Corrupt(ID): The oracle returns d_{ID} for the identity ID. Note that if $ID = TA$ then this method returns the private key sk associated with the trust authority TA. This oracle can only be queried for situations where TA is "honest". If $ID = TA$ then TA is labelled "corrupt".
- Encrypt(m_0, m_1): The oracle returns $C^* \overset{\$}{\leftarrow} \texttt{Encrypt}(C^*, PK, P^*, m_b)$ where PK is the set of public keys associated with trust authorities $TA \in C^*$ and $b \overset{\$}{\leftarrow} \{0, 1\}$. This oracle can only be queried once and only if $|m_0| = |m_1|$.

The attacker is forbidden from corrupting an identity $ID \in_* P^*$ under a trust authority $TA \in C^*$. The attacker's advantage is defined to be

$$Adv_{\mathcal{A}}^{\texttt{sID}}(k) = |\Pr[b' = 1 \mid b = 1] - \Pr[b' = 1 \mid b = 0]|.$$

We define extended notions of security in the usual way. The IND-CPA notion of security is identical to the sID-IND-CPA notion of security except that there is no $\mathcal{A}_0$ algorithm. The algorithm $\mathcal{A}_1$ takes 1^k as input and the encryption oracle changes so that it works as follows:

- Encrypt(C^*, P^*, m_0, m_1): The oracle returns $C^* \overset{\$}{\leftarrow} \texttt{Encrypt}(C^*, PK, P^*, m_b)$ where PK is the set of public keys associated with trust authorities $TA \in C^*$ and $b \overset{\$}{\leftarrow} \{0, 1\}$. This oracle can only be queried once, only if $|m_0| = |m_1|$, and only on coalitions C^* where every $TA \in C^*$ is honest.

The IND-CCA2 notion of security is identical to the IND-CPA notion of security except that $\mathcal{A}_1$ has access to a decryption oracle:

- Decrypt(C, ID, C): This oracle checks whether the coalition key c_{ID} has been defined for the coalition C (via a CoalitionUpdate oracle query). If not, the oracle returns $\perp$. Otherwise, the oracle returns $\texttt{Decrypt}(ID, c_{ID}, C)$. This oracle can only be queried on identities for which the trust authority $TA = ID_0$ is honest.

The attacker is forbidden from submitting (C^*, ID, C^*) to the decryption oracle for any identity $ID \in_* P^*$.

We note that this model allows for "rogue TAs" whose parameters are generated maliciously, rather than by the CreateTA oracle, as there is no requirement that C contain TA identities generated by the CreateTA oracle *except* for the coalition submitted to the Encrypt oracle. The SubmitTA oracle allows the attacker to define a public key for a rogue TA although this public key is only used by the CoalitionBroadcast oracle. We also note that the inability to query an oracle to obtain the coalition key c_{ID} does not represent a weakness in the model (assuming that c_{ID} and d_{ID} are secured in a similar manner) as c_{ID} can always be formed from d_{ID} and the public value v.

3   Boneh-Boyen MTA-WIBE

We present a selective-identity IND-CPA secure MTA-WIBE based on the Boneh-Boyen MTA-WIBE. The scheme is given in Figure 1. Our scheme makes use

Setup(1^k):

  $g_1, g_2, u_{i,j} \xleftarrow{\$} \mathbb{G}^*$ for $0 \leq i \leq L$, $j \in \{0,1\}$

  $param \leftarrow (g_1, g_2, u_{0,0}, \ldots, u_{L,1})$

  Return $param$

CreateTA(TA):

  $\alpha \xleftarrow{\$} \mathbb{Z}_p$

  $pk \leftarrow g_1^\alpha$; $sk \leftarrow g_2^\alpha$

  Return (pk, sk)

CoalitionBroadcast($TA, sk, \mathcal{C}, PK$):

  For each $TA_j \in \mathcal{C}$:

    $r_j \xleftarrow{\$} \mathbb{Z}_p$

    $w_{j,0} \leftarrow g_2^\alpha (u_{0,0} \cdot u_{0,1}^{TA_j})^{r_j}$

    $w_{j,1} \leftarrow g_1^{r_j}$

    $w_j \leftarrow (w_{j,0}, w_{j,1})$

  $W \leftarrow \{w_j \ : \ TA_j \in \mathcal{C} \setminus \{TA\}\}$

  Return W

CoalitionUpdate($TA, sk, \mathcal{C}, PK, \hat{W}$):

  Parse $\hat{W}$ as $\{w_j \ : \ TA_j \in \mathcal{C}\}$

  Parse w_j as $(w_{j,0}, w_{j,1})$

  $v_0 \leftarrow \prod_{TA_j \in \mathcal{C} \setminus \{TA\}} w_{j,0}$

  $v_1 \leftarrow \prod_{TA_j \in \mathcal{C} \setminus \{TA\}} w_{j,1}$

  $v \leftarrow (v_0, v_1)$

  Return v

CoalitionExtract(d_{ID}, v):

  Parse v as (v_0, v_1)

  Parse d_{ID} as $(h, a_0, \ldots, a_k)$

  $h' \leftarrow h \cdot v_0$

  $a_0' \leftarrow a_0 \cdot v_1$

  Return $c_{ID} \leftarrow (h', a_0', a_1, \ldots, a_k)$

Extract(ID, d_{ID}, ID'):

  If $ID = \varepsilon$ then

    $r_0, r_1 \xleftarrow{\$} \mathbb{Z}_p$

    $h \leftarrow g_2^\alpha (u_{0,0} \cdot u_{0,1}^{ID_0})^{r_0} (u_{1,0} \cdot u_{1,1}^{ID_1})^{r_1}$

    $a_0 \leftarrow g_1^{r_0}$; $a_1 \leftarrow g_1^{r_1}$

    Return (h, a_0, a_1)

  Else

    Parse d_{ID} as $(h, a_0, \ldots, a_k)$

    $r_{k+1} \xleftarrow{\$} \mathbb{Z}_p$

    $h' \leftarrow h(u_{k+1,0} u_{k+1,1}^{ID'})^{r_{k+1}}$

    $a_{k+1} \leftarrow g_1^{r_{k+1}}$

    Return $(h', a_0, \ldots, a_{k+1})$

Encrypt($\mathcal{C}, PK, P, m$):

  $t \xleftarrow{\$} \mathbb{Z}_p$

  $C_1 \leftarrow g_1^t$

  For each $i \in W(P)$ set $C_{2,i} \leftarrow (u_{i,0}^t, u_{i,1}^t)$

  For each $i \in \bar{W}(P)$ set $C_{2,i} \leftarrow (u_{i,0} \cdot u_{i,1}^{P_i})^t$

  $C_3 \leftarrow m \cdot e(\prod_{TA_j \in \mathcal{C}} pk_j, g_2)^t$

  Return $(C_1, C_{2,1}, \ldots, C_{2,\ell}, C_3)$

Decrypt(ID, c_{ID}, C):

  Parse c_{ID} as $(h, a_0, \ldots, a_\ell)$

  Parse C as $(C_1, C_{2,1}, \ldots, C_{2,\ell}, C_3)$

  For each $i \in W(P)$ then

    Parse $C_{2,i}$ as $(\tilde{u}_0, \tilde{u}_1)$

    $C_{2,i}' \leftarrow \tilde{u}_0 \cdot \tilde{u}_1^{ID_i}$

  For each $i \in \bar{W}(P)$ set $C_{2,i}' \leftarrow C_{2,i}$

  $m' \xleftarrow{\$} C_3 \cdot \prod_{i=1}^\ell e(a_i, C_{2,i}') / e(C_1, h)$

  Return m'

Fig. 1. The Boneh-Boyen MTA-WIBE. Recall that any identity ID has $ID_0 = TA$. The Extract algorithm differentiates between initial key extraction by the TA and hierarchical extraction by a user. The Decrypt algorithm assumes that the depth of the decryption key and the depth of the ciphertext are equal. If the depth of the decryption key is shorter than the depth of the ciphertext, then the user can extract a key of a correct length and use the decryption algorithm.

of two prime-order groups $(\mathbb{G}, \mathbb{G}_T)$ and an efficiently computable bilinear map $e : \mathbb{G} \times \mathbb{G} \to \mathbb{G}_T$. We assume that the size of the prime p is determined by the security parameter k.

We prove this algorithm secure in the sID-IND-CPA security model. The intuition behind the proof is that any coalition of trust authorities can be viewed as an extended hierarchy with a "ghost" trust authority at the top level. Each actual trust authority is represented as a first-level identity under this ghost TA and, through communication with the other trust authorities in the coalition, is able to determine a private key for their first-level identity under the ghost TA. More specifically, if we consider a coalition $\mathcal{C} = \{TA_1, \dots, TA_n\}$ in which each TA has a private key $sk_i = g_2^{\alpha_i}$, then the ghost TA will have a private key $g_2^{\sum \alpha_i}$. Upon forming the coalition, the trust authority TA_j receives the messages

$$w_{i,j,0} \leftarrow g_2^{\alpha_i}(u_{0,0} \cdot u_{0,1}^{TA_j})^{r_i} \qquad w_{i,j,1} \leftarrow g_1^{r_i}$$

from each $TA_i \in \mathcal{C} \setminus \{TA_j\}$. This allows TA_j to form the private key

$$h \leftarrow g_2^{\sum_i \alpha_i}(u_{0,0} \cdot u_{0,1}^{TA_j})^{\sum_{i \neq j} r_i} \qquad a_1 \leftarrow g_1^{\sum_{i \neq j} r_i}$$

which is precisely the key that would be obtained if the ghost TA were to distribute a private key to the identity TA_j. The security of the multi-TA scheme then essentially follows from the security of the single-TA WIBE scheme, although care must be taken to show that the broadcast messages $w_{i,j}$ and v_i do not leak information about the private keys to the attacker.

We prove this theorem in two steps. The first step removes the wildcards to form an sID-IND-CPA secure MTA-HIBE (i.e. a WIBE scheme which doesn't support wildcards).

Theorem 1. *Suppose that there exists a PPT attacker $\mathcal{A}$ against the sID-IND-CPA security of the multi-TA Boneh-Boyen WIBE with advantage $Adv_{\mathcal{A}}^{WIBE}(k)$. Then there exists a PPT attacker $\mathcal{B}$ against the sID-IND-CPA security of the multi-TA Boneh-Boyen HIBE with advantage $Adv_{\mathcal{B}}^{HIBE}(k) = Adv_{\mathcal{A}}^{WIBE}(k)$.*

Theorem 1 is proven using the projection technique of Abdalla *et al.* [1]. For completeness, the proof is given in Appendix B. The more interesting step is to show that the HIBE is secure. This is shown relative to the DBDH assumption:

Definition 1. *Let $(\mathbb{G}, \mathbb{G}_T)$ be groups of cyclic groups of prime order $p(k)$ with a bilinear map e and let g be a generator of $\mathbb{G}$. Let D_k be the distribution $\boldsymbol{x} \leftarrow (g, g^a, g^b, g^c, e(g,g)^{abc})$ for $a, b, c \xleftarrow{\$} \mathbb{Z}_p$. Let R_k be the distribution $\boldsymbol{x} \leftarrow (g, g^a, g^b, g^c, Z)$ for $a, b, c \xleftarrow{\$} \mathbb{Z}_p$ and $Z \xleftarrow{\$} \mathbb{G}_T$. An algorithm $\mathcal{A}$ has advantage*

$$Adv_{\mathcal{A}}^{DBDH}(k) = |\Pr[\mathcal{A}(\boldsymbol{x}) = 1 \mid \boldsymbol{x} \xleftarrow{\$} D_k] - \Pr[\mathcal{A}(\boldsymbol{x}) = 1 \mid \boldsymbol{x} \xleftarrow{\$} R_k]|.$$

The DBDH assumption holds if every PPT attacker has negligible advantage.

Theorem 2. *Suppose that there exists a PPT attacker $\mathcal{A}$ against the sID-IND-CPA security of the Boneh-Boyen HIBE that makes at most q_K Corrupt oracle queries and has advantage $Adv_{\mathcal{A}}^{HIBE}(k)$. Then there exists a PPT algorithm $\mathcal{B}$ that solves the DBDH problem with advantage $Adv_{\mathcal{B}}^{BDDH}(k) \geq Adv_{\mathcal{A}}^{HIBE}(k)/2 - q_K/2p$.*

Proof We directly describe the algorithm $\mathcal{B}$ against the DBDH problem:

1. $\mathcal{B}$ receives the input (g, g^a, g^b, g^c, Z).

2. $\mathcal{B}$ runs $\mathcal{A}_0$ to obtain the challenge coalition $TA^* = \{TA_1^*, \ldots, TA_{n^*}^*\}$ and the challenge identity $ID^* = (ID_0^*, \ldots, ID_{\ell^*}^*)$ where $ID_0^* = TA_1^*$ (wlog).

3. If $\ell^* < L$ then $\mathcal{B}$ randomly generates $ID_{\ell^*+1}^*, \ldots, ID_L^* \xleftarrow{\$} \mathbb{Z}_p$.

4. $\mathcal{B}$ computes the challenge parameters

$$
\begin{aligned}
g_1 &\leftarrow g \quad\quad g_2 \leftarrow g^b \quad\quad k_{i,j}, \alpha_j \xleftarrow{\$} \mathbb{Z}_p^* \text{ for } 0 \le i \le L, j \in \{0,1\} \\
pk_1 &\leftarrow g^a / g^{\sum_{j=2}^{n^*} \alpha_j} \quad\quad pk_j \leftarrow g^{\alpha_j} \text{ and } sk_j \leftarrow (g^b)^{\alpha_j} \text{ for } 2 \le j \le n^* \\
u_{i,0} &\leftarrow g_1^{k_{i,0}} \cdot (g^a)^{-ID_i^* k_{i,1}} \quad\quad u_{i,1} \leftarrow (g^a)^{k_{i,1}} \quad\quad \text{for } 0 \le i \le L
\end{aligned}
$$

5. $\mathcal{B}$ runs $\mathcal{A}_1$ on the input $(g_1, g_2, u_{0,0}, u_{0,1}, \ldots, u_{L,0}, u_{L,1}, PK)$ where $PK = (pk_1, \ldots, pk_{n^*})$. If $\mathcal{A}_1$ makes an oracle query, then $\mathcal{B}$ answers queries as follows:

  – CreateTA: $\mathcal{B}$ generates $\alpha_{TA} \xleftarrow{\$} \mathbb{Z}_p$ and returns the public key $g_1^{\alpha_{TA}}$, while storing α_{TA} for future use.

Note that $\mathcal{B}$ knows the private key for all TAs except TA_1^*. Hence, we only have to show how to simulate the remaining oracles for TA_1.

  – SubmitTA: $\mathcal{B}$ ignores any queried made to this oracle (as the Boneh-Boyen scheme does not make use of public key values in the CoalitionBroadcast algorithm and the challenge coalition $\mathcal{C}^*$ must be entirely honest).

  – Corrupt: Suppose $\mathcal{A}$ requests the decryption key for $(TA_1^*, ID_1 \ldots, ID_\ell)$. If ID is not ancestor of $(TA_1^*, ID_1^*, \ldots, ID_L^*)$, then there exists an index $1 \le \mu \le \ell$ such that $ID_\mu \ne ID_\mu^*$. $\mathcal{B}$ generates $r_1, \ldots, r_\mu \xleftarrow{\$} \mathbb{Z}_p$ and computes the decryption key $(h, a_0, \ldots, a_\mu)$ for $(ID_0, \ldots, ID_\mu)$ as

$$
h \leftarrow g_2^{-\frac{k_{\mu,0}}{k_{\mu,1}(ID_\mu - ID_\mu^*)}} \cdot g_2^{-\sum_{j=2}^{n^*} \alpha_j} \cdot \prod_{i=0}^{\mu} \left(u_{i,0} \cdot u_{i,1}^{ID_i} \right)^{r_i}
$$

$$
a_i \leftarrow g_1^{r_i} \text{ for } 0 \le i \le \mu - 1
$$

$$
a_\mu \leftarrow g_2^{-\frac{1}{k_{\mu,1}(ID_\mu - ID_\mu^*)}} \cdot g_1^{r_j} .
$$

  $\mathcal{B}$ computes the decryption key for ID using the key derivation algorithm and returns the result. If no such μ exists (i.e. if ID is an ancestor of $(TA_1^*, ID_1^*, \ldots, ID_L^*)$ then $\mathcal{B}$ aborts .

  – CoalitionBroadcast: Suppose that $\mathcal{A}$ requests that TA_1^* sends messages to the coalition $\mathcal{C}$. $\mathcal{B}$ generates $r_1 \xleftarrow{\$} \mathbb{Z}_p$ and computes for each $TA_i \in \mathcal{C} \setminus \{TA_1^*\}$

$$
w_{i,0} \leftarrow g_2^{-\frac{k_{1,0}}{k_{1,1}(TA_i - TA_1^*)}} \cdot g_2^{-\sum_{j=2}^{n^*} \alpha_j} \cdot \left(u_{1,0} \cdot u_{1,1}^{TA_i} \right)^{r_1}
$$

$$
w_{i,1} \leftarrow g_2^{-\frac{1}{k_{1,1}(TA_i - TA_1^*)}} g_1^{r_1}
$$

  and sets $w_j \leftarrow (w_{j,0}, w_{j,1})$. $\mathcal{B}$ returns the list $\{w_j : TA_j \in \mathcal{C} \setminus \{TA_1^*\}\}$.

  – CoalitionUpdate: The output of this oracle can be returned directly as it is independent of any private key values.

– Encrypt: Suppose $\mathcal{A}_1$ makes the oracle query on two equal-length messages (m_0, m_1). $\mathcal{B}$ chooses a bit $b \xleftarrow{\$} \{0, 1\}$ and computes the ciphertext

$$C^* \leftarrow (g^c, (g^c)^{k_{1,0}}, \ldots, (g^c)^{k_{\ell^*,0}}, m_b \cdot Z).$$

$\mathcal{A}_1$ terminates with the output of a bit b'.
6. If $b = b'$ then $\mathcal{B}$ outputs 1. Otherwise, outputs 0.

The Corrupt oracle works perfectly provided that $\mathcal{A}_1$ does not abort, which can only occur if $\mathcal{A}_1$ makes query on an identity ID which is not an ancestor of ID^* but is an ancestor of $(ID_0^*, \ldots, ID_L^*)$. This can only occur if $\ell > \ell^*$ and $ID_{\ell^*+1} = ID_{\ell^*+1}^*$, which occurs with probability $1/p$ as this value is information theoretically hidden from $\mathcal{A}$. Hence, the probability that this does not occur in the entire execution of $\mathcal{A}$ is q_K/p where q_K is the number of queries to the Corrupt oracle. We note that the corrupt oracle gives correct responses for queries since

$$sk_1 \left(u_{j,0} \cdot u_{j,1}^{ID_j} \right)^r = g_2^{\frac{-k_{j,0}}{k_{j,1}(ID_j - ID_j^*)}} \cdot g_2^{-\sum_{i=2}^{n^*} \alpha_i} \qquad \text{for} \qquad r = -\frac{b}{k_{j,1}(ID_j - ID_j^*)}.$$

A similar calculation shows that the CoalitionBroadcast algorithm gives correct broadcast messages for TA_1^*. All other oracles that $\mathcal{B}$ provides correctly simulate the security model for $\mathcal{A}$.

If $Z = e(g, g)^{abc}$ then the challenge ciphertext is a correct encryption of m_b. This is because an encryption using the random value c would have

$$C_1 = g_1^c = g^c$$
$$C_{2,i} = (u_{i,0} \cdot u_{i,1}^{ID_i^*})^c = (g^c)^{k_{i,0}} \qquad \text{for } 0 \le i \le \ell^*$$
$$C_3 = m_b \cdot e(\textstyle\prod_{i=0}^{n^*} pk_i, g_2)^c = m_b \cdot e(g^a, g^b)^c = m_b \cdot e(g, g)^{abc}$$

The probability that $\mathcal{B}$ outputs 1 in this situation is the probability that $b = b'$ in the sID-IND-CPA game for the attacker $\mathcal{A}$. This probability can be shown to be $(Adv_{\mathcal{A}}^{\text{HIBE}}(k) - 1)/2$. If Z is random then the challenge ciphertext information theoretically hides b and so the probability that $\mathcal{B}$ outputs 1 in this situation is $1/2$. This completes the proof. □

4   Strengthened Security Results

4.1   IND-CPA Security

We may prove the security of the Boneh-Boyen scheme in the (non-selective-identity) IND-CPA model by hashing all identities before use. The proof of this fact mirrors the proof in Abdalla et al. [1] (in the random oracle model).

Setup'(1^k):
  $param \xleftarrow{\$} \text{Setup}(1^k)$
  $\sigma \xleftarrow{\$} \mathcal{G}(1^k)$
  $param' \leftarrow (param, \sigma)$
  Return $param'$

Encode(P, α):
  Parse P as $(P_0, \ldots, P_\ell)$
  For $i = 0, \ldots, \ell$, $P_i' \leftarrow P_i$
  For $i = \ell + 1, \ldots, L$, $P_i' \leftarrow$ "$-$"
  $P_{L+1}' \leftarrow \alpha$
  Return P'

Encode'(P, ID, α):
  For $i = 1, \ldots, |P| - |ID|$
    If $P_{|ID|+i} \neq *$ then $ID_i' \leftarrow P_{|ID|+i}$
    If $P_{|ID|+i} = *$ then $ID_i' \leftarrow 1^k$
  For $i = 1, \ldots, L - |P|$
    $ID_{|P|-|ID|+i} \leftarrow$ "$-$"
  $ID_{L-|ID|+1} \leftarrow \alpha$
  Return ID'

CoalitionExtract'(d_{ID}, v):
  $c_{ID} \leftarrow (d_{ID}, v)$
  Return c_{ID}

Encrypt'$(\mathcal{C}, PK, P, m)$:
  $(K, com, dec) \xleftarrow{\$} \mathcal{S}(1^k, \sigma)$
  $P' \leftarrow \text{Encode}(P, com)$
  $m' \leftarrow (m, dec)$
  $C' \xleftarrow{\$} \text{Encrypt}(\mathcal{C}, PK, P', m')$
  $\tau \leftarrow \text{MAC}_K(\mathcal{C}\|P\|C')$
  Return $(com, \mathcal{C}, P, C', \tau)$

Decrypt'(c_{ID}, C):
  Parse C as $(com, \mathcal{C}, P, C', \tau)$
  Parse c_{ID} as (d_{ID}, v)
  $ID' \leftarrow \text{Encode'}(P, ID, com)$
  $d' \xleftarrow{\$} \text{Extract}(ID, d_{ID}, ID')$
  $c' \leftarrow \text{CoalitionUpdate}(d', v)$
  $(m, dec) \xleftarrow{\$} \text{Decrypt}(c', C')$
  $K \leftarrow \mathcal{R}(\sigma, com, dec)$
  If $\text{MAC}_K(\mathcal{C}\|P\|C') \neq \tau$ then return $\bot$
  Else return m

Fig. 2. The Boneh-Katz transform for a MTA-WIBE. Any algorithm of Π' not explicitly defined in this figure is identical to the corresponding algorithm in Π. The Encode algorithm turns an ℓ level pattern into an $L + 1$ level pattern. The Encode' algorithm computes the extension to ID required to turn an identity which matches P into an identity which matches Encode(P, α).

4.2   IND-CCA2 Security

We may transform an IND-CPA MTA-WIBE scheme into an IND-CCA2 MTA-WIBE scheme using the CHK transform [6] in a manner similar to that described in Abdalla *et al.* [1]. However, we will describe an alternative transformation based on the Boneh-Katz (BK) transform [5]. This gives a new and more efficient method to transform IND-CPA secure WIBEs into IND-CCA2 secure WIBEs. For the specific MTA-WIBE scheme presented in Section 3, there may be more efficient IND-CCA2 constructions; however, we believe that the BK transformation in this section is of independent interest and provides the most efficient generic currently-known method to construct IND-CCA2 WIBEs and MTA-WIBEs from IND-CPA schemes.

Boneh-Katz transforms an MTA-WIBE Π into a new MTA-WIBE Π' using a MAC algorithm MAC and an "encapsulation" scheme $(\mathcal{G}, \mathcal{S}, \mathcal{R})$. The encapsulation scheme has a key generation algorithm $\sigma \xleftarrow{\$} \mathcal{G}(1^k)$, commitment algorithm $(K, com, dec) \xleftarrow{\$} \mathcal{S}(1^k, \sigma)$, and a decommitment algorithm $\mathcal{D}(\sigma, com, dec)$ which outputs either a bitstring K or the error symbol $\bot$. We assume that $K \in \{0, 1\}^k$.

We require that if $(K, com, dec) \overset{\$}{\leftarrow} \mathcal{S}(1^k, \sigma)$ then $\mathcal{D}(\sigma, com, dec) = K$. We also require that the scheme is hiding in the sense that all PPT attackers $\mathcal{A}$ have negligible advantage:

$$\left| \Pr\left[\mathcal{A}(1^k, \sigma, com, K_b) = b : \begin{array}{c} \sigma \overset{\$}{\leftarrow} \mathcal{G}(1^k); \; K_0 \overset{\$}{\leftarrow} \{0,1\}^k \\ (K_1, com, dec) \overset{\$}{\leftarrow} \mathcal{S}(1^k, \sigma); \; b \overset{\$}{\leftarrow} \{0,1\} \end{array} \right] - \frac{1}{2} \right|$$

We further require that the encapsulation scheme is binding in the sense that all PPT attackers $\mathcal{A}$ have negligible advantage:

$$\Pr\left[\mathcal{R}(\sigma, com, dec') \notin \{\perp, K\} : \begin{array}{c} \sigma \overset{\$}{\leftarrow} \mathcal{G}(1^k); \; (K, com, dec) \overset{\$}{\leftarrow} \mathcal{S}(1^k, \sigma) \\ dec' \overset{\$}{\leftarrow} \mathcal{A}(1^k, \sigma, K, com, dec) \end{array} \right]$$

Lastly, we assume that the decommitments dec^* are always of some fixed size (which may depend on k). The security notions for a MAC scheme are given in Appendix A.2. The transform of Π into Π' is given in Figure 2. We assume that "$-$" represents some fixed, publicly-known allowable identity for the CPA scheme; we will deliberately exclude "$-$" from the space of allowable identities in the CCA scheme.

Theorem 3. *Suppose that the Π is an IND-CPA secure MTA-WIBE, MAC is an unforgeable MAC scheme, and $(\mathcal{G}, \mathcal{S}, \mathcal{R})$ is a hiding and binding encapsulation algorithm. Then the MTA-WIBE Π' produced by the BK transform is IND-CCA2 secure.*

The proof strategy is similar to that of Boneh and Katz [5] but has to deal with technical details introduced by the trust authorities and the WIBE scheme. A full proof is given in Appendix C

Acknowledgements

This research was sponsored by the US Army Research Laboratory and the UK Ministry of Defence and was accomplished under Agreement Number W911NF-06-3-0001. The views and conclusions contained in this document are those of the authors and should not be interpreted as representing the official policies, either expressed or implied, of the US Army Research Laboratory, the US Government, the UK Ministry of Defence, or the UK Government. The US and UK Governments are authorized to reproduce and distribute reprints for Government purposes notwithstanding any copyright notation hereon. The research was conducted while the second author was visiting The Graduate Center of the City University of New York. The authors would like to thank the reviewers for their comments on the paper.

References

1. Abdalla, M., Catalano, D., Dent, A.W., Malone-Lee, J., Neven, G., Smart, N.P.: Identity-based encryption gone wild. In: Bugliesi, M., Preneel, B., Sassone, V., Wegener, I. (eds.) ICALP 2006. LNCS, vol. 4052, pp. 300–311. Springer, Heidelberg (2006)

2. Abdalla, M., Kiltz, E., Neven, G.: Generalized key delegation for hierarchical identity-based encryption. In: Biskup, J., López, J. (eds.) ESORICS 2007. LNCS, vol. 4734, pp. 139–154. Springer, Heidelberg (2007)
3. Boklan, K.D., Klagsbrun, Z., Paterson, K.G., Srinivasan, S.: Flexible and secure communications in an identity-based coalition environment. In: Proc. IEEE Military Communications Conference - MILCOM 2008 (2008)
4. Boneh, D., Boyen, X.: Efficient selective-ID secure identity based encryption without random oracles. In: Cachin, C., Camenisch, J. (eds.) EUROCRYPT 2004. LNCS, vol. 3027, pp. 223–238. Springer, Heidelberg (2004)
5. Boneh, D., Katz, J.: Improved efficiency for CCA-secure cryptosystems built using identity-based encryption. In: Menezes, A. (ed.) CT-RSA 2005. LNCS, vol. 3376, pp. 87–103. Springer, Heidelberg (2005)
6. Canetti, R., Halevi, S., Katz, J.: Chosen-ciphertext security from identity-based encryption. In: Cachin, C., Camenisch, J. (eds.) EUROCRYPT 2004. LNCS, vol. 3027, pp. 207–222. Springer, Heidelberg (2004)
7. Chatterjee, S., Sarkar, P.: Multi-receiver identity-based key encapsulation with shortened ciphertext. In: Barua, R., Lange, T. (eds.) INDOCRYPT 2006. LNCS, vol. 4329, pp. 394–408. Springer, Heidelberg (2006)
8. Dodis, Y., Fazio, N.: Public key broadcast encryption for stateless receivers. In: Feigenbaum, J. (ed.) DRM 2002. LNCS, vol. 2696, pp. 61–80. Springer, Heidelberg (2003)
9. Horwitz, J., Lynn, B.: Towards hierarchical identity-based encryption. In: Knudsen, L. (ed.) EUROCRYPT 2002. LNCS, vol. 2332, pp. 466–481. Springer, Heidelberg (2002)
10. Park, J.H., Kim, K.T., Lee, D.H.: Cryptanalysis and improvement of a multi-receiver identity-based key encapsulation at INDOCRYPT'06. In: ASIAN ACM Symposium on Information, Computer and Communications Security – ASIA CCS 2008, pp. 373–380. ACM Press, New York (2008)
11. Paterson, K.G., Srinivasan, S.: Security and anonymity of identity-based encryption with multiple trusted authorities. In: Galbraith, S.D., Paterson, K.G. (eds.) Pairing 2008. LNCS, vol. 5209, pp. 354–375. Springer, Heidelberg (2008)
12. Shamir, A.: Identity-based cryptosystems and signature schemes. In: Blakely, G.R., Chaum, D. (eds.) CRYPTO 1984. LNCS, vol. 196, pp. 47–53. Springer, Heidelberg (1985)

A   Standard Definitions

A.1   Algorithms and Assignment

Throughout this article, $y \leftarrow x$ denotes the assignment of the value x to the variable y and $y \xleftarrow{\$} S$ denotes the assignment of a uniform random element of the finite set S to the variable y. If $\mathcal{A}$ is a probabilistic algorithm, then $y \xleftarrow{\$} \mathcal{A}(x)$ denotes the assignment of the output of the algorithm $\mathcal{A}$ run on the input x to the variable y when $\mathcal{A}$ is computed using a fresh set of random coins. We write $y \leftarrow \mathcal{A}(x)$ if $\mathcal{A}$ is deterministic.

A.2 MAC Algorithms

A MAC algorithm is a deterministic polynomial-time algorithm MAC. It takes as input a message $m \in \{0,1\}^*$ and a symmetric key $K \in \{0,1\}^k$, and outputs a tag $\tau \leftarrow \text{MAC}_K(m)$. It should be infeasible for a PPT attacker $\mathcal{A}$ to win the unforgeability game: (1) the challenger generates a key $K \xleftarrow{\$} \{0,1\}^k$; (2) the attacker outputs a forgery $(m^*, \tau^*) \xleftarrow{\$} \mathcal{A}(1^k)$. During its execution the attacker can query a MAC oracle with a message m and will receive $\text{MAC}_K(m)$. The attacker wins if $\text{MAC}_K(m^*) = \tau^*$ and m^* was never queried to the MAC oracle. The attackers probability of winning is written $Adv_{\mathcal{A}}^{\text{MAC}}(k)$.

B Security Proof for BB-WIBE to BB-HIBE Reduction

Proof of Theorem 1

We directly describe the algorithm $\mathcal{B}$ which breaks the HIBE using the algorithm $\mathcal{A}$ as a subroutine. Before we begin, we define some useful notation. If $P = (P_1, \ldots, P_k)$ is a pattern, then

$$W(P) = \{1 \leq i \leq k : P_i = *\} \quad \text{and} \quad W(P_{\leq j}) = \{1 \leq i \leq \min\{j, k\} : P_i = *\}.$$

The algorithm $\mathcal{B}$ runs as follows:

1. $\mathcal{B}$ runs $\mathcal{A}_0$ on the security parameter. $\mathcal{A}_0$ responds by outputting a description of the challenge coalition $TA^* = (TA_1^*, \ldots, TA_n^*)$ and the challenge pattern $P^* = (P_1^*, \ldots, P_{\ell^*}^*)$. Let π be a map which identifies the number of non-wildcard entries in the first i layers of P^*, i.e. $\pi(i) = i - |W(P_{\leq i}^*)|$.
   $\mathcal{B}$ outputs the challenge coalition TA^* and the challenge identity $\hat{ID}^* = (\hat{ID}_1^*, \ldots, \hat{ID}_{\pi(\ell^*)}^*)$ where $\hat{ID}_{\pi(i)}^* = P_i^*$ for $i \notin W(P^*)$.
2. $\mathcal{B}$ responds with HIBE parameters $param = (\hat{g}_1, \hat{g}_2, \hat{u}_{1,0}, \ldots, \hat{u}_{L,1})$. $\mathcal{B}$ generates WIBE parameters as follows:

$$
\begin{aligned}
&(g_1, g_2) \leftarrow (\hat{g}_1, \hat{g}_2) \\
&u_{i,j} \leftarrow \hat{u}_{\pi(i),j} && \text{for } i \notin W(P^*), j \in \{0,1\} \\
&u_{i,j} \leftarrow g_1^{\beta_{i,j}} && \text{for } i \in W(P^*), j \in \{0,1\} \text{ where } \beta_{i,j} \xleftarrow{\$} \mathbb{Z}_p \\
&u_{i,j} \leftarrow \hat{u}_{i-|W(P^*)|,j} && \text{for } i \in \{\ell^* + 1, \ldots, L\}, j \in \{0,1\}.
\end{aligned}
$$

3. $\mathcal{B}$ executes $\mathcal{A}_1$ on the public parameters $(g_1, g_2, u_{0,0}, \ldots, u_{L,1})$. $\mathcal{A}$ may make the following oracle queries:
   - CreateTA: $\mathcal{B}$ forwards this request to its own oracle and returns the response.
   - SubmitTA: $\mathcal{B}$ may ignore these queries as the CoalitionBroadcast algorithm does not depend upon individual TA's public keys.
   - CoalitionBroadcast: $\mathcal{B}$ forwards this request to its own oracle and returns the response.
   - CoalitionUpdate: $\mathcal{B}$ forwards this request to its own oracle and returns the response.

- **Corrupt**: To extract a decryption key for an identity $ID = (ID_1, \ldots, ID_\ell)$ which does not match the challenge pattern, $\mathcal{B}$ computes the projection of the identity onto the HIBE identity space to give a projected identity $\hat{ID} = (\hat{ID}_1 \ldots, \hat{ID}_{\hat{\ell}})$.

  - If $\ell \leq \ell^*$ then $\hat{\ell} \leftarrow \pi(\ell)$ and $\hat{ID}_{\pi(i)} \leftarrow ID_i$ for $i \notin W(P^*_{\leq \ell})$. Since ID does not match the challenge pattern for the WIBE, $\hat{ID}$ does not match the challenge identity for the HIBE. $\mathcal{B}$ queries its Corrupt oracle on $\hat{ID}$ and receives $(\hat{h}, \hat{a}_0, \ldots, \hat{a}_{\hat{\ell}})$ in response. $\mathcal{B}$ now "retrofits" to find a complete key, by setting

$$
\begin{aligned}
a_0 &\leftarrow \hat{a}_0 \\
a_i &\leftarrow \hat{a}_{\pi(i)} && \text{for } 1 \leq i \leq \ell \text{ and } i \notin W(P^*_{\leq \ell}) \\
a_i &\leftarrow g_1^{r_i} && \text{for } 1 \leq i \leq \ell \text{ and } i \in W(P^*_{\leq \ell}) \text{ where } r_i \xleftarrow{\$} \mathbb{Z}_p \\
h &\leftarrow \hat{h} \prod_{i=1, i \in W(P^*_{\leq \ell})}^{\ell} (u_{i,0} \cdot u_{i,1}^{ID_i})^{r_i}
\end{aligned}
$$

    and returning the key $(h, a_0, \ldots, a_\ell)$.

  - If $\ell > \ell^*$, then $\hat{\ell} = \ell - |W(P^*)|$, $\hat{ID}_{\pi(i)} \leftarrow ID_i$ for $1 \leq i \leq \ell^*$ and $i \notin W(P^*)$, and $\hat{ID}_{i-|W(P^*)|} \leftarrow ID_i$ for $\ell^* < i \leq \ell$. Since ID does not match the challenge pattern for the WIBE, $\hat{ID}$ does not match the challenge identity for the HIBE. $\mathcal{B}$ queries its Corrupt oracle on $\hat{ID}$ and receives $(\hat{h}, \hat{a}_0, \ldots, \hat{a}_{\hat{\ell}})$ in response. $\mathcal{B}$ now "retro-fits" to find a complete key, by setting

$$
\begin{aligned}
a_0 &\leftarrow \hat{a}_0 \\
a_i &\leftarrow \hat{a}_{\pi(i)} && \text{for } 1 \leq i \leq \ell^* \text{ and } i \notin W(P^*) \\
a_i &\leftarrow g_1^{r_i} && \text{for } 1 \leq i \leq \ell^* \text{ and } i \in W(P^*) \text{ where } r_i \xleftarrow{\$} \mathbb{Z}_p \\
a_i &\leftarrow \hat{a}_{i-|W(P^*)|} && \text{for } \ell^* < i \leq \ell \\
h &\leftarrow \hat{h} \prod_{i=1, i \in W(P^*)}^{\ell^*} (u_{i,0} \cdot u_{i,1}^{ID_i})^{r_i}
\end{aligned}
$$

    and returning the key $(h, a_0, \ldots, a_\ell)$.

- **Encrypt**: $\mathcal{A}$ outputs two equal-length messages (m_0, m_1). $\mathcal{B}$ queries its own encryption oracle on the messages (m_0, m_1) and receives the ciphertext $(C_1^*, \hat{C}_{2,1}^*, \ldots, \hat{C}_{2,\pi(\ell^*)}^*, C_3^*)$. $\mathcal{B}$ retro-fits this to form the challenge ciphertext for $\mathcal{A}$ by setting

$$
\begin{aligned}
C_{2,i}^* &\leftarrow \hat{C}_{2,\pi(i)}^* && \text{for } 1 \leq i \leq \ell^*, i \notin W(P^*) \\
C_{2,i}^* &\leftarrow (C_1^{*\beta_{i,0}}, C_1^{*\beta_{i,1}}) && \text{for } 1 \leq i \leq \ell^*, i \in W(P^*).
\end{aligned}
$$

$\mathcal{A}_1$ terminates with the output of a bit b'.

4. $\mathcal{B}$ outputs the bit b'.

The algorithm $\mathcal{B}$ correctly simulates the oracles to which $\mathcal{A}$ has access; furthermore, $\mathcal{B}$ wins the HIBE game if and only if $\mathcal{A}$ wins the game. Hence, the theorem is proven. $\qquad\square$

C Security Proof for the BK Transform

Proof of Theorem 3

Our proof proceeds through a series of games. Let W_i be the event that the attacker $\mathcal{A}$ outputs $b' = b$ in Game i and let starred values denote values computed during the computation of the challenge ciphertext. Let Game 1 be the normal IND-CCA2 game for $\mathcal{A}$. Hence,

$$Adv_{\mathcal{A}}^{\mathsf{CCA}}(k) = 2 \cdot |\Pr[W_1] - 1/2|.$$

Let Game 2 be the same as Game 1 except that $\mathcal{A}$ is deemed to lose if it submits a ciphertext (com^*, P, C, τ) such that the decommitment value dec' recovered during the decryption process satisfies $\mathcal{R}(\sigma, com^*, dec') \notin \{\bot, K^*\}$. It is easy to show that there exists a PPT algorithm $\mathcal{B}$ such that $|\Pr[W_1] - \Pr[W_2]| \leq Adv_{\mathcal{B}}^{\mathsf{bind}}(k)$.

Let Game 3 be identical to Game 2 except that the encryption oracle computes $m'^* \leftarrow (m_b, 0^{|dec^*|})$ rather than $m'^* \leftarrow (m_b, dec^*)$. Let E_2 be the event that $\mathcal{A}$ submits a ciphertext $(com^*, \mathcal{C}, P, C', \tau)$ to the decryption oracle with $\mathrm{MAC}_{K^*}(\mathcal{C}\|P\|C') = \tau$ in Game 2. Let E_3 be the event that $\mathcal{A}$ submits a ciphertext $(com^*, \mathcal{C}, P, C', \tau)$ to the decryption oracle with $\mathrm{MAC}_{K^*}(\mathcal{C}\|P\|C') = \tau$ in Game 3. There exists an algorithm $\mathcal{B}^*$ against the IND-CPA security of Π such that $|\Pr[E_3] - \Pr[E_2]| \leq Adv_{\mathcal{B}^*}^{\mathsf{CPA}}(k)$. The attacker $\mathcal{B}^*(param)$ is defined as follows:

1. $\sigma \xleftarrow{\$} \mathcal{G}(1^k)$ and $(K^*, com^*, dec^*) \xleftarrow{\$} \mathcal{S}(1^k, \sigma)$.
2. $param' \leftarrow (param, \sigma)$.
3. Run $b' \xleftarrow{\$} \mathcal{A}(param')$. Suppose $\mathcal{A}$ makes an oracle query.
   - If $\mathcal{A}$ makes a CreateTA, SubmitTA, CoalitionBroadcast, Coalition Update, CoalitionExtract or Corrupt query, then $\mathcal{B}^*$ passes the query to its own oracle and returns the result.
   - If $\mathcal{A}$ makes an encryption oracle query on the equal-length messages (m_0, m_1), the pattern P^*, and the coalition C^* then $\mathcal{B}^*$ computes $P'^* \leftarrow$ Encode(P^*, com^*), $d \xleftarrow{\$} \{0,1\}$, $m'_0 \leftarrow (m_d, dec^*)$, $m'_1 \leftarrow (m_d, 0^{|dec^*|})$, and queries its encryption oracle on (m'_0, m'_1), the pattern P'^*, and the coalition C^*. It receives C'^* from its oracle, and computes $\tau^* \leftarrow \mathrm{MAC}_{K^*}(C^*\|P^*\|C'^*)$. It returns $(com^*, C^*, P^*, C'^*, \tau^*)$.
   - If $\mathcal{A}$ makes a decryption query on $(com, \mathcal{C}, P, C', \tau)$ with $com \neq com^*$ for the identity ID and the coalition $\mathcal{C}$, then $\mathcal{B}^*$ computes $P' \leftarrow$ Encode (P, com), replaces the wildcards in P' with 1^k to form the identity ID' and requests the decryption key $d_{ID'}$ for ID'. Since $\mathcal{A}$ can only make decryption queries for coalitions for which the adjustment parameter v is known, $\mathcal{B}^*$ forms the decryption key $c' \xleftarrow{\$}$ CoalitionExtract$(d_{ID'}, v)$. $\mathcal{B}^*$ can use this key to decrypt C', and decrypt the rest of the ciphertext as normal.
   - If $\mathcal{A}$ makes a decryption query on $(com^*, \mathcal{C}, P, C', \tau)$, then $\mathcal{B}^*$ checks whether $\mathrm{MAC}_{K^*}(\mathcal{C}\|P\|C') = \tau$. If so, $\mathcal{B}^*$ outputs 1 and terminates. Otherwise, $\mathcal{B}$ returns $\bot$ to $\mathcal{A}$.
4. $\mathcal{B}^*$ outputs 0

This attacker is legal since it only queries the decryption oracle on identities with $com \neq com^*$. If $b = 0$ then $\mathcal{B}^*$ outputs 1 whenever E_2 occurs. If $b = 1$ then $\mathcal{B}^*$ outputs 1 whenever E_3 occurs. Hence, $|Pr[E_3] - \Pr[E_2]| \leq Adv^{\mathrm{CPA}}_{\mathcal{B}^*}(k)$.

There exists an attacker $\mathcal{B}'$ such that $|\Pr[W_3|\neg E_3] - \Pr[W_2|\neg E_2]| \leq Adv^{\mathrm{CPA}}_{\mathcal{B}'}(k)$. The attacker $\mathcal{B}'(param)$ is defined as follows:

1. $\sigma \overset{\$}{\leftarrow} \mathcal{G}(1^k)$ and $(K^*, com^*, dec^*) \overset{\$}{\leftarrow} \mathcal{S}(1^k, \sigma)$.
2. $param' \leftarrow (param, \sigma)$.
3. Run $d' \overset{\$}{\leftarrow} \mathcal{A}(param')$. Suppose $\mathcal{A}$ makes an oracle query.
   - If $\mathcal{A}$ makes a CreateTA, SubmitTA, CoalitionBroadcast, Coalition Update, CoalitionExtract or Corrupt query, then $\mathcal{B}$ passes the query to its own oracle and returns the result.
   - If $\mathcal{A}$ makes an encryption oracle query on the equal-length messages (m_0, m_1) and the pattern P^*, then $\mathcal{B}$ computes $P'^* \leftarrow \text{Encode}(P^*, com^*)$, $d \overset{\$}{\leftarrow} \{0, 1\}$, $m_0' \leftarrow (m_d, dec^*)$, $m_1' \leftarrow (m_d, 0^{|dec^*|})$, and queries its encryption oracle on (m_0', m_1') and the pattern P'. It receives C'^* from its oracle, and computes $\tau^* \leftarrow \text{MAC}_{K^*}(C^* \| P'^* \| C'^*)$. It returns $(com^*, C^*, P^*, C'^*, \tau^*)$.
   - If $\mathcal{A}$ makes a decryption query on (com, C, P, C', τ) with $com \neq com^*$ for the identity ID and the coalition $\mathcal{C}$, then $\mathcal{B}$ computes $P' \leftarrow \text{Encode}(P, com)$, replaces the wildcards in P' with 1^k to form the identity ID' and requests the decryption key $d_{ID'}$ for ID'. Since $\mathcal{A}$ can only make decryption queries for coalitions for which the adjustment parameter v is known, $\mathcal{B}$ forms the decryption key $c' \overset{\$}{\leftarrow} \text{CoalitionExtract}(d_{ID'}, v)$. $\mathcal{B}$ can use this key to decrypt C', and decrypt the rest of the ciphertext as normal.
   - If $\mathcal{A}$ makes a decryption query on $(com^*, \mathcal{C}, P, C', \tau)$, then $\mathcal{B}$ returns $\bot$.
4. If $d = d'$ then $\mathcal{B}'$ returns 1, else it returns 0.

This is a legal attacker and $|\Pr[W_3|\neg E_3] - \Pr[W_2|\neg E_2]| \leq Adv^{\mathrm{CPA}}_{\mathcal{B}'}(k)$. A simple probability argument can be used to show that:

$$|\Pr[W_3] - \Pr[W_2]| \leq 2 \cdot Adv^{\mathrm{CPA}}_{\mathcal{B}^*}(k) + Adv^{\mathrm{CPA}}_{\mathcal{B}'}(k) + \Pr[E_3].$$

Next, let Game 4 be identical to Game 3 except that the key K^* used in the encryption algorithm (and to determine if ciphertexts should be rejected) is randomly chosen from $\{0, 1\}^k$. There exists an attacker $\mathcal{B}^\dagger$ against the hiding property of the encapsulation algorithm such that $|\Pr[W_4] - \Pr[W_3]| \leq 2 \cdot Adv^{\mathrm{hide}}_{\mathcal{B}^\dagger}(k)$. Let E_4 be the event that $\mathcal{A}$ submits a ciphertext $(com^*, \mathcal{C}, P, C', \tau)$ to the decryption oracle with $\text{MAC}_{K^*}(\mathcal{C} \| P \| C') = \tau$ in Game 4. Again, we have $|\Pr[E_4] - \Pr[E_3]| \leq 2 \cdot Adv^{\mathrm{hide}}_{\mathcal{B}^\dagger}(k)$.

Finally, let Game 5 be identical to Game 4 except that (a) the attacker loses if it queries the decryption oracle on a ciphertext $(com^*, \mathcal{C}, P, C', \tau)$ before it queries the encryption oracle, and (b) the attacker returns $\bot$ whenever the attacker queries the decryption oracle on a ciphertext $(com^*, \mathcal{C}, P, C', \tau)$ after it queries the encryption oracle. There exists an algorithm $\mathcal{B}''$ against the

MAC algorithm such that $|\Pr[W_5] - \Pr[W_4]| \le q_D Adv_{\mathcal{B}''}^{\text{MAC}}(k) + \gamma(k)$ where $\gamma(k)$ is the maximum probability that a randomly generated com^* is any fixed binary value. As a byproduct, we also obtain $\Pr[E_4] \le q_D Adv_{\mathcal{B}''}^{\text{MAC}}(k)$.

We can show a direct reduction from Game 5 to the underlying IND-CPA security of Π. There exists an algorithm $\mathcal{B}^\sharp$ such that $2 \cdot |\Pr[W_5] - 1/2| = Adv_{\mathcal{B}^\sharp}^{\text{CPA}}(k)$. This algorithm simply translates decryption oracle queries made by $\mathcal{A}$ against the MTA-WIBE scheme into translates decryption oracles made by $\mathcal{B}^\sharp$ against the tag-based encryption scheme (for ciphertexts with $com \ne com^*$) or returns $\perp$ (for ciphertexts with $com = com^*$). All decryption oracle queries made by $\mathcal{B}^\sharp$ are legal as the weak selective-tag IND-CPA security model allows for decryption oracle queries for tags $com \ne com^*$. This concludes the proof. $\qquad\square$

Security of Sequential Multiple Encryption

Atsushi Fujioka[1], Yoshiaki Okamoto[2], and Taiichi Saito[2]

[1] NTT Information Sharing Platform Laboratories,
3-9-11 Midori-cho, Musashino-shi, Tokyo 180-8585, Japan
fujioka.atsushi@lab.ntt.co.jp
[2] Tokyo Denki University,
2-2 Kanda Nishiki-cho, Chiyoda-ku, Tokyo 101-8457, Japan
{okamoto@crypt.,taiichi@}c.dendai.ac.jp

Abstract. This paper analyzes the security of sequential multiple encryptions based on asymmetric key encryptions, and shows that a sequential construction of secure multiple encryptions exists.

The sequential multiple encryption can be proved to be indistinguishable against chosen ciphertext attacks for multiple encryptions (IND-ME-CCA), where the adversary can access to the decryption oracle of the multiple encryption, even when all the component encryptions of the multiple encryption are indistinguishable against chosen plaintext attacks (IND-CPA). We present an extended security notion of sequential multiple encryptions, in which the adversary is allowed to decrypt component encryptions in addition to access to the decryption oracle of the multiple encryption, and show that our constructed scheme satisfies it.

Keywords: multiple encryption, sequential construction, random oracle model, Fujisaki-Okamoto conversion.

1 Introduction

Multiple encryption, which encrypts a message several times with different keys or algorithms, has been applied to many communication systems in order to enhance the security of their encryption schemes in total. The idea was first seen in "product ciphers" by Shannon [28] and has often appeared in research such as that on "cascade ciphers" [14,22]. In addition to these works, several papers [23,1] discuss the security of multiple encryptions built from *symmetric key encryptions*.

Although multiple encryption schemes based on *asymmetric key encryptions* are used in many practical systems, their security has not been thoroughly investigated until a recent work by Zhang, Hanaoka, Shikata, and Imai [30]. They defined security for multiple encryption and presented generic constructions secure in the random oracle model [2]. Dodis and Katz independently investigated and proposed stronger definitions to capture a general framework of multiple encryptions and presented generic constructions that satisfied the security definitions [12]. Their constructed encryptions are secure in the standard model.

M. Abdalla and P.S.L.M. Barreto (Eds.): LATINCRYPT 2010, LNCS 6212, pp. 20–39, 2010.

These results are significant because multiple encryptions are basic components for designing other cryptographic applications: key-insulated encryption [13], broadcast encryption [11], threshold encryption [9,15,10], MIX-net [7,19], and so on.

These important works on the security of multiple encryptions based on asymmetric key encryptions arose from a consideration that a natural construction of multiple encryption cannot retain its security even when all the component encryptions of the multiple encryption are secure. However, it is worth noting that this does not mean all natural constructions of multiple encryptions are insecure.

In this paper, we analyze the security of multiple encryptions based on asymmetric key encryptions. We propose a secure natural construction of multiple encryptions. Our constructed multiple encryptions satisfy the existing security definition in [30]. In addition, we propose a stronger definition which is similar to those discussed in [12] and prove that the constructed schemes also satisfy this definition.

1.1 Background

CCA Security for Multiple Encryption. A multiple encryption scheme constructed by combining different encryption schemes based on different cryptographic assumptions should provide long-term security because at least some of the component encryption schemes might remain unbroken and secure for long periods. However, long-term security does not rule out the possibility that several secret keys might be compromised, some component schemes collapse, or some assumptions be broken, during long periods.

Multiple encryption should satisfy the chosen-ciphertext security, the standard notion of security for asymmetric key encryption schemes (IND-CCA) [25], and in addition is required to be secure against the possibility of the above danger. This consideration leads to the chosen-ciphertext security notion extended for multiple encryption (IND-ME-CCA) proposed in [30]. This IND-ME-CCA model allows the adversary to access not only the decryption oracle for multiple encryption but also all secret keys except one, which serves to illustrate both the chosen-ciphertext attack and secret key exposure.

Dodis and Katz independently defined several security notions of multiple encryption in [12], and among the security definitions, the wMCCA security is equivalent to the above IND-ME-CCA security.

Sequential Natural Constructions. In [30], Zhang et al. pointed out that straightforward constructions (called "natural constructions") of multiple encryptions produce *insecure* multiple encryptions in the IND-ME-CCA model even if all the component encryptions are IND-CCA secure.

Let Enc_i be an IND-CCA encryption algorithm and pk_i be the encryption key for Enc_i. The *sequential* natural construction is as follows: given a message m to be multiple-encrypted, a user sets $c_0 = m$, sequentially encrypts $c_i = \mathsf{Enc}_i(pk_i, c_{i-1})$ from $i = 1$ to n, and outputs the final c_n as a ciphertext of the multiple encryption where n is the number of the component encryptions used for constructing the multiple encryption. Here the notation $\mathsf{Enc}(pk, m)$ means a probabilistic encryption that takes as inputs a public key pk and a message m and internally uses randomness. Hereafter, when we need to explicitly describe randomness, we adopt the notation $\mathsf{Enc}(pk, m; r)$ where r is a random string and thus Enc is a deterministic algorithm.

Decrypt-then-Encrypt-again Attack. Multiple encryption based on the sequential "natural construction" is shown to be insecure with regard to IND-ME-CCA in the following attack [30]. Suppose the adversary is given the challenge ciphertext c^*. Under the IND-ME-CCA model, it is possible to assume that the adversary has the secret key sk_n corresponding to pk_n of the last component encryption. The adversary decrypts c^* with sk_n, obtains $c_{n-1} = \mathsf{Dec}_n(sk_n, c^*)$, and encrypts c_{n-1} again to obtain a new ciphertext $c' = \mathsf{Enc}_n(pk_n, c_{n-1})$. Because Enc_n is an IND-CCA scheme, $c^* \neq c'$ holds with overwhelming probability. Then, the adversary can ask c' to the decryption oracle (of the multiple encryption) and receive a message m', which is equal to the message of the challenge c^*. This means that the multiple encryption on the above sequential natural construction is insecure in the IND-ME-CCA model. We call this kind of attack a *decrypt-then-encrypt-again attack*.

Sequential Constructions. Zhang et al. propose a sequential construction of multiple encryption secure in the IND-ME-CCA model. The brief description of the scheme is as follows[1]. Let m be a message to be encrypted. Set $c_0 = m$, compute $c_{i,1} = \mathsf{Enc}_i(pk_i, r_i; H_i(m, r_1, \ldots, r_n))$, $c_{i,2} = G_i(r_i) \oplus c_{i-1}$, and $c_i = (c_{i,1}, c_{i,2})$ repeatedly for $i = 1$ to n, and then, obtain the ciphertext $c = c_n$.

In their construction, all randomness $r_1, \ldots, r_n$ are generated before all component encryptions, and besides the immediately previous output ciphertext, all the randomness and the message are used in each component encryption. If an adversary decrypts c and encrypts the decrypted message again with different randomness, the resulting ciphertext would be invalid and could not be accepted by the decryption oracle. Thus the multiple encryption prevents the decrypt-then-encrypt-again attack.

Parallel Constructions. Zhang et al. have presented a generic *parallel* construction of IND-ME-CCA secure multiple encryption, in which all message pieces split by the all-or-nothing transform [26,6] are encrypted in parallel [30]. Dodis and Katz have presented a framework of parallel construction allowing a threshold transform, which is an extension of all-or-nothing transforms, and proposed the stronger definitions (MCCA and sMCCA) for multiple encryption based on the parallel construction [12]. They used secret sharing schemes [27,4] as threshold transforms, and presented generic parallel constructions of MCCA or sMCCA secure multiple encryptions in the standard model. Cui, Kobara, and Imai [8]

---

[1] As the sequential construction in [30] is incomplete, we obtained the correct description from one of the authors [29].

presented an efficient construction of parallel multiple encryptions that achieves the security defined in [12] in the random oracle model.

While an adversary in the IND-ME-CCA (=wMCCA) model can obtain only plaintext recovered from the whole ciphertext of multiple encryption, the MCCA model enables an adversary to access a decryption oracle that outputs the split pieces of the plaintext (not the entire plaintext) as the answer to the whole ciphertext. The sMCCA model also enables an adversary to access a decryption oracle that outputs the split pieces of the plaintext as the answer to a piece of ciphertext. Note that while IND-ME-CCA and wMCCA models are applicable to both parallel and sequential constructions, MCCA and sMCCA models are defined only for parallel construction.

1.2   Our Contributions

As shown above, parallel constructions of multiple encryption have been thoroughly studied. In contrast, little research on sequential constructions of multiple encryption has been done except for insecurity in sequential natural constructions. However, sequential constructions have several advantages over parallel constructions.

In sequential construction, the task of creating a ciphertext may be securely distributed to multiple entities even connected via insecure communication channels because only encrypted data are transmitted through the channels. To capture this security in future, this paper treats, as the first step, a weaker situation where the adversary is passive in encryption phase. Encryption and decryption in sequential construction require less memory than those in parallel construction. Zhang et al. [30] discussed that sequential construction has an advantage in ciphertext size over parallel construction. It is thus important to investigate sequential multiple encryptions and to clarify security conditions.

This paper addresses the question of whether all sequential "natural constructions" of multiple encryptions are insecure; we answer in the negative. We present a secure sequential multiple encryption, which, to our best knowledge, is the first concrete scheme that has the same features as the schemes by sequential natural constructions.

The constructed multiple encryptions achieve the IND-ME-CCA security in the random oracle model [2] when all the component encryptions of the multiple encryptions are IND-CPA secure [18]. We define a stronger security notion for sequential multiple encryptions, IND-sME-CCA, similar to sMCCA for parallel constructions, and prove that an IND-sME-CCA secure multiple encryption is possible in the random oracle model if all the component encryptions are IND-CCA secure.

Sequential Multiple Encryption. We call a multiple encryption *sequential* if it satisfies the following properties:

1. The encryption operation of the multiple encryption is composed of a chain of sequential encryption operations.

2. Each output of a component encryption algorithm becomes the input for the next component encryption algorithm.
3. The output of the last component encryption algorithm is the ciphertext of the multiple encryption.
4. Each encryption depends only on the immediately previous output ciphertext, but not the other ciphertexts or randomness generated in the previous component encryptions.

The *sequential multiple encryption* captures the widely shared features of sequential "natural construction". We note that the sequential construction proposed in [30] does not satisfy the fourth property because the component encryptions require not only the immediately previous ciphertext but also the message and all the random strings used in all component encryption algorithms.

Sequential multiple encryption offers a practical advantage in implementation: computation of each encryption can be sequentially performed. Because each component encryption needs only the immediately previous ciphertext but not the other data used in the other component encryptions, each computation requires less memory than the other constructions. Thus, the sequential multiple encryptions are suitable for devices with low memory, such as smart cards and cellular phones.

Bound Randomness Construction. We briefly present a construction of sequential multiple encryption that we discuss later in detail. Let $(\mathsf{Enc}_1, \ldots, \mathsf{Enc}_n)$ be a sequence of encryption algorithms and H_i $(2 \le i \le n)$ be hash functions. The multiple encryption for a plaintext m is performed as follows: $c_1 = \mathsf{Enc}_1(pk_1, m; r)$, $c_i = \mathsf{Enc}_i(pk_i, c_{i-1}; H_i(c_{i-1}))$ $(2 \le i \le n)$, $c = c_n$, and c is the resulting ciphertext. Note that randomness in each component encryption except the first one is bound with a hash value.

In the random oracle model, this multiple encryption is proved to be IND-ME-CCA secure or to satisfy stronger security described below when the first component encryption Enc_1 is secure with regard to IND-CCA and the other component encryptions Enc_i are secure with regard to IND-CPA, and H_i $(2 \le i \le n)$ are considered as random oracles. Note that using the Fujisaki-Okamoto conversion [16], this secure multiple encryption also can be constructed only from IND-CPA secure encryptions.

In our construction, each component encryption is computed in a deterministic manner except for the first one; namely, the computations do not use internal randomness. Because computation of each encryption other than the first is deterministic, it is clear that the decrypt-then-encrypt-again attack cannot be applied to our constructed scheme.

Stronger Security Model. Dodis and Katz introduced the security definitions for multiple encryption, the MCCA security and the sMCCA security, which are stronger than the IND-ME-CCA (=wMCCA) security [12]. The MCCA security and the sMCCA security are defined only for parallel constructions.

We introduce another security definition for sequential multiple encryption, the IND-sME-CCA security, which is stronger than the IND-ME-CCA security and is similar to the sMCCA security for parallel construction. Moreover, we show that the constructed sequential multiple encryption is IND-sME-CCA secure if all the building block encryptions are IND-CCA secure.

The sMCCA and IND-sME-CCA models are similar in that adversaries in both models are allowed to access decryption oracles of component encryptions. However they are different in constraints of input to the decryption oracles.

Organization. **Section 2** explains public key encryption and multiple encryption, and defines their security notions. **Section 3** describes a construction of sequential multiple encryption schemes, and discusses the security of constructed schemes. Comparison and Conclusion are provided in **Section 4** and **5**. **Appendix** gives detailed proofs regarding the security results discussed in **Section 3**.

2   Definitions

Throughout this paper, all security definitions are considered in *the random oracle model* [2], in which a random oracle is a random function that anyone can access. We regard hash functions used in our encryption schemes as random oracles.

Public Key Encryption and Multiple Encryption. We review the definitions of public key encryption and multiple encryption.

Let k be a security parameter. A *public key encryption scheme* $\mathcal{E}_i = (\mathsf{KGen}_i, \mathsf{Enc}_i, \mathsf{Dec}_i)$ consists of three probabilistic polynomial-time algorithms. The key generation algorithm KGen_i takes as input 1^k and outputs a public key pk_i and a secret key sk_i. The encryption algorithm Enc_i takes as inputs pk_i, a message $m \in \{0,1\}^*$ and a random string $r \in \{0,1\}^{rlen_i(k)}$ and outputs a ciphertext $c \in \{0,1\}^*$ where $rlen_i(k)$ is a polynomial in k that gives the upper bound of the length of a random string used in the encryption algorithm Enc_i. The decryption algorithm Dec_i takes as inputs sk_i and a ciphertext $c' \in \{0,1\}^*$ and outputs the plaintext $m' \in \{0,1\}^*$ or $\perp$. These algorithms are assumed to satisfy $\mathsf{Dec}_i(sk_i, \mathsf{Enc}_i(pk_i, m; r)) = m$ for any m and r and for any output (pk_i, sk_i) of KGen_i.

Let $\mathcal{E}_1, \ldots, \mathcal{E}_n$ be public key encryption schemes ($n \geq 2$). A *multiple encryption scheme* $\mathcal{ME}^n = (\mathsf{MKGen}^n, \mathsf{MEnc}^n, \mathsf{MDec}^n)$ composed of $\mathcal{E}_1, \ldots, \mathcal{E}_n$ is specified by three probabilistic polynomial-time algorithms. The key generation algorithm MKGen^n takes as input 1^k, runs $(pk_i, sk_i) = \mathsf{KGen}_i(1^k)$ for all i, and outputs a public key $PK^n = (pk_1, \ldots, pk_n)$ and a secret key $SK^n = (sk_1, \ldots, sk_n)$. The encryption algorithm MEnc^n takes as inputs PK^n, a message $m \in \{0,1\}^*$, and a random string $r \in \{0,1\}^{rlen^n(k)}$ and outputs a ciphertext $c \in \{0,1\}^*$ using $\mathsf{Enc}_1, \ldots, \mathsf{Enc}_n$ where $rlen^n(k)$ is a polynomial in k that gives the upper bound of the length of a random string used in the encryption algorithm MEnc^n. The decryption algorithm MDec^n takes as inputs SK^n and a ciphertext c' and outputs the plaintext m' using $\mathsf{Dec}_1, \ldots, \mathsf{Dec}_n$. These algorithms are assumed to satisfy $\mathsf{MDec}^n(SK^n, \mathsf{MEnc}^n(PK^n, m; r)) = m$ for any m and r and for any output (PK^n, SK^n) of MKGen^n.

In most schemes of public key encryption and multiple encryption, Dec_i and MDec^n are deterministic.

IND-CCA Security and IND-CPA Security. We review the standard security notions for public key encryption: the IND-CCA [25] security and the IND-CPA [18] security.

We define the IND-CCA security for public key encryption scheme $\mathcal{E}_i$ based on the following IND-CCA game between a challenger and adversary $A := (A_1, A_2)$. **[Setup]:** The challenger takes a security parameter k, runs the key generation algorithm $(pk_i, sk_i) = \mathsf{KGen}_i(1^k)$, and gives the adversary A_1 the public key pk_i. **[Phase 1]:** The adversary A_1 issues hash queries σ and decryption queries c' to hash oracles $H_j(\cdot)$ and a decryption oracle $\mathsf{Dec}_i(sk_i, \cdot)$ to obtain the hash value $H_j(\sigma)$ and the decrypted message $\mathsf{Dec}_i(sk_i, c')$, respectively. It finally gives the challenger two messages x_0, x_1, such that $|x_0| = |x_1|$, and some information s. **[Challenge]:** The challenger randomly chooses $r \in \{0,1\}^{rlen_i(k)}$ and $b \in \{0,1\}$ and gives the adversary A_2 a challenge ciphertext $c^* = \mathsf{Enc}_i(pk_i, x_b; r)$ with s. **[Phase 2]:** The adversary A_2 issues hash queries and decryption queries as same as **Phase 1**. The decryption queries must differ from the challenge ciphertext c^*. **[Guess]:** The adversary A_2 finally outputs a guess $b' \in \{0,1\}$ and wins the game if $b = b'$.

We define the advantage of A in the IND-CCA game as $Adv_{\mathcal{E}_i, A}^{ind\text{-}cca}(1^k) = 2\Pr[b = b'] - 1$, where the probability is taken over the random coins used by the challenger and A. We say that the public key encryption $\mathcal{E}_i$ is IND-CCA *secure* if, for any probabilistic polynomial-time adversary A, the function $Adv_{\mathcal{E}_i, A}^{ind\text{-}cca}(1^k)$ is negligible in k.

The IND-CPA security is a weaker security notion than the IND-CCA. IND-CPA security for $\mathcal{E}_i$ is based on the same game as IND-CCA security except for, in **Phase 1** and **Phase 2**, where the adversary A cannot access the decryption oracle. We define the advantage of A in the IND-CPA game as $Adv_{\mathcal{E}_i, A}^{ind\text{-}cpa}(1^k) = 2\Pr[b = b'] - 1$, where the probability is taken over the random coins used by the challenger and A. We say that the public key encryption $\mathcal{E}_i$ is IND-CPA *secure* if, for any probabilistic polynomial-time adversary A, the function $Adv_{\mathcal{E}_i, A}^{ind\text{-}cpa}(1^k)$ is negligible in k.

Security for Multiple Encryption. We review IND-ME-CCA security, which is security for multiple encryption [30] and can be applied to *sequential* multiple encryption. In addition, we introduce IND-sME-CCA security, which is an extension of IND-ME-CCA security and can be defined *only* for sequential, not parallel, multiple encryptions. A similar security notion for parallel multiple encryptions is defined as sMCCA in [12], and both sMCCA and IND-sME-CCA adversaries are allowed to access a decryption oracle for a component encryption $\mathcal{E}_\ell$. However they are different in restriction of input to the decryption oracles. In the sM-CCA model, the adversary is not allowed to ask the ciphertext shares generated by splitting the challenge ciphertext. On the other hand, in the IND-sME-CCA model, the adversary is not allowed to ask the intermediate ciphertexts that appear while sequentially decrypting the challenge ciphertext by each component decryption.

We describe the definition of the IND-ME-CCA security for multiple encryption scheme $\mathcal{ME}^n$ based on the following IND-ME-CCA game between a challenger and adversary $A := (A_1, A_2)$. [**Setup**]: The challenger takes a security parameter k, runs the key generation algorithm $(PK^n, SK^n) = \text{MKGen}^n(1^k)$, chooses $\ell \in \{1, \ldots, n\}$, sets $SK_\ell^n = (sk_1, \ldots, sk_{\ell-1}, sk_{\ell+1}, \ldots, sk_n)$ and gives the adversary A_1 the public key PK^n and SK_ℓ^n. [**Phase 1**]: The adversary A_1 issues hash queries σ and decryption queries c' to hash oracles $H_j(\cdot)$ and a decryption oracle $\text{MDec}^n(SK^n, \cdot)$ to obtain the hash value $H_j(\sigma)$ and the decrypted message $\text{MDec}^n(SK^n, c')$, respectively. It finally gives the challenger two messages x_0, x_1, such that $|x_0| = |x_1|$, and some information s. [**Challenge**]: The challenger randomly chooses $r \in \{0, 1\}^{rlen^n(k)}$ and $b \in \{0, 1\}$ and gives the adversary A_2 a challenge ciphertext $c^* = \text{MEnc}^n(PK^n, x_b; r)$ with s. [**Phase 2**]: The adversary A_2 issues hash queries and decryption queries. The decryption queries must differ from the challenge ciphertext c^*. [**Guess**]: The adversary A_2 finally outputs a guess $b' \in \{0, 1\}$ and wins the game if $b = b'$.

We define the advantage of A in the IND-ME-CCA game as $Adv_{\mathcal{ME}^n, A}^{ind\text{-}me\text{-}cca}(1^k) = 2\Pr[b = b'] - 1$, where the probability is taken over the random coins used by the challenger and A. We say that the multiple encryption $\mathcal{ME}^n$ is IND-ME-CCA *secure* if, for any probabilistic polynomial-time adversary A, the function $Adv_{\mathcal{ME}^n, A}^{ind\text{-}me\text{-}cca}(1^k)$ is negligible in k.

In this paper, we use this definition of the IND-ME-CCA security, which is slightly different from the original one in [30]. In latter, the adversary can adaptively request the secret keys but in former, the adversary in our definition is given the secret keys statically. However, it is easy to prove that they are *polynomially equivalent*.

We define IND-sME-CCA security for sequential multiple encryption scheme $\mathcal{ME}^n$ constructed from public key encryptions $\mathcal{E}_1, \ldots, \mathcal{E}_n$. Note that in sequential multiple encryption, a valid ciphertext c' can be decrypted in such a way that we set $c_n' = c'$, repeat decrypting $c_{i-1}' = \text{Dec}_i(sk_i, c_i')$ for $i = n$ to 1, and output c_0' as the decrypted message. Using the ℓ-th element c_ℓ' in the sequence $(c_1', \ldots, c_n')$, we define a constraint of inputs for the decryption oracle.

The IND-sME-CCA security for $\mathcal{ME}^n$ is based on the same game as IND-ME-CCA except that the adversary can access another decryption oracle $\text{Dec}_\ell(sk_\ell, \cdot)$ in addition to $\text{MDec}^n(SK^n, \cdot)$ and is not allowed to ask to the decryption oracle the ℓ-th ciphertext that appears in the above sequential decryption of the challenge ciphertext c^*. Namely, the decryption oracle $\text{Dec}_\ell(sk_\ell, \cdot)$ does not accept as input the ℓ-th element c_ℓ^* in the sequence $(c_1^*, \ldots, c_n^*)$ such that $c_n^* = c^*$ and $c_{i-1}^* = \text{Dec}_i(sk_i, c_i^*)$ $(2 \leq i \leq n)$.

We define the advantage of A in the IND-sME-CCA game as $Adv_{\mathcal{ME}^n, A}^{ind\text{-}sme\text{-}cca}(1^k) = 2\Pr[b = b'] - 1$, where the probability is taken over the random coins used by the challenger and A. We say that the multiple encryption $\mathcal{ME}^n$ is IND-sME-CCA *secure* if, for any probabilistic polynomial-time adversary A, the function $Adv_{\mathcal{ME}^n, A}^{ind\text{-}sme\text{-}cca}(1^k)$ is negligible in k.

γ-Uniformity. In [16,17], Fujisaki and Okamoto propose γ-uniformity for evaluating the probability that a ciphertext is generated in the probabilistic encryption of a fixed message. It is known that any IND-CPA secure encryption has negligible γ-uniformity in the security parameter k.

Let k be the security parameter and $\mathcal{E} = (\mathsf{KGen}, \mathsf{Enc}, \mathsf{Dec})$ be a public key encryption. For given $x \in \{0,1\}^*$, $y \in \{0,1\}^*$ and pk generated by $\mathsf{KGen}(1^k)$, let $g(x,y)$ denote $\Pr[r \leftarrow \{0,1\}^{rlen(k)} : y = \mathsf{Enc}(pk, x; r)]$. We say Enc is γ-uniform if $g(x,y) \leq \gamma$ for any $x \in \{0,1\}^*$, $y \in \{0,1\}^*$ and $pk \leftarrow \mathsf{KGen}(1^k)$.

Hash Function. A hash function H_h is a polynomial-time algorithm that is parameterized by an index $h \in \{0,1\}^{ilen(k)}$ and on arbitrary long input m outputs $rlen(k)$ bit string $H_h(m)$, where $ilen(k)$ and $rlen(k)$ are polynomials in k.

3   Security of Sequential Multiple Encryption

3.1   Bound Randomness Construction

We describe a construction of our sequential multiple encryption scheme.

Let $\mathcal{E}_i = (\mathsf{KGen}_i, \mathsf{Enc}_i, \mathsf{Dec}_i)$ $(1 \leq i \leq n, \ n \geq 2)$ be public key encryption schemes and H_{h_i} $(2 \leq i \leq n)$ be hash functions from $\{0,1\}^*$ to $\{0,1\}^{rlen_i(k)}$ where h_i is the index of the hash function taken from $\{0,1\}^{ilen_i(k)}$, $ilen_i(k)$ is the length of the index, and $rlen_i(k)$ is the upper bound of the length of a random string used in the encryption algorithm Enc_i. We assume that the public key encryption schemes and the hash functions accept arbitrary length input. This assumption is reasonable because almost practical public key encryptions can be transformed into the ones allowing arbitrary length input, e.g., by using the Fujisaki-Okamoto integration.

Our multiple encryption scheme $\mathcal{ME}^n = (\mathsf{MKGen}^n, \mathsf{MEnc}^n, \mathsf{MDec}^n)$ is constructed as follows:

Key-Generation MKGen^n: The input is 1^k (k is a security parameter).
Step 1: Run KGen_i on input 1^k to generate (pk_i, sk_i) from $i = 1$ to n.
Step 2: Randomly choose indices $h_i \in \{0,1\}^{ilen_i(k)}$ from $i = 2$ to n and set $H^n = (h_2, \ldots, h_n)$.
Step 3: Set $PK^n = (pk_1, \ldots, pk_n)$ and $SK^n = (sk_1, \ldots, sk_n)$.
Step 4: Return (PK^n, SK^n, H^n).
The public key of multiple encryption $\mathcal{ME}^n$ is PK^n, and the secret key is SK^n.

Encryption MEnc^n: The inputs are a public key PK^n, indices of hash functions H^n, a message m, and a random string $r \in \{0,1\}^{rlen^n(k)}$ where $rlen^n(k) = rlen_1(k)$.
Step 1: Parse PK^n as $(pk_1, \ldots, pk_n)$ and H^n as $(h_2, \ldots, h_n)$.
Step 2: Run $\mathsf{Enc}_1(pk_1, m; r)$ to obtain c_1.
Step 3: Run, from $i = 2$ to n, each encryption algorithm as $c_i = \mathsf{Enc}_i(pk_i, c_{i-1}; H_{h_i}(c_{i-1}))$.
Step 4: Set $c = c_n$ and return c.
The output ciphertext of m is c.

Decryption MDec^n: The inputs are a secret key SK^n, indices of hash functions H^n and a ciphertext c'.

Step 1: Parse SK^n as $(sk_1, \ldots, sk_n)$ and H^n as $(h_2, \ldots, h_n)$.

Step 2: Set $c'_n = c'$.

Step 3: Repeat the following from $i = n$ to 2:

Run each decryption algorithm as $c'_{i-1} = \mathsf{Dec}_i(sk_i, c'_i)$, check whether $c'_i = \mathsf{Enc}_i(pk_i, c'_{i-1}; H_{h_i}(c'_{i-1}))$ holds, and if it does not hold, return $\perp$ and stop.

Step 4: Run the final decryption $m' = \mathsf{Dec}_1(sk_1, c'_1)$ and return m'.

The decrypted message is m'.

This completes the description of the sequential multiple encryption scheme.

3.2 IND-ME-CCA Security

The following theorem holds for the security of our multiple encryption scheme $\mathcal{ME}^n$. Assume that n ($n \geq 2$) is fixed and independent of the security parameter k.

Theorem 1. *Suppose that $\mathcal{E}_1$ is an* IND-CCA *secure public key encryption and that $\mathcal{E}_2, \ldots, \mathcal{E}_n$ are* IND-CPA *secure public key encryptions ($n \geq 2$). Then, $\mathcal{ME}^n$ by the bound randomness construction is an* IND-ME-CCA *secure multiple encryption in the random oracle model.*

The multiple encryption $\mathcal{ME}^n$ is constructed by combining IND-CCA secure encryption $\mathcal{E}_1$ and IND-CPA secure encryptions $\mathcal{E}_2, \ldots, \mathcal{E}_n$. To prove that this $\mathcal{ME}^n$ is IND-ME-CCA secure, we need to show that $Adv_{\mathcal{ME}^n, A}^{ind\text{-}me\text{-}cca}(1^k)$ is negligible, i.e., we have to show that the success probability of any IND-ME-CCA adversary given $n-1$ secret keys $SK_\ell^n = (sk_1, \ldots, sk_{\ell-1}, sk_{\ell+1}, \ldots, sk_n)$ is negligible for any $\ell \in \{1, \ldots, n\}$.

We assume for contradiction that there is a probabilistic polynomial-time adversary with non-negligible success probability in the IND-ME-CCA game given secret keys $SK_\ell^n = (sk_1, \ldots, sk_{\ell-1}, sk_{\ell+1}, \ldots, sk_n)$. Then we show that (1) when $SK_1^n = (sk_2, \ldots, sk_n)$ (not including sk_1) is given, such an IND-ME-CCA adversary is straightforwardly reduced to an adversary for $\mathcal{E}_1$ in the IND-CCA game (shown in **Lemma 1**) and (2) when $SK_\ell^n = (sk_1, \ldots, sk_{\ell-1}, sk_{\ell+1}, \ldots, sk_n)$ (including sk_1) is given, such an IND-ME-CCA adversary is reduced to an adversary for $\mathcal{E}_\ell$ in the IND-CPA game (shown in **Lemma 2**), where $2 \leq \ell \leq n$. The existence of constructed adversaries for $\mathcal{E}_1$ and $\mathcal{E}_\ell$ ($2 \leq \ell \leq n$) contradicts the assumptions. Thus the following **Lemma 1** and **Lemma 2** prove **Theorem 1**.

Lemma 1. *Let k be the security parameter. Suppose that $A := (A_1, A_2)$ is a probabilistic polynomial-time* IND-ME-CCA *adversary for the constructed $\mathcal{ME}^n$ with non-negligible success probability in k and is given $n-1$ secret keys $SK_1^n = (sk_2, \ldots, sk_n)$. Then there is a probabilistic polynomial-time* IND-CCA *adversary $B := (B_1, B_2)$ for $\mathcal{E}_1$ with non-negligible success probability in k.*

This lemma shows that the IND-ME-CCA security, in which an IND-ME-CCA adversary is given the secret keys $SK_1^n = (sk_2, \ldots, sk_n)$, is reduced to the IND-CCA security of $\mathcal{E}_1$.

We describe the strategy to prove the lemma below. We give the full proof in **Appendix**.

Sketch of Proof.
We construct an IND-CCA adversary $B := (B_1, B_2)$, which uses A as a blackbox and also simulates the challenger for the adversary A in the IND-ME-CCA game and the random oracles $H_{h_2}, \ldots, H_{h_n}$ in the following straightforward way.

Given pk_1, the adversary B generates pairs (pk_i, sk_i) of public and secret keys of $\mathcal{E}_i$ for all i $(2 \leq i \leq n)$ and feeds $PK^n = (pk_1, \ldots, pk_n)$, $SK_1^n = (sk_2, \ldots, sk_n)$, and $H^n = (h_2, \ldots, h_n)$ to the IND-ME-CCA adversary A. B responds to H_{h_i} queries while maintaining hash tables in the usual manner. For $MDec^n$ queries, B decrypts the ciphertext with the decryption algorithms for $\mathcal{E}_i$ with sk_i and checks the validity for all i $(2 \leq i \leq n)$. If the ciphertext passes all the checks, B queries the decrypted value to the outer decryption oracle of $\mathcal{E}_1$, receives an answer, and sends it to A. The challenge message pair (x_0, x_1) received from A is output to the challenger as is. Given the challenge ciphertext, B encrypts it with $(pk_2, \ldots, pk_n)$ and feeds the final ciphertext to A. The guessed value b' received from A is output as is.

This simulation succeeds with overwhelming probability.

Lemma 2. *Let k be the security parameter. Suppose that $A := (A_1, A_2)$ is a probabilistic polynomial-time IND-ME-CCA adversary for the constructed $\mathcal{ME}^n$ with non-negligible success probability in k and is given $n-1$ secret keys $SK_\ell^n = (sk_1, \ldots, sk_{\ell-1}, sk_{\ell+1}, \ldots, sk_n)$ $(2 \leq \ell \leq n)$. Suppose that $\mathsf{Enc}_1, \ldots, \mathsf{Enc}_n$ are γ-uniform with γ negligible in k. Then there is a probabilistic polynomial-time IND-CPA adversary $C := (C_1, C_2)$ for $\mathcal{E}_\ell$ with non-negligible success probability in k.*

This lemma shows that the IND-ME-CCA security, in which an IND-ME-CCA adversary is given the secret keys $SK_\ell^n = (sk_1, \ldots, sk_{\ell-1}, sk_{\ell+1}, \ldots, sk_n)$ $(2 \leq \ell \leq n)$, is reduced to the IND-CPA security of $\mathcal{E}_\ell$.

We describe the strategy to prove the lemma below. We give a detailed proof in **Appendix**.

Sketch of Proof.
We construct an IND-CPA adversary $C := (C_1, C_2)$ for $\mathcal{E}_\ell$ $(2 \leq \ell \leq n)$, which uses A as a blackbox and also simulates the challenger for the adversary A in the IND-ME-CCA game and the random oracles $H_{h_2}, \ldots, H_{h_n}$ as follows.

Given pk_ℓ, the adversary C generates pairs (pk_i, sk_i) of public and secret keys of $\mathcal{E}_i$ for all i $(1 \leq i \leq n, i \neq \ell)$ and feeds $PK^n = (pk_1, \ldots, pk_n)$, $SK_\ell^n = (sk_1, \ldots, sk_{\ell-1}, sk_{\ell+1}, \ldots, sk_n)$, and $H^n = (h_2, \ldots, h_n)$ to the IND-ME-CCA adversary A. C responds to H_{h_i} queries while maintaining the hash tables $\mathcal{T}_i$. C receives a message pair (x_0, x_1) from A, creates two messages (x_0', x_1') as $c_{b,0} = x_b$, $c_{b,1} = \mathsf{Enc}_1(pk_1, c_{b,0}; r_b)$, $c_{b,j} = \mathsf{Enc}_j(pk_j, c_{b,j-1}; H_{h_j}(c_{b,j-1}))$ $(2 \leq j \leq \ell - 1)$ and $x_b' = c_{b,\ell-1}$ $(b \in \{0, 1\})$ where r_0, r_1 are randomly and uniformly taken from

$\{0,1\}^{rlen_1(k)}$, and gives (x'_0, x'_1) to the challenger in the IND-CPA game for $\mathcal{E}_\ell$. C obtains a challenge ciphertext c^*_ℓ and creates a challenge ciphertext c^*_n in the IND-ME-CCA game as $c^*_j = \mathsf{Enc}_j(pk_j, c^*_{j-1}; H_{h_j}(c^*_{j-1}))$ $(\ell + 1 \leq j \leq n)$. The guessed value b' received from A is output as is.

Since we cannot use any outer decryption oracle, we simulate the MDec^n oracle utilizing the hash tables $\mathcal{T}_i$ as follows. Suppose that A makes an MDec^n query c'_n. If there are $(c'_{n-1}, \tau_n) \in \mathcal{T}_n$ such that $c'_n = \mathsf{Enc}_n(pk_n, c'_{n-1}; \tau_n)$, and $(c'_{i-1}, \tau_i) \in \mathcal{T}_i$ such that $c'_i = \mathsf{Enc}_i(pk_i, c'_{i-1}; \tau_i)$ for all i $(2 \leq i \leq n - 1)$, C decrypts c'_1 with sk_1 and returns the obtained message to A. C can correctly answer and the simulation succeeds. If there are no such entries in the hash tables, C returns $\perp$.

We cannot correctly answer for the H_{h_ℓ} query x'_b because we do not know the hash value $H_{h_\ell}(x'_b)$ used in the generation of the challenge ciphertext. However, when A makes an H_{h_ℓ} query x'_b coincident with x'_0 or x'_1, the simulator C stops the simulation and judges the corresponding b to be equal to a random coin flipped by the challenger. Intuitively speaking, this judgment is correct with high probability because, if the challenger chooses b, there is no chance that A knows $x'_{\bar{b}}$, where $\bar{b}$ denotes the bit complement of b. Note that this comes from the γ-uniformity of $\mathcal{E}_1$.

3.3   IND-ME-CCA Security from IND-CCA Encryptions

Using the Fujisaki-Okamoto conversion [16], an IND-CPA secure public key encryption scheme $\mathsf{Enc}(pk, m; r)$ can be converted to an IND-CCA secure public key encryption scheme $\overline{\mathsf{Enc}}(pk, m; r) = \mathsf{Enc}(pk, m\|r; H(m\|r))$, where $x\|y$ denotes the concatenation of x and y.

Combining **Theorem 1** and the result for the Fujisaki-Okamoto conversion, we obtain the following theorem, which implies that IND-ME-CCA secure multiple encryption can be constructed only from IND-CCA encryptions.

Theorem 2. *We can construct an* IND-ME-CCA *secure multiple encryption in the random oracle model from* n IND-CPA *secure public key encryptions* $(n \geq 2)$.

3.4   IND-sME-CCA Security

We here discuss the IND-sME-CCA security of our multiple encryption scheme.

The following theorem holds for the security of our multiple encryption $\mathcal{ME}^n$ for $n \geq 2$.

Theorem 3. *Suppose that* $\mathcal{E}_1, \ldots, \mathcal{E}_n$ *are* IND-CCA *secure public key encryptions* $(n \geq 2)$. *Then, the constructed* $\mathcal{ME}^n$ *is* IND-sME-CCA *secure in the random oracle model.*

Sketch of Proof.

The proof in the case that an adversary is given secret keys $(sk_2, \ldots, sk_n)$ and allowed to access the decryption oracle $\mathsf{Dec}_1(sk_1, \cdot)$ is essentially the same as in **Lemma 1**. The IND-sME-CCA security also is reduced to the IND-CCA security of $\mathcal{E}_1$.

We discuss the other case, in which an adversary is given secret keys $(sk_1, \ldots, sk_{\ell-1}, sk_{\ell+1}, \ldots, sk_n)$ $(2 \leq \ell \leq n)$ and allowed to access the decryption oracle $\mathsf{Dec}_\ell(sk_\ell, \cdot)$. The simulation in this case is almost the same as in the above case except for the hash oracle simulation in **Phase 2**. The simulator creates two messages (x_0', x_1') as $c_{b,0} = x_b$, $c_{b,1} = \mathsf{Enc}_1(pk_1, c_{b,0}; r_b)$, $c_{b,j} = \mathsf{Enc}_j(pk_j, c_{b,j-1};$ $H_{h_i}(c_{b,j-1}))$ $(2 \leq j \leq \ell - 1)$, and $x_b' = c_{b,\ell-1}$ $(b \in \{0,1\})$ from two messages (x_0, x_1) that the IND-sME-CCA adversary outputs where r_0, r_1 are randomly and uniformly taken from $\{0,1\}^{rlen_1(k)}$, gives (x_0', x_1') to the challenger in the IND-CCA game for $\mathcal{E}_\ell$ to obtain a challenge ciphertext c_ℓ^*, and creates a challenge ciphertext c_n^* in the IND-sME-CCA game from c_ℓ^* as $c_j^* = \mathsf{Enc}_j(pk_j, c_{j-1}^*;$ $H_{h_j}(c_{j-1}^*))$ $(\ell + 1 \leq j \leq n)$. In the simulation of the hash oracles, if the simulator receives $x_{b'}'$ for some $b' \in \{0,1\}$, it stops simulation and outputs the corresponding b'. This simulation succeeds with overwhelming probability because if the challenger chooses $b \in \{0,1\}$, the adversary has no chance to know $x_{\bar{b}}'$, where $\bar{b}$ denotes the bit complement of b. Note that this comes from the γ-uniformity of $\mathcal{E}_1$.

We will give the detailed proof in the full version of the paper.

3.5   Properties

We discuss several properties of our sequential multiple encryption.

Sequential Multiple Encryption. We show that the constructed multiple encryption schemes are *sequential*. It is obvious to satisfy the first, second and third properties of sequential multiple encryption in **Section 1.2**. The fourth property is also satisfied because each component encryption is computed as $c_i = \mathsf{Enc}_i(pk_i, c_{i-1}; H_{h_i}(c_{i-1}))$; namely, the inputs to Enc_i are computed from only the immediately previous output ciphertext c_{i-1} and the public key pk_i. Note that each component encryption algorithm except the first one does not need a random string.

Security of Component Encryptions. An IND-ME-CCA secure multiple encryption can be constructed from one IND-CCA secure encryption scheme and the other IND-CPA secure encryption schemes. The first component encryption is the most important since only it is required to use randomness and to be the most secure (IND-CCA secure). In contrast, the other components are allowed to be less secure (IND-CPA secure) than the first one, and, surprisingly, do not use randomness in contrast to the first component.

Note that, by using the Fujisaki-Okamoto conversion [16], IND-ME-CCA secure multiple encryption and IND-sME-CCA secure multiple encryption can be constructed only from IND-CPA secure encryption schemes.

Similarity to Fujisaki-Okamoto Conversion. The proposed construction uses a method that converts a probabilistic encryption $\mathsf{Enc}(pk, m; r)$ to a deterministic encryption $\overline{\mathsf{Enc}}(pk, m) = \mathsf{Enc}(pk, m; H(m))$ using a hash function H

in such a way that a message m is encrypted with the hash value $H(m)$ of m instead of random r. We see that each component encryption except the first one has the form $\overline{\mathsf{Enc}}_i(pk_i, m) = \mathsf{Enc}_i(pk_i, m; H_i(m))$, in which randomness is bound with the hash value $H_i(m)$ of m. We note that a variant of the conversion can be seen in the Fujisaki-Okamoto conversion [16], which converts the IND-CPA secure scheme $\mathsf{Enc}(pk, m; r)$ to the IND-CCA secure $\overline{\mathsf{Enc}}(pk, m; r) = \mathsf{Enc}(pk, m||r; H(m||r))$, where $x||y$ denotes the concatenation of x and y.

Drawback. In our multiple encryption scheme, while only the first component encryption utilizes randomness, the other components encryptions runs in deterministic manner. Because the output c_i of the i-th component encryption is uniquely determined by the input c_{i-1} and anyone can compute c_i from c_{i-1}, anyone can link c_i and c_{i-1}. Thus our multiple encryption scheme cannot provide *unlinkability* required for the MIX-net [7,19,21,20].

Usage of Single Algorithm. In the construction of $\mathcal{ME}^n$, $n-1$ hash functions H_{h_i} are parameterized by $n-1$ indices h_i. We can construct the hash functions H_{h_i} from a single hash function H by letting $H_{h_i}(x)$ be $H(h_i||x)$. This minimizes the number of random oracles.

Regarding to component encryption schemes, they all may be distinct. When a single encryption is used for all component encryptions, we can use a notation $E_{pk_i}(x; r)$ instead of $\mathsf{E}_i(pk_i, x; r)$.

4   Comparison

4.1   Efficiency Comparison

Here, we discuss efficiency of the constructed multiple encryption scheme.

Let $\mathcal{E}_i$ be a public key encryption scheme and c_i denote a ciphertext $c_i = \mathcal{E}_i(pk, m)$ of a message m. The overhead OH_i of $\mathcal{E}_i$ is defined as $\mathrm{OH}_i = |c_i| - |m|$ where $|m|$ is the plaintext size and $|c_i|$ is the ciphertext size. In most practical public key encryptions, OH_i depends only on the security parameter k. Here we assume that all overheads OH_i of $\mathcal{E}_i$ is equal to OH.

In parallel multiple encryption, a plaintext m is processed as follows. m is split into multiple pieces $(m_1, \ldots, m_n)$, m_i's are encrypted in parallel, $c_i = \mathcal{E}_i(pk_i, m_i)$, and $c = (c_1, \ldots, c_n)$ is an output ciphertext. When the splitting algorithm is the all-or-nothing transform [26,6], then $\sum |m_i| \geq |m|$ holds. Since $|c| = \sum |c_i|$ and $|c_i| = \mathrm{OH} + |m_i|$, the ciphertext size of parallel multiple encryption $|c|$ is $n\mathrm{OH} + \sum |m_i|$ and is not over $n\mathrm{OH} + |m|$. When the splitting algorithm is usual secret sharing, the ciphertext size of parallel multiple encryption $|c|$ is less than or equal to $n\mathrm{OH} + n|m|$.

In our sequential multiple encryptions, a plaintext m is processed as follows: $c_0 = m$, $c_i = \mathsf{Enc}_i(pk_i, c_{i-1})$ ($1 \leq i \leq n$), and $c = c_n$. Since $|c_i| = \mathrm{OH} + |c_{i-1}|$, the ciphertext size of our sequential multiple encryption $|c|$ is $n\mathrm{OH} + |m|$. Consequently our sequential multiple encryption is comparable with or more efficient than parallel multiple encryption in ciphertext size when OH_i depends only on the security parameter k but does not depend on $|m|$.

In addition, each component encryption can be processed only with the previous output ciphertext as our multiple encryption is sequential. This feature is suitable for devices with low memory, such as smart cards and cellular phones.

4.2   Comparison with Onion-Security

Onion routing is a technology for building anonymous channels. In an onion routing system, a sender encrypts a message with multiple public keys of onion routers to generate a ciphertext "onion". Each onion router decrypts an incoming message, and sends the message part in the decrypted message to the next onion router indicated in the destination part. A security of Onion routing (Onion-security) is formally defined by Camenisch and Lysyanskaya [5].

The ciphertext "onion" of Onion routing can be thought as a ciphertext of multiple encryption. Both in the security definitions of Onion routing and multiple encryption, adversaries can access to oracles that decrypt ciphertexts.

However, since the aim of Onion routing and multiple encryption are quite different, the goals of their security definitions also differ. The onion-security captures a property that an adversary cannot correctly guess relations between incoming messages and outgoing messages at onion routers, and a property that each onion router cannot knows the whole route path of any onion. On the other hand, these properties are not required in security definitions of multiple encryption (IND-ME-CCA and IND-sME-CCA).

5   Conclusion

We constructed a sequential multiple encryption scheme, which has an advantage in that it requires small memory space for computing encryption and decryption. We also proved the security of the constructed multiple encryption.

The constructed multiple encryption, with the first component encryption IND-CCA secure and the other IND-CPA secure, was proved IND-ME-CCA secure. This result is similar to the security of "cascade cipher" in that both say the security of the whole scheme strongly depends on that of the first component.

We presented the extended security, IND-sME-CCA, of multiple encryption and showed that our sequential multiple encryption, with all component encryptions IND-CCA secure, is IND-sME-CCA secure.

The proposed construction can be seen as a "natural" construction combining one IND-CCA secure encryption and the other IND-CPA or IND-CCA secure encryptions, and the constructed multiple encryption is proved IND-ME-CCA or IND-sME-CCA secure. Therefore, we are able to say that a sequential "natural" multiple encryption is still secure.

As a future work, we have a security proof without random oracles. A generalization of the bound randomness construction such as $\mathsf{Enc}_i(pk_i, f(x); g(x))$, where f is a functions and g is a pseudorandom deterministic functions, may help us to prove the security of the resulting multiple encryption scheme in the standard mode.

Acknowledgments. We would like to thank Rui Zhang, Kazukuni Kobara and Yang Cui for their valuable information. We also would like to thank anonymous referees for their comments that helped us to improve this paper.

References

1. Aiello, W., Bellare, M., Di Crescenzo, G., Venkatesan, R.: Security Amplification by Composition: The Case of Doubly-Iterated, Ideal Ciphers. In: Krawczyk, H. (ed.) CRYPTO 1998. LNCS, vol. 1462, pp. 390–407. Springer, Heidelberg (1998)
2. Bellare, M., Rogaway, P.: Random Oracles are Practical: A Paradigm for Designing Efficient Protocols. In: 1st ACM Conference on Computer and Communications Security, pp. 62–73. ACM, New York (1993)
3. Bellare, M., Desai, A., Pointcheval, D., Rogaway, P.: Relations among Notions of Security for Public-Key Encryption Schemes. In: Krawczyk, H. (ed.) CRYPTO 1998. LNCS, vol. 1462, pp. 26–45. Springer, Heidelberg (1998)
4. Blakley, G.R.: Safeguarding Cryptographic Keys. In: 1979 AFIPS National Computer Conference, vol. 48, pp. 313–317. AFIPS Press (1979)
5. Camenisch, J., Lysyanskaya, A.: A Formal Treatment of Onion Routing. In: Shoup, V. (ed.) CRYPTO 2005. LNCS, vol. 3621, pp. 169–187. Springer, Heidelberg (2005)
6. Canetti, R., Dodis, Y., Halevi, S., Kushilevitz, E., Sahai, A.: Exposure-Resilient Functions and All-Or-Nothing Transforms. In: Preneel, B. (ed.) EUROCRYPT 2000. LNCS, vol. 1807, pp. 453–469. Springer, Heidelberg (2000)
7. Chaum, D.: Untraceable Electronic Mail, Return Addresses, and Digital Pseudonyms. ACM Commun. 24(2), 84–88 (1981)
8. Cui, Y., Kobara, K., Imai, H.: Efficient Multiple Encryption from OW-PCA Primitives. In: 2006 International Symposium on Information Theory and its Applications, SITA, pp. 502–506 (2006)
9. Desmedt, Y.: Society and Group Oriented Cryptography: A New Concept. In: Pomerance, C. (ed.) CRYPTO 1987. LNCS, vol. 293, pp. 120–127. Springer, Heidelberg (1988)
10. Desmedt, Y., Frankel, Y.: Threshold Cryptosystems. In: Brassard, G. (ed.) CRYPTO 1989. LNCS, vol. 435, pp. 307–315. Springer, Heidelberg (1990)
11. Dodis, Y., Fazio, N.: Public Key Broadcast Encryption for Stateless Receivers. In: Feigenbaum, J. (ed.) DRM 2002. LNCS, vol. 2696, pp. 61–80. Springer, Heidelberg (2003)
12. Dodis, Y., Katz, J.: Chosen-Ciphertext Security of Multiple Encryption. In: Kilian, J. (ed.) TCC 2005. LNCS, vol. 3378, pp. 188–209. Springer, Heidelberg (2005)
13. Dodis, Y., Katz, J., Xu, S., Yung, M.: Key-Insulated Public Key Cryptosystems. In: Knudsen, L.R. (ed.) EUROCRYPT 2002. LNCS, vol. 2332, pp. 65–82. Springer, Heidelberg (2002)
14. Even, S., Goldreich, O.: On the Power of Cascade Ciphers. ACM Trans. Computer Systems 3(2), 108–116 (1985)
15. Frankel, Y.: A Practical Protocol for Large Group Oriented Networks. In: Quisquater, J.-J., Vandewalle, J. (eds.) EUROCRYPT 1989. LNCS, vol. 434, pp. 56–61. Springer, Heidelberg (1990)
16. Fujisaki, E., Okamoto, T.: How to Enhance the Security of Public-Key Encryption at Minimum Cost. In: Imai, H., Zheng, Y. (eds.) PKC 1999. LNCS, vol. 1560, pp. 53–68. Springer, Heidelberg (1999)

17. Fujisaki, E., Okamoto, T.: Secure Integration of Asymmetric and Symmetric Encryption Schemes. In: Wiener, M.J. (ed.) CRYPTO 1999. LNCS, vol. 1666, pp. 537–554. Springer, Heidelberg (1999)
18. Goldwasser, S., Micali, S.: Probabilistic Encryption. J. Comput. Syst. Sci. 28(2), 270–299 (1984)
19. Goldschlag, D., Reed, M., Syverson, P.: Onion Routing. ACM Commun. 42(2), 39–41 (1999)
20. Golle, P., Zhong, S., Boneh, D., Jakobsson, M., Juels, A.: Optimistic Mixing for Exit-Polls. In: Zheng, Y. (ed.) ASIACRYPT 2002. LNCS, vol. 2501, pp. 451–465. Springer, Heidelberg (2002)
21. Jakobsson, M., Juels, A.: An Optimally Robust Hybrid Mix Network. In: 20th Annual ACM Symposium on Principles of Distributed Computing, pp. 284–292. ACM, New York (2001)
22. Maurer, U.M., Massey, J.L.: Cascade Ciphers: The Importance of Being First. J. Cryptology 6(1), 55–61 (1993)
23. Merkle, R.C., Hellman, M.E.: On the Security of Multiple Encryption. ACM Commun. 24(7), 465–467 (1981)
24. Naor, M., Yung, M.: Public-Key Cryptosystems Provably Secure against Chosen Ciphertext Attacks. In: 22nd Annual ACM Symposium on Theory of Computing, pp. 427–437. ACM, New York (1990)
25. Rackoff, C., Simon, D.: Non-Interactive Zero-Knowledge Proof of Knowledge and Chosen Ciphertext Attack. In: Feigenbaum, J. (ed.) CRYPTO 1991. LNCS, vol. 576, pp. 433–444. Springer, Heidelberg (1992)
26. Rivest, R.L.: All-Or-Nothing Encryption and the Package Transform. In: Biham, E. (ed.) FSE 1997. LNCS, vol. 1267, pp. 210–218. Springer, Heidelberg (1997)
27. Shamir, A.: How to Share a Secret. ACM Commun. 22(11), 612–613 (1979)
28. Shannon, C.E.: Communication Theory of Secrecy Systems. Bell Systems Technical Journal 28, 656–715 (1949)
29. Zhang, R.: *private communication*, August 5 (2009)
30. Zhang, R., Hanaoka, G., Shikata, J., Imai, H.: On the Security of Multiple Encryption or CCA-security+CCA-security=CCA-security? In: Bao, F., Deng, R.H., Zhou, J. (eds.) PKC 2004. LNCS, vol. 2947, pp. 360–374. Springer, Heidelberg (2004)

A   Proofs of Lemmas

A.1   Proof of Lemma 1

We prove **Lemma 1**. We construct an IND-CCA adversary $B := (B_1, B_2)$, which uses A as a blackbox and also simulates the challenger for the adversary A in the IND-ME-CCA game and the random oracles H_{h_i} as follows.

Setup: The challenger in the IND-CCA game for $\mathcal{E}_1$ runs $\mathsf{KGen}_1(1^k)$, obtains (pk_1, sk_1), and inputs pk_1 to B_1. Then B_1 runs $\mathsf{KGen}_i(1^k)$ to generate (pk_i, sk_i) for i $(2 \leq i \leq n)$, randomly choose $h_i \in \{0,1\}^{ilen_i(k)}$ for i $(2 \leq i \leq n)$, and gives the public key $PK^n = (pk_1, \ldots, pk_n)$ of $\mathcal{ME}^n$, secret keys $SK_1^n = (sk_2, \ldots, sk_n)$ of $\mathcal{E}_2, \ldots, \mathcal{E}_n$, and indices of hash functions $H^n = (h_2, \ldots, h_n)$ to an adversary A in the IND-ME-CCA game for $\mathcal{ME}^n$.

H_{h_i} **queries:** B simulates the random oracle H_{h_i} maintaining a query-answer list T_i as follows. At the start of simulation, the list T_i is set as empty. For a query σ from A, if σ has not been asked, B chooses τ randomly and uniformly from $\{0,1\}^{rlen_i(k)}$, answers τ to A_1, and puts (σ,τ) on T_i. Otherwise, B answers τ' such that $\sigma = \sigma'$ and $(\sigma',\tau') \in T_i$.

MDec^n queries: When A_1 makes an MDec^n query c'_n, B decrypts $c'_{i-1} = \mathsf{Dec}_i(sk_i, c'_i)$ with sk_i for all i $(2 \le i \le n)$. If $c'_i = \mathsf{Enc}_i(pk_i, c'_{i-1}; H_{h_i}(c'_{i-1}))$ does not hold for some i, B answers A_1 with $\perp$. If all checks pass, B sends c'_1 to the outer decryption oracle of $\mathcal{E}_1$, receives an answer m', and answers A_1 with m'.

Challenge: At the end of **Phase 1**, A_1 outputs two messages to be challenged (x_0, x_1). Then B_1 passes (x_0, x_1) to the challenger for the IND-CCA game for $\mathcal{E}_1$. The challenger randomly chooses $b \in \{0,1\}$ and $r \in \{0,1\}^{rlen_1(k)}$, creates a challenge ciphertext $c_1^* = \mathsf{Enc}_1(pk_1, x_b; r)$ from two received messages (x_0, x_1), and inputs c_1^* as a challenge to adversary B_2.

At the start of **Phase 2**, after receiving c_1^*, B_2 creates c_n^* as $c_i^* = \mathsf{Enc}_i(pk_i, c_{i-1}^*; H_{h_i}(c_{i-1}^*))$ $(2 \le i \le n)$. Then, B_2 inputs c_n^* to A_2 as a challenge ciphertext of $\mathcal{ME}^n$.

Guess: At the end of **Phase 2**, A_2 outputs b' as an answer to the challenge in the IND-ME-CCA game. Then, B_2 receives b' and outputs it as B_2's answer to the challenge in the IND-CCA game.

The challenge ciphertext c_1^* in the IND-CCA game is transformed into the challenge ciphertext c_n^* in the IND-ME-CCA game through the deterministic processes $c_i^* = \mathsf{Enc}_i(pk_i, c_{i-1}^*; H_{h_i}(c_{i-1}^*))$ $(2 \le i \le n)$. In the IND-ME-CCA game, the MDec^n query c'_n must differ from the challenge c_n^*. If c'_n is a valid ciphertext, it has to satisfy $c'_i = \mathsf{Enc}_i(pk_i, c'_{i-1}; H_{h_i}(c'_{i-1}))$ for some $(c'_1, \ldots, c'_{n-1})$. Then we see that c'_1 is not equal to c_1^*. Therefore the decrypted c'_1 satisfies the constraint in the IND-CCA game and can be sent to the outer decryption oracle of $\mathcal{E}_1$ in the IND-CCA game.

The simulation is perfect and then the success probability of B is equal to that of A. B also runs in polynomial time since A does. We have thus proved **Lemma 1**. $\qquad\qquad\square$

A.2   Proof of Lemma 2

We now prove **Lemma 2**.

We construct an IND-CPA adversary $C := (C_1, C_2)$, which uses A as a black-box and also simulates the challenger for the adversary A in the IND-ME-CCA game and the random oracles H_{h_i} as follows.

Setup: The challenger in the IND-CPA game for $\mathcal{E}_\ell$ $(2 \le \ell \le n)$ runs $\mathsf{KGen}_\ell(1^k)$, obtains (pk_ℓ, sk_ℓ), and inputs pk_ℓ to C_1. Then C_1 runs $\mathsf{KGen}_i(1^k)$ to generate (pk_i, sk_i) for i $(1 \le i \le n,\ i \ne \ell)$, randomly choose $h_i \in \{0,1\}^{ilen_i(k)}$ for i $(2 \le i \le n)$, and gives the public key $PK^n = (pk_1, \ldots, pk_n)$ of $\mathcal{ME}^n$, secret keys

$SK_\ell^n = (sk_1, \ldots, sk_{\ell-1}, sk_{\ell+1}, \ldots, sk_n)$ of $\mathcal{E}_1, \ldots, \mathcal{E}_{\ell-1}, \mathcal{E}_{\ell+1}, \ldots, \mathcal{E}_n$, and indices of hash functions $H^n = (h_2, \ldots, h_n)$ to an adversary A in the IND-ME-CCA game for $\mathcal{ME}^n$.

MDec^n queries: When A makes an MDec^n query c'_n, C searches the hash lists $\mathcal{T}_i$ to find entries $(c'_{i-1}, \tau_i) \in \mathcal{T}_i$ such that $c'_i = \mathsf{Enc}_i(pk_i, c'_{i-1}; \tau_i)$ for all i ($2 \le i \le n$). If such entries is found, C decrypts $m' = \mathsf{Dec}_1(sk_1, c'_1)$ and answers A with m'. Otherwise, C answers A with $\bot$.

Challenge: At the end of **Phase 1**, A_1 outputs two messages (x_0, x_1) to be challenged in the IND-ME-CPA game. C_1 creates two messages (x'_0, x'_1) as $c_{b,0} = x_b$, $c_{b,1} = \mathsf{Enc}_1(pk_1, c_{b,0}; r_b)$, $c_{b,j} = \mathsf{Enc}_j(pk_j, c_{b,j-1}; H_{h_j}(c_{b,j-1}))$ ($2 \le j \le \ell - 1$) and $x'_b = c_{b,\ell-1}$ ($b \in \{0,1\}$), and passes (x'_0, x'_1) to the challenger in the IND-CPA game for $\mathcal{E}_\ell$ where r_0, r_1 are randomly and uniformly taken from $\{0,1\}^{rlen_1(k)}$.

The challenger receives two messages (x'_0, x'_1), randomly chooses $b \in \{0,1\}$ and $r' \in \{0,1\}^{rlen_2(k)}$, creates a challenge ciphertext $c^*_\ell = \mathsf{Enc}_\ell(pk_\ell, x'_b; r')$ of $\mathcal{E}_\ell$ in the IND-CPA game, and returns c^*_ℓ to C_2.

At the start of **Phase 2**, C_2 receives c^*_ℓ, creates a challenge ciphertext c^*_n in the IND-ME-CCA game as $c^*_j = \mathsf{Enc}_j(pk_j, c^*_{j-1}; H_{h_j}(c^*_{j-1}))$ ($\ell + 1 \le j \le n$) and inputs c^*_n to A_2 as a challenge ciphertext of $\mathcal{ME}^n$ in the IND-ME-CCA game.

H_{h_i} queries: C simulates the random oracles H_{h_i} maintaining a query-answer list $\mathcal{T}_i$ as B in **Lemma 1** except when A makes an H_{h_ℓ} query equal to the above x'_0 or x'_1. If A makes such an H_{h_ℓ} query equal to x'_b for some $b \in \{0,1\}$, C stops A and, without going to **Guess**, outputs the corresponding b as an answer in the IND-CPA game.

Guess: At the end of **Phase 2**, A_2 outputs b' as an answer to the challenge in the IND-ME-CCA game. Then C_2 outputs b' as C_2's answer to the challenge in the IND-CPA game.

MDec^n Oracle Simulation. We use the assumption that the encryptions Enc_i's are γ-uniform and γ is negligible in k.

Suppose that A makes an MDec^n query c'_n. If there are entries $(c'_{i-1}, \tau_i) \in \mathcal{T}_i$ such that $c'_i = \mathsf{Enc}_i(pk_i, c'_{i-1}; \tau_i)$ for all i ($2 \le i \le n$), C gives a correct answer and the simulation succeeds. If there are no such hash table entries, C is designed to answer $\bot$.

Let t be the maximum number of i such that there is not any entry $(c'_{i-1}, \tau_i) \in \mathcal{T}_i$ such that $c'_i = \mathsf{Enc}_i(pk_i, c'_{i-1}; \tau_i)$. If C's response of $\bot$ is not correct, c'_n must be a valid ciphertext and then must have the form $c'_t = \mathsf{Enc}_t(pk_t, u; H_{h_t}(u))$ of some u. However, such u has not been recorded in $\mathcal{T}_t$; namely, the value of $H_{h_t}(u)$ has not been determined yet. Thus, since a value $H_{h_t}(u)$ is randomly determined after the query u, the probability that $c'_t = \mathsf{Enc}_t(pk_t, u; H_{h_t}(u))$ holds is less than or equal to γ (the γ-uniformity of Enc_t). Hence, the probability that C's MDec^n oracle simulation is not correct is not over γ and thus is negligible.

This construction of the MDec^n oracle is similar to the knowledge extractor for the plaintext-aware encryption generated by the Fujisaki-Okamoto conversion [16]. In fact, the knowledge extractor is constructed using the property that it is infeasible to construct a valid ciphertext without knowing the corresponding plaintext and its hash value.

H_{h_ℓ} Oracle Simulation. We use the assumption that the encryption Enc_1 is γ-uniform and γ is negligible in k.

In the simulation of the random oracle H_{h_ℓ}, if A makes an H_{h_ℓ} query x'_b coincident with x'_0 or x'_1, the simulator C judges the corresponding b to be equal to the random coin flipped by the challenger. Intuitively, this judgment is correct with high probability because, if the challenger chooses b, there is no chance that A knows $x'_{\bar{b}}$ where $\bar{b}$ denotes the bit complement of b.

Suppose that the challenger in the IND-CPA game chooses b. A certainly knows $x_{\bar{b}}$ since A itself creates (x_0, x_1). However, A does not see $x'_{\bar{b}}$ created from $c_{b,1} = \mathsf{Enc}_1(pk_1, x_{\bar{b}}; r_{\bar{b}})$, and thus A's view is independent of the random $r_{\bar{b}}$ for generating $x'_{\bar{b}}$. Furthermore, since Enc_1 is γ-uniform and γ is negligible, any ciphertext of a fixed message appears only with negligible probability. Therefore the probability of A guessing $x'_{\bar{b}}$ and asking it as an H_{h_ℓ} query is negligible.

This simulation of the H_{h_ℓ} oracle is also similar to the random oracle simulation in the security proof of the Fujisaki-Okamoto conversion, which converts the IND-CPA secure encryption $\mathsf{Enc}(pk, m; r)$ to the IND-CCA secure $\mathsf{Enc}(pk, m\|r; H(m\|r))$. In the random oracle simulation, if a hash query $x_b\|r_b$ is received, the simulator judges the corresponding b to be equal to the random coin in the challenge. Since the simulator's view is independent of $r_{\bar{b}}$, the probability that $x_{\bar{b}}\|r_{\bar{b}}$ is asked as a hash query is negligible.

The detailed estimates of probabilities will appear in the full version of the paper.

Mediated Traceable Anonymous Encryption

Malika Izabachène[1], David Pointcheval[2], and Damien Vergnaud[2]

[1] Université de Versailles, 45 avenue des États-Unis, 78035 Versailles, France
[2] École normale supérieure-CNRS-INRIA, 45 rue d'Ulm, 75320 Paris Cedex 05, France

Abstract. The notion of *key privacy* for asymmetric encryption schemes was formally defined by Bellare, Boldyreva, Desai and Pointcheval in 2001: it states that an eavesdropper in possession of a ciphertext is not able to tell which specific key, out of a set of known public keys, is the one under which the ciphertext was created. Since anonymity can be misused by dishonest users, some situations could require a tracing authority capable of revoking key privacy when illegal behavior is detected. Prior works on *traceable anonymous encryption* miss a critical point: an encryption scheme may produce a covert channel which malicious users can use to communicate illegally using ciphertexts that trace back to nobody or, even worse, to some honest user.

In this paper, we examine subliminal channels in the context of traceable anonymous encryption and we introduce a new primitive termed *mediated traceable anonymous encryption* that provides confidentiality and anonymity while preventing malicious users to embed subliminal messages in ciphertexts. In our model, all ciphertexts pass through a *mediator* (or possibly several successive mediators) and our goal is to design protocols where the absence of covert channels is guaranteed as long as the mediator is honest, while semantic security and key privacy hold even if the mediator is dishonest.

We give security definitions for this new primitive and constructions meeting the formalized requirements. Our generic construction is fairly efficient, with ciphertexts that have logarithmic size in the number of group members, while preventing collusions. The security analysis requires classical complexity assumptions in the standard model.

1 Introduction

Motivation. The notion of *key privacy* for (asymmetric) encryption schemes was formally defined by Bellare, Boldyreva, Desai and Pointcheval [2]. The motivation for this security notion is anonymous communication, where eavesdroppers are prevented from learning the identities of the communicating parties, and namely the target recipient of a ciphertext. Since people are more and more concerned about all their actions being linkable to each other (or even worse, to their identity), key privacy is obviously a very attractive notion from the user's point of view. However, some organizations and governments are concerned about how anonymity can be abused by criminals, and the key privacy property can potentially be dangerous against public safety. Therefore anonymity revocation should be available when illegal behavior is detected, as provided by group signatures [8].

M. Abdalla and P.S.L.M. Barreto (Eds.): LATINCRYPT 2010, LNCS 6212, pp. 40–60, 2010.

This motivates the notion of *traceable anonymous encryption* in which an adversary cannot determine which user's public key has been used to generate the ciphertext that it sees while a trusted third party (given some trapdoor information) is able to revoke anonymity and thus to trace back to the intended recipient. Some work dealt with such a property, but to the best of our knowledge, a critical point was missed: an encryption scheme may contain a steganographic channel (or a covert channel) which malicious users can use to communicate illegally using ciphertexts that trace back to nobody, or even worse to some honest user. More precisely, still using the official scheme, it may be possible to encrypt a message to a user A (the official target recipient for the tracing authority) so that the randomness is used for transmitting some extra information to a user B, that would not be traced as a possible recipient.

For instance, in 2007, Kiayias, Tsiounis and Yung [17] presented *group encryption*, a cryptographic primitive which can be seen as the encryption analogue of a *group signature* [8]. It provides semantic security, anonymity and a way for the *group manager* to revoke anonymity of ciphertexts. However, it makes use of zero-knowledge proofs to determine whether a ciphertext is valid or not. As a consequence, an invalid ciphertext can be used to transmit some information. Above all, subliminal channels (available in the randomness) can be exploited to send some information in addition to a clean message, or even to frame an honest user.

Let us consider the following example: in 2000, Sako [20] proposed a novel approach to achieve bid secrecy in auction protocols. Her technique consists in expressing each bid as an encryption of a *known* message, with a key corresponding to the value of the bid. Therefore, what needs to be hidden in the ciphertext is not the message, but the key itself; the use of traceable anonymous encryption (e.g. group encryption) seems very promising for such applications (the bid itself being identified using the tracing procedure). However, one major concern in auction protocols is the problem of collusion between bidders and it is highly desirable to prevent bidders from engaging in such collaborative bidding strategies. Unfortunately, no known construction of traceable anonymous encryption is free of covert channels and the main purpose of the present paper is precisely to propose a new cryptographic primitive addressing this issue. Recently, Abdalla, Bellare and Neven [1] introduced the concept of *robust encryption* in which it is hard to produce a ciphertext that is valid for two different users. They showed that if the anonymous encryption scheme used in Sako's protocol is not robust then the auction protocol does not achieve *fairness* (*i.e.* a cheating bidder can place a bid that he can open later to an arbitrary value). The primitive we propose in this paper permits to achieve simultaneously fairness and collusion-freeness in Sako's protocol.

Contributions. We introduce a new primitive which we call *mediated traceable anonymous encryption* and that provides confidentiality and anonymity while preventing malicious users to embed subliminal messages in ciphertexts, which would allow to transmit information to a recipient that would remain perfectly anonymous, or even worse to frame an honest user.

In order to provide semantic security, asymmetric encryption has to be probabilistic, and randomness can be used as a covert channel. We will thus have to avoid the users to control the randomness used in the ciphertext. We introduce a *mediator* that is not provided with any secret information, but whose role —similar to the warden model introduced by Simmons [21]— is to add more randomness to each ciphertext so that any hidden message is smothered. It is worth noting that —contrary to the group encryption primitive— the mediator only checks the syntactic validity of the ciphertext but it does not verify the soundness of any complex proof. We can even iterate the re-randomization process by several *mediators* to be sure that any ciphertext has been re-randomized at least once.

Another point for traceability, it is impossible to get it without assuming that users (recipients) are registered in the system, since registered users only can be traced. As for (dynamic) group signatures [3], we also introduce a trusted party termed the *issuer* that registers new users. One may wonder whether the issuer has to be trusted or not with respect to the semantic security property, since he might know all the decryption keys of the system: one does not really care about that since one can use its own additional encryption scheme to encrypt the plaintext before re-encrypting using our traceable encryption primitive.

It is relatively easy to design an anonymous encryption scheme that provides traceability or the absence of steganographic channel, but the task is more challenging if we want to achieve both simultaneously. Indeed, the existence of the tracing procedure implies that a ciphertext contains (at least implicitly) some information about the recipient, but this value can be used to transmit one bit of covert information. For instance, a Boneh-Franklin [6] identity-based variant of the ElGamal universal re-encryption scheme [14] cannot be used to achieve covert-free traceable anonymous encryption, since it turns out that the re-randomization preserves some predicates that can be used to transfer some information.

In this paper we propose a formal definition of *Mediated Traceable Anonymous Encryption Scheme* ($\mathcal{M}$TAES) and a security model capturing the (seemingly contradictory) following security notions:

1. *subliminal channel freeness:* After re-randomization, no information at all can be extracted from a ciphertext that does not trace back to a user registered to the issuer. We thus assume that the communication network guarantees that any ciphertext will go through a mediator. In practice, we can assume that in a specific network, all the routers implement the mediator re-randomization, which enforces the use of our scheme by all the users, and which guarantees that all the ciphertexts are re-randomized at least once. Then, packets that do not follow the encryption rules are made random;

2. The tracing trapdoor information does not allow the *opener* to violate the semantic security of ciphertexts nor to issue valid decryption keys (*i.e.* to play the role of the issuer);

3. The ciphertext remains confidential and anonymous even with respect to the mediator (*i.e.* we only rely on the mediator to guarantee the absence of

covert channels in ciphertexts, by properly re-randomizing the ciphertexts), or any collusion of users and the mediator. As already said, multiple re-randomizations are even possible by various independent mediators.

We propose efficient constructions of $\mathcal{M}$TAES in the standard model, which security relies on DDH-like assumptions. The first one does not split the roles of the issuer and the opener and can be applied in any group where the DDH assumption holds while the second scheme makes use of (Type-2 or Type-3 [12]) pairing-friendly groups, with asymmetric pairing where the XDH and the (asymmetric[1]) DBDH assumptions hold, to separate the two authority roles (and then achieve the second above property). The two first schemes lead to ciphertexts that are linear in the number of registered users. This is not very practical, but they are fully-collusion secure. Using public collusion-secure codes (e.g. IPP codes [15]), better efficiency can be achieved: we provide a generic construction, with (almost) logarithmic ciphertexts.

2   Security Model

2.1   Syntactic Definitions

In this section, we give the formal definitions of our new concept: the *Mediated Traceable Anonymous Encryption*, which involves two trusted authorities, an *issuer* for adding new members to the system, and an *opener* for revoking anonymity; and a non-trusted authority, the *mediator* that systematically re-randomizes all its inputs, without any private information. There even can be several independent mediators. Mediators will be assumed to be honest (but possibly curious, and thus definitely not trusted): for the subliminal-channel freeness security notion we will define later, it is clear that in case of collusion with the last mediator, this strong security level cannot be achieved.

Definition 1 (Mediated Traceable Anonymous Encryption Schemes).
*A $\mathcal{M}$TAES is a tuple of efficient algorithms or protocols (*GSetup, Join, Encrypt, ReRand, Decrypt, Trace, Judge*) such that:*

- GSetup(λ) $\rightarrow$ (mpk, msk, sk$_O$)*: This is a randomized algorithm run by a trusted party that, on input of a security parameter λ, produces three keys consisting of a group public key* mpk*, a manager's secret key* msk *and an opening key* sk$_O$*; It also generates a data structure $\mathcal{L}$, called a registration list which is initially empty.*
- Join(*id*, mpk, msk) $\rightarrow$ (pk$_{id}$, sk$_{id}$) *takes a bit-string identity* id*, the group public key* mpk *and the manager's secret key* msk *as inputs. It outputs a pair of member keys* (pk$_{id}$, sk$_{id}$) *associated to* id*, and updates the registration list $\mathcal{L}$ with the pair* (id, pk$_{id}$)*.*
- Encrypt(mpk, pk$_{id}$, m) $\rightarrow$ C *takes as input the group public key* mpk*, a user public key* pk$_{id}$ *and a message* m*, and outputs a pre-ciphertext* C*.*

---

[1] The asymmetric DBDH assumption [10] reduces to the classical DBDH assumption [6] in the case of Type-3 bilinear structures [12].

- ReRand(mpk, C) → C' *takes as input the group public key* mpk *and a pre-ciphertext* C, *and outputs a randomized ciphertext* C'. *Note that it may be applied again on a re-randomized ciphertext.*
- Decrypt(mpk, sk$_{id}$, C) → m *takes as input the group public key* mpk, *a member secret key* sk$_{id}$, *as well as a* ciphertext C, *then it outputs a message, or* ⊥ *in case of invalid ciphertext.*
- Trace(mpk, sk$_O$, $\mathcal{L}$, C) → (id, Π): *This is a deterministic algorithm that on input the group public key* mpk, *the opening key* sk$_O$, *the registration list* $\mathcal{L}$ *and a ciphertext* C, *outputs a user identity* id *(equivalently, the public key* pk*) and a proof* Π *for the judge, otherwise* ⊥ *in case of failure.*
- Judge(mpk, $\mathcal{L}$, C, id, Π): *This is a deterministic algorithm that on input the group public key* mpk, *the registration list* $\mathcal{L}$, *a ciphertext in* C, *a user identity* id *and a proof* Π *checks whether* Π *indeed proves that* id *is the target recipient of the ciphertext* C *(or one of them, in case of collusion).*

Random tapes have been omitted in the notations, for the sake of clarity, but in some cases, they may be explicit: Join(id, mpk, msk; r), Encrypt(mpk, pk$_{id}$, m; r) *or* ReRand(mpk, C; r).

2.2 Security Notions

In any group protocol, where each user owns a private key, collusions have to be dealt with: a collusion of users may help them to manufacture a new pair (pk, sk) associated to no user, or to an honest user. The latter case should be unlikely. The tracing algorithm should thus (in case the ciphertext "contains" some information) either output the identity of the target receiver if this is a well-formed ciphertext to this user, or the identity of one of the colluders who helped to manufacture the target public key. If the pre-ciphertext does not target any public key (nobody can be traced) then we want the re-randomization to cancel any information. Collusion will be modeled by corrupt queries, that will provide the secret keys of the corrupted users to the adversary. Then, from all these keys, the adversary will be allowed to do anything it wants to transfer some information, in an untraceable way.

As a consequence, in the security model we provide the adversary with two oracles: a restricted Join oracle (denoted Join*) that just outputs the public keys, and a Corrupt oracle that outputs the user's secret key. Corrupted users are then registered in the *corruption list* $\mathcal{C}$, initially empty:

- Join*(id) → pk$_{id}$, takes as input an identity, and then runs Join(id, mpk, msk) to get (pk$_{id}$, sk$_{id}$), but outputs pk$_{id}$ only. Note that the registration list $\mathcal{L}$ has been updated by the Join procedure;
- Corrupt(id) → sk$_{id}$ takes as input a registered identity, and outputs the secret key corresponding to pk$_{id}$. It also updates the corruption list $\mathcal{C}$ with (id, pk$_{id}$).

We then denote by $\mathcal{LU}$ the list of registered identities, and by $\mathcal{CU}$ the list of the corrupted users, whereas $\mathcal{L}$ and $\mathcal{C}$ also contain keys. We additionally define a predicate Traceable($\mathcal{U}$, C), where $\mathcal{U}$ is a list of identities and C a pre-ciphertext, that tests whether the tracing algorithm, run on the global parameters and a re-randomization of C, outputs an identity id $\in \mathcal{U}$ with a convincing proof Π.

Since we are dealing with anonymity and traceability, we should address full-anonymity and chosen-ciphertext security, providing access to the opening oracle and to the decryption oracle respectively. But due to the inherent malleability of such a re-randomizable encryption scheme, some constraints are required. This is discussed in the full version [16]. In this section, we focus on the basic anonymity (without opening oracle access) and the chosen-plaintext security (without decryption oracle access).

In order to avoid the opener to frame an honest user, as the recipient of a ciphertext that is not aimed to him, we can rely on an additional Public Key Infrastructure (PKI), in which each user owns a pair of public/private key, and signs $\mathsf{pk}_{\mathsf{id}}$ when it receives the associated secret key $\mathsf{sk}_{\mathsf{id}}$. This signature can be added to the registration list $\mathcal{L}$. We thus trust the link between an identity id and the associated public key. And we will use both in an indifferentiable way.

SEMANTIC SECURITY. The main security notion for an encryption scheme is of course the semantic security of the ciphertext (after re-randomization), that is formalized by the indistinguishability of the two experiments (for $b = 0, 1$) presented Fig. 1(a). As usual, the adversary has to guess which plaintext has been encrypted in the challenge ciphertext. Note that we provide the opening key sk_O to the adversary, which models a collusion with the opener. We restrict the adversary to use a valid (registered) public key, since otherwise no one can decrypt the ciphertext. We are thus only interested in the privacy of real ciphertexts. We define the advantage of $\mathcal{A}$ in breaking the semantic security by its advantage:

$$\mathsf{Adv}^{\mathsf{rind}}_{\mathcal{M}\mathrm{TAES},\mathcal{A}}(\lambda) = \Pr[\mathsf{Exp}^{\mathsf{rind}-1}_{\mathcal{M}\mathrm{TAES},\mathcal{A}}(\lambda) = 1] - \Pr[\mathsf{Exp}^{\mathsf{rind}-0}_{\mathcal{M}\mathrm{TAES},\mathcal{A}}(\lambda) = 1].$$

We define a weaker version, where the opening key is not provided to the adversary (which is useful when we cannot separate the issuing and opening/tracing roles, as in our first simple scheme below):

$$\mathsf{Adv}^{\mathsf{weak-rind}}_{\mathcal{M}\mathrm{TAES},\mathcal{A}}(\lambda) = \Pr[\mathsf{Exp}^{\mathsf{weak-rind}-1}_{\mathcal{M}\mathrm{TAES},\mathcal{A}}(\lambda) = 1] - \Pr[\mathsf{Exp}^{\mathsf{weak-rind}-0}_{\mathcal{M}\mathrm{TAES},\mathcal{A}}(\lambda) = 1].$$

As usual, we denote by $\mathsf{Adv}_{\mathcal{M}\mathrm{TAES}}(\lambda, \tau)$, for any security notion, the best advantage any adversary can get within time τ. Furthermore, we may add an extra parameter ω, when we limit the number of Corrupt-queries. This will be useful for schemes that are not fully-collusion secure (see Section 4), but ω-resilient: the security holds if the number of Corrupt-queries is less than ω.

The above security notion is about the re-randomized ciphertext, and thus for an adversary that does not have access to the pre-ciphertext before re-randomization. We thus define the same security notion about the pre-ciphertext characterized by the advantages $\mathsf{Adv}^{\mathsf{ind}}_{\mathcal{M}\mathrm{TAES},\mathcal{A}}(\lambda)$ and $\mathsf{Adv}^{\mathsf{weak-ind}}_{\mathcal{M}\mathrm{TAES},\mathcal{A}}(\lambda)$. It is clear that the latter security notions (before re-randomization) are stronger than the former, and address the case where the mediator is honest but curious:

Theorem 2. *For any scheme* $\mathcal{M}\mathrm{TAES}$ *and any time bound* τ,

$$\mathsf{Adv}^{\mathsf{rind}}_{\mathcal{M}\mathrm{TAES}}(\lambda, \tau) \leq \mathsf{Adv}^{\mathsf{ind}}_{\mathcal{M}\mathrm{TAES}}(\lambda, \tau) \qquad \mathsf{Adv}^{\mathsf{weak-rind}}_{\mathcal{M}\mathrm{TAES}}(\lambda, \tau) \leq \mathsf{Adv}^{\mathsf{weak-ind}}_{\mathcal{M}\mathrm{TAES}}(\lambda, \tau)$$

Experiment $\mathsf{Exp}^{\mathsf{rind}-b}_{\mathcal{MTAES},\mathcal{A}}(\lambda)$
  $(\mathsf{mpk},\mathsf{msk},\mathsf{sk}_O) \leftarrow \mathsf{GSetup}(\lambda)$
  $\mathcal{A}^{\mathsf{Join}^*(\cdot),\mathsf{Corrupt}(\cdot)}(\mathsf{mpk},\mathsf{sk}_O)$
    $\rightarrow (\mathsf{pk}, m_0, m_1, s)$
  $C \leftarrow \mathsf{Encrypt}(\mathsf{mpk},\mathsf{pk}, m_b)$
  $C^* \leftarrow \mathsf{ReRand}(\mathsf{mpk}, C)$
  $b' \leftarrow \mathcal{A}^{\mathsf{Join}^*(\cdot),\mathsf{Corrupt}(\cdot)}(s, C^*)$
  IF $\mathsf{pk} \notin \mathcal{L}\backslash\mathcal{C}$ RETURN 0
  ELSE RETURN b'

Experiment $\mathsf{Exp}^{\mathsf{ranon}-b}_{\mathcal{MTAES},\mathcal{A}}(\lambda)$
  $(\mathsf{mpk},\mathsf{msk},\mathsf{sk}_O) \leftarrow \mathsf{GSetup}(\lambda)$
  $\mathcal{A}^{\mathsf{Join}^*(\cdot),\mathsf{Corrupt}(\cdot)}(\mathsf{mpk})$
    $\rightarrow (\mathsf{pk}_0, \mathsf{pk}_1, m, s)$
  $C \leftarrow \mathsf{Encrypt}(\mathsf{mpk},\mathsf{pk}_b, m)$
  $C^* \leftarrow \mathsf{ReRand}(\mathsf{mpk}, C)$
  $b' \leftarrow \mathcal{A}^{\mathsf{Join}^*(\cdot),\mathsf{Corrupt}(\cdot)}(s, C^*)$
  IF $\mathsf{pk}_0 \notin \mathcal{L}\backslash\mathcal{C}$
    OR $\mathsf{pk}_1 \notin \mathcal{L}\backslash\mathcal{C}$ RETURN 0
    ELSE RETURN b'

Experiment $\mathsf{Exp}^{\mathsf{ind}-b}_{\mathcal{MTAES},\mathcal{A}}(\lambda)$
  $(\mathsf{mpk},\mathsf{msk},\mathsf{sk}_O) \leftarrow \mathsf{GSetup}(\lambda)$
  $\mathcal{A}^{\mathsf{Join}^*(\cdot),\mathsf{Corrupt}(\cdot)}(\mathsf{mpk},\mathsf{sk}_O)$
    $\rightarrow (\mathsf{pk}, m_0, m_1, s)$
  $C^* \leftarrow \mathsf{Encrypt}(\mathsf{mpk},\mathsf{pk}, m_b)$
  $b' \leftarrow \mathcal{A}^{\mathsf{Join}^*(\cdot),\mathsf{Corrupt}(\cdot)}(s, C^*)$
  IF $\mathsf{pk} \notin \mathcal{L}\backslash\mathcal{C}$ RETURN 0
  ELSE RETURN b'

Experiment $\mathsf{Exp}^{\mathsf{anon}-b}_{\mathcal{MTAES},\mathcal{A}}(\lambda)$
  $(\mathsf{mpk},\mathsf{msk},\mathsf{sk}_O) \leftarrow \mathsf{GSetup}(\lambda)$
  $\mathcal{A}^{\mathsf{Join}^*(\cdot),\mathsf{Corrupt}(\cdot)}(\mathsf{mpk})$
    $\rightarrow (\mathsf{pk}_0, \mathsf{pk}_1, m, s)$
  $C^* \leftarrow \mathsf{Encrypt}(\mathsf{mpk},\mathsf{pk}_b, m)$
  $b' \leftarrow \mathcal{A}^{\mathsf{Join}^*(\cdot),\mathsf{Corrupt}(\cdot)}(s, C^*)$
  IF $\mathsf{pk}_0 \notin \mathcal{L}\backslash\mathcal{C}$
    OR $\mathsf{pk}_1 \notin \mathcal{L}\backslash\mathcal{C}$ RETURN 0
    ELSE RETURN b'

(a) Semantic Security

(b) Anonymity

Experiment $\mathsf{Exp}^{\mathsf{correct}}_{\mathcal{MTAES},\mathcal{A}}(\lambda)$
  $(\mathsf{mpk},\mathsf{msk},\mathsf{sk}_O) \leftarrow \mathsf{GSetup}(\lambda)$
  $\mathcal{A}^{\mathsf{Join}^*(\cdot),\mathsf{Corrupt}(\cdot)}(\mathsf{mpk})$
    $\rightarrow (\mathsf{pk}, m, r, r')$
  $C \leftarrow \mathsf{Encrypt}(\mathsf{mpk},\mathsf{pk}, m; r)$
  $C^* \leftarrow \mathsf{ReRand}(\mathsf{mpk}, C; r')$
  IF $\mathsf{pk} \notin \mathcal{L}$ RETURN 0
  IF $\mathsf{pk} \neq \mathsf{Trace}(\mathsf{mpk},\mathsf{sk}_O,\mathcal{L}, C^*)$
    RETURN 1
  IF $\mathsf{Decrypt}(\mathsf{mpk},\mathsf{sk}, C^*) \neq m$
    (where sk associated to pk) RETURN 1
  ELSE RETURN 0

Experiment $\mathsf{Exp}^{\mathsf{subF}-b}_{\mathcal{MTAES},\mathcal{A}}(\lambda)$
  $(\mathsf{mpk},\mathsf{msk},\mathsf{sk}_O) \leftarrow \mathsf{GSetup}(\lambda)$
  $\mathcal{A}^{\mathsf{Join}^*(\cdot),\mathsf{Corrupt}(\cdot)}(\mathsf{mpk})$
    $\rightarrow (C_0, C_1, s)$
  $C^* \leftarrow \mathsf{ReRand}(\mathsf{mpk}, C_b)$
  $b' \leftarrow \mathcal{A}^{\mathsf{Join}^*(\cdot),\mathsf{Corrupt}(\cdot)}(s, C^*)$
  IF $\mathsf{Traceable}(\mathcal{CU}, C_0)$
    AND $\mathsf{Traceable}(\mathcal{CU}, C_1)$ RETURN 0
  ELSE RETURN b'

(c) Correctness

(d) Subliminal-Channel Freeness

Experiment $\mathsf{Exp}^{\mathsf{priv}-b}_{\mathcal{MTAES},\mathcal{A}}(\lambda)$
  $(\mathsf{mpk},\mathsf{msk},\mathsf{sk}_O) \leftarrow \mathsf{GSetup}(\lambda)$
  $\mathcal{A}^{\mathsf{Join}^*(\cdot),\mathsf{Corrupt}(\cdot)}(\mathsf{mpk})$
    $\rightarrow (\mathsf{pk}_0, \mathsf{pk}_1, m_0, m_1, s)$
  $C^* \leftarrow \mathsf{Encrypt}(\mathsf{mpk},\mathsf{pk}_d, m_d)$
  $b' \leftarrow \mathcal{A}^{\mathsf{Join}^*(\cdot),\mathsf{Corrupt}(\cdot)}(s, C^*)$
  IF $\mathsf{pk}_0 \notin \mathcal{L}\backslash\mathcal{C}$
    OR $\mathsf{pk}_1 \notin \mathcal{L}\backslash\mathcal{C}$ RETURN 0
  ELSE RETURN b'

Experiment $\mathsf{Exp}^{\mathsf{unlink}-b}_{\mathcal{MTAES},\mathcal{A}}(\lambda)$
  $(\mathsf{mpk},\mathsf{msk},\mathsf{sk}_O) \leftarrow \mathsf{GSetup}(\lambda)$
  $\mathcal{A}^{\mathsf{Join}^*(\cdot),\mathsf{Corrupt}(\cdot)}(\mathsf{mpk})$
    $\rightarrow (C, s)$
  $C'_0 \leftarrow \mathsf{ReRand}(\mathsf{mpk}, C)$
  $C'_1 \overset{R}{\leftarrow} \mathcal{C}, \ C^* \leftarrow C'_b$
  $b' \leftarrow \mathcal{A}^{\mathsf{Join}^*(\cdot),\mathsf{Corrupt}(\cdot)}(s, C^*)$
  IF $\mathsf{Traceable}(\mathcal{CU}, C'_0)$ RETURN 0
  ELSE RETURN b'

(e) Privacy

(f) Ciphertext Unlinkability

Fig. 1. Experiments for Security Notions

ANONYMITY. Our goal in this work is anonymity of the recipient (a.k.a. key privacy [2]), we formalize it as usual by the indistinguishability of the two experiments presented Fig. 1(b): the adversary has to guess which public key has been used to generate the challenge ciphertext. Again, we restrict the adversary to use valid (registered) public keys. We define the advantage of $\mathcal{A}$ in breaking the anonymity (after re-randomization or before) by:

$$\mathsf{Adv}^{(r)\mathsf{anon}}_{\mathcal{M}\text{TAES},\mathcal{A}}(\lambda) = \Pr[\mathsf{Exp}^{(r)\mathsf{anon}-1}_{\mathcal{M}\text{TAES},\mathcal{A}}(\lambda) = 1] - \Pr[\mathsf{Exp}^{(r)\mathsf{anon}-0}_{\mathcal{M}\text{TAES},\mathcal{A}}(\lambda) = 1].$$

Theorem 3. *For any scheme* $\mathcal{M}$TAES *and any time bound* τ, $\mathsf{Adv}^{\mathsf{ranon}}_{\mathcal{M}\text{TAES}}(\lambda, \tau) \leq \mathsf{Adv}^{\mathsf{anon}}_{\mathcal{M}\text{TAES}}(\lambda, \tau)$.

CORRECTNESS. Of course, an encryption scheme that is non-decryptable could be secure (semantically secure and anonymous). We thus need the scheme to be both decryptable and traceable: a well-formed ciphertext should be decryptable by the target recipient (using sk associated to the target pk, both generated by the Join oracle), and should be traced (with high probability) to this recipient by the opener. No adversary should be able to win the correctness game (see Fig. 1(c)) with significant advantage:

$$\mathsf{Adv}^{\mathsf{correct}}_{\mathcal{M}\text{TAES},\mathcal{A}}(\lambda) = \Pr[\mathsf{Exp}^{\mathsf{correct}}_{\mathcal{M}\text{TAES},\mathcal{A}}(\lambda) = 1].$$

SUBLIMINAL-CHANNEL FREENESS. Let us remind that our ultimate goal is that either the ciphertext can be traced to a corrupted user (under the control of the adversary), or the adversary cannot transfer any information. This is modeled by the *subliminal-channel freeness property* (see Fig. 1(d)): the adversary generates two pre-ciphertexts C_0 and C_1, with which it tries to transmit some information. If they are well-formed, and really trace to corrupted users, then this is normal that the information is transferred and so the adversary does not win (hence the two tests with the predicate Traceable). The challenger provides a re-randomized version of one of them to the adversary, and the latter has to guess which one: it has no bias unless some information leaks in the re-randomized ciphertext. As a consequence, subliminal-channel freeness is quantified by

$$\mathsf{Adv}^{\mathsf{subF}}_{\mathcal{M}\text{TAES},\mathcal{A}}(\lambda) = \Pr[\mathsf{Exp}^{\mathsf{subF}-1}_{\mathcal{M}\text{TAES},\mathcal{A}}(\lambda) = 1] - \Pr[\mathsf{Exp}^{\mathsf{subF}-0}_{\mathcal{M}\text{TAES},\mathcal{A}}(\lambda) = 1].$$

We note that for this security notion, the adversary generates the ciphertext itself, and is thus allowed to generate ill-formed ciphertexts, contrarily to the previous security notions. In such a case, only, it wins if it manages to transmit some information. We now provide two additional one that will imply the above ones.

PRIVACY. This privacy notion (see Fig. 1(e)) encompasses both semantic security (plaintext-privacy) and anonymity (key-privacy) before re-randomization, and thus even with respect to the mediator:

$$\mathsf{Adv}^{\mathsf{priv}}_{\mathcal{M}\text{TAES},\mathcal{A}}(\lambda) = \Pr[\mathsf{Exp}^{\mathsf{priv}-1}_{\mathcal{M}\text{TAES},\mathcal{A}}(\lambda) = 1] - \Pr[\mathsf{Exp}^{\mathsf{priv}-0}_{\mathcal{M}\text{TAES},\mathcal{A}}(\lambda) = 1].$$

CIPHERTEXT-UNLINKABILITY. Then, we want that either the pre-ciphertext sent to the mediator has a well identified target recipient, or the re-randomization cancel any information: unless the ciphertext traces back to a user controlled by the adversary, or the re-randomized ciphertext is unlinkable to the input pre-ciphertext, and thus indistinguishable with a truly random ciphertext (in the Real-or-Random sense) – (see Fig. 1(f)):

$$\mathsf{Adv}^{\mathsf{unlink}}_{\mathcal{M}\mathrm{TAES},\mathcal{A}}(\lambda) = \Pr[\mathsf{Exp}^{\mathsf{unlink}-1}_{\mathcal{M}\mathrm{TAES},\mathcal{A}}(\lambda) = 1] - \Pr[\mathsf{Exp}^{\mathsf{unlink}-0}_{\mathcal{M}\mathrm{TAES},\mathcal{A}}(\lambda) = 1].$$

2.3   Relations between the Security Notions

In this section, we state that the later security notions imply the former, and the proofs can be found in the full version [16].

Theorem 4. *For any scheme* $\mathcal{M}\mathrm{TAES}$ *and any time bound* τ,

$$\mathsf{Adv}^{\mathsf{weak-ind}}_{\mathcal{M}\mathrm{TAES}}(\lambda,\tau) \le \mathsf{Adv}^{\mathsf{priv}}_{\mathcal{M}\mathrm{TAES}}(\lambda,\tau) \qquad \mathsf{Adv}^{\mathsf{anon}}_{\mathcal{M}\mathrm{TAES}}(\lambda,\tau) \le \mathsf{Adv}^{\mathsf{priv}}_{\mathcal{M}\mathrm{TAES}}(\lambda,\tau)$$
$$\mathsf{Adv}^{\mathsf{priv}}_{\mathcal{M}\mathrm{TAES}}(\lambda,\tau) \le \mathsf{Adv}^{\mathsf{weak-ind}}_{\mathcal{M}\mathrm{TAES}}(\lambda,\tau) + \mathsf{Adv}^{\mathsf{anon}}_{\mathcal{M}\mathrm{TAES}}(\lambda,\tau).$$

Theorem 5. *For any scheme* $\mathcal{M}\mathrm{TAES}$ *and any time bound* τ,

$$\mathsf{Adv}^{\mathsf{subF}}_{\mathcal{M}\mathrm{TAES}}(\lambda,\tau) \le \frac{1}{2} \times \mathsf{Adv}^{\mathsf{unlink}}_{\mathcal{M}\mathrm{TAES}}(\lambda,\tau).$$

3   Our Scheme

First, we present a simple scheme achieving the above security requirements. This scheme inherits the properties of some combination of broadcast encryption and re-randomizable techniques. It fulfills the strongest properties of privacy and un-linkabillity under the sole DDH assumption, but with the restriction that the same trapdoor is used for both decrypting and tracing ciphertexts. We then show how we can separate these capabilities, under the XDH [5] and the (asymmetric) DBDH [10] assumptions. These classical assumptions are reviewed in the full version [16]. We here use classical advantage notations for all the decisional problems.

3.1   Description of the Scheme $\mathcal{M}\mathrm{TAES}_1$

- GSetup(λ): The GSetup algorithm takes as input a security parameter λ. It defines a cyclic group $\mathbb{G}$ of prime order q, in which the DDH assumption holds, in some basis g. We denote $\mathbb{G}^* = \mathbb{G}\backslash\{1\}$, the subset of elements of order exactly q. It chooses random scalars $x_1, \ldots, x_t \in \mathbb{Z}_q^*$ with t the maximum number of registered users. It sets the master secret key and the opening key as $\mathsf{msk} = \mathsf{sk}_O = (x_1, x_2, \ldots, x_t)$ and the group public key $\mathsf{mpk} = (y_1 = g^{x_1}, \ldots, y_t = g^{x_t})$. It also sets the registration list $\mathcal{L}$ to empty.
- Join(id, mpk, msk): The id is assumed to be an integer between 1 and t. This algorithm thus outputs $\mathsf{sk}_{\mathsf{id}} = x_{\mathsf{id}}$ as the secret key of user id, whereas the public key is y_{id}. It adds the pair (id, $\mathsf{pk}_{\mathsf{id}} = y_{\mathsf{id}}$) in the list $\mathcal{L}$.

- Encrypt(mpk, i, m): To encrypt a message $m \in \mathbb{G}$ under a public key $\mathsf{pk}_i = y_i$, we choose two random scalars $r, s \in \mathbb{Z}_q^*$ and compute $(A_1, A_2, B_1, B_2) = (g^r, m \cdot y_i^r, g^s, y_i^s)$.
- ReRand(mpk, C): To re-randomize a pre-ciphertext in $(\mathbb{G}^*)^4$, we first choose $4t$ random scalars r_j, r_j' and s_j, s_j' in $\mathbb{Z}_q^*$, for $j = 1, \cdots, t$ and compute t sub-ciphertexts as follows:

$$C_{1,j} \leftarrow A_1 \cdot B_1^{r_j'} \cdot g^{r_j} \qquad\qquad C_{2,j} \leftarrow A_2 \cdot B_2^{r_j'} \cdot y_j^{r_j}$$
$$D_{1,j} \leftarrow B_1^{s_j'} \cdot g^{s_j} \qquad\qquad D_{2,j} \leftarrow B_2^{s_j'} \cdot y_j^{s_j}.$$

Then, we obtain a sequence C of t tuples $(C_{1,j}, C_{2,j}, D_{1,j}, D_{2,j})$ for $j = 1, \ldots, t$. Note that the second halves of the tuples allow to re-randomize again the ciphertext, with $4t$ random scalars a_j, a_j' and b_j, b_j':

$$C_{1,j}' \leftarrow C_{1,j} \cdot D_{1,j}^{a_j'} \cdot g^{a_j} \qquad\qquad C_{2,j}' \leftarrow C_{2,j} \cdot D_{2,j}^{a_j'} \cdot y_j^{a_j}$$
$$D_{1,j}' \leftarrow D_{1,j}^{b_j'} \cdot g^{b_j} \qquad\qquad D_{2,j}' \leftarrow D_{2,j}^{b_j'} \cdot y_j^{b_j}.$$

- Decrypt(mpk, i, C): To decrypt a ciphertext for user i, using the secret key x_i, we compute $m \leftarrow C_{2,i} \cdot C_{1,i}^{-x_i}$. Note that user i can check whether he really is the target recipient: $D_{2,i} \stackrel{?}{=} D_{1,i}^{x_i}$.
- Trace(msk, $\mathcal{L}, \mathsf{sk}_O, C$): To trace the recipient of a ciphertext C, parse C as $(C_{1,i}, C_{2,i}, D_{1,i}, D_{2,i})_{i=1,\ldots,t}$ and check whether $g, y_i, D_{1,i}, D_{2,i}$ is a DDH-tuple for one of the index i (which would correspond to a registered user in the list $\mathcal{L}$). If such an index is found, we provide a non-interactive zero-knowledge proof of validity Π showing the existence of $x_i \in \mathbb{Z}_q$ such that $y_i = g^{x_i}$ and $D_{2,i} = D_{1,i}^{x_i}$; otherwise we output an error symbol $\perp$. Note that the same can be done on (g, y_i, B_1, B_2) from the pre-ciphertext.
- Judge(mpk, $\mathcal{L}, C, \mathsf{id}, \Pi$): This algorithm checks whether the proof Π is valid wrt $\mathcal{L}, C, \mathsf{id}$.

3.2 Security Analysis

CORRECTNESS. First, one should note that after re-randomization, a ciphertext for $\mathsf{pk}_i = y_i$ looks like

$$C_{1,j} \leftarrow A_1 \cdot B_1^{r_j'} \cdot g^{r_j} = g^{r+s \cdot r_j' + r_j} \qquad C_{2,j} \leftarrow A_2 \cdot B_2^{r_j'} \cdot y_j^{r_j} = m \cdot y_i^{r+s \cdot r_j'} \cdot y_j^{r_j}$$
$$D_{1,j} \leftarrow B_1^{s_j'} \cdot g^{s_j} = g^{s \cdot s_j' + s_j} \qquad D_{2,j} \leftarrow B_2^{s_j'} \cdot y_j^{s_j} = y_i^{s \cdot s_j'} \cdot y_j^{s_j},$$

where r, s are the random values chosen by the sender, whereas r_j', s_j' and the r_j, s_j are chosen by the re-randomizer for $j = 1, \ldots, t$. If $y_i \in \mathcal{L}$, and thus $y_i = g^{x_i}$, then

$$C_{1,i} = g^{r+s \cdot r_i' + r_i} \qquad\qquad C_{2,i} = m \cdot y_i^{r+s \cdot r_i' + r_i} = m \cdot C_{1,i}^{x_i}$$
$$D_{1,i} = g^{s \cdot s_i' + s_i} \qquad\qquad D_{2,i} = y_i^{s \cdot s_i' + s_i} = D_{1,i}^{x_i}.$$

Using the secret key $\mathsf{sk}_i = x_i$, we immediately get m by computing $C_{2,i} \cdot C_{1,i}^{-x_i}$. A similar computation on $D_{1,i}$ and $D_{2,i}$ traces back user i. For any index $j \neq i$ (or if $y_i = g^{x_i} \notin \mathcal{L}$), with $\delta_j = x_j - x_i \neq 0$,

$$C_{1,j} = g^{r+s\cdot r'_j+r_j} \qquad C_{2,j} = m \cdot g^{x_i(r+s\cdot r'_j)+x_j r_j} = m \cdot C_{1,j}^{x_j} \cdot g^{(r+s\cdot r'_j)\delta_j}$$

$$D_{1,j} = g^{s\cdot s'_j+s_j} \qquad D_{2,j} = g^{x_i\cdot s\cdot s'_j+x_j s_j} = D_{1,j}^{x_j} \cdot g^{\delta_j s s'_j}.$$

Then, the tuple $(C_{1,j}, C_{2,j}, D_{1,j}, D_{2,j})$ follows a distribution statistically close to random in $\mathbb{G}^4$, since s and s'_j are non-zero. It thus contains no information on m and i. We will formally justify that in the following.

PRIVACY. The privacy property implies both semantic security and anonymity of pre-ciphertexts. We obtain the following result, whose proof can be found in the full version [16]:

Theorem 6. *Our scheme* $\mathcal{M}\text{TAES}_1$ *proposed in Section 3.1 fulfills the privacy property under the* DDH *assumption:*

$$\mathsf{Adv}^{\mathsf{priv}}_{\mathcal{M}\text{TAES}_1}(\lambda, \tau) \leq 2t \cdot \mathsf{Adv}^{\mathsf{ddh}}_{\mathbb{G}}(\tau + 2\tau_{\mathsf{exp}}),$$

where τ_{exp} *denotes an upper bound on the time computation for one exponentiation.*

UNLINKABILITY. In order to get the subliminal-channel freeness, we will prove the unlinkability, which holds under the DDH assumption too (the proof can be found in the full version [16]):

Theorem 7. *Our scheme* $\mathcal{M}\text{TAES}_1$ *proposed in Section 3.1 is unlinkable under the* DDH *assumption:*

$$\mathsf{Adv}^{\mathsf{unlink}}_{\mathcal{M}\text{TAES}_1}(\lambda, \tau) \leq 2(t+1) \cdot \mathsf{Adv}^{\mathsf{ddh}}_{\mathbb{G}}(\tau + 2\tau_{\mathsf{exp}}),$$

where τ_{exp} *denotes an upper bound on the time computation for one exponentiation.*

3.3   Two-Level Scheme $\mathcal{M}\text{TAES}_2$

In the previous scheme $\mathcal{M}\text{TAES}_1$, the same key is used for both the join and the tracing procedures, hence it achieves the weak security level only. In this section, we separate these two capabilities in $\mathcal{M}\text{TAES}_2$, making use of a so-called Type-2 or Type-3 pairing-friendly structure [12]. It consists in a tuple $(\mathbb{G}_1, \mathbb{G}_2, \mathbb{G}_T, q, e, g_1, g_2)$ where e is an admissible bilinear map [6], g_1, g_2 and $G = e(g_1, g_2)$ are generators of $\mathbb{G}_1$, $\mathbb{G}_2$ and $\mathbb{G}_T$ respectively (and additionally there exist an efficiently computable isomorphism $\psi : \mathbb{G}_2 \to \mathbb{G}_1$ in the case of Type-2 structure). We consider structures in which the XDH (*i.e.* the DDH assumption in $\mathbb{G}_1$) and the (asymmetric) DBDH[2] [10] assumptions can be made (*e.g.*, using Weil or Tate pairings on certain MNT curves as defined in [18], these assumptions seem reasonable).

---

[2] Our scheme actually relies on a weaker *mixed* assumption which states that given $g_1^a, g_2^a, e(g_1, g_2)^b$ and $e(g_1, g_2)^c$, it is intractable to decide whether $c \overset{?}{=} ab \bmod q$.

Description.

- GSetup(λ): The GSetup algorithm takes as input a security parameter λ and generates parameters for a bilinear structure $(\mathbb{G}_1, \mathbb{G}_2, \mathbb{G}_T, q, e, g_1, g_2)$ As before, the master secret key is set to be a sequence of t random scalars in $\mathbb{Z}_q^*$, $\mathsf{msk} = (x_1, x_2, \ldots, x_t)$, and the group public key is defined by

$$\mathsf{mpk} = \begin{pmatrix} g_1, g_2, G, (y_1 = g_1^{x_1}, \ldots, y_t = g_1^{x_t}), \\ (Y_1 = e\,(g_1^{x_1}, g_2), \ldots, Y_t = e\,(g_1^{x_t}, g_2)) \end{pmatrix}.$$

  The opening key consists of the sequence $\mathsf{sk}_O = (h_1 = g_2^{x_1}, \cdots, h_t = g_2^{x_t})$. This algorithm also sets the registration list $\mathcal{L}$ to empty.
- Join(id, mpk, msk): As before, this algorithm outputs x_{id} as the secret key $\mathsf{sk}_{\mathsf{id}}$ of user id, whereas the public key is $(y_{\mathsf{id}}, Y_{\mathsf{id}})$. It also adds the pair (id, $\mathsf{pk}_{\mathsf{id}} = (y_{\mathsf{id}}, Y_{\mathsf{id}})$) in the list $\mathcal{L}$. (Note that y_{id} would be enough in the public key, and in the master public key, but the use of Y_{id} will simplify the notations).
- Encrypt(mpk, i, m): To encrypt a message $m \in \mathbb{G}_T$ under a public key $\mathsf{pk}_i = (y_i, Y_i)$, one first chooses two random scalars $r, s \in \mathbb{Z}_q^*$ and then computes $(A_1, A_2, B_1, B_2) = (G^r, m \cdot Y_i^r, g_1^s, y_i^s)$.
- ReRand(mpk, C): To re-randomize a pre-ciphertext, one first chooses $4t$ random scalars r_j, r_j' and s_j, s_j' in $\mathbb{Z}_q^*$ for $j = 1, \cdots, t$ and computes t sub-ciphertexts as follows:

$$C_{1,j} \leftarrow A_1 \cdot e\,(B_1, g_2)^{r_j'} \cdot G^{r_j} \qquad C_{2,j} \leftarrow A_2 \cdot e\,(B_2, g_2)^{r_j'} \cdot Y_j^{r_j}$$
$$D_{1,j} \leftarrow B_1^{s_j'} \cdot g_1^{s_j} \qquad\qquad D_{2,j} \leftarrow B_2^{s_j'} \cdot y_j^{s_j}.$$

  Then, we obtain a sequence C of t tuples $(C_{1,j}, C_{2,j}, D_{1,j}, D_{2,j})$ for $j = 1, \ldots, t$. Note that the second halves of the tuples allow to re-randomize again the ciphertext, as in $\mathcal{M}\mathrm{TAES}_1$.
- Decrypt(mpk, i, C): To decrypt a ciphertext for user i, using the secret key x_i, we compute $m \leftarrow C_{2,i} \cdot C_{1,i}^{-x_i}$.
- Trace(msk, $\mathcal{L}$, sk_O, C): To trace the recipient of a given ciphertext C, check whether $(g_1, y_i, D_{1,i}, D_{2,i})$ is a DDH-tuple in $\mathbb{G}_1$ for some registered user i in the list $\mathcal{L}$, by testing whether $e\,(D_{2,i}, g_2) = e\,(D_{1,i}, h_i)$. If no such one is found, we output $\perp$ otherwise, we provide a non-interactive zero-knowledge proof of validity, Π showing the existence of $x_i \in \mathbb{Z}_q$ such that $h_i = g_2^{x_i}$ and $D_{2,i} = D_{1,i}^{x_i}$.
- Judge(mpk, $\mathcal{L}$, C, id, Π): This algorithm checks whether the proof Π is valid wrt $\mathcal{L}$, C, id.

Security Properties. Granted the richer structure, and both the XDH and the DBDH assumptions, this scheme achieves all the expected security properties: anonymity, indistinguishability (even given access to the opening/tracing key) and unlinkability. The proof can be found in the full version [16].

Theorem 8. *Our scheme* $\mathcal{M}\text{TAES}_2$ *proposed in Section 3.3 is anonymous, indistinguishable and unlinkable under the* XDH *assumption (the* DDH *assumption in* $\mathbb{G}_1$*), and the* DBDH *assumption:*

$$\mathsf{Adv}^{\mathsf{anon}}_{\mathcal{M}\text{TAES}_2}(\lambda, \tau), \mathsf{Adv}^{\mathsf{unlink}}_{\mathcal{M}\text{TAES}_2}(\lambda, \tau) \leq 2t \cdot \mathsf{Adv}^{\mathsf{xdh}}_{\mathcal{BS}}(\tau + 2\tau_{\mathsf{exp}})$$
$$\mathsf{Adv}^{\mathsf{ind}}_{\mathcal{M}\text{TAES}_2}(\lambda, \tau) \leq t \cdot \mathsf{Adv}^{\mathsf{dbdh}}_{\mathcal{BS}}(\tau),$$

where τ_{exp} *denotes an upper bound on the time computation for one exponentiation.*

3.4   Protection against the Issuer

As the Private Key Generator (PKG) in Identity Based-Encryption, the issuer can be involved in malicious activities since it knows all users' registered secret keys. We can easily prevent the issuer from breaking the semantic security of a ciphertext sent to a specific user by first encrypting the message with an appropriate encryption scheme (for which the issuer does not know the decryption keys) and then re-encrypt (component by component) the ciphertext with our *mediated traceable anonymous encryption scheme*: If the global ciphertext is not traceable, then the underlying ciphertext will be totally random, and thus, no information will be transmitted.

More precisely, for such a technique to be applied with our schemes, we need an underlying ElGamal [11] encryption scheme in $\mathbb{G}$ for $\mathcal{M}\text{TAES}_1$ (or $\mathbb{G} = \mathbb{G}_T$ for $\mathcal{M}\text{TAES}_2$). For encrypting a message $m \in \mathbb{G}$, one gets the recipient's ElGamal public key, and applies the ElGamal encryption of m: it gets $(c_1, c_2) \in \mathbb{G}^2$. Thereafter, c_1 and c_2 are independently re-encrypted under our $\mathcal{M}\text{TAES}_1$ scheme, using the recipient registered key. One could use another encryption scheme, different or stronger than ElGamal. The unique constraint is that the underlying encryption scheme should produce a ciphertext in $\mathbb{G}^k$, for some k, so that it can thereafter be re-encrypted by our $\mathcal{M}\text{TAES}$'s.

4   An ω-Resilient Generic Construction

In this section, we propose a generic scheme that is *ω-resilient*, which means that the malicious adversary can corrupt up to a maximum of ω users adaptively and thus possess the ω corresponding private keys. However, it cannot obtain any information relevant to ciphertexts that are encrypted for public keys not within the corrupt users. For a fixed ω, our construction is fairly efficient, with ciphertexts that have logarithmic size in the number of group members (instead of linear with the two previous proposals $\mathcal{M}\text{TAES}_1$ and $\mathcal{M}\text{TAES}_2$). However, tracing might fail (with small probability, depending on the code). Our construction relies on well-known tools, namely *collusion-secure codes* and *homomorphic encryption schemes* that generalize the protocols from the previous section.

4.1   Collusion-Secure Codes

Our construction makes use of ω-*traceable* codes [22], in the same vein as the collusion-secure codes proposed by Boneh and Shaw [7] as a method of digital fingerprinting while preventing a collusion of a specified size ω from framing a user not in the coalition, but furthermore allowing the traceability of a traitor from a word generated by the coalition. We consider a code $\mathcal{C}$ of length ℓ on an alphabet T, with $\#T = t$ (*i.e.* $\mathcal{C} \subseteq T^\ell$) and we call it an (n, ℓ, t)-code if $\#\mathcal{C} = n$. The elements of $\mathcal{C}$ are called *codewords*.

For any subset of codewords $\mathcal{C}_0 \subset \mathcal{C}$, we define the set of descendants of $\mathcal{C}_0$ (*a.k.a.* the feasible set), denoted $\mathsf{Desc}(\mathcal{C}_0) = \{x \in T^\ell : x_i \in \{a_i : a \in \mathcal{C}_0\}, 1 \leq i \leq \ell\}$. We now recall the following definitions concerning non-frameability and traceability of codes. Let $\mathcal{C}$ be an (n, ℓ, t)-code and ω any integer such that $n > t \geq \omega \geq 1$.

Definition 9. $\mathcal{C}$ *is an* ω-frameproof *code if for any subset* $\mathcal{C}_0 \subset \mathcal{C}$ *such that* $\#\mathcal{C}_0 \leq \omega$, $\mathsf{Desc}(\mathcal{C}_0) \cap \mathcal{C} = \mathcal{C}_0$.

Optimal explicit constructions of ω-frameproof codes are known for small coalitions [4]. Wang and Xing [24] provided explicit constructions of ω-frameproof codes based on algebraic curves over finite fields; they obtain infinite classes of such (n, ℓ, t)-codes with $\ell = O(\log n)$ for fixed t and ω.

However, a frameproof-code just guarantees that no coalition (not too large) can produce a codeword of a user not in the coalition. But in the fingerprinting setting and for traitor tracing [9], we furthermore want a tracing algorithm $\mathsf{Trace}_\mathcal{C}$ which, on input a word x generated by the coalition, outputs a member of the coalition $\mathcal{C}_0$:

Definition 10. *Let* $\varepsilon > 0$. *An* $(n, \ell, \omega, t, \varepsilon)$-*collusion-secure code is an* (n, ℓ, t)-*code for which there exists a (probabilistic) tracing algorithm* $\mathsf{Trace}_\mathcal{C}$ *satisfying the following condition: for any* $\mathcal{C}_0 \subset \mathcal{C}$ *such that* $\#\mathcal{C}_0 \leq \omega$, *and any* $x \in \mathsf{Desc}(\mathcal{C}_0)$, $\Pr[\mathsf{Trace}_\mathcal{C}(x) \in \mathcal{C}_0] > 1 - \varepsilon$.

Such codes with efficient tracing algorithms were proposed with $\ell = O(\log n)$ [23].

4.2   Homomorphic Encryption

Homomorphic encryption is a form of encryption where one can perform a group operation on the plaintexts by performing a (possibly different) algebraic operation on the ciphertexts. More formally, a $\mathbb{H}$-homomorphic encryption scheme is a tuple of efficient algorithms $(\mathsf{Setup}, \mathsf{Kg}, \mathsf{Encrypt}, \odot, \mathsf{Decrypt})$ such that $(\mathsf{Setup}, \mathsf{Kg}, \mathsf{Encrypt}, \mathsf{Decrypt})$ is an encryption scheme with message space a group $\mathbb{H}$ and $\odot$ is an algorithm (written infix style) that takes two elements in Encrypt's codomain and outputs an element of Encrypt's codomain such that for all messages $m, m' \in \mathbb{H}$ and any matching key pair $(\mathsf{pk}, \mathsf{sk})$, we have:

$$\mathsf{Decrypt}(\mathsf{Encrypt}(m, \mathsf{pk}) \odot \mathsf{Encrypt}(m', \mathsf{pk}), \mathsf{sk}) = m \cdot m' \in \mathbb{H}. \qquad (1)$$

Examples of homomorphic cryptosystems are due to ElGamal [11], Golwasser-Micali [13] and Paillier [19]. Note that (1) further implies the existence of an efficient function that allows exponentiation of ciphertexts (using a *square-and-multiply* algorithm): $\mathsf{Encrypt}(m, \mathsf{pk})^{\odot^r} = \mathsf{Encrypt}(m, \mathsf{pk}) \odot \cdots \odot \mathsf{Encrypt}(m, \mathsf{pk})$ (*r* times). Our construction relies on a pair of encryption schemes that are compatible for two algebraic operations $\odot$ and $\otimes$ in the following way:

Definition 11. *Let $\mathbb{H}_1$ and $\mathbb{H}_2$ be two abelian groups of prime order q and let $\varphi : \mathbb{H}_2 \to \mathbb{H}_1$ be a group homomorphism. A $(\mathbb{H}_1, \mathbb{H}_2, \varphi)$-compatible encryption scheme is a tuple of (probabilistic) polynomial-time algorithms (Setup, Kg, $\mathsf{Encrypt}_1$, $\mathsf{Encrypt}_2$,$\odot$,$\otimes$, $\mathsf{Decrypt}_1$, $\mathsf{Decrypt}_2$) such that:*

- Setup(λ) $\to$ params: *this algorithm is run by a (trusted) party that, on input of a security parameter λ, produces a set* params *of common public parameters.*
- Kg(params) $\to$ $(\mathsf{pk}, \mathsf{sk}^{(1)}, \mathsf{sk}^{(2)})$: *on input of public parameters* params, *all parties use this randomized algorithm to generate a private/public key pair $(\mathsf{pk}, \mathsf{sk}^{(1)}, \mathsf{sk}^{(2)})$. We denote Kg_i for $i \in \{1, 2\}$ the algorithm that executes Kg but only returns $(\mathsf{pk}, \mathsf{sk}^{(i)})$.*
- $(\mathsf{Setup}, \mathsf{Kg}_1, \mathsf{Encrypt}_1, \mathsf{Decrypt}_1)$ *is an encryption scheme with message space $\mathbb{H}_1$.*
- $(\mathsf{Setup}, \mathsf{Kg}_2, \mathsf{Encrypt}_2, \odot, \mathsf{Decrypt}_2)$ *is a $\mathbb{H}_2$-homomorphic encryption scheme, but for which we ask for the decryption algorithm to output $\varphi(m) \in \mathbb{H}_1$ only (and not $m \in \mathbb{H}_2$ itself).*
- $\otimes$ *is an algorithm (written infix style) that on input an $\mathsf{Encrypt}_1$-ciphertext and an $\mathsf{Encrypt}_2$-ciphertext outputs an $\mathsf{Encrypt}_1$-ciphertext such that for all messages $m_1 \in \mathbb{H}_1$ and $m_2 \in \mathbb{H}_2$ and any matching key pair $(\mathsf{pk}, \mathsf{sk}^{(1)}, \mathsf{sk}^{(2)})$, we have: $\mathsf{Decrypt}_1(\mathsf{Encrypt}_1(m_1, \mathsf{pk}) \otimes \mathsf{Encrypt}_2(m_2, \mathsf{pk}), \mathsf{sk}^{(1)}) = m_1 \cdot \varphi(m_2) \in \mathbb{H}_1$.*

Remark 12. Any $\mathbb{G}$-homomorphic encryption gives rise to a $(\mathbb{H}_1 = \mathbb{G}, \mathbb{H}_2 = \mathbb{G}, \mathsf{id})$-compatible encryption scheme in the trivial way (*i.e.* with $\otimes = \odot$). In a bilinear structure $\mathcal{BS} = (\mathbb{G}_1, \mathbb{G}_2, \mathbb{G}_T, q, e, g_1, g_2)$, a non-straightforward $(\mathbb{H}_1 = \mathbb{G}_T, \mathbb{H}_2 = \mathbb{G}_1, \varphi : y \mapsto e(y, g_2))$-compatible encryption scheme is the one we implicitly use in the construction of the scheme $\mathcal{M}\mathsf{TAES}_2$ (see the full version [16]):

- Setup generates the parameters for an appropriate bilinear structure $\mathcal{BS} = (\mathbb{G}_1, \mathbb{G}_2, \mathbb{G}_T, q, e, g_1, g_2)$ where g_1, g_2 and $G = e(g_1, g_2)$ are generators of $\mathbb{G}_1$, $\mathbb{G}_2$ and $\mathbb{G}_T$ respectively;
- Kg picks at random a scalar $x \in \mathbb{Z}_q^*$ and outputs a triple $(\mathsf{pk}, \mathsf{sk}^{(1)}, \mathsf{sk}^{(2)}) = (y = g_1^x, x, h = g_2^x)$;
- $(\mathsf{Setup}, \mathsf{Kg}_2, \mathsf{Encrypt}_2, \odot, \mathsf{Decrypt}_2)$ is the ElGamal encryption scheme in the group $\mathbb{G}_1$: it performs the encryption of $m \in \mathbb{G}_1$ as $C = (c_1, c_2) = (m \cdot \mathsf{pk}^r, g_1^r) \in \mathbb{G}_1^2$, for a random $r \overset{R}{\leftarrow} \mathbb{Z}_q^*$, and the knowledge of $\mathsf{sk}^{(2)}$ allows to recover $\varphi(m) \in \mathbb{G}_T$ from C as: $\varphi(m) = e(c_1, g_2) / e\left(c_2, \mathsf{sk}^{(2)}\right)$. The operation $\odot$ is the component-wise product in $\mathbb{G}_1^2$.

- (Setup, Kg_1, $\mathsf{Encrypt}_1$, $\mathsf{Decrypt}_1$) is the ElGamal encryption scheme in the group $\mathbb{G}_T$ with public key $Y = e\,(\mathsf{pk}, g_2) = \varphi(\mathsf{pk})$;
- The operation $\otimes : \mathbb{G}_T^2 \times \mathbb{G}_1^2 \longrightarrow \mathbb{G}_T^2$ is: $(Y_1, Y_2) \otimes (z_1, z_2) = (Y_1 \cdot e\,(z_1, g_2)\,, Y_2 \cdot e\,(z_2, g_2))$.

Notation. Let $\mathbb{H}$ be a finite group.

- We denote $\mathsf{Split}_{\mathbb{H}}$ the probabilistic algorithm that on input $m \in \mathbb{H}$ and $\ell \geq 1$, picks uniformly at random $m_1, \ldots, m_{\ell-1} \in \mathbb{H}$, sets $m_\ell = m/(m_1 \ldots m_{\ell-1})$ and outputs the vector $\boldsymbol{m} = (m_1, \ldots, m_\ell) = \mathsf{Split}_{\mathbb{H}}(m, \ell)$.
- For an encryption scheme (Setup, Kg, Encrypt, Decrypt) with domain $\mathbb{H}$, we denote $\mathsf{Encrypt}^{(\ell)}$ the algorithm that takes as input $\boldsymbol{m} = (m_1, \ldots, m_\ell) \in \mathbb{H}^\ell$ and $\mathbf{pk} = (\mathsf{pk}_1, \ldots, \mathsf{pk}_\ell)$ and returns the vector $\boldsymbol{c} = \mathsf{Encrypt}(\boldsymbol{m}, \mathbf{pk})$ defined as the coordinate-wise encryption of $\boldsymbol{m}$ under the public-key $\mathbf{pk}$. Similarly, we denote $\mathsf{Decrypt}^{(\ell)}$ the algorithm that given a vector of ciphertexts $\boldsymbol{c}$ and a vector of secret keys $\mathbf{sk} = (\mathsf{sk}_1, \ldots, \mathsf{sk}_\ell)$, parses $\boldsymbol{c}$ as $\boldsymbol{c} = (c_1, \ldots, c_\ell)$ (where each c_i is a ciphertext), outputs $\bot$ if $\mathsf{Decrypt}(c_i, \mathsf{sk}_i) = \bot$ for some $i \in \{1, \ldots, \ell\}$ and $\prod_{i=1}^{\ell} \mathsf{Decrypt}(c_i, \mathsf{sk}_i) \in \mathbb{H}$, otherwise.
  In particular, for any vector of matching key pairs $(\mathbf{pk}, \mathbf{sk})$, for any $m \in \mathbb{H}$, and any integer $\ell \geq 1$, we have:

$$\mathsf{Decrypt}^{(\ell)}\left(\mathsf{Encrypt}^{(\ell)}(\mathsf{Split}_{\mathbb{H}}(m, \ell), \mathbf{pk}), \mathbf{sk}\right) = m.$$

- If (Setup, Kg, Encrypt, Decrypt) is a $\mathbb{H}$-homomorphic encryption scheme, we denote $\odot$ the coordinate-wise product defined on the codomain of $\mathsf{Encrypt}^{(\ell)}$. If (Setup, Kg, $\mathsf{Encrypt}_1$, $\mathsf{Encrypt}_2$, $\odot$, $\otimes$, $\mathsf{Decrypt}_1$, $\mathsf{Decrypt}_2$) is a $(\mathbb{H}_1, \mathbb{H}_2, \varphi)$-compatible encryption scheme, we also denote $\otimes$ the coordinate-wise operation defined on the cartesian product of the $\mathsf{Encrypt}_1^{(\ell)}$-ciphertexts and the $\mathsf{Encrypt}_2^{(\ell)}$-ciphertexts.

4.3   Description of the Scheme $\mathcal{M}\text{TAES}_3^\ell$

Let $\ell \geq 1$ be an integer, let $\mathbb{H}_1$ and $\mathbb{H}_2$ be two abelian groups of prime order q and let the map $\varphi : \mathbb{H}_2 \to \mathbb{H}_1$ be a group homomorphism. Let the system (Setup, Kg, $\mathsf{Encrypt}_1$, $\mathsf{Encrypt}_2$, $\odot$, $\otimes$, $\mathsf{Decrypt}_1$, $\mathsf{Decrypt}_2$) be a $(\mathbb{H}_1, \mathbb{H}_2, \varphi)$-compatible encryption scheme and $\mathcal{C}$ a $(n, \ell, \omega, t, \varepsilon)$-collusion-secure code of length ℓ on the alphabet $T = \{1, \ldots, t\}$. The following construction describes the generic scheme $\mathcal{M}\text{TAES}_3^\ell$:

- GSetup(λ): The GSetup algorithm takes as input a security parameter λ. It executes Setup(λ) and given the common public parameters params, it runs $t\ell$ times Kg(params) and gets $t\ell$ triples $(\mathsf{pk}_{i,j}, \mathsf{sk}_{i,j}^{(1)}, \mathsf{sk}_{i,j}^{(2)})$ for $(i, j) \in \{1, \ldots, \ell\} \times \{1, \ldots, t\}$. It sets the group public key, the opening key and the master secret key:

$$\mathsf{mpk} = \begin{pmatrix} \mathsf{pk}_{1,1} & \mathsf{pk}_{1,2} & \cdots & \mathsf{pk}_{1,t} \\ \mathsf{pk}_{2,1} & \mathsf{pk}_{2,2} & \cdots & \mathsf{pk}_{2,t} \\ \vdots & \vdots & \vdots & \\ \mathsf{pk}_{\ell,1} & \mathsf{pk}_{\ell,2} & \cdots & \mathsf{pk}_{\ell,t} \end{pmatrix}, \qquad \mathsf{sk}_O = \begin{pmatrix} \mathsf{sk}_{1,1}^{(2)} & \mathsf{sk}_{1,2}^{(2)} & \cdots & \mathsf{sk}_{1,t}^{(2)} \\ \mathsf{sk}_{2,1}^{(2)} & \mathsf{sk}_{2,2}^{(2)} & \cdots & \mathsf{sk}_{2,t}^{(2)} \\ \vdots & \vdots & \vdots & \\ \mathsf{sk}_{\ell,1}^{(2)} & \mathsf{sk}_{\ell,2}^{(2)} & \cdots & \mathsf{sk}_{\ell,t}^{(2)} \end{pmatrix}$$

$$\mathsf{msk} = \begin{pmatrix} \mathsf{sk}_{1,1}^{(1)} & \mathsf{sk}_{1,2}^{(1)} & \cdots & \mathsf{sk}_{1,t}^{(1)} \\ \mathsf{sk}_{2,1}^{(1)} & \mathsf{sk}_{2,2}^{(1)} & \cdots & \mathsf{sk}_{2,t}^{(1)} \\ \vdots & \vdots & \vdots & \\ \mathsf{sk}_{\ell,1}^{(1)} & \mathsf{sk}_{\ell,2}^{(1)} & \cdots & \mathsf{sk}_{\ell,t}^{(1)} \end{pmatrix}$$

It also outputs the registration list $\mathcal{L}$ that is initially empty.

- Join(id, mpk, msk): This algorithm encodes the id into the public key, $\mathsf{pk}_{\mathsf{id}} = c = (c_1 c_2 \ldots c_\ell) \in \mathcal{C}$, where for each i, $c_i \in \{1, \ldots, t\}$, and outputs $\mathsf{sk}_c^{(1)} = (\mathsf{sk}_{1,c_1}^{(1)}, \ldots, \mathsf{sk}_{\ell,c_\ell}^{(1)})$ the secret key of user id. It furthermore adds the pair $(\mathsf{id}, \mathsf{pk}_{\mathsf{id}})$ in the list $\mathcal{L}$.

- Encrypt(mpk, c, m): To encrypt a message $m \in \mathbb{H}_1$ under a public key $\mathsf{pk}_{\mathsf{id}} = c$, the algorithm computes $\boldsymbol{A} = \mathsf{Encrypt}_1^{(\ell)}(\mathsf{Split}_{\mathbb{H}_1}(m, \ell), \mathbf{pk}_c)$ and $\boldsymbol{B} = \mathsf{Encrypt}_2^{(\ell)}((1_{\mathbb{H}_2}, \ldots, 1_{\mathbb{H}_2}), \mathbf{pk}_c)$ where $\mathbf{pk}_c = (\mathsf{pk}_{1,c_1}, \ldots, \mathsf{pk}_{\ell,c_\ell})$ and outputs $C = (\boldsymbol{A}, \boldsymbol{B})$.

- ReRand(mpk, C): To re-randomize a pre-ciphertext $C = (\boldsymbol{A}, \boldsymbol{B})$, the algorithm picks at random t vectors $\boldsymbol{r}_j, \boldsymbol{s}_j \in (\mathbb{Z}_q^*)^\ell$ for $j \in \{1, \ldots, t\}$, generates $\boldsymbol{u} = \mathsf{Split}_{\mathbb{H}_2}(1, \ell)$ and $\boldsymbol{v} = \mathsf{Split}_{\mathbb{H}_2}(1, \ell)$ and computes t vectors of ciphertexts as follows:

$$\boldsymbol{C}_j \leftarrow \boldsymbol{A} \otimes (\boldsymbol{B}^{\odot^{\boldsymbol{r}_j}} \odot \mathsf{Encrypt}_2^{(\ell)}(\boldsymbol{u}, \mathbf{pk}_j)) \quad \boldsymbol{D}_j \leftarrow \boldsymbol{B}^{\odot^{\boldsymbol{s}_j}} \odot \mathsf{Encrypt}_2^{(\ell)}(\boldsymbol{v}, \mathbf{pk}_j),$$

for $j \in \{1, \ldots, t\}$ and $\mathbf{pk}_j = (\mathsf{pk}_{1,j}, \ldots, \mathsf{pk}_{\ell,j})$. It outputs the $2t\ell$ vector $C' = (\boldsymbol{C}_1, \ldots, \boldsymbol{C}_t, \boldsymbol{D}_1, \ldots, \boldsymbol{D}_t)$.

- Decrypt(mpk, i, C): To decrypt a ciphertext $C = (\boldsymbol{C}_1, \ldots, \boldsymbol{C}_t, \boldsymbol{D}_1, \ldots, \boldsymbol{D}_t)$ for the public key $\mathbf{pk}_c$, using the secret key $\mathbf{sk}_c^{(1)}$, the algorithm computes $\mathsf{Decrypt}_1^{(\ell)}((C_{1,c_1}, \ldots, C_{\ell,c_\ell}), \mathbf{sk}_c^{(1)})$.

- Trace(msk, $\mathcal{L}, \mathsf{sk}_O, C$): To trace a user wrt a given ciphertext C, parse C as $(\boldsymbol{C}_1, \ldots, \boldsymbol{C}_t, \boldsymbol{D}_1, \ldots, \boldsymbol{D}_t)$ and decrypts $\boldsymbol{D}_c = (D_{1,c_1}, \ldots, D_{\ell,c_\ell})$ with the decryption algorithm $\mathsf{Decrypt}_2^{(\ell)}$ for all the secret keys $\mathbf{sk}_c^{(2)}$ (where c draws all the domain $\{1, \ldots, t\}^\ell$). If for one of the vector c, the decryption leads to $\varphi(1_{\mathbb{H}_2}) = 1_{\mathbb{H}_1}$, then the algorithm executes $\mathsf{Trace}_C(c)$ and if it returns a codeword v, it provides a non-interactive zero-knowledge proof of validity Π showing that $\mathsf{Decrypt}_2^{(\ell)}(\boldsymbol{D}_c, \mathbf{sk}_c^{(2)}) = 1_{\mathbb{H}_1}$ and that $\mathsf{Trace}_C(c) = v$. Otherwise, it outputs an error symbol $\bot$.

- Judge(mpk, $\mathcal{L}, C, \mathsf{id}, \Pi$): This algorithm checks whether the proof Π is valid wrt $\mathcal{L}, C, \mathsf{id}$.

Remark 13. If we instantiate the scheme $\mathcal{M}\mathrm{TAES}_3^1$ with the ElGamal homomorphic encryption scheme in a group $\mathbb{G}$ (*resp.* with the $(\mathbb{G}_T, \mathbb{G}_1, \varphi : y \mapsto e(y, g_2))$-compatible encryption scheme in a bilinear structure $(\mathbb{G}_1, \mathbb{G}_2, \mathbb{G}_T, q, e, g_1, g_2)$, described in Remark 12) and the code $\mathcal{C} = \{1,\ldots,t\} = T$, we obtain the scheme $\mathcal{M}\text{TAES}_1$ (*resp.* the scheme $\mathcal{M}\text{TAES}_2$) described in the Section 3.

4.4   Security Analysis

Let us explain why this scheme works, and which security level it provides.

Correctness. Since $\boldsymbol{B} = \mathsf{Encrypt}_2^{(\ell)}((1_{\mathbb{H}_2},\ldots,1_{\mathbb{H}_2}),\mathsf{pk}_c)$, for any random $r \in (\mathbb{Z}_q^*)^\ell$, $\mathsf{Decrypt}_1^{(\ell)}(\boldsymbol{B}^{\odot^r},\mathsf{pk}_c) = 1_{\mathbb{H}_2}$ and therefore

$$\mathsf{Decrypt}_1^{(\ell)}(\boldsymbol{B}^{\odot^r} \odot \mathsf{Encrypt}^{(\ell)}(u,\mathsf{pk}_c),\mathsf{sk}_c) = 1_{\mathbb{H}_2}.$$

The extracted ciphertext $(C_{1,c_1},\ldots,C_{\ell,c_\ell})$ is $\boldsymbol{A}\otimes(\boldsymbol{B}^{\odot^r}\odot\mathsf{Encrypt}^{(\ell)}(u,\mathsf{pk}_c))$ with $r = (r_{c_1},\ldots,r_{c_\ell})$ and thus $\mathsf{Decrypt}_1^{(\ell)}\left((C_{1,c_1},\ldots,C_{\ell,c_\ell}),\mathsf{sk}_c^{(1)}\right) = m \in \mathbb{H}_1$. Note that because of the code, tracing may fail with some small probability ε.

Semantic Security and Privacy. We now prove that if the basic construction $\mathcal{M}\text{TAES}_3^1$ is semantically secure (*resp.* anonymous or private) then for any integer $\ell \geq 1$ and any ω-collusion secure code $\mathcal{C}$, the scheme $\mathcal{M}\text{TAES}_3^\ell$ is ω-resilient semantically secure (*resp.* ω-resilient anonymous or ω-resilient private).

Theorem 14. *Let $\ell \geq 1$ be an integer and let $\mathcal{C}$ be an $(n,\ell,\omega,t,\varepsilon)$-secure code. Our scheme $\mathcal{M}\text{TAES}_3^\ell$ fulfills the ω-resilient (strong) semantic security property if and only if our scheme $\mathcal{M}\text{TAES}_3^1$ fulfills the (strong) semantic security property:*

$$\mathsf{Adv}_{\mathcal{M}\text{TAES}_3^\ell}^{\mathsf{ind}}(\lambda,\tau,\omega) \leq n \times \mathsf{Adv}_{\mathcal{M}\text{TAES}_3^1}^{\mathsf{ind}}(\lambda,\tau + t\ell\tau_{\mathsf{Kg}}),$$

where τ_{Kg} denotes an upper bound on the time computation for execution of the Kg algorithm.

Proof. Let us consider an adversary $\mathcal{A}$ against the ω-resilient (strong) semantic security of $\mathcal{M}\text{TAES}_3^\ell$. We construct an adversary $\mathcal{B}$ against the (strong) semantic security of $\mathcal{M}\text{TAES}_3^1$.

KEY GENERATION. The adversary $\mathcal{B}$ simulates the GSetup algorithm by using params, the common parameters received from its own challenger as the common parameters given to $\mathcal{A}$. In addition, $\mathcal{B}$ receives from its challenger a list of public keys $(\mathsf{pk}_1,\ldots,\mathsf{pk}_\ell)$ as well as the second-level matching secret keys $(\mathsf{sk}_1^{(2)},\ldots,\mathsf{sk}_\ell^{(2)})$ for the scheme $\mathcal{M}\text{TAES}_3^1$. The algorithm then uniformly picks at random a vector $(a_1,\ldots,a_\ell) \in \mathcal{C} \subset \{1,\ldots,t\}^\ell$ and sets $(\mathsf{pk}_{i,a_i},\mathsf{sk}_{i,a_i}^{(1)},\mathsf{sk}_{i,a_i}^{(2)}) \leftarrow (\mathsf{pk}_i,\perp,\mathsf{sk}_i^{(2)})$ for $i \in \{1,\ldots,\ell\}$. It then executes $(t-1)\ell$ times the key generation algorithm $\mathsf{Kg}(\lambda)$ and gets $(t-1)\ell$ triples $(\mathsf{pk}_{i,j},\mathsf{sk}_{i,j}^{(1)},\mathsf{sk}_{i,j}^{(2)})$, for $(i,j) \in \{1,\ldots,\ell\} \times \{1,\ldots,t\}$ but $j \neq a_i$. It sets the group public key, the opening key and the master secret key as in the real scheme. The algorithm $\mathcal{B}$ runs $\mathcal{A}$ on input params, mpk and sk_O.

$\textsf{Join}^{*}$ AND $\textsf{Corrupt}$ QUERIES. When $\mathcal{A}$ asks a $\textsf{Join}^{*}$ query for user j, $\mathcal{B}$ encodes the id into the public key, $\textsf{pk}_{\textsf{id}} = \boldsymbol{c} = (c_1 c_2 \ldots c_\ell) \in \mathcal{C}$, where $c_i \in \{1, \ldots, t\}$. It furthermore adds the pair $(\textsf{id}, \textsf{pk}_{\textsf{id}})$ in the list $\mathcal{L}$.

When $\mathcal{A}$ asks a $\textsf{Corrupt}$ query for user j with identity $\textsf{id} = \boldsymbol{c}$, $\mathcal{B}$ outputs $(\textsf{sk}_1^{(1)}, \ldots, \textsf{sk}_\ell^{(1)})$ possibly by asking to its own $\textsf{Corrupt}$ oracle the keys $\textsf{sk}_{i,a_i}^{(1)}$ it does not know. It furthermore adds the pair $(\textsf{id}, \textsf{pk}_{\textsf{id}})$ in the list $\mathcal{C}$. If the adversary $\mathcal{A}$ wants to corrupt player $(a_1, \ldots, a_\ell)$, then $\mathcal{B}$ aborts. Otherwise, thanks to the ω-collusion security of the code $\mathcal{C}$, we know the ω corruptions cannot involve all the coordinates of the challenge code $(a_1, \ldots, a_\ell)$, otherwise the latter would be in the feasible set, which would contradict the frameproof-property: $\mathcal{B}$ will query its $\textsf{Corrupt}$ oracle at most $\ell - 1$ times. Then, $\textsf{pk}_I$ has not been corrupted, for some index I.

CHALLENGE CIPHERTEXT. Eventually, $\mathcal{A}$ outputs a public key $\textsf{pk}_{\textsf{id}}$ and two messages m_0 and m_1 (and possibly some state information s). With probability greater than $1/n$ (which automatically includes the fact that $(a_1, \ldots, a_\ell)$ has not been asked as a $\textsf{Corrupt}$-query), we have $\textsf{id} = (a_1, \ldots, a_\ell)$. If this is not the case, $\mathcal{B}$ aborts. As said above, we know that $\textsf{sk}_{I,a_I}^{(1)}$ has not been queried to $\mathcal{B}$'s $\textsf{Corrupt}$ oracle. The algorithm $\mathcal{B}$ then computes $\boldsymbol{u} = (u_1, \ldots, u_\ell) = \textsf{Split}_{\mathbb{H}_1}(1, \ell)$ and for $j \in \{1, \ldots, \ell\} \setminus \{I\}$, $c_j^\star = \textsf{Encrypt}_1(u_j, \textsf{pk}_{a_j})$. It then sends to its own challenger $(\textsf{pk}_I = \textsf{pk}_{a_I}, u_I \cdot m_0, u_I \cdot m_1)$ and receives the encryption $c_I^\star$ of $u_I m_b$ for a random $b \in \{0, 1\}$ under the public key pk_I. The algorithm $\mathcal{B}$ sends $\boldsymbol{c}^\star = (c_1^\star, \ldots, c_\ell^\star)$ to $\mathcal{A}$. This is a valid encryption of m_b: $\mathcal{A}$ outputs a bit $b^\star$ that $\mathcal{B}$ forwards to its own challenger.

CONCLUSION. Globally, the running time of $\mathcal{B}$ is the same as $\mathcal{A}$ (and the real challenger) plus the time to execute $(t-1)\ell$ times $\textsf{Kg}$ and its success probability is identical to the one of $\mathcal{A}$ when the guess for $(a_1, \ldots, a_\ell)$ has been correct (which happens with probability greater than $1/n$). This concludes the proof of (strong) semantic security.   □

Theorem 15. *Let $\ell \geq 1$ be an integer and let $\mathcal{C}$ be an $(n, \ell, \omega, t, \varepsilon)$-secure code. Our scheme $\mathcal{M}\textsc{Taes}_3^\ell$ fulfills the ω-resilient privacy property if and only if our scheme $\mathcal{M}\textsc{Taes}_3^1$ fulfills the privacy property*

$$\textsf{Adv}^{\textsf{priv}}_{\mathcal{M}\textsc{Taes}_3^\ell}(\lambda, t, \omega) \leq n \times \textsf{Adv}^{\textsf{priv}}_{\mathcal{M}\textsc{Taes}_3^1}(\lambda, \tau + t\ell\tau_{\textsf{Kg}}),$$

where $\tau_{\textsf{Kg}}$ denotes an upper bound on the time computation for execution of the $\textsf{Kg}$ algorithm.

Proof (Sketch). The proof is very close to the previous one. In the *Challenge ciphertext* phase, the adversary $\mathcal{A}$ outputs a tuple $(\textsf{pk}_0, \textsf{pk}_1, m_0, m_1, s)$, and we know that the two (which are possibly the same) public keys are not corrupted. Again, still with probability greater than $1/n$, the above simulation worked and there is I such that $\textsf{pk}_{a_I}$ has not been queried to $\mathcal{B}$'s $\textsf{Corrupt}$ oracle.   □

This theorem implies the anonymity property.

Unlinkability. Finally, we also state that if the basic construction $\mathcal{M}\text{TAES}_3^1$ is unlinkable then for any integer $\ell \geq 1$ and any ω-secure code $\mathcal{C}$ the scheme $\mathcal{M}\text{TAES}_3^\ell$ is ω-resilient unlinkable. The proof can be found in the full version [16].

Theorem 16. *Let $\ell \geq 1$ be an integer and let $\mathcal{C}$ be an $(n, \ell, \omega, t, \varepsilon)$-secure code. Our scheme $\mathcal{M}\text{TAES}_3^\ell$ is ω-resilient unlinkable if and only if our scheme $\mathcal{M}\text{TAES}_3^1$ is unlinkable.*

Acknowledgments. This work was supported by the French ANR-07-SESU-008-01 PAMPA Project and the European Commission through the ICT Program under Contract ICT-2007-216646 ECRYPT II. The authors thank Julien Cathalo for his participation and contributions in the early stage of this work.

References

1. Abdalla, M., Bellare, M., Neven, G.: Robust encryption. In: Micciancio, D. (ed.) TCC 2010. LNCS, vol. 5978, pp. 480–497. Springer, Heidelberg (2010)
2. Bellare, M., Boldyreva, A., Desai, A., Pointcheval, D.: Key-privacy in public-key encryption. In: Boyd, C. (ed.) ASIACRYPT 2001. LNCS, vol. 2248, pp. 566–582. Springer, Heidelberg (2001)
3. Bellare, M., Shi, H., Zhang, C.: Foundations of group signatures: The case of dynamic groups. In: Menezes, A. (ed.) CT-RSA 2005. LNCS, vol. 3376, pp. 136–153. Springer, Heidelberg (2005)
4. Blackburn, S.R.: Perfect hash families: Probabilistic methods and explicit constructions. J. Comb. Theory, Ser. A 92(1), 54–60 (2000)
5. Boneh, D., Boyen, X., Shacham, H.: Short group signatures. In: Franklin, M. (ed.) CRYPTO 2004. LNCS, vol. 3152, pp. 41–55. Springer, Heidelberg (2004)
6. Boneh, D., Franklin, M.K.: Identity-based encryption from the Weil pairing. In: Kilian, J. (ed.) CRYPTO 2001. LNCS, vol. 2139, pp. 213–229. Springer, Heidelberg (2001)
7. Boneh, D., Shaw, J.: Collusion-secure fingerprinting for digital data (extended abstract). In: Coppersmith, D. (ed.) CRYPTO 1995. LNCS, vol. 963, pp. 452–465. Springer, Heidelberg (1995)
8. Chaum, D., van Heyst, E.: Group signatures. In: Davies, D.W. (ed.) EUROCRYPT 1991. LNCS, vol. 547, pp. 257–265. Springer, Heidelberg (1991)
9. Chor, B., Fiat, A., Naor, M.: Tracing traitors. In: Desmedt, Y. (ed.) CRYPTO 1994. LNCS, vol. 839, pp. 257–270. Springer, Heidelberg (1994)
10. Ducas, L.: Anonymity from asymmetry: New constructions for anonymous HIBE. In: Pieprzyk, J. (ed.) CT-RSA 2010. LNCS, vol. 5985, pp. 148–164. Springer, Heidelberg (2010)
11. El Gamal, T.: A public key cryptosystem and a signature scheme based on discrete logarithms. In: Blakely, G.R., Chaum, D. (eds.) CRYPTO 1984. LNCS, vol. 196, pp. 10–18. Springer, Heidelberg (1985)
12. Galbraith, S.D., Paterson, K.G., Smart, N.P.: Pairings for cryptographers. Discrete Applied Mathematics 156(16), 3113–3121 (2008)
13. Goldwasser, S., Micali, S.: Probabilistic encryption. Journal of Computer and System Sciences 28(2), 270–299 (1984)

14. Golle, P., Jakobsson, M., Juels, A., Syverson, P.F.: Universal re-encryption for mixnets. In: Okamoto, T. (ed.) CT-RSA 2004. LNCS, vol. 2964, pp. 163–178. Springer, Heidelberg (2004)
15. Hollmann, H.D.L., van Lint, J.H., Linnartz, J.-P., Tolhuizen, L.M.G.M.: On codes with identifiable parent property. J. Comb. Theory, Ser. A 82, 121–133 (1998)
16. Izabachène, M., Pointcheval, D., Vergnaud, D.: Traceable anonymous encryption. In: Abdalla, M., Barreto, P.S.L.M. (eds.) LATINCRYPT 2010. LNCS, vol. 6212, pp. 40–60. Springer, Heidelberg (2010)
17. Kiayias, A., Tsiounis, Y., Yung, M.: Group encryption. In: Kurosawa, K. (ed.) ASIACRYPT 2007. LNCS, vol. 4833, pp. 181–199. Springer, Heidelberg (2007)
18. Miyaji, A., Nakabayashi, M., Takano, S.: New explicit conditions of elliptic curve traces for FR-reduction. IEICE Trans. Fundamentals E84-A(5), 1234–1243 (2001)
19. Paillier, P.: Public-key cryptosystems based on composite degree residuosity classes. In: Stern, J. (ed.) EUROCRYPT 1999. LNCS, vol. 1592, pp. 223–238. Springer, Heidelberg (1999)
20. Sako, K.: An auction protocol which hides bids of losers. In: Imai, H., Zheng, Y. (eds.) PKC 2000. LNCS, vol. 1751, pp. 422–432. Springer, Heidelberg (2000)
21. Simmons, G.J.: The prisoners' problem and the subliminal channel. In: Chaum, D. (ed.) Advances in Cryptology – CRYPTO'83, pp. 51–67. Plenum Press, New York (1984)
22. Staddon, J., Stinson, D.R., Wei, R.: Combinatorial properties of frameproof and traceability codes. IEEE Transactions on Information Theory 47(3), 1042–1049 (2001)
23. van Trung, T., Martirosyan, S.: New constructions for IPP codes. Des. Codes Cryptography 35(2), 227–239 (2005)
24. Wang, H., Xing, C.: Explicit constructions of perfect hash families from algebraic curves over finite fields. J. Comb. Theory, Ser. A 93(1) (2001)

Starfish on Strike

Daniel J. Bernstein[1], Peter Birkner[2], and Tanja Lange[3]

[1] Department of Mathematics, Statistics, and Computer Science (M/C 249)
University of Illinois at Chicago, Chicago, IL 60607–7045, USA
djb@cr.yp.to
[2] Laboratoire PRiSM, Université de Versailles Saint-Quentin-en-Yvelines, France
pbirkner@fastmail.fm
[3] Department of Mathematics and Computer Science
Technische Universiteit Eindhoven, P.O. Box 513, 5600 MB Eindhoven, Netherlands
tanja@hyperelliptic.org

Abstract. This paper improves the price-performance ratio of ECM, the elliptic-curve method of integer factorization. In particular, this paper constructs "$a = -1$" twisted Edwards curves having $\mathbf{Q}$-torsion group $\mathbf{Z}/2 \times \mathbf{Z}/4$, $\mathbf{Z}/8$, or $\mathbf{Z}/6$ and having a known non-torsion point; demonstrates that, compared to the curves used in previous ECM implementations, some of the new curves are more effective at finding small primes despite being faster; and precomputes particularly effective curves for several specific sizes of primes.

Keywords: Factorization, ECM, elliptic-curve method, curve selection, Edwards coordinates, twisted Edwards curves, Suyama curves.

1 Introduction

ECM, Lenstra's elliptic-curve method of integer factorization [11], does not find the secret prime factors of an RSA modulus as quickly as the number-field sieve (NFS) does. However, ECM is an increasingly important tool *inside* NFS as a method of finding many smaller primes.

This paper proposes a new two-part strategy to choose curves in ECM. We have implemented the strategy as a patch to the state-of-the-art "EECM-MPFQ" software, and demonstrated through extensive computer experiments that the new strategy achieves better ECM price-performance ratios than anything in the previous literature.

1.1. Background: Edwards curves in ECM. Edwards curves were first described by Edwards in [7]. Bernstein and Lange [5] gave inversion-free formulas for addition and doubling, showing that Edwards curves allow faster scalar multiplication than all other known curve shapes.

Permanent ID of this document: 44c7b02bb6796bb931f85794f77ef1b0. Date of this document: 2010.06.01. This work has been supported in part by the European Commission through the IST Programme under Contract ICT–2007–216676 ECRYPT II, and in part by the National Science Foundation under grant ITR–0716498.

M. Abdalla and P.S.L.M. Barreto (Eds.): LATINCRYPT 2010, LNCS 6212, pp. 61–80, 2010.
© Springer-Verlag Berlin Heidelberg 2010

Edwards curves save time in many applications in cryptography and number theory — provided that the underlying curve is allowed to have a point of order 4. This 4-torsion requirement does not sound troublesome for ECM: the conventional wisdom is that torsion points increase the chance of factorization. This conventional wisdom is based on the heuristic that, for a curve having a torsion group of size r, the group order modulo p has the same smoothness probability as an integer divisible by r in the Hasse interval $[p + 1 - 2\sqrt{p}, p + 1 + 2\sqrt{p}]$, or equivalently an integer in $[(p + 1 - 2\sqrt{p})/r, (p + 1 + 2\sqrt{p})/r]$, so increasing r increases the smoothness chance. For more details on this heuristic and the extent to which it holds, see [4, Section 9].

Bernstein, Birkner, Lange, and Peters demonstrated in [4] the speed of Edwards curves inside ECM. The same paper introduced new small-coefficient high-torsion positive-rank Edwards curves and reported measurements of the effectiveness of two representative curves, i.e., the success chance of the curves at finding primes of various sizes. One curve was the smallest-coefficient positive-rank Edwards curve having torsion group isomorphic to $\mathbf{Z}/12$; the other, $\mathbf{Z}/2 \times \mathbf{Z}/8$. Those curves turned out to be simultaneously faster and more effective than the standard ECM choices described in detail in [17], namely Montgomery curves (specifically Suyama curves) for stage 1 and Weierstrass curves for stage 2.

Twisted Edwards curves $ax^2 + y^2 = 1 + dx^2y^2$ were introduced in [3] as a generalization of Edwards curves; they do not necessarily have a point of order 4. For a twisted Edwards curve with $a = -1$ and negative d the affine graph looks like the following:

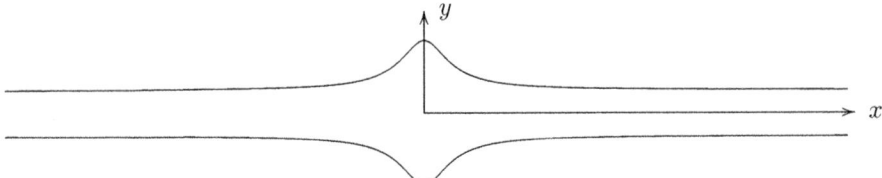

To visualize the behavior at infinity we map a sphere to $\mathbf{P}^2(\mathbf{R})$, rotate the sphere to an angle that makes the relevant points at infinity visible at the same time as $(0, 0)$, and then project the front half of the sphere onto a circle. This first picture shows that there is a single point at infinity and that the curve has two different tangent lines at this point — but only the second picture shows the true nature of things:

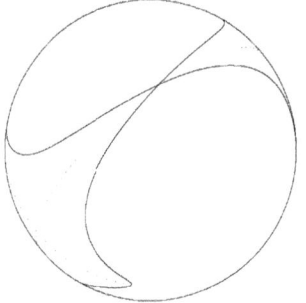

Clearly our all-time-favorite starfish has gone on strike! This might explain the results of [4] that curves over $\mathbf{Q}$ with $a = -1$ cannot have 12 or more rational torsion points. Twisted Edwards curves with this parameter choice are refusing to work for ECM!

The interest in curves with $a = -1$ comes from a curve-addition speedup found by Hisil et al. in [9]. The addition formulas in [9] use 9$\mathbf{M}$ for $a = 1$ but only 8$\mathbf{M}$ for $a = -1$, where $\mathbf{M}$ is the cost of a field multiplication; these formulas hold the speed records for elliptic-curve addition, and one might even speculate that they are optimal. The speed of *doubling* is unaffected by $a = -1$, and scalar multiplication (using standard "window" methods) consists *asymptotically* of 100% doublings and 0% additions; however, additions are a significant fraction of the cost of ECM stage 1, as illustrated by [4, Table 4.1], and are even more important for ECM stage 2.

Unfortunately [4] showed that there are no twisted Edwards curves with $a = -1$ and torsion group isomorphic to $\mathbf{Z}/10$, or to $\mathbf{Z}/12$, or to $\mathbf{Z}/2 \times \mathbf{Z}/8$, or (even for general a) to $\mathbf{Z}/2 \times \mathbf{Z}/6$.

1.2. Contributions of this paper. It is natural to ask whether the speedup in curve additions might be worth a sacrifice in size of the torsion subgroup. To answer this question we first construct twisted Edwards curves with $a = -1$, with positive rank, and with 8 or 6 $\mathbf{Q}$-rational torsion points, and we then carry out extensive computer experiments to analyze the effectiveness of the curves at finding various sizes of primes. The constructions cover three torsion groups, discussed in Sections 3, 4, and 5; for each torsion group we give a fast search method for small-coefficient curves, an explicit infinite family of suitable curves, and the best curves we found. Section 7 compares our curves to previous curves.

We were initially hoping, and were pleased to discover, that the speedup in curve additions *is* worthwhile. Some of our $a = -1$ curves are the new price-performance leaders for ECM: they cost fewer modular multiplications per prime found than the curves used in [12], [13], [17], and [4]. The loss of effectiveness, compared to previous curves with 12 or 16 torsion points, is outweighed by the $a = -1$ gain in speed.

We were surprised to learn that some of our $a = -1$ curves are *more effective* than previous curves with 12 or 16 torsion points. These curves establish new price-performance records for ECM in Montgomery form, even without the Edwards speedups and without the $a = -1$ speedups. In twisted Edwards form, with $a = -1$, these curves require fewer modular multiplications than previous curves *and* find more primes. Evidently the starfish has found a better job working for smaller torsion!

1.3. Sizes of primes used in our paper. We do not claim to be able to *prove* the effectiveness of our curves except through computation. There is a common belief that one can estimate the effectiveness of a curve E by counting the average number of powers of 2 and 3 in $\#E(\mathbf{F}_p)$, as in [13], [17], [2], etc.; but this belief cannot be correct, because it suggests that our curves have, at best, the *same* effectiveness as previous $\mathbf{Z}/12$ curves.

To ensure the comprehensiveness of our computations we try a huge number of curves on *all* b-bit primes, for various values of b. Of course, the cost of this computation increases exponentially with b, and this paper reports results only for $15 \le b \le 26$, but these results are enough to demonstrate the impact of the ECM variations considered in this paper.

We do not claim that ECM is useful for $b = 15$; presumably Pollard's rho method is better at that size. We also do not claim that our quantitative improvements are independent of b; it seems obvious that the gains decrease slowly with b. We are continuing our computations and do not anticipate problems pushing the computations past $b = 30$, i.e., solidly into the range where ECM is used in cryptanalysis.

2 Summary of Results on Points of Small Order

Let k be a field of characteristic different from 2. A twisted Edwards curve over k has the form $E : ax^2 + y^2 = 1 + dx^2y^2$, for some $a, d \in k \setminus \{0\}$ with $a \ne d$. The Edwards addition law is given by

$$(x_1, y_1), (x_2, y_2) \mapsto \left(\frac{x_1 y_2 + y_1 x_2}{1 + dx_1 x_2 y_1 y_2}, \frac{y_1 y_2 - ax_1 x_2}{1 - dx_1 x_2 y_1 y_2} \right).$$

See [6] for a simple definition of a group law on the completed twisted Edwards curve

$$\overline{E}_{E,a,d} = \{((X : Z), (Y : T)) \in \mathbf{P}^1 \times \mathbf{P}^1 : aX^2T^2 + Y^2Z^2 = Z^2T^2 + dX^2Y^2\}.$$

We abbreviate $((x_1 : 1), (y_1 : 1))$ as (x_1, y_1).

We describe points of small order in the special case $a = -1$; see [4, Sections 2 and 3] for proofs in the general case. The picture in the previous section shows the case of $a = -1$ and $d < 0$. The three points $(0, -1)$ and $((1 : 0), (1 : \pm\sqrt{-d}))$ have order 2, so $E(\mathbf{Q})$ contains a subgroup isomorphic to $\mathbf{Z}/2 \times \mathbf{Z}/2$ if and only if $-d$ is a square. Points of order 4 doubling to $(0, -1)$ are $(\pm\sqrt{-1}, 0)$ (which do not exist over $\mathbf{Q}$) and $((1 : \pm\sqrt{d}), (1 : 0))$ which exist if and only if d is a square. Over $\mathbf{Q}$, the values of d and $-d$ cannot simultaneously be squares, so the only way that $\mathbf{Z}/2 \times \mathbf{Z}/4$ can be achieved is with points of order 4 doubling to $((1 : 0), (1 : \pm\sqrt{-d}))$. These are $(\pm\sqrt[4]{-1/d}, \pm\sqrt[4]{-1/d})$. Order-8 points doubling to $((1 : \pm\sqrt{d}), (1 : 0))$ are of the form $(x_8, \pm 1/(x_8\sqrt{d}))$, where $d = 1/(x_8^4 + 2x_8^2)$.

Note that there is no other way a twisted Edwards curve with $a = -1$ can have torsion group isomorphic to $\mathbf{Z}/8$: There is only one element of order 2 in $\mathbf{Z}/8$, so $-d$ must not be a square. The only points of order 4 are $((1 : \pm\sqrt{d}), (1 : 0))$, so d must be a square and any point of order 8 must double to $((1 : \pm\sqrt{d}), (1 : 0))$.

If $y_3 \in \mathbf{Q} \setminus \{-2, -1/2, 0, 1\}$ and $x_3 \in \mathbf{Q}$ satisfy the equation $x_3^2 = y_3^2 + 2y_3$ then the twisted Edwards curve $-x^2 + y^2 = 1 + dx^2y^2$ over $\mathbf{Q}$, where $d = -(2y_3 + 1)/(x_3^2 y_3^2)$, has $(\pm x_3, y_3)$ as points of order 3 and $(\pm x_3, -y_3)$ as points of order 6.

3   Torsion Group Isomorphic to $\mathbf{Z}/2 \times \mathbf{Z}/4$

In this section we present two approaches to finding curves with torsion group isomorphic to $\mathbf{Z}/2 \times \mathbf{Z}/4$. In the first we find curves with non-torsion points of small height; in the second we present a family of such curves for which d and the coordinates of a non-torsion point are parameterized in terms of points on a related elliptic curve, the "generating curve". We then study the effectiveness of the curves in finding primes.

3.1. Finding curves with small parameters. To find curves with torsion group isomorphic to $\mathbf{Z}/2 \times \mathbf{Z}/4$ and rank at least 1 we need to choose d so that $d = -e^4$ for some $e \in \mathbf{Q}$ and so that there exists a point which has infinite order. All points of finite order are listed in the previous section, so this task amounts to putting $d = -a^4/b^4$ for some positive a, b, and letting the coordinates of the non-torsion point be $x_1 = b/c$ and $y_1 = b/f$ for $c \neq \pm f$ and $c, f \neq 0$. Such points correspond to solutions of $(c^2 + b^2)(f^2 - b^2) = a^4 - b^4$. We iterated over many small pairs (a, b) and tested for each divisor A_1 of $a^4 - b^4$ whether $A_1 - b^2$ and $(a^4 - b^4)/A_1 + b^2$ are squares; after testing fewer than 10^{10} divisors we had found 793 different curves.

3.2. Infinite families. The point $Q = (36, -864/5)$ is a non-torsion point on the curve C in the following theorem. Almost all $(u, v) = [i]Q$ satisfy the hypotheses and generate curves with torsion group $\mathbf{Z}/2 \times \mathbf{Z}/4$ and rank at least 1.

Theorem 3.3. *Let* (u, v) *with* $u \neq -324/25, (25v - 1944)/30, -(25v + 1944)/270, -5v/24, (-25v + 972)/45$ *or* $(25v - 3888)/180$ *be a rational point on the elliptic curve* $C : V^2 = U^3 - 11664U/25$ *over* $\mathbf{Q}$. *Define* $e = (270u + 25v + 1944)/(30u - 25v + 1944)$ *and* $y_1 = (30u - 25v + 1944)^2/(-625v^2 + 77760v + 1250u^3 + 24300u^2 - 3779136)$. *Then the twisted Edwards curve* $E : -x^2 + y^2 = 1 - e^4 x^2 y^2$ *has torsion group* $\mathbf{Z}/2 \times \mathbf{Z}/4$ *and* $(1/3, y_1)$ *is a non-torsion point on the curve.*

Proof. For $u \neq -324/25, (25v - 1944)/30, -(25v + 1944)/270, -5v/24$ the value e is defined and not equal to $0, \pm 1$. The twisted Edwards curve E has the desired torsion group, because $a = -1$, $d = -e^4$ for some rational e and d is different from 0 and -1.

If we require $d = -e^4$ and that $x = 1/3$ is the x-coordinate of a point on E we obtain $-1/9 + y_1^2 = 1 - (1/9)e^4 y_1^2$ which is a quadratic equation in y_1 with the two solutions $y_1 = \pm 10/\sqrt{90 + 10e^4}$. These solutions are rational only if $90 + 10e^4 = r^2$. This defines an elliptic curve which is isomorphic to C : $V^2 = U^3 - 11664U/25$ and every point (u, v) on C gives a solution, namely $e = (270u + 25v + 1944)/(30u - 25v + 1944)$ and $y_1 = (30u - 25v + 1944)^2/(-625v^2 + 77760v + 1250u^3 + 24300u^2 - 3779136)$. This solution has been constructed to have $(1/3, y_1)$ on the curve.

Section 2 lists all torsion points. The point $(1/3, y_1)$ is a non-torsion point, unless $e = \pm 3$, i.e., unless $u = (-25v + 972)/45$ or $(25v - 3888)/180$.   □

It is possible to obtain more elliptic families by choosing different values for the x-coordinate of the non-torsion point. Several, but not all, choices lead to parameterizing curves of rank > 0.

Table 3.1. Number of b-bit primes found by various curves having torsion group $\mathbf{Z}/2 \times \mathbf{Z}/4$ and having $a = -1$, using standard EECM parameters. The "bits" column is b. The "#1" column specifies a non-torsion point (x_1, y_1) on the curve that, out of a pool of 1000 curves, was most effective at finding b-bit primes; and the number of b-bit primes found by that curve. The "#2" column provides similar data for the second-best curve out of the same pool. The "#1000" column provides similar data for the worst curve out of the same pool. If $[i]$ appears in place of (x_1, y_1) then it means the curve generated by Theorem 3.3 using $[i](36, -864/5)$. The "ratio" column is the #1 number of primes divided by the #1000 number of primes.

bits	#1	#2	#3	#250	#500	#750	#1000	ratio
15	$\left(\frac{12}{91}, \frac{27}{29}\right)$ 1089	$\left(\frac{23}{14}, \frac{49}{578}\right)$ 1060	$\left(\frac{27}{11}, \frac{5}{13}\right)$ 1057	$\left(\frac{1448}{2151}, \frac{1448}{3697}\right)$ 1006	$[72]$ 990	$\left(\frac{1}{8}, \frac{196}{689}\right)$ 978	$\left(\frac{47}{129}, \frac{47}{89}\right)$ 933	1.16720
16	$\left(\frac{27}{11}, \frac{5}{13}\right)$ 1564	$\left(\frac{12}{343}, \frac{1404}{1421}\right)$ 1564	$\left(\frac{12}{41}, \frac{16}{461}\right)$ 1546	$\left(\frac{57}{176}, \frac{703}{1252}\right)$ 1449	$\left(\frac{178}{729}, \frac{445}{477}\right)$ 1428	$\left(\frac{1122}{949}, \frac{187}{2405}\right)$ 1408	$\left(\frac{21}{38}, \frac{7}{34}\right)$ 1345	1.16283
17	$\left(\frac{12}{343}, \frac{1404}{1421}\right)$ 2985	$\left(\frac{27}{11}, \frac{5}{13}\right)$ 2928	$\left(\frac{12}{91}, \frac{27}{29}\right)$ 2895	$\left(\frac{949}{1122}, \frac{73}{1110}\right)$ 2742	$[17]$ 2712	$[135]$ 2686	$\left(\frac{304}{44187}, \frac{76}{85}\right)$ 2593	1.15118
18	$\left(\frac{27}{11}, \frac{5}{13}\right)$ 5575	$\left(\frac{12}{343}, \frac{1404}{1421}\right)$ 5529	$\left(\frac{13}{16}, \frac{64}{233}\right)$ 5433	$[18]$ 5163	$\left(\frac{888}{539}, \frac{111}{401}\right)$ 5117	$\left(\frac{237}{518}, \frac{79}{241}\right)$ 5076	$\left(\frac{133}{219}, \frac{665}{877}\right)$ 4939	1.12877
19	$\left(\frac{12}{343}, \frac{1404}{1421}\right)$ 10200	$\left(\frac{27}{11}, \frac{5}{13}\right)$ 9770	$\left(\frac{3}{14}, \frac{1}{17}\right)$ 9629	$\left(\frac{1173}{161896}, \frac{391}{392}\right)$ 9271	$\left(\frac{9}{13}, \frac{405}{12277}\right)$ 9212	$\left(\frac{946}{11529}, \frac{473}{1017}\right)$ 9160	$\left(\frac{154}{309}, \frac{154}{339}\right)$ 9004	1.13283
20	$\left(\frac{12}{343}, \frac{1404}{1421}\right)$ 15486	$\left(\frac{27}{11}, \frac{5}{13}\right)$ 14845	$\left(\frac{63}{20}, \frac{1}{244}\right)$ 14537	$\left(\frac{19}{1328}, \frac{19}{10064}\right)$ 13785	$\left(\frac{119}{62}, \frac{119}{194}\right)$ 13706	$[168]$ 13634	$\left(\frac{539}{1278}, \frac{539}{1154}\right)$ 13379	1.15749
21	$\left(\frac{12}{343}, \frac{1404}{1421}\right)$ 22681	$\left(\frac{27}{11}, \frac{5}{13}\right)$ 21745	$\left(\frac{3}{14}, \frac{1}{17}\right)$ 21428	$[29]$ 20095	$\left(\frac{106}{555}, \frac{106}{771}\right)$ 19979	$\left(\frac{28}{101}, \frac{1456}{2777}\right)$ 19886	$\left(\frac{7}{6}, \frac{7}{1385}\right)$ 19475	1.16462
22	$\left(\frac{12}{343}, \frac{1404}{1421}\right)$ 46150	$\left(\frac{27}{11}, \frac{5}{13}\right)$ 43916	$\left(\frac{3}{14}, \frac{1}{17}\right)$ 43482	$\left(\frac{583}{391986}, \frac{583}{585}\right)$ 41185	$\left(\frac{2755}{10816}, \frac{551}{676}\right)$ 40993	$\left(\frac{59}{133}, \frac{59}{377}\right)$ 40843	$\left(\frac{371}{768}, \frac{371}{5440}\right)$ 40410	1.14204
23	$\left(\frac{12}{343}, \frac{1404}{1421}\right)$ 82743	$\left(\frac{27}{11}, \frac{5}{13}\right)$ 77161	$\left(\frac{3}{14}, \frac{1}{17}\right)$ 76640	$[45]$ 72681	$\left(\frac{671}{234}, \frac{671}{11169}\right)$ 72475	$\left(\frac{2}{309}, \frac{26}{519}\right)$ 72293	$\left(\frac{237}{24256}, \frac{79}{164}\right)$ 71612	1.15543
24	$\left(\frac{12}{343}, \frac{1404}{1421}\right)$ 187596	$\left(\frac{27}{11}, \frac{5}{13}\right)$ 177237	$\left(\frac{12}{91}, \frac{27}{29}\right)$ 176170	$[74]$ 167895	$\left(\frac{8}{39}, \frac{1352}{1385}\right)$ 167509	$\left(\frac{96}{41}, \frac{864}{1241}\right)$ 167209	$\left(\frac{68}{609}, \frac{17}{105}\right)$ 166251	1.12839
25	$\left(\frac{12}{343}, \frac{1404}{1421}\right)$ 311864	$\left(\frac{27}{11}, \frac{5}{13}\right)$ 293153	$\left(\frac{12}{91}, \frac{27}{29}\right)$ 289748	$\left(\frac{20}{11}, \frac{80}{10909}\right)$ 277183	$\left(\frac{119}{11649}, \frac{119}{339}\right)$ 276546	$\left(\frac{959}{3655}, \frac{959}{3845}\right)$ 276098	$\left(\frac{231}{5780}, \frac{231}{289}\right)$ 274946	1.13427
26	$\left(\frac{12}{343}, \frac{1404}{1421}\right)$ 480006	$\left(\frac{27}{11}, \frac{5}{13}\right)$ 451692	$\left(\frac{12}{91}, \frac{27}{29}\right)$ 446071	$\left(\frac{133}{2419}, \frac{95}{101}\right)$ 424437	$\left(\frac{1199}{13392}, \frac{1199}{1233}\right)$ 423131	$\left(\frac{322}{251}, \frac{161}{353}\right)$ 422585	$\left(\frac{12}{731}, \frac{27}{29}\right)$ 420891	1.14045

3.4. Effectiveness. We modified the EECM-MPFQ software from [4] to test 1000 curves having torsion group $\mathbf{Z}/2 \times \mathbf{Z}/4$ and having $a = -1$. These 1000 curves include the 793 small-coefficient curves mentioned above, and an additional 207 curves generated modulo n from the infinite family stated in Theorem 3.3.

For each $b \in \{15, 16, 17, 18, 19, 20, 21, 22, 23, 24, 25, 26\}$ we tried all 1000 of these curves on all b-bit primes, i.e., all primes between 2^{b-1} and 2^b. To simplify comparisons we used the EECM parameters B_1, d_1 suggested in [4, Table 10.1]: specifically, $(16, 60)$ for $b \in \{15, 16\}$; $(27, 60)$ for $b = 17$; $(27, 90)$ for $b = 18$;

$(37, 90)$ for $b \in \{19, 20, 21\}$; $(47, 120)$ for $b = 22$; $(64, 120)$ for $b = 23$; $(81, 210)$ for $b = 24$; and $(97, 210)$ for $b \in \{25, 26\}$.

Table 3.1 shows that curves with this torsion group vary quite dramatically in effectiveness (number of primes found). The improvement from the worst curve to the best curve fluctuates somewhat with b, hinting at interactions between curve effectiveness and parameter choice, but is typically around 15%; see the "ratio" column in the table. This improvement is not merely a matter of luck: in particular, the interesting curve $-x^2 + y^2 = 1 - (77/36)^4 x^2 y^2$, with torsion group $\mathbf{Z}/2 \times \mathbf{Z}/4$ and non-torsion point $(12/343, 1404/1421)$, easily outperforms the other 999 curves for $b \geq 19$, for example finding 46150 primes for $b = 22$.

For comparison, [4] reported finding 46323 of the 22-bit primes using the curve $x^2 + y^2 = 1 - (24167/25)x^2 y^2$ with torsion group $\mathbf{Z}/12$ and non-torsion point $(5/23, -1/7)$. Switching to our curve $-x^2 + y^2 = 1 - (77/36)^4 x^2 y^2$ produces only a tiny decrease in effectiveness, 0.4%, while reducing the total ECM stage-1-and-stage-2 cost from $1016\mathbf{M} + 276\mathbf{S}$ to $970\mathbf{M} + 276\mathbf{S}$, a speedup of nearly 4%. This is only the beginning of the comparison between $a = -1$ and $a = 1$: we have identified better $\mathbf{Z}/12$ curves, and better $\mathbf{Z}/2 \times \mathbf{Z}/8$ curves, but as described in subsequent sections we have also identified better $a = -1$ curves.

4   Torsion Group Isomorphic to Z/8

We start this section by giving a parameterization of all curves having torsion group isomorphic to $\mathbf{Z}/8$ and then show how to construct these curves and how effective they are.

Theorem 4.1. *If $u \in \mathbf{Q} \setminus \{0\}$ then the twisted Edwards curve $E : -x^2 + y^2 = 1 + dx^2 y^2$ over $\mathbf{Q}$, where*

$$x_8 = \frac{2u^2 - 1}{2u}, \qquad y_8 = \frac{2u^2 + 1}{2u}, \qquad d = \frac{16u^4}{(4u^4 - 1)^2},$$

has (x_8, y_8) as a point of order 8 and has torsion group isomorphic to $\mathbf{Z}/8$.

Conversely, every twisted Edwards curve over $\mathbf{Q}$ with $a = -1$ and torsion group isomorphic to $\mathbf{Z}/8$ is expressible in this way.

The parameters $u, -u, 1/(2u)$, and $-1/(2u)$ give the same value of d and they are the only values giving this d.

Proof. Note that $d = ((4u^2)/(4u^4 - 1))^2$ is a square, that $1/(x_8^4 + 2x_8^2) = (2u)^4/((2u^2 - 1)^4 + 2(2u^2 - 1)^2(2u)^2) = d$, and that $1/(x_8\sqrt{d}) = (2u(4u^4 - 1))/(4u^2(2u^2 - 1)) = (2u^2 + 1)/(2u) = y_8$. By Section 2, the curve E has (x_8, y_8) as a point of order 8, and has torsion group isomorphic to $\mathbf{Z}/8$.

Conversely, assume that a twisted Edwards curve with $a = -1$ has torsion group isomorphic to $\mathbf{Z}/8$ and has a point of order 8. So the curve can be expressed in this form for some $x_8 \in \mathbf{Q} \setminus \{0\}$ such that $d = 1/(x_8^4 + 2x_8^2)$ is a square in $\mathbf{Q}$. In other words, x_8 is a root of $x_8^4 + 2x_8^2 - 1/d$. Put $x_8^2 = T$, then T is a root of $T^2 + 2T - 1/d$ which means that $(d + 1)/d$ is a square, i.e. that $d + 1$ is also a square. Thus $1, d$, and $d+1$ form a Pythagorean triple and can be parameterized as $d = (r^2 - 1)^2/(2r)^2$ and $d + 1 = (r^2 + 1)^2/(2r)^2$ for $r \neq 0$. The solutions for T are then $2/(r^2 - 1)$ and $-2r^2/(r^2 - 1)$. Obviously only one of them can be positive for each choice of r, in particular the first one requires $r^2 > 1$ while the second one requires $r^2 < 1$; changing r to $1/r$ changes from one value to the other and if one is a square for r_1 then the other one becomes one for $1/r_1$; d is left invariant by this change.

It is thus sufficient to restrict to one case, so request that $2/(r^2 - 1)$ is a square in $\mathbf{Q}$, i.e. $r^2 = 2s^2 + 1$. Define u as the slope of the line between $(1, 0)$ and (r, s): i.e., $u = s/(r - 1)$. Substitute $s = u(r - 1)$ into $r^2 = 2s^2 + 1$ to obtain $r = (2u^2 + 1)/(2u^2 - 1)$. This gives $d = (r^2 - 1)^2/(2r)^2 = (2u^2 - 1)^2((2u^2 + 1)^2 - (2u^2 - 1)^2)^2/(4(2u^2 + 1)^2(2u^2 - 1)^4) = 16u^4/(4u^4 - 1)^2$, $T = 2/(r^2 - 1) = 2(2u^2 - 1)^2/((2u^2 + 1)^2 - (2u^2 - 1)^2) = (2u^2 - 1)^2/(4u^2)$, i.e. $x_8 = (2u^2 - 1)/(2u)$, and $y_8 = 2u(4u^4 - 1)/((2u^2 - 1)4u^2) = (2u^2 + 1)/(2u)$.

The numerator of $(d(u) - d(v))$ factors as $(u - v)(u + v)(uv - 1/2)(uv + 1/2)(u^2 + v^2)(u^2v^2 + 1/4)$ showing that if v is any of the listed values $u, -u, 1/(2u)$, and $-1/(2u)$ then $d(v) = d(u)$. Conversely, if v is not one of those values then none of the factors $u - v, u + v, uv - 1/2$, and $uv + 1/2$ are 0 so $d(v) \neq d(u)$. □

4.2. Finding curves with small parameters.

Theorem 4.1 gives a complete parameterization of all twisted Edwards curves with $a = -1$ and torsion subgroup isomorphic to $\mathbf{Z}/8$. To find such curves of rank at least 1, i.e. with some point (x_1, y_1) which is not a point of finite order, write $u = a/b$, $x_1 = (2a^2 - b^2)/e$, and $y_1 = (2a^2 + b^2)/f$ where a, b, e, f are non-zero integers. Then a, b, e, f satisfy

$$((2a^2 - b^2)^2 + e^2)((2a^2 + b^2)^2 - f^2) = (2ab)^4.$$

We searched for solutions by considering a range of positive integers a and integers $1 < b < a\sqrt{2}$; this ensures $u > 1/\sqrt{2}$ which does not lose any generality by Theorem 4.1. For each (a, b) we enumerated all divisors of $(2ab)^4$, subtracted $(2a^2 - b^2)^2$ from each divisor, and searched for squares. As one would expect from the degree of the equation, this search was less productive than the search in Section 3: after a comparably fast test of $10^{10.66}$ divisors we had found just 3 curves, such as the curve $-x^2 + y^2 = 1 + (784/2337)^2x^2y^2$ with non-torsion point $(8/49, 2337/2303)$.

4.3. Infinite families.

The following theorem, applied to multiples of the non-torsion point $(4, -16)$ on the specified curve, produces infinitely many curves with positive rank and torsion group isomorphic to $\mathbf{Z}/8$.

Theorem 4.4. *Let (r, s) be a rational point with $r, s \neq 0$ and $s \neq \pm 4r$ on the elliptic curve $S^2 = R^3 + 48R$ over $\mathbf{Q}$. Let $u = 2r/s$, $v = (2r^3 - s^2)/s^2$ and $d = (16u^4)/(4u^4 - 1)^2$. The twisted Edwards curve $-x^2 + y^2 = 1 + dx^2y^2$ has torsion subgroup $\mathbf{Z}/8$ and $(x_1, y_1) = (2u^2, (4u^4 - 1)/v)$ as a non-torsion point.*

Proof. The conditions on r and s ensure that d is defined and $\neq 0, -1$; Theorem 4.1 shows that the torsion group equals $\mathbf{Z}/8$.

Table 4.1. Number of b-bit primes found by various curves having torsion group $\mathbf{Z}/8$ and having $a = -1$, using standard EECM parameters. Columns are defined as in Table 3.1, except that if $[i]$ appears in place of (x_1, y_1) then it means the curve generated by Theorem 4.4 using $[i](4, -16)$.

bits	#1	#2	#3	#250	#500	#750	#1000	ratio
15	[455] 1113	[763] 1108	[903] 1106	[580] 1059	[773] 1042	[73] 1026	[86] 973	1.14388
16	[899] 1636	[986] 1633	[880] 1626	[641] 1549	[648] 1523	[269] 1500	$(\frac{133}{156}, \frac{697}{528})$ 1397	1.17108
17	[954] 2986	[985] 2970	[314] 2957	[830] 2878	[305] 2847	[641] 2817	[23] 2716	1.09941
18	[583] 5506	[585] 5487	[891] 5468	[722] 5356	[84] 5318	[57] 5281	[483] 5116	1.07623
19	[506] 9859	[825] 9821	[844] 9813	[932] 9652	[233] 9603	[256] 9551	[32] 9349	1.05455
20	$(\frac{27692}{361875}, \frac{362933}{352275})$ 14823	[456] 14696	[765] 14675	[394] 14432	[466] 14370	[565] 14305	[475] 14053	1.05479
21	$(\frac{27692}{361875}, \frac{362933}{352275})$ 21637	[670] 21499	[904] 21467	[128] 21157	[549] 21069	[604] 20983	[69] 20636	1.04851
22	$(\frac{27692}{361875}, \frac{362933}{352275})$ 43760	[903] 43454	[704] 43411	[105] 43018	[690] 42888	[801] 42779	[893] 42331	1.03376
23	$(\frac{27692}{361875}, \frac{362933}{352275})$ 76798	[887] 76675	[668] 76484	[989] 75983	[555] 75809	[87] 75640	[43] 75044	1.02337
24	$(\frac{27692}{361875}, \frac{362933}{352275})$ 176146	[970] 174926	[554] 174911	[15] 174235	[791] 173994	[986] 173767	[47] 172910	1.01871
25	$(\frac{27692}{361875}, \frac{362933}{352275})$ 291211	[655] 289378	[713] 289365	[950] 287993	[176] 287690	[247] 287384	[330] 286355	1.01696
26	$(\frac{27692}{361875}, \frac{362933}{352275})$ 447683	[793] 443619	[457] 443432	[490] 442162	[468] 441787	[585] 441398	[721] 439094	1.01956

If we require $d = (16u^4)/(4u^4 - 1)^2$ as in Theorem 4.1 and $x_1 = 2u^2$ then y_1 has to satisfy $y_1^2 = (4u^4 - 1)^2(1 + 4u^4)/((4u^4 - 1)^2 - 64u^8) = (4u^4 - 1)^2/(-12u^4 + 1)$. So $-12u^4 + 1$ must be a rational square. This leads to the elliptic curve $v^2 = -12u^4 + 1$, which is isomorphic to the Weierstrass curve $C : S^2 = R^3 + 48R$ via $u = 2R/S$ and $v = (2R^3 - S^2)/S^2$. Any point (r, s) on C gives a point $(x_1, y_1) = (2u^2, (4u^4 - 1)/v)$ on the twisted Edwards curve.

Since $u \neq 0$ also $x_1 \neq 0$ and then $x_8 = x_1$ implies $2u^2 = \pm(2u^2 - 1)/(2u)$ which is excluded by $s \neq \pm 4r$. This means that (x_1, y_1) is different from all torsion points listed in Section 2. $\square$

4.5. Effectiveness. We tried 1000 curves having torsion group $\mathbf{Z}/8$ and having $a = -1$, and measured their effectiveness by the procedures described in Section 3. Table 4.1 reports the results. There is again a clear curve #1 whose performance cannot be explained by random fluctuation. The average effectiveness of $\mathbf{Z}/8$ curves is higher than the average effectiveness of $\mathbf{Z}/2 \times \mathbf{Z}/4$ curves, but the variation is smaller, and the best $\mathbf{Z}/8$ curve is not as good as the best $\mathbf{Z}/2 \times \mathbf{Z}/4$ curve.

5 Torsion Group Isomorphic to Z/6

The structure of this section follows closely that of the previous one.

Theorem 5.1. *If $u \in \mathbf{Q} \setminus \{0, \pm 1\}$ then the twisted Edwards curve $-x^2 + y^2 = 1 + dx^2y^2$ over $\mathbf{Q}$, where*

$$x_3 = \frac{u^2 - 1}{2u}, \quad y_3 = \frac{(u-1)^2}{2u}, \quad d = -16\frac{u^3(u^2 - u + 1)}{(u-1)^6(u+1)^2},$$

has (x_3, y_3) as a point of order 3 and has torsion group isomorphic to $\mathbf{Z}/6$. Conversely, every twisted Edwards curve over $\mathbf{Q}$ with $a = -1$ and a point of order 3 arises in this way.

The parameters u and $1/u$ give the same value of d.

Proof. For $u \in \mathbf{Q} \setminus \{0, \pm 1\}$ the value d is defined and not equal to 0 or -1. Use $-x_3^2 + y_3^2 = -\frac{(u^2-1)^2}{(2u)^2} + \frac{(u-1)^4}{(2u)^2} = \frac{-4u^3 + 8u^2 - 4u}{(2u)^2} = -\frac{2(u-1)^2}{2u} = -2y_3$ to see that (x_3, y_3) is a point of order 3. Further observe that

$$-\frac{2y_3 + 1}{x_3^2 y_3^2} = -\frac{(2(u-1)^2 + 2u)(2u)^4}{2u(u^2-1)^2(u-1)^4} = \frac{16u^3(u^2 - u + 1)}{(u+1)^2(u-1)^6} = d.$$

Furthermore $y_3 \notin \{-2, -1/2, 0, 1\}$ since $u \in \mathbf{Q} \setminus \{0, \pm 1\}$. By Section 2, the twisted Edwards curve $-x^2 + y^2 = 1 + dx^2y^2$ over $\mathbf{Q}$ has (x_3, y_3) as a point of order 3 and has torsion group isomorphic to $\mathbf{Z}/6$.

Conversely, let $x_3^2 = y_3^2 + 2y_3$, then $1 = (y_3+1)^2 - x_3^2 = (y_3 + 1 - x_3)(y_3 + 1 + x_3)$. Splitting 1 as $u \cdot 1/u$ gives $(y_3 + 1 + x_3) = u$ and $(y_3 + 1 - x_3) = 1/u$ and thus $2(y_3 + 1) = u + 1/u$ and $2x_3 = u - 1/u$. The value for d follows from $d = -(2y_3 + 1)/(x_3^2 y_3^2)$.

The numerator of $(d(u) - d(v))$ factors as $(u - v)(uv - 1)$ times a polynomial of degree 6 in u and v which does not factor over $\mathbf{Q}$, showing there are no other rational transformations leaving d invariant that work independently of u. □

5.2. Finding curves with small parameters. Theorem 5.1 gives a complete parameterization of all Edwards curves with torsion group isomorphic to $\mathbf{Z}/6$. Write $u = a/b$ for integers a, b satisfying $0 < |b| < a$, so $|u| > 1$ ensuring that d is defined and avoiding repetitions of d by Theorem 5.1. Define $e = (a^2 - b^2)/x_1$ and $f = -(a-b)^2/y_1$, with integers $e \neq f$. Any solution to $-x_1^2 + y_1^2 = 1 + dx_1^2 y_1^2$ corresponds to a point (a, b, e, f) on

$$((a^2 - b^2)^2 + e^2)((a-b)^4 - f^2) = (a^2 + b^2)^3(b^2 - 4ab + a^2).$$

We searched for solutions following the same strategy as in the previous sections and within $10^{10.7}$ divisors had found 12 curves.

5.3. Infinite families. Suyama [15] presented a rational family of Montgomery curves with torsion containing $\mathbf{Z}/6$. All Suyama curves can be translated to twisted Edwards curves as shown in [4] but here we additionally require $a = -1$. We now present an elliptic family that is a subfamily of Suyama's construction and satisfies $a = -1$.

Theorem 5.4. *Let (u, v) be a rational point with $u, v \neq 0$ and $u \neq 1/96, 1/192,$ $-1/384, 1/576$ on the curve $C : V^2 = U^3 - U^2/2304 - 5U/221184 + 1/28311552.$ Define $\sigma = (1 - 96u)/(96u)$ and $r = v/u^2$. Define $\alpha = \sigma^2 - 5$ and $\beta = 4\sigma$. Define $d = (\beta + \alpha)^3(\beta - 3\alpha)/(r(\beta - \alpha))^2$. Then the twisted Edwards curve $-x^2 + y^2 = 1 + dx^2y^2$ has torsion group isomorphic to $\mathbf{Z}/6$ and a non-torsion point (x_1, y_1) with $x_1 = 2r\sigma/((\sigma - 1)(\sigma + 5)(\sigma^2 + 5))$ and $y_1 = (\alpha^3 - \beta^3)/(\alpha^3 + \beta^3)$. A point of order 3 is given by $(x_3, y_3) = (-r/((\sigma - 1)(\sigma + 5)), (\alpha - \beta)/(\alpha + \beta))$.*

Proof. The twisted Edwards curves $-c^2x^2 + y^2 = 1 + dx^2y^2$ and $-\bar{x}^2 + \bar{y}^2 = 1 + (d/c^2)\bar{x}^2\bar{y}^2$ are isomorphic with $\bar{x} = cx$. By Theorem 7.6 of [4] the Edwards curves corresponding to Suyama curves have $a = (\beta - \alpha)^3(3\alpha + \beta)$ and $d = (\beta + \alpha)^3(\beta - 3\alpha)$. To get an isomorphic curve with $a = -1$ we thus need that $(\beta - \alpha)(3\alpha + \beta)$ is the negative of a rational square. Expanding gives $3\sigma^4 - 8\sigma^3 - 46\sigma^2 + 40\sigma + 75 = r^2$. This defines an elliptic curve isomorphic to C : $V^2 = U^3 - U^2/2304 - 5U/221184 + 1/28311552$, with $\sigma = -(U - 1/96)/U$ and $r = V/U^2$. The values for x_1, y_1, and d in terms of s and t follow from $c = r(\beta - \alpha)$ and the expressions in [4].

By the conditions on u, v all expressions are defined and $d \neq 0, -1$; furthermore (x_1, y_1) does not match any of the points of finite order. To verify the statements on (x_3, y_3) observe that $-x_3^2 + y_3^2 = 1 + dx_3^2y_3^2$ and that $-x_3^2 + y_3^2 = -2y_3$, showing that the point is on the curve and has order 3.   □

The elliptic curve C from the proof has rank 1 and torsion subgroup isomorphic to $\mathbf{Z}/2 \times \mathbf{Z}/2$. A non-torsion point is given by $Q = (1/192, 1/4608)$, so (u, v) can be chosen as a multiple $[i]Q$ of Q with $i > 1$. One can also add points of order 2 to these multiples; in particular, $(1/1152, 7/55296)$ is $-Q$ plus a point of order 2, and generates $\sigma = 11$, a Suyama case that has already drawn attention for being more effective than typical Suyama curves, as discussed in [2].

5.5. Effectiveness. We tried 1000 curves having torsion group $\mathbf{Z}/6$ and having $a = -1$, and measured their effectiveness as in Sections 3 and 4. Table 5.1 shows that these curves are extremely effective, even better than the $\mathbf{Z}/12$ curve measured in [4]. See Sections 6 and 7 for further discussion.

6 Effectiveness for $\mathbf{Z}/12$ and $\mathbf{Z}/2 \times \mathbf{Z}/8$

This paper proposes that the ECM curves used to find b-bit primes should be selected by precomputing the most effective curves. Of course, this proposal is not limited to the fast $a = -1$ curves analyzed in this paper; one can instead precompute, e.g., the most effective $\mathbf{Z}/2 \times \mathbf{Z}/8$ curve.

Table 5.1. Number of b-bit primes found by various curves having torsion group $\mathbf{Z}/6$ and having $a = -1$, using standard EECM parameters. Columns are defined as in Table 3.1, except that if $[i]$ appears in place of (x_1, y_1) then it means the curve generated by Theorem 5.4 from $[i](1/192, 1/4608)$.

bits	#1	#2	#3	#250	#500	#750	#1000	ratio
15	[58] 1175	[348] 1173	[853] 1172	[850] 1128	[799] 1116	[74] 1104	$(\frac{176}{321},\frac{2}{123})$ 1051	1.11798
16	[519] 1779	[532] 1772	[711] 1751	[170] 1695	[38] 1677	[460] 1656	$(\frac{864}{403},\frac{343}{143})$ 1546	1.15071
17	[745] 3355	[868] 3343	[971] 3341	[539] 3253	[425] 3226	[166] 3202	$(\frac{176}{321},\frac{2}{123})$ 3010	1.11462
18	[424] 6223	[310] 6209	[18] 6209	[379] 6104	[634] 6067	[463] 6034	$(\frac{147}{1696},\frac{14336}{10229})$ 5729	1.08623
19	[615] 10809	$(\frac{825}{2752},\frac{1521}{1504})$ 10802	[96] 10771	[175] 10640	[375] 10593	[497] 10538	$(\frac{864}{403},\frac{343}{143})$ 10301	1.04932
20	[932] 16328	[94] 16289	[785] 16287	[334] 16106	[107] 16037	[466] 15969	$(\frac{176}{321},\frac{2}{123})$ 15399	1.06033
21	$(\frac{825}{2752},\frac{1521}{1504})$ 24160	[982] 24119	[265] 24113	[194] 23821	[669] 23735	[869] 23654	$(\frac{749}{3420},\frac{17199}{122324})$ 22790	1.06011
22	$(\frac{336}{527},\frac{80}{67})$ 48424	$(\frac{825}{2752},\frac{1521}{1504})$ 48378	[306] 48357	[565] 47982	[960] 47867	[474] 47749	$(\frac{147}{1696},\frac{14336}{10229})$ 45828	1.05665
23	$(\frac{336}{527},\frac{80}{67})$ 83943	[604] 83417	[879] 83360	[861] 82907	[658] 82755	[3] 82593	$(\frac{864}{403},\frac{343}{143})$ 81114	1.03488
24	$(\frac{825}{2752},\frac{1521}{1504})$ 193069	[119] 192831	[90] 192667	[618] 191776	[728] 191526	[513] 191288	$(\frac{147}{1696},\frac{14336}{10229})$ 188198	1.02588
25	$(\frac{825}{2752},\frac{1521}{1504})$ 318865	[290] 318680	[149] 318605	[453] 317555	[708] 317228	[217] 316924	$(\frac{176}{321},\frac{2}{123})$ 311394	1.02399
26	$(\frac{825}{2752},\frac{1521}{1504})$ 493470	$(\frac{336}{527},\frac{80}{67})$ 493015	[337] 492320	[303] 490886	[198] 490477	[577] 490104	$(\frac{176}{321},\frac{2}{123})$ 480263	1.02750

We carried out computations for 1000 curves having $\mathbf{Z}/2 \times \mathbf{Z}/8$ torsion with $a = 1$, and 1000 curves having $\mathbf{Z}/12$ torsion with $a = 1$. For $\mathbf{Z}/2 \times \mathbf{Z}/8$ we used 975 curves from the (rank-1 elliptic) Atkin–Morain family [1], translated to Edwards form in [4, Theorem 7.3], and 25 small-coefficient curves from [4, Section 8]. For $\mathbf{Z}/12$ we used 922 curves from a (rank-1 elliptic) family introduced by Montgomery in [12], translated analogously to Edwards form, and 78 small-coefficient curves from [4, Section 8].

The results appear in Tables 6.1 and 6.2. It is clear from the tables that $\mathbf{Z}/12$ $a = 1$ is very close in effectiveness to $\mathbf{Z}/6$ $a = -1$, while $\mathbf{Z}/2 \times \mathbf{Z}/8$ $a = 1$ is noticeably worse: for example, the median $\mathbf{Z}/2 \times \mathbf{Z}/8$ curve finds 46501 22-bit primes, the median $\mathbf{Z}/12$ curve finds 47521 22-bit primes, and the median $\mathbf{Z}/6$ curve finds 47687 22-bit primes.

Recall that the small-coefficient $\mathbf{Z}/12$ curve measured in [4] finds only 46323 22-bit primes. The $\mathbf{Z}/12$ median reported here is dominated by the infinite family

Table 6.1. Number of b-bit primes found by various curves having torsion group $\mathbf{Z}/2 \times \mathbf{Z}/8$ and having $a = 1$, using standard EECM parameters. Columns are defined as in Table 3.1.

bits	#1	#2	#3	#250	#500	#750	#1000	ratio
	[792]	[921]	[389]	[364]	[647]	[608]	$(\frac{29573281}{31533721}, \frac{29573281}{79031041})$	
15	1165	1164	1163	1112	1096	1082	1014	1.14892
	[642]	[915]	[855]	[537]	[532]	[467]	$(\frac{305}{851}, \frac{305}{319})$	
16	1726	1723	1716	1653	1634	1612	1506	1.14608
	[920]	[931]	[908]	[694]	[929]	[103]	$(\frac{89623}{51987}, \frac{33019}{31961})$	
17	3176	3163	3161	3045	3016	2988	2838	1.11910
	[758]	[22]	[906]	[868]	[297]	[392]	$(\frac{4913}{377}, \frac{51}{19})$	
18	5804	5781	5779	5665	5630	5588	5298	1.09551
	[955]	[370]	[871]	[564]	[700]	[747]	[2]	
19	10644	10635	10625	10439	10384	10333	10046	1.05953
	[942]	[350]	[707]	[654]	[426]	[596]	$(\frac{1025}{1032}, \frac{41}{265})$	
20	15980	15893	15870	15668	15607	15538	15096	1.05856
	[943]	[316]	[369]	[43]	[764]	[443]	$(\frac{1009}{15801}, \frac{41369}{41441})$	
21	23369	23354	23347	23081	22998	22903	22070	1.05886
	[846]	[724]	[869]	[743]	[430]	[46]	$(\frac{86866}{18259}, \frac{8481}{4001})$	
22	46990	46977	46964	46620	46501	46377	45299	1.03733
	[972]	[590]	[261]	[483]	[367]	[919]	$(\frac{18096}{9793}, \frac{62959}{30191})$	
23	83712	83706	83691	83181	83005	82828	81505	1.02708
	[95]	[485]	[950]	[637]	[239]	[116]	$(\frac{29573281}{31533721}, \frac{29573281}{79031041})$	
24	189700	189678	189660	188973	188724	188502	185854	1.02069
	[657]	[723]	[667]	[938]	[629]	[328]	$(\frac{7825}{12866}, \frac{22223}{27025})$	
25	313857	313718	313600	312577	312253	311942	308060	1.01882
	[594]	[269]	[638]	[801]	[887]	[631]	$(\frac{28577}{34343}, \frac{527}{943})$	
26	483474	483440	483431	482285	481868	481471	474443	1.01903

of $\mathbf{Z}/12$ curves, and it turns out that the average curves in that family are more effective than most of the small-coefficient $\mathbf{Z}/12$ curves. A similar effect occurs for $\mathbf{Z}/2 \times \mathbf{Z}/8$. Countering this effect is a speedup mentioned in [4]: additions of small-coefficient base points are much faster than additions of general points. In this paper we ignore this speedup and count multiplications by small coefficients as if they were as expensive as full multiplications.

7   Comparison

Among all of the 5000 curves measured here, the overall winner in effectiveness for 22-bit primes is the curve $-x^2 + y^2 = 1 - (6517/196608)x^2y^2$, with torsion group $\mathbf{Z}/6$ and non-torsion point $(336/527, 80/67)$. The runner-up for 22-bit primes is the curve $-x^2 + y^2 = 1 - (13312/18225)x^2y^2$, with torsion group $\mathbf{Z}/6$ and non-torsion point $(825/2752, 1521/1504)$. Compared to the $\mathbf{Z}/12$ curve measured in [4], both of these curves find 4% more primes and gain a further 4%

Table 6.2. Number of b-bit primes found by various curves having torsion group $\mathbf{Z}/12$ and having $a = 1$, using standard EECM parameters. Columns are defined as in Table 3.1.

bits	#1	#2	#3	#250	#500	#750	#1000	ratio
15	[636] 1208	[872] 1206	[840] 1206	[516] 1158	[539] 1141	[218] 1120	$(\frac{1159}{191}, \frac{3971}{33239})$ 1039	1.16266
16	[903] 1829	[884] 1808	[662] 1807	[385] 1721	[684] 1690	[170] 1656	$(\frac{514917}{463733}, \frac{507}{277})$ 1509	1.21206
17	[780] 3394	[893] 3371	[850] 3360	[686] 3264	[172] 3229	[15] 3193	$(\frac{424}{18299}, \frac{316}{34075})$ 3011	1.12720
18	[878] 6261	[671] 6218	[666] 6215	[678] 6076	[99] 6032	[82] 5986	$(\frac{2511}{4931}, \frac{549}{3301})$ 5684	1.10151
19	[799] 10882	[918] 10846	[696] 10846	[203] 10643	[539] 10582	[253] 10525	$(\frac{2223}{1165}, \frac{3887}{4055})$ 10181	1.06885
20	[918] 16276	[811] 16275	[719] 16273	[536] 16052	[165] 15977	[441] 15890	$(\frac{1817}{4267}, \frac{2401}{10081})$ 15313	1.06289
21	[772] 23991	[663] 23970	$(\frac{285}{293}, \frac{153}{569})$ 23965	[386] 23687	[449] 23590	[737] 23476	$(\frac{15375}{31217}, \frac{149609}{124766})$ 22714	1.05622
22	[861] 48076	[400] 48028	[648] 48020	[923] 47651	[421] 47521	[11] 47367	$(\frac{4272}{3007397}, \frac{80}{323})$ 45987	1.04543
23	$(\frac{1856}{1735}, \frac{396}{445})$ 83563	[662] 83242	[888] 83196	[799] 82643	[858] 82439	[695] 82260	$(\frac{217}{2687}, \frac{8649}{8599})$ 80858	1.03345
24	$(\frac{285}{293}, \frac{153}{569})$ 192256	[705] 191836	[673] 191693	[275] 190997	[161] 190725	[907] 190459	$(\frac{31293}{105533}, \frac{160003}{307178})$ 187647	1.02456
25	$(\frac{285}{293}, \frac{153}{569})$ 317527	[556] 317372	[575] 317368	[371] 316185	[463] 315835	[457] 315485	$(\frac{192061}{196355}, \frac{2775125}{13288277})$ 310830	1.02155
26	$(\frac{285}{293}, \frac{153}{569})$ 491042	$(\frac{1856}{1735}, \frac{396}{445})$ 490405	[85] 489815	[865] 488399	[695] 487954	[278] 487484	$(\frac{2349}{199}, \frac{11907}{21733})$ 480509	1.02192

from the $a = -1$ speedup, for an overall improvement of 8% in price-performance ratio. Our best $\mathbf{Z}/12$ curves close only about half of the gap.

It is easy to point to algebraic reasons for the effectiveness of $\mathbf{Z}/6$ $a = -1$ curves. Like all Suyama curves these curves have order divisible by 12 modulo any prime. For primes $p \in 1 + 4\mathbf{Z}$ more is true, thanks to $a = -1$: the point $(\sqrt{-1}, 0)$ is defined over $\mathbf{F}_p$ and has order 4; if d is a square then there are extra points of order 2 and 4; and if d is a 4th power then there is full 4-torsion. These reasons suggest that the $\mathbf{Z}/6$ curves with $a = -1$ are more effective than most Suyama curves, and *as effective* as $\mathbf{Z}/12$ curves, but do not explain why the curves are *more effective* than $\mathbf{Z}/12$ curves.

Figure 7.1 plots the price-performance ratio of all 5000 curves for $b = 15$: the number of multiplications per prime found (but counting all multiplications in stage 1 and stage 2 even for primes that actually skip stage 2), as in [4]. Figures 7.2, 7.3, and 7.4 plot data for $b \in \{15, 16, 17, 18, 19, 20, 21, 22, 23, 24, 25, 26\}$. These plots are directly comparable to the "ratio" column in [4, Table 10.1],

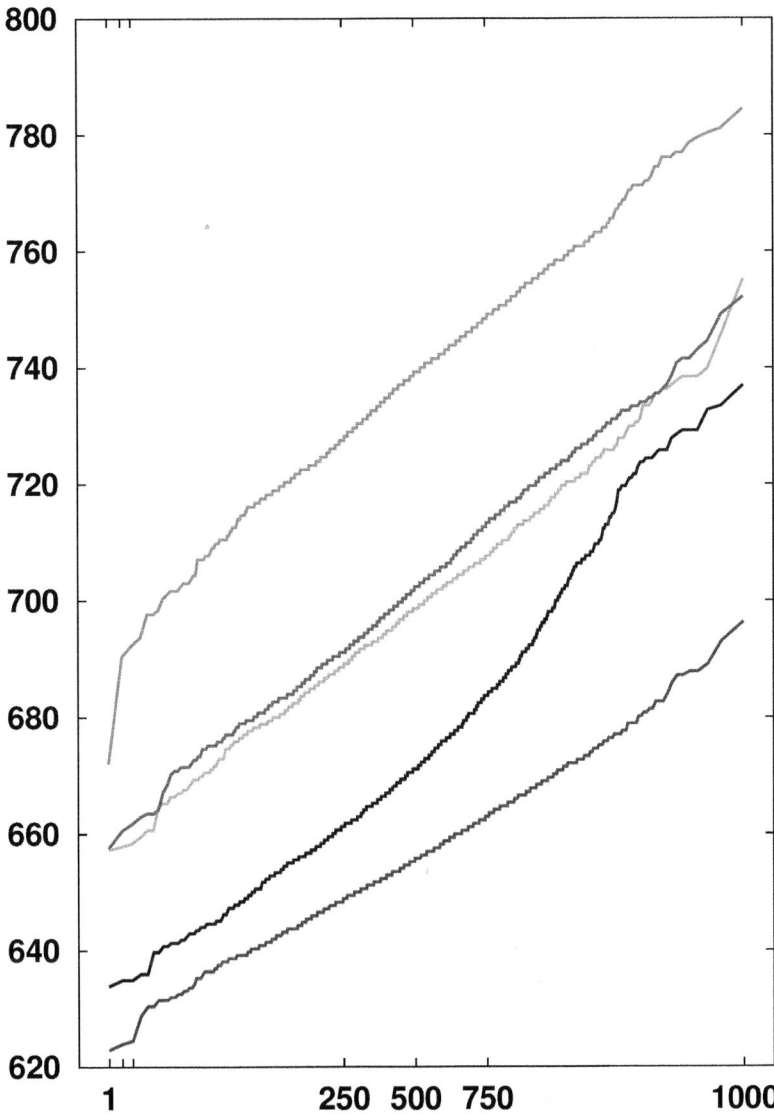

Fig. 7.1. Cost ratio for finding b-bit primes for $b = 15$. The horizontal axis is the curve number c within a pool of 1000 curves, with the most effective curve on the left and the least effective curve on the right. Horizontal tic marks appear at $c \in \{1, 2, 3, 250, 500, 750, 1000\}$. The horizontal scale is $\mathrm{erf}^{-1}((c - 500)/501)$, so a normal distribution would appear as approximately a straight line. The vertical axis is the total number of multiplications and squarings used in stage 1 and stage 2 of EECM with standard parameters, times the total number of b-bit primes, divided by the number of b-bit primes found by the curve. The five graphs are, from top to bottom in the middle, (green) $\mathbf{Z}/2 \times \mathbf{Z}/4$ with $a = -1$; (magenta) $\mathbf{Z}/8$ with $a = -1$; (cyan) $\mathbf{Z}/2 \times \mathbf{Z}/8$ with $a = 1$; (blue) $\mathbf{Z}/12$ with $a = 1$; and (red) $\mathbf{Z}/6$ with $a = -1$.

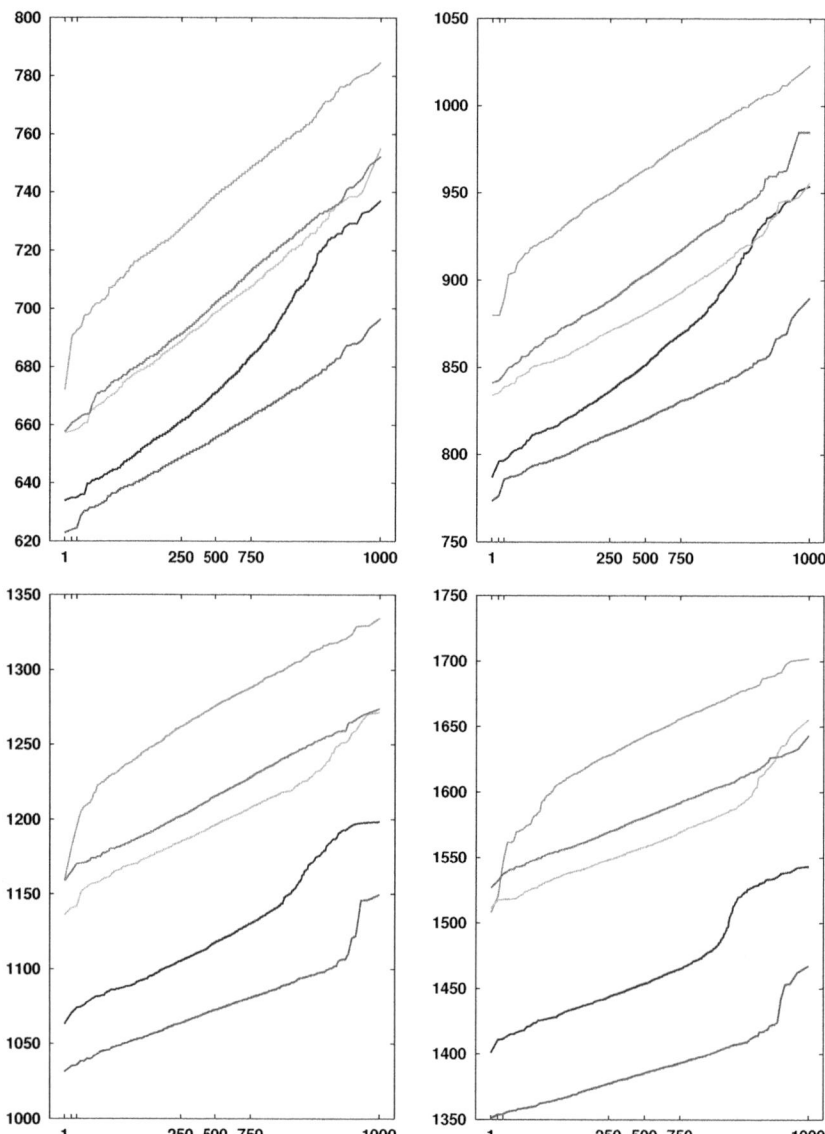

Fig. 7.2. Cost ratio for finding b-bit primes for $b \in \{15, 16, 17, 18\}$. See Figure 7.1 for explanation.

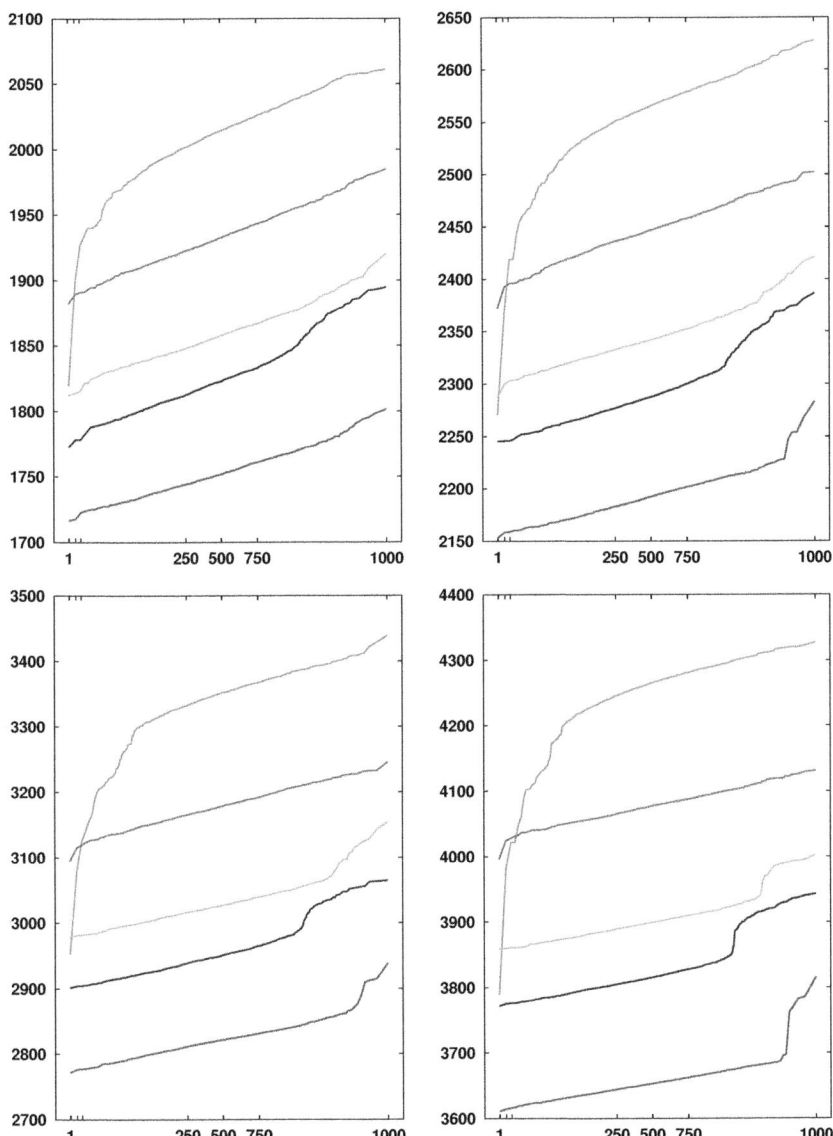

Fig. 7.3. Cost ratio for finding b-bit primes for $b \in \{19, 20, 21, 22\}$. See Figure 7.1 for explanation.

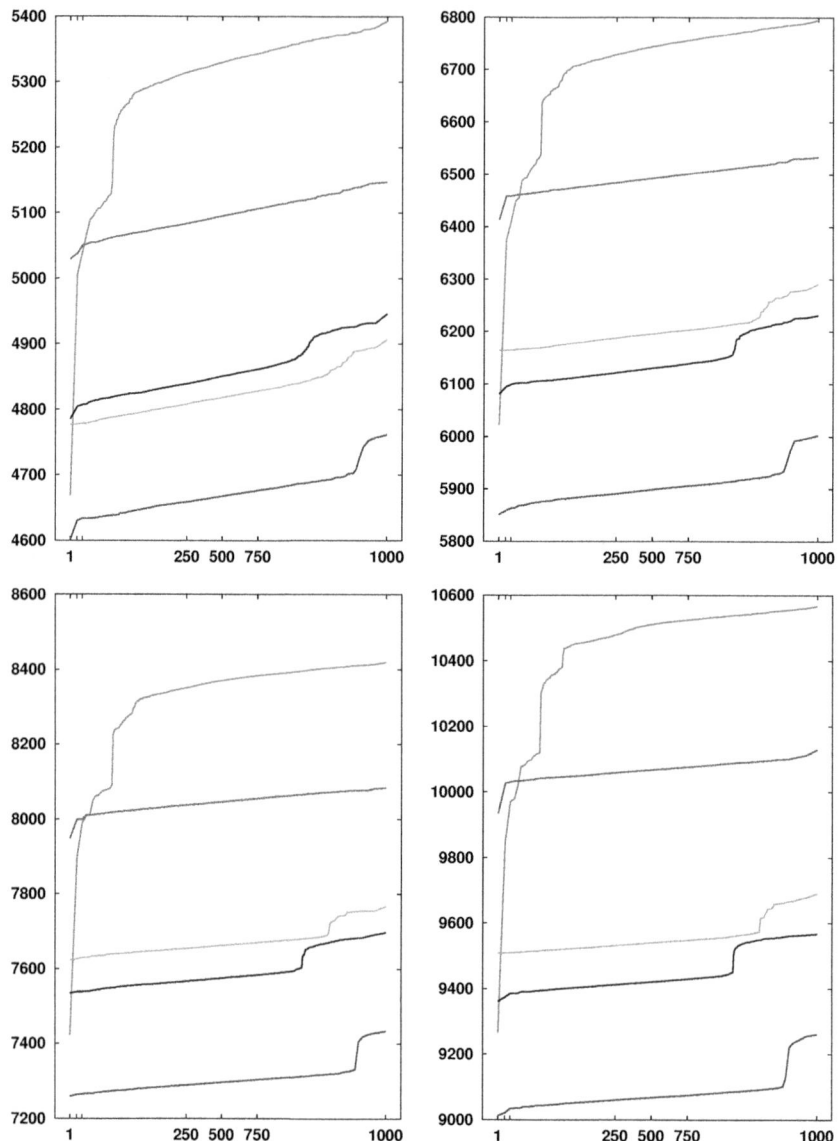

Fig. 7.4. Cost ratio for finding b-bit primes for $b \in \{23, 24, 25, 26\}$. See Figure 7.1 for explanation. The graph for $b = 23$ has $\mathbf{Z}/2 \times \mathbf{Z}/8$ below $\mathbf{Z}/12$.

reporting (e.g.) 1519.3 multiplications for $b = 18$ and 3914.1 multiplications for $b = 22$. The "bumps" on the sides of several graphs are not random: they illustrate the family effects mentioned above.

7.1. Further computations. We plan to extend our precomputations to other choices of EECM-MPFQ parameters (B_1, d_1), to larger values of b, and to a larger pool of curves for each b. We expect that our continuing computations will gradually identify better and better curves for each b, mostly by luck for smaller values of b but also by locating special curves such as $-x^2 + y^2 = 1 - (13312/18225)x^2y^2$. Rather than constantly updating this paper we will maintain a web page showing the best results. Some of the other $\mathbf{Z}/2 \times \mathbf{Z}/8$ families listed in [13] have rank 1; our guess is that none of the families will be competitive with $\mathbf{Z}/6$ but we plan to check this through computation.

Note that each of the curves we consider can be efficiently computed modulo any desired n. The expense of this computation is at most the cost of a small number of additions (modulo n) on a parameterizing elliptic curve. This cost is noticeable only for very small b; it decreases rapidly as b increases.

ECM is normally applied as part of a series of computations: typically $p - 1$, then $p + 1$, then one ECM curve, then another ECM curve, etc. We plan to compute the best ECM curve for primes not found by the $p - 1$ method, the best ECM curve for primes not found by the first curve, etc. Note that there are some known correlations between ECM curves; for example, $\mathbf{Z}/12$ prefers to find primes in $1 + 3\mathbf{Z}$, while $\mathbf{Z}/2 \times \mathbf{Z}/8$ prefers to find primes in $2 + 3\mathbf{Z}$. Our greedy approach might not be optimal but we expect it to produce noticeably better ECM sequences than choosing curves independently.

References

[1] Atkin, A.O.L., Morain, F.: Finding suitable curves for the elliptic curve method of factorization. Mathematics of Computation 60, 399–405 (1993) ISSN 0025–5718. MR 93k:11115,
http://www.lix.polytechnique.fr/~morain/Articles/articles.english.html
Citations in this document: §6

[2] Bărbulesc, R.: Familles de courbes adaptées à la factorisation des entiers (2009), http://hal.inria.fr/inria-00419218/PDF/Familles_version2.pdf Citations in this document: §1.3, §5.3

[3] Bernstein, D.J., Birkner, P., Joye, M., Lange, T., Peters, C.: Twisted Edwards curves. In: Vaudenay, S. (ed.) AFRICACRYPT 2008 [16]. LNCS, vol. 5023, pp. 389–405. Springer, Heidelberg (2008),http://eprint.iacr.org/2008/013 Citations in this document: §1.1

[4] Bernstein, D.J., Birkner, P., Lange, T., Peters, C.: ECM using Edwards curves (24 January 2010 version) (2010), http://eprint.iacr.org/2008/016 Citations in this document: §1.1, §1.1, §1.1, §1.1, §1.1, §1.2, §2, §3.4, §3.4, §3.4, §5.3, §5.3, §5.3, §5.5, §6, §6, §6, §6, §6, §7, §7, §7

[5] Bernstein, D.J., Lange, T.: Faster addition and doubling on elliptic curves. In: Kurosawa, K. (ed.) ASIACRYPT 2007 [10]. LNCS, vol. 4833, pp. 29–50. Springer, Heidelberg (2007),http://cr.yp.to/papers.html#newelliptic Citations in this document: §1.1

[6] Bernstein, D.J., Lange, T.: A complete set of addition laws for incomplete Edwards curves (2009),http://eprint.iacr.org/2009/580 Citations in this document: §2

[7] Edwards, H.M.: A normal form for elliptic curves. Bulletin of the American Mathematical Society 44, 393–422 (2007),
http://www.ams.org/bull/2007-44-03/S0273-0979-07-01153-6/home.html
Citations in this document: §1.1

[8] Hess, F., Pauli, S., Pohst, M. (eds.): ANTS 2006. LNCS, vol. 4076. Springer, Heidelberg (2006) ISBN 3-540-36075-1. See [17]

[9] Hisil, H., Wong, K.K.-H., Carter, G., Dawson, E.: Twisted Edwards curves revisited. In: Asiacrypt 2008 [14] (2008), http://eprint.iacr.org/2008/522 Citations in this document: §1.1, §1.1

[10] Kurosawa, K. (ed.): ASIACRYPT 2007. LNCS, vol. 4833. Springer, Heidelberg (2007), See [5]

[11] Lenstra Jr., H.W.: Factoring integers with elliptic curves. Annals of Mathematics 126, 649–673 (1987) ISSN 0003–486X. MR 89g:11125,
http://links.jstor.org/sici?sici=0003-486X(198711)2:126:3
<649:FIWEC>2.0.CO;2-V Citations in this document: §1

[12] Montgomery, P.L.: Speeding the Pollard and elliptic curve methods of factorization. Mathematics of Computation 48, 243–264 (1987) ISSN 0025–5718. MR 88e:11130, http://links.jstor.org/sici?sici=0025-5718(198701)48:177<243:STPAEC>2.0.CO;2-3 See [15] Citations in this document: §1.2, §6

[13] Montgomery, P.L.: An FFT extension of the elliptic curve method of factorization, Ph.D. thesis, University of California at Los Angeles (1992), ftp://ftp.cwi.nl/pub/pmontgom/ucladissertation.psl.gz Citations in this document: §1.2, §1.3, §7.1

[14] Pieprzyk, J. (ed.): ASIACRYPT 2008. LNCS, vol. 5350. Springer, Heidelberg (2008) ISBN 978-3-540-89254-0. See [9]

[15] Suyama, H.: Informal preliminary report (8), cited in [12] (1985), Citations in this document: §5.3

[16] Vaudenay, S. (ed.): AFRICACRYPT 2008. LNCS, vol. 5023. Springer, Heidelberg (2008) ISBN 978-3-540-68159-5. See [3]

[17] Zimmermann, P., Dodson, B.: 20 Years of ECM. In: ANTS 2006 [8], pp. 525–542 (2006), Citations in this document: §1.1, §1.2, §1.3

Estimating the Size of the Image of Deterministic Hash Functions to Elliptic Curves

Pierre-Alain Fouque and Mehdi Tibouchi[*]

École normale supérieure
Département d'informatique, équipe de cryptographie
45, rue d'Ulm, F-75230 Paris CEDEX 05, France
{pierre-alain.fouque,mehdi.tibouchi}@ens.fr

Abstract. Let E be a non-supersingular elliptic curve over a finite field $\mathbb{F}_q$. At CRYPTO 2009, Icart introduced a deterministic function $\mathbb{F}_q \rightarrow E(\mathbb{F}_q)$ which can be computed efficiently, and allowed him and Coron to define well-behaved hash functions with values in $E(\mathbb{F}_q)$. Some properties of this function rely on a conjecture which was left as an open problem in Icart's paper. We prove this conjecture below as well as analogues for other hash functions.

Keywords: Elliptic Curves, Function Fields, Hash Functions.

1 Introduction

In cryptography, it has been an open problem for a long time to transform a random value in $\mathbb{F}_q$ into a random point on an elliptic curve in a deterministic and efficient manner. Such transformations f are called hash functions since they have been used, say in the context of identity-based encryption [1,7], by first hashing an identity into a random value in $\mathbb{F}_q$ using a standard cryptographic hash function h and then applying such a transformation to get a point on the curve: $H(m) = f(h(m))$. They have also applications in password-based authentication schemes [3]. However, only probabilistic solutions were known before 2006.

The usual solution before 2006 was to take $x \in \mathbb{F}_q$ and check whether this value corresponds to a valid abscissa of a point on the elliptic curve. If not, try another abscissa until one of them works. Consequently, random bits are needed to perform this random search and the running time cannot be bounded and cannot be constant. The main drawback of this approach is that for password-based authentication schemes, an adversary can perform timing attacks and off-line computations in exhaustive search attacks [2]. Some passwords do not need to be tested if the number of iterations of the probabilistic process is not the correct one. Indeed, security proofs for password-based authentication schemes rely on the fact that only on-line attacks are possible and each try allows to

---

[*] This research was carried out while the second author was visiting the Okamoto Research Laboratory at the NTT Information Sharing Platform (Tokyo, Japan).

M. Abdalla and P.S.L.M. Barreto (Eds.): LATINCRYPT 2010, LNCS 6212, pp. 81–91, 2010.

remove a small constant number of passwords, ideally one. Other cryptographic solutions have been proposed to avoid the random process but they made the protocol more complex. One of these is to apply the protocol twice, once with the original curve and in parallel on one of the twisted curves of the original curve. Now, any value in $\mathbb{F}_q$ corresponds either to an abscissa of the original curve or of the associated twisted curve since the two curves represent a distinct union of $\mathbb{F}_q$. Finally, it is worth noticing that the function $h(m) \cdot G$ were G is a generator of the point group of the curve is not a secure solution since the discrete log of the point is known and this makes most protocols insecure.

Deterministic functions. To construct such function, Shallue and van de Woestijne at ANTS 2006 [11] proposed a deterministic algorithm based on Skalba's inequality. The running time of this function is $O(\log^4 q)$. Later, a generalization for hyper-elliptic curve was proposed by Ulas [13]. At CRYPTO 2009, Icart [9] proposed another more efficient technique in $O(\log^3 q)$. Finally, Brier *et al.* [4] propose another technique based on a variant of the Shallue-Woestijne-Ulas (SWU) function, and explain how to construct secure hash functions to elliptic curves based on Icart's function or SWU.

Ideally, it would be nice if the image of the hash function was the whole curve, and if the distribution on the points was statistically close to uniform. In order to prove such results, it is interesting to know how many points there are in the image. Icart showed a coarse bound for his function f: $q/4 \leq \#f(\mathbb{F}_q) \leq q$. He conjectured that

$$\left| \#f(\mathbb{F}_q) - \frac{5q}{8} \right| \leq \lambda\sqrt{q}$$

for some constant λ but left this conjecture as an open problem. Similar statements can be formulated about the size of the image of other hash functions, such as the characteristic 2 version of Icart's function, or the simplified version of SWU proposed by Brier *et al.*.

Related Work. Very recently and independently of our work, Farashahi, Shparlinski and Voloch have also analyzed Icart's function in the case of finite fields of odd characteristic, using Chebotarev theorem in [8] as we did. However, our paper also covers the case of even characteristic for Icart function which is interesting in a cryptographic point of view and the simplified version of SWU which is important in the new paper of Brier *et al.* [4].

It is interesting to note that, depending on the particular function we consider, the number of points in the image varies according to some Galois group associated with the function.

Organization of the paper. In section 2, we describe Icart's hash function and his conjecture. Then, we prove the conjecture for curves of odd characteristic, of characteristic 2 and finally for the variant of SWU.

2 Preliminaries

2.1 Icart's Function

Let $\mathbb{F}_q$ be a finite field of characteristic > 3 and E an elliptic curve over $\mathbb{F}_q$. E can be represented as the union of its neutral element O and the set of points (x, y) in the affine plane over $\mathbb{F}_q$ such that:

$$y^2 = x^3 + ax + b$$

for some suitable constants $a, b \in \mathbb{F}_q$ satisfying $4a^3 + 27b^2 \neq 0$ (non-singularity).

When $q - 1$ is not divisible by 3, these curves are supersingular for $a = 0$. In all other cases, Icart [9] defines the following function $f_{a,b} \colon \mathbb{F}_q \to E(\mathbb{F}_q)$. He sets $f_{a,b}(0) = O$ and for all $u \neq 0$, $f_{a,b}(u) = (x, y)$ with:

$$x = \left(v^2 - b - \frac{u^6}{27}\right)^{1/3} + \frac{u^2}{3}$$
$$y = ux + v$$

where $v = (3a - u^4)/(6u)$. This function is shown to be well-defined and easily computed in deterministic polynomial time. Moreover, if (x, y) is a point in $E(\mathbb{F}_q)$, then $f_{a,b}(u) = (x, y)$ if and only if u satisfies the quartic equation

$$u^4 - 6xu^2 + 6yu - 3a = 0$$

2.2 Icart's Conjecture

In [9], Icart conjectures that the image of $f_{a,b}$ contains $(5/8) \cdot \#E(\mathbb{F}_q) + O(q^{1/2})$ points of the curve. In view of the previous equation, and since the curve itself has $\#E(\mathbb{F}_q) = q + O(q^{1/2})$ points in $\mathbb{F}_q$, this conjecture can be stated as follows.

Conjecture 1 (Icart). Let $K = \mathbb{F}_q(x, y) = \mathbb{F}_q(x)[Y]/(Y^2 - x^3 - ax - b)$ be the function field of E, and P the polynomial in $K[u]$ defined by $P(u) = u^4 - 6xu^2 + 6yu - 3a$. Let further N be the number of points in $E(\mathbb{F}_q)$ at which the reduction of P has a root in $\mathbb{F}_q$. Then

$$N = \frac{5}{8}q + O(q^{1/2})$$

The next section is devoted to the proof of this conjecture.

3 Proof of Icart's Conjecture

3.1 Genericity of P

Proposition 1. *Let again $K = \mathbb{F}_q(x, y)$ be the function field of E. The polynomial $P(u) = u^4 - 6xu^2 + 6yu - 3a \in K[u]$ is irreducible over K, and its Galois group is S_4.*

Proof. Introduce the resolvent cubic of P, whose roots in an algebraic closure are $(r_i + r_j)(r_k + r_l)$ for all permutations (i, j, k, l) of $(1, 2, 3, 4)$, with $r_1, \ldots, r_4$ the roots of P:[1]

$$C(u) = u^3 + 12xu^2 + (36x^2 + 12a)u + 36y^2$$
$$= u^3 + 12xu^2 + (36x^2 + 12a)u + 36(x^3 + ax + b) \in \mathbb{F}_q(x)$$

According to classical facts about the quartic equation (see Appendix A), it suffices to prove that P and C are irreducible over K, and that their common discriminant

$$\Delta = -432(9x^6 + 18ax^4 + 90bx^3 - 39a^2x^2 - 54abx + 16a^3 + 81b^2)$$

is not a square in K. Moreover, we can prove these assertions after extending the field of scalars to $F = \bar{\mathbb{F}}_q$. Indeed, if they hold over F, they clearly hold *a fortiori* over $\mathbb{F}_q$. The following three lemmas conclude the proof.

Lemma 1. *The resolvent cubic $C(u)$ is irreducible over $F(x, y)$.*

Proof. This amounts to showing that $C(u)$ has no root in $F(x, y)$. Note first that it is actually sufficient to prove it has no root in $F(x)$. Indeed, if it is irreducible in $F(x)$ but has a root in $F(x, y)$, the degree of the algebraic extension $F(x, y)/F(x)$ must be divisible by $\deg C(u) = 3$. But this extension is quadratic: hence a condraction.

Let then f/g be a root of C in $F(x)$, with f and g coprime polynomials. Multiplying the equation $C(f/g) = 0$ by g^3, we get

$$f^3 = g \cdot \left(-12xf^2 - (36x^2 + 12a)fg - 36(x^3 + ax + b)g^2 \right)$$

Thus g divides f^3, and since it is coprime to f, it must be constant. Without loss of generality, we thus have $g = 1$ and

$$f^3 + 12xf^2 + (36x^2 + 12a)f + 36(x^3 + ax + b) = 0$$

Let $m = \deg f$. Then the terms in the previous sum are of respective degrees $3m$, $2m + 1$, $m + 2$, 3. If $m \geq 2$, the sum is thus of degree $3m$, and if $m \leq 0$, it is of degree 3: in neither case can it be 0. The only possibility is thus $m = 1$ and $f = \alpha x + \beta$. We get

$$(\alpha^3 + 12\alpha^2 + 36\alpha + 36)x^3 + 3\beta(\alpha^2 + 8\alpha + 12)x^2 +$$
$$(3\alpha\beta^2 + 12a\alpha + 12\beta^2 + 36a)x + (\beta^3 + 12a\beta + 36b) = 0$$

in $F(x)$. Suppose $\beta \neq 0$. Since the coefficients of x^3 and x^2 must be zero, this gives $\alpha^3 + 12\alpha^2 + 36\alpha + 36 = \alpha^2 + 8\alpha + 12 = 0$, which is impossible, since the polynomials $X^3 + 12X^2 + 36X + 36$ and $X^2 + 8X + 12$ are coprime. Hence $\beta = 0$, and thus $\alpha^3 + 12\alpha^2 + 36\alpha + 36 = 12a(\alpha + 3) = 0$, which is similarly seen to be impossible (as $a \neq 0$). This completes the proof.

---

[1] Some texts use the resolvent whose roots are the $r_i r_j + r_k r_l$. This is of course equivalent, as both sets of roots have the same Galois action.

Lemma 2. *The discriminant Δ is not a square in $F(x, y)$.*

Proof. Again, we will show that it is sufficient to prove that Δ is not a square in $F(x)$. Indeed, suppose that Δ is not a square in $F(x)$ but becomes a square in $F(x, y)$. Since the extension is quadratic, this gives $F(x, y) = F(x, \sqrt{\Delta})$. In particular, if λ is a root of $X^3 + aX + b$ in F, the extension $F(x, \sqrt{\Delta})/F(x)$ must be ramified at $(x - \lambda)$. In other words, if we specialize $\Delta(x)$ at $x = \lambda$, we must get 0. But

$$(\lambda - 3b/a)\Delta(\lambda) = 16 \cdot 432(\lambda - 3b/a)(3a^2\lambda^2 + 9ab\lambda - a^3)$$
$$= 16 \cdot 432\big[3a^2(\lambda^3 + a\lambda + b) - (4a^3 + 27b^2)\lambda\big]$$
$$= -16 \cdot 432(4a^3 + 27b^2)\lambda \neq 0$$

since the characteristic does not divide 6 and $a \neq 0$. Hence a contradiction.

It remains to prove that Δ is not a square in $F(x)$, or equivalently in $F[x]$ (since $F[x]$ is integrally closed). A square root of Δ in $F[x]$ must have the form $S = \sqrt{-432} \cdot (3x^3 + rx^2 + sx + t)$. The coefficient of x^5 in S^2 must be 0, hence $r = 0$. The coefficient of x^4 must be $18a$, hence $s = 3a$. But then the coefficient of x^2 is equal to both $9a^2$ and $-39a^2$, which is a contradiction since $48a^2 \neq 0$. This completes the proof.

Lemma 3. *The polynomial P is irreducible over $F(x, y)$.*

Proof. Let σ be the non trivial Galois automorphism of the extension $F(x, y)/F(x)$ $(\sigma(y) = -y)$. If $P(u)$ decomposes as a product of non constant factors in $F(x, y)[u]$, then its norm $P_0(u) = P(u)P(u)^\sigma$ is reducible over $F(x)$. We will show that this is not the case. Note first that $P_0(u)$ can be written as $Q_0(u^2)$, where

$$Q_0(v) = v^4 - 12xv^3 + (36x^2 - 6a)v^2 - 36(x^3 + b)v + 9a^2$$

Now $Q_0(v)$ is easily seen to be an irreducible polynomial of $F(x)[v]$. Indeed, if it had a root $f/g \in F(x)$, the rational function f/g would be constant, which is clearly impossible. And if it decomposes as a product of degree 2 factors $Q_0 = (v^2 + rv + s)(v^2 + r'v + s')$, these factors are in $F[x]$ (integrally closed domain). Since $ss' = 9a^2$, both s and s' are constant. Then, since the coefficient of v^2, $rr' + s + s'$, is of degree 2, r and r' are both of degree at most 2. But then so is $rs' + r's$, which is the coefficient of v in Q_0, namely $-36(x^3 + b)$, hence a contradiction.

Now let w be a root of P_0 in the separable closure of $F(x)$, and let $L = F(x, w)$, $L' = F(x, w^2)$. L' is a subfield of L, and a rupture field of Q_0. In particular $[L : F(x)] = [L : L'] \cdot [L' : F(x)] = 4[L : L']$. Since the polynomial P_0 is even, $-w$ is another root of P_0. As $w \notin F(x)$, $w \mapsto -w$ defines a non trivial $F(x)$-automorphism of L. This automorphism fixes L', so $[L : L'] \geq 2$. This gives $[L : F(x)] \geq 8$, and thus P_0 must have an irreducible factor of degree ≥ 8. In other words, P_0 is irreducible over $F(x)$ as required.

3.2   Applying Chebotarev

Now that Proposition 1 is established, Conjecture 1 readily follows from effective versions of the Chebotarev Density Theorem for function fields. One such version is [6, Proposition 6.4.8], from which one can easily deduce:

Theorem 1 (Chebotarev). *Let K be an extension of $\mathbb{F}_q(x)$ of degree $d < \infty$ and L a Galois extension of K of degree $m < \infty$. Assume $\mathbb{F}_q$ is algebraically closed in L, and fix some subset $\mathscr{S}$ of $\mathrm{Gal}(L/K)$ stable under conjugation. Let $s = \#\mathscr{S}$ and $N(\mathscr{S})$ the number of places v of K of degree 1, unramified in L, such that the Artin symbol $\left(\frac{L/K}{v}\right)$ (defined up to conjugation) is in $\mathscr{S}$. Then*

$$\left| N(\mathscr{S}) - \frac{s}{m}q \right| \leq \frac{2s}{m}\big((m + g_L) \cdot q^{1/2} + m(2g_K + 1) \cdot q^{1/4} + g_L + dm\big)$$

where g_K and g_L are the genera of the function fields K and L.

Proof (of Conjecture 1). In our case, K is the function field of E and L the splitting field of $P(u)$. In particular, $d = 2$, $m = \#S_4 = 24$ and $g_K = 1$. We consider the subset $\mathscr{S} \subset \mathrm{Gal}(L/K) = S_4$ consisting of permutations with at least one fixed point—these are the conjugates of (1), (12) and (123), and there are $s = 1 + 6 + 8 = 15$ of them. Hence $s/m = 15/24 = 5/8$.

The places v of K of degree 1 correspond to points of $E(\mathbb{F}_q)$ (in the projective plane), and for a point $(x_0, y_0) \in E(\mathbb{F}_q)$ not at infinity, saying that $v = (x - x_0)$ has its Artin symbol in $\mathscr{S}$ means that the reduction of $P(u)$ at (x_0, y_0) is a polynomial over $\mathbb{F}_q$ which decomposes into a products of factors at least one of which is of degree 1 (it splits completely if the symbol is (1), decomposes as two linear factors and a quadratic if it is (12) and a product of a linear factor and a cubic if it is (123) up to conjugation).

In other words, $N(\mathscr{S})$ is the same as N in the statement of Conjecture 1 up to a constant number accounting for ramified places (at most 12 since Δ is a polynomial of degree 6 in x) and the point at infinity. We then get

$$\left| N - \frac{5}{8}q \right| \leq \frac{5}{4}\big((24 + g_L) \cdot q^{1/2} + 72q^{1/4} + g_L + 48\big) + 12 + 1$$

To bound g_L, note again that there are at most 12 ramified points, and the ramification index is at most $\deg P_0 = 4$ at each of them. The Riemann-Hurwitz formula thus gives

$$2 - 2g_L \geq 24(2 - 2g_K) - 12 \cdot (4 - 1) \quad \text{i.e.} \quad g_L \leq 17$$

and thus

$$\left| N - \frac{5}{8}q \right| \leq \frac{5}{4}\big(41q^{1/2} + 72q^{1/4} + 76\big)$$

In particular, $N = (5/8)q + O(q^{1/2})$. Concretely, for all $q \geq 2^{19}$, we have

$$\left| N - \frac{5}{8}q \right| \leq 55q^{1/2} \tag{1}$$

4   Analogue in Characteristic 2

In [9], Icart also introduces a variant of his function for elliptic curves over finite fields $\mathbb{F}_q$ of even characteristic, i.e. $q = 2^n$. Such an elliptic curve has the form

$$y^2 + xy = x^3 + ax^2 + b$$

with $a, b \in \mathbb{F}_q$, $b \neq 0$. Icart's function for such a curve E is defined when n is odd as

$$f_{a,b} \colon \mathbb{F}_q \to E(\mathbb{F}_q)$$
$$u \mapsto (x, ux + v^2)$$

where $v = a + u + u^2$ and $x = (v^4 + v^3 + b)^{1/3} + v$. It is shown that $u \in \mathbb{F}_q$ maps to $(x, y) \in E(\mathbb{F}_q)$ if and only if $P(u) = 0$, where $P \in K[u]$ is defined as

$$P(u) = u^4 + u^2 + xu + (a^2 + y)$$

Using this result, we can prove the following analogue of Icart's conjecture.

Proposition 2. *The number of points N in the image of $f_{a,b}$ satisfies:*

$$N = \frac{3}{4}q + O(q^{1/2})$$

where the implied constant in the big-O is universal.

The proof is identical to the one in §3.2. The only difference is that the Galois group of P is A_4 instead of S_4, which leads to the constant $3/4$ instead of $5/8$ (as there are $1 + 8 = 9$ permutations out of 12 in A_4 which have at least one fixed point). Let us prove this fact now.

Proposition 3. *The polynomial $P(u) = u^4 + u^2 + xu + (a^2 + y) \in K[u]$ is separable and irreducible over K, and its Galois group is A_4.*

Proof. Since $P' = x$ is a unit in $K[u]$, P is certainly separable. Now, the relevant case of [5, Theorem 13.1.1] is easily seen to hold in any characteristic for separable polynomials, so it remains to prove that P is irreducible, that its resolvent cubic C is irreducible, and that their common discriminant Δ is a square in K.

Note first that $\Delta = x^4$, so the last point is obvious. Further, we have $C(u) = u^3 + u^2 + x^2$. If this polynomial had a root in $\mathbb{F}_q(x)$, it would be a polynomial of $\mathbb{F}_q[x]$ dividing x^2 by integral closure, which is clearly impossible. Therefore, $C(u)$ is irreducible over $\mathbb{F}_q(x)$, and also over K by the same degree argument as in the proof of Lemma 1: namely, if $C(u)$ had a root in K, $[K : \mathbb{F}_q(x)] = 2$ would be divisible by $\deg C(u) = 3$, a contradiction.

Finally, let us prove that P is irreducible. Let first σ be the non-trivial Galois automorphism of $K/\mathbb{F}_q(x)$, namely $y \mapsto y + x$, and set $P_0 = PP^\sigma \in \mathbb{F}_q(x)$. It suffices to prove that P_0 is irreducible over $\mathbb{F}_q(x)$. We have

$$P_0 = (u^8 + u^4) + x(u^4 + u^2) + x^2(u^2 + u) + (x^3 + a^2x^2 + a^2x + a^4 + b) = Q_0(u^2 + u)$$

where $Q_0(v) = v^4 + xv^2 + x^2v + (x^3 + a^2x^2 + a^2x + a^4 + b)$.

If Q_0 has a root over $\mathbb{F}_q(x)$, it is in fact in $\mathbb{F}_q[x]$, which is not possible by inspection of the degrees of the four terms in the sum. Similarly, if Q_0 can be written as a product of factors of degree 2, we have $Q_0 = (v^2 + r + s)(v^2 + r + s')$ with r, s and s' are all in $\mathbb{F}_q[x]$ (with r appearing in both factors by inspection of the degree 3 coefficient of Q_0). We get $\deg(ss') = 3$, so the polynomial $s + s'$ must be of degree at least 2. Since $r(s + s') = x^2$, this implies that r is constant. But then the relation $s + s' + r^2 = x$ gives a contradiction. Therefore Q_0 is irreducible over $\mathbb{F}_q(x)$.

Then, let w be a root of P_0 in the separable closure of $\mathbb{F}_q(x)$, and set $L = \mathbb{F}_q(x, w)$, $L' = \mathbb{F}_q(x, w + w^2)$. Like in the proof of Lemma 3, we have a tower of extensions $\mathbb{F}_q(x) \subset L' \subset L$, and L' is a rupture field of Q_0, so $[L : \mathbb{F}_q(x)] = 4[L : L']$. Furthermore, since $P_0(u + 1) = P(u)$, $w \mapsto w + 1$ is a non-trivial L'-automorphism of L, which gives $[L : \mathbb{F}_q(x)] \geq 8$ and hence, P_0 is irreducible over $\mathbb{F}_q(x)$, which concludes the proof.

We can again give concrete bounds. With the notations of §3.2, we have $d = 2$, $m = 12$, $s = 8$, $g_K = 1$ and there is exactly one ramified point corresponding to $x = 0$. The Riemann-Hurwitz formula then gives $g_L \leq 2$, and thus:

$$\left| N - \frac{3}{4}q \right| \leq 21q^{1/2} + 54q^{1/4} + 42$$

In particular, for $q > 2^{16}$ we get

$$\left| N - \frac{3}{4}q \right| \leq 25q^{1/2} \tag{2}$$

5   Analogue for the Simplified Shallue-Woestijne-Ulas Algorithm

The first deterministic algorithm for hashing to elliptic curves was introduced by Shallue and van de Woestijne in [11]. It was later generalized and simplified by Ulas in [13]. Brier *et al.* [4] describe a further simplification of the Shallue-Woestijne-Ulas (SWU) algorithm for elliptic curves over fields $\mathbb{F}_q$ with $q \equiv 3 \pmod 4$, based on the following result.

Theorem 2 ([4], Th. 5). *Let $\mathbb{F}_q$ be a finite field and $g(x) := x^3 + ax + b$, where $ab \neq 0$. Consider the following rational functions.*

$$X_2(u) = -\frac{b}{a}\left(1 + \frac{1}{u^4 - u^2}\right), \quad X_3(u) = -u^2 X_2(u), \quad Z(u) = u^3 g\big(X_2(u)\big)$$

Then we have $Z(u)^2 = -g\big(X_2(u)\big) \cdot g\big(X_3(u)\big)$.

If $q \equiv 3 \pmod 4$, -1 is a quadratic non-residue in $\mathbb{F}_q$. Therefore, for each u, exactly one of $g\big(X_2(u)\big)$ and $g\big(X_3(u)\big)$ is a square. This leads to the following deterministic algorithm mapping elements in $\mathbb{F}_q$ to points on the curve $E_{a,b}$: $y^2 = x^3 + ax + b$.

Simplified SWU algorithm.

Input: $\mathbb{F}_q$ such that $q > 3$ and $q \equiv 3 \pmod 4$, parameters a, b such that $ab \neq 0$, and input $u \in \mathbb{F}_q$.

Output: $(x, y) \in E_{a,b}(\mathbb{F}_q)$.

1. $\alpha \leftarrow -u^2$
2. $X_2 \leftarrow -\frac{b}{a}\left(1 + \frac{1}{\alpha^2+\alpha}\right)$
3. $X_3 \leftarrow \alpha \cdot X_2$
4. $h_j \leftarrow X_j^3 + aX_j + b, \; j = 2, 3$
5. If h_2 is a square, return $(X_2, h_2^{(q+1)/4})$; otherwise, return $(X_3, -h_3^{(q+1)/4})$.

This algorithm is a slightly modified version of the one described in [4] §5.5. The only difference is the minus sign in $(X_3, -h_3^{(q+1)/4})$, which ensures that, up to three possible exceptions (points with a zero x-coordinate), the set of points obtained when $g(X_2(u))$ is a square is disjoint from the set of points obtained when $g(X_3(u))$ is a square (which improves the size of the image over the original version). Thus, the image of this function $\mathbb{F}_q \to E_{a,b}(\mathbb{F}_q)$ is the (almost disjoint) union of the sets I_2 and I_3 defined by

$$I_j = \left\{(x, y) \in E_{a,b}(\mathbb{F}_q) \mid \exists u \in \mathbb{F}_q, \; x = X_j(u) \text{ and } y = (-1)^j \sqrt{g(x)}\right\}$$

(where $\sqrt{\cdot}$ denotes the standard square root in $\mathbb{F}_q$, obtained by exponentiation by $(q+1)/4$). Again disregarding at most three points, I_j consists of half the points on the curve with an x-coordinate of the form $X_j(u)$ for some u. Therefore, if N is the number of points in the image of the algorithm and N_j denotes the number of points with an x-coordinate of the form $X_j(u)$, we get

$$N = \frac{N_2 + N_3}{2} + O(1)$$

and the implied constant is at most 6. We deduce the following result.

Proposition 4. *The number of points N in the image of the simplified SWU algorithm satisfies:*

$$N = \frac{3}{8}q + O(q^{1/2})$$

where the implied constant in the big-O is universal.

Proof. The proof is again similar to the previous ones. What we actually show is that $N_j = (3/8)q + O(q^{1/2})$ for $j = 2, 3$, using the Chebotarev density theorem again. Note that for all $u \in \mathbb{F}_q \setminus \{-1, 0, 1\}$, we have

$$x = X_2(u) \iff u^4 - u^2 + \frac{1}{\omega} = 0$$
$$x = X_3(u) \iff u^4 - \omega u^2 + \omega = 0$$

where $\omega = \frac{a}{b}x + 1$. Hence, denoting by $K = \mathbb{F}_q(x, y)$ the function field of $E_{a,b}$, it suffices to prove that the polynomials $P_2(u) = u^4 - u^2 + 1/\omega$ and $P_3(u) =$

$u^4 - \omega u^2 + \omega$ are irreducible and have Galois group D_8 (the 8-element dihedral group, viewed as a transitive subgroup of S_4) over K. Indeed, D_8 has 8 elements, 3 of which have a fixed point: the same technique as in §3.2 then gives the desired estimates for N_2 and N_3.

In view of [10, Theorems 2 and 3], a polynomial $P(u) = u^4 - ru^2 + s \in K[u]$ is irreducible with Galois group D_8 if and only if none of s, $\delta = r^2 - 4s$ or $s\delta$ are squares in K. For P_2, we have $(s, \delta, s\delta) = \frac{1}{\omega^2}(\omega, \omega(\omega - 4), \omega - 4)$, and for P_3, $(s, \delta, s\delta) = (\omega, \omega(\omega - 4), \omega^2(\omega - 4))$. Thus, all we have to prove is that ω, $\omega - 4$ and $\omega(\omega - 4)$ are not squares in K. This is obvious in $\mathbb{F}_q(x)$ (since these are polynomials of $\mathbb{F}_q[x]$ which are not square), and extends to K by a ramification argument as in the proof of Lemma 2.

6   Conclusion

In this paper, we provide a technique to analyze the image of some hash functions mapping elements of $\mathbb{F}_q$ to elliptic curves $E(\mathbb{F}_q)$. It relies on the Chebotarev density theorem in function fields, and in order to apply it, we need to prove the irreducibility of some related polynomial and compute its Galois group.

The same technique should apply similarly to any deterministic, algebraic hash function to curves of any genus. Depending on the particular hash function under consideration, the Galois group varies and the Chebotarev density theorem yields different results accordingly.

Acknowledgements

We would like to thank Jean-Sébastien Coron and Thomas Icart for suggesting this problem to us, and both of them as well as Éric Brier, Igor Shparlinski, Go Yamamoto and an anonymous referee for helpful comments.

References

1. Boneh, D., Franklin, M.K.: Identity-based encryption from the Weil pairing. In: Kilian, J. (ed.) CRYPTO 2001. LNCS, vol. 2139, pp. 213–229. Springer, Heidelberg (2001)
2. Boyd, C., Montague, P., Nguyen, K.Q.: Elliptic curve based password-authenticated key exchange protocols. In: Varadharajan, V., Mu, Y. (eds.) ACISP 2001. LNCS, vol. 2119, pp. 487–501. Springer, Heidelberg (2001)
3. Boyko, V., MacKenzie, P.D., Patel, S.: Provably secure password-authenticated key exchange using Diffie-Hellman. In: Preneel, B. (ed.) EUROCRYPT 2000. LNCS, vol. 1807, pp. 156–171. Springer, Heidelberg (2000)
4. Brier, E., Coron, J.-S., Icart, T., Madore, D., Randriam, H., Tibouchi, M.: Efficient indifferentiable hashing to elliptic curves. In: Proceedings of CRYPTO 2010. LNCS. Springer, Heidelberg (2010)
5. Cox, D.A.: Galois theory. Series in Pure Mathematics. Wiley, Chichester (2004)
6. Fried, M.D., Jarden, M.: Field arithmetic, 2nd edn. Ergebnisse der Mathematik und ihre Grenzgebiete, vol. 11. Springer, Heidelberg (2002)

7. Gentry, C., Silverberg, A.: Hierarchical ID-based cryptography. In: Zheng, Y. (ed.) ASIACRYPT 2002. LNCS, vol. 2501, pp. 548–566. Springer, Heidelberg (2002)
8. Farashahi, R.R., Shparlinski, I., Voloch, J.F.: On hashing into elliptic curves. J. Math. Crypt. 3(10), 353–360 (2009)
9. Icart, T.: How to hash into elliptic curves. In: Halevi, S. (ed.) CRYPTO 2009. LNCS, vol. 5677, pp. 303–316. Springer, Heidelberg (2009)
10. Kappe, L.C., Warren, B.: An elementary test for the Galois group of a quartic polynomial. Amer. Math. Monthly, Mathematical Association of America 96(2), 133–137 (1989)
11. Shallue, A., van de Woestjine, C.: Construction of rational points on elliptic curves over finite fields. In: Hess, F., Pauli, S., Pohst, M. (eds.) ANTS 2006. LNCS, vol. 4076, pp. 510–524. Springer, Heidelberg (2006)
12. Skałba, M.: Points on elliptic curves over finite fields. Acta Arith. IMPAN 117, 293–301 (2005)
13. Ulas, M.: Rational points on certain hyperelliptic curves over finite fields. Bull. Polish Acad. Sci. Math. IMPAN 55, 97–104 (2007)

A   Galois Groups of Quartics

In this appendix, we recall some classical results regarding the computation of Galois groups of quartic polynomials. The reader is refered to texts like [5, Theorem 13.1.1] and [10] for details.

Let F be any field, and $P(x) = x^4 + a_1 x^3 + a_2 x^2 + a_3 x + a_4 \in F[x]$ an irreducible, separable polynomial of degree 4. Let further $\Delta \in F$ be its discriminant, and

$$C(x) = x^3 - 2a_2 x^2 + (a_2^2 + a_1 a_3 - 4a_4)x + (a_3^2 + a_1^2 a_4 - a_1 a_2 a_3)$$

its resolvent cubic. Then the Galois group G of P is conjugate to:

- S_4 if C is irreducible and Δ is not a square in F;
- A_4 if C is irreducible and Δ is a square in F;
- $V_4 = \mathbb{Z}/2\mathbb{Z} \times \mathbb{Z}/2\mathbb{Z}$ if C is reducible and Δ is a square in F;
- D_8 or $\mathbb{Z}/4\mathbb{Z}$ otherwise.

Furthermore, when P is an irreducible biquadratic polynomial (i.e. $a_1 = a_3 = 0$) in odd characteristic, its Galois group can be determined by inspection of its coefficients. It is conjugate to:

- V_4 if a_4 is a square in F;
- $\mathbb{Z}/4\mathbb{Z}$ if $a_4(a_2^2 - 4a_4)$ is a square in F;
- D_8 if neither a_4 nor $a_4(a_2^2 - 4a_4)$ are squares in F.

Fixed Argument Pairings

Craig Costello* and Douglas Stebila

Information Security Institute, Queensland University of Technology,
Brisbane, Queensland, Australia
craig.costello@qut.edu.au, douglas@stebila.ca

Abstract. A common scenario in many pairing-based cryptographic protocols is that one argument in the pairing is fixed as a long term secret key or a constant parameter in the system. In these situations, the runtime of Miller's algorithm can be significantly reduced by storing precomputed values that depend on the fixed argument, prior to the input or existence of the second argument. In light of recent developments in pairing computation, we show that the computation of the Miller loop can be sped up by up to 37% if precomputation is employed, with our method being up to 19.5% faster than the previous precomputation techniques.

Keywords: Pairings, Miller's algorithm, Tate pairing, ate pairing, precomputation.

1 Introduction

Boneh and Franklin were among the first to present a pairing-based cryptosystem in 2001, when they exploited the powerful bilinearity property of pairings to construct the first efficient and provably secure identity-based encryption (IBE) scheme [9], answering an open question first posed by Shamir in 1984 [44]. Boneh and Franklin's discovery, alongside Joux's one round tripartite key agreement protocol [29], were major breakthroughs that gave rise to the now thriving field of pairing-based cryptography and a vast array of new pairing-based primitives that followed, including short signatures [11], hierarchical encryption [23], group signatures [8], ring signatures [10], identity-based key agreement schemes [45,13,33], an IBE scheme secure in the standard model [47], as well as generalizations of IBE such as attribute-based encryption [24,31].

The computation of pairings via Miller's algorithm [35] was initially too slow for them to be considered practically viable, but this did not remain the case for long. Much research has concentrated on achieving pairings at high security levels that are efficient enough for industrial applications. Although use of the Weil pairing was initially proposed, it quickly became evident that the computation of the Tate pairing was much faster in practice [9,21,22,4]. A decade after their introduction into cryptosystems, the computation of a pairing has accelerated

---

* Acknowledges funding from the Queensland Government Smart State PhD Scholarship.

M. Abdalla and P.S.L.M. Barreto (Eds.): LATINCRYPT 2010, LNCS 6212, pp. 92–108, 2010.

from older implementations that took a few minutes [34], to current state-of-the-art implementations that take only a few milliseconds [25,1,37]. Many of the avenues for improving the computation speed of cryptographic pairings on elliptic curves have been somewhat exhausted:

- the Miller loop has been truncated to optimal lengths [3,28,32,46,27];
- improvements inside the Miller iterations, such as denominator elimination, have been thoroughly explored [4,5];
- the choice of the groups $\mathbb{G}_1$ and $\mathbb{G}_2$ as the two eigenspaces of the Frobenius endomorphism is now standard [28,18];
- there is now a flexible array of curve constructions that facilitate fast implementations [20];
- different elliptic curve representations and coordinates systems have been explored in efforts to reduce the field operations encountered when computing the Miller functions [2,16,17]; and
- many other improvements have become standard in optimal or restricted implementations, such as compressed pairings [39,36], optimized field constructions [30,6], fast hashing [40], and fast final exponentiation [41] techniques.

While these techniques have allowed for relatively fast implementations of pairings, there are still some possible improvements that are yet to be explored to their full potential. In this paper we explore one such technique: the implementation of pairings with one argument fixed, which allow for improvements in runtime performance based on precomputations. In the pairing $e(R, S)$ of two points R and S on an elliptic curve, we call the argument R *fixed* if it is constant in terms of the corresponding protocol that employs the pairing, for example, R is a long-term private key that is "paired" with ephemeral or dynamic values (different S values) at runtime.

Scott [38] was the first to comment on the possibility of exploiting the nature of a fixed argument R, suggesting to precompute all multiples of the point R required in the Miller loop. Scott *et al.* [42] took this idea further by also precomputing the gradients, λ_i, of each of the line functions that arise in the Miller iterations, since these are also values depending solely on the first argument R. Essentially, this means that the coefficients of the affine Miller functions have been computed in advance and are just "waiting" as indeterminate functions until S is known, so that they can be evaluated and used to update the Miller function.

We adopt this same approach by performing all computations that are solely dependent on the fixed argument R, and storing these before the second argument S is available. Since R-dependent computations can be performed once only and stored in the long term, it is only the subsequent S-dependent computations that affect the runtime of the pairing algorithm. The question that we address in this paper arises naturally: *are there further R-dependent (pre)computations that can be done to reduce the workload encountered when the dynamic second argument S is known?*

In light of recent developments in pairing computation [14,15], we address this question by considering another: *is it computationally cheaper to evaluate a function before operating on its result, or can it be advantageous to operate on the indeterminate function before evaluating it?*

When neither of the pairing arguments are fixed, the results in [14] and [15] show that many cases of pairing implementations favour the latter. In the case of fixed argument pairings, this becomes even more evident when we observe that any computations on the indeterminate Miller functions are entirely R-dependent and can be done in advance. We show that for both the Tate and ate pairings, the Miller loop can be computed with between 25 and 37% fewer field multiplications (or squarings) if an optimal amount of precomputation is performed in the fixed argument, compared to the case when no precomputation is performed.

The rest of this paper is organized as follows. In Section 2, we present background information on computing pairings using Miller's algorithm. In Section 3, we separate the R-dependent precomputations from the S-dependent dynamic computations in preparation for Section 4, where we present our main technical innovation: we show how to merge multiple iterations of the loop in Miller's algorithm in the precomputation stage to reduce the cost of the S-dependent computations. Section 5 presents the optimal number of iterations to merge for various security levels, and Section 6 lists a number of cryptosystems which can benefit from our techniques. We conclude in Section 7.

2   Preliminaries

Let E be an elliptic curve defined over a large prime field $\mathbb{F}_p$ which is given by the short Weierstrass equation $E : y^2 = x^3 + ax + b$, the identity element of which is denoted by $\mathcal{O}$. Let r be a large prime and let $E[r]$ be the group of points with order r (the r-torsion) on E. Let $k > 1$ be the smallest integer such that $r \mid p^k - 1$; we call k the *embedding degree*. Let π_p be the p-power Frobenius endormorphism on E. The two eigenspaces of π_p, restricted to the r-torsion on E, form two linearly independent groups of order r, written as $\mathbb{G}_1 = E[r] \cap \ker(\pi_p - [1])$ and $\mathbb{G}_2 = E[r] \cap \ker(\pi_p - [p])$. The group $\mathbb{G}_1$ is defined over the base field $\mathbb{F}_p$, whilst the group $\mathbb{G}_2$ is defined over the full extension field $\mathbb{F}_{p^k}$.

A bilinear pairing e of two points $R, S \in E$ can be computed as

$$e(R, S) = f_{m,R}(S)^{(p^k - 1)/r},$$

where $m \in \mathbb{Z}$, and $f_{m,R}$ is a function with divisor $\mathrm{div}(f_{m,R}) = m(R) - ([m]R) - (m-1)(\mathcal{O})$. For our purposes, k will always be even, which allows us to write the function $f_{m,R}$ as a polynomial in x and y so that $f_{m,R}(x, y)$ is evaluated at the coordinates of the point S when the pairing is computed. For the Tate pairing, the first argument R comes from $\mathbb{G}_1$ and the second argument S comes from $\mathbb{G}_2$, whilst the ate pairing takes $R \in \mathbb{G}_2$ and $S \in \mathbb{G}_1$. In either case, the function $f_{m,R}(S)$ evaluates as an element of the finite field $\mathbb{F}_{p^k}$, and this value is raised to the power $(p^k - 1)/r$ in the "final exponentiation" stage. The function $f_{m,R}$ is called the *Miller function*, since it is constructed in a double-and-add like fashion using Miller's algorithm, which is described in Algorithm 1.

Algorithm 1. Miller's affine double-and-add algorithm with denominator elimination

Input: $R = (x_R, y_R)$, $S = (x_S, y_S)$, $m = (m_{l-1}...m_1, m_0)_2$.
Output: $f_{m,R}(S) \leftarrow f$.

1: $T \leftarrow R$, $f \leftarrow 1$.
2: **for** i from $l - 2$ to 0 **do**
3:     Compute $g(x, y) = y - y_T + \lambda(x_T - x)$, where λ is the gradient of the tangent line to T.
4:     $T \leftarrow [2]T = [2](x_T, y_T)$.
5:     $g \leftarrow g(x_S, y_S)$.
6:     $f \leftarrow f^2 \cdot g$.
7:     **if** $m_i \neq 0$ **then**
8:         Compute $g(x, y) = y - y_T + \lambda(x_T - x)$, where λ is the gradient of the line joining T and R.
9:         $T \leftarrow T + R$.
10:         $g \leftarrow g(x_S, y_S)$.
11:         $f \leftarrow f \cdot g$.
12:     **end if**
13: **end for**
14: **return** f.

If we were to discard lines 5 and 10 of Algorithm 1, the output would be an indeterminate function $f_{m,R}(x, y)$ of degree m, rather than a field element $f_{m,R}(x_S, y_S) \in \mathbb{F}_{p^k}$. The reason we include lines 5 and 10 and evaluate the intermediate functions in each iteration is because m is usually quite large (for example, no smaller than 2^{20}), and storing so many coefficients is infeasible; memory constraints force us to evaluate the g functions as we go.

Modern pairing implementations make use of the twisted curve E' of E, to define a group $\mathbb{G}'_2 \in E'$ that is isomorphic to $\mathbb{G}_2 \in E$, but is defined over a smaller subfield $\mathbb{F}_{p^e}$ of $\mathbb{F}_{p^k}$. We let $\psi : E' \to E$ be the twisting isomorphism from E' to E, so that $\psi(\mathbb{G}'_2) = \mathbb{G}_2$. A point $P \in \mathbb{G}_2$ is usually written as $P = P' \cdot \alpha$, where $P' \in \mathbb{G}'_2$ is defined over $\mathbb{F}_{p^e}$ and α is an algebraic element used in the twisting isomorphism (cf. [28,17]). In both the Tate and ate pairings, such points in $\mathbb{G}_2$ are often multiplied by elements in the base field $\mathbb{F}_p$, and because of the representation of $\mathbb{G}_2$ over the twisted curve, these multiplications are counted as e multiplications in the base field.

To count field multiplications and squarings across the different fields employed in pairing computations, we use $\mathbf{m}_i$ and $\mathbf{s}_i$ to respectively denote a multiplication and a squaring in the field $\mathbb{F}_{p^i}$. We maintain generality (across both Tate and ate like pairings) by assuming that the first argument R is written as an element of $\mathbb{F}_{p^u}$ and that the second argument S is written as an element of $\mathbb{F}_{p^v}$, where it is understood that the Tate pairing has $(u, v) = (1, e)$ and that the ate pairing has $(u, v) = (e, 1)$. In both cases, the argument defined over $\mathbb{F}_{p^k}$ is actually treated as an element of $\mathbb{F}_{p^e}$ using $\mathbb{G}'_2$.

3 R-Dependent versus S-Dependent Computations

We begin by separating the R-dependent (fixed) computations from the S-dependent (dynamic) computations. Our goal is to minimize the computational complexity of the S-dependent computations.

When the first argument in the pairing, R, is a fixed or constant parameter in a protocol, Scott et al. [42] propose precomputing and storing all the multiples of R (the T values in Algorithm 1) and all of the gradients (the λ values) in each of the Miller lines (the functions g). This is essentially the same as writing each of the Miller lines as $g(x,y) = y - \lambda x - c$, where $c = y_T - \lambda x_T$ is precomputed and stored alongside λ (see Algorithm 1). We prefer to precompute and store (λ, c) at each iteration, rather than (x_T, y_T, λ), since this saves an extra multiplication (λ by x_T) at runtime and only requires the storage of two values for each iteration, as well as somewhat simplifying the description of what the precomputation achieves. Namely, we do not store the multiples of the point R, since they are not necessarily required once S is input. Instead, we compute all of the R-dependent coefficients of the Miller line functions that are required, in complete preparation for the "arrival" of the argument S.

In this light, fixing one argument in the pairing allows us to split Miller's algorithm into two parts. The first part involves all of the R-dependent (pre)computations that can be performed in advance: computing a set of indeterminate Miller lines defined by (λ, c). The second part involves all of the S-dependent computations, namely those which cannot be performed until the argument S is known. We describe the R-dependent precomputations in Algorithm 2 and the S-dependent dynamic computations in Algorithm 3. For ease of exposition, we assume from here on that the Miller lines are of the form $g(x,y) = y + \tilde{\lambda} x + \tilde{c}$, instead of the usual $g(x,y) = y - \lambda x - c$, by taking $\tilde{\lambda} = -\lambda$ and $\tilde{c} = -c$, and make an abuse of notation by relabeling and writing $g(x,y) = y + \lambda x + c$ from now on. We use #DBL and #ADD in both algorithms to denote the number of doublings and additions, respectively, that occur in the run of Miller's algorithm. Clearly, #DBL $= l - 1$ (from Algorithm 1) and #ADD is equal to the number of non-zero bits in the binary representation of the loop parameter m (excluding the most significant bit). We also write the binary representation of m from $m = (m_{l-1}...m_1, m_0)_2$ to $m = (\tilde{m}_0, \tilde{m}_1...\tilde{m}_{\#DBL-1}, \tilde{m}_{\#DBL})_2$, so that $\tilde{m}_0$ is now the most significant bit, and Miller's algorithm proceeds from $\tilde{m}_1$ to $\tilde{m}_{\#DBL}$; we relabel so that $m = (m_0, m_1...m_{\#DBL-1}, m_{\#DBL})_2$ from now on.

It is important to note that we are solely focussed on minimizing the computational complexity of the algorithm that is S-dependent. We are assuming that the R-dependent precomputations are carried out well in advance on a platform that is not too restricted (within reason) with computational time. For example, in pairings where both arguments are dynamic, one would never compute the Miller point operations and the Miller line functions in affine coordinates, as this involves costly field inversions. Such pairings always resort to avoiding these inversions by using projective coordinates, but in these cases the Miller lines that arise are almost always (cf. [17]) of the form $g(x,y) = g_x \cdot x + g_y \cdot y + g_0$. Employing

Algorithm 2. R-dependent precomputations

Input: $R = (x_R, y_R)$, $m = (m_0, m_1...m_{\#\text{DBL}-1}, m_{\#\text{DBL}})_2$.
Output: $G_{\text{DBL}} = \{(\lambda_1, c_1), (\lambda_2, c_2), ..., (\lambda_{\#\text{DBL}}, c_{\#\text{DBL}})\}$ and
$\quad\quad G_{\text{ADD}} = \{(\lambda'_1, c'_1), (\lambda'_2, c'_2), ..., (\lambda'_{\#\text{ADD}}, c'_{\#\text{ADD}})\}$.

1: $T \leftarrow R$, $G_{\text{DBL}} \leftarrow \{\emptyset\}$, $G_{\text{ADD}} \leftarrow \{\emptyset\}$.
2: **for** i from 1 to $\#\text{DBL}$ **do**
3: $\quad\quad$ Compute λ_i and c_i, such that $y + \lambda_i x + c_i$ is the line tangent to T.
4: $\quad\quad T \leftarrow [2]T$.
5: $\quad\quad$ Append (λ_i, c_i) to G_{DBL}.
6: $\quad\quad$ **if** $m_i \neq 0$ **then**
7: $\quad\quad\quad\quad$ Compute λ'_i and c'_i, such that $y + \lambda'_i x + c'_i$ is the line joining T and R.
8: $\quad\quad\quad\quad T \leftarrow T + R$.
9: $\quad\quad\quad\quad$ Append (λ'_i, c'_i) to G_{ADD}.
10: $\quad\quad$ **end if**
11: **end for**
12: **return** $G_{\text{DBL}}, G_{\text{ADD}}$.

Algorithm 3. S-dependent computations

Input: $S = (x_S, y_S)$, $m = (m_0, m_1...m_{\#\text{DBL}-1}, m_{\#\text{DBL}})_2$, G_{DBL} and G_{ADD} (from Algorithm 2).
Output: $f_{m,R}(S) \leftarrow f$.

1: $f \leftarrow 1$, $\text{count}_{\text{ADD}} \leftarrow 1$.
2: **for** i from 1 to $\#\text{DBL}$ **do**
3: $\quad\quad$ Compute $g \leftarrow (y_S + \lambda_i x_S + c_i)$.
4: $\quad\quad f \leftarrow f^2 \cdot g$.
5: $\quad\quad$ **if** $m_i \neq 0$ **then**
6: $\quad\quad\quad\quad$ Compute $g \leftarrow (y_S + \lambda'_{\text{count}_{\text{ADD}}} x_S + c'_{\text{count}_{\text{ADD}}})$.
7: $\quad\quad\quad\quad \text{count}_{\text{ADD}} \leftarrow \text{count}_{\text{ADD}} + 1$.
8: $\quad\quad\quad\quad f \leftarrow f \cdot g$.
9: $\quad\quad$ **end if**
10: **end for**
11: **return** f.

projective coordinates would certainly reduce the computational time spent performing the R-dependent precomputations, but this would produce slightly more complicated Miller lines (the extra coefficient g_y in front of y), and would inevitably slow down the dynamic computations involving S. In the theme of this paper then, we opt for affine coordinates throughout, with the ultimate goal of minimizing the S-dependent runtime. We do point out however, that the methods in this paper are entirely compatible with an implementation where the precomputation complexity might still be somewhat crucial, in which case the precomputation could be performed in projective coordinates. In such cases, one would split the algorithm and the analogous computational cost analysis described in [15].

Table 1. The complexity of S-dependent computations and storage requirements for Miller's double-and-add routine

Iteration	R-dependent values	Storage $\in \mathbb{F}_{p^u}$	S-dependent computations	Dynamic costs
1	λ_1, c_1	2	$\lambda_1 \cdot x_S, f \leftarrow f^2, f \leftarrow f \cdot g$	$\mathbf{em}_1 + \mathbf{s}_k + \tilde{\mathbf{m}}_k$
2	λ_2, c_2	2	$\lambda_2 \cdot x_S, f \leftarrow f^2, f \leftarrow f \cdot g$	$\mathbf{em}_1 + \mathbf{s}_k + \tilde{\mathbf{m}}_k$
$\vdots$	$\vdots$	$\vdots$	$\vdots$	$\vdots$
i	λ_i, c_i	2	$\lambda_i \cdot x_S, f \leftarrow f^2, f \leftarrow f \cdot g$	$\mathbf{em}_1 + \mathbf{s}_k + \tilde{\mathbf{m}}_k$
$\vdots$	$\vdots$	$\vdots$	$\vdots$	$\vdots$
#DBL	$\lambda_{\#\text{DBL}}, c_{\#\text{DBL}}$	2	$\lambda_{\#\text{DBL}} \cdot x_S, f \leftarrow f^2, f \leftarrow f \cdot g$	$\mathbf{em}_1 + \mathbf{s}_k + \tilde{\mathbf{m}}_k$

In Table 1, we present the S-dependent dynamic computational complexity in a typical iteration of Algorithm 3, ignoring the cost of the precomputations in Algorithm 2.

Table 1 also includes the storage requirements for the Miller lines in each iteration. We do not include the extra storage and S-dependent computations required for the addition steps in our analysis, since additions only occur a small number of times in state-of-the-art implementations that make use of well-chosen, low Hamming-weight loop parameters. In each iteration, the multiplication of the Miller function f by the update g is counted as $\tilde{\mathbf{m}}_k$, where $\tilde{\mathbf{m}}_k$ is actually less than a general $\mathbf{m}_k$, since the updates g are sparse. The complexity of $\tilde{\mathbf{m}}_k$ compared with $\mathbf{m}_k$ depends on the degree of the twist and the nature of the field construction.

The R-dependent precomputations described above are somewhat natural in the context of fixed argument pairings. In the next section, we investigate whether more precomputation can be done to reduce the overall S-dependent complexity (the total of all the entries in the "Dynamic costs" column).

4   Further Precomputations: Merging n Iterations at a Time

It was shown very recently [14,15] that speedups in pairing computations can be achieved if the Miller lines for consecutive iterations are combined before they are evaluated at the second argument of the pairing. In [15], speedups were achieved by developing a general algorithm for merging n consecutive iterations. This involves multiplying n Miller lines together, each of which is raised to a different exponent depending on how many field squarings it would otherwise encounter in the standard Miller routine, given as

$$G_n(x, y) = \prod_{i=1}^{n} g_i(x, y)^{2^{n-i}}. \tag{1}$$

The technique in [14] is much the same, except the formulas for the above line product were presented in (slightly faster) explicit formulas, depending on the shape of the curve employed.

Our approach is analogous to that of [15], where we derive an algorithm to give $G_n(x, y)$ in its general form. We note two important differences between the results herein, and those in [15]. Firstly, the Miller lines in this paper are given in affine form, and so the general product in (1) will have a slightly different form. Secondly, the only computational costs we are concerned with are the dynamic S-dependent costs. This means that the (potentially very expensive) computational costs associated with building up the combined products in (1) can be ignored when determining the optimal number of lines to combine.

We start the discussion by determining the nature of the function $G_n(x, y)$, since the $G_n(x, y)$ products will be evaluated at S, and this is the first S-dependent cost incurred in each of the n-at-a-time iterations. We reiterate that the cost associated with building the indeterminate $G_n(x, y)$ functions is ignored since the coefficients of these functions are solely R-dependent. We assume that $G_n(x, y)$ is reduced modulo the curve equation $y^2 = h(x)$, so that the result will always be (at most) linear in y, given as

$$G_n(x, y) = f_n(x) + g_n(x)y, \tag{2}$$

(where $f_n(x)$ and $g_n(x)$ are not to be confused with the f and g functions described in the algorithms in the previous sections). The following lemma can be used to determine the exact degree of $f_n(x)$ and $g_n(x)$ for all n.

Lemma 1. *Let $y^2 = h(x)$ define an elliptic curve, where $h(x)$ is a monic polynomial with $\deg(h) = 3$. Let n consecutive affine Miller doubling updates be given by $g_1(x, y) = y + \lambda_1 x + c_1,..., g_n(x, y) = y + \lambda_n x + c_n$. If G_n is defined as in Equation (1), then $G_n(x, y)$ takes the form*

$$G_n(x, y) = f_n(x) + g_n(x)y,$$

where $g(x)$ is a monic polynomial such that $\deg(g_n) = \deg(f_n) - 1$.

Proof. When $n = 1$, we have $G_1(x, y) = g_1(x, y) = y + \lambda_1 x + c_1 = f_1(x) + g_1(x)y$, where $f_1(x) = \lambda_1 x + c$ and $g_1(x) = 1$, so that $\deg(g_1) = \deg(f_1) - 1$ and $g_1(x)$ is trivially monic.

For induction, assume $G_k = f_k(x) + g_k(x)y$, where $\deg(g_k) = \deg(f_k) - 1$ and g_k is monic. G_{k+1} is computed as

$$\begin{aligned}
G_{k+1} &= G_k^2 \cdot g_{k+1} \\
&= \left(f_k(x) + g_k(x)y\right)^2 \cdot \left(y + \lambda_{k+1}x + c_{k+1}\right) \\
&= \left(f_k(x)^2 + 2f_k(x)g_k(x)y + g_k(x)^2 h(x)\right)(y + \lambda_{k+1}x + c_{k+1}) \\
&= f_{k+1}(x) + g_{k+1}(x)y,
\end{aligned}$$

where

$$f_{k+1}(x) = 2f_k(x)g_k(x)h(x) + \big(f_k(x)^2 + g_k(x)^2 h(x)\big)\big(\lambda_{k+1}x + c_{k+1}\big)$$

and

$$g_{k+1}(x) = f_k(x)^2 + g_k(x)^2 h(x) + 2f_k(x)g_k(x)\big(\lambda_{k+1}x + c_{k+1}\big).$$

The degree of $f_{k+1}(x)$ is easily seen to be $\deg(f_{k+1}) = \deg(f_k) + \mathrm{def}(g_k) + \deg(h) = \deg(f_k) + (\deg(f_k) - 1) + 3 = 2 \cdot \deg(f_k) + 2$, and the degree of $g_{k+1}(x)$ is $2 \cdot \deg(g_k) + \deg(h) = 2 \cdot \deg(f_k) + 1$, so that $\deg(g_{k+1}) = \deg(f_{k+1}) - 1$. Lastly, $g_k(x)^2 h(x)$ is the only expression contributing to $g_{k+1}(x)$ whose degree is the same as the degree of $g_{k+1}(x)$, and $g_k(x)^2 h(x)$ is clearly monic (since both $g_k(x)$ and $h(x)$ are monic), so $g_{k+1}(x)$ is also monic.   □

To determine the degrees of f_n and g_n, we couple the initial values, $\deg(f_1) = 1$ and $\deg(g_1) = 0$, with the conditions $\deg(f_{k+1}) = 2 \cdot \deg(f_k) + 2$ and $\deg(g_{k+1}) = 2 \cdot \deg(f_k) + 1$; hence

$$\deg(f_n) = 3 \cdot (2^{n-1} - 1) + 1 \qquad \text{and} \qquad \deg(g_n) = 3 \cdot (2^{n-1} - 1), \qquad (3)$$

agreeing with the analogous result for projective coordinates in [15, Eq. (10)].

Since we are combining n iterations into one, the R-dependent precomputation stage of the pairing algorithm will now involve two sub-algorithms. Firstly, Algorithm 2 will precompute the (λ, c) and (λ', c') pairs as usual. Then, another sub-algorithm will be called to combine these pairs (which define lines $g(x, y) = y + \lambda x + c$), combining n at a time into products of the form in (2), the degrees of which are described in (3). Since this sub-algorithm deals with n of the $\lfloor \log_2(m) \rfloor$ standard Miller iterations at a time, it will involve $\lfloor \log_{2^n}(m) \rfloor$ iterations.

For exactly the same reason, the modified S-dependent evaluation stage of the pairing algorithm will now also involve $\lfloor \log_{2^n}(m) \rfloor$ iterations. We now turn to determining the cost of each of these dynamic iterations. Each of the $G_{n(i)}$ takes the form $G_{n(i)}(x, y) = f_{n(i)}(x) + g_{n(i)}(x)y$, containing $\deg(f_n) + 1 + \deg(g_n) = 2 \cdot \deg(f_n) = 6 \cdot (2^{n-1} - 1) + 2$ non-trivial coefficients, since g_n is monic. Thus, for each $1 \le i \le \lfloor \log_{2^n}(m) \rfloor$, we must store $6 \cdot (2^{n-1} - 1) + 2$ elements in $\mathbb{F}_{p^u}$. Apart from the constant term of $f_{n(i)}(x)$, every one of these $6 \cdot (2^{n-1} - 1) + 2$ non-trivial coefficients is multiplied by a product of the coordinates of S, each multiplication of which costs $e\mathbf{m}_1$. Thus, the cost of evaluating $G_{n(i)}$ at S is $[6 \cdot (2^{n-1} - 1) + 1]e\mathbf{m}_1$. We summarize the S-dependent "per-iteration" costs in Table 2. Importantly, we note that each of the n-at-a-time iterations will also involve n squarings of the Miller function f, as well as one (rather than n) multiplication of f by $G(S)$ (see [14,15]). For $n > 1$, this multiplication becomes a general full extension field multiplication $\mathbf{m}_k$, rather than the $\tilde{\mathbf{m}}_k$ that is reported for $n = 1$, since $G(S)$ is no longer sparse.

Each of the $\lfloor \log_{2^n}(m) \rfloor$ iterations requires the computation of $f_{n(1)}(S_x)$ and $g_{n(1)}(S_x) \cdot S_y$. Thus, each iterate requires the same products of S_x^i and $S_x^j S_y$, where $2 \le i \le \deg(f_n)$ and $1 \le j \le \deg(g_n)$, and these products, which are dependent on the dynamic input, are *precomputed* before the first iteration. We use

Table 2. The complexity of S-dependent computations and storage requirements for n combined iterations

Iterations	R-dependent values	Storage $\in \mathbb{F}_{p^u}$	S-dependent computations		Dynamic costs
1	coefficients of	$6(2^{n-1} - 1)$	$f_{n(1)}(S), g_{n(1)}(S)$	$(6(2^{n-1} - 1) + 1)\mathbf{em}_1$	
$\downarrow$	$f_{n(1)}, g_{n(1)}$	$+2$	$f \leftarrow f^{2^n}$	$n\mathbf{s}_k$	
n			$f \leftarrow f \cdot G(S)$	$\mathbf{m}_k$	
$n+1$	coefficients of	$6(2^{n-1} - 1)$	$f_{n(2)}(S), g_{n(2)}(S)$	$(6(2^{n-1} - 1) + 1)\mathbf{em}_1$	
$\downarrow$	$f_{n(2)}, g_{n(2)}$	$+2$	$f \leftarrow f^{2^n}$	$n\mathbf{s}_k$	
$2n$			$f \leftarrow f \cdot G(S)$	$\mathbf{m}_k$	
$\vdots$	$\vdots$	$\vdots$	$\vdots$		$\vdots$
$in+1$	coefficients of	$6(2^{n-1} - 1)$	$f_{n(i)}(S), g_{n(i)}(S)$	$(6(2^{n-1} - 1) + 1)\mathbf{em}_1$	
$\downarrow$	$f_{n(i)}, g_{n(i)}$	$+2$	$f \leftarrow f^{2^n}$	$n\mathbf{s}_k$	
$(i+1)n$			$f \leftarrow f \cdot G(S)$	$\mathbf{m}_k$	
$\vdots$	$\vdots$	$\vdots$	$\vdots$		$\vdots$

the term precomputed here carefully, since these S-dependent precomputations are not to be confused with the R-dependent precomputations that don't contribute to the complexity at runtime. Where possible, we would like to use field squarings to determine the S_x^i and $S_x^j S_y$ terms, rather than the slightly more expensive field multiplications. We can compute the S_x^i terms, which range from S_x^2 to $S_x^{\deg(f_n)}$, where $2 \leq i \leq 2^{\lfloor \log_2(\deg(f_n)) \rfloor}$, using one field squaring each (cf. [14, §5.2]). The remaining S_x^i terms, where $i > 2^{\lfloor \log_2(\deg(f_n)) \rfloor}$, are computed using $(\deg(f_n) - 2^{\lfloor \log_2(\deg(f_n)) \rfloor})$ field multiplications. These multiplications and squarings occur in the field $\mathbb{F}_{p^v}$, so that the total dynamic cost of obtaining S_x^i for $2 \leq i \leq \deg(f_n)$ is

$$(2^{\lfloor \log_2(\deg(f_n)) \rfloor} - 1)\mathbf{s}_v + (\deg(f_n) - 2^{\lfloor \log_2(\deg(f_n)) \rfloor})\mathbf{m}_v.$$

To compute the $S_x^j S_y$ products, where $1 \leq j \leq \deg(g_n)$, we require $\deg(g_n)$ multiplications[1] since we already have all of the S_x^j. Each of these multiplications occur in $\mathbb{F}_{p^v}$, so that the total cost of the S-dependent precomputation is given by adding $\deg(g_n)\mathbf{m}_v = (\deg(f_n) - 1)\mathbf{m}_v$ to the previous cost, giving

$$(2^{\lfloor \log_2(\deg(f_n)) \rfloor} - 1)\mathbf{s}_v + (2 \cdot \deg(f_n) - 2^{\lfloor \log_2(\deg(f_n)) \rfloor} - 1)\mathbf{m}_v.$$

Substituting $\deg(f_n) = 3(2^{n-1}-1)+1$ (from (3)) into the above equation requires the evaluation of $2^{\lfloor \log_2(3(2^{n-1}-1)+1) \rfloor}$. To simplify this expression we rewrite the index as $\lfloor \log_2(2^n + 2^{n-1} - 2) \rfloor = n$, so that the total number of S-dependent computations simplifies to

$$(2^n - 1)\mathbf{s}_v + (2^{n+1} - 5)\mathbf{m}_v. \tag{4}$$

---

[1] This is the cheapest way to compute these products, as trying to use field squarings to form the products would require us to compute $S_x^j S_y = ((S_x^j + S_y)^2 - S_x^{2j} + S_y^2)$; even though we have S_y^2 via the curve equation, the squaring $(S_x^j + S_y)^2$ would require a full extension field squaring.

Table 3. The total storage requirements and S-dependent complexity for a fixed argument pairing

n	Storage $\in \mathbb{F}_{p^u}$	S-dependent costs
1	$2\lfloor \log_2 m \rfloor$	$\lfloor \log_2(m) \rfloor (\mathbf{em}_1 + \mathbf{s}_k + \tilde{\mathbf{m}}_k)$
≥ 2	$\lfloor \log_{2^n} m \rfloor (6(2^{n-1} - 1) + 2)$	$\lfloor \log_{2^n}(m) \rfloor ((6(2^{n-1} - 1) + 1)\mathbf{em}_1 + n\mathbf{s}_k + \mathbf{m}_k)$ $+(2^n - 1)\mathbf{s}_v + (2^{n+1} - 5)\mathbf{m}_v$

From Table 2, each of the iterations costs $\big([6 \cdot (2^{n-1} - 1) + 2]\mathbf{em}_1 + n\mathbf{s}_k + \mathbf{m}_k\big)$. Summing this cost over the $\lfloor \log_{2^n}(m) \rfloor$ iterations, and adding the S-dependent precomputation in (4), gives the total S-dependent computation complexity as

$$\lfloor \log_{2^n}(m) \rfloor \big([6 \cdot (2^{n-1} - 1) + 1]\mathbf{em}_1 + n\mathbf{s}_k + \mathbf{m}_k\big) + (2^n - 1)\mathbf{s}_v + (2^{n+1} - 5)\mathbf{m}_v. \tag{5}$$

We summarize the total storage and the total costs for all n in Table 3. Once more, we reiterate that the total complexity is independent of the field containing the first argument, $\mathbb{F}_{p^u}$, and is only dependent on the field containing the second argument, $\mathbb{F}_{p^v}$. Interestingly, this means that even if the ate and Tate pairings had equal loop lengths, a fixed argument ate pairing ($v = 1$) will still perform faster than a fixed argument Tate pairing ($v = e$) in general. As far as storage goes, the ate pairing will require storing values in the field $\mathbb{F}_{p^e}$, whilst the Tate pairing will store values in the base field $\mathbb{F}_p$. However, because of the shorter loop lengths achieved in the ate pairing, the total storage needed in the ate pairing may still end up being less than for the Tate pairing. Unlike the speedups achieved in [14] and [15] which mainly benefit the Tate pairing, it is clear that our techniques will also speed up the ate pairing when a fixed argument can be exploited. In the next section, we use the complexities in Table 3 to determine the optimal amount of precomputation for implementations over various embedding degrees.

5   Optimising n

With the ultimate goal of minimizing the dynamic computations incurred in a pairing with a fixed argument, we use the total complexities for the Miller loop in Table 3 to determine the best value of n for both the Tate and ate pairings at different security levels. In Table 4, we summarize our results for a variety of common security levels (taken from [20]) and embedding degrees, for both the Tate and ate pairings. At each security level, we list:

- the optimal[2] length of the Miller loop (m_{Tate} and m_{ate}, respectively) for both pairings (taken from [17]);
- the optimal value of n, the number of iterations to merge, based on the analysis in Section 4;

---

[2] These loop lengths are commonly $m_{Tate} = \log(r)/2$ and $m_{ate} = \log(r)/\phi(k)$, corresponding to the twisted ate [28] and optimal ate [46] pairings respectively.

Table 4. The optimal number of iterations to merge (n), the resulting S-dependent base field operation counts $(\#\mathbf{m}_1)$, and the percentage speedup compared to previous precomputation (pre.) [42] and no precomputation (no pre.) techniques, for a variety of security levels and embedding degrees (k).

Security (bits)	r (bits)	k	Best ρ	$\mathbb{F}_p$ (bits)	$\mathbb{F}_{p^e}$ (bits)	$\mathbb{F}_{p^k}$ (bits)	Pairing	m	n	$\#\mathbf{m}_1$	% Speedup pre.	% Speedup no pre.
80	160	6	2.000	320	320	1920	Tate	80	2	1843	7.8	37.1
							ate	80	2	1846	7.7	37.0
		8	1.500	240	480	1920	Tate	120	2	5069	11.2	30.8
							ate	120	2	5058	11.4	30.9
112	224	12	1.000	224	448	2688	Tate	112	3	7308	11.8	29.5
							ate	56	3	3646	12.0	29.7
		16	1.250	280	1120	4480	Tate	112	2	13460	14.6	25.9
							ate	28	2	3346	15.1	26.3
128	256	12	1.000	256	512	3072	Tate	128	3	8263	12.7	30.3
							ate	64	2	4198	11.3	29.2
		16	1.250	320	1280	4096	Tate	128	2	15368	14.7	26.0
							ate	32	2	3823	15.1	26.3
		18	1.333	342	1026	4608	Tate	128	3	13590	13.6	28.5
							ate	43	3	4697	11.1	26.5
192	384	18	1.333	512	1536	6912	Tate	192	3	20173	14.2	29.3
							ate	64	3	6881	12.5	27.6
		24	1.250	478	1912	9216	Tate	192	3	34540	18.2	30.4
							ate	48	3	8577	18.7	30.9
256	512	32	1.125	576	4608	16384	Tate	256	3	87876	17.9	25.7
							ate	32	3	10777	19.5	27.1
		36	1.167	598	3588	18432	Tate	264	3	102960	18.2	29.5
							ate	43	3	13202	16.1	27.7

- the overall cost of S-dependent dynamic Miller loop doubling operations in terms of base field $(\mathbb{F}_p)$ multiplications, assuming that $s_1 = 0.8m_1$, and counting multiplications in fields with extension degrees of the form $k = 2^i 3^j$, as $\mathbf{m}_k = 3^i 5^j \mathbf{m}_1$ (cf. [30]);
- the percentage reductions in Miller loop operations between an optimal n implementation (this paper) and (i) the previous precomputation methods [42] (which correspond to $n = 1$ herein), (ii) no precomputation, but with optimal delayed multiplications [14].

We point out that these percentage speedups are based on the computation of the Miller loop only, and do not take into account the fixed cost of the final exponentation, so that the relative speedups for the entire pairing computation will be less than those reported in Table 4.

In Figure 1(a), we show the operation count (in terms of number of base field multiplications) for the entire S-dependent dynamic Miller loop doubling operations in the Tate and ate pairings for a curve with $r = 256$ and $k = 12$ based on the analysis in Section 4, as well as the precomputation storage costs in terms

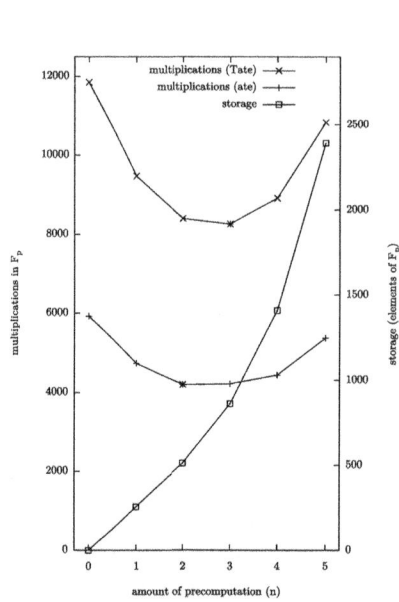

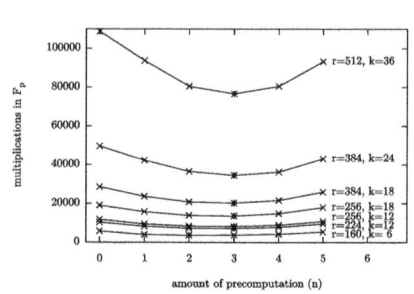

(b) Tate pairing multiplication costs with different r and k for various n.

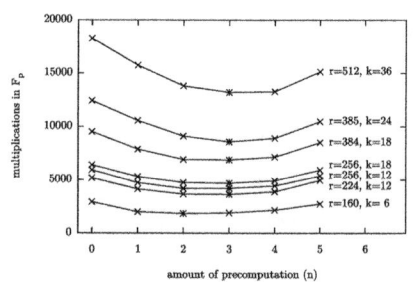

(a) Tate and ate pairing multiplication vs. storage costs with $r = 256$ and $k = 12$ for various n.

(c) ate pairing multiplication costs with different r and k for various n.

Fig. 1. S-dependent costs for various n values for the Tate and ate pairings

Table 5. Fixed arguments in various pairing-based cryptosystems

	# pairings	fixed arguments	# pairings	fixed arguments
Public key encryption		Encryption		Decryption
Boyen-Mei-Waters [12]	0		1	2nd
ID-based encryption		Encryption		Decryption
Boneh-Franklin [9]	1	2nd	1	1st
Boneh-Boyen [7]	0		1	2nd
Waters [47]	0		2	both in 2nd
Attribute-based encr.		Encryption		Decryption
GPSW [24, §4]	0		≤ #attr.	all in 1st
LOSTW [31, §2]	0		≤ 2 · #attr.	all in 2nd
ID-based signatures		Signing		Verification
Waters [47]	0		2	1 in 2nd
ID-based key exchange		Initiator		Responder
Smart-1 [45]	2	1 in 1st, 1 in 2nd	2	1 in 1st, 1 in 2nd
Chen-Kudla [13]	1	1st	1	2nd
McCullagh-Barreto [33]	1	2nd	1	2nd

of number of base field elements, for various amounts of precomputation; $n = 0$ corresponds to no precomputation, while $n \geq 1$ corresponds to the complexity from Table 3. The optimal amount of precomputation for this case occurs at $n = 3$, at which point the precomputation storage costs are 860 base field elements, which is not too prohibitive for many applications.

Figure 1(b) shows the base field multiplication costs for the S-dependent dynamic Miller loop doubling operations in a Tate pairing for a variety of subgroup sizes and embedding degrees based on the amount (n) of precomputation. With the exception of the $r = 160$ case, the optimal n is 3, meaning for those cases we should use precomputation to merge 3 iterations of the Miller loop at a time, as described in Section 4. Figure 1(c) shows the same costs in an ate pairing.

6   Applications

There are many pairing-based cryptosystems that can benefit from precomputation when one of the arguments is fixed. In Table 5, we have listed some pairing-based cryptosystems that have fixed arguments and hence which can benefit from the improvements in this paper.

In some cases, such as the Boneh-Franklin identity-based encryption scheme [9] or the Chen-Kudla identity-based key agreement protocol [13], one party computes a pairing where the first argument is fixed while the other party computes a pairing where the second argument is fixed; here, our technique can only be applied to speed up one party's pairing computation.

In others cases, such as the McCullagh-Barreto identity based key agreement protocol [33], the two parties employing the cryptosystem can both benefit because they each compute pairings where the fixed value appears in the same argument of the pairing. Our speed-up is also applicable to attribute-based encryption schemes such as those of Goyal et al. [24, §4] and Lewko et al. [31, §2] which perform a large number of pairings (one or two for each attribute used in decryption), as in these schemes the second arguments in all these pairing computations are long-term values (fixed across multiple runs of the protocol, though not all identical within a single run of the protocol).

7   Conclusions

We have shown how using precomputation to merge iterations of the Miller loop in Tate and ate pairings can reduce the cost of the dynamic running time when computing a pairing with one fixed argument and one dynamic argument. This improves the runtime cost by between 25% and 37% when compared to a pairing computation with no precomputation, and up to 19.5% when compared to previous precomputation techniques. While the precomputation stage is somewhat expensive compared to the cost of pairing computation, it can still be run quite quickly (in a few seconds or less) on modern computers, and the amount of precomputation storage required is not prohibitive for many settings. Given the wide variety of pairing-based cryptosystems where one argument (say, a long-term private key or system parameter) is fixed across many protocol runs, we believe our techniques have wide applicability.

References

1. Aranha, D.F., López, J., Hankerson, D.: High-speed parallel software implementation of the η_T pairing. In: Pieprzyk, J. (ed.) CT-RSA 2010. LNCS, vol. 5985, pp. 89–105. Springer, Heidelberg (2010)
2. Arene, C., Lange, T., Naehrig, M., Ritzenthaler, C.: Faster pairing computation. Cryptology ePrint Archive, Report 2009/155 (2009)
3. Barreto, P.S.L.M., Galbraith, S.D., O'Eigeartaigh, C., Scott, M.: Efficient pairing computation on supersingular abelian varieties. Designs, Codes and Cryptography 42(3), 239–271 (2007)
4. Barreto, P.S.L.M., Kim, H.Y., Lynn, B., Scott, M.: Efficient algorithms for pairing-based cryptosystems. In: Yung, M. (ed.) CRYPTO 2002. LNCS, vol. 2442, pp. 354–368. Springer, Heidelberg (2002)
5. Barreto, P.S.L.M., Lynn, B., Scott, M.: Efficient implementation of pairing-based cryptosystems. J. Cryptology 17(4), 321–334 (2004)
6. Benger, N., Scott, M.: Constructing tower extensions for the implementation of pairing-based cryptography. In: Hasan, Helleseth (eds.) [26],
7. Boneh, D., Boyen, X.: Efficient selective-ID secure identity-based encryption without random oracles. In: Cachin, C., Camenisch, J. (eds.) EUROCRYPT 2004. LNCS, vol. 3027, pp. 223–238. Springer, Heidelberg (2004), doi:10.1007/b97182
8. Boneh, D., Boyen, X., Shacham, H.: Short group signatures. In: Franklin (ed.) [19], pp. 41–55.
9. Boneh, D., Franklin, M.: Identity-based encryption from the Weil pairing. In: Kilian, J. (ed.) CRYPTO 2001. LNCS, vol. 2139, pp. 213–229. Springer, Heidelberg (2001)
10. Boneh, D., Gentry, C., Lynn, B., Shacham, H.: Aggregate and verifiably encrypted signatures from bilinear maps. In: Biham, E. (ed.) EUROCRYPT 2003. LNCS, vol. 2656, pp. 416–432. Springer, Heidelberg (2003)
11. Boneh, D., Lynn, B., Shacham, H.: Short signatures from the Weil pairing. J. Cryptology 17(4), 297–319 (2004)
12. Boyen, X., Mei, Q., Waters, B.: Direct chosen ciphertext security from identity-based techniques. In: Meadows, C., Syverson, P. (eds.) Proc. 12th ACM Conference on Computer and Communications Security (CCS), pp. 320–329. ACM, New York (2005)
13. Chen, L., Kudla, C.: Identity based authenticated key agreement protocols from pairings. In: Proceedings 16th IEEE Computer Security Foundations Workshop (CSWF-16), pp. 219–233. IEEE, Los Alamitos (2003)
14. Costello, C., Boyd, C., Nieto, J.M.G., Wong, K.K.H.: Avoiding full extension field arithmetic in pairing computations. In: Bernstein, D.J., Lange, T. (eds.) AFRICACRYPT 2010. LNCS, vol. 6055, pp. 203–224. Springer, Heidelberg (2010)
15. Costello, C., Boyd, C., Nieto, J.M.G., Wong, K.K.H.: Delaying mismatched field multiplications in pairing computations. In: Hasan, Helleseth (eds.) [26]
16. Costello, C., Hisil, H., Boyd, C., Nieto, J.M.G., Wong, K.K.H.: Faster pairings on special Weierstrass curves. In: Shacham, Waters (eds.) [43], pp. 89–101

17. Costello, C., Lange, T., Naehrig, M.: Faster pairing computations on curves with high-degree twists. In: Nguyen, P.Q., Pointcheval, D. (eds.) PKC 2010. LNCS, vol. 6056, pp. 224–242. Springer, Heidelberg (2010)
18. Devegili, A.J., Scott, M., Dahab, R.: Implementing cryptographic pairings over Barreto-Naehrig curves. In: Takagi, T., Okamoto, T., Okamoto, E., Okamoto, T. (eds.) Pairing 2007. LNCS, vol. 4575, pp. 197–207. Springer, Heidelberg (2007)
19. Franklin, M.K. (ed.): CRYPTO 2004. LNCS, vol. 3152. Springer, Heidelberg (2004)
20. Freeman, D., Scott, M., Teske, E.: A taxonomy of pairing-friendly elliptic curves. J. Cryptology 23(2), 224–280 (2010)
21. Galbraith, S.D.: Supersingular curves in cryptography. In: Boyd, C. (ed.) ASIACRYPT 2001. LNCS, vol. 2248, pp. 495–513. Springer, Heidelberg (2001)
22. Galbraith, S.D., Harrison, K., Soldera, D.: Implementing the Tate pairing. In: Fieker, C., Kohel, D.R. (eds.) ANTS 2002. LNCS, vol. 2369, pp. 324–337. Springer, Heidelberg (2002)
23. Gentry, C., Silverberg, A.: Hierarchical ID-based cryptography. In: Zheng, Y. (ed.) ASIACRYPT 2002. LNCS, vol. 2501, pp. 548–566. Springer, Heidelberg (2002)
24. Goyal, V., Pandey, O., Sahai, A., Waters, B.: Attribute-based encryption for fine-grained access control of encrypted data. In: Wright, R., De Capitani de Vimercati, S., Shmatikov, V. (eds.) Proc. 13th ACM Conference on Computer and Communications Security (CCS), pp. 89–98. ACM, New York (2006)
25. Hankerson, D., Menezes, A.J., Scott, M.: Software implementation of pairings. In: Joye, M., Neven, G. (eds.) Identity-Based Cryptography, pp. 188–206. IOS Press, Amsterdam (2008)
26. Hasan, A.M., Helleseth, T. (eds.): WAIFI 2010. LNCS, vol. 6087. Springer, Heidelberg (2010)
27. Hess, F.: Pairing lattices. In: Galbraith, S.D., Paterson, K.G. (eds.) Pairing 2008. LNCS, vol. 5209, pp. 18–38. Springer, Heidelberg (2008)
28. Hess, F., Smart, N.P., Vercauteren, F.: The eta pairing revisited. IEEE Transactions on Information Theory 52(10), 4595–4602 (2006)
29. Joux, A.: A one round protocol for tripartite Diffie-Hellman. In: Bosma, W. (ed.) ANTS 2000. LNCS, vol. 1838, pp. 385–394. Springer, Heidelberg (2000)
30. Koblitz, N., Menezes, A.: Pairing-based cryptography at high security levels. In: Smart, N.P. (ed.) Cryptography and Coding 2005. LNCS, vol. 3796, pp. 13–36. Springer, Heidelberg (2005)
31. Lewko, A., Okamoto, T., Sahai, A., Takashima, K., Waters, B.: Fully secure functional encryption: Attribute-based encryption and (hierarchical) inner product encryption. In: Gilbert, H. (ed.) EUROCRYPT 2010. LNCS, vol. 6110, pp. 62–91. Springer, Heidelberg (2010)
32. Matsuda, S., Kanayama, N., Hess, F., Okamoto, E.: Optimised versions of the ate and twisted ate pairings. In: Galbraith, S.D. (ed.) Cryptography and Coding 2007. LNCS, vol. 4887, pp. 302–312. Springer, Heidelberg (2007)
33. McCullagh, N., Barreto, P.S.: A new two-party identity-based authenticated key agreement. In: Menezes, A. (ed.) CT-RSA 2005. LNCS, vol. 3376, pp. 262–274. Springer, Heidelberg (2005)
34. Menezes, A.J.: Elliptic Curve Public Key Cryptosystems. Kluwer Academic Publishers, Dordrecht (1993)
35. Miller, V.S.: The Weil pairing, and its efficient calculation. Journal of Cryptology 17, 235–261 (2004)
36. Naehrig, M., Barreto, P.S.L.M., Schwabe, P.: On compressible pairings and their computation. In: Vaudenay, S. (ed.) AFRICACRYPT 2008. LNCS, vol. 5023, pp. 371–388. Springer, Heidelberg (2008)

37. Naehrig, M., Niederhagen, R., Schwabe, P.: New software speed records for cryptographic pairings. Cryptology ePrint Archive, Report 2010/186 (2010)
38. Scott, M.: Implementing cryptographic pairings. In: Takagi, T., Okamoto, T., Okamoto, E., Okamoto, T. (eds.) Pairing 2007. LNCS, vol. 4575, pp. 177–196. Springer, Heidelberg (2007)
39. Scott, M., Barreto, P.S.L.M.: Compressed pairings. In: Franklin (ed.) [19], pp. 140–156
40. Scott, M., Benger, N., Charlemagne, M., Perez, L.J.D., Kachisa, E.J.: Fast hashing to G_2 on pairing-friendly curves. In: Shacham, Waters (eds.) [43], pp. 102–113
41. Scott, M., Benger, N., Charlemagne, M., Perez, L.J.D., Kachisa, E.J.: On the final exponentiation for calculating pairings on ordinary elliptic curves. In: Shacham, Waters (eds.) [43], pp. 78–88
42. Scott, M., Costigan, N., Abdulwahab, W.: Implementing cryptographic pairings on smartcards. In: Goubin, L., Matsui, M. (eds.) CHES 2006. LNCS, vol. 4249, pp. 134–147. Springer, Heidelberg (2006)
43. Shacham, H., Waters, B. (eds.): Pairing 2009. LNCS, vol. 5671. Springer, Heidelberg (2009)
44. Shamir, A.: Identity-based cryptosystems and signature schemes. In: Goos, G., Hartmanis, J. (eds.) CRYPTO 1984. LNCS, vol. 196, pp. 47–53. Springer, Heidelberg (1985)
45. Smart, N.P.: Identity-based authenticated key agreement protocol based on Weil pairing. Electronics Letters 38(13), 630–632 (2002)
46. Vercauteren, F.: Optimal pairings. IEEE Transactions on Information Theory 56(1), 455–461 (2010)
47. Waters, B.: Efficient identity-based encryption without random oracles. In: Cramer, R. (ed.) EUROCRYPT 2005. LNCS, vol. 3494, pp. 114–127. Springer, Heidelberg (2005)

New Software Speed Records for Cryptographic Pairings⋆

Michael Naehrig[1], Ruben Niederhagen[2,3], and Peter Schwabe[3]

[1] Microsoft Research, One Microsoft Way, Redmond, WA 98052, USA
mnaehrig@microsoft.com
[2] Department of Electrical Engineering
National Taiwan University, 1 Section 4 Roosevelt Road, Taipei 106-70, Taiwan
ruben@polycephaly.org
[3] Department of Mathematics and Computer Science
Technische Universiteit Eindhoven, P.O. Box 513, 5600 MB Eindhoven, Netherlands
peter@cryptojedi.org

Abstract. This paper presents new software speed records for the computation of cryptographic pairings. More specifically, we present details of an implementation which computes the optimal ate pairing on a 257-bit Barreto-Naehrig curve in only 4,470,408 cycles on one core of an Intel Core 2 Quad Q6600 processor.

This speed is achieved by combining 1.) state-of-the-art high-level optimization techniques, 2.) a new representation of elements in the underlying finite fields which makes use of the special modulus arising from the Barreto-Naehrig curve construction, and 3.) implementing arithmetic in this representation using the double-precision floating-point SIMD instructions of the AMD64 architecture.

Keywords: Pairings, Barreto-Naehrig curves, ate pairing, AMD64 architecture, modular arithmetic, SIMD floating-point instructions.

1 Introduction

The use of pairings in cryptography has enabled practical realizations of numerous protocols. The implementation of such protocols demands the ability to efficiently compute the pairing while guaranteeing a required level of security. Most cryptographic pairings are derived from the Tate pairing on elliptic curves.

Since the introduction of Miller's algorithm [26,27] for computing pairings on elliptic curves, a lot of research has been devoted to finding the most efficient Tate-pairing variants for different security levels by constructing suitable pairing-friendly elliptic curves [18] and by making specific choices for the groups and parameters involved in the computation [7,8]. Several variants of the Tate pairing

---

⋆ This work has been supported in part by the European Commission through the ICT Programme under Contract ICT–2007–216499 CACE, and through the ICT Programme under Contract ICT-2007-216646 ECRYPT II. Permanent ID of this document: 4d8d6cd8dc32f9524bb84bbe9c148076. Date: May 28, 2010.

M. Abdalla and P.S.L.M. Barreto (Eds.): LATINCRYPT 2010, LNCS 6212, pp. 109–123, 2010.
© Springer-Verlag Berlin Heidelberg 2010

have been proposed like the eta, ate and twisted ate pairings [6,23], the R-ate [24] and optimal ate pairings [32] (see also [5]), often increasing the computational efficiency over that of their predecessors. Overall, these improvements have led to a remarkable increase in the efficiency of pairing-based protocols. Still, new protocols including the computation of a large number of pairings or pairing products [13,21] demand even faster pairings.

Pairing-based protocols involve elliptic-curve point groups as well as subgroups of the multiplicative group of a finite field. To achieve most efficient implementations, it is desirable to choose parameters such that the discrete logarithm problems in all groups have roughly the same difficulty.

At the 128-bit security level, a nearly optimal choice for a pairing-friendly curve is a Barreto-Naehrig (BN) curve [9] over a prime field of size roughly 256 bits with embedding degree $k = 12$. According to [4], such a curve achieves 128 bits of security, while according to [15] this is 124 bits. This paper describes a constant-time implementation of an optimal ate pairing on a BN curve over a prime field $\mathbb{F}_p$ of size 257 bits. The prime p is given by the BN polynomial parametrization $p = 36u^4 + 36u^3 + 24u^2 + 6u + 1$, where $u = v^3$ and $v = 1966080$. The curve equation is $E : y^2 = x^3 + 17$.

We are the first to propose a software pairing implementation exploiting the polynomial parametrization of the prime p to speed up the underlying field arithmetic. For most pairing-friendly curves, the primes defining the base field are constructed using polynomial parametrizations. These parametrizations have been used to speed up the final exponentiation [31], but so far have not been successfully exploited for field arithmetic in software. Nevertheless, Fan, Vercauteren, and Verbauwhede [16] use the polynomial shape of the prime p to achieve computational speedups in hardware.

To maximize reusability of our results we put all software[1] described in this paper into the public domain.

Comparison to previous work. There exist several descriptions and benchmarks of software implementations of cryptographic pairings. Implementations targeting the 128-bit security level usually use 256-bit BN curves.

The software presented in [22] takes 10,000,000 cycles to compute the R-ate pairing over a 256-bit BN curve on one core of an Intel Core 2 processor; the same computation on one core of an AMD Opteron processor also takes 10,000,000 cycles. Unpublished benchmarks of a newer version of that software (included in the Miracl library [25]) are claimed to take 7,850,000 cycles on an Intel Core 2 Duo T5500 processor [30]. The software presented in [29] takes 29,650,000 cycles to compute the ate pairing over a 256-bit BN curve on one core of a Core 2 Duo processor. Software presented in [19] takes 23,319,673 cycles to compute the ate pairing over a 256-bit BN curve on one core of an Intel Core 2 Duo processor; another implementation described in the same paper takes 14,429,439 to compute the ate pairing on two cores of an Intel Core 2 Duo processor.

The software presented in this paper computes the optimal ate pairing in $4,470,408$ cycles on one core of an Intel Core 2 Quad Q6600 processor and is

---

[1] Available at http://www.cryptojedi.org/crypto/#dclxvi

thus more than twice as fast as the fastest previously published result and more than 40 percent faster than other unpublished results we are aware of. We are not aware of any other software implementation of a cryptographic pairing at the 128-bit security level that achieves speeds of 7,850,000 cycles or faster on any AMD64 processor.

Organization of the paper. In Section 2 we give a short review of the optimal ate pairing for BN curves. Section 3 collects state-of-the-art high-level optimization techniques for the computation of cryptographic pairings on BN curves from the literature as we use them in our software. Section 4 describes our new approach to represent elements of the underlying finite field $\mathbb{F}_p$ and algorithms to perform arithmetic using this representation in $\mathbb{F}_p$ and $\mathbb{F}_{p^2}$. In Section 5 we explain how we use the double-precision floating-point SIMD instructions of the AMD64 instruction set (SSE, SSE2, SSE3) to efficiently implement these algorithms. Section 6 gives benchmarking results of our software on different microarchitectures.

2   An Optimal Ate Pairing over Barreto-Naehrig Curves

For a Barreto-Naehrig (BN) curve, the most efficient pairings are the R-ate pairing [24] and optimal ate pairings [32]. In this section, we provide the basic background and notation, and describe the algorithm for an optimal ate pairing that is used in our implementation.

Let $E : y^2 = x^3 + b$ be a BN curve over the prime field $\mathbb{F}_p$. This means that there is a $u \in \mathbb{Z}$ such that both p and n, given by

$$p = p(u) = 36u^4 + 36u^3 + 24u^2 + 6u + 1,$$
$$n = n(u) = 36u^4 + 36u^3 + 18u^2 + 6u + 1,$$

are prime. The number of $\mathbb{F}_p$-rational points on E is $\#E(\mathbb{F}_p) = n$, and E has embedding degree $k = 12$ with respect to n. We denote by $\mathcal{O}$ the point at infinity, i.e. the neutral element of the group operation on E. For $m \in \mathbb{Z}$, we write $[m]$ for the multiplication-by-m map on E.

Let ϕ_p be the p-power Frobenius endomorphism on E and $E[n]$ the n-torsion subgroup of E. We define $G_1 = E[n] \cap \ker(\phi_p - [1]) = E(\mathbb{F}_p)$, $G_2 = E[n] \cap \ker(\phi_p - [p]) \subseteq E(\mathbb{F}_{p^{12}})[n]$, $G_3 = \mu_n$, where $\mu_n \subset \mathbb{F}_{p^{12}}^*$ is the group of n-th roots of unity.

An optimal ate pairing on E is given in [32] as

$$a_{\mathrm{opt}} : G_2 \times G_1 \to G_3, \ (Q, P) \mapsto \left(f_{6u+2,Q}(P) \cdot g_{6u+2,Q}(P)\right)^{(p^{12}-1)/n},$$

where $g_{6u+2,Q}(P) = l_{Q_3,-Q_2}(P) \cdot l_{-Q_2+Q_3,Q_1}(P) \cdot l_{Q_1-Q_2+Q_3,[6u+2]Q}(P)$ with $Q_1 = \phi_p(Q)$, $Q_2 = \phi_p^2(Q)$, and $Q_3 = \phi_p^3(Q)$. The value $l_{R,S}(P) \in \mathbb{F}_{p^{12}}$ is the function of the line through the points R and S on the curve, evaluated at P.

There is no need to compute Q_3. Instead, $g_{6u+2,Q}(P)$ can be replaced by

$$h_{6u+2,Q}(P) = l_{[6u+2]Q,Q_1}(P) \cdot l_{[6u+2]Q+Q_1,-Q_2}(P).$$

The reason for this is that for BN curves $Q_1 - Q_2 + Q_3 + [6u + 2]Q = \mathcal{O}$, which can be easily derived from Lemma 2.17 in [28]. By writing down the divisors of the functions $g_{6u+2,Q}$ and $h_{6u+2,Q}$, it can be seen that they only differ by vertical line functions. When evaluated at P, such line functions produce values in proper subfields of $\mathbb{F}_{p^{12}}$ that are mapped to 1 by the final exponentiation.

Algorithm 1. Optimal ate pairing on BN curves for $u > 0$

Input: $P \in G_1$, $Q \in G_2$, $m_{\mathrm{opt}} = 6u + 2 = (1, m_{s-1}, \ldots, m_0)_2$.
Output: $a_{\mathrm{opt}}(Q, P)$.
1: $R \leftarrow Q$, $f \leftarrow 1$
2: **for** $(i \leftarrow s - 1; \; i \geq 0; \; i - -)$ **do**
3:      $f \leftarrow f^2 \cdot l_{R,R}(P)$, $R \leftarrow [2]R$
4:      **if** $(m_i = 1)$ **then**
5:          $f \leftarrow f \cdot l_{R,Q}(P)$, $R \leftarrow R + Q$
6:      **end if**
7: **end for**
8: $Q_1 = \phi_p(Q)$, $Q_2 = \phi_{p^2}(Q)$
9: $f \leftarrow f \cdot l_{R,Q_1}(P)$, $R \leftarrow R + Q_1$
10: $f \leftarrow f \cdot l_{R,-Q_2}(P)$, $R \leftarrow R - Q_2$
11: $f \leftarrow f^{p^6 - 1}$
12: $f \leftarrow f^{p^2 + 1}$
13: $f \leftarrow f^{(p^4 - p^2 + 1)/n}$
14: **return** f

Algorithm 1 shows how $a_{\mathrm{opt}}(Q, P)$ can be computed in the case $u > 0$. Lines 2 to 7 are called the Miller loop. It contains doubling steps in Line 3 and addition steps in Line 5. The value $h_{6u+2,Q}(P)$ is multiplied to the result of the Miller loop in Lines 8 to 10 by two addition steps. Lines 11 to 13 together carry out the final exponentiation to the power $(p^{12} - 1)/n$, where Lines 11 and 12 comprise its easy part. It can be done by applying the p^6-power Frobenius automorphism on $\mathbb{F}_{p^{12}}$, a single inversion and a multiplication in $\mathbb{F}_{p^{12}}$. Line 13 represents the hard part of the final exponentiation.

As usual [9,23,14], we use a sextic twist $E' : y^2 = x^3 + b/\xi$ defined over $\mathbb{F}_{p^2}$ to represent the points in G_2 by points on the twist using the twist isomorphism $\psi : E' \rightarrow E$, $(x', y') \mapsto (\omega^2 x', \omega^3 y')$. The element $\xi \in \mathbb{F}_{p^2}$ (neither a cube nor a square in $\mathbb{F}_{p^2}$) is chosen such that the twist has the right order, i.e. it holds $n \mid \#E'(\mathbb{F}_{p^2})$. The field $\mathbb{F}_{p^{12}}$ is generated over $\mathbb{F}_{p^2}$ by ω via the irreducible polynomial $X^6 - \xi$, i.e. $\omega^6 = \xi$.

The map ψ induces a group isomorphism between $G_2' = E'(\mathbb{F}_{p^2})[n]$ and G_2. So, all points $R \in G_2$ should be seen as being represented by a corresponding point $R' \in G_2'$, i.e. $R = \psi(R')$. All curve arithmetic is done on the twist and intermediate results can be kept in their representation on E'. This means that all curve arithmetic requires $\mathbb{F}_{p^2}$-arithmetic only. Arithmetic in $\mathbb{F}_{p^{12}}$ is also based on arithmetic in $\mathbb{F}_{p^2}$. Overall, there are no $\mathbb{F}_p$ computations other than those involved in $\mathbb{F}_{p^2}$ computations during the optimal-ate-pairing algorithm. Thus an improvement of $\mathbb{F}_{p^2}$-arithmetic–even without improving $\mathbb{F}_p$-arithmetic–leads to an improvement of all parts of the computation.

3 High-Level Techniques: Field Extensions, Miller Loop and Final Exponentiation

In this section, we describe the high-level structure of our implementation. We use state-of-the-art optimization techniques from the literature for this implementation level. Our focus is on the construction of the higher degree field extensions such as $\mathbb{F}_{p^6}$ and $\mathbb{F}_{p^{12}}$, the Miller loop to compute $f_{6u+2,Q}(P)$, the function value $h_{6u+2,Q}(P)$ and the structure of the final exponentiation.

The construction of field extensions and the efficiency of the optimal ate pairing depend on the chosen curve parameters. Since our new base-field representation needs the parameter u to be a third power $u = v^3$, we are strongly restricted in the choice of curves. Field multiplications and squarings in $\mathbb{F}_{p^{12}}$ are very expensive, so another important condition on u is that $6u + 2$ should have a Hamming weight as low as possible, to save as many addition steps during the Miller loop as possible.

Our specific choice here is $u = v^3$ with $v = 1966080$. This value provided the lowest Hamming weight for $6u + 2$ among all possibilities for u a third power that gave primes p of 256 or 257 bits. All ideas in this paper also work for other choices of v, but possibly lead to less efficient implementations.

3.1 Field Extensions

The above choice for u implies $p \equiv 1 \pmod 4$ which unfortunately means that the field extension $\mathbb{F}_{p^2}$ can not be constructed using $\sqrt{-1}$. Instead we use $\mathbb{F}_{p^2} = \mathbb{F}_p(i)$, where $i^2 = -7$. The value ξ to construct the twist and higher-degree extensions is $\xi = i + 6$.

On top of the quadratic extension we build the field $\mathbb{F}_{p^{12}}$ as a tower, first $\mathbb{F}_{p^6} = \mathbb{F}_{p^2}(\tau)$ with $\tau^3 = \xi$ and then $\mathbb{F}_{p^{12}} = \mathbb{F}_{p^6}(\omega)$ with $\omega^2 = \tau$. This is the same construction as in [14] and we follow [14] in implementing the extension field arithmetic.

3.2 Miller Loop

The value $6u + 2$ determines the number of doubling and addition steps in the Miller loop of the optimal ate pairing. The number of doubling steps is 65. The Hamming weight of $6u + 2$ is 9, so there are 8 addition steps. Throughout the pairing computation we use the group G_2' to represent points in G_2. We use Jacobian coordinates for the curve arithmetic in G_2'. In particular, for the doubling and addition steps, we use the formulas given by Arène et al. in [3]. The points in G_1, at which line functions are evaluated, are kept in affine coordinates.

The multiplication of the intermediate variable f with the line function values in the Miller loop is done via a special multiplication function exploiting the fact that line function values are sparse elements of $\mathbb{F}_{p^{12}}$, where only half of the coefficients over $\mathbb{F}_{p^2}$ are different from zero.

After the Miller loop, the points Q_1 and Q_2 are computed by applying the p-power and the p^2-power Frobenius endomorphisms. We do two final addition steps with Q_1 and $-Q_2$, respectively, to multiply the result of the Miller loop by the function value $h_{6u+2,Q}(P)$.

3.3   Final Exponentiation

The final exponentiation in our implementation is done as indicated in Lines 11 to 13 of Algorithm 1. It is divided into the easy part (Lines 11, 12) and the hard part (Line 13). The easy part has low computational costs compared to the hard part. Raising the element to the power $p^6 - 1$ is simply a conjugation in the extension $\mathbb{F}_{p^{12}}/\mathbb{F}_{p^6}$ and a single division in $\mathbb{F}_{p^{12}}$. The exponentiation by $p^2 + 1$ is done by applying the p^2-power Frobenius automorphism and one multiplication.

For the hard part, we use the method proposed by Scott et al. in [31]. The main advantage here is that the exponentiation is essentially split into three exponentiations by the sparse exponent u. For our choice the Hamming weight of u is 8. The final result is then obtained by applying the Frobenius automorphism and by using the polynomial representation in u of the fixed exponent $(p^4 - p^2 + 1)/n$.

Note that after the easy part of the final exponentiation, the resulting element in $\mathbb{F}_{p^{12}}$ lies in the cyclotomic subgroup of $\mathbb{F}_{p^{12}}^*$, i.e. the subgroup of order $\Phi_{12}(p) = p^4 - p^2 + 1$, where Φ_{12} is the 12-th cyclotomic polynomial. Granger and Scott [20] recently showed how to exploit this fact to obtain very efficient squaring formulas for such elements. We use these formulas during the hard part of the final exponentiation.

4   Mid-Level Techniques: Arithmetic in $\mathbb{F}_{p^2}$ and $\mathbb{F}_p$

This section explains the new approach for representing integers modulo p where p is given by the BN polynomial $36u^4 + 36u^3 + 24u^2 + 6u + 1$. Inspired by Bernstein's implementation of Curve25519 [12], we suggest to split such an integer into 12 coefficients each of which will be stored in a double-precision floating-point variable in the software implementation. We now give the details of our approach.

4.1   Representing Base Field Elements

Elements in the base field $\mathbb{F}_p$ are integers modulo the prime $p = 36u^4 + 36u^3 + 24u^2 + 6u + 1$ for some $u \in \mathbb{Z}$. The technique in this section does not depend on the specific fixed value for u that we chose in our implementation. We only need to make the assumption that there exists an integer $v \in \mathbb{Z}$ with $u = v^3$. Furthermore, let $\delta = \sqrt[6]{6}$. Then we have $(\delta v x)^3 = \sqrt{6}ux^3$.

We represent integers by polynomials in the ring

$$R = \mathbb{Z}[x] \cap \overline{\mathbb{Z}}[\delta vx],$$

where $\overline{\mathbb{Z}}$ denotes the ring of algebraic integers in $\mathbb{C}$. Note that the ring homomorphism $R \mapsto \mathbb{Z}$, $F \mapsto f = F(1)$ is surjective and thus we may represent an integer f by any polynomial F in the preimage of f under the above map. The product of two integers can be computed by multiplying the corresponding polynomials in R and evaluating the product at 1.

Since δ is an algebraic integer, we see that the polynomial

$$P = 36u^4x^{12} + 36u^3x^9 + 24u^2x^6 + 6ux^3 + 1$$
$$= (\delta vx)^{12} + \delta^3(\delta vx)^9 + 4(\delta vx)^6 + \delta^3(\delta vx)^3 + 1$$

is an element of R representing the prime p.

Let $\alpha = \delta vx$. Any integer f can be represented by a polynomial $F \in R$ with $F(1) = f$ of the following form:

$$\begin{aligned}
F &= f_0 + f_1\delta^5\alpha + f_2\delta^4\alpha^2 + f_3\delta^3\alpha^3 + f_4\delta^2\alpha^4 + f_5\delta\alpha^5 \\
&\quad + f_6\alpha^6 + f_7\delta^5\alpha^7 + f_8\delta^4\alpha^8 + f_9\delta^3\alpha^9 + f_{10}\delta^2\alpha^{10} + f_{11}\delta\alpha^{11} \\
&= f_0 + f_1 \cdot 6(vx) + f_2 \cdot 6(vx)^2 + f_3 \cdot 6(vx)^3 + f_4 \cdot 6(vx)^4 \\
&\quad + f_5 \cdot 6(vx)^5 + f_6 \cdot 6(vx)^6 + f_7 \cdot 36(vx)^7 + f_8 \cdot 36(vx)^8 \\
&\quad + f_9 \cdot 36(vx)^9 + f_{10} \cdot 36(vx)^{10} + f_{11} \cdot 36(vx)^{11},
\end{aligned}$$

where $f_i \in \mathbb{Z}$ for all i. The integer f corresponds to the vector of coefficients $(f_0, f_1, \ldots, f_{11})$ of F.

4.2   Multiplication Modulo p

Multiplication modulo p in the new representation is done in two stages, first a polynomial multiplication of the two polynomials representing the integers and second a reduction step.

Let $f, g \in \mathbb{Z}$ be two integers with corresponding polynomials $F, G \in R$ and coefficient vectors $(f_0, f_1, \ldots, f_{11})$ and $(g_0, g_1, \ldots, g_{11})$. The product $H = FG$ then has coefficient vector $(h_0, h_1, \ldots, h_{22})$ and has the form $H = h_0 + h_1\delta^5\alpha + \cdots + h_{21}\delta^2\alpha^{21} + h_{22}\delta\alpha^{22}$.

We next represent the result of the multiplication by a polynomial of degree 11 which has 12 coefficients. For the degree-reduction, we use the polynomial P representing the BN prime p. Reducing polynomials modulo P corresponds to reducing the corresponding integers modulo p. We have $P = \alpha^{12} + \delta^3\alpha^9 + 4\alpha^6 + \delta^3\alpha^3 + 1$, thus we can use the equation

$$\alpha^{12} = -\delta^3\alpha^9 - 4\alpha^6 - \delta^3\alpha^3 - 1$$

to reduce the degree of H. The degree reduction is given in Algorithm 2.

Algorithm 2. Degree reduction after polynomial multiplication

---

Input: Coefficient vector $(h_0, h_1, \ldots, h_{22}) \in \mathbb{Z}^{23}$ of $H \in R$ with $H(1) = h$.

Output: Reduced coefficient vector $(h'_0, h'_1, \ldots, h'_{11})$ of H' with $H'(1) = h$.

1: $h'_0 \leftarrow h_0 - h_{12} + 6h_{15} - 2h_{18} - 6h_{21}$

2: $h'_1 \leftarrow h_1 - h_{13} + h_{16} - 2h_{19} - h_{22}$

3: $h'_2 \leftarrow h_2 - h_{14} + h_{17} - 2h_{20}$

4: $h'_3 \leftarrow h_3 - h_{12} + 5h_{15} - h_{18} - 8h_{21}$

5: $h'_4 \leftarrow h_4 - 6h_{13} + 5h_{16} - 6h_{19} - 8h_{22}$

6: $h'_5 \leftarrow h_5 - 6h_{14} + 5h_{17} - 6h_{20}$

7: $h'_6 \leftarrow h_6 - 4h_{12} + 18h_{15} - 3h_{18} - 30h_{21}$

8: $h'_7 \leftarrow h_7 - 4h_{13} + 3h_{16} - 3h_{19} - 5h_{22}$

9: $h'_8 \leftarrow h_8 - 4h_{14} + 3h_{17} - 3h_{20}$

10: $h'_9 \leftarrow h_9 - h_{12} + 2h_{15} + h_{18} - 9h_{21}$

11: $h'_{10} \leftarrow h_{10} - 6h_{13} + 2h_{16} + 6h_{19} - 9h_{22}$

12: $h'_{11} \leftarrow h_{11} - 6h_{14} + 2h_{17} + 6h_{20}$

13: **return** $(h'_0, h'_1, \ldots, h'_{11})$.

Polynomial multiplication and degree reduction make the coefficients grow in their absolute value. Whenever the coefficients get too large we need to do a coefficient reduction. For that we use Algorithm 3. We address the relevant bounds on the coefficients and how to guarantee them in Section 5.1. After the reduction, we have

$$h_0, h_6 \in [-|3v|, |3v|), \quad h_1, h_3, h_4, h_7, h_9, h_{10} \in [-|v/2|, |v/2|),$$

the coefficients h_2, h_5, h_8, h_{11} may have an absolute value only slightly larger than $|v/2|$. The function rnd in Algorithm 3 denotes rounding to the nearest integer.

5 Low-Level Techniques: Using SIMD Floating-Point Arithmetic

Implementations of large-integer arithmetic on 64-bit processors usually decompose a large integer into limbs of 64 bits. Arithmetic is then performed using fast 64-bit integer-multiply and -add instructions [1,25,2]. For our implementation we do not make use of these instructions but instead use double-precision floating-point arithmetic. Many modern microprocessors including all microprocessors implementing the AMD64 architecture have very fast floating-point units. This is due to the fact that the performance of many applications such as image and video processing relies on fast floating-point arithmetic rather than integer processing and that many CPU benchmarks focus on the speed of floating-point operations.

It has been shown before that one can use these fast floating-point units for high-speed cryptography and for arithmetic on large integers, see for example Bernstein in [12] and [11]. In contrast to the implementation in [12] which uses 80-bit floating-point values (with a 64-bit mantissa), we decided to use 64-bit

---

Algorithm 3. Coefficient reduction

Input: Coefficient vector $(h_0, h_1, \ldots, h_{11}) \in \mathbb{Z}^{12}$ of $H \in R$ with $H(1) = h$.
Output: Reduced coefficient vector $(h'_0, h'_1, \ldots, h'_{11})$ of H' with $H'(1) = h$.
1: $r \leftarrow \mathrm{rnd}(h_1/v), h_1 \leftarrow h_1 - rv, h_2 \leftarrow h_2 + r$
2: $r \leftarrow \mathrm{rnd}(h_4/v), h_4 \leftarrow h_4 - rv, h_5 \leftarrow h_5 + r$
3: $r \leftarrow \mathrm{rnd}(h_7/v), h_7 \leftarrow h_7 - rv, h_8 \leftarrow h_8 + r$
4: $r \leftarrow \mathrm{rnd}(h_{10}/v), h_{10} \leftarrow h_{10} - rv, h_{11} \leftarrow h_{11} + r$
5: $r \leftarrow \mathrm{rnd}(h_2/v), h_2 \leftarrow h_2 - rv, h_3 \leftarrow h_3 + r$
6: $r \leftarrow \mathrm{rnd}(h_5/v), h_5 \leftarrow h_5 - rv, h_6 \leftarrow h_6 + r$
7: $r \leftarrow \mathrm{rnd}(h_8/v), h_8 \leftarrow h_8 - rv, h_9 \leftarrow h_9 + r$
8: $r \leftarrow \mathrm{rnd}(h_{11}/v), h_{11} \leftarrow h_{11} - rv$
9: $h_9 \leftarrow h_9 - r$
10: $h_6 \leftarrow h_6 - 4r$
11: $h_3 \leftarrow h_3 - r$
12: $h_0 \leftarrow h_0 - r$
13: $r \leftarrow \mathrm{rnd}(h_0/(6v)), h_0 \leftarrow h_0 - r \cdot 6v, h_1 \leftarrow h_1 + r$
14: $r \leftarrow \mathrm{rnd}(h_3/v), h_3 \leftarrow h_3 - rv, h_4 \leftarrow h_4 + r$
15: $r \leftarrow \mathrm{rnd}(h_6/(6v)), h_6 \leftarrow h_6 - r \cdot 6v, h_7 \leftarrow h_7 + r$
16: $r \leftarrow \mathrm{rnd}(h_9/v), h_9 \leftarrow h_9 - rv, h_{10} \leftarrow h_{10} + r$
17: $r \leftarrow \mathrm{rnd}(h_1/v), h_1 \leftarrow h_1 - rv, h_2 \leftarrow h_2 + r$
18: $r \leftarrow \mathrm{rnd}(h_4/v), h_4 \leftarrow h_4 - rv, h_5 \leftarrow h_5 + r$
19: $r \leftarrow \mathrm{rnd}(h_7/v), h_7 \leftarrow h_7 - rv, h_8 \leftarrow h_8 + r$
20: $r \leftarrow \mathrm{rnd}(h_{10}/v), h_{10} \leftarrow h_{10} - rv, h_{11} \leftarrow h_{11} + r$
21: **return** $(h'_0, h'_1, \ldots, h'_{11})$.

---

floating-point values (with a 53-bit mantissa). This allows us to use the single-instruction multiple-data (SIMD) instructions of the SSE2 and SSE3 instruction set operating on double-precision (64-bit) floating-point values.

These instructions perform two double-precision floating-point operations at once on two independent inputs layed out in 128-bit vector registers called XMM registers. The AMD64 architecture defines 16 architectural XMM registers. For example the instruction addpd %xmm1, %xmm2 takes the low 64 bits from register %xmm1 and the low 64 bits of register %xmm2, adds them as double-precision floating-point values and stores the result in the low 64 bits of register %xmm2; at the same time it takes the high 64 bits from register %xmm1 and the high 64 bits of register %xmm2, adds them as double-precision floating-point values and stores the result in the high 64 bits of register %xmm2.

The most important SSE2 instructions for our implementation are the addpd and the mulpd instructions. The Intel Core 2 processors (both, 65 nm and 45 nm models) can issue up to one mulpd and one addpd instruction per cycle and thus execute 4 floating-point operations in one cycle. However, it can not execute 2 mulpd or 2 addpd instructions in the same cycle (for details see [17]). To arrange data in the XMM vector registers our implementation requires additional non-arithmetic instructions such as shufpd, unpckhpd and unpcklpd. In the implementation of the squaring in $\mathbb{F}_{p^2}$ we also need the addsd instruction which adds the low double values of two XMM registers and leaves the high double value of the destination register unchanged.

Note that all arithmetic instructions only have 2 operands, one of the inputs is overwritten by the output. This sometimes requires additional mov instructions to copy data to other registers or memory.

5.1 Avoiding Overflows

Double-precision floating point registers hold real numbers of the form $2^e f$, with $f \in \{-2^{53} - 1, \ldots, 2^{53} - 1\}$ and $e \in \{-1022, \ldots, 1023\}$. The result of an operation on two such numbers is guaranteed to be exact if it is in $\{-2^{53} - 1, \ldots, 2^{53} - 1\}$, otherwise the result value may *overflow*. To make sure that such overflows do not occur, we cannot simply run the code on some inputs and check whether it produces the correct results; we have to make sure that an overflow cannot occur for any valid inputs.

We first implemented all algorithms in the C++ programming language (not using SIMD instructions) and replace the double data type by a self-written class CheckDouble to represent 64-bit floating-point values. This class performs all arithmetic operations on a member variable d of type double. Furthermore it stores the "worst-case" absolute value of the mantissa m in a member variable of type uint64_t which is updated with each operation. Before actually performing an operation it checks whether the worst-case result overflows; if it does, the program is aborted. Updating m is straight-forward: Multiplying (d_1, m_1) and (d_2, m_2) yields $(d_1 d_2, m_1 m_2)$, adding (d_1, m_1) and (d_2, m_2) yields $(d_1 + d_2, m_1 + m_2)$, and subtracting (d_1, m_1) from (d_2, m_2) yields $(d_2 - d_1, m_1 + m_2)$. The only divisions are by the constants v and $6v$, for those divisions it is safe to set the result to $(d/v, |m/v|)$ or $(d/6v, |m/6v|)$ respectively. The remainder of a (rounding) division by v is always between $-|v/2|$ and $|v/2|$, so we can just set the maximal mantissa to $|v/2|$ when computing the remainder of a division by v. Analgously, the maximal mantissa of the remainder of a division by $6v$ is $|3v|$.

For all constants involved in the pairing computation we can initialize the maximal mantissa with the actual value. For the inputs to the pairing we assume that they are worst-case output of the reduction described in Algorithm 3.

In order to obtain the targeted performance we replaced the CheckDouble class again by the double data type and re-implemented the speed-critical functions in the qhasm programming language [10] using SIMD instructions where possible. The operations on double-precision floating-point values in this qhasm implementation are the same as in the C version for which we automatically verified that no overflows can occur. Tools to verify this property on the assembly level would be very helpful but we do not know of such tools. The resulting software has passed a bilinearity and non-degeneracy test on 1,000,000 random inputs, each test involving 3 pairing computations.

5.2 Implementation of Field-Arithmetic Operations

The 12 coefficients $f_0, \ldots, f_{11}$ of a polynomial F representing an element $f \in \mathbb{F}_p$ (see Section 4) are stored consecutively in a double array of size 12. The 24 coefficients $g_0, \ldots, g_{11}$ and $h_0, \ldots, h_{11}$ representing an element $(gi + h) \in \mathbb{F}_{p^2}$ are stored interleaved in a `double` array of size 24 as $(h_0, g_0 | h_1, g_1 | \ldots | h_{11}, g_{11})$. In the following descriptions, all SIMD instructions operate on every two adjacent double values of this representation. Observe that the implementations do not minimize the number of *instructions* but try to minimize the number of *cycles*.

$\mathbb{F}_{p^2} \times \mathbb{F}_{p^2}$ **multiplication.** Multiplication of $ai + b$ and $ci + d$, layed out in memory as $op_1 = (b_0, a_0 | \ldots | b_{11}, a_{11})$ and $op_2 = (d_0, c_0 | \ldots | d_{11}, c_{11})$, is done by duplicating $b_0, \ldots, b_{11}$ to obtain

$$t_1 = (b_0, b_0 | b_1, b_1 | \ldots | b_{11}, b_{11}).$$

We then perform a digit-sliced multiplication of t_1 and op_2 to obtain

$$t_2 = (bd_0, bc_0 | \ldots | bd_{22}, bc_{22}).$$

In a second step we duplicate $a_0, \ldots, a_{11}$, obtain

$$t_1 = (a_0, a_0 | a_1, a_1 | \ldots | a_{11}, a_{11}),$$

multiply digit-sliced with op_2 and obtain

$$t_3 = (ad_0, ac_0 | \ldots | ad_{22}, ac_{22}).$$

We then multiply the high double values of t_3 by $i^2 = -7$ and obtain

$$t_3 = (ad_0, -7ac_0 | \ldots | ad_{22}, -7ac_{22}).$$

Swapping in t_3 yields

$$t_3 = (-7ac_0, ad_0 | \ldots | -7ac_{22}, ad_{22}).$$

Finally we add t_3 to t_2 and apply polynomial reduction (Algorithm 2) and coefficient reduction (Algorithm 3) to obtain interleaved coefficients of $(ai+b)(ci+d) = ((ad + bc)i + (bd - 7ac))$. During this computation we keep values in XMM registers as much as possible.

The parallel digit-sliced multiplication uses the schoolbook algorithm resulting in 144 multiplications (`mulpd`), 121 additions (`addpd`), and 10 more multiplications by 6 (`mulpd`). We experimented with Karatsuba multiplication but did not gain any performance – we are planning to further examine possible speedups by using Karatsuba multiplication.

Computing the rounded quotient and the remainder in the coefficient reduction could be done using multiplication by $1/v$, using the `roundpd` instruction on the result, multiplying by v and subtracting the result from the original value to obtain the remainder. As the `roundpd` instruction is part of the SSE4.1 instruction set which is not available on 65 nm Core 2 processors and all AMD processors we decided to implement rounding as addition and subsequent subtraction of a constant as explained for example by Bernstein in [11].

$\mathbb{F}_{p^2}$ **squaring.** When squaring an element $ai + b \in \mathbb{F}_{p^2}$, layed out in memory as $op_1 = (b_0, a_0 | \dots | b_{11}, a_{11})$, we swap the coefficients to obtain

$$t_1 = (a_0, b_0 | \dots | a_{11}, b_{11}).$$

We then copy t_1 and apply the addsd instruction with op_1 to obtain

$$t_2 = (a_0 + b_0, b_0 | \dots | a_{11} + b_{11}, b_{11}).$$

Then we multiply the low double values in t_1 by $i^2 = -7$ and obtain

$$t_1 = (-7a_0, b_0 | \dots | -7a_{11}, b_{11}).$$

Applying the addsd instruction on t_1 and op_1 yields

$$t_1 = (b_0 - 7a_0, b_0 | \dots | b_{11} - 7a_{11}, b_{11}).$$

Now we use digit-sliced multiplication on t_1 and t_2 to obtain

$$r = (((b - 7a)(a + b))_0, ab_0 | \dots | ((b - 7a)(a + b))_{22}, ab_{22}).$$

Copying r and duplicating the high double values yields

$$d = (ab_0, ab_0 | \dots | ab_{22}, ab_{22}).$$

Multiplying the low double values in d by $-i^2 - 1 = 6$ yields

$$d = (6ab_0, ab_0 | \dots | 6ab_{22}, ab_{22}), \text{ and}$$

adding d to r and applying polynomial reduction and coefficient reduction yields the coefficients of the result $(2ab)i + (b^2 - 7a^2)$.

$\mathbb{F}_{p^2} \times \mathbb{F}_p$ **multiplication.** Evaluating the line functions requires multiplications of an element of $\mathbb{F}_{p^2}$ with an element of $\mathbb{F}_p$. This is implemented using the same parallel schoolbook multiplication which is used in the $\mathbb{F}_{p^2} \times \mathbb{F}_{p^2}$ multiplication. This requires first duplicating the coefficients of the $\mathbb{F}_p$ element in memory.

$\mathbb{F}_{p^2}$ **short coefficient reduction.** Additions, subtractions and multiplications with small constants in $\mathbb{F}_{p^2}$ can all be implemented using 12 SIMD instructions. They produce results which may have coefficients that are too large to go as input into a multiplication but are still so small that they do not require the full-fledged coefficient reduction from Algorithm 3. If the output of an addition or subtraction is used as input to a multiplication we apply a short coefficient reduction which first carries from f_{11} to f_0, f_3, f_6 and f_9. Then it carries from all odd coefficients $f_1, f_3, \dots, f_9$ and then from all even coefficients $f_0, f_2, \dots, f_{10}$.

$\mathbb{F}_p$ **inversion.** The final exponentiation involves one inversion in $\mathbb{F}_{p^{12}}$. This can be computed with only one inversion in $\mathbb{F}_p$ and several multiplications as described in, e.g., [22, Sec. 2]. We implement inversion in $\mathbb{F}_p$ as exponentiation with $p - 2$ using a simple square-and-multiply algorithm. There exist certainly faster methods to compute inverses in $\mathbb{F}_p$, but this way we can easily ensure constant-time behaviour of the inversion and the single inversion in $\mathbb{F}_{p^2}$ accounts for less than 3 percent of the total computation time.

6   Benchmarking Results

This section gives benchmarking results of the pairing computation on different microarchitectures. All benchmarks were obtained by iteratively calling the function to benchmark and a function reading the CPU cycle counter 1000 times and then computing the median of the differences of every two consecutive cycle counts. The call to the function reading the cycle counter and the loop control incurs some overhead so Table 2 also gives the cycles obtained when no function is called between two consecutive cycle counts. The counts for the Miller loop in Table 2 include the two final addition steps in the optimal ate pairing before the final exponentiation.

Table 1. Machines used for benchmarking

Name	Affiliation	CPU	OS	Compiler
latour	Eindhoven University of Technology	Intel Core 2 Quad Q6600 2394 MHz	Linux 2.6.28	gcc 4.3.3
behemoth	National Taiwan University	Intel Core 2 Quad Q9550 2830 MHz	Linux 2.6.27	gcc 4.3.2
dragon	National Taiwan University	Intel Xeon E5504 2000 MHz	Linux 2.6.27	gcc 3.4.6
mace	University of Illinois at Chicago	AMD Athlon 64 X2 3800+ 2000 MHz	Linux 2.6.31	gcc 4.4.1
chukonu	University of Illinois at Chicago	AMD Phenom II X4 955 3210.298 MHz	Linux 2.6.31	gcc 4.4.1

Table 2. Cycle counts of relevant operations on different machines. Parameters: $p = 36u^4 + 36u^3 + 24u^2 + 6u + 1$, with $u = v^3$ and $v = 1966080$, BN curve: $y^2 = x^3 + 17$ over $\mathbb{F}_p$.

	latour	behemoth	dragon	mace	chukonu
no function	72	34	24	11	75
$\mathbb{F}_{p^2} \times \mathbb{F}_{p^2}$ multiplication	693	672	676	1732	737
$\mathbb{F}_{p^2}$ squaring	558	510	504	1220	606
$\mathbb{F}_{p^2} \times \mathbb{F}_p$ multiplication	432	391	388	977	434
$\mathbb{F}_{p^2}$ short coefficient reduction	144	110	84	195	152
$\mathbb{F}_{p^2}$ inversion	127071	126718	134524	339835	127067
Miller loop	2,267,811	2,320,908	2,365,812	5,666,343	2,506,893
optimal ate pairing	4,470,408	4,480,716	4,736,408	10,961,234	4,989,872

Acknowledgements. We thank Tanja Lange and the anonymous referees for their valuable comments that helped us improve the paper.

References

1. The GNU MP bignum library, http://gmplib.org/ (accessed March 31, 2010)
2. MPFQ - a finite field library, http://mpfq.gforge.inria.fr/ (accessed March 31, 2010)

3. Arène, C., Lange, T., Naehrig, M., Ritzenthaler, C.: Faster pairing computation. Cryptology ePrint Archive, Report 2009/155, to appear in the Journal of Number Theory (2010), http://eprint.iacr.org/2009/155/

4. Barker, E., Barker, W., Burr, W., Polk, W., Smid, M.: Recommendation for key management - part 1: General (revised). Published as NIST Special Publication 800-57 (2007), http://csrc.nist.gov/groups/ST/toolkit/documents/SP800-57Part1_3-8-07.pdf

5. Barreto, P.S.L.M.: A survey on craptological pairing algorithms. Journal of Craptology 7 (2010), http://www.anagram.com/~jcrap/Volume_7/Pairings.pdf

6. Barreto, P.S.L.M., Galbraith, S.D., Ó' hÉigeartaigh, C., Scott, M.: Efficient pairing computation on supersingular abelian varieties. Designs, Codes and Cryptography 42(3), 239–271 (2007)

7. Barreto, P.S.L.M., Kim, H.Y., Lynn, B., Scott, M.: Efficient algorithms for pairing-based cryptosystems. In: Yung, M. (ed.) CRYPTO 2002. LNCS, vol. 2442, pp. 354–368. Springer, Heidelberg (2002)

8. Barreto, P.S.L.M., Lynn, B., Scott, M.: Efficient implementation of pairing-based cryptosystems. Journal of Cryptology 17(4), 321–334 (2004)

9. Barreto, P.S.L.M., Naehrig, M.: Pairing-friendly elliptic curves of prime order. In: Preneel, B., Tavares, S. (eds.) SAC 2005. LNCS, vol. 3897, pp. 319–331. Springer, Heidelberg (2006)

10. Bernstein, D.J.: qhasm: tools to help write high-speed software, http://cr.yp.to/qhasm.html (accessed March 31, 2010)

11. Bernstein, D.J.: Floating-point arithmetic and message authentication, Document ID: dabadd3095644704c5cbe9690ea3738e (2004), http://cr.yp.to/papers.html#hash127

12. Bernstein, D.J.: Curve25519: new Diffie-Hellman speed records. In: Yung, M., Dodis, Y., Kiayias, A., Malkin, T.G. (eds.) PKC 2006. LNCS, vol. 3958, pp. 207–228. Springer, Heidelberg (2006) Document ID: 4230efdfa673480fc079449d90f322c0, http://cr.yp.to/papers.html#curve25519

13. Boneh, D., Di Crescenzo, G., Ostrovsky, R., Persiano, G.: Public key encryption with keyword search. In: Cachin, C., Camenisch, J.L. (eds.) EUROCRYPT 2004. LNCS, vol. 3027, pp. 506–522. Springer, Heidelberg (2004)

14. Devegili, A.J., Scott, M., Dahab, R.: Implementing cryptographic pairings over Barreto-Naehrig curves. In: Takagi, T., Okamoto, T., Okamoto, E., Okamoto, T. (eds.) Pairing 2007. LNCS, vol. 4575, pp. 197–207. Springer, Heidelberg (2007)

15. Smart, N. (ed): ECRYPT2 yearly report on algorithms and keysizes (2008-2009). Technical report, ECRYPT II – European Network of Excellence in Cryptology, EU FP7, ICT-2007-216676 (2009) (published as deliverable D.SPA.7), http://www.ecrypt.eu.org/documents/D.SPA.7.pdf

16. Fan, J., Vercauteren, F., Verbauwhede, I.: Faster $\mathbb{F}_p$-arithmetic for cryptographic pairings on Barreto-Naehrig curves. In: Clavier, C., Gaj, K. (eds.) CHES 2009. LNCS, vol. 5747, pp. 240–253. Springer, Heidelberg (2009), http://www.cosic.esat.kuleuven.be/publications/article-1256.pdf

17. Fog, A.: Software optimization ressources (2010), http://www.agner.org/optimize/ (accessed March 31, 2010)

18. Freeman, D., Scott, M., Teske, E.: A taxonomy of pairing-friendly elliptic curves. Journal of Cryptology 23(2), 224–280 (2010)

19. Grabher, P., Großschädl, J., Page, D.: On software parallel implementation of cryptographic pairings. In: Avanzi, R.M., Keliher, L., Sica, F. (eds.) SAC 2008. LNCS, vol. 5381, pp. 34–49. Springer, Heidelberg (2009)

20. Granger, R., Scott, M.: Faster squaring in the cyclotomic subgroup of sixth degree extensions. In: Nguyen, P., Pointcheval, D. (eds.) PKC 2010. LNCS, vol. 6056, pp. 209–223. Springer, Heidelberg (2010), http://eprint.iacr.org/2009/565/

21. Groth, J., Sahai, A.: Efficient non-interactive proof systems for bilinear groups. In: Smart, N.P. (ed.) EUROCRYPT 2008. LNCS, vol. 4965, pp. 415–432. Springer, Heidelberg (2008)

22. Hankerson, D., Menezes, A., Scott, M.: Software implementation of pairings. In: Joye, M., Neven, G. (eds.) Identity-Based Cryptography. IOS Press, Amsterdam (2008), http://www.math.uwaterloo.ca/~ajmeneze/publications/pairings_software.pdf

23. Heß, F., Smart, N.P., Vercauteren, F.: The eta pairing revisited. IEEE Transactions on Information Theory 52, 4595–4602 (2006)

24. Lee, E., Lee, H.-S., Park, C.-M.: Efficient and generalized pairing computation on abelian varieties. Cryptology ePrint Archive, Report 2008/040 (2008), http://eprint.iacr.org/2008/040/

25. Shamus Software Ltd. Multiprecision integer and rational arithmetic C/C++ library, http://www.shamus.ie/ (accessed March 31, 2010)

26. Miller, V.S.: Short programs for functions on curves (Unpublished manuscript) (1986), http://crypto.stanford.edu/miller/miller.pdf

27. Miller, V.S.: The Weil pairing, and its efficient calculation. Journal of Cryptology 17, 235–261 (2004)

28. Naehrig, M.: Constructive and Computational Aspects of Cryptographic Pairings. PhD thesis, Technische Universiteit Eindhoven (2009), http://www.cryptojedi.org/users/michael/data/thesis/2009-05-13-diss.pdf

29. Naehrig, M., Barreto, P.S.L.M., Schwabe, P.: On compressible pairings and their computation. In: Vaudenay, S. (ed.) AFRICACRYPT 2008. LNCS, vol. 5023, pp. 371–388. Springer, Heidelberg (2008)

30. Scott, M.: Personal communication (March 2010)

31. Scott, M., Benger, N., Charlemagne, M., Dominguez Perez, L.J., Kachisa, E.J.: On the final exponentiation for calculating pairings on ordinary elliptic curves. In: Shacham, H. (ed.) Pairing 2009. LNCS, vol. 5671, pp. 78–88. Springer, Heidelberg (2009)

32. Vercauteren, F.: Optimal pairings. IEEE Transactions on Information Theory 56(1) (2010)

Accelerating Lattice Reduction with FPGAs

Jérémie Detrey[1], Guillaume Hanrot[2], Xavier Pujol[2], and Damien Stehlé[3]

[1] CARAMEL project-team, LORIA, INRIA / CNRS / Nancy Université,
Campus Scientifique, BP 239 F-54506 Vandœuvre-lès-Nancy Cedex, France
[2] ÉNS Lyon, Université de Lyon, Laboratoire LIP, CNRS-ENSL-INRIA-UCBL,
46 Allée d'Italie, 69364 Lyon Cedex 07, France
[3] CNRS, Macquarie University and University of Sydney,
Dpt. of Mathematics and Statistics, University of Sydney NSW 2006, Australia
jeremie.detrey@loria.fr,
{guillaume.hanrot,xavier.pujol,damien.stehle}@ens-lyon.fr

Abstract. We describe an FPGA accelerator for the Kannan–Fincke–Pohst enumeration algorithm (KFP) solving the Shortest Lattice Vector Problem (SVP). This is the first FPGA implementation of KFP specifically targeting cryptographically relevant dimensions. In order to optimize this implementation, we theoretically and experimentally study several facets of KFP, including its efficient parallelization and its underlying arithmetic. Our FPGA accelerator can be used for both solving stand-alone instances of SVP (within a hybrid CPU–FPGA compound) or myriads of smaller dimensional SVP instances arising in a BKZ-type algorithm. For devices of comparable costs, our FPGA implementation is faster than a multi-core CPU implementation by a factor around 2.12.

Keywords: FPGA, Euclidean Lattices, Shortest Vector Problem.

1 Introduction

Given $\mathbf{b}_1, \ldots, \mathbf{b}_d \in \mathbb{R}^n$ linearly independent, the spanned lattice $L[(\mathbf{b}_i)_i]$ is the set of all integer linear combinations of the $\mathbf{b}_i$'s, *i.e.*, $L = \sum_i \mathbb{Z}\mathbf{b}_i$. The $\mathbf{b}_i$'s are called a basis of L. The lattice L is discrete, and thus contains a vector of minimal non-zero Euclidean norm. This norm, denoted by $\lambda(L)$, is referred to as the lattice minimum. The Shortest Vector Problem (SVP) consists in finding such a vector given a basis. Its decisional variant (given a basis and $r > 0$, decide whether $\lambda \leq r$) is known to be NP-hard under randomized reductions [2]. When SVP is deemed to be hard to solve, the relaxed problem γ-SVP may be considered: given a basis of L, find $\mathbf{b} \in L \setminus \mathbf{0}$ such that $\|\mathbf{b}\| \leq \gamma \cdot \lambda(L)$.

Lattices have repeatedly occurred in cryptography since the beginning of the 1980s [36,32]. In some cases, such as for most lattice attacks on variants of RSA [9,27], solving $2^{O(d)}$-SVP suffices. This is achieved with the LLL polynomial-time algorithm [24]. Here we are interested in the cases where γ-SVP needs to be solved for a rather small γ (*e.g.*, polynomial in d). These include the lattice attacks against knapsack-based cryptosystems [38,33], NTRU [21,22], and

M. Abdalla and P.S.L.M. Barreto (Eds.): LATINCRYPT 2010, LNCS 6212, pp. 124–143, 2010.
© Springer-Verlag Berlin Heidelberg 2010

lattice-based cryptosystems [16,3,35,43,5,15,28,39,49]. Lattice-based cryptosystems are becoming increasingly popular, thanks to their promising asymptotic complexities, their unmatched levels of provable security and their apparent resistance to quantum computers. Another attractive feature is that lattices can be used to build complex cryptographic functions, such as identity-based encryption [15,7,1] and fully homomorphic encryption [14,48,10]. A major challenge in lattice-based cryptography consists in assessing its practicality: To provide meaningful security parameters, it is crucial to determine the practical limits of the best known attacks, namely, γ-SVP solvers. The present article is a step forward in that direction.

The known algorithms (*e.g.*, [44,12]) for solving γ-SVP all rely on an SVP solver that is used for smaller-dimensional projected sublattices. Our main contribution is to describe the first FPGA implementation of the Kannan–Fincke–Pohst enumeration algorithm (KFP) for SVP [11,23]. KFP exhaustively looks for all integer points within high-dimensional ellipsoids, by visiting all the nodes of a huge tree. The asymptotically best known KFP-based SVP solver is Kannan's algorithm, which requires a polynomial space and has been shown in [19] to run in time $d^{\frac{d}{2e}(1+o(1))}$. (For the sake of simplicity, we omit terms polynomial in n and the bit-sizes of the input matrix entries.) In 2001, Ajtai *et al.* [4] invented a probabilistic Monte Carlo SVP solver with time and space complexities $2^{O(d)}$. This algorithm was progressively improved in [42,37,30] and the currently most efficient variant [41] runs in time and space bounded by $2^{2.47d}$ and $2^{1.24d}$, respectively. Finally, Micciancio and Voulgaris [29] recently described yet another SVP solver, which is deterministic and has time and space complexities $2^{O(d)}$. Although asymptotically weaker, KFP remains the currently fastest one in practice for all handleable dimensions, even if heuristic variants are considered [30,13].

FPGAs are a particularly appropriate platform for KFP, as little memory is required, the inputs and outputs are negligible compared to the internal computational effort, KFP is highly parallelizable, and FPGAs can take advantage of the possibility of using low-precision arithmetic. In order to maximize the efficiency of our implementation, we introduce a number of algorithmic improvements which may also prove useful for other architectures. Firstly, we propose a quasi-optimal parallelization technique for KFP; this is a non-trivial task, as the sizes of the subtrees of the KFP tree may be extremely unbalanced. Secondly, we adapt and extend the results of [40] to show that the underlying arithmetic operations can be performed with low-precision fixed-point arithmetic. Thirdly, we do not implement KFP fully on FPGA, but introduce instead a hybrid CPU–FPGA algorithm: since the KFP tree typically has an exponentially large middle section, the top and bottom layers of the tree are handled on CPU, which allows us to significantly decrease the memory requirements.

We compared our FPGA implementation to the one from the fplll library [6], which is currently the best available software implementation of KFP. We also took into account the recent algorithmic improvement of [13, App. D]. Our hardware device was a Xilinx Virtex-5 SXT 35 FPGA with a speed grade of -1, at a unit price of approximately US\$460. The software benchmarks were run on an

Intel Core 2 Quad Q9550 at 2.83 GHz, which costs around US\$275. Our FPGA implementation achieves a traversal rate of $2.50 \cdot 10^8$ tree nodes per second in dimension 64, whereas our corresponding software traversal rate is $1.76 \cdot 10^7$ per CPU core, or equivalently $7.03 \cdot 10^7$ when using the four available cores. The cost-normalized speed-up is thus around 2.12. These figures imply that KFP may heuristically solve SVP up to dimension 110 in less than 40 hours, using a single FPGA device (with the extreme pruning strategy from [13]).

Implications for lattice-based cryptography. The dimensions considered in lattice-based cryptosystems are significantly beyond the above figures. However, solving γ-SVP for a moderate approximation factor γ often suffices to break them. As already mentioned, the known algorithms for solving γ-SVP all rely on an SVP solver, which is by far the main contributor to the cost. In practice, (*e.g.*, in NTL [47]), one uses the heuristic BKZ algorithm [45] and the underlying SVP solver is KFP. To further speed up KFP within BKZ, it is classical to prune the KFP tree [45,46,13]. For instance, pruning is available in NTL [47] and Magma [26]. Our FPGA implementation can be trivially modified to handle pruning. In our experiments, we considered KFP without pruning, to concentrate on the gains solely due to the FPGA implementation. There is no *a priori* reason why the speed-ups should not add up as well.

Related works. Recently, Hermans *et al.* [20] described a parallel version of KFP and implemented it on GPUs. According to their benchmarks, an Nvidia GeForce GTX 280 GPU yields a 5-fold acceleration against a single core of an Intel Core 2 Extreme QX9650 at 3 GHz which processes $1.25 \cdot 10^7$ nodes per second.[1] Their full system (one QX9650 CPU and four GTX 280 GPUs) is estimated at US\$2200 and is said to deliver a speed-up of 24 against a single QX9650 core, thus tallying a traversal rate of $3.00 \cdot 10^8$ nodes per second, or equivalently $1.36 \cdot 10^5$ nodes per second per dollar after normalizing by the system cost. Besides cryptology, KFP is also common-place in communications theory, in particular for MIMO wireless communications [31,51], in which field it is known as sphere decoding. In this context, KFP has been implemented on ASICs (see, *e.g.*, [18,50]). However, these implementations do not seem relevant for cryptographic applications, as they are optimized for much smaller dimensions.

Road-map. In Section 2, we give the necessary background on the KFP algorithm. Our parallel variant is described in Section 3, and the use of low-precision fixed-point arithmetic is investigated in Section 4. Finally, we describe our FPGA implementation and provide the reader with implementation results in Section 5.

Notations. The canonical inner product of $\mathbf{x}, \mathbf{y} \in \mathbb{R}^n$ will be denoted by $\langle \mathbf{x}, \mathbf{y} \rangle$. If the vectors $\mathbf{b}_1, \ldots, \mathbf{b}_d \in \mathbb{R}^n$ are linearly independent, we define their Gram–Schmidt basis by $\mathbf{b}_i^* = \mathbf{b}_i - \sum_{j<i} \mu_{i,j} \mathbf{b}_j^*$ for $i \leq d$, where $\mu_{i,j} = \frac{\langle \mathbf{b}_i, \mathbf{b}_j^* \rangle}{\langle \mathbf{b}_j^*, \mathbf{b}_j^* \rangle}$. It

---

[1] Note that what is defined as a node in this paper differs by a factor 2 from the "enumeration step" metric in [20]; the latter (see [20, Sec. 3.1, second paragraph]) indeed counts each node twice, once when traversed downwards, once when traversed upwards during the enumeration.

can be readily checked that this basis is orthogonal, so that $\|\sum_{i\le d} u_i \mathbf{b}_i^*\|^2 = \sum_{i\le d} u_i^2 \|\mathbf{b}_i^*\|^2$, for any $u_1, \ldots, u_d \in \mathbb{R}$. We shall denote by γ_d Hermite's constant for dimension d. The inequality $\gamma_d \le (d+1)/4$ classically holds for all d.

Experiments. In our experiments, we used the "knapsack" random lattice bases from [17], as described in [34]. The bit-sizes of the non-trivial entries was set to $\approx 100 \cdot d$, where d is the dimension. For BKZ-reduction, we used the implementation contained in [47], whereas [6] was used for LLL-reduction and KFP.

Code distribution. We plan to make the codes mentioned in Sections 3, 4, and 5 publicly available.

2   The KFP Enumeration Algorithm

We assume the reader is familiar with the elementary aspects on Euclidean lattices, and refer to [25] for an introduction. In this section, we recall the basic enumeration algorithm for solving SVP.

2.1   Reminders on the KFP Enumeration Algorithm

Consider a d-dimensional lattice $L \subseteq \mathbb{R}^n$ with basis $(\mathbf{b}_1, \ldots, \mathbf{b}_d)$. We want to find a shortest nonzero vector of L. In the context of KFP, this is performed by enumerating all points of L within a ball with radius $\sqrt{A}$ centered at $\mathbf{0}$, where A is an estimate for $\lambda(L)^2$. For instance, A can be set to Minkowski's bound $\gamma_d(\det L)^{2/d}$ or to $\min \|\mathbf{b}_i\|$; we shall discuss the choice of A in Section 2.3. If a vector of norm $\le \sqrt{A}$ is found during the enumeration, the bound A is updated accordingly in a dynamic way. Consider a lattice vector $\sum_{i\le d} x_i \mathbf{b}_i$. We have

$$\left\| \sum_{i=1}^{d} x_i \mathbf{b}_i \right\|^2 = \left\| \sum_{i=1}^{d} x_i \left(\mathbf{b}_i^* + \sum_{j=1}^{i-1} \mu_{i,j} \mathbf{b}_j^* \right) \right\|^2 = \sum_{j=1}^{d} \left(x_j + \sum_{i=j+1}^{d} \mu_{i,j} x_i \right)^2 \|\mathbf{b}_j^*\|^2. \quad (1)$$

This equation implies that for any $(x_1, \ldots, x_d)$ such that $\sum_{i=1}^{d} x_i \mathbf{b}_i$ is a solution to the problem, one should have $x_d^2 \|\mathbf{b}_d^*\|^2 \le A$. As x_d is an integer, only a finite number of x_d's satisfy this inequality. Furthermore, for each of those values of x_d, we must have

$$\sum_{j=1}^{d-1} \left(x_j + \mu_{d,j} x_d + \sum_{i=j+1}^{d-1} \mu_{i,j} x_i \right)^2 \|\mathbf{b}_j^*\|^2 \le A - x_d^2 \|\mathbf{b}_d^*\|^2.$$

This corresponds to a new enumeration problem, in dimension $d-1$ and centered at $-x_d \sum_{j<d} \mu_{d,j} \mathbf{b}_j^*$ rather than at $\mathbf{0}$, which is solved recursively. This recursive description builds a tree, where the first (or top) level of the tree is labeled by the possible values for (x_d), the second level by the possible values for the pair (x_{d-1}, x_d), etc.

For the sake of further description of optimizations, it is however better to reformulate this algorithm in a sequential form. Also, Schnorr and Euchner [45] suggested an optimization regarding the order in which the nodes are considered. The key idea is that very short vectors should be sought in an aggressive way, so as to quickly decrease the initial bound A. Eq. (1) suggests that the values $x_i \approx \left\lceil -\sum_{j=i+1}^{d} x_j \mu_{j,i} \right\rceil$ are most likely to yield a short vector.

Unrolling the depth-first traversal of the tree then yields the algorithm of Figure 1.

Inputs: A positive real A, $(\mu_{i,j})_{1 \leq j < i \leq d}$, $(\|\mathbf{b}_i^*\|^2)_{1 \leq i \leq d}$.

Output: The coordinates of a nonzero shortest vector of L with respect to the basis $(\mathbf{b}_1, \ldots, \mathbf{b}_d)$.

1. $\mathbf{x}[1..d] \leftarrow (0, 0, \ldots, 0)$, $\delta\mathbf{x}[1..d] \leftarrow (0, 0, \ldots, 0)$, $\delta^2\mathbf{x}(1..d) \leftarrow (-1, -1, \ldots, -1)$.
2. $\mathbf{c}[1..d] \leftarrow (0, \ldots, 0)$, $\ell[1..d+1] \leftarrow (0, \ldots, 0)$, $\mathbf{y}[1..d] \leftarrow (0, \ldots, 0)$.
3. $i \leftarrow d$, $S \leftarrow \emptyset$.
4. Repeat
5. $\quad y_i \leftarrow |x_i - c_i|$; $\ell_i \leftarrow \ell_{i+1} + \|\mathbf{b}_i^*\|^2 y_i^2$.
6. $\quad$ If $\ell_i \leq A$ and $i = 1$ then
7. $\quad\quad$ If $\ell_1 \neq 0$ then $(S, A) \leftarrow (\mathbf{x}, \ell_1)$.
8. $\quad$ If $\ell_i \leq A$ and $i > 1$ then
9. $\quad\quad i \leftarrow i - 1, c_i \leftarrow -\sum_{j=i+1}^{d} x_j \mu_{j,i}, x_i \leftarrow \lfloor c_i \rceil, \delta x_i \leftarrow 0$.
10. $\quad\quad$ If $c_i < x_i$ then $\delta^2 x_i \leftarrow 1$, else $\delta^2 x_i \leftarrow -1$.
11. $\quad$ Else
12. $\quad\quad i \leftarrow i + 1$.
13. $\quad\quad$ If $i > d$ then return S.
14. $\quad\quad \delta^2 x_i \leftarrow -\delta^2 x_i$; $\delta x_i \leftarrow -\delta x_i + \delta^2 x_i$; $x_i \leftarrow x_i + \delta x_i$.

Fig. 1. The KFP enumeration algorithm

During the execution of the algorithm, the depth of the current node in the tree is $d - i + 1$, and the value ℓ_i is equal to the part of the sum of the right hand side of Eq. (1) corresponding to indices i to d. Entering Step 9 starts the exploration of a new subtree; then, exiting Step 12 with the same value of i marks the end of the exploration of this subtree.

Recently, Gama *et al.* [13, App. D] described a variant of the algorithm of Figure 1 that leads to run-times being decreased by up to 40%. The idea consists in storing all partial sums of the c_i's of Step 9, and maintaining a table of indices which tell which partial sums remain relevant at any given moment. The speed-up is greatest if the index i stays long within a small interval, since then most of the sum of Step 9 is already known and does not need being recomputed. A drawback of this improvement, especially for memory-limited hardware devices, is that it requires more memory: $\Theta(d^2)$ partial sums need to be stored.

2.2 Heuristic Analysis of the Enumeration Algorithm

We shall now overview some elements of the analysis of the enumeration algorithm. These are important to understand the shape of the enumeration tree, and, among others, to devise a parallelization strategy. Understanding the overall shape of the enumeration tree also proves useful in finding the right global computational architecture for dealing with enumeration problems. In this analysis, we shall ignore aspects related to the dynamic evolution of the bound A.

The following lemma provides a geometric characterization of points encountered in the tree. Here and in the sequel, we denote by Π_k the projection orthogonally to the span of $\mathbf{b}_1, \ldots, \mathbf{b}_{d-k}$. We have $\Pi_k(\mathbf{b}_j) = \mathbf{b}_j - \sum_{l=1}^{d-k} \mu_{l,j} \mathbf{b}_l^*$ for any $j > d - k$.

Lemma 1. *At depth k in the tree, we consider all points $\sum_{j=d-k+1}^{d} x_j \mathbf{b}_j$ such that*

$$\left\| \sum_{j=d-k+1}^{d} x_j \Pi_k(\mathbf{b}_j) \right\|^2 \leq A.$$

Stated differently, the points considered are points of the projected lattice $\Pi_k(L)$ within the k-dimensional closed ball $\mathcal{B}_k(\mathbf{0}, \sqrt{A})$ with radius $\sqrt{A}$. A classical principle due to Gauss provides a (usually good) heuristic estimate for the number of these points, namely:

$$|\Pi_k(L) \cap \mathcal{B}_k(\mathbf{0}, \sqrt{A})| \approx \frac{\mathrm{vol}\, \mathcal{B}_k(\mathbf{0}, \sqrt{A})}{\det \Pi_k(L)} = \frac{\pi^{k/2} A^{k/2}}{\Gamma(k/2 + 1) \prod_{l=d-k+1}^{d} \|\mathbf{b}_l^*\|}$$

$$\approx \frac{(2e\pi A/k)^{k/2}}{\prod_{l=d-k+1}^{d} \|\mathbf{b}_l^*\|}.$$

This suggests the following estimate for the number of nodes of a subtree at depth k:

$$\mathcal{C}(x_{d-k+1}, \ldots, x_d) := \sum_{j \leq d-k} \frac{(2e\pi \ell_k/j)^{j/2}}{\prod_{l=d-k-j+1}^{d-k} \|\mathbf{b}_l^*\|}.$$

For $k = d$, we obtain an estimate for the full enumeration:

$$\mathcal{C} := \sum_{j \leq d} \frac{(2e\pi A/j)^{j/2}}{\prod_{l=d-j+1}^{d} \|\mathbf{b}_l^*\|}.$$

These estimates strongly depend on the $\|\mathbf{b}_i^*\|$'s: they have a major influence on the shape and size of the enumeration tree. For extremely reduced bases, for example HKZ-reduced, these estimates predict that the width of the tree at depth k is roughly $2^{O(d)} d^{\frac{k}{2} \log \frac{d}{k}}$ (see [19]): the top and bottom of the tree are small, whereas the width is reached by the middle layers (it is obtained for $k \approx d/e$). If the reduction is weaker, *e.g.*, with BKZ-reduction, then the tree is even more unbalanced, with a very wide middle section, and tiny top and bottom. This is a general fact: most of the points encountered are "dead-ends" of the enumeration tree (*i.e.*, most of the paths followed from the root end before reaching level d of the tree). We refer to Appendix A for a figure showing the number of nodes per level on typical examples.

2.3   Choosing the Initial Parameter A

The cost of KFP greatly depends on the initial choice for A. If the minimum $\lambda(L)$ is already known, the optimal choice is $A = \lambda(L)^2$. If unknown, two main approaches can be considered: use an upper bound, or start from a lower bound and increase it until a solution is found.

In the first case, an option is to set $A = \min_i \|b_i\|^2$. If the basis is nearly HKZ-reduced, this might be the most efficient choice as it will be very close to $\lambda(L)^2$. However, in the worst-case, the gap between $\min_i \|b_i\|^2$ and $\lambda(L)$ grows with the dimension. A second option consists in using the inequality $\lambda(L) \leq \sqrt{\gamma_d}(\det L)^{1/d}$. When the dimension is not too small, this gives a more accurate estimate for $\lambda(L)$. However, the exact values of γ_d are unknown in general, and using known upper bounds on γ_d is likely to provide a value for A that is a constant factor too large. If so, the cost of the enumeration will be exponentially larger than the optimal.

Another possibility consists in starting with $A = \min_i \|b_i^*\|^2$, which is a lower bound for $\lambda(L)^2$. If the algorithm fails because A is too small, we try again with a larger value of A such that the heuristic cost is multiplied by 2. As we have seen, the cost can be estimated efficiently with the Gaussian heuristic. This strategy ensures that the overall cost is no more than four times the optimal cost. Since we are mostly interested in the case where d is rather large, we may use the asymptotic lower bound $\gamma_d \gtrsim \frac{d}{2\pi e}$ (see [8, Ch. 1, Eq. (48)]), and set $A = \frac{d}{2\pi e}(\det L)^{2/d}$. The latter should be a rather tight estimate for $\lambda(L)^2$, for somewhat random lattices. If no solution is found for this value of A, we increase A as explained above.

3   Parallel Implementation

The enumeration algorithm is typical example where the main problem can be decomposed in lots of small, independent subproblems, which pleads for a study of their parallelization. One might naively fix a level i of the tree and dispatch all subtrees with root at level i. However, the shape of the tree is not adapted to this approach: such subtasks are of too uneven a size. For instance, if the level is close to the root of the tree, the size of the largest task is of the order of magnitude of the whole computation. Furthermore, if the level i is lower, the number of tasks increases exponentially, which leads to a large number of threads, and to a quick growth of the communication cost. A better strategy is obtained by dispatching the subtasks in a dynamic way:

– Fix a computational granularity level (*e.g.*, around 1 second);
– Start the enumeration on a master machine;
– Whenever entering Step 9, estimate the cost of the corresponding subtree using the heuristic described in Section 2.2:
   • if it is below the granularity level, affect this task to an available slave machine and jump to Step 13,
   • otherwise continue handling the tree on the master machine.

Note that with this strategy, there is no lower bound on the size of a task. However, each node has a small number of children (typically less than 10), which implies that a non-negligible fraction of the tasks will have a non-negligible cost. This ensures that the overall communication cost is low. If the granularity level is high, further care should be taken so that each subprocess can receive a signal whenever the value of A is updated (Step 7). Conversely, if the granularity level is sufficiently low (*i.e.*, the communication cost is higher), it suffices to provide the new A only to the new threads.

We performed experiments to assess the accuracy of the gaussian heuristic, and refer to Appendix B for a detailed account. Typically, for $d = 64$, we observe that the relative error of the gaussian heuristic for any subtree whose number of nodes is more than 10^6 is less than 0.1%. We coded the above parallelization technique in MPI/C++. The code achieves quasi-optimal parallelization. With a single CPU core (Intel Core 2 Quad Q9550 at 2.83 GHz), the average traversal rate is $1.27 \cdot 10^7$ KFP nodes per second without the recent optimisation of [13, App. D], and $1.76 \cdot 10^7$ with it (in dimension 64). With 10 CPU cores (plus a master which only commands the slaves), these traversal rates are multiplied by approximately 9.7.

4   Arithmetic Aspects of KFP

In KFP, the quantities $(\mu_{i,j}, \|b_i^*\|^2, \ell_i, A)$ are all rational, so, in theory, all computations could be performed exactly. However, the bit-sizes of these numbers can be as large as $\Theta(d \log(\max_i \|b_i\|))$, which implies a large arithmetic overhead. In practice, approximate arithmetic such as fixed-point or floating-point is used instead.

4.1   Fixed-Point Arithmetic

A fixed-point number of precision p is a real number that can be written as $m \cdot 2^{-p}$ with $m \in \mathbb{Z}$. Any real number can be rounded to the nearest fixed-point number with an absolute error $\leq 2^{-p-1}$. Additions and subtractions of fixed-point numbers can be performed exactly, but the result of multiplications and divisions must be rounded. From an implementation point of view, fixed-point arithmetic is equivalent to integer arithmetic.

In software, floating-point arithmetic is more common than fixed-point arithmetic: it is standardized and available in hardware on most general-purpose CPUs, enabling reliable and efficient implementations. However, since there are no embedded floating-point operators on FPGA, and as we also want to keep the circuit as small as possible, fixed-point arithmetic is the natural choice. Additionally, the resource usage of the implementation of KFP on the FPGA directly depends on the precision of the fixed-point arithmetic: The size of the data grows linearly with the precision, and the size of multipliers grows quadratically (although the granularity for multipliers is larger). Therefore we want to determine the smallest precision for which the result is still meaningful.

In fixed-point arithmetic, the bit-size comes from two components: the (logarithm of the) magnitude of the numbers we want to represent, and the precision. Here, most of the variables (x_i, δx_i, $\delta^2 x_i$, μ_{ij}, and c_i) have rather small magnitudes. The norm $\|\boldsymbol{b}_i^*\|$ is not bounded, but the ratio between $\max_i \|\boldsymbol{b}_i^*\|$ and $\min_i \|\boldsymbol{b}_i^*\|$ is $2^{O(d)}$ provided that the input is (at least) LLL-reduced and $\|\boldsymbol{b}_d^*\| \leq \|\boldsymbol{b}_1^*\|$. The LLL-reduction of the input basis can be done efficiently and we can remove the last vector of the basis until the second condition is fulfilled (it cannot be used in an integer linear combination that leads to a shortest non-zero lattice vector). If the input basis is scaled so that $1/2 \leq \max_i \|\boldsymbol{b}_i^*\| < 1$, then all variables can be represented in fixed-point arithmetic.

4.2   Numerical Accuracy

The numerical behaviour of a floating-point version KFP has been studied in [40]. The main result of this article is that a precision of roughly $0.8d$ bits suffices to ensure the correctness when the input is LLL-reduced with quasi-optimal factors. The proof consists in bounding the magnitudes of all x_i's, y_i's and c_i's and then analyzing the accuracy of all computations. It can readily be adapted to fixed-point arithmetic. However, for several reasons, this worst-case analysis is far from being tight for the considered lattices and bases.

A possible way to decrease the required precision, already mentioned in [40], consists in replacing the static error analysis by a dynamic algorithm which uses the exact $\|\boldsymbol{b}_i^*\|$'s of the input to compute an *a priori* error bound for this input. Also, as the $\mu_{i,j}$'s and $\|\boldsymbol{b}_i^*\|^2$'s are used many times but computed only once, we assume that they are computed exactly and then rounded. We call this the *a priori adaptive precision strategy*.

Over-estimating the $|x_i|$'s significantly contributes to the computed sufficient precision being large. The bound for the $|x_i|$'s derives from the triangular inequality $|\sum \mu_{i,j} x_j| \leq \sum |\mu_{i,j} x_j|$, which is very loose in practice. For instance, on BKZ-40-reduced random knapsack lattices of dimension 64, we typically obtain $|x_i| \leq 2^{26}$. However, the worst-case for 20 lattices of the same form is $|x_i| = 54 \leq 2^6$. We develop the following strategy to exploit the latter observation: Let X be fixed (*e.g.*, $X = 2^7$); We assume that $|x_i| \leq X$ and then bound the accuracy of ℓ_i; During the execution of KFP, we compare all $|x_i|$'s to X and check that it is valid. This strategy allows us to guarantee the validity of the computation *a posteriori*. In practice, this means that we have to detect overflows in the computation of $|x_i|$'s (provided that X is set to a power of 2).

It remains to explain how to estimate the error on the ℓ_i's. It can be done via a uniform estimate (a bound of $(d + 1 - i)(2YXd + Y^2 + Y + 1)2^{-p-1}$, where $Y := (\min_i \|\boldsymbol{b}_i^*\|)^{-1} + Xd \cdot 2^{-p-1}$, can be achieved), but this leads to a significant increase of A and/or the precision, hence of the computing time. Instead, we use the algorithm of Figure 2, which takes the above improvements into account. This gives what we call the *a posteriori adaptive precision strategy*.

Lemma 2. *The algorithm of Figure 2 (executed with rounding mode set to "towards $+\infty$") returns a valid bound for the error on all the ℓ_i's.*

Inputs: The Gram–Schmidt vectors b_i^*, an upper bound X on the $|x_i|$'s.
Output: An error bound on all ℓ_i.
1. $\delta_l \leftarrow 0, \varepsilon \leftarrow 2^{-p-1}$.
2. For $i = d$ downto 1
3. $Y \leftarrow \|b_i^*\|^{-1}$,
4. $\delta_y \leftarrow X(d-i)\varepsilon$,
5. $\delta_{ry} \leftarrow (Y + \delta_y + 1)\varepsilon + \|b_i^*\|^2 \delta_y$,
6. $\delta_{ryy} \leftarrow (Y + \delta_y)\delta_{ry} + \|b_i^*\|\delta_y + \varepsilon$,
7. $\delta_\ell \leftarrow \delta_\ell + \delta_{ryy}$.
8. Return δ_ℓ.

Fig. 2. Bounding the numerical error on the computed ℓ_i's

The proof is given in Appendix C. In the examples we studied, this gave an upper bound of the order of 10^{-2}. Once we have bounded the error on ℓ_i by $\Delta_{\max}$, we follow the same strategy as in [40] to compute a guaranteed solution: add $\Delta_{\max}$ to the chosen bound A, and round it to fixed-point with rounding towards $+\infty$. This should be done every time A is updated.

Under the above conditions, one can prove that the shortest vector will be considered by the algorithm. However, one more modification is required if one really wants a shortest non-zero vector as *an output* of the algorithm: because of the errors on the ℓ_i's, one might incorrectly believe that a vector b is shorter than the current optimum b'. Hence, when Step 7 of the algorithm is entered, the norm of b should be recomputed exactly and compared to A. Since our FPGA implementation is targeted at dealing with the intermediate levels of the enumeration tree, this computation will in practice be done in software. Note that in the context of KFP being used within BKZ, finding a vector whose norm deviates from the optimal value only because of numerical inaccuracies is deemed sufficient (see, *e.g.*, NTL's BKZ [47]).

In the table below, we compare the sufficient precisions we obtain with the three analyses, for several dimensions of interest. The first row gives a bound valid for any LLL-reduced basis (with the same parameters as in [40]). To compute the first two rows, the bound X in the algorithm is replaced by a bound which depends on i, and which is computed by using the triangular inequality and the upper bound Y. For the last row, we took $X = 2^7$, which was checked valid in dimensions 40 and 64, and conjectured to hold for dimension 80. Each given *a priori* and *a posteriori* bound is the maximum that we obtained for 10 independent samples.

Dimension	40	64	80
Sufficient precision in the worst case	36	52	63
A priori adaptive precision	27	36	42
A posteriori adaptive precision	21	23	24

5   An FPGA-Based Accelerator for KFP

From the intrinsic parallelism of KFP along with its fairly limited accuracy requirements, as per Sections 3 and 4, respectively, FPGAs look like a perfectly suitable target architecture for implementing fast and cost-efficient accelerators for short-vector enumeration in lattices. In the following, in order to assess the validity of this observation, we present the design of such an accelerator and provide the reader with performance estimations.

5.1   Choice of the Target FPGA

Since we are aiming at a high-performing implementation in order to demonstrate the relevance of FPGAs as enumeration accelerators, we choose to target our implementation at a particular FPGA family. Despite losing in portability and a slightly higher design effort, this enables us to fully exploit and benefit from all the available FPGA resources.

Considering the KFP algorithm given in Figure 1, two main bottlenecks can be identified:

- first, its relatively high memory requirements: the storage necessary for the Gram–Schmidt matrix and for the local variables quickly becomes critical when considering a circuit with several KFP instances running in parallel; and
- second, the fixed-point multiplications, which are the main source of computations in KFP: two products need be performed at Step 5, and $d - i$ are required to compute c_i in Step 9.

Furthermore, other criteria have to be taken into account when choosing the suitable FPGA, such as the overall logic density (*i.e.*, the number of available logic and routing elements), the achievable performance (*i.e.*, the maximum clock frequency), and, last but not least, the actual cost of the device. Indeed, if we are to draw a fair comparison between FPGAs and CPUs when it comes to running KFP, we have to benchmark equally priced systems.

For all of the aforementioned reasons, we opted for the Xilinx Virtex-5 SXT family of FPGAs [52], and more specifically for the smallest one of the range, namely the XC5VSX35T, at the slowest speed grade (-1). For a unit price of US\$460,[2] this FPGA combines 168 18-kbit RAM blocks, 192 DSP blocks (each comprising a 25-by-18-bit signed multiplier and a 48-bit adder/accumulator) and 5 440 logic slices (each comprising four 6-to-1-bit look-up tables, or LUTs, and four 1-bit flip-flops), which suits reasonably well our requirements.

5.2   Main Architecture of the Accelerator

As the KFP enumeration algorithm lends itself quite well to parallelization, as discussed in Section 3, a natural idea to implement it in hardware is to have

---

[2] As per http://www.nuhorizons.com/

several small "cores" running in parallel, each one traversing a distinct subtree of the whole enumeration tree. Those subtrees are dispatched to the cores through a shared bus, and the found short vectors are collected and sent back to the host by a dedicated I/O controller.

By enumerating vectors in the corresponding subtree, each KFP core handles subproblems of fixed dimension d. We set the bound $d \leq 64$, as this seems sufficient to accelerate the fat section of the enumeration tree in dimensions up to 100–120 (which is achievable with [13]). This means that the bottom layer considered in the KFP core is higher than the bottom layer of the overall tree: the subtrees possibly found below the subtree handled by the KFP core are sent back to the host and processed in software. Due to the extreme unbalanced-ness of the KFP tree, if the interval of dimensions handled by the KFP core is chosen carefully, then very few such subtrees will be found.

In the context of BKZ-type algorithms, the accelerator can be used to handle many different blocks in parallel. The BKZ blocks need not be of dimension 64: smaller dimensions can be handled on 64-dimensional KFP cores by simply setting the superfluous Gram–Schmidt coefficients to 0.

Finally, in order to maximize to computational power of the accelerator (which is directly proportional to the number of KFP cores that can fit on the FPGA), the resource usage of the bus and of the I/O controller should be kept as low as possible. However, since this part of the circuit is also highly dependent on the type of connectivity between the FPGA and the host, we have not implemented it yet, focusing primarily our efforts on designing efficient KFP cores.

5.3   Storing the Gram–Schmidt Matrix

As previously mentioned, a critical issue of KFP lies in its memory require-ments, and more especially in the quadratic storage space required for the Gram–Schmidt matrix. Indeed, when enumerating vectors in dimension d, one needs to store all the $\mu_{j,i}$ coefficients for $1 \leq i < j \leq d$, as all of them will take part in the computation of the c_i's at Step 9 of the algorithm in Figure 1. This represents $d(d-1)/2$ coefficients that have to be stored on the circuit and can be accessed independently by each KFP core.

The adopted solution is also the simplest one, and is perfectly suited to low-dimensional lattices ($d \leq 64$) and to memory-rich FPGAs. The idea here is to make use of the available dual-port RAM blocks on the FPGA to build a ROM for the Gram–Schmidt matrix coefficients. On the Virtex-5 FPGA we considered, those RAM blocks are 18 kbits large and can be configured as 16k × 1-, 8k × 2-, 4k × 4-, 2k × 9- or 1k × 18-bit true dual-port memories. Additionally, two adjacent 18-kbit blocks can be combined to form a 36-kbit RAM block, supporting from 32k × 1- to 1k × 36-bit dual-port memories. The coefficients of the Gram–Schmidt matrix can then be stored on several of such RAM blocks, their actual number depending on the required dimension d and precision p. In some case, a small amount of extra logic might also be necessary to multiplex several memories. Moreover, since the RAM blocks are dual-ported, they allow such a Gram–Schmidt matrix ROM to be shared between two KFP cores.

For instance, for a lattice of dimension $d = 64$ and taking $p = 24$ bits of precision for the $\mu_{i,j}$'s, the ROM would require a storage capacity of $d(d-1)/2 = 2\,016$ words of 24 bits each. This can be achieved by means of one 36-kbit RAM block (*i.e.*, two 18-kbit blocks) configured as a 2k × 18-bit memory and one 18-kbit RAM block configured as a 2k × 9-bit memory.

5.4   Architecture of a KFP Core

The basic processing unit of our accelerator is the KFP core, which runs the enumeration algorithm depicted in Figure 1 on a subtree of the whole enumeration tree. Each such core is based on a fixed-point multiplier–accumulator, which is in charge of computing the ℓ_i's (Step 5) and the c_i's (Step 9). This multiplier is coupled with a register-file responsible for storing all the local variables. Finally, a small control automaton ensures the correct execution of the algorithm, keeping track of the current level i and coordinates x_i, δx_i, and $\delta^2 x_i$, computing the corresponding addresses for accessing the registered data, and multiplexing the inputs to be fed to the multiplier.

Since the overall performance of the accelerator is directly proportional to the number of KFP cores that can fit on the FPGA, it is crucial to streamline their architecture as much as possible without impacting too much on their standalone performance. To that intent, we make extensive use of the available FPGA-specific embedded features, such as DSP blocks for the fixed-point multiplier–accumulator and RAM blocks for the register file. Not only does this allow us to fully exploit most of the available resources on the FPGA, but, since these embedded blocks can usually be clocked at much higher frequencies than the logic cells, keeping the logic usage to its bare minimum is also key to designing a high-performing accelerator.

Following this rationale, the fixed-point multiplier is implemented by means of two adjacent DSP48E blocks. Thanks to their versatility, these blocks support the two modes of operation required by the KFP algorithm:

– Cascading the two DSP blocks yields a 34×24-bit unsigned multiplier, which can be used to compute successively the two products $y_i \times \|\mathbf{b}_i^*\|^2$ and $y_i \times \|\mathbf{b}_i^*\|^2 y_i$, for precisions p up to 24 bits. Indeed, since the $\mathbf{b}_i$'s are scaled (as per Section 4.1), the squared norm $\|\mathbf{b}_i^*\|^2$ is lower than 1 and therefore fits in p bits. Furthermore, concerning y_i, 34 bits are more than enough since its integer part, bounded by $|\delta x_i|/2$, will never exceed a few bits in practice.

   Finally, one can see that if $\|\mathbf{b}_i^*\|^2 y_i \geq 1$ then $\|\mathbf{b}_i^*\|^2 y_i^2 \geq 1 > A$. Thus, if the first product is greater than 1, we need not compute the second one, as ℓ_i will exceed the bound A and the enumeration will go up one level in the tree. Conversely, if this product is lower than 1, then it fits on p bits and can be fed back to the multiplier in order to compute the second product.

   Additionally, rounding the two products to p fractional bits, along with adding ℓ_{i+1}, is achieved using the cascaded 48-bit adders available in the DSP blocks. The comparison against the bound A is also carried out by these adders.

So as to ensure a high operating frequency, the two DSP blocks are pipelined with a latency of 3 clock cycles. Taking the cascading latency of 1 extra cycle into account, each 34×24-bit product is performed in 4 cycles. The squared norm ℓ_i is then computed in 9 clock cycles, plus 1 additional cycle for obtaining the difference $\ell_i - A$.

— The computation of c_i at Step 9 only requires one DSP block, configured as a 25×18-bit signed multiplier–accumulator. For each product of the sum, the first operand is the p-bit Gram–Schmidt coefficient $\mu_{j,i}$, sign-extended to 25 bits, and the second operand is the corresponding x_j, which fits in the available 18 bits, as discussed in Section 4.2. The 48-bit accumulator embedded in the DSP block is wide enough to accommodate c_i and can also be initialized to a particular value $c_i^{(0)}$ in order to avoid having to explicitly compute the last terms of the sum, when dealing with subtrees for which the last coordinates are fixed.

A 3-cycle-deep pipelining is also used in this mode of operation. Furthermore, the products being all independent, it is possible to schedule one such product per clock cycle. The computation of c_i (i.e., accumulating $d-i$ products) thus requires $2 + d - i$ clock cycles.

As far as the KFP core register file is concerned, the most suitable solution is to use an embedded 18-kbit RAM block configured as a 512×36-bit simple dual-port memory with independent read and write ports. The widest data to be stored in these registers are the c_i's, which have a p-bit fractional part and an integer part the size of the x_i's. The precision $p = 24$ bits therefore leaves up to 12 bits for the x_i's, which is enough in practice, as per Section 4.2.

The variables to be stored in this register file are the ℓ_i's, the c_i's, the $c_i^{(0)}$'s, the triples $(x_i, \delta x_i, \delta^2 x_i)$, the bound A, along with the constants $\|\mathbf{b}_i^*\|^2$. Each cluster of d variables is aligned on 64-word boundaries, for simpler register address computation.

Finally, as most computations and storage tasks are handled by the DSP and RAM blocks, respectively, the purpose of the control unit is mostly to feed the proper control signals to those embedded blocks. However, some computations are still directly carried out by the control unit:

— The computation of $y_i = |x_i - c_i|$ at Step 5 is performed by a carry-propagate subtracter. Indeed, noticing that the sign of $x_i - c_i$ is given by $\delta^2 x_i$, it is possible to control the subtracter to compute either $x_i - c_i$ or $c_i - x_i$ according to the sign of $\delta^2 x_i$ at no additional cost.

— Updating the coordinates at Step 14 is also very efficient, provided that we use a slightly different update algorithm. Defining the variables $\tilde{\delta} x_i$ and $\tilde{\delta}^2 x_i$ such that $\tilde{\delta} x_i = |\delta x_i|$ and $\tilde{\delta}^2 x_i = (-1)^{\tilde{\delta}^2 x_i}$, we have the following equivalent coordinate update method:

$$x_i \leftarrow x_i + (-1)^{\tilde{\delta}^2 x_i} \tilde{\delta} x_i \ ; \ \ \tilde{\delta} x_i \leftarrow \tilde{\delta} x_i + 1 \ ; \ \ \tilde{\delta}^2 x_i \leftarrow \text{NOT } \tilde{\delta}^2 x_i.$$

This solution is much better suited to hardware implementation, as computing $x_i \pm \tilde{\delta} x_i$ only requires a single adder/subtracter controlled by $\tilde{\delta}^2 x_i$, whereas computing $-\delta x_i + \delta^2 x_i$ as in the original KFP algorithm involvesan extra carry propagation. Additionally, the proposed method lends itself more naturally to a parallel implementation of the three affectations.

5.5   Performance Estimations

As mentioned previously, we implemented a VHDL description of our KFP accelerator on a Xilinx Virtex-5 SXT 35 FPGA with a speed grade of -1. We present here results from the post-place-and-route area and timing estimations given by the Xilinx ISE 10.1 toolchain.

On the considered FPGA, a single KFP core designed for dimension $d = 64$ and precision $p = 24$ bits then requires 1 18-kbit RAM block, 2 DSP blocks, 274 LUTs, and 101 flip-flops (not counting the extra memory and logic used to store the Gram–Schmidt coefficients). Such a core can be clocked at an operating frequency of 250 MHz and processes a valid level-i node of the enumeration tree in $34 + d - i$ cycles: $20 + d - i$ cycles when going down to its first child and 14 cycles when coming back up from its last child. For a 64-dimensional lattice and assuming that the average node depth is 32, this yields a processing time of 264 ns per node or, equivalently, a traversal rate of 3.79 million visited nodes per second per KFP core.

It turns out that exactly 66 such cores can fit on the XC5VSX35T FPGA without lowering the clock frequency. The total resource usage is then 165 out of the 168 available 18-kbit RAM blocks (98%), 132 out of 192 DSP blocks (68%), 19 217 out of 21 760 LUTs (88%), and 6 733 out of 21 760 flip-flops (30%).[3] These figures are satisfactory, as we observe a well-balanced usage of the FPGA resources: our careful design strategy, matching closely the architecture of the FPGA, really pays off at this point.

Finally, those 66 KFP cores deliver a total traversal rate of $2.50 \cdot 10^8$ nodes per second. This result has however to be taken with some caution, as our implementation does not take the I/O controller overhead into account. Nevertheless, we are quite confident that a carefully designed and lightweight I/O controller would not have too adverse an impact on the accelerator performance.

Of course, this rate of $2.50 \cdot 10^8$ traversed nodes per second is only achieved when all of the 66 KFP cores are busy. If the main KFP problem is not properly splitted into large enough sub-instances, the cores would spend too much time performing I/Os and would therefore be completely underexploited, rendering the whole approach pointless. However, since typical dimension-64 KFP trees have several billion nodes, this should ensure keeping the communication costs negligible, even when restricted to using high-latency I/Os such as USB.

6   Conclusion

We have presented a first attempt at speeding up vector enumeration in Euclidean lattices by means of a dedicated FPGA accelerator. Even though the KFP algorithm lends itself particularly well to parallelization, adapting it to fully take

---

[3] Actually, the FPGA is even more congested, as 5 303 out of the 5 440 available logic slices (97%) are occupied, due to some LUT/flip-flop packing issues.

advantage of the FPGA's specificities requires particular care in ensuring the validity of the drastic arithmetic choices (limited precision and fixed-point instead of floating-point) and in designing the actual circuit with efficiency in mind.

The proposed accelerator achieves a cost-normalized traversal rate of $5.43 \cdot 10^5$ visited nodes per second per dollar in dimension 64, against a rate of $2.55 \cdot 10^5$ for a multi-core software implementation on an Intel Core 2 Quad Q9550 processor, thus yielding a speed-up of 2.12. The performance of our FPGA accelerator is even better compared to that of the GPU implementation proposed in [20] which delivers a total traversal rate of $1.36 \cdot 10^5$ nodes per second per dollar.

All in all, it appears that, thanks to our implementation, FPGAs qualify as a perfectly relevant architecture for accelerating lattice reduction, thus calling for further investigations in that direction.

Acknowledgments. The authors would like to thank Jens Hermans and Michael Schneider for helpful discussions, the anonymous reviewers for their valuable comments, and Florent de Dinechin for fruitful discussions when this work was initiated. The last author was partly supported by the ARC Discovery Grant DP0880724 "Integral lattices and their theta series".

References

1. Agrawal, S., Boneh, D., Boyen, X.: Efficient lattice (H)IBE in the standard model. In: Gilbert, H. (ed.) EUROCRYPT 2010. LNCS, vol. 6110, pp. 553–572. Springer, Heidelberg (2010)
2. Ajtai, M.: The shortest vector problem in L_2 is NP-hard for randomized reductions (extended abstract). In: Proc. of STOC, pp. 284–293. ACM, New York (1998)
3. Ajtai, M., Dwork, C.: A public-key cryptosystem with worst-case/average-case equivalence. In: Proc. of STOC, pp. 284–293. ACM, New York (1997)
4. Ajtai, M., Kumar, R., Sivakumar, D.: A sieve algorithm for the shortest lattice vector problem. In: Proc. of STOC, pp. 601–610. ACM, New York (2001)
5. Arbitman, Y., Dogon, G., Lyubashevsky, V., Micciancio, D., Peikert, C., Rosen, A.: SWIFFTX: a proposal for the SHA-3 standard. Submission to NIST (2008), http://www.eecs.harvard.edu/~alon/PAPERS/lattices/swifftx.pdf
6. Cadé, D., Pujol, X., Stehlé, D.: fplll - a floating-point LLL implementation, http://perso.ens-lyon.fr/damien.stehle
7. Cash, D., Hofheinz, D., Kiltz, E., Peikert, C.: Bonsai trees, or how to delegate a lattice basis. In: Gilbert, H. (ed.) EUROCRYPT 2010. LNCS, vol. 6110, pp. 523–552. Springer, Heidelberg (2010)
8. Conway, J.H., Sloane, N.J.A.: Sphere Packings, Lattices and Groups. Springer, Heidelberg (1988)
9. Coppersmith, D.: Small solutions to polynomial equations, and low exponent RSA vulnerabilities. J. Cryptology 10(4), 233–260 (1997)
10. van Dijk, Gentry, C., Halevi, S., Vaikuntanathan, V.: Fully homomorphic encryption over the integers. In: Gilbert, H. (ed.) Advances in Cryptology – EUROCRYPT 2010. LNCS, vol. 6110, pp. 24–43. Springer, Heidelberg (2010)
11. Fincke, U., Pohst, M.: A procedure for determining algebraic integers of given norm. In: van Hulzen, J.A. (ed.) ISSAC 1983 and EUROCAL 1983. LNCS, vol. 162, pp. 194–202. Springer, Heidelberg (1983)
12. Gama, N., Nguyen, P.Q.: Finding short lattice vectors within Mordell's inequality. In: Proc. of STOC, pp. 207–216. ACM, New York (2008)

13. Gama, N., Nguyen, P.Q., Regev, O.: Lattice enumeration using extreme pruning. In: Gilbert, H. (ed.) EUROCRYPT 2010. LNCS, vol. 6110, pp. 257–278. Springer, Heidelberg (2010)
14. Gentry, C.: Fully homomorphic encryption using ideal lattices. In: Proc. of STOC, pp. 169–178. ACM, New York (2009)
15. Gentry, C., Peikert, C., Vaikuntanathan, V.: Trapdoors for hard lattices and new cryptographic constructions. In: Proc. of STOC, pp. 197–206. ACM, New York (2008)
16. Goldreich, O., Goldwasser, S., Halevi, S.: Public-key cryptosystems from lattice reduction problems. In: Kaliski Jr., B.S. (ed.) CRYPTO 1997. LNCS, vol. 1294, pp. 112–131. Springer, Heidelberg (1997)
17. Goldstein, D., Mayer, A.: On the equidistribution of Hecke points. Forum Mathematicum 15, 165–189 (2003)
18. Guo, Z., Nilsson, P.: VLSI architecture of the soft-output sphere decoder for MIMO systems. In: Proc. of MWSCAS, vol. 2, pp. 1195–1198. IEEE, Los Alamitos (2005)
19. Hanrot, G., Stehlé, D.: Improved analysis of Kannan's shortest lattice vector algorithm. In: Menezes, A. (ed.) CRYPTO 2007. LNCS, vol. 4622, pp. 170–186. Springer, Heidelberg (2007)
20. Hermans, J., Schneider, M., Buchmann, J., Vercauteren, F., Preneel, B.: Parallel shortest lattice vector enumeration on graphics cards. In: Bernstein, D.J., Lange, T. (eds.) AFRICACRYPT 2010. LNCS, vol. 6055, pp. 52–68. Springer, Heidelberg (2010)
21. Hoffstein, J., Pipher, J., Silverman, J.H.: NTRU: A ring-based public key cryptosystem. In: Buhler, J.P. (ed.) ANTS 1998. LNCS, vol. 1423, pp. 267–288. Springer, Heidelberg (1998)
22. Howgrave-Graham, N.: A hybrid lattice-reduction and meet-in-the-middle attack against NTRU. In: Menezes, A. (ed.) CRYPTO 2007. LNCS, vol. 4622, pp. 150–169. Springer, Heidelberg (2007)
23. Kannan, R.: Improved algorithms for integer programming and related lattice problems. In: Proc. of STOC, pp. 99–108. ACM, New York (1983)
24. Lenstra, A.K., Lenstra Jr., H.W., Lovász, L.: Factoring polynomials with rational coefficients. Math. Ann. 261, 515–534 (1982)
25. Lovász, L.: An Algorithmic Theory of Numbers, Graphs and Convexity. SIAM, cBMS-NSF Regional Conference Series in Applied Mathematics (1986)
26. Magma: The Magma computational algebra system, http://magma.maths.usyd.edu.au/magma/
27. May, A.: Using LLL-reduction for solving RSA and factorization problems: A survey. In: [32] (2009)
28. Micciancio, D., Regev, O.: Lattice-based cryptography. In: Bernstein, D.J., Buchmann, J., Dahmen, E. (eds.) Post-Quantum Cryptography, pp. 147–191. Springer, Heidelberg (2009)
29. Micciancio, D., Voulgaris, P.: A deterministic single exponential time algorithm for most lattice problems based on Voronoi cell computations. To appear in the proceedings of STOC 2010 (2010)
30. Micciancio, D., Voulgaris, P.: Faster exponential time algorithms for the shortest vector problem. In: Proc. of SODA, pp. 1468–1480. SIAM, Philadelphia (2010)
31. Mow, W.H.: Maximum likelihood sequence estimation from the lattice viewpoint. IEEE TIT 40, 1591–1600 (1994)
32. Nguyen, P.Q., Vallée, B.: The LLL algorithm, survey and applications. Information Security and Cryptography. Springer, Heidelberg (2010)

33. Nguyen, P.Q., Stehlé, D.: Floating-point LLL revisited. In: Cramer, R. (ed.) EUROCRYPT 2005. LNCS, vol. 3494, pp. 215–233. Springer, Heidelberg (2005)

34. Nguyen, P.Q., Stehlé, D.: LLL on the average. In: Hess, F., Pauli, S., Pohst, M. (eds.) ANTS 2006. LNCS, vol. 4076, pp. 238–256. Springer, Heidelberg (2006)

35. Nguyen, P.Q., Stern, J.: Cryptanalysis of the Ajtai-Dwork cryptosystem. In: Krawczyk, H. (ed.) CRYPTO 1998. LNCS, vol. 1462, pp. 223–242. Springer, Heidelberg (1998)

36. Nguyen, P.Q., Stern, J.: The two faces of lattices in cryptology. In: Silverman, J.H. (ed.) CaLC 2001. LNCS, vol. 2146, pp. 146–180. Springer, Heidelberg (2001)

37. Nguyen, P.Q., Vidick, T.: Sieve algorithms for the shortest vector problem are practical. J. Mathematical Cryptology 2(2) (2008)

38. Odlyzko, A.M.: The rise and fall of knapsack cryptosystems. In: Proceedings of Cryptology and Computational Number Theory. Proceedings of Symposia in Applied Mathematics, vol. 42, pp. 75–88. AMS (1989)

39. Peikert, C.: Public-key cryptosystems from the worst-case shortest vector problem. In: Proc. of STOC, pp. 333–342. ACM, New York (2009)

40. Pujol, X., Stehlé, D.: Rigorous and efficient short lattice vectors enumeration. In: Pieprzyk, J. (ed.) ASIACRYPT 2008. LNCS, vol. 5350, pp. 390–405. Springer, Heidelberg (2008)

41. Pujol, X., Stehlé, D.: Solving the shortest lattice vector problem in time $2^{2.465n}$. Cryptology ePrint Archive, Report 2009/605 (2009), http://eprint.iacr.org/2009/605

42. Regev, O.: Lattices in computer science (2004). lecture notes of a course given at the Tel. Aviv. University, http://www.cs.tau.ac.il/~odedr/teaching/lattices_fall_2004/

43. Regev, O.: On lattices, learning with errors, random linear codes, and cryptography. In: Proc. of STOC, pp. 84–93. ACM, New York (2005)

44. Schnorr, C.P.: A hierarchy of polynomial lattice basis reduction algorithms. Theor. Comput. Sci. 53, 201–224 (1987)

45. Schnorr, C.P., Euchner, M.: Lattice basis reduction: improved practical algorithms and solving subset sum problems. Math. Programming 66, 181–199 (1994)

46. Schnorr, C.P., Hörner, H.H.: Attacking the Chor-Rivest cryptosystem by improved lattice reduction. In: Guillou, L.C., Quisquater, J.-J. (eds.) EUROCRYPT 1995. LNCS, vol. 921, pp. 1–12. Springer, Heidelberg (1995)

47. Shoup, V.: NTL, Number Theory C++ Library, http://www.shoup.net/ntl/

48. Smart, N.P., Vercauteren, F.: Fully homomorphic encryption with relatively small key and ciphertext sizes. In: Nguyen, P.Q., Pointcheval, D. (eds.) PKC 2010. LNCS, vol. 6056, pp. 420–443. Springer, Heidelberg (2010)

49. Stehlé, D., Steinfeld, R., Tanaka, K., Xagawa, K.: Efficient public key encryption based on ideal lattices. In: Matsui, M. (ed.) ASIACRYPT 2009. LNCS, vol. 5912, pp. 617–635. Springer, Heidelberg (2009)

50. Studer, C., Burg, A., Bölcskei, H.: Soft-output sphere decoding: Algorithms and VLSI implementation. IEEE Journal on Selected Areas in Communications 26(2), 290–300 (2008)

51. Viterbo, E., Boutros, J.: A universal lattice code decoder for fading channels. IEEE TIT 45, 1639–1642 (1999)

52. Xilinx: Virtex-5 family overview, http://www.xilinx.com/support/documentation/virtex-5.htm

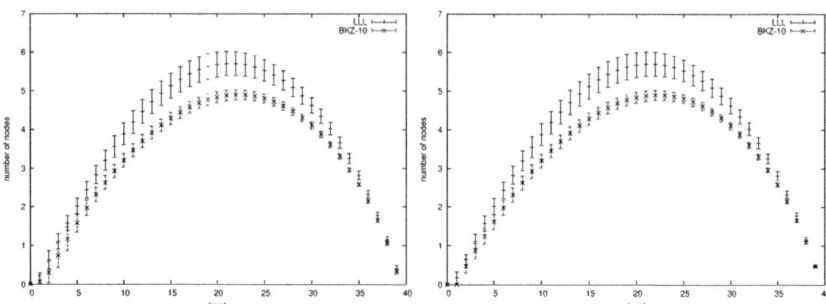

Fig. 3. Number of nodes per level in KFP, dimension 40: experimental (left), Gaussian estimate (right)

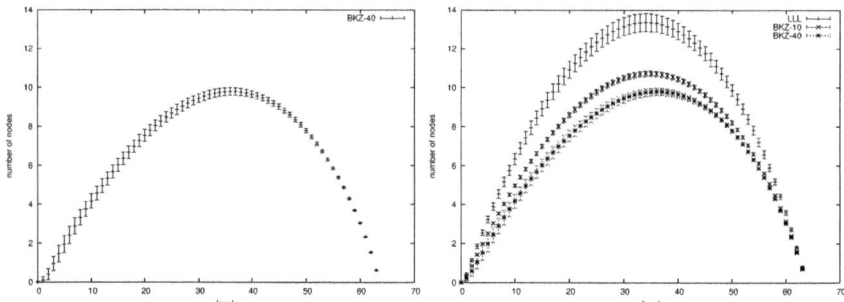

Fig. 4. Number of nodes per level in KFP, dimension 64: experimental (left), Gaussian estimate (right)

A   Shape of the KFP Tree

In Figures 3, 4, we compare the Gaussian approximation and the actual number of KFP-nodes per level on the same type of bases, using similar reductions. Note that for dimension 64, only the BKZ-40 preprocessing allows for enumeration in a reasonable amount of time, explaining the fact that the left graphics only has one curve.

B   Performance of the Software Implementation of KFP

The tables below give the number of nodes treated per second of our software implementations of the KFP algorithm on an Intel Core 2 Quad Q9550 at 2.83 GHz, with or without the optimization described in [13, App. D]. These data have been obtained via the enumeration of 32 different lattices; we provide the average number of nodes per second and the standard deviation.

We also provide data regarding parallelization. The granularity level has been set to $2 \cdot 10^7$ nodes. The left diagram shows the number of subtrees of the enumeration that have (estimated via the Gaussian heuristic) size $\leq 2 \cdot 10^7$ and whose father has (estimated) size $> 2 \cdot 10^7$; we call these subtrees *slave subtrees*.

dim.	avg. # nodes	std. dev.
40	1.48238e+07	273330
48	1.40783e+07	176269
56	1.3272e+07	134886
64	1.26201e+07	128941

dim.	avg. # nodes	std. dev.
40	1.72778e+07	281925
48	1.73586e+07	96808.5
56	1.74355e+07	127681
64	1.75637e+07	179223

Fig. 5. Number of nodes per second in software, unoptimized version (left) versus optimized (right)

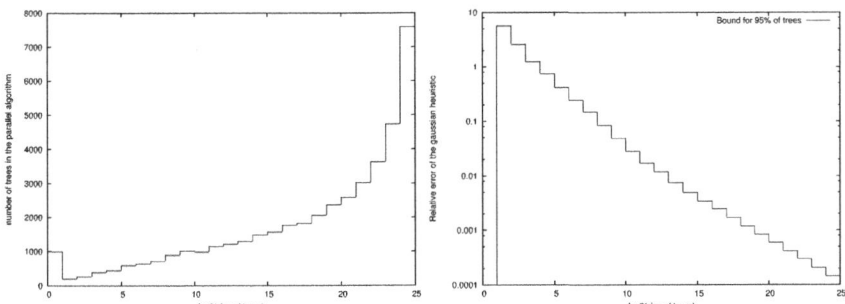

Fig. 6. Left: number of unique subtrees of a given size; right: validity of the Gaussian approximation as a function of tree size

The right diagram shows that the Gaussian heuristic remains extremely reliable in this context: for 95% of trees of size 2^{15}, it estimates the correct size within a factor < 1.01.

The latter shows that the size of tasks is rather well estimated (mainly, no "large" subtree is mistakenly handled as a small one), whereas the former shows that most of the tasks below a given granularity level are in fact of size close to that granularity level: the parallelization proposed is extremely close to splitting the tree into pieces of equal sizes.

C   Proof of Lemma 2

For any quantity α, we denote its fixed-point evaluation by $\bar{\alpha}$. We also define $\Delta\alpha = |\alpha - \bar{\alpha}|$. Let $\varepsilon = 2^{-p-1}$, where p is the precision of the fixed-point arithmetic. The Gram–Schmidt coefficients can be computed exactly in software and then rounded, which ensures that $\Delta\mu_{i,j} \leq \varepsilon$ and $\Delta(\|b_i^*\|^2) \leq \varepsilon$.

This implies that $\Delta y_i \leq (d - i - 1)X\varepsilon$. We now consider an iteration of KFP where $\ell_i \leq A$ (≤ 1). This implies that $y_i \leq \|b_i^*\|^{-1}$, which gives $\|b_i^*\|^2 y_i \leq \|b_i^*\|$ and $\bar{y}_i \leq \|b_i^*\|^{-1} + \Delta y_i$. The product $\|b_i^*\|^2 y_i^2$ is computed as $(\|b_i^*\|^2 \times y_i) \times y_i$, and we thus bound the error on this product in two steps:

$$\Delta(r_i y_i) \leq \varepsilon + \bar{y}_i \varepsilon + r_i \Delta y_i,$$
$$\Delta(r_i y_i^2) \leq \varepsilon + \bar{y}_i \Delta(y_i r_i) + r_i y_i \Delta y_i.$$

Finally, for all i we have $\Delta\ell_i \leq \sum_{j=i}^{d} \Delta(r_j y_j^2)$. The correctness of the algorithm of Figure 2 derives from those inequalities.

Efficient Software Implementation of Binary Field Arithmetic Using Vector Instruction Sets

Diego F. Aranha[1], Julio López[1], and Darrel Hankerson[2]

[1] University of Campinas
{dfaranha,jlopez}@ic.unicamp.br
[2] Auburn University
hankedr@auburn.edu

Abstract. In this paper we describe an efficient software implementation of characteristic 2 fields making extensive use of vector instruction sets commonly found in desktop processors. Field elements are represented in a split form so performance-critical field operations can be formulated in terms of simple operations over 4-bit sets. In particular, we detail techniques for implementing field multiplication, squaring, square root extraction and present a constant-memory lookup-based multiplication strategy. Our representation makes extensive use of the *parallel table lookup* (PTLU) instruction recently introduced in popular desktop platforms and follows the trend of accelerating implementations of cryptography through PTLU-style instructions. We present timings for several binary fields commonly employed for curve-based cryptography and illustrate the presented techniques with executions of the ECDH and ECDSA protocols over binary curves at the 128-bit and 256-bit security levels standardized by NIST. Our implementation results are compared with publicly available benchmarking data.

1 Introduction

Arithmetic in binary fields has significant cryptographic interest and finds several applications such as providing the underlying layer for arithmetic in elliptic curves – among them the highly efficient Koblitz family of anomalous binary curves [1] – and building blocks for the construction of symmetric ciphers [2], bilinear maps [3] and post-quantum cryptographic schemes [4,5]. At the same time, modern processors are increasingly receiving new parallelism resources in the form of advanced vector processing units. Employing these resources in an efficient way is crucial to improve the performance of binary field arithmetic and consequently the performance of several cryptographic primitives.

As the main contribution, this work presents a high-speed software implementation of binary field arithmetic particularly appropriate for vector processors. Field arithmetic is expressed in terms of operations easily translated to contemporary vector instruction sets with a clear emphasis in arithmetic of 4-bit granularity to make proper use of the recently introduced powerful *parallel table lookup* (PTLU) instructions [6]. The presented techniques are compatible with

M. Abdalla and P.S.L.M. Barreto (Eds.): LATINCRYPT 2010, LNCS 6212, pp. 144–161, 2010.

the most efficient algorithms known for binary field arithmetic using a polynomial basis [7,8] and with several of the implementation optimizations proposed in the literature [9]. These algorithms and optimizations can thus be seen in a new light under the framework we develop. Using the new PTLU instructions, we derive a new implementation strategy for binary field multiplication entirely based on table lookups. This strategy does not precompute tables and consequently consumes less memory than standard approaches: a single table of constants must be kept so memory consumption apart from space for temporary results is constant. The efficiency of our techniques and corresponding implementations is illustrated with performance figures for arithmetic in fields ranging from $\mathbb{F}_{2^{113}}$ to $\mathbb{F}_{2^{1223}}$ defined with square root friendly polynomials or NIST standard polynomials. Timings are also provided for key agreement and signature protocols at the two security levels adopted as standard for secure elliptic curve cryptography by the Brazilian National Public Key Infrastructure. We also present timings for curves supported by the eBACS [10] benchmarking project. The target platforms are several versions of the Intel Core microarchitecture.

The results of this work can improve the performance of cryptographic primitives employing binary field arithmetic in vector processors. The introduced techniques may also be important for exploring trade-offs occurring in the design of hardware arithmetic units or to optimize software implementations of other small-characteristic fields such as the ternary fields used in pairing-based cryptography [3]. Furthermore, our results follow the recent trend of optimizing implementations of cryptography through PTLU instructions [6,11] and pose an interesting question about which operations should be supported by vector arithmetic units from a cost-benefit point of view.

This paper is organized as follows. Section 2 presents target platform characteristics. Section 3 presents our formulation and the techniques employed for efficient binary field arithmetic. Section 4 discusses experimental results for field and elliptic curve arithmetic and comparison with related work. The final section concludes the paper.

2   Platform Model

We assume that the target platform is equipped with a set of vector instructions, also called SIMD (Single Instruction, Multiple Data) because they operate in several data objects simultaneously. Currently, the most popular SIMD instruction sets are the Intel Streaming SIMD Extensions [12] and the AltiVec extensions introduced by Apple and IBM in the Power architecture specification [13]. Present technology provides instructions for orthogonal manipulation of 8, 16, 32 or 64-bit objects stored inside 128-bit architectural registers, but recently announced improvements in the form of Intel AVX and AMD SSE5 [14] extensions will support 256-bit registers in the future along with new operations like a native binary field multiplier [15].

To abstract the specific details of the underlying platform, vector instructions will be represented as mnemonics denoting a subset of operations supported in most instruction sets. Table 1 presents the mnemonics and the corresponding instructions in the SSE and AltiVec families, and thus shows the generality of our platform model. Experimental results will be provided only for SSSE3-capable Core 2/i7 platforms, however. In Table 1, memory access operations assume that memory addresses are always aligned in 16-byte boundaries so the faster load/store instructions can be used. Mnemonics for memory operations are reserved for loading/storing vector registers from/to word arrays. Bitwise shift instructions do not propagate bits between contiguous 32/64-bit data objects, requiring additional shifts and additions to be used as 128-bit bitwise shifts. Bytewise shift instructions (i.e. the shift amount is a multiple of 8) work across an entire vector register. We explicitly differentiate between bitwise and bytewise shifts because bytewise shifts may have smaller latencies in some vector instruction sets. Note that conventional shift mnemonics ($\ll, \gg$) are reserved for bitwise shifts of 64-bit words. Interleaving instructions alternately take bytes from the lower or higher parts of two registers to produce the output register. Two powerful instructions are discussed in more detail:

Memory alignment instructions extract a 128-bit section from the concatenation of two 128-bit registers, working as a fast shift with propagation of shifted out bytes between two vector registers.

Byte shuffling instructions take as inputs registers of bytes $r_a = (a_0, a_1, \ldots, a_{15})$ and $r_b = (b_0, b_1, \ldots, b_{15})$ and produce as result a permuted vector represented by the 16-byte register $r_c = (a_{b_0 \bmod 16}, a_{b_1 \bmod 16}, \ldots, a_{b_{15} \bmod 16})$. An often-missed use of these instructions is to perform 16 simultaneous lookups in a 16-byte lookup table, working as a legitimate PTLU instruction. This can be easily done by storing the lookup table in r_a and the lookup indexes in r_b and allows one to efficiently evaluate any function with 4-bit input and 8-bit output in parallel.

Table 1. Relevant vector instructions for the implementation of binary field arithmetic

Mnemonic	Description	SSE	AltiVec
load,store	Memory load/store	MOVDQA	LVX
$\ll_{\uparrow 8}, \gg_{\uparrow 8}$	32/64-bit bitwise shifts	PSLLQ,PSRLQ	VSLW,VSRW
$\ll_8, \gg_8$	128-bit bytewise shift	PSLLDQ,PSRLDQ	VPERM
$\oplus, \wedge, \vee$	Bitwise XOR,AND,OR	PXOR,PAND,POR	VAND,VOR,VXOR
interlo,interhi	Byte interleaving	PUNPCKLBW,PUNPCKHBW	VMRGLB,VMRGHB
$\triangleleft$	Memory alignment	PALIGNR	LVSL+VPERM,LVSR+VPERM
shuffle,lookup	Byte shuffling	PSHUFB	VPERM

There is a visible recent effort from processor manufacturers to increase the performance and flexibility of shuffle instructions. Intel introduced a *Super Shuffle Engine* in the Core 2 45nm microarchitecture to reduce the latency of the PSHUFB instruction from 3 cycles to 1 cycle and doubled the throughput of this instruction in the Core i7 microarchitecture. AMD plans to introduce a new permutation instruction capable of operating at bit level with opcode PPERM in the upcoming SSE5 instruction set.

3   Binary Field Representation and Arithmetic

In this section we will represent the elements of the binary field $\mathbb{F}_{2^m}$ using a polynomial basis. Let $f(z)$ be an irreducible binary polynomial of degree m. The elements of $\mathbb{F}_{2^m}$ are the binary polynomials of degree at most $m-1$. A field element $a(z) = \sum_{i=0}^{m-1} a_i z^i$ is associated with the binary vector $a = (a_{m-1}, \ldots, a_1, a_0)$ of length m. In a software implementation, these bit coefficients are typically packed and stored in a compact array $(a[0], \ldots, a[n-1])$ of n W-bit words, where W is the word size of the processor. For simplicity, it is assumed that n is even. We will instead use a split representation where a polynomial $a \in \mathbb{F}_{2^m}$ is divided into two polynomials:

$$a_L = \sum_{\substack{0 \leq i < m, \\ 0 \leq i \bmod 8 \leq 3}} a_i z^i, \quad a_H = \sum_{\substack{0 \leq i < m, \\ 4 \leq i \bmod 8 \leq 7}} a_i z^{i-4},$$

where a_L stores the low-order 4-bits of the contiguous bytes storing a in memory, and a_H stores the high-order 4-bits of the contiguous bytes storing a in memory. Using this representation, $a(z)$ can be simply written as:

$$a(z) = a_H(z) z^4 + a_L(z).$$

This representation allows performance-critical field operations to be formulated in terms of operations in groups of 4 bits (*nibbles*), taking advantage of the 4-bit granularity PTLU instructions. To minimize memory consumption, the algorithms will always receive the operands in the compact representation, convert them to the split representation using simple bit masks and return as result a field element stored in the compact form. In the following sections, algorithms for efficient squaring, square root extraction and multiplication using the split representation will be discussed.

3.1   Squaring

Since squaring in $\mathbb{F}_{2^m}$ is a linear map, the square of a field element $a(z)$ represented in split form is:

$$a(z)^2 = (a_H(z) z^4 + a_L(z))^2 = a_H(z)^2 z^8 + a_L(z)^2.$$

Algorithmically, this means we can compute the $a(z)^2$ by adding the squares of a_L and a_H with an 8-bit offset. Squaring a_L and a_H in turn can be computed by the conventional method of inserting a zero bit between each pair of consecutive bits on their binary representations through a 16-byte table lookup [16]. Since these two polynomials have coefficients stored in 4-bit sets, the table lookups can be executed simultaneously using PTLU instructions. The proposed optimization is shown in Algorithm 1. The algorithm receives a field element a stored in a compact vector of n 64-bit words (or $\frac{n}{2}$ 128-bit values) and at each iteration of the algorithm, a 128-bit value $a[2i]$ is loaded from memory and converted to the split representation by a bit mask. Each group of nibbles is then expanded from 4 bits to 8 bits by a parallel table lookup. The final 8-bit offset addition is implemented by interleaving instructions which pick alternately the lower or higher bytes of a_L or a_H to form two consecutive 128-bit values $(t[2i], t[2i + 1])$ produced as the result. The polynomial stored into t can be reduced modulo $f(z)$ to produce the final result $c(z)$.

Algorithm 1. Proposed optimization for the implementation of squaring in $\mathbb{F}_{2^m}$

Input: $a(z) = a[0..n - 1]$.
Output: $c(z) = c[0..n - 1] = a(z)^2 \bmod f(z)$.
 1: $\diamond$ Store in *table* the squares $u(z)^2$ of all 4-bit polynomials $u(z)$.
 2: $table \leftarrow$ (0x5554515045044140, 0x1514111005040100)
 3: $mask \leftarrow$ (0x0F0F0F0F0F0F0F0F, 0x0F0F0F0F0F0F0F0F)
 4: **for** $i \leftarrow 0$ **to** $\frac{n}{2} - 1$ **do**
 5:     $a_0 \leftarrow load(a[2i])$
 6:     $\diamond$ Convert to split representation.
 7:     $a_L \leftarrow a_0 \wedge mask$
 8:     $a_H \leftarrow a_0 \gg_{\dagger 8} 4, a_H \leftarrow a_H \wedge mask$
 9:     $\diamond$ Perform parallel table lookups.
10:     $a_L \leftarrow lookup(table, a_L), a_H \leftarrow lookup(table, a_H)$
11:     $\diamond$ Simulate addition with 8-bit offset.
12:     $t[2i] \leftarrow interlo(a_L, a_H)$
13:     $t[2i + 1] \leftarrow interhi(a_L, a_H)$
14: **end for**
15: **return** $c = t \bmod f(z)$

3.2   Square Root

Square root extraction is an important operation for fast implementations of point halving [17] and the n_T pairing [3]. Square root is the inverse of squaring and consequently it is also a linear map. Using the split representation, we have:

$$\sqrt{a(z)} = \sqrt{a_H(z)z^4 + a_L(z)} = \sqrt{a_H(z)} \cdot z^2 + \sqrt{a_L(z)}.$$

Given an element $a(z) \in \mathbb{F}_{2^m}$, the field element $c(z)$ such that $c(z)^2 = a(z) \bmod f(z)$ can be computed by the expression $c(z) = a_{even}(z) + \sqrt{z} \cdot a_{odd}(z) \bmod f(z)$, where $a_{even}(z)$ represents the concatenation of even coefficients of $a(z)$, $a_{odd}(z)$ represents the concatenation of odd coefficients of $a(z)$ and $\sqrt{z}$ is a constant depending on the irreducible polynomial $f(z)$ [17]. When f is chosen as a square root friendly polynomial [18], $\sqrt{z}$ has a sparse format and multiplication by this constant can be implemented with cheap shifted additions and no further reduction. For several of the NIST-standardized polynomials (e.g., $\mathbb{F}_{2^{283}}$ and $\mathbb{F}_{2^{571}}$), however, this is not the case and multiplication by $\sqrt{z}$ can be computed by a half-precision multiplication. A common optimization technique to treat this case is to precompute a multiplication table for $\sqrt{z}$.

Considering the above, the split representation induces a square root algorithm where $\sqrt{a_L(z)}$ and $\sqrt{a_H(z)}$ are computed separately and added with a 2-bit offset:

$$\sqrt{a(z)} = \sqrt{a_H(z)}z^2 + \sqrt{a_L(z)}$$
$$= \sqrt{z} \cdot (a_{L_{odd}}(z) + a_{H_{odd}}(z)z^2) + a_{L_{even}}(z) + a_{H_{even}}(z)z^2.$$

Algorithm 2 presents our implementation of this method with vector instructions. The algorithm processes 128 bits of a in each iteration and progressively separates the coefficients of $a[2i]$ into even or odd coefficients. First, a permutation mask is used to divide $a[2i]$ in bytes of odd index and bytes of even index. This trick makes the final step easier. The bytes with even indexes are stored in the lower 64-bit part of a_0 and the bytes with odd indexes are stored in the higher 64-bit part of a_0. The high and low nibbles of a_0 are then split into a_L and a_H and additional lookup tables are applied to further separate the bits of a_L and a_H into $(a_{L_{odd}}(z), a_{L_{even}}(z), a_{H_{odd}}(z)z^2, a_{H_{even}}(z)z^2)$. Note that the 2-bit offset (or z^2 factor) is embedded in the $sqrt_H$ lookup table. At the end of the 128-bit section, a_0 stores the interleaving of coefficients from a_L and a_H packed into 4-bit sets. The remaining instructions in the 128-bit section separate the even and odd coefficients into u and v, which can be reordered and multiplied by $\sqrt{z}$. We implement these final steps in 64-bit mode to avoid expensive shifts in 128-bit mode.

3.3 Multiplication

In this section, we discuss two strategies for implementing multiplication induced by the split representation.

Single Operand in Split Representation

If the multiplier is represented in split form, the following expression for multiplication is obtained:

$$a(z) \cdot b(z) = b(z) \cdot (a_H(z)z^4 + a_L(z)) = b(z)z^4 a_H(z) + b(z)a_L(z). \tag{1}$$

The full multiplication result can then be obtained by adding the partial results of two smaller multiplications with a 4-bit offset. Since multiplication in a binary field rarely enjoys native support in common processors, one of the fastest ways of implementing multiplication with a polynomial basis is through the precomputation-based algorithm proposed by López and Dahab [7]. For computing $a(z) \cdot b(z)$, this algorithm builds a table of products of small polynomials of degree less than w by the full field element $b(z)$ and scans operand $a(z)$ in sets of w bits of each word at a time adding the intermediate results left-shifted by multiples of w. A common implementation choice is to use $w = 4$. The core operation of this algorithm is simulating a fast way of multiplying a small polynomial

---

Algorithm 2. Proposed optimization for square root in $\mathbb{F}_{2^m}$.

Input: $a(z) = a[0..n-1]$, exponents m and t of trinomial $f(z)$.

Output: $c(z) = c[0..n-1] = a(z)^{\frac{1}{2}} \bmod f(z)$.

1: $\diamond$ Permutation mask to divide a 128-bit value in bytes with odd and even indexes.
2: $perm \leftarrow (\texttt{0x0F0D0B0907050301}, \texttt{0x0E0C0A0806040200})$
3: $\diamond$ Table to divide a low nibble in bits with odd and even indexes.
4: $sqrt_L \leftarrow (\texttt{0x3332232231302120}, \texttt{0x1312030211100100})$
5: $\diamond$ Table to divide a high nibble in bits with odd and even indexes ($sqrt_L \lll_8 2$).
6: $sqrt_H \leftarrow (\texttt{0xCCC88C88C4C08480}, \texttt{0x4C480C0844400400})$
7: $\diamond$ Bit masks to convert to split representation.
8: $mask_L \leftarrow (\texttt{0x0F0F0F0F0F0F0F0F}, \texttt{0x0F0F0F0F0F0F0F0F})$
9: $mask_H \leftarrow (\texttt{0xF0F0F0F0F0F0F0F0}, \texttt{0xF0F0F0F0F0F0F0F0})$
10: $a_{even} \leftarrow 0, a_{odd} \leftarrow 0$
11: **for** $i \leftarrow 0$ **to** $\frac{n}{2} - 1$ **do**
12:    $a_0 \leftarrow load(a[2i])$
13:    $a_0 \leftarrow shuffle(a_0, perm)$
14:    $\diamond$ Convert permuted vector to split representation.
15:    $a_L \leftarrow a_0 \wedge mask_L$
16:    $a_H \leftarrow a_0 \wedge mask_H, a_H \leftarrow a_H \ggg_8 4$
17:    $\diamond$ Extract $(a_{L_{odd}}(z) + a_{L_{even}(z)})$ in a_L and $(a_{H_{odd}}(z)z^2 + a_{H_{even}(z)}z^2)$ in a_H.
18:    $a_L \leftarrow lookup(sqrt_L, a_L), a_H \leftarrow lookup(sqrt_H, a_H)$
19:    $\diamond$ Compute $(a_{L_{odd}}(z) + a_{L_{even}(z)} + a_{H_{odd}}(z)z^2 + a_{H_{even}(z)}z^2)$.
20:    $a_0 \leftarrow a_L \oplus a_H$
21:    $\diamond$ Compute $u = a_{L_{even}}(z) + a_{H_{even}}(z)z^2$ and $v = a_{L_{odd}}(z) + a_{H_{odd}}(z)z^2$.
22:    $a_L \leftarrow a_0 \wedge mask_L, a_H \leftarrow a_0 \wedge mask_H$
23:    $u \leftarrow store(a_L)$
24:    $v \leftarrow store(a_H)$
25:    $\diamond$ From now on, operate in 64-bit registers.
26:    $a_{even} \leftarrow a_{even} + (u[0] \vee (u[1] \ll 4))$
27:    $a_{odd} \leftarrow a_{odd} + (v[1] \vee (v[0] \gg 4))$
28: **end for**
29: **return** $c(z) = a_{even} + \sqrt{z} \cdot a_{odd} \bmod f(z)$

---

by a full field element using a lookup table. This allows the implementation to employ the XOR instruction with highest granularity included in the target platform, heavily benefiting from vector instruction sets. When left-shifts by 4 bits are expensive, as is the case with the target platform, a variant is also provided in [7] which employs two precomputation tables: one for $b(z)$ and other for $b(z)z^4$. This variant is clearly induced by Equation 1 and its implementation with vector registers is presented in Algorithm 3. In our implementation, all the shifted additions are done in registers to avoid costly memory operations and left-shifts by 4 bits are completely eliminated in favor of left-shifts by 8 bits. Recall that shifts by multiples of 8 bits can use the convenient and faster memory-alignment instructions. Operand a is scanned in 128-bit intervals to avoid 64-bit shifts of the partial result stored in registers.

Algorithm 3. LD multiplication implemented with n 128-bit registers.

Input: $a(z) = a[0..n-1], b(z) = b[0..n-1]$.
Output: $c(z) = c[0..n-1] = a(z) \cdot b(z)$.
Note: m_i denotes the vector of $\frac{n}{2}$ 128-bit registers $(r_{(i-1+n/2)}, \ldots, r_i)$.

1: Compute $T_0(u) = u(z) \cdot b(z), T_1(u) = u(z) \cdot (b(z)z^4)$ for all $u(z)$ of degree < 4.
2: $(r_{n-1} \ldots, r_0) \leftarrow 0$
3: **for** $k \leftarrow 56$ **downto** 0 **by** 8 **do**
4:    **for** $j \leftarrow 1$ **to** $n-1$ **by** 2 **do**
5:       $\diamond$ Process implictly 4 bits of a_L and then 4 bits of a_H.
6:       Let $u = (u_3, u_2, u_1, u_0)$, where u_t is bit $(k+t)$ of $a[j]$.
7:       $m_{(j-1)/2} \leftarrow m_{(j-1)/2} \oplus T_0(u)$
8:       Let $v = (v_3, v_2, v_1, v_0)$, where v_t is bit $(k+t+4)$ of $a[j]$.
9:       $m_{(j-1)/2} \leftarrow m_{(j-1)/2} \oplus T_1(v)$
10:    **end for**
11:    $(r_{n-1} \ldots, r_0) \leftarrow (r_{n-1} \ldots, r_0) \lhd 8$
12: **end for**
13: **for** $k \leftarrow 56$ **downto** 0 **by** 8 **do**
14:    **for** $j \leftarrow 0$ **to** $n-2$ **by** 2 **do**
15:       $\diamond$ Process implictly 4 bits of a_L and then 4 bits of a_H.
16:       Let $u = (u_3, u_2, u_1, u_0)$, where u_t is bit $(k+t)$ of $a[j]$.
17:       $m_{j/2} \leftarrow m_{j/2} \oplus T_0(u)$
18:       Let $v = (v_3, v_2, v_1, v_0)$, where v_t is bit $(k+t+4)$ of $a[j]$.
19:       $m_{j/2} \leftarrow m_{j/2} \oplus T_1(v)$
20:    **end for**
21:    **if** $k > 0$ **then** $(r_{n-1} \ldots, r_0) \leftarrow (r_{n-1} \ldots, r_0) \lhd 8$
22: **end for**
23: **return** $c = (r_{n-1} \ldots, r_0) \bmod f(z)$

Both Operands in Split Representation

If both multiplicand and multiplier are represented in split form, the following expression is obtained:

$$a(z) \cdot b(z) = (b_H(z)z^4 + b_L(z)) \cdot (a_H(z)z^4 + a_L(z)).$$

Due to the sparseness of the split representation, a direct software implementation of this formula would lead to 4 applications of Algorithm 3. By using Karatsuba [19], we can lower the number of applications to 3:

$$a(z) \cdot b(z) = a_H b_H z^8 + [(a_H + a_L)(b_H + b_L) + a_H b_H + a_L b_L] z^4 + a_L b_L.$$

This can be improved by observing that a multiplication in split representation can be seen as a series of products of polynomials of degree less than w by a sparse polynomial with coefficients grouped in sets of size w. Products of a small polynomial by small sets of coefficients can be efficiently computed through table lookups and, moreover, by choosing $w = 4$ we can implement the 4-bit granular multiplication by simultaneous table lookups. Replacing lookups in a precomputation table (as in Algorithm 3) by lookups in a constant table leads to reduced memory consumption and increased arithmetic density. Higher arithmetic density has lower dependency on the performance of the memory subsystem and is consequently more attractive for implementation in vector processors. Unfortunately, there is no easy way of storing the table of constants without using memory and our approach does not benefit heavily of the feature. Algorithm 4 presents our shuffle-based approach to multiplication with the auxiliary function M_{split} defined in Algorithm 5. The disadvantage of this approach in comparison with [7] is that the core operation is sparser: now we multiply a small polynomial by a sparse field element, requiring more executions of this core operation to achieve the result. A fast shuffle instruction is thus required to implement this strategy in a competitive way. It is important to note that this approach is not immune to cache latency effects, since lookups using 4-bit sets of a on a table of constants stored into memory are still required. This is also the reason why operand a is processed in 64-bit mode inside M_{split}: quick access to these sets must be provided. Operand a is scanned in offsets a multiple of 8 so there is no need to apply masks to explicitly obtain a_L and a_H.

Algorithm 4. Left-to-right shuffle-based multiplication in $\mathbb{F}_{2^m}$.

Input: $a(z) = a[0..n-1], b(z) = b[0..n-1]$.
Output: $c(z) = c[0..n-1] = a(z) \cdot b(z)$.

1: ◇ Bit mask to convert to split representation.
2: $mask \leftarrow$ (0x0F0F0F0F0F0F0F0F, 0x0F0F0F0F0F0F0F0F)
3: ◇ Prepare operands $a_L(z)$ and $b_L(z)$ in split representation.
4: **for** $i \leftarrow 0$ to $\frac{n}{2} - 1$ **do** $b_H[i] \leftarrow load(b[2i])$, $b_L[i] = b_H[i] \wedge mask$, $a_L[i] = a[i]$
5: ◇ Compute $a_L(z)b_L(z)$.
6: $(m_L[n-1], \ldots, m_L[0]) \leftarrow M_{split}(a_L, b_L)$
7: ◇ Prepare operands $a_H(z)$ and $b_H(z)$ in split representation.
8: **for** $i \leftarrow 0$ to $\frac{n}{2} - 1$ **do** $b_H[i] \leftarrow (b_H[i] \gg_{\dagger 8} 4) \wedge mask$, $a_H[i] \leftarrow a[i] \gg 4$
9: ◇ Compute $a_H(z)b_H(z)$.
10: $(m_H[n-1], \ldots, m_H[0]) \leftarrow M_{split}(a_H, b_H)$
11: ◇ Prepare operands $(a_L(z) + a_H(z))$ and $(b_L(z) + b_H(z))$ in split representation.
12: **for** $i \leftarrow 0$ to $\frac{n}{2} - 1$ **do** $b_M[i] \leftarrow b_H[i] \oplus b_L[i]$, $a_M[i] = a_L[i] \oplus a_H[i]$
13: ◇ Compute $(a_L(z) + a_H(z))(b_L(z) + b_H(z))$.
14: $(m[n-1], \ldots, m[0]) \leftarrow M_{split}(a_M, b_M)$
15: ◇ Compute $(a_L(z) + a_H(z))(b_L(z) + b_H(z)) + a_L(z)b_L(z) + a_H(z)b_H(z)$.
16: **for** $i \leftarrow 0$ to $n-1$ **do**
17:     $m[i] \leftarrow m[i] \oplus (m_L[i] \oplus m_H[i])$
18: **end for**
19: ◇ Multiply $[(a_L(z) + a_H(z))(b_L(z) + b_H(z)) + a_L(z)b_L(z) + a_H(z)b_H(z)]$ by z^4.
20: $(m[n-1], \ldots, m[0]) \leftarrow (m[n-1], \ldots, m[0]) \ll_{\dagger 8} 4$
21: ◇ Multiply $a_H(z)b_H(z)$ by z^8.
22: $(m_H[n-1], \ldots, m_H[0]) \leftarrow (m_H[n-1], \ldots, m_H[0]) \triangleleft 8$
23: ◇ Compute $a_H b_H z^8 + [(a_H + a_L)(b_H + b_L) + a_H b_H + a_L b_L] z^4 + a_L b_L$.
24: **for** $i \leftarrow 0$ to $n-1$ **do**
25:     $m[i] \leftarrow m[i] \oplus (m_L[i] \oplus m_H[i])$
26: **end for**
27: **return** $c = (m[n-1], \ldots, m[0]) \mod f(z)$

Algorithm 5. Auxiliary multiplication function $M_{split}(a, b)$.

Input: Operands a, b in split representation.
Output: Result $a \cdot b$ stored in registers $(r_{n-1} \ldots, r_0)$.

1: ⋄ Table of constants storing all products of 4-bit × 4-bit polynomials.
2: $table[0] \leftarrow$ (0x0000000000000000, 0x0000000000000000)
3: $table[1] \leftarrow$ (0x0F0E0D0C0B0A0908, 0x0706050403020100)
4: $table[2] \leftarrow$ (0x1E1C1A1816141210, 0x0E0C0A0806040200)
5: $table[3] \leftarrow$ (0x111217141D1E1B18, 0x090A0F0C05060300)
6: $table[4] \leftarrow$ (0x3C3834302C282420, 0x1C1814100C080400)
7: $table[5] \leftarrow$ (0x3336393C27222D28, 0x1B1E11140F0A0500)
8: $table[6] \leftarrow$ (0x22242E283A3C3630, 0x12141E180A0C0600)
9: $table[7] \leftarrow$ (0x2D2A232431363F38, 0x15121B1C090E0700)
10: $table[8] \leftarrow$ (0x7870686058504840, 0x3830282018100800)
11: $table[9] \leftarrow$ (0x777E656C535A4148, 0x3F362D241B120900)
12: $table[10] \leftarrow$ (0x666C72784E445A50, 0x363C22281E140A00)
13: $table[11] \leftarrow$ (0x69627F74454E5358, 0x313A272C1D160B00)
14: $table[12] \leftarrow$ (0x44485C5074786C60, 0x24283C3014180C00)
15: $table[13] \leftarrow$ (0x4B46515C7F726568, 0x232E3934171A0D00)
16: $table[14] \leftarrow$ (0x5A544648626C7E70, 0x2A243638121C0E00)
17: $table[15] \leftarrow$ (0x555A4B4469667778, 0x2D22333C111E0F00)
18: $(r_{n-1} \ldots, r_0) \leftarrow 0$
19: **for** $k \leftarrow 56$ **downto** 0 **by** 8 **do**
20:     **for** $j \leftarrow 1$ **to** $n - 1$ **by** 2 **do**
21:         Let $u = (u_3, u_2, u_1, u_0)$, where u_t is bit $(k + t)$ of $a[j]$.
22:         **for** $i \leftarrow 0$ **to** $\frac{n}{2} - 1$ **do** $r_i \leftarrow r_i \oplus shuffle(table[u], b[i])$
23:     **end for**
24:     $(r_{n-1} \ldots, r_0) \leftarrow (r_{n-1} \ldots, r_0) \lhd 8$
25: **end for**
26: **for** $k \leftarrow 56$ **downto** 0 **by** 8 **do**
27:     **for** $j \leftarrow 0$ **to** $n - 2$ **by** 2 **do**
28:         Let $u = (u_3, u_2, u_1, u_0)$, where u_t is bit $(k + t)$ of $a[j]$.
29:         **for** $i \leftarrow 0$ **to** $\frac{n}{2} - 1$ **do** $r_i \leftarrow r_i \oplus shuffle(table[u], b[i])$
30:     **end for**
31:     **if** $k > 0$ **then** $(r_{n-1} \ldots, r_0) \leftarrow (r_{n-1} \ldots, r_0) \lhd 8$
32: **end for**

3.4   Modular Reduction and Inversion

Efficient modular reduction and inversion do not benefit from the split representation. The performance of both operations heavily depend on the performance of shifting and *ad-hoc* optimizations. For this reason, we only provide some of the general guidelines that were followed for the implementation of modular reduction for all the considered different choices of irreducible polynomial $f(z) = z^m + r(z)$:

- If $f(z)$ is a trinomial and $m - deg(r) \geq 128$, modular reduction should be implemented in 128-bit mode because of the small number of shifts required. Bytewise shifts should be used whenever possible. One example of modular reduction implemented with this guideline can be found in [9].

- If $f(z)$ is a pentanomial or if the degree of $r(z)$ is too big to satisfy the previous criteria, but still $m - deg(r) \geq 64$, modular reduction should be implemented in 64-bit mode but processing two words in parallel with 128-bit registers when possible.
- Consecutive writes can be accumulated into registers before being written to memory to avoid redundant memory writes.
- If the number of 128-bit digits n required to store a field element is small, squaring and multiplication results can be stored and immediately reduced using registers instead of using arrays. This optimization also reduces redundant memory operations for reloading and reducing an intermediate value.

For inversion in $\mathbb{F}_{2^m}$, the Extended Euclidean Algorithm variant for polynomials [16] can be implemented in 64-bit mode to make use of flexible shifts by arbitrary amounts. Our implementation of inversion was focused only in correctness and did not receive the amount of attention dedicated to the performance-critical operations.

4   Experimental Results

We now present and discuss our timings for finite field arithmetic and elliptic curve arithmetic.

4.1   Finite Field Arithmetic

We implemented arithmetic in the binary fields $\mathbb{F}_{2^m}$, $m \in \{113, 127, 163, 233, 239, 251, 283, 409, 571\}$, using the non-square root friendly polynomials defined by NIST or the Standards for Efficient Cryptography Group (SECG) [20] or the ECRYPT Benchmarking of Cryptographic Systems (eBACS) project [10]; and using the independent square root friendly polynomials given in [18,21,22]. All our choices for defining polynomials can be found in Table 2.

The C programming language was used in conjunction with compiler intrinsics for accessing vector instructions. The chosen compiler was GCC version 4.1.2 with backports from 4.3 because in our experiments it generated the fastest code from vector intrinsics, as already observed in [22]. Compiler flags included optimization level -O2, loop unrolling and tuning with the -march=core2 switch. Considered target platforms are the Core 2 65nm (Core 2 I), Core 2 45nm (Core 2 II) and Core i7 45nm microarchitectures, represented by a mobile Intel Core 2 T7200 2.0GHz, a Xeon X3320 2.5GHz and a Core i7 860 2.8GHz, respectively. Finite field arithmetic was implemented as an arithmetic backend of the RELIC toolkit [23] and the library was used for testing and benchmarking.

Table 3 presents our results for finite field arithmetic. The operations considered are squaring, multiplication, square root extraction and inversion. The standard polynomials are used in all operations with the exception of square root modulo a friendly polynomial. The differences between our implementations in the various microarchitectures can be explained by the lower cost of the bytewise shift and shuffle instructions after the introduction of the *Super Shuffle*

Table 2. Different choices of irreducible binary polynomials $f(z)$ of degree m. Polynomials are classified into Standard (as defined by NIST, SECG or eBACS) or square root friendly (SQRTF).

m	$f(z)$	$\sqrt{z} \bmod f(z)$	Type
113	$z^{113} + z^9 + 1$	$z^{57} + z^5$	SQRTF
127	$z^{127} + z^{63} + 1$	$z^{64} + z^{32}$	SQRTF
163	$z^{163} + z^7 + z^6 + z^3 + 1$	79 terms	Standard
	$z^{163} + z^{57} + z^{49} + z^{29} + 1$	$z^{82} + z^{29} + z^{25} + z^{15}$	SQRTF
233	$z^{233} + z^{74} + 1$	$z^{228} + z^{191} + z^{154} + z^{117} + z^{69} + z^{32}$	SQRTF
	$z^{233} + z^{159} + 1$	$z^{117} + z^{80}$	SQRTF
239	$z^{239} + z^{158} + 1$	$z^{199} + z^{120} + z^{118} + z^{39}$	Standard
	$z^{239} + z^{81} + 1$	$z^{120} + z^{41}$	SQRTF
251	$z^{251} + z^7 + z^4 + z^2 + 1$	166 terms	Standard
	$z^{251} + z^{89} + z^{81} + z^3 + 1$	$z^{126} + z^{45} + z^{41} + z^2$	SQRTF
283	$z^{283} + z^{12} + z^7 + z^5 + 1$	68 terms	Standard
	$z^{283} + z^{97} + z^{89} + z^{87} + 1$	$z^{142} + z^{49} + z^{45} + z^{44}$	SQRTF
409	$z^{409} + z^{87} + 1$	$z^{205} + z^{44}$	SQRTF
571	$z^{571} + z^{10} + z^5 + z^2 + 1$	273 terms	Standard
	$z^{571} + z^{193} + z^{185} + z^5 + 1$	$z^{286} + z^{97} + z^{93} + z^3$	SQRTF
1223	$z^{1223} + z^{255} + 1$	$z^{612} + z^{128}$	SQRTF

Engine by Intel in the first release of the 45nm microarchitecture. Timings for the Core i7 are a little faster or competitive with timings for the Core 2 45nm architecture up to $m = 251$. For the bigger fields, minor compiler decisions focusing on Core 2 scheduling characteristics decrease performance in Core i7. To date, no released GCC version has specific tuning for the Core i7 microarchitecture. Our implementation shows some interesting results:

1. PTLU-based approaches like squaring, square root extraction and shuffle-based multiplication are significantly faster in the latest microarchitectures. The increased throughput of PTLU instructions is visible in simple operations like squaring and square root extraction and on the small field multipliers. Square root extraction modulo friendly polynomials is the only PTLU-based approach that benefits from increased throughput in all field sizes. This happens because of its the lower dependence on memory performance compared to squaring or shuffle-based multiplication, since square root does not rely on a table of constants stored into memory and has a higher arithmetic density between fetching the operands and storing the results. Nevertheless, these approaches will likely benefit from future enhancements to the flexibility or speed of PTLU instructions.

2. Squaring and square root extraction with a friendly $f(z)$ are formulated and computed very efficiently using shuffling, producing multiplication-to-squaring ratios as high as 34. Table lookups are so fast that performance is mainly dependent on the choice of $f(z)$ and the resulting form of $\sqrt{z}$, as we can see in two cases: (i) comparing squaring in $\mathbb{F}_{2^{251}}$ and in $\mathbb{F}_{2^{409}}$, where the former requires the expansion of two vector registers, but expansion of three

vector registers and reduction modulo a trinomial in the latter is cheaper; (ii) comparing square root with friendly $f(z)$ between $\mathbb{F}_{2^{571}}$ and $\mathbb{F}_{2^{1223}}$, where the former has half the field size, but the nice form of $\sqrt{z}$ in the latter makes square root extraction faster. Square root in field $\mathbb{F}_{2^{1223}}$ on the Core i7 is indeed an extreme example of this, since it is competitive with square root modulo friendly polynomials in much smaller fields.

3. Shuffle-based multiplication strategy (Algorithm 4) gets a significant speed improvement with faster shuffle instructions. However, memory access for addressing the table of 16 constants acts as a bottleneck for further improvements in the Core i7 architecture where shuffle throughput is doubled. A faster way to address this table must be made available so the higher arithmetic density can be explored without memory performance interference. It is still surprising that this algorithm requiring three times the number of operations of conventional López-Dahab multiplication (Algorithm 3) is only 50%-90% slower in the microarchitectures where shuffling is faster.

Our results lack a full comparison with other works because we were not able to find published timings for the same combinations of parameters and architectures using vector instruction sets. Comparing with the results given by [21] for a 64-bit C-only implementation of arithmetic in $\mathbb{F}_{2^{127}}$ on a Core 2 65nm machine: (i) both López-Dahab and shuffle-based multiplication approaches are faster by 25% and 3% than the reported 270 cycles, respectively, because of the higher addition granularity and fast shifting by 8 bits; (ii) square root extraction is 64% faster due to the way PTLU instructions are employed; (iii) inversion is 17% slower because it was not considered performance-critical in this work. The improvement with vector registers is still less than what could be expected by doubling the register size, but this can be explained in terms of arithmetic density: López-Dahab multiplication benefits from larger ratios between field size and register size. We also refer the reader to [9] for a comparison of our implementation of arithmetic in $\mathbb{F}_{2^{1223}}$ using similar techniques with an efficient implementation of this field reported in [24].

A full comparison can however be provided in the fields $\mathbb{F}_{2^{113}}$ and $\mathbb{F}_{2^{251}}$ employed for curve-based key exchange benchmarking in the eBACS project [10]. We present in Table 4 timings obtained by the eBACS 64-bit version of the $\mathbf{mp}\mathbb{F}_q$ library [25] distributed as part of SUPERCOP version 20100509. This version employs the SSE2 vector instruction set inside the multiplier and relies on automatic tuning of the multiplication code. These timings were measured through the simple integration of $\mathbf{mp}\mathbb{F}_q$ as an arithmetic backend of RELIC so that the same compiling, testing and benchmarking procedures could be used. Comparison of results in Tables 3 and 4 for the corresponding fields favor our approaches with the exception of López-Dahab Multiplication in $\mathbb{F}_{2^{113}}$ on Core 2 I. Speedups range from 8% to 84%. This gives an idea of the improvements of our approach over the previous state-of-the-art in efficient implementations of finite field arithmetic using vector instructions. Note that although our code was handwritten, most of it closely follows the described algorithms. There is no obstacle to automatically generate an implementation with comparable performance.

Table 3. Timings in cycles for our implementation of binary field arithmetic arithmetic in Intel platforms Core 2 65nm (Core 2 I), Core 2 45nm (Core 2 II) and Core i7 45nm. Square root friendly polynomials are only used when explicitly stated (or when the standard polynomial is also square root friendly). Results are the average of 10^4 executions of each algorithm with random inputs.

	Platform and field size					
	Core 2 I	Core 2 II	Core i7	Core 2 I	Core 2 II	Core i7
Field operation	$m = 113$			$m = 127$		
Squaring	34	25	24	25	16	16
Square root with standard f	-	-	-	-	-	-
Square root with friendly f	27	23	22	22	19	17
López-Dahab multiplication	147	127	116	200	179	165
Shuffle-based multiplication	257	187	176	262	191	169
Inversion	3675	3593	3446	4096	4042	3894
	$m = 163$			$m = 233$		
Squaring	60	49	48	50	36	34
Square root with standard f	195	163	167	128	124	117
Square root with friendly f	99	89	84	92	76	74
López-Dahab multiplication	240	218	216	276	241	246
Shuffle-based multiplication	506	336	313	695	429	403
Inversion	5984	5948	5756	9986	9922	10074
	$m = 239$			$m = 251$		
Squaring	53	43	47	72	59	58
Square root with standard f	113	104	94	258	237	231
Square root with friendly f	94	77	71	109	99	88
López-Dahab multiplication	284	251	261	350	325	323
Shuffle-based multiplication	686	441	412	738	468	475
Inversion	10259	10150	10101	10816	10471	10761
	$m = 283$			$m = 409$		
Squaring	73	58	55	67	52	50
Square root with standard f	309	278	292	171	155	135
Square root with friendly f	131	106	103	171	155	135
López-Dahab multiplication	418	397	400	751	690	715
Shuffle-based multiplication	1084	664	647	2239	1234	1265
Inversion	13522	13301	13608	23199	23050	24012
	$m = 571$			$m = 1223$		
Squaring	124	95	94	160	108	110
Square root with standard f	844	827	849	-	-	-
Square root with friendly f	211	191	174	166	140	114
López-Dahab multiplication	1247	1173	1197	4030*	3785*	3912*
Shuffle-based multiplication	4105	2163	2285	12204*	7219*	7367*
Inversion	38404	38173	40226	149763	149589	161577

(*) Karatsuba at depth 1 was used at the top level.

4.2   Elliptic Curve Arithmetic

The performance obtained by our efficient implementation is illustrated with some executions of the Elliptic Curve Diffie-Hellman (ECDH) and Elliptic Curve

Table 4. Timings in cycles of the $\mathbf{mp}\mathbb{F}_q$ library for binary field arithmetic arithmetic in Intel platforms Core 2 65nm (Core 2 I), Core 2 45nm (Core 2 II) and Core i7 45nm. Using notation of Table 3, results of square root extraction correspond to the square root friendly polynomial in $\mathbb{F}_{2^{113}}$ and to the standard polynomial in $\mathbb{F}_{2^{251}}$. Results are the average of 10^4 executions of each algorithm with random inputs.

	Platform and field size					
	Core 2 I	Core 2 II	Core i7	Core 2 I	Core 2 II	Core i7
Field operation	$m = 113$			$m = 251$		
Squaring	38	40	36	106	103	102
Square root	144	141	128	557	552	526
Multiplication	135	139	129	490	489	458
Inversion	5497	5435	5430	18425	16502	17907

Digital Signature Algorithm (ECDSA) protocols [26]. We have selected fast algorithms for elliptic curve arithmetic in three situations: multiplying a random point P by a scalar k, multiplying the generator G by a scalar k and simultaneously multiplying two points P and Q by scalars k and l to obtain $kP + lQ$. Our implementation uses mixed addition with projective coordinates [27], given that the multiplication-to-inversion ratio is between 22 and 41.

For multiplying a random point by a scalar, we choose Solinas' τ-adic non-adjacent form (TNAF) representation [28] with $w = 4$ for Koblitz curves (4-TNAF method with 4 precomputation points) and the method due to López and Dahab [29] for random binary curves. We did not implement point halving [17] because NIST field definitions are not optimal for square root computation, although conversion to the friendly representations used in Table 3 would be practical in some scenarios. For multiplying the generator, we employ the 6-TNAF method for Koblitz curves; and for generic curves, we employ the Comb method [30] with 256 precomputed points. For simultaneous multiplication, we implement the interleaving method with 4-TNAFs for Koblitz curves and with 4-NAFs (*width-4 non-adjacent form*) for generic curves [31].

Table 5 presents our timings for elliptic curve arithmetic using the fastest finite field implementations presented in the previous section. We provide timings for curves at the 128-bit and 256-bit security levels defined by NIST as reference for future implementations. The eBACS [10] website currently reports timings for key exchange of 855000, 748000 and 755000 cycles on platforms Core 2 I (`latour`), Core 2 II (`needme`) and Core i7 (`dragon`) respectively using CURVE2251. We improve these timings by 27%-30% with our implementation of CURVE2251 and show that we can instead compute key exchanges in curve NIST-B283 with performance comparable to the eBACS results. Bernstein [32] describes a bitsliced implementation of 251-bit binary Edwards curves (BBE) that computes a batch of 1024 point multiplications in parallel taking in average 314000 cycles per scalar multiplication in a Core 2 I (`latour`) platform. A question left open is the speed of a bitsliced approach using special curves. The straight-line requirements noted in [32] are naturally compatible with reducing side-channel exposure, but these do not appear to be compatible with traditional approaches on Koblitz curves. As a reference point, our results show that it's possible to match BBE's performance with a conventional implementation using the Koblitz curve SECG-K239 if one is willing to accept the following trade-offs: (i) allow curves with special algebraic structures; (ii) relax side-channel resistance; and (iii) lower the security level to a 239-bit curve. In order to comply with the security requirements in [32] while keeping the flexibility a non-bitsliced implementation provides, currently the best choice for binary curves is to use our implementation of CURVE2251 with the added performance impact.

Table 5. Timings given in 10^3 cycles for elliptic curve operations inside executions of the ECDH and ECDSA protocols measured in Intel platforms Core 2 65nm (Core 2 I), Core 2 45nm (Core 2 II) and Core i7 45nm. Results are the average of 10^4 executions of each algorithm with random inputs.

Curve	Key Exchange (kP)			Sign (kG) + Verify $(kG + lP)$		
	Core 2 I	Core 2 II	Core i7	Core 2 I	Core 2 II	Core i7
SECG-K239	270	247	260	196 + 419	175 + 384	184 + 400
CURVE2251	594	535	537	172 + 926	157 + 850	157 + 852
NIST-K283	411	378	386	298 + 632	270 + 586	275 + 599
NIST-B283	858	785	793	225 + 1212	210 + 1120	212 + 1140
NIST-K571	1782	1617	1656	1295 + 2840	1159 + 2580	1185 + 2645
NIST-B571	4754	4310	4440	1225 + 6206	1126 + 5683	1145 + 5822

5   Conclusion

In this work, we proposed novel techniques for exploring parallelism during the implementation of binary fields in computers equipped with modern vector instruction sets. It was made clear that field arithmetic can be efficiently formulated and implemented using these instructions. A competitive shuffle-based implementation of multiplication was introduced and our results show that it has two main requirements: (i) the availability of fast shuffle instructions; (ii) an efficient table addressing mechanism avoiding memory accesses completely. If both requirements can be satisfied in a low-cost way, we pose an interesting question on the design of future vector arithmetic units: is there a real need for a native binary field multiplier from a cost-benefit perspective? Supporting a single fast shuffle instruction can be cheaper and may allow very efficient implementations of the performance-critical operations in $\mathbb{F}_{2^m}$ and other fields of cryptographic interest such as $\mathbb{F}_{3^m}$.

We illustrated our implementation results with timings for ECDSA and ECDH protocols in two different NIST-standardized security levels, showing that a random point multiplication at the 128-bit security level can be computed in 411000 cycles in an Intel Core 2 65nm architecture. A comparison of our results with benchmark data from the eBACS project shows that our implementation of CURVE2251 is up to 30% faster. The timings on SECG-K239 provide a reference point for future comparisons with batch methods such as [32] under the assumption that the interest is in the fastest point multiplication on standardized curves over binary fields. This comparison will be interesting to revisit once the effects of the to-be-released native multiplier [15] and the AVX extensions [14] are evaluated in both implementations.

Acknowledgements

We would like to thank the anonymous reviewers for pointing out useful suggestions on how to compare our preliminary results with related work; and CNPq, CAPES and FAPESP, which support authors Diego F. Aranha and Julio López.

References

1. Koblitz, N.: CM-Curves with Good Cryptographic Properties. In: Feigenbaum, J. (ed.) CRYPTO 1991. LNCS, vol. 576, pp. 279–287. Springer, Heidelberg (1992)
2. Daemen, J., Rijmen, V.: The Design of Rijndael. Springer, New York (2002)
3. Barreto, P.S.L.M., Galbraith, S., hÉigeartaigh, C.O., Scott, M.: Efficient Pairing Computation on Supersingular Abelian Varieties. Designs, Codes and Cryptography 42(3), 239–271 (2007)
4. Misoczki, R., Barreto, P.S.L.M.: Compact McEliece Keys from Goppa Codes. In: Jacobson Jr., M.J., Rijmen, V., Safavi-Naini, R. (eds.) SAC 2009. LNCS, vol. 5867, pp. 376–392. Springer, Heidelberg (2009)
5. Chen, A.T., Chen, M.S., Chen, T.R., Cheng, C.M., Ding, J., Kuo, E.H., Lee, F.S., Yang, B.Y.: SSE Implementation of Multivariate PKCs on Modern x86 CPUs. In: Clavier, C., Gaj, K. (eds.) CHES 2009. LNCS, vol. 5747, pp. 33–48. Springer, Heidelberg (2009)
6. Fiskiran, A.M., Lee, R.B.: Fast Parallel Table Lookups to Accelerate Symmetric-Key Cryptography. In: International Symposium on Information Technology: Coding and Computing (ITCC 2005), vol. 1, pp. 526–531. IEEE, Los Alamitos (2005)
7. López, J., Dahab, R.: High-Speed Software Multiplication in $GF(2^m)$. In: Roy, B.K., Okamoto, E. (eds.) INDOCRYPT 2000. LNCS, vol. 1977, pp. 203–212. Springer, Heidelberg (2000)
8. Hankerson, D., López, J., Menezes, A.: Software Implementation of Elliptic Curve Cryptography over Binary Fields. In: Paar, C., Koç, Ç.K. (eds.) CHES 2000. LNCS, vol. 1965, pp. 1–24. Springer, Heidelberg (2000)
9. Aranha, D.F., López, J., Hankerson, D.: High-Speed Parallel Software Implementation of the η_T Pairing. In: Pieprzyk, J. (ed.) CT-RSA 2010. LNCS, vol. 5985, pp. 89–105. Springer, Heidelberg (2010)
10. Bernstein, D.J., Lange, T. (ed.): eBACS: ECRYPT Benchmarking of Cryptographic Systems, http://bench.cr.yp.to (accessed May 25, 2010)
11. Hilewitz, Y., Yin, Y.L., Lee, R.B.: Accelerating the Whirlpool Hash Function Using Parallel Table Lookup and Fast Cyclical Permutation. In: Nyberg, K. (ed.) FSE 2008. LNCS, vol. 5086, pp. 173–188. Springer, Heidelberg (2008)
12. Intel: Intel Architecture Software Developer's Manual: Instruction Set Reference, vol. 2 (2002), http://www.intel.com
13. Diefendorff, K., Dubey, P.K., Hochsprung, R., Scales, H.: AltiVec Extension to PowerPC Accelerates Media Processing. IEEE Micro 20(2), 85–95 (2000)
14. AMD Technology: AMD64 Architecture Programmer's Manual: 128-bit and 256-bit XOP, FMA4 and CVT16 Instruction, vol. 6,
http://support.amd.com/us/Processor_TechDocs/43479.pdf

15. Gueron, S., Kounavis, M.E.: Carry-Less Multiplication and Its Usage for Computing The GCM Mode. White paper, http://software.intel.com/
16. Hankerson, D., Menezes, A.J., Vanstone, S.: Guide to Elliptic Curve Cryptography. Springer, Secaucus (2003)
17. Fong, K., Hankerson, D., López, J., Menezes, A.: Field Inversion and Point Halving Revisited. IEEE Transactions on Computers 53(8), 1047–1059 (2004)
18. Avanzi, R.M.: Another Look at Square Roots (and Other Less Common Operations) in Fields of Even Characteristic. In: Adams, C.M., Miri, A., Wiener, M.J. (eds.) SAC 2007. LNCS, vol. 4876, pp. 138–154. Springer, Heidelberg (2007)
19. Karatsuba, A., Ofman, Y.: Multiplication of Many-Digital Numbers by Automatic Computers. Doklady Akad. Nauk SSSR (145), 293–294 (1962) Translation in Physics-Doklady 7, 595–596 (1963)
20. Certicom Research: SEC 2: Recommended Elliptic Curve Domain Parameters, http://www.secg.org (2000)
21. Hankerson, D., Karabina, K., Menezes, A.: Analyzing the Galbraith-Lin-Scott Point Multiplication Method for Elliptic Curves over Binary Fields. IEEE Transactions on Computers 58(10), 1411–1420 (2009)
22. Hankerson, D., Menezes, A., Scott, M.: Software Implementation of Pairings. In: Identity-Based Cryptography, pp. 188–206. IOS Press, Amsterdam (2008)
23. Aranha, D.F., Gouvêa, C.P.L.: RELIC is an Efficient LIbrary for Cryptography, http://code.google.com/p/relic-toolkit/
24. Beuchat, J., López-Trejo, E., Martínez-Ramos, L., Mitsunari, S., Rodríguez-Henríquez, F.: Multi-core Implementation of the Tate Pairing over Supersingular Elliptic Curves. In: Garay, J.A., Miyaji, A., Otsuka, A. (eds.) CANS 2009. LNCS, vol. 5888, pp. 413–432. Springer, Heidelberg (2009)
25. Gaudry, P., Thomé, E.: The mpFq library and implementing curve-based key exchanges. In: Software Performance Enhancement of Encryption and Decryption (SPEED 2007), pp. 49–64 (2009), http://www.hyperelliptic.org/SPEED/record.pdf
26. Certicom Research: SEC 1: Elliptic Curve Cryptography (2000), http://www.secg.org
27. López, J., Dahab, R.: Improved Algorithms for Elliptic Curve Arithmetic in $GF(2^n)$. In: Tavares, S.E., Meijer, H. (eds.) SAC 1998. LNCS, vol. 1556, pp. 201–212. Springer, Heidelberg (1999)
28. Solinas, J.A.: Efficient Arithmetic on Koblitz Curves. Designs, Codes and Cryptography 19(2-3), 195–249 (2000)
29. López, J., Dahab, R.: Fast Multiplication on Elliptic Curves over $GF(2^m)$ without Precomputation. In: Koç, Ç.K., Paar, C. (eds.) CHES 1999. LNCS, vol. 1717, pp. 316–327. Springer, Heidelberg (1999)
30. Lim, C.H., Lee, P.J.: More Flexible Exponentiation with Precomputation. In: Desmedt, Y. (ed.) CRYPTO 1994. LNCS, vol. 839, pp. 95–107. Springer, Heidelberg (1994)
31. Gallant, R., Lambert, R., Vanstone, S.: Faster Point Multiplication on Elliptic Curves with Efficient Endomorphisms. In: Kilian, J. (ed.) CRYPTO 2001. LNCS, vol. 2139, pp. 190–200. Springer, Heidelberg (2001)
32. Bernstein, D.J.: Batch Binary Edwards. In: Halevi, S. (ed.) CRYPTO 2009. LNCS, vol. 5677, pp. 317–336. Springer, Heidelberg (2009)

Communication Optimal Multi-valued Asynchronous Broadcast Protocol

Arpita Patra* and C. Pandu Rangan**

Dept of Computer Science and Engineering
IIT Madras, Chennai India 600036
{arpitapatra10,prangan55}@gmail.com

Abstract. Broadcast (BC) is considered as the most fundamental primitive for fault-tolerant distributed computing and cryptographic protocols. An important and practical variant of BC is Asynchronous BC (known as A-cast). An A-cast protocol enables a specific party called sender (possibly corrupted) to send some message identically to a set of parties despite the presence of an adversary who may corrupt some of the parties in a malicious manner.

Though the existing protocol for A-cast is designed for a single bit message, in real life applications typically A-cast is invoked on long message (whose size can be in gigabytes) rather than on single bit. Therefore, it is important to design efficient multi-valued A-cast protocols (i.e protocols with long message) which extract several advantages offered by directly dealing with long messages and are far better than multiple invocations to existing protocols for single bit. In this paper, we design highly efficient, *communication optimal*[1], optimally resilient[2] multi-valued A-cast protocol for long messages, based on access to the existing A-cast protocol for short messages. Our protocol also provides better communication complexity than existing protocol for A-cast.

Keywords: A-cast, Asynchronous, Multi-valued, Unbounded Computing Power, Byzantine.

1 Introduction

The problem of Broadcast (BC) was introduced in [17] and since then it have emerged as one of the most fundamental problems in distributed computing. It has been used as building block for several important secure distributed computing tasks such as Secure Multiparty Computation (MPC) [3,8], Verifiable

* Financial Support from Microsoft Research India Acknowledged.
** Work Supported by Project No. CSE/05-06/076/DITX/CPAN on Protocols for Secure Communication and Computation Sponsored by Department of Information Technology, Government of India.

[1] A communication optimal protocol achieves a communication complexity that is minimal and that no other protocol can improve.
[2] A protocol that allows maximum fault tolerance.

Secret Sharing (VSS) [9,11,3] etc. In practice, BC is used in almost any task that involves multiple parties, like voting, bidding, secure function evaluation, threshold key generation etc.

A BC protocol is executed among a set $\mathcal{P}$ of n parties, who are connected to each other by pairwise secure channel. In brief, a BC protocol allows a special party in $\mathcal{P}$, called sender, to send some message identically to all other parties in $\mathcal{P}$, such that even when the sender is corrupted, all honest parties in $\mathcal{P}$ output the same message. The challenge lies in achieving the above task despite the presence of t faulty parties in $\mathcal{P}$ (possibly including the sender), who may deviate from the protocol arbitrarily.

In is known that A-cast protocol is possible tolerating t faulty parties in $\mathcal{P}$ iff $n = 3t+1$ [16,13]. Thus any A-cast designed with $n = 3t+1$, is said to be *optimally resilient*. The BC have been investigated extensively in various models, characterized by the synchrony of the network, privacy of the channels, computational power of the faulty parties and many other parameters [12,5,7,16,13]. But most of the emphasis was on the study of BC in synchronous settings [12,13]. But the limitations with the BC protocol in synchronous settings are that they assume that the delay in the transmission of every message in the network is bounded by a fixed constant. Though these protocols are theoretically impressive, the above assumption is a very strong assumption in practice. This is because a delay in the transmission of even a single message may hamper the overall property of the protocol. Therefore, BC in asynchronous network, known as A-cast has been introduced and studied in the literature [1,18,5,6]. In this paper, we study A-cast problem, specifically the communication complexity of the problem. In the sequel, we first present the model that we use for our work and the formal definitions of A-cast. Subsequently, we will present the literature survey on A-cast. Lastly, we will elaborate on our contribution in this paper.

1.1   Model

In this paper, we follow the network model of [5]. Specifically, our A-cast protocol is carried out among a set of n parties, say $\mathcal{P} = \{P_1, \ldots, P_n\}$, where every two parties are directly connected by a secure channel and t out of the n parties can be under the influence of a *computationally unbounded Byzantine (active) adversary*, denoted as $\mathcal{A}_t$. We assume $n = 3t + 1$ which is the minimum number of parties required to design any A-cast protocol [16,13]. The adversary $\mathcal{A}_t$, completely dictates the parties under its control and can force them to deviate from the protocol in any arbitrary manner. Moreover, we assume $\mathcal{A}_t$ to be *rushing* [10], who may first listen all the messages sent to the corrupted parties by the honest parties, before allowing the corrupted parties to send their messages. The parties not under the influence of $\mathcal{A}_t$ are called *honest or uncorrupted*.

The underlying network is asynchronous, where the communication channels between the parties have arbitrary, yet finite delay (i.e. the messages are guaranteed to reach eventually). To model this, $\mathcal{A}_t$ is given the power to schedule the delivery of *all* messages in the network. However, $\mathcal{A}_t$ can *only schedule* the messages communicated between honest parties, without having any access to them.

In asynchronous network, the inherent difficulty in designing a protocol comes from the fact that when a party does not receive an expected message then he cannot decide whether the sender is corrupted (and did not send the message at all) or the message is just delayed. So a party can not wait to consider the values sent by all parties, as waiting for all of them could turn out to be endless. Hence the values of up to t (potentially honest) parties may have to be ignored. Due to this the protocols in asynchronous network are generally involved in nature and require new set of primitives and techniques. For comprehensive introduction to asynchronous protocols and network, see [7].

1.2   Definitions

We now formally define A-cast and its variant.

Definition 1 (A-cast [7]). *Let Π be a protocol executed among the set of parties $\mathcal{P}$ and initiated by a special party caller sender $S \in \mathcal{P}$, having input m (the message to be sent). Π is an A-cast protocol tolerating $\mathcal{A}_t$ if the following hold, for every behavior of $\mathcal{A}_t$ and every input m:*

1. **Termination:**
   (a) If S is honest, then all honest parties in $\mathcal{P}$ will eventually terminate Π;
   (b) If any honest party terminates Π, then all honest parties will eventually terminate Π.
2. **Correctness:**
   (a) If the honest parties terminate Π, then they do so with a common output m^*;
   (b) Furthermore, if the sender S is honest then $m^* = m$.

We now define (ϵ, δ)-A-cast protocol, where both ϵ and δ are negligibly small values and are called as error probabilities of the A-cast protocol.

Definition 2 ((ϵ, δ)-A-cast). *An A-cast protocol Π is called (ϵ, δ)-A-cast protocol if :*

1. *Π satisfies **Termination** described in Definition 1, except with an error probability of ϵ and*
2. *Conditioned on the event that every honest party terminates Π, Π satisfies **Correctness** property described in Definition 1, except with error probability δ.*

Both A-cast and (ϵ, δ)-A-cast can be executed for long messages. A-cast and (ϵ, δ)-A-cast for long messages are referred as *multi-valued* A-cast and *multi-valued* (ϵ, δ)-A-cast respectively.

Now we discuss about what we mean by negligible and how we bound the error probabilities of a protocol by some desired negligibly small values. The discussion is presented for ϵ and it will hold for δ without any modification.

By negligible it means that ϵ is exponentially small in n i.e $\epsilon \leq \frac{1}{2^n}$ or $\epsilon \leq \frac{1}{2^{\alpha n}}$ for some integer α greater than or equal to one. Now to bound the error probability of a protocol by some desired value of ϵ, we have to choose an appropriate finite field over which all the computations of the protocol should be carried out. We say that the protocol should operate on finite Galois field $\mathbb{F} = GF(2^\kappa)$ where the κ has to be chosen based on the desired value for ϵ and the relation between ϵ and κ. Here κ is called as the error parameter. The working of a protocol will decide the relationship between κ and ϵ. Now since any (ϵ, δ)-A-cast protocol has two error probabilities, we will get two values of κ: (a) one value of κ will be obtained from the desired value for ϵ and the relation between ϵ and κ (b) the other value of κ will be obtained from the desired value for δ and the relation between δ and κ. Then we take the maximum of the two values of κ as the final value for κ. The final value for κ will consequently determine the field $\mathbb{F}$ over which the protocol should work to bound the error probabilities of the protocol by desired values of ϵ and δ. Lastly, from $\epsilon \leq \frac{1}{2^{\alpha n}}$, we may conclude that $n = \mathcal{O}(\log \frac{1}{\epsilon})$. Similarly, we will have $n = \mathcal{O}(\log \frac{1}{\delta})$

1.3 The History of A-cast

The only known protocol for A-cast is due to Bracha [5] and the protocol is a $(0, 0)$-A-cast protocol. The $(0, 0)$-A-cast protocol of [5] is *optimally resilient* (i.e designed with $n \geq 3t + 1$) and it requires a communication complexity of $\mathcal{O}(n^2)$ bits to A-cast a *single bit* message in constant running time. To the best of our knowledge, there is no (ϵ, δ)-A-cast protocol for non-zero ϵ and/or δ.

1.4 Multi-valued A-cast

A-cast is one of the most important primitives in asynchronous distributed computing. However, in real-life applications typically A-cast protocols are invoked on *long messages* (whose size can be in gigabytes) rather than on single bit. Even in asynchronous MPC (AMPC) [4], where typically lot of A-cast invocations are required, many of the invocations can be parallelized and optimized to a single invocation with a long message. Hence A-cast protocols with long message, called *multi-valued* A-cast, are very relevant to many real life situations. The existing protocol for A-cast [5] is designed for single bit message. A naive approach to design multi-valued A-cast for $\ell > 1$ bit message is to parallelize ℓ invocations of existing A-cast protocol dealing with single bit. This approach requires a communication complexity that is ℓ times the communication complexity of the existing protocols for single bit and hence is not very efficient.

In synchronous network, researchers have tried to design multi-valued BC protocol by making use of existing BC protocol for small message, as a black-box. Turpin and Coan [19] are the first to report a multi-valued BC protocol based on the access to a BC protocol for short message (a brief description of how the reduction works can be found in [14,13]). Recently, following the same approach, Fitzi et al. [14] have designed *communication optimal* BC protocols for large message. While all existing synchronous BC protocols required a communication cost of $\Omega(\ell n^2)$ bits, the BC protocols of [14] require a communication complexity of $\mathcal{O}(\ell n + poly(n, \kappa))$ bits for an ℓ bit message. For a sufficiently large ℓ, the communication complexity expression reduces to $\mathcal{O}(n\ell)$, which is a clear improvement over $\Omega(\ell n^2)$. Moreover, in [14] the authors have shown that their BC protocols are *communication optimal* for large ℓ. However, the BC protocol of [14] involve a negligible error probability of $2^{-\Omega(\kappa)}$ in **Correctness**.

Designing *communication optimal* multi-valued A-cast protocols for large message based on the application of existing A-cast protocols for smaller message was left as an interesting open question in [14].

1.5   Our Contribution

In this paper, we solve the open question posed in [14], by designing communication optimal, optimally resilient, multi-valued A-cast protocol for long message, using the existing A-cast protocol for short message as black-box. To the best of our knowledge, ours is the first ever attempt to design multi-valued A-cast protocol. In summary, our contribution is: A *communication optimal* (ϵ, δ)-A-cast protocol with $n = 3t + 1$ that requires a communication complexity of $\mathcal{O}(\ell n + n^4 \log n + n^3 \kappa)$ bits for an ℓ bit message. Our A-cast protocol uses the existing A-cast protocol of [5] as a black box for smaller size message. For sufficiently large ℓ (i.e., $\ell = \omega(n^2(n \log n + \kappa)))$, the communication complexity of our protocol is $\mathcal{O}(\ell n)$ bits, which is strictly better than the only known A-cast protocol of [5] in terms of communication complexity.

In [14], it is shown that any BC protocol in synchronous networks with $t \in \Omega(n)$, requires a communication complexity of $\Omega(n\ell)$ bits for an ℓ bit message. Obviously, this lower bound holds for asynchronous networks as well. Now it is easy to see that our protocols for A-cast is *communication optimal* for any $\ell = \omega(n^2(n \log n + \kappa))$.

To bound the error probability of **Termination** by ϵ and **Correctness** by δ, our protocols for A-cast works over a finite Galois field $\mathbb{F}$ with $\mathbb{F} = GF(2^\kappa)$, where κ has to be determined using the relations $\epsilon \geq \frac{n\ell 2^{-\kappa}}{\kappa}$ and $\delta \geq \frac{n^2 \ell 2^{-\kappa}}{\kappa}$. We assume that $\ell = poly(\kappa, n)$. Now any field element from field $\mathbb{F}$ can be represented by κ bits. In order to bound the error probability of our A-cast protocol by some specific values of ϵ and δ, we find out the *minimum* value of κ that satisfies $\epsilon \geq \frac{n\ell 2^{-\kappa}}{\kappa}$ and the *minimum* value of κ that satisfies $\delta \geq \frac{n^2 \ell 2^{-\kappa}}{\kappa}$. Then we take the maximum of the two values of κ as the final value for κ. The final value for κ will consequently determine the field $\mathbb{F}$ over which the protocol should work.

1.6   The Road-Map

Section 2 presents our (ϵ, δ)-A-cast protocol. Inside section 2, we present the tools that are used to design our A-cast protocol. Finally, we conclude this paper with concluding remarks and open problems in section 3.

2   Communication Optimal (ϵ, δ)-**A-cast** Protocol

Here we present our (ϵ, δ)-A-cast protocol with $n = 3t + 1$, called Optimal-A-cast. The protocol allows a party $S \in \mathcal{P}$ to identically send his message $m \in \{0, 1\}^\ell$, to every (honest) party in $\mathcal{P}$. Now before presenting our protocol, we briefly describe existing tools used in it.

2.1   Tools Used

Bracha's A-cast Protocol: Here, we recall Bracha's $(0,0)$-A-cast protocol from [7] and present it in Fig. 1. The current description of the protocol is taken from [7]. For convenience, we denote the protocol of [5] as Bracha-A-cast$(S, \mathcal{P}, M)$, where M is the message that the sender S wants to send and $|M| \geq 1$ (in bits).

Bracha-A-cast$(S, \mathcal{P}, M)$

Code for the sender S (with input M): only S executes this code

1. Send message (MSG, M) privately to all the parties.

Code for party P_i: every party in $\mathcal{P}$ executes this code

1. Upon receiving a message (MSG, M), send $(ECHO, M)$ privately to all parties.
2. Upon receiving $n - t$ messages $(ECHO, M')$ that agree on the value of M', send $(READY, M')$ privately to all the parties.
3. Upon receiving $t + 1$ messages $(READY, M')$ that agree on the value of M', send $(READY, M')$ privately to all the parties.
4. Upon receiving $n - t$ messages $(READY, M')$ that agree on the value of M', send (OK, M') privately to all the parties, accept M' as the output message and terminate the protocol.

Fig. 1. Bracha's A-cast Protocol with $n = 3t + 1$

Theorem 1 ([7]). *Protocol* Bracha-A-cast *privately communicates* $\mathcal{O}(|M|n^2)$ *bits to A-cast an* $|M|$ *bit message.*

Notation 1 (Notation for Using Bracha's A-cast) *In the rest of the paper, we use the following convention: By saying that 'P_i* Bracha-A-casts M', *we mean that P_i as a sender, initiates* Bracha-A-cast$(P_i, \mathcal{P}, M)$. *Then by saying that 'P_j receives M from the* Bracha-A-cast *of P_i', we mean that P_j terminates the execution of* Bracha-A-cast$(P_i, \mathcal{P}, M)$, *with M as the output.*

Hash Function: A *keyed* hash function $\mathcal{U}_\kappa$ maps arbitrary strings in $\{0,1\}^*$ to κ bit string with the help of a κ bit random key. So $\mathcal{U}_\kappa : \{0,1\}^* \to \{0,1\}^\kappa$. The function $\mathcal{U}_\kappa$ can be implemented as follows: Let m and r be the input to $\mathcal{U}_\kappa$, where m is a ℓ bit string that need to be hashed/mapped and r is the hash key selected from $\mathbb{F}$. Without loss of generality, we assume that $\ell = \text{poly}(\kappa)$. Then m is interpreted as a polynomial $f_m(x)$ over $\mathbb{F}$, where the degree of $f_m(x)$ is $\lceil \ell/\kappa \rceil - 1$. For this, m is divided into blocks of κ bits and each block of κ bits is interpreted as an element from $\mathbb{F}$. Then these field elements are considered as the coefficients of $f_m(x)$ over $\mathbb{F}$. Finally, $\mathcal{U}_\kappa(m, r) = f_m(r)$. It is easy to see that $f_m(r)$ belongs to $\mathbb{F}$.

Theorem 2 (Collision Theorem [14]). *Let m_1 and m_2 be two different ℓ bit messages. Then the probability that $\mathcal{U}_\kappa(m_1, r) = \mathcal{U}_\kappa(m_2, r)$ for a randomly chosen hash key r is $\frac{\ell 2^{-\kappa}}{\kappa}$ (which is $\leq \frac{\epsilon}{n}$ OR $\leq \frac{\delta}{n^2}$).*

Proof: Assume that m_1 and m_2 are represented by polynomials $f_1(x)$ and $f_2(x)$ respectively, each having degree $\lceil \ell/\kappa \rceil - 1$. Now $\mathcal{U}_\kappa(m_1, r) = \mathcal{U}_\kappa(m_2, r)$ implies that $f_1(r) = f_2(r)$ holds for random r. We now compute the error probability with which the above event i.e $f_1(r) = f_2(r)$ may happen. First, we note that polynomials $f_1(x)$ and $f_2(x)$ may intersect each other (i.e they evaluate to the same value) in at most $\lceil \ell/\kappa \rceil - 1$ values which is same as the degree of the polynomials. Now if the randomly selected r happens to be one among these $\lceil \ell/\kappa \rceil - 1$ values, then the event $f_1(r) = f_2(r)$ and consequently $\mathcal{U}_\kappa(m_1, r) = \mathcal{U}_\kappa(m_2, r)$ will hold. But the event that r is one among these $\lceil \ell/\kappa \rceil - 1$ values can happen with error probability $(\lceil \ell/\kappa \rceil - 1) \frac{1}{|\mathbb{F}|} \approx \frac{\ell 2^{-\kappa}}{\kappa}$ (which is $\leq \frac{\epsilon}{n}$ OR $\leq \frac{\delta}{n^2}$). Hence the theorem. $\square$

Finding (n, t)-star Structure in a Graph: We now describe an existing solution for a graph theoretic problem, called finding (n, t)-star in an undirected graph $G = (V, E)$.

Definition 3 ((n, t)-star[7,2]). *Let G be an undirected graph with the n parties in $\mathcal{P}$ as its vertex set. We say that a pair $(\mathcal{C}, \mathcal{D})$ of sets with $\mathcal{C} \subseteq \mathcal{D} \subseteq \mathcal{P}$ is an (n, t)-star in G, if: (i) $|\mathcal{C}| \geq n - 2t$; (ii) $|\mathcal{D}| \geq n - t$; (iii) for every $P_j \in \mathcal{C}$ and every $P_k \in \mathcal{D}$ the edge (P_j, P_k) exists in G.*

Following an idea of [15], Ben-Or et. al. [2] have presented an elegant and efficient algorithm for finding a (n, t)-star in a graph of n nodes, *provided that the graph contains a clique of size $n - t$*. The algorithm, called Find-STAR outputs either a (n, t)-star or the message star-Not-Found. Whenever, the input graph contains a clique of size $n - t$, Find-STAR will always output a (n, t)-star in the graph. Actually, algorithm Find-STAR takes the complementary graph $\overline{G}$ of G as input and tries to find (n, t)-$\overline{\text{star}}$ in $\overline{G}$, where (n, t)-$\overline{\text{star}}$ is a pair $(\mathcal{C}, \mathcal{D})$ of sets with $\mathcal{C} \subseteq \mathcal{D} \subseteq \mathcal{P}$, satisfying the following conditions: (a) $|\mathcal{C}| \geq n - 2t$; (b) $|\mathcal{D}| \geq n - t$; (c) There are no edges between the nodes in $\mathcal{C}$ and nodes in $\mathcal{C} \cup \mathcal{D}$ in $\overline{G}$. Clearly, a pair $(\mathcal{C}, \mathcal{D})$ representing an (n, t)-$\overline{\text{star}}$ in $\overline{G}$, is an (n, t)-star in G. Recasting the task of Find-STAR in terms of complementary graph $\overline{G}$, we say that Find-STAR outputs either a (n, t)-$\overline{\text{star}}$, or a message star-Not-Found. Whenever, *the input graph $\overline{G}$ contains an independent set of size $n - t$*, Find-STAR always outputs an (n, t)-$\overline{\text{star}}$. For simple notation, we denote $\overline{G}$ by H. The algorithm Find-STAR is presented in Fig. 2 and its properties are mentioned in the sequel for ready access.

Lemma 1 ([7]). *If Find-STAR outputs $(\mathcal{C}, \mathcal{D})$ on input graph H, then $(\mathcal{C}, \mathcal{D})$ is an (n, t)-$\overline{\text{star}}$ in H.*

Lemma 2 ([7]). *Let H be a graph with $\mathcal{P}$ as its vertex set, containing an independent set of size $n - t$. Then algorithm Find-STAR always outputs an (n, t)-$\overline{\text{star}}$, say $(\mathcal{C}, \mathcal{D})$, in H.*

Algorithm Find-STAR(H)

1. Find a maximum matching M in H. Let N be the set of matched nodes (namely, the endpoints of the edges in M), and let $\overline{N} = \mathcal{P} \setminus N$.
2. Compute output as follows (which could be either (n,t)-$\overline{\text{star}}$ or a message star-Not-Found):
   (a) Let $T = \{P_i \in \overline{N} | \exists P_j, P_k \text{ s.t } (P_j, P_k) \in M \text{ and } (P_i, P_j), (P_i, P_k) \in E\}$. T is called the set of triangle-heads.
   (b) Let $\mathcal{C} = \overline{N} \setminus T$.
   (c) Let B be the set of matched nodes that have neighbors in $\mathcal{C}$. So $B = \{P_j \in N | \exists P_i \in \mathcal{C} \text{ s. t. } (P_i, P_j) \in E\}$.
   (d) Let $\mathcal{D} = \mathcal{P} \setminus B$. If $|\mathcal{C}| \geq n - 2t$ and $|\mathcal{D}| \geq n - t$, output $(\mathcal{C}, \mathcal{D})$. Otherwise, output star-Not-Found.

Fig. 2. Algorithm For Finding (n,t)-star

Lemma 3 ([7]). *The computational complexity of Algorithm Find-STAR is polynomial.*

2.2   Protocol Optimal-A-cast

We now present our (ϵ, δ)-A-cast protocol called Optimal-A-cast. Protocol Optimal-A-cast consists of the following three phases:

1. **Distribution Phase:** Here S sends the message to all the parties in $\mathcal{P}$.
2. **Verification & Agreement on CORE Phase:** Here the parties jointly perform some computation in order to verify the consistency of the messages received from S. In case of successful verification, the honest parties agree on a set of at least $n - t = 2t + 1$ parties called $CORE$, such that *the honest parties in $CORE$ have received same message from S with very high probability.*
3. **Output Phase:** Here the (honest) parties in $CORE$ propagate the common message held by them (which they have received from S) to all other (honest) parties in $\mathcal{P} \setminus CORE$.

Informal Description of First Two Phases: Informally, in **Distribution Phase**, S sends his message m to every party in $\mathcal{P}$. In **Verification & Agreement on CORE Phase**, party P_i on receiving a message, say m_i from S, computes n hash values of m_i corresponding to n *distinct random hash keys*, say $r_{i1}, \ldots, r_{in}$ chosen from $\mathbb{F}$. To enable P_j to check whether P_j's received message m_j is same as P_i's received message m_i, party P_i privately sends r_{ij} and $\mathcal{V}_{ij} = \mathcal{U}_\kappa(m_i, r_{ij})$ to P_j. Party P_j, on receiving these values from P_i, checks whether $\mathcal{V}_{ij} = \mathcal{U}_\kappa(m_j, r_{ij})$ (for honest S and P_i, it should hold). P_j Bracha-A-casts a confirmation signal $\text{OK}(P_j, P_i)$ if the above check passes. Now based on the confirmation signals, a graph with the parties in $\mathcal{P}$ as vertex set is formed and applying Find-STAR on the graph, an (n,t)-star $(\mathcal{C}, \mathcal{D})$ is obtained. The $(\mathcal{C}, \mathcal{D})$ is then agreed among all the parties and $\mathcal{D}$ component of it is taken as $CORE$.

Achieving the agreement (among the honest parties) on a common $(\mathcal{C}, \mathcal{D})$ is a bit tricky in asynchronous network. Even though the *confirmations* are Bracha-A-casted by parties, parties may end up with different versions of $(\mathcal{C}, \mathcal{D})$ while attempting to generate them locally, due to the asynchronous nature of the network. We solve this problem by asking S to first compute $(\mathcal{C}, \mathcal{D})$ after receiving enough *confirmations* and then Bracha-A-cast $(\mathcal{C}, \mathcal{D})$. After receiving $(\mathcal{C}, \mathcal{D})$ from the Bracha-A-cast of S, individual party checks if the received $(\mathcal{C}, \mathcal{D})$ is indeed a valid (n, t)-star and then sets $CORE = \mathcal{D}$. The protocols for **Distribution Phase** and **Verification & Agreement on CORE Phase** are presented in Fig. 3. Before outlining **Output Phase**, we prove Lemma 4-6.

Lemma 4. *For a pair of honest parties (P_i, P_j), if P_i Bracha-A-casts $\mathsf{OK}(P_i, P_j)$ and P_j Bracha-A-casts $\mathsf{OK}(P_j, P_i)$, then $m_i = m_j$, except with error probability of at most $\frac{\epsilon}{n}$ or $\frac{\delta}{n^2}$.*

Proof. It is easy to see that the lemma is true without any error if S is honest. So we prove the lemma when S is corrupted. Since an honest P_i Bracha-A-casted $\mathsf{OK}(P_i, P_j)$ and an honest P_j Bracha-A-casted $\mathsf{OK}(P_j, P_i)$, it must be the case that the tests $\mathcal{V}_{ji} \stackrel{?}{=} \mathcal{U}_\kappa(m_i, r_{ji})$ and $\mathcal{V}_{ij} \stackrel{?}{=} \mathcal{U}_\kappa(m_j, r_{ij})$ have passed for P_i and P_j, respectively. By **Collision Theorem** (see Theorem 2), the above statement implies that $m_i = m_j$, except with probability at most $\frac{\epsilon}{n}$ or $\frac{\delta}{n^2}$, as the hash keys r_{ij} and r_{ji} are completely random and unknown to corrupted S.   □

Lemma 5. *If S is honest, then the (honest) parties will eventually agree on CORE of size at least $2t + 1$. Moreover, if one honest party decides on CORE, then every honest party will eventually decide on same CORE even for a corrupted S.*

Proof. An honest S will send identical m to every party in $\mathcal{P}$. Hence for every pair of honest parties (P_i, P_j), P_i and P_j will eventually Bracha-A-cast $\mathsf{OK}(P_i, P_j)$ and $\mathsf{OK}(P_j, P_i)$, respectively. Hence the nodes corresponding to honest parties will eventually form a clique (independent set) of size at least $2t+1$ in G_i $(\overline{G_i})$ graphs of every honest P_i. However, it may be possible that some corrupted parties are also present in the clique. But what ever may be the case, by Lemma 2, S will eventually find an (n, t)-star $(\mathcal{C}, \mathcal{D})$ in G_S and will Bracha-A-cast the same. Now by the property of Bracha-A-cast, eventually every honest party P_i will receive $(\mathcal{C}, \mathcal{D})$ from S and also the OK signals such that $(\mathcal{C}, \mathcal{D})$ will be a valid (n, t)-star in G_i. Hence every honest party will agree on $(\mathcal{C}, \mathcal{D})$ and therefore will agree on $CORE = \mathcal{D}$ as well.

For the second part of lemma, suppose some honest party P_i has decided on a $CORE$. This implies that P_i has received $(\mathcal{C}, \mathcal{D})$ from the Bracha-A-cast of S, such that $(\mathcal{C}, \mathcal{D})$ is a valid (n, t)-star in G_i. By the property of Bracha-A-cast, the same will eventually happen for every other honest P_j, who will eventually receive $(\mathcal{C}, \mathcal{D})$ from S and the corresponding OK signals such that $(\mathcal{C}, \mathcal{D})$ becomes a valid (n, t)-star in graph G_j.   □

First two Phases of Protocol Optimal-A-cast$(S, \mathcal{P}, m, \epsilon, \delta)$

Protocol Distribution$(S, \mathcal{P}, m, \epsilon, \delta)$: Distribution Phase

Code for S: Send m to every $P_i \in \mathcal{P}$ over the private channels.

Protocol Verification$(S, \mathcal{P}, m, \epsilon, \delta)$: Verification & Agreement on CORE Phase

i. **Code for P_i**: This code will be executed by every party in $\mathcal{P}$, including S.

1. Wait to receive a message containing ℓ bits from S. Denote it by m_i.
2. Upon receiving m_i, choose n random, distinct hash keys $(r_{i1}, \ldots, r_{in})$ from $\mathbb{F}$. For $j = 1, \ldots, n$, compute $\mathcal{V}_{ij} = \mathcal{U}_\kappa(m_i, r_{ij})$ and send $(r_{ij}, \mathcal{V}_{ij})$ to party P_j.
3. Upon receiving $(r_{ji}, \mathcal{V}_{ji})$ from P_j, check whether $\mathcal{V}_{ji} \overset{?}{=} \mathcal{U}_\kappa(m_i, r_{ji})$. If yes, then Bracha-A-cast $\mathsf{OK}(P_i, P_j)$.
4. Construct an undirected graph G_i with $\mathcal{P}$ as vertex set. Add an edge (P_j, P_k) in G_i upon receiving
   (a) $\mathsf{OK}(P_k, P_j)$ from the Bracha-A-cast of P_k and
   (b) $\mathsf{OK}(P_j, P_k)$ from the Bracha-A-cast of P_j.

ii. **Code for S**: This code will be executed only by S.

1. For every new receipt of some $\mathsf{OK}(*, *)$ from some Bracha-A-cast, update G_S. If a new edge is added to G_S, then execute Find-STAR$(\overline{G_S})$ on current G_S. If this is the first time when Find-STAR$(\overline{G_S})$ returns an (n, t)-star $(\mathcal{C}, \mathcal{D})$, then stop any further computation and Bracha-A-cast $(\mathcal{C}, \mathcal{D})$. Finally assign $CORE = \mathcal{D}$ and $\overline{CORE} = \mathcal{P} \setminus CORE$. If no (n, t)-star is found so far, then wait to receive more $\mathsf{OK}(*, *)$'s and repeat the above computation until an (n, t)-star is obtained.

iii. **Code for P_i**: This code will be executed by every party in $\mathcal{P}$, including S.

1. Wait to receive $(\mathcal{C}, \mathcal{D})$ from the Bracha-A-cast of S such that $|\mathcal{C}| \geq n - 2t$ and $|\mathcal{D}| \geq n - t$.
2. After receiving $(\mathcal{C}, \mathcal{D})$, wait to receive all $\mathsf{OK}(*, *)$'s and keep updating G_i, until $(\mathcal{C}, \mathcal{D})$ becomes a valid (n, t)-star in G_i. After that, assign $CORE = \mathcal{D}$ and $\overline{CORE} = \mathcal{P} \setminus CORE$.
3. Assign $m^* = m_i$ if $P_i \in CORE$. Here m^* is the message which will be agreed upon by all the honest parties in $\mathcal{P}$ at the end of Optimal-A-cast.

Fig. 3. Protocols for First Two Phases of Optimal-A-cast: **Distribution Phase** and **Verification & Agreement on CORE Phase**

Lemma 6. *All honest parties in CORE (if it is constructed) will possess same message m^*, except with error probability at most ϵ or $\frac{\delta}{n}$. Moreover if S is honest then $m^* = m$.*

Proof: It is trivial to show that if S is honest then every honest party in $CORE$ will possess $m^* = m$. So we consider the case when S is corrupted. Recall that $CORE = \mathcal{D}$ for an (n, t)-star $(\mathcal{C}, \mathcal{D})$. By property of (n, t)-star, $|\mathcal{C}| \geq n - 2t$ which is at least $t + 1$ in our case. So there is at least one honest party in $\mathcal{C}$, say P_i. Now the honest P_i has edges with every party in $\mathcal{D}$ which implies that P_i's message m_i is equal to the message m_j of every honest P_j in $\mathcal{D}$ which in turn implies that all the honest parties in $\mathcal{D}$ or $CORE$ possess same message.

We now estimate the error probability of the above event. From Lemma 4, P_i's message m_i is identical to the message m_j of an honest party P_j in $\mathcal{D}$, except with probability at most $\frac{\epsilon}{n}$ or $\frac{\delta}{n^2}$. Therefore, P_i's message m_i is identical to the messages of all the honest parties in $\mathcal{D}$, except with probability at most $|H|\frac{\epsilon}{n}$ or $|H|\frac{\delta}{n^2}$, where H is the set of honest parties in $\mathcal{D}$. Now since $|H| \geq n - 2t = t + 1$, we have $|H|\frac{\epsilon}{n} \approx \epsilon$ and $|H|\frac{\delta}{n^2} \approx \frac{\delta}{n}$. This proves that honest parties in $\mathcal{D} = CORE$ hold common m^*, except with probability at most ϵ or $\frac{\delta}{n}$.   □

Informal Description of **Output Phase***:* Once the parties agree on $CORE$, with all honest parties in it holding some common m^*, we need to ensure that m^* propagates to all (honest) parties in $\overline{CORE} = \mathcal{P} \setminus CORE$, in order to reach agreement on m^*. This is achieved in **Output Phase** (presented in Fig. 4) with the help of the parties in $CORE$. A simple solution could be to ask each party in $CORE$ to send his m^* to all the parties in $\overline{CORE}$, who can wait to receive $t + 1$ same m^* and then accept m^* as the message. This solution will work as there are at least $t + 1$ honest parties in $CORE$. But clearly, this requires a communication complexity of $\mathcal{O}(\ell n^2)$ bits (which violates out promised bound for Optimal-A-cast). Hence, we adopt a technique proposed in [14] for designing a BA protocol in synchronous settings with $n = |\mathcal{P}| = 2t + 1$ parties. Now the technique proposed in [14] requires a set of parties, say $\mathcal{H} \subset \mathcal{P}$ such that all the honest parties in $\mathcal{H}$ hold the same message and the majority of the parties in $\mathcal{H}$ are honest. Under this condition the technique allows the set of honest parties in $\mathcal{P} \setminus \mathcal{H}$ to obtain the common message of the honest parties in $\mathcal{H}$ with a communication cost of $\mathcal{O}(\ell n)$ bits. In our context $CORE$ has all the properties of $\mathcal{H}$. Hence we adopt the technique of [14] in our context in the following way: Every $P_i \in CORE$ sets $d = t + 1$ and $c = \lceil \frac{\ell+1}{d} \rceil$ and transforms his message m^* into a polynomial $p(x)$ of degree $d - 1$ over $GF(2^c)$. Now if somehow a party $P_j \in \overline{CORE}$ receives d values on $p(x)$, then he can interpolate $p(x)$ and receive m^*. For this, party $P_i \in CORE$ sends i^{th} value on $p(x)$, namely $p_i = p(i)$ to every $P_j \in \overline{CORE}$. As the corrupted parties in $CORE$ may send wrong p_i, party P_j should be able to detect correct values. For this, every party $P_i \in CORE$ also sends hash values of $(p_1, \ldots, p_n)$ for a random hash key to every $P_j \in \overline{CORE}$. Now P_j can detect 'clean' (or correct) values with the help of the hash values and eventually P_j will receive d 'clean' values (possibly from $d = t + 1$ honest parties in $CORE$) using which he can compute m^*.

Last phase of Protocol Optimal-A-cast$(S, \mathcal{P}, m, \epsilon, \delta)$

Protocol Output$(S, \mathcal{P}, m, \epsilon, \delta)$: Output Phase

i. **Code for P_i:** Every party in $\mathcal{P}$ will execute this code.

1. If $P_i \in CORE$, do the following to help the parties in $\overline{CORE}$ to compute m^*:
   (a) Set $d = t + 1$ and $c = \lceil \frac{\ell+1}{d} \rceil$.
   (b) Interpret m^* as a polynomial $p(x)$ of degree $d - 1$ over $GF(2^c)$. For this, divide m^* into blocks of c bits and interpret each block as an element from $GF(2^c)$. These elements from $GF(2^c)$ are the coefficients of $p(x)$.
   (c) Send $p_i = p(i)$ to every $P_j \in \overline{CORE}$, where p_i is computed over $GF(2^c)$.
   (d) For every $P_j \in \overline{CORE}$, choose a random distinct hash key R_{ij} from $\mathbb{F}$ and send $(R_{ij}, \mathcal{X}_{ij1}, \ldots, \mathcal{X}_{ijn})$ to P_j, where for $k = 1, \ldots, n$, $\mathcal{X}_{ijk} = \mathcal{U}_\kappa(p_k, R_{ij})$. Here, to compute $\mathcal{X}_{ijk}$, interpret p_k as a c bit string.
   (e) Terminate this protocol with m^* as output.
2. If $P_i \in \overline{CORE}$, do the following to compute m^*:
   (a) Call p_k received from party $P_k \in CORE$ as 'clean' if there are at least $t + 1$ P_j's in $CORE$, corresponding to which $\mathcal{X}_{jik} = \mathcal{U}_\kappa(p_k, R_{ji})$ holds, where $(R_{ji}, \mathcal{X}_{ji1}, \ldots, \mathcal{X}_{jin})$ is received from $P_j \in CORE$.
   (b) Wait to receive d 'clean' p_k's and upon receiving, interpolate $d - 1$ degree polynomial $p(x)$ using those 'clean' values, interpret m^* from $p(x)$ and terminate this protocol with m^* as output.

Fig. 4. Protocol for Last Phase of Optimal-A-cast: **Output Phase**

Lemma 7. *If the parties agree on $CORE$, then every honest party in $\mathcal{P}$ will eventually terminate protocol* **Output**, *except with probability at most ϵ.*

Proof: We show that the lemma holds without any error probability when S is honest and with error probability ϵ, when S is corrupted.

1. *S is honest:* Let E_{CORE} and $E_{\overline{CORE}}$ be the events that the honest parties in $CORE$ and $\overline{CORE}$ (respectively) terminate. We show that $Prob(E_{CORE}) = Prob(E_{\overline{CORE}}) = 1$. From the steps of the protocol Output, the parties in $CORE$ will always terminate after performing the steps as mentioned in step 1(a)-1(d) of the protocol. Hence $Prob(E_{CORE}) = 1$ holds.
   To show that $Prob(E_{\overline{CORE}}) = 1$, consider an honest party P_i in $\overline{CORE}$. Clearly, P_i will terminate if it receives $d = t + 1$ 'clean' values eventually. To assert that P_i will indeed receive $d = t + 1$ 'clean' values, we first show that the value p_k received from every honest P_k in $CORE$ will be considered as 'clean' by P_i. Consequently, since there are $t + 1$ honest parties in $CORE$, P_i will eventually receive $t + 1$ 'clean' values even though the corrupted parties in $CORE$ never send any value to P_i. As the honest parties in $CORE$ have common m^*, they will generate same $p(x)$ and therefore same $p_k = p(k)$. Hence, $\mathcal{X}_{jik} = \mathcal{U}_\kappa(p_k, R_{ji})$ will hold, with respect to $(R_{ji}, \mathcal{X}_{jik})$ of every honest P_j in $CORE$. As there at least $d = t + 1$ honest parties in $CORE$,

this proves that p_k received from honest $P_k \in CORE$ will be considered as 'clean' by P_i. This proves $Prob(E_{\overline{CORE}}) = 1$.
Finally, we have

$$Prob(\text{Every honest party in } \mathcal{P} \text{ terminates}) = Prob(E_{CORE} \cap E_{\overline{CORE}})$$
$$= Prob(E_{CORE}) \cdot Prob(E_{\overline{CORE}})$$
$$= 1 \cdot 1 = 1$$

2. *S is Corrupted:* Here we show that $Prob(E_{CORE}) = 1$ and $Prob(E_{\overline{CORE}}) = (1-\epsilon)$. Consequently, we will have $Prob(\text{Every honest party in } \mathcal{P} \text{ terminates}) = 1 \cdot (1-\epsilon) = (1-\epsilon)$. As in the case of *honest S*, the parties in $CORE$ will always terminate even when S is corrupted. This asserts that $Prob(E_{CORE}) = 1$. But on the other hand, here $Prob(E_{\overline{CORE}}) = (1 - \epsilon)$. The reason is: From the previous case (i.e. when S is honest), if all the honest parties in $CORE$ holds common m^*, then $Prob(E_{\overline{CORE}}) = 1$ holds; but the parties in $CORE$ holds common m^*, except with probability ϵ (from Lemma 6). So, we have $Prob(E_{\overline{CORE}}) = Prob(\text{honest parties in } CORE \text{ hold common } m^*) \cdot Prob(E_{\overline{CORE}} \mid \text{honest parties in } CORE \text{ hold common } m^*) = (1 - \epsilon) \cdot 1 = (1 - \epsilon)$. Hence, every honest party in $\mathcal{P}$ will eventually terminate protocol Output, except with probability at most ϵ.

Hence the lemma.   □

Lemma 8. *Conditioned on the event that all the honest parties terminate Output, every honest party in $\mathcal{P}$ will output m^* in protocol Output, except with probability at most δ. Moreover, if S is honest then $m^* = m$.*

Proof. We consider the following cases, namely (a) when S is honest and (b) when S is corrupted.

- *S is honest:* Consider the following two events, E_{CORE} and $E_{\overline{CORE}}$, where E_{CORE} is the event that *all the honest parties in $CORE$ output same m^** and $E_{\overline{CORE}}$ is the event that *all the honest parties in $\overline{CORE}$ output same $m^* = m$*. We now assert that $Prob(E_{CORE}) = 1$ and $Prob(E_{\overline{CORE}}|E_{CORE}) = (1 - \delta)$.
  1. $Prob(E_{CORE}) = 1$: This follows from Lemma 6. Moreover, here $m^* = m$, where m is the message of S.
  2. $Prob(E_{\overline{CORE}}|E_{CORE}) = (1 - \delta)$: Here we show that every honest $P_i \in \overline{CORE}$ will output m^*, except with probability $\frac{\delta}{n}$. This will assert that all the honest parties in $\overline{CORE}$ will output same m^*, except with error probability $|\overline{H}|\frac{\delta}{n}$ where $\overline{H}$ is the set of honest parties in $\overline{CORE}$. As $|\overline{H}|\frac{\delta}{n}$ can be at most t, we have $|\overline{H}|\frac{\delta}{n} \approx \delta$.

     So let $P_i \in \overline{CORE}$ be an honest party. Now the p_k value of each honest $P_k \in CORE$ will be eventually considered as 'clean' value by honest P_i. This is because there are at least $t+1$ honest parties in $CORE$, who hold same m^* and therefore same $p(x)$ (and hence $p(k)$) when S is honest. So $\mathcal{X}_{jik} = \mathcal{U}_\kappa(p_k, R_{ji})$ will hold, with respect to $(R_{ji}, \mathcal{X}_{jik})$ of every honest P_j in $CORE$. A corrupted $P_k \in CORE$ may send $\overline{p_k} \neq p_k$ to P_i, but $\overline{p_k}$ will not be considered as a 'clean' value with probability at least $(1 - \frac{\delta}{n^2})$. This is because, in order to be considered as 'clean' value, $\overline{p_k}$ should satisfy $\mathcal{X}_{jik} = \mathcal{U}_\kappa(\overline{p_k}, R_{ji})$ with respect to $(R_{ji}, \mathcal{X}_{jik})$ of at least $t + 1$ P_j's from $CORE$. The test will fail with respect to an honest party from $CORE$ with probability $\frac{c2^{-\kappa}}{\kappa} \approx \frac{\delta}{n^3}$ according to **Collision Theorem** (see Theorem 2; putting $\ell = c$, where $c = \lceil \frac{l+1}{d} \rceil = \lceil \frac{l+1}{t} \rceil$). Thus though the test may pass with respect to all corrupted parties in $CORE$ (at most t), the test will fail for every honest party from $CORE$ with probability $(1 - \frac{\delta}{n^3})^{|H|}$, where H is the set of honest parties in $CORE$. Now since $|H|$ can be $\Theta(t)$, we have $(1 - \frac{\delta}{n^3})^{|H|} \approx (1 - |H| \frac{\delta}{n^3}) \approx (1 - \frac{\delta}{n^2})$. Now the probability that none of the wrong $\overline{p_k} \neq p_k$ sent by corrupted P_ks in $CORE$ will be considered as 'clean' by honest P_i is $(1 - \frac{\delta}{n^2})^{\Theta(t)} \approx (1 - \Theta(t) \frac{\delta}{n^2}) \approx (1 - \frac{\delta}{n})$ (as there can be at most $\Theta(t)$ corrupted parties in $CORE$). Hence, honest P_i will reconstruct $p(x)$ using d 'clean' values (which he is bound to get eventually), except with probability $\frac{\delta}{n}$.

It is easy to see that $m^* = m$ here.

Finally, we have

$$
\begin{aligned}
Prob(\text{Each honest party in } \mathcal{P} \text{ holds } m^*) &= Prob(E_{CORE} \cap E_{\overline{CORE}}) \\
&= Prob(E_{CORE}) \cdot Prob(E_{\overline{CORE}} | E_{CORE}) \\
&= 1 \cdot (1 - \delta) = (1 - \delta)
\end{aligned}
$$

- *S is corrupted:* Here also we consider same two events E_{CORE} and $E_{\overline{CORE}}$ and show that $Prob(E_{CORE}) = (1 - \frac{\delta}{n})$ and $Prob(E_{\overline{CORE}} | E_{CORE}) = (1 - \delta)$.
  1. $Prob(E_{CORE}) = (1 - \frac{\delta}{n})$: Follows from Lemma 6.
  2. $Prob(E_{\overline{CORE}} | E_{CORE}) = (1 - \delta)$: Follows from the case when S is honest.

So we have, $Prob(\text{ Every honest party in } \mathcal{P} \text{ holds } m^*) = (1 - \frac{\delta}{n}) \cdot (1 - \delta) \approx (1 - \delta)$.

Hence the lemma holds irrespective of when S is honest or corrupted.   □

Now our new (ϵ, δ)-A-cast protocol called Optimal-A-cast is presented in Fig. 5.

Optimal-A-cast$(S, \mathcal{P}, m, \epsilon, \delta)$

1. Execute Distribution$(S, \mathcal{P}, m, \delta, \epsilon)$;
2. Execute Verification$(S, \mathcal{P}, m, \epsilon, \delta)$;
3. Execute Output$(S, \mathcal{P}, m, \epsilon, \delta)$.
4. Terminate Optimal-A-cast after terminating Output.

Fig. 5. Protocol Optimal-A-cast: Communication Optimal A-cast protocol

We now prove the properties of protocol Optimal-A-cast.

Theorem 3. *Protocol Optimal-A-cast is a (ϵ, δ)-A-cast protocol with $\epsilon \geq \frac{n\ell 2^{-\kappa}}{\kappa}$ and $\delta \geq \frac{n^2 \ell 2^{-\kappa}}{\kappa}$.*

Proof: **Termination: Termination (a)** is asserted as follows: If S is honest then by Lemma 5 all honest parties will agree on $CORE$ eventually and by Lemma 7, every honest party in $\mathcal{P}$ will terminate eventually. Now **Termination (b)** is proved as follows: If an honest party terminates protocol Optimal-A-cast, then it implies that it has terminated Output which in turn implies it has agreed on some $CORE$. Now by Lemma 5, if some honest party agrees on some $CORE$, then every other honest party will agree on the same $CORE$ eventually. Now by Lemma 7, if every honest party agrees on $CORE$, then all the honest party will terminate Output (and thus Optimal-A-cast), except with probability ϵ.

Correctness: Completely follows from Lemma 8. $\square$

Theorem 4. *Optimal-A-cast requires a private communication of $\mathcal{O}(\ell n + n^4 + n^3 \kappa)$ bits.*

Proof: Protocol Distribution requires ℓn bits of private communication. Protocol Verification requires $\mathcal{O}(n^2 \kappa)$ bits of private communication. Protocol Verification also requires $\mathcal{O}(n^2 \log n)$ bits of Bracha-A-cast (this is because there can be at most $\mathcal{O}(n^2)$ OK signals and each of them contains identities of two parties; since the identity of every party can be represented by $\log n$ bits, each OK signal can be represented by $\mathcal{O}(\log n)$ bits) which in turn requires $\mathcal{O}(n^4 \log n)$ bits of private communication. So Verification privately communicates $\mathcal{O}(n^2 \kappa + n^4 \log n)$ bits. Protocol Output requires $\mathcal{O}(n^2 c + n^3 \kappa)$ bits of private communication. Now $\mathcal{O}(n^2 c + n^3 \kappa) = \mathcal{O}(n\ell + n^3 \kappa)$ as $c = \lceil \frac{\ell+1}{d} \rceil = \lceil \frac{\ell+1}{t+1} \rceil$ and $n = \Theta(t)$. So protocol Optimal-A-cast requires a private communication of $\mathcal{O}(\ell n + n^4 \log n + n^3 \kappa)$ bits. $\square$

3 Conclusion and Open Problems

In this paper, we present a communication optimal, optimally resilient A-cast protocol for sufficiently long message. Designing communication optimal A-cast protocol for all values of ℓ is left as an interesting open question.

Acknowledgement. We would like to thank Ashish Choudhury for several helpful discussions.

References

1. Ben-Or, M.: Another Advantage of Free Choice: Completely Asynchronous Agreement Protocols. In: PODC, pp. 27–30. ACM Press, New York (1983)
2. Ben-Or, M., Canetti, R., Goldreich, O.: Asynchronous Secure Computation. In: STOC, pp. 52–61. ACM Press, New York (1993)

3. Ben-Or, M., Goldwasser, S., Wigderson, A.: Completeness Theorems for Non-Cryptographic Fault-Tolerant Distributed Computation (Extended Abstract). In: STOC, pp. 1–10. ACM Press, New York (1988)

4. BenOr, M., Kelmer, B., Rabin, T.: Asynchronous Secure Computations with Optimal Resilience. In: PODC, pp. 183–192. ACM Press, New York (1994)

5. Bracha, G.: An Asynchronous $\lfloor(n-1)/3\rfloor$-resilient Consensus Protocol. In: PODC, pp. 154–162. ACM Press, New York (1984)

6. Bracha, G., Toueg, S.: Asynchronous Consensus and Broadcast Protocols. J. ACM 32(4), 824–840 (1985)

7. Canetti, R.: Studies in Secure Multiparty Computation and Applications. PhD thesis, Weizmann Institute, Israel (1995)

8. Chaum, D., Crpeau, C., Damgård, I.: Multiparty Unconditionally Secure Protocols (Extended Abstract). In: STOC, pp. 11–19. ACM Press, New York (1988)

9. Chor, B., Goldwasser, S., Micali, S., Awerbuch, B.: Verifiable Secret Sharing and Achieving Simultaneity in the Presence of Faults (Extended Abstract). In: STOC, pp. 383–395. ACM Press, New York (1985)

10. Cramer, R., Damgård, I., Dziembowski, S., Hirt, M., Rabin, T.: Efficient Multiparty Computations Secure Against an Adaptive Adversary. In: Stern, J. (ed.) EUROCRYPT 1999. LNCS, vol. 1592, pp. 311–326. Springer, Heidelberg (1999)

11. Dolev, D., Dwork, C., Waarts, O., Yung, M.: Perfectly Secure Message Transmission. JACM 40(1), 17–47 (1993)

12. Fischer, M.J.: The Consensus Problem in Unreliable Distributed Systems (A Brief Survey). In: FCT, pp. 127–140 (1983)

13. Fitzi, M.: Generalized Communication and Security Models in Byzantine Agreement. PhD thesis, ETH Zurich (2002)

14. Fitzi, M., Hirt, M.: Optimally Efficient Multi-valued Byzantine Agreement. In: PODC, pp. 163–168. ACM Press, New York (2006)

15. Garey, M.R., Johnson, D.S.: Computers and Intractability: A Guide to the Theory of NP-Completeness. W.H. Freeman, New York (1979)

16. Lynch, N.A.: Distributed Algorithms. Morgan Kaufmann, San Francisco (1996)

17. Pease, M., Shostak, R.E., Lamport, L.: Reaching Agreement in the Presence of Faults. JACM 27(2), 228–234 (1980)

18. Rabin, M.O.: Randomized Byzantine Generals. In: FOCS, pp. 403–409. IEEE Computer Society Press, Los Alamitos (1983)

19. Turpin, R., Coan, B.A.: Extending Binary Byzantine Agreement to Multivalued Byzantine Agreement. Information Processing Letters 18(2), 73–76 (1984)

On the Impossibility of Batch Update
for Cryptographic Accumulators

Philippe Camacho and Alejandro Hevia

Dept. of Computer Science, University of Chile,
Blanco Encalada 2120, 3er piso, Santiago, Chile
{pcamacho,ahevia}@dcc.uchile.cl

Abstract. A cryptographic accumulator is a scheme where a set of elements is represented by a single short value. This value, along with another value called witness, allows to prove membership into the set. If new values are added or existent values are deleted from the accumulator, then the accumulated value changes and the witnesses need to be updated. In their survey on accumulators [6], Fazio and Nicolosi noted that Camenisch and Lysyanskaya's construction [3] was such that the time to update a witness after m changes to the accumulated value was proportional to m. They posed the question whether *batch update* was possible, namely if a cryptographic accumulator where the time to update witnesses is independent from the number of changes in the accumulated set exists. Recently, Wang et al. answered positively by giving a construction for an accumulator with *batch update* [9,10]. In this work, we show that the construction is not secure by exhibiting an attack. Moreover, we prove it cannot be fixed. If the accumulated value has been updated m times then the time to update a witness must be at least $\Omega(m)$ in the worst case.

Keywords: cryptographic accumulators, batch update.

1   Introduction

An accumulator is a scheme that hashes elements of a set X into a single, short size value called the *accumulated value*. Then it is possible to prove membership into X of an element x using a verification algorithm that takes as input the accumulated value, the element x, and some value called *witness*. The first construction of such scheme is due to Benaloh and De Mare [2]. Several improvements later followed, including the work of Camenisch and Lysyanskaya [3] who showed how to build dynamic accumulators (where the accumulated set can evolve), and how to use them as a tool to efficiently implement anonymous credentials. In their survey on accumulators [6], Fazio and Nicolosi pointed out that, in Camenisch and Lysyanskaya's construction, the time to recompute the witnesses once the accumulated set has been modified was proportional to m, the number of changes of the accumulated set. This raised a natural question:
"Is it possible to construct dynamic accumulators in which the update of several witnesses can be performed in constant (independently of m) time?"

M. Abdalla and P.S.L.M. Barreto (Eds.): LATINCRYPT 2010, LNCS 6212, pp. 178–188, 2010.
© Springer-Verlag Berlin Heidelberg 2010

Wang et al. [9,10] answered positively this question by showing a construction that allows *batch update*. Unfortunately, we show that this construction is not secure. Moreover, we prove that there is no way to fix Wang et al.'s accumulator by giving a lower bound of $\Omega(m)$ in the time required to update witnesses after m updates.

RELATED WORK. The first construction for cryptographic accumulators with *batch update* was given in [9] and later revised in [10]. The existence of accumulators with *batch update* seems to have been taken for granted, and in fact assumed to exist in subsequent work. Damgård and Triandopoulos [5] cite their availability as an example of an accumulator construction based on the Paillier cryptosystem. Camenisch et al. [4] also mentioned Wang et al.'s accumulator and claim to support *batch update*. If we consider strictly Fazio and Nicolosi's definition however, this is not the case, as the witness update algorithm in [4] performs a number of operations proportional to the combined size of the set of added elements and removed elements.

We remark that our impossibility result also apply to any batch update variant of the accumulator schemes proposed in [5,7], which allow both membership and non-membership proofs.

ORGANIZATION OF THE PAPER. First, in Section 2, we briefly recall the notion of a dynamic accumulator, and Section 3 we outline Wang et al.'s construction [9,10]. Our attack is described next in Section 4. The general impossibility result is then presented in Section 5. Finally, we conclude in section 6.

2 Dynamic Accumulators

In this section, we briefly review the notion of dynamic accumulators.

SYNTAX. Accumulator schemes consider two types of participants: a *manager* who initializes the parameters, and computes the accumulated value as well as the witnesses; and *users*, whose role is to verify the membership of elements in the (accumulated) set and possibly ask the *manager* to insert/delete elements in the set.

Definition 1. *[3] Let $k \in \mathbb{N}$ be the security parameter. An accumulator scheme $\mathfrak{Acc}$ consists of the following algorithms.*

- KeyGen(1^k): *This probabilistic algorithm takes k in unary as input and returns a pair of public and private keys (PK, SK), and the initial accumulated value for the empty set $Acc_\emptyset$.*
- AccVal($X, Acc_\emptyset, PK, [SK]$): *Given a finite set of elements X (of at most polynomial size in k), a public key, and the initial accumulated value $Acc_\emptyset$, this algorithm returns the accumulated value Acc_X corresponding to the set X. Depending on the implementation, the secret key SK may also be given as optional parameter, often to improve the efficiency[1].*

---

[1] The secret key may also be an optional parameter in the algorithms WitGen, AddEle, DelEle, and UpdWitGen.

- Verify(x, w, Acc_X, PK): *Given an element x, a witness w, an accumulated value Acc_X, and a public key PK, this deterministic algorithm returns* Yes *if the verification is successful, meaning that $x \in X$, or $\perp$ otherwise. This algorithm is run by a* user.
- WitGen$(x, Acc_X, PK, [SK])$: *This algorithm returns a witness w associated to the element x of the set X represented by Acc_X.*
- AddEle$(x, Acc_X, PK, [SK])$: *This algorithm computes the new accumulated value $Acc_{X \cup \{x\}}$ obtained after the insertion of x into set X.*
- DelEle$(x, Acc_X, PK, [SK])$: *This algorithm computes the new accumulated value $Acc_{X \setminus \{x\}}$ obtained by removing the element x from the accumulated set X.*
- UpdWitGen$(X, X', PK, [SK])$: *Suppose the set X is transformed into the set X' after several updates (insertions/deletions). The algorithm UpdWitGen returns the information $Upd_{X,X'}$ required to update all the witnesses (using the algorithm UpdWit) of the elements of X that are still in X'. This algorithm is run by the* manager.
- UpdWit$(w_x, Acc_X, Acc_{X'}, Upd_{X,X'}, PK)$: *This algorithm recomputes the witness w_x for some element x that remains in the set X'. It takes as parameters an existent witness w_x with respect to set X (represented by the accumulated value Acc_X), some update information $Upd_{X,X'}$, and the public key PK. It returns a new witness w'_x for the element x with respect to the new set X' represented by some accumulated value $Acc_{X'}$. This algorithm is run by the* user.

The above definition is slightly more general than the one proposed by Camenisch and Lysyanskaya [3] as it does not depend on how these algorithms are implemented, and it explicitly includes the update algorithms UpdWit and UpdWitGen in the syntax.

CORRECTNESS. The correctness property of an accumulator scheme simply says that if an element x belongs to the accumulated set X and if the corresponding witness w has been computed using WitGen or UpdWitGen, UpdWit then the verification process should pass. Although the notion of correctness for accumulators with *batch update* was informally used before, it appears it has not been formalized until now. If $\mathsf{Alg}(\cdot)$ is a possibly probabilistic algorithm, and a a parameter, let $\{\mathsf{Alg}(a)\}$ be the set of all possible values output by running algorithm Alg with argument a.

Definition 2. *(Correctness) Let X, Y be sets, Acc_X, Acc_Y their respective associated accumulated values, PK a public key, SK the corresponding private key, and $y \in X \bigcap Y$. Let w_y a value (witness) that satisfies either*

- $w_y \in \{\mathsf{WitGen}(y, Acc_Y, PK, SK)\}$, *or*
- $w_y \in \{\mathsf{UpdWit}(w'_y, Acc_X, Acc_Y, Upd_{X,Y}, PK)\}$ *where w'_y is witness of y with respect to Acc_X, and $Upd_{X,Y} \in \{\mathsf{UpdWitGen}(X, Y, PK, SK)\}$.*

We say that an accumulator scheme $\mathfrak{Acc}$ is correct if and only if for every such y, w_y, X, and Y, it holds that Verify$(y, w_y, Acc_Y, PK) =$ Yes.

SECURITY. The security of an accumulator scheme is captured by an experiment where the adversary plays the role of a *user* and attempts to forge a witness (i.e. finding a valid witness for an element that does not belong to the set) while having access to an oracle that implements the operations relative to the *manager*. Such adversary must succeed with at most negligible probability on the security parameter. The definition proposed in [9] is built on the one of [3] and includes the new algorithms AddEle,DelEle (for sets) and UpdWit that are run by the oracle (*manager*).

Definition 3. *([3,9]) Let $\mathfrak{Acc}$ be an accumulator scheme. We consider the notion of security denoted $\mathcal{UF}\text{-}\mathcal{ACC}$ described by the following experiment: on input the security parameter k, the adversary $\mathcal{A}$ has access to an oracle $\mathcal{O}(\cdot)$ that replies to queries by playing the role of the accumulator manager. Using the oracle, the adversary can insert and delete a polynomial number of elements of his choice. The oracle $\mathcal{O}(\cdot)$ replies with the new accumulated value. The adversary can also ask for witness computations or update information. Finally, the adversary is required to output a pair (x, w). The advantage of the adversary $\mathcal{A}$ is defined by:*

$$Adv^{\mathcal{UF}\text{-}\mathcal{ACC}}_{\mathfrak{Acc}}(\mathcal{A}) = \Pr\left[\,\mathsf{Verify}(x, w, Acc_X, PK) = \mathsf{Yes} \wedge x \notin X\,\right]$$

where PK is the public key generated by KeyGen, and Acc_X is the accumulated value of the resulting accumulated set X. The scheme $\mathfrak{Acc}$ is said to be secure if for every probabilistic polynomial time adversary $\mathcal{A}$ we have

$$Adv^{\mathcal{UF}\text{-}\mathcal{ACC}}_{\mathfrak{Acc}}(\mathcal{A}) = \mathsf{neg}(k)$$

where $\mathsf{neg} : \mathbb{N} \to \mathbb{R}^+$ is some negligible function.

BATCH UPDATE. As originally proposed [6], the *batch update* property for an accumulator scheme states that each *user* should be able to update each of its witness using the algorithm UpdWit in time independent from the number of changes (additions and deletions) to the accumulated set.

Definition 4. *(Batch update for accumulator schemes). Let $k \in \mathbb{N}$ be a security parameter and let $\mathfrak{Acc}$ be an accumulator scheme. Also, let X_i be a set of accumulated values at some time i, and $U_i \subset X_i$ be a set of elements for which some user $\mathcal{U}$ holds valid witnesses. Suppose that after $m > 0$ updates (insertions or deletions) to set X_i, the new accumulated set is X_{i+m} and the associated accumulated value is $Acc_{X_{i+m}}$. We say that $\mathfrak{Acc}$ has the batch update property if given some information $Upd_{X_i, X_{i+m}}$, user $\mathcal{U}$ running UpdWit can recompute a valid witness for any element in $U_i \bigcap X_{i+m}$ in constant time (with respect to m), or equivalently, time $\mathcal{O}(k)$.*

3   Wang et al.'s Construction

In this section, we briefly recall Wang et al.'s accumulator with *batch update* [9,10]. The first version of their work [9] suffered from two correctness problems which were later fixed [10]. Below we review the improved version [10].

SYNTAX. The algorithms of Wang et al.'s scheme slightly deviate from the general syntax of section 2 as they allow to add and delete sets of more than one element to the accumulator. Moreover the algorithms AddEle and AccVal are randomized which means that the accumulated value does not only depend on the elements of the set, contrary to the definition of Fazio and Nicolosi [6]. The general idea however remains the same. The syntax from [9] can be found in the Appendix A.1.

CONSTRUCTION. Wang et al.'s accumulator relies on the Paillier cryptosystem [8] which we recall in Appendix A.2. In the following, λ will denote the value $lcm(p-1, q-1)$ where $n = pq$ is a product of large-enough safe primes p, q, and $F : u \to \frac{u-1}{n}$ is Paillier's L function [8].

- KeyGen(1^k): Given the security parameter k in unary, compute a safe-prime product $n = pq$ that is k-bits long and create an empty set V. Let $\mathcal{C} = \mathbb{Z}_{n^2}^* \setminus \{1\}$ and $T' = \{3, ..., n^2\}$. Let $\beta \xleftarrow{R} \mathbb{Z}_{\varphi(n^2)}^*$ and $\sigma \xleftarrow{R} \mathbb{Z}^+$ be two random numbers. The public key PK is set to (n, β) and the private key SK to (σ, λ). The output is the parameter $\mathcal{P} = (PK, SK)$.
- AccVal($X, \mathcal{P}$): Given a set $X = \{c_1, ..., c_m\}$ with $X \subset \mathcal{C}$, and the parameter $\mathcal{P}$, take $c_{m+1} \xleftarrow{R} \mathcal{C}$ and compute

$$x_i = F(c_i^\lambda \bmod n^2) \bmod n \quad (\text{for } i = 1, ..., m+1)$$
$$Acc_X = \sigma \sum_{i=1}^{m+1} x_i \bmod n$$
$$y_i = c_i^{\lambda \sigma \beta^{-1}} \bmod n^2 \quad (\text{for } i = 1, ..., m+1)$$
$$a_c = \Pi_{i=1}^{m+1} y_i \bmod n^2$$

Output the accumulated value Acc_X and the auxiliary information a_c.
- WitGen($a_c, X, \mathcal{P}$): Given the auxiliary information a_c, a set $X = \{c_1, ..., c_m\}$, and the parameter $\mathcal{P}$, choose uniformly at random a set of m numbers $T = \{t_1, ..., t_m\} \subset T' \setminus \{\beta\}$ (for $i = 1, ..., m$) and compute

$$w_i = a_c c_i^{-t_i \beta^{-1}} \bmod n^2 \quad (\text{for } i = 1, ..., m)$$

Output the witness $W_i = (w_i, t_i)$ for c_i (for $i = 1, ..., m$).
- AddEle($X^\oplus, a_c, Acc_X, \mathcal{P}$): Given a set $X^\oplus = \{c_1^\oplus, ..., c_l^\oplus\}(X^\oplus \subseteq \mathcal{C} \setminus X)$, to be inserted, the auxiliary information a_c, the accumulated value Acc_X, and the parameter $\mathcal{P}$, choose $c_{l+1}^\oplus \xleftarrow{R} \mathcal{C}$ and a set of l numbers $T^\oplus = \{t_1^\oplus, ..., t_l^\oplus\} \xleftarrow{R} T' \setminus (T \cup \{\beta\})$, and compute

$$x_i^\oplus = F((c_i^\oplus)^\lambda \bmod n^2) \bmod n \quad (\text{for } i = 1, ..., l+1)$$
$$Acc_{X \cup X^\oplus} = Acc_X + \sigma \sum_{i=1}^{l+1} x_i^\oplus \bmod n$$
$$y_i^\oplus = (c_i^\oplus)^{\lambda \sigma \beta^{-1}} \bmod n^2 \quad (\text{for } i = 1, ..., l+1)$$
$$a_u = \Pi_{i=1}^{l+1} y_i^\oplus \bmod n^2$$
$$w_i^\oplus = a_c a_u (c_i^\oplus)^{-t_i^\oplus \beta^{-1}} \bmod n^2 \quad (\text{for } i = 1, ..., l)$$

Set $a_c = a_c a_u \bmod n^2$, $T = T \cup T^\oplus$, and $V = V \cup \{a_u\}$. Then output the new accumulated value $Acc_{X \cup X^\oplus}$ corresponding to the set $X \cup X^\oplus$, the witness

$W_i^\oplus = (w_i^\oplus, t_i^\oplus)$ for the new added elements $c_i^\oplus$ (for $i = 1, ..., l$), and the auxiliary information a_u and a_c.

- DelEle($X^\ominus, a_c, Acc_X, \mathcal{P}$): Given a set $X^\ominus = \{c_1^\ominus, ..., c_l^\ominus\}$ ($X^\ominus \subset X$) to be deleted, the auxiliary information a_c, the accumulated value Acc_X, and the parameter $\mathcal{P}$, choose $c_{l+1}^\ominus \xleftarrow{R} \mathcal{C}$ and compute

$$x_i^\ominus = F((c_i^\ominus)^\lambda \bmod n^2) \bmod n \ \ (\text{for } i = 1, ..., l+1)$$
$$Acc_{X \setminus X^\ominus} = Acc_X - \sigma \sum_{i=1}^{l} x_i^\ominus + \sigma x_{l+1}^\ominus \bmod n$$
$$y_i^\ominus = (c_i^\ominus)^{\lambda \sigma \beta^{-1}} \bmod n^2 \ \ (\text{for } i = 1, ..., l+1)$$
$$a_u = y_{l+1}^\ominus \Pi_{j=1}^{l} (y_j^\ominus)^{-1} \bmod n^2$$

Set $a_c = a_c a_u \bmod n^2$ and $V = V \cup \{a_u\}$. Then output the new accumulated value $Acc_{X \setminus X^\ominus}$ corresponding to the set $X \setminus X^\ominus$ and the auxiliary information a_u and a_c.

- Verify(c, W, Acc_X, PK): Given an element c, its witness $W = (w, t)$, the accumulated value Acc_X, and the public key PK, test whether $\{c, w\} \subset \mathcal{C}, t \in T'$ and $F(w^\beta c^t \bmod n^2) \equiv Acc_X (\bmod n)$. If so, output Yes, otherwise output $\perp$.

- UpdWit(W_i, a_u, PK) : Given the witness W_i, the auxiliary information a_u and the public key PK, compute $w_i' = w_i a_u \bmod n^2$ then output the new witness $W_i' = (w_i', t_i)$ for the element c_i.

In the following section we show that Wang et al.'s construction is not secure.

4   An Attack on the Accumulator with Batch Update of Wang et al.

4.1   Problems with the Proof

A security proof for the scheme was presented in the original paper[2] by Wang et al. [9]. In this work, a security reduction is presented assuming the *Extended Strong RSA assumption* (or *es-RSA*), also proposed in [9] as an analogous to the *Strong RSA assumption* [1] but relative to modulus n^2 instead of n. Unfortunately, there are two main problems in the proof. First, it states that adversary $\mathcal{B}$ must "run the KeyGen algorithm" which means it knows the factorization of the product $n = pq$, or at least has the knowledge of $\varphi(n^2)$ and $\lambda = lcm(p-1, q-1)$ since $\beta = \sigma \lambda \bmod n^2$ (see [9]). Therefore, it is not clear how the reduction to break the *es-RSA* assumption can be achieved.

The second problem is that, to break the *es-RSA* assumption, $\mathcal{B}$ needs to find non trivial values (y, s) such that $y^s = x \bmod n^2$ where x is given as input to $\mathcal{B}$. This value x does not seem to be mentioned in the proof.

---

[2] As mentioned before, the subsequent paper [10] fixes two correctness flaws in [9] but does not give a new security proof. The attack we consider however is relative to the improved version [10].

4.2   Description of the Attack

In order to show that the construction is not secure, i.e., the proof of security cannot be fixed, we present an attack. This attack considers the updated scheme [10]. The idea is simply to delete an element from the set, and then update the witness of this element with the update information obtained by the execution of the algorithm DelEle. We then observe that this new witness is a valid one for the deleted element, which of course should not happen. We start with the set $X = \{c_1\}$ for some c_1, and let $x_1 = F(c_1^\lambda \bmod n^2) \bmod n$. Then, a random element c_* is chosen and $x_* = F(c_*^\lambda \bmod n^2) \bmod n$ is computed. The accumulated value is set to $v = \sigma(x_1 + x_*) \bmod n$. The witness value $W_1 = (w_1, t_1)$ for c_1 is defined by $w_1 = a_c c_1^{-t_1 \beta^{-1}} \bmod n^2$ where $a_c = y_* y_1 \bmod n^2$, $y_1 = c_1^{\lambda \sigma \beta^{-1}} \bmod n^2$, $y_* = c_*^{\lambda \sigma \beta^{-1}} \bmod n^2$, and t_1 is random.

Then the adversary asks the manager to delete element c_1. This means that the new accumulated value is $v' = v - \sigma x_1 + \sigma(x_{**}) \bmod n = \sigma(x_* + x_{**}) \bmod n$ where $x_{**} = F(c_{**}^\lambda \bmod n^2) \bmod n$ and c_{**} is random. The auxiliary value a_u used to update the witnesses is $a_u = y_{**} y_1^{-1} \bmod n^2$ where $y_{**} = c_{**}^{\lambda \sigma \beta^{-1}} \bmod n^2$. So, by updating the witness w_1 with a_u we obtain $w_1' = a_u w_1 \bmod n^2 = y_{**} y_1^{-1} y_* y_1 c_1^{-t_1 \beta^{-1}} \bmod n^2 = y_{**} y_* c_1^{-t_1 \beta^{-1}} \bmod n^2$. Then $w_1'^\beta c_1^{t_1} \equiv (y_{**} y_* c_1^{-t_1 \beta^{-1}})^\beta c_1^{t_1} \bmod n^2 = (y_{**} y_*)^\beta \bmod n^2 = (c_{**} c_*)^{\lambda \sigma} \bmod n^2$. It follows that

$$F(w_1'^\beta c_1^{t_1} \bmod n^2) \equiv F((c_{**} c_*)^{\lambda \sigma} \bmod n^2) \bmod n$$
$$\equiv \sigma(F(c_{**}^\lambda \bmod n^2) + F(c_*^\lambda \bmod n^2)) \bmod n$$
$$\equiv \sigma(x_* + x_{**}) \bmod n$$
$$\equiv v' \bmod n$$

This shows that (w_1', t_1) is a valid witness for the deleted element x_1. Therefore the scheme is not secure. Indeed the problem is simply that the information a_u allows to update *every* old witness including w_1 for which such an update should not be possible.

5   A Lower Bound for Updating the Witnesses

The attack of the last section is an indication that the proposed construction may have some design flaws. In this section, we show that the problem indeed is more fundamental and the *batch update* property is essentially unrealizable. We argue this by presenting a lower bound on the size of $Upd_{X,X'}$, the information needed to update the witnesses after m changes (more precisely deletions). Any deterministic[3] update algorithm UpdWit must at least read $Upd_{X,X'}$, and so it also bounds the running time of any such algorithm. In the following theorem log refers to the logarithm in base two function.

---

[3] For simplicity, in the proof we focus on deterministic update (UpdWit) and verification (Verify) algorithms. This is in fact the case for the construction of [10]. We believe the result can be extended to the probabilistic case but the proof becomes more involved.

Theorem 1. *Let $\mathfrak{Acc}$ be a secure accumulator scheme with deterministic* UpdWit *and* Verify *algorithms. For an update involving m delete operations in a set of N elements, the size of the information $Upd_{X,X'}$ required by the algorithm* UpdWit *is $\Omega(m \log \frac{N}{m})$. In particular if $m = \frac{N}{2}$ we have $|Upd_{X,X'}| = \Omega(m) = \Omega(N)$.*

Proof. The idea of the proof is that the update information must encode a minimum amount of information in order for the accumulator scheme to be correct and secure. We prove this by considering a theoretical game between the accumulator manager and some user U. In the game, starting from an accumulated set X, the accumulator manager updates the accumulator in a way that is not known to user U (namely, the manager deletes some elements in an arbitrary set $X_d \subset X$) while still providing the update information $Upd_{X,X'}$ to U, where $X' = X \setminus X_d$. We prove that, as long as the scheme is correct and secure, there is a simple strategy that allows the user U to recover the exact changes made by the manager, that is, the set of deleted elements X_d. We conclude that the information provided by the manager to the user must at least encode a description of set X_d. Details follow.

Consider the following game. The set accumulated in some point of the time is $X = \{x_1, x_2, ..., x_N\}$, and the corresponding accumulated value is Acc_X. We suppose the user possesses all the witnesses for each element in X and knows the accumulated value. Then m DelEle operations are performed, that is the new set obtained is $X' = X \setminus X_d$ where $X_d = \{x_{i_1}, x_{i_2}, ..., x_{i_m}\}$. The manager computes the new accumulated value $Acc_{X'}$ and sends it to the user along with the update information $Upd_{X,X'}$ required to update all the witnesses that are still in X'.

Armed with this update information $Upd_{X,X'}$ and the new accumulated value $Acc_{X'}$, user U is able to reconstruct the set X_d of deleted elements as follows: for each element in X, the user checks if the corresponding witness can be successfully updated using algorithm UpdWit with input $Upd_{X,X'}$. More specifically, the user computes $w'_x = \mathsf{UpdWit}(w_x, Upd_{X,X'}, PK)$ and checks whether or not w'_x is a valid witness. If not, that is, if $\mathsf{Verify}(x, w'_x, Acc_{X'}, PK) = \perp$, then the element x must have been deleted from X. Note that this condition is necessary otherwise it would contradict the scheme's correctness (there would be elements in X' for which an updated witness cannot be computed) or the scheme's security (it would be possible to update witnesses for deleted elements).

Hence, the user must be able to recompute the set of deleted elements X_d only from values $Upd_{X,X'}$ and $Acc_{X'}$. We therefore conclude that $(Upd_{X,X'}, Acc_{X'})$ must contain at least the information required to encode any subset with m elements of a set containing N elements. There are $\binom{N}{m}$ such subsets, so the minimum amount of information required is $\log \binom{N}{m}$ bits. Since $\log(\binom{N}{m}) \geq m \log \frac{N}{m}$ we obtain that $|(Acc_{X'}, Upd_{X,X'})| = \Omega(m \log \frac{N}{m})$. Given that $|Acc_{X'}|$ must be sufficiently short (say, at least $\mathcal{O}(\log(N))$, as otherwise the accumulated value is not longer a "short representation" of the set, and the scheme is not really useful), we conclude that $|Upd_{X,X'}| = \Omega(m \log \frac{N}{m})$. The result then follows.

Given a the security parameter k, the above theorem says that any update algorithm must take time at least $\mathcal{O}(m) = \mathcal{O}(N) = \mathcal{O}(p(k)) = \omega(k)$ for some polynomial p, in order to *read* the input. This goes beyond $\mathcal{O}(k)$, the desired "constant time" in the number of changes. Interestingly, even if the number of *expensive operations* (say, $\mathcal{O}(k^3)$ modular exponentiations) of UpdWit were sublinear in the size of the update information $Upd_{X,X'}$, the overall complexity of the update operation would still be dominated by the time $\mathcal{O}(p(k))$ to read the update information (and the accumulated value).

Corollary 1. *Cryptographic accumulators with* batch update *(and deterministic update and verification) do not exist.*

6   Conclusion

This result shows that the *batch update* property as proposed in [6] essentially cannot be obtained, as the time to update all the witnesses cannot be linear in the security parameter k, i.e $\mathcal{O}(k)$, but it must be at least $\mathcal{O}(p(k)) = \omega(k)$ for some polynomial p. Notice that our lower bound is not tight since Camenisch and Lysyanskaya's accumulator requires $\mathcal{O}(p(k) \cdot k)$ time to update the witnesses after $\mathcal{O}(p(k))$ changes. Nonetheless, in principle, it leaves some (potential) room to improve their construction by at most a factor of k.

Finally, one may consider getting around this impossibility result by not allowing deletions in the set. Unfortunately, such an accumulator can be trivially implemented by signing the elements of the set, as in this case there is no replay-attack. The witness for every element consists in its signature under the manager's private key, and clearly needs not to be updated.

Acknowledgments

The authors wish to thank the anonymous reviewers for their helpful comments and suggestions. Alejandro Hevia gratefully acknowledges the support of CONICYT via FONDECYT No. 1070332.

References

1. Barić, N., Pfitzmann, B.: Collision-free accumulators and fail-stop signature schemes without trees. In: Fumy, W. (ed.) EUROCRYPT 1997. LNCS, vol. 1233, pp. 480–494. Springer, Heidelberg (1997)
2. Benaloh, J.C., de Mare, M.: One-way accumulators: A decentralized alternative to digital signatures. In: Helleseth, T. (ed.) EUROCRYPT 1993. LNCS, vol. 765, pp. 274–285. Springer, Heidelberg (1994)
3. Camenisch, J., Lysyanskaya, A.: Dynamic accumulators and application to efficient revocation of anonymous credentials. In: Yung, M. (ed.) CRYPTO 2002. LNCS, vol. 2442, pp. 61–76. Springer, Heidelberg (2002)
4. Camenisch, J., Kohlweiss, M., Soriente, C.: An accumulator based on bilinear maps and efficient revocation for anonymous credentials. In: Jarecki, S., Tsudik, G. (eds.) PKC 2009. LNCS, vol. 5443, pp. 481–500. Springer, Heidelberg (2009)

5. Damgård, I., Triandopoulos, N.: Supporting non-membership proofs with bilinear-map accumulators. Cryptology ePrint Archive, Report 2008/538 (2008)
6. Fazio, N., Nicolosi, A.: Cryptographic accumulators: Definitions, constructions and applications. Technical report (2002)
7. Li, J., Li, N., Xue, R.: Universal accumulators with efficient nonmembership proofs. In: Katz, J., Yung, M. (eds.) ACNS 2007. LNCS, vol. 4521, pp. 253–269. Springer, Heidelberg (2007)
8. Paillier, P.: Public-key cryptosystems based on composite degree residuosity classes. In: Stern, J. (ed.) EUROCRYPT 1999. LNCS, vol. 1592, pp. 223–238. Springer, Heidelberg (1999)
9. Wang, P., Wang, H., Pieprzyk, J.: A new dynamic accumulator for batch updates. In: Qing, S., Imai, H., Wang, G. (eds.) ICICS 2007. LNCS, vol. 4861, pp. 98–112. Springer, Heidelberg (2007)
10. Wang, P., Wang, H., Pieprzyk, J.: Improvement of a dynamic accumulator at ICICS 07 and its application in multi-user keyword-based retrieval on encrypted data. In: Proceedings of IEEE Asia-Pacific Services Computing Conference - APSCC, pp. 1381–1386 (2008)

A   Appendix

A.1   Syntax of Wang et al.'s Accumulator

Definition 5. *([9]) Let k be the security parameter. A dynamic accumulator with batch update $\mathfrak{Acc}_{\mathfrak{BU}}$ consists of the following algorithms:*

- KeyGen(1^k): *Is a probabilistic algorithm that takes as input the security parameter k in unary and returns a parameter $\mathcal{P} = (PK, SK)$ where PK is the public key and SK is the private key[4].*
- AccVal($X, \mathcal{P}$): *Is a probabilistic algorithm that computes an accumulated value. It takes as input the set $X = \{c_1, ..., c_m\}$ and the parameter $\mathcal{P}$ and returns an accumulated value Acc_X along with some auxiliary information a_c that will be used by other algorithms.*
- Verify(x, W, Acc_X, PK): *This deterministic algorithm checks whether an element x belongs to the set X represented by the accumulated value Acc_X using the witness W and the public key PK. It returns Yes whether the witness W for x is valid or $\perp$ otherwise.*
- AddEle($X^{\oplus}, a_c, Acc_X, \mathcal{P}$): *This probabilistic algorithm adds some new elements to the accumulated value. The input values are the set of new elements to add $X^{\oplus} = \{c_1^{\oplus}, ..., c_l^{\oplus}\}$, the auxiliary information a_c, the accumulated value Acc_X and the parameter $\mathcal{P}$. The returned values are $Acc_{X \cup X^{\oplus}}$ the accumulated value corresponding to the set $X \cup X^{\oplus}$, a witnesses $\{W_1^{\oplus}, ..., W_l^{\oplus}\}$ associated to the inserted elements $\{c_1^{\oplus}, ..., c_l^{\oplus}\}$, and the auxiliary information a_c, a_u, that will be used for future update operations.*

---

[4] In the original paper, the authors mention another parameter M which is an upper bound to the number of elements that can be accumulated. In order to simplify the notations, we omit it and recall that this upper bound must be a polynomial in k.

- DelEle($X^{\ominus}, a_c, Acc_X, \mathcal{P}$): *This probabilistic algorithm is analogous to* AddEle *and allows to delete a set of elements $X^{\ominus}$. The input values are the set of elements to delete $X^{\ominus} = \{c_1^{\ominus}, ..., c_l^{\ominus}\}$, the auxiliary information a_c, the accumulated value Acc_X and the parameter $\mathcal{P}$. The returned values are $Acc_{X\setminus X^{\ominus}}$ the accumulated value corresponding to the set $X \setminus X^{\ominus}$, and the auxiliary information a_c, a_u, that will be used for future update operations.*
- WitGen($a_c, X, \mathcal{P}$): *This probabilistic algorithm creates a witness for every element in the set X. It takes as input an auxiliary information a_c, the set X and the parameter $\mathcal{P}$.*
- UpdWit(W_i, a_u, PK) : *This deterministic algorithm updates witnesses for the elements accumulated Acc_X and that are still accumulated in $Acc_{X'}$ (the new set after update). The inputs are W_i, the witness to update, the auxiliary information a_u and the public key PK. It returns an updated witness W_i' that allows to prove that c_i is still accumulated in the new accumulated value $Acc_{X'}$.*

Note that in this definition UpdWitGen does not appear. The reason is that in Wang et al.'s construction, the update information required to recompute the witnesses is generated by algorithms AddEle and DelEle.

A.2   Paillier Cryptosystem

The Paillier cryptosystem [8] consists of the following three algorithms.

- KeyGen: let $n = pq$ be a RSA modulus, with p, q large prime integers. Let g an integer multiple of n modulo n^2. The public key is defined by $PK = (n, g)$ and the private key by $SK = \lambda = \lambda(n) = lcm(p - 1, q - 1)$.
- Encrypt: let $M \in \mathbb{Z}_n$ be a plaintext message and r a random element in $\mathbb{Z}_n^*$, the encrypted message is $c = g^M r^n \bmod n^2$.
- Decrypt: to recover M from ciphertext c, compute $M = \frac{F(c^\lambda \bmod n^2)}{F(g^\lambda \bmod n^2)} \bmod n$ where $F : u \rightarrow \frac{u-1}{n}$ takes as argument elements from the set $S_n = \{u < n^2 | u = 1 \bmod n\}$.

The homomorphic property of the Paillier cryptosystem follows from the fact that $\forall x, y \in S_n$ and $\sigma \in \mathbb{Z}^+$:

$$F((x.y)^\lambda \bmod n^2) \bmod n = F(x^\lambda \bmod n^2) + F(y^\lambda \bmod n^2) \bmod n$$
$$F(x^{\sigma\lambda} \bmod n^2) \bmod n = \sigma F(x^\lambda \bmod n^2) \bmod n$$

On the Round Complexity of Zero-Knowledge Proofs Based on One-Way Permutations

S. Dov Gordon[1], Hoeteck Wee[2,*], David Xiao[3,**], and Arkady Yerukhimovich[1]

[1] Dept. of Computer Science, University of Maryland, College Park MD 20742, USA
[2] Dept. of Computer Science, Queens College, CUNY, Flushing NY 11367, USA
[3] LRI, Université Paris-Sud, 91405 Orsay Cedex, France

Abstract. We consider the following problem: can we construct constant-round zero-knowledge proofs (with negligible soundness) for **NP** assuming only the existence of one-way permutations? We answer the question in the negative for fully black-box constructions (using only black-box access to both the underlying primitive and the cheating verifier) that satisfy a natural restriction on the "adaptivity" of the simulator's queries. Specifically, we show that only languages in **coAM** have constant-round zero-knowledge proofs of this kind. We also give strong evidence that we are unlikely to find fully black-box constructions of constant-round zero knowledge proofs for **NP**, even without this restriction on adaptivity.

Keywords: constant-round zero-knowledge proofs, black-box separations.

1 Introduction

A *zero-knowledge proof* is a protocol wherein one party, the prover, convinces another party, the verifier, of the validity of an assertion while revealing no additional knowledge. Introduced by Goldwasser, Micali and Rackoff in the 1980s [18], zero-knowledge proofs have played a central role in the design and study of cryptographic protocols. In these applications, the main measure of efficiency is the *round complexity* of the proof system, and it is important to construct constant-round zero-knowledge protocols for **NP** (with negligible soundness) under minimal assumptions. In many cases, a computational zero-knowledge argument system (where both the zero-knowledge and soundness guarantees hold against computationally bounded adversaries) suffices, and we know how to construct such protocols for **NP** under the minimal assumption of one-way functions [9,29]. However, in this work, we focus on computational zero-knowledge proof systems, where the soundness guarantee must hold against computationally unbounded adversaries.

---

* Part of this research was completed while a post-doc at Columbia University. Supported in part by NSF CAREER Award CNS-0953626.
** Part of this reseach was completed while a student at Princeton University.

A common intuition in constructing zero knowledge protocols (typically based on some form of commitments) is that statistical (resp. computational) soundness corresponds to using a statistically (resp. computationally) binding commitment, while statistical (resp. computational) zero knowledge corresponds to using statistically (computationally) hiding commitments. One might also expect that the round complexity of the resulting zero knowledge protocol is roughly the same as the round complexity of the underlying commitment scheme.

However, the best known construction of computational zero-knowledge proofs from one-way permutations has $\omega(1)$ rounds [16,7], and the minimal assumption from which we know how to construct constant-round computational zero-knowledge proofs for **NP** is constant-round statistically *hiding* commitments [14,35], which seem to be a stronger assumption than one-way permutations [37,21]. There are no known constructions of constant-round computational zero knowledge proofs from constant-round statistically *binding* commitments. We note that the latter may be constructed from one-way permutations [7] and one-way functions [28,24]. This raises the following intriguing open problem:

> Can we base constant-round zero-knowledge proofs for **NP** on the existence of one-way permutations?

We briefly survey what's known in this regard for constant-round black-box zero-knowledge protocols (that is, those using a black-box simulation strategy). We clarify that while we do know of non-black-box zero-knowledge protocols [2,20], these protocols are all zero-knowledge arguments and not proofs.

Unconditional Constructions. The only languages currently known to have constant-round zero-knowledge proofs from assumptions weaker than statistically hiding commitment schemes are those that admit statistical zero-knowledge proofs, which do not require any computational assumption at all. Even though this includes languages believed to be outside of **BPP** such as graph isomorphism and graph non-isomorphism [16,6], all languages with statistical zero knowledge proofs lie in **AM ∩ coAM** [1,11] (and therefore do not include all of **NP** unless the polynomial hierarchy collapses).

Lower Bounds. Goldreich and Krawczyk [15] showed that 3-round zero-knowledge protocols and public-coin constant-round zero-knowledge protocols with black-box simulators exist only for languages in **BPP**. Katz [26] showed that 4-round zero-knowledge proofs only exist for languages in **MA ∩ coMA**. Haitner et al. [21] ruled out fully black-box constructions of constant-round statistically hiding commitment schemes (in fact, any $O(n/\log n)$-round protocol) from one-way permutations, which means that we are unlikely to obtain constant-round zero-knowledge proofs from one-way permutations via the approach in [14]. More recently, Haitner et al. [23] established a partial converse to [14], namely that any constant-round zero-knowledge proof for **NP** that remains zero-knowledge under parallel composition implies the existence of constant-round statistically hiding commitments. Unlike the case for stand-alone zero-knowledge, we do not know if there exists a $\omega(1)$-round zero-knowledge proof system for **NP** that remains zero-knowledge under parallel composition, assuming only the existence of one-way permutations. Indeed, zero-knowledge under parallel composition appears to be a qualitively much stronger security guarantee than stand-alone zero-knowledge.

1.1   Our Result

In this work, we establish new barriers towards constructing zero-knowledge proof systems from one-way permutations for all of **NP**:

> **Main Theorem (informal).** Only languages in **AM** ∩ **coAM** admit a fully black-box construction of zero-knowledge proofs starting from one-way permutations where the construction relies on a black-box simulation strategy with constant adaptivity.

A fully black-box construction (c.f. [34,25]) is one that not only relies on a black-box simulation strategy, but where the protocol relies on black-box access to the underlying primitive. Adaptivity is a measure of how much the black-box simulator relies on responses from previous queries to the cheating verifier in order to generate new queries. We point out that all known constructions of black-box simulators achieve adaptivity that is linear in the round complexity of the protocol and therefore constant adaptivity is a fairly natural restriction for constant-round protocols. Apart from the restriction on adaptivity, this is essentially the best one could hope for in lieu of various positive results mentioned earlier:

- Our result only applies to constant-round protocols – running the $O(\log n)$-fold parallel repetition of Blum's Hamiltonicity protocol [7] sequentially yields a $\omega(1)$-round black-box zero-knowledge proof system for **NP**.
- Our result applies only to proofs, but not arguments – there exists a fully black-box construction of constant-round computational zero-knowledge arguments with constant adaptivity from one-way functions for all of **NP**. [10,32].
- We have unconditional constructions of constant-round statistical black-box zero-knowledge proofs for graph isomorphism and graph non-isomorphism, languages which are in **AM∩coAM** but are commonly believed to lie outside **BPP**.

Limitations of Our Impossibilty Result. Our impossibilty result imposes three main restrictions on the construction: black-box simulation strategy, black-box access to the one-way permutation, and bounded adaptivity of the black-box simulator, amongst which adaptivity appears to be the greatest limitation. Our current ability to prove general lower bounds for zero-knowledge (without limitation to black-box simulation) is relatively limited [17,4]; moreover, non-black-box simulation strategies so far only yield arguments and not proof systems. In the context of zero-knowledge protocols, there is no indication whether non-black-box access to the underlying primitive has an advantage over black-box access to the primitive.

Extensions to Higher Adaptivity. The formal statement of our result (Theorem 2) is slightly more general than stated above and, in particular, allows us to obtain non-trivial consequences even when the simulator's adaptivity is polynomial.

> **Generalized Main Theorem (informal).** If a language L admits a fully black-box construction of zero-knowledge proofs starting from one-way permutations where the construction relies on a black-box simulation strategy with adaptivity t, then both L and $\overline{L}$ have $O(t)$-round public coin interactive proofs where the honest prover strategy can be implemented in $\mathbf{BPP^{NP}}$.

For the case $t = O(1)$ this is just our main theorem. If we now let L be an **NP**-complete language, then for $t = O(\log n)$ this implies a collapse in the *quasi-polynomial hierarchy* [33], which one can view as a weakened version of a collapse in the polynomial hierarchy. For $t = o(n)$ this would improve on the best known round complexity for an interactive protocol for a **coNP**-complete language (the best known is linear [27]), and even for $t = \mathrm{poly}(n)$ this would improve on the best known honest prover complexity for an interactive protocol for a **coNP**-complete language (the best known is $\mathbf{P^{\#P}}$ [27]). We view these results as evidence that such constructions will be hard to find.

1.2   Proof Overview

Recall that we start out with a constant-round zero-knowledge proof system $(\mathcal{P}, \mathcal{V})$ with constant adaptivity for a language L and we want to show that L lies in $\mathbf{AM} \cap \mathbf{coAM}$. The high level strategy is to extend the Goldreich-Krawczyk lower bound for constant-round public-coin protocols [15] to the private-coin setting. Following [15] (also [30,26,23]), we consider a cheating verifier $\mathcal{V}^*_{\mathsf{GK}}$ that "resamples" new messages that are distributed identically to the real verifier's messages (conditioned upon the partial transcript) every time it is rewound. We will need to address the fact that we do not know how to simulate such a $\mathcal{V}^*_{\mathsf{GK}}$ efficiently for general private-coin protocols. The computational complexity of $\mathcal{V}^*_{\mathsf{GK}}$ comes up in two ways in [15]: first to deduce that the zero-knowledge property holds against such a $\mathcal{V}^*_{\mathsf{GK}}$, and second to derive an efficient **AM** protocol for the underlying language L and its complement $\overline{L}$.

To address the first issue, we rely on a result of Haitner et al. [21], which, roughly speaking, demonstrates the existence of a one-way permutation π secure in the presence of a $\mathcal{V}^*_{\mathsf{GK}}$ oracle (as long as the zero-knowledge protocol has bounded round complexity, which is the case here). We will then instantiate the zero-knowledge protocol $(\mathcal{P}, \mathcal{V})$ with the permutation π. This will remain zero-knowledge against the cheating verifier $\mathcal{V}^*_{\mathsf{GK}}$ since π is one-way against $\mathcal{V}^*_{\mathsf{GK}}$. Following [15,26,23], we may then deduce a $\mathbf{BPP}^{\pi, \mathcal{V}^*_{\mathsf{GK}}}$ algorithm for L. (Such a statement was obtained independently by Pass and Venkitasubramaniam [31].) Along the way, we will exploit (as with [26,23]) the fact that $(\mathcal{P}, \mathcal{V})$ is a proof system as we need soundness to hold against a cheating prover that is able to simulate $\mathcal{V}^*_{\mathsf{GK}}$.

Next, we will essentially show that $\mathbf{BPP}^{\pi,\mathcal{V}_{\mathsf{GK}}^*} \subseteq \mathbf{AM} \cap \mathbf{coAM}$ from which our main result follows. Since L already has a constant-round proof system by assumption[1], $L \in \mathbf{AM}$. Thus, it suffices to show that $\mathbf{BPP}^{\pi,\mathcal{V}_{\mathsf{GK}}^*} \subseteq \mathbf{coAM}$. We do this by constructing a $\mathbf{AM}$ protocol for $\overline{L}$ where the strategy is to have the $\mathbf{AM}$ prover and verifier jointly simulate π and $\mathcal{V}_{\mathsf{GK}}^*$. In more detail, the $\mathbf{AM}$ verifier will pick the permutation π at random from a space of $\mathrm{poly}(T^m)$ permutations, where T is an upper bound on the running time of the reduction in the zero-knowledge protocol and m is the round complexity of the protocol; this turns out to suffice as a one-way permutation for the result in [21].[2] Next, we will have the $\mathbf{AM}$ prover and verifier jointly simulate each oracle computation of $\mathcal{V}_{\mathsf{GK}}^*$ using a (constant-round public-coin) random sampling protocol from [22]. Note that naively having the $\mathbf{AM}$ prover perform the computation of $\mathcal{V}_{\mathsf{GK}}^*$ fails for two reasons: a cheating $\mathbf{AM}$ prover may resample messages from a distribution different from the uniform distribution, and may not answer all of the $\mathcal{V}_{\mathsf{GK}}^*$ queries "independently". Finally, we rely on the constant adaptivity requirement of $(\mathcal{P},\mathcal{V})$ to partially parallelize the executions of the random sampling protocol, so that the final protocol for $\overline{L}$ has constant round complexity.

As mentioned previously, in a recent work, Pass et al. [31] independently obtained results similar to ours. They also show that any language L for which there exists a fully black-box construction of constant-round zero-knowledge proofs from one-way functions is in $\mathbf{BPP}^{\pi,\mathcal{V}_{\mathsf{GK}}^*}$. Their techniques for doing this are different from ours. They use a generic transformation from private-coin protocols into $\mathcal{V}_{\mathsf{GK}}^*$-relativized public-coin protocols, upon which the result then follows from the (relativized) lower bound for constant-round public-coin protocols in [15]. They then argue that if such proofs exist for all of $\mathbf{NP}$, this would imply unlikely properties for the complexity class $\mathbf{BPP}^{\pi,\mathcal{V}_{\mathsf{GK}}^*}$. Our techniques, on the other hand, allow us to relate the existence of such proofs to old questions in complexity such as whether $\mathbf{NP} \subseteq \mathbf{coAM}$ or whether $\mathbf{coNP}$ has interactive proofs with a $\mathbf{BPP}^{\mathbf{NP}}$ prover, whereas $\mathbf{BPP}^{\pi,\mathcal{V}_{\mathsf{GK}}^*}$ is a new and less well-understood notion.

2 Preliminaries

2.1 Definitions

We let $[m] = \{1,\ldots,m\}$. For a random variable X, we let $x \leftarrow_{\mathrm{R}} X$ denote that x is sampled according to X. For a set S, we let $x \leftarrow_{\mathrm{R}} U_S$ denote x sampled according to the uniform distribution over S. We say that an event occurs with negligible probability if it occurs with probabilty $n^{-\omega(1)}$, and it occurs with overwhelming probability if it occurs with probability $1 - n^{-\omega(1)}$, where n is the input length.

---

[1] We can instantiate the protocol $(\mathcal{P},\mathcal{V})$ for L with the identity permutation for this purpose.

[2] Having the $\mathbf{AM}$ verifier sample a random permutation "on the fly" does not work because the permutation π needs to be defined everywhere for $\mathcal{V}_{\mathsf{GK}}^*$ to be well-defined.

Definition 1. *A permutation* $\pi : \{0,1\}^n \to \{0,1\}^n$ *is* T-*hard if for any circuit* C *of size at most* T, *and for* y *chosen uniformly at random,* $\Pr[C(y) = \pi^{-1}(y)] \leq \frac{1}{T}$, *where the probability is taken over the choice of* y. *If, given* x, $\pi(x)$ *is also efficiently computable then we call such a permutation a* one way permutation *(OWP).*

Definition 2. *Let* Π_n *be the set of all permutations from* $\{0,1\}^n \to \{0,1\}^n$. *Then, using the notation of [12], we define* $\Pi_{k,n} \subseteq \Pi_n$ *as* $\{\pi_{k,n} \mid \pi_{k,n}(a,b) = (\pi_k(a), b)$ *for some* $\pi_k \in \Pi_k\}$ *In other words, a uniform element of* $\Pi_{k,n}$ *is a random permutation on the first* k *bits, and fixes the last* $n - k$ *bits.*

Complexity Classes. We let $\mathbf{AM}[k]$ denote the class of languages that have $O(k)$-round public-coin interactive protocols (recall that public-coins are equivalent to private coins by [19]). Namely:

Definition 3. $L \in \mathbf{AM}[k]$ *if there is a* $O(k)$-*round public-coin interactive proof between an efficient verifier* $\mathcal{V}$ *and an all-powerful prover* $\mathcal{P}$ *such that:*

- *For all* $x \in L$, $\mathcal{V}$ *always accepts when interacting with* $\mathcal{P}$.
- *For all* $x \notin L$ *and all possibly cheating prover strategies* $\mathcal{P}^*$, $\mathcal{V}$ *accepts when interacting with* $\mathcal{P}^*$ *with only negligible probability.*

We let $\mathbf{AM} = \mathbf{AM}[O(1)]$. We say that a protocol $(\mathcal{P}, \mathcal{V})$ has an *honest prover strategy* of complexity $\mathcal{C}$ if the prover algorithm can be implemented by a machine in the class $\mathcal{C}$. We recall that $\mathbf{coNP}$ is in $\mathbf{AM}[n]$ with an honest prover strategy complexity of $\mathbf{P}^{\#\mathbf{P}}$ [27], and it is an open question whether the round complexity or the honest prover strategy complexity can be improved.

For any oracle $\mathcal{O}$, we let $\mathbf{BPP}^{\mathcal{O}[k]}$ denote the class of languages that are decidable by efficient randomized algorithms using at most k rounds of adaptive queries to an oracle $\mathcal{O}$. One round of adaptivity is a set of queries $x_1, \ldots, x_k$ the algorithm asks to the oracle such that the x_i can only depend on oracle answers to queries asked in previous rounds.

2.2   Zero-Knowledge

In what follows we define a fully black-box construction of weak computational zero knowledge (CZK) from one way permutations. For a more general definition of CZK we refer the reader to previous literature [13]. As usual, we let $\mathsf{negl}(n)$ be some function such that $\mathsf{negl}(n) < \frac{1}{p(n)}$ for all polynomials $p(n)$.

Notation: We will use the following notation for interactive protocols. For any interactive protocol between a prover P and a verifier V, we let $2m$ denote the total number of rounds of communication, where a round consists of one message, either from P to V or from V to P. We let α_i denote the ith message sent from P to V, and β_i the ith response from V to P. Note that α_i is sent in round $2i - 1$ and β_i is sent in round $2i$. Also, having P always send the first message is without loss of generality as we can set $\alpha_1 = \bot$ to model a proof where V goes first. For $i \in \{1 \ldots, m\}$, we let $\alpha_{[i]} = (\alpha_1, \ldots, \alpha_i)$. Let $V = (V_1, \ldots V_m)$ be the decomposition of V into its next-message functions. Here $V_i(x, \alpha_{[i]}, \omega)$ outputs β_i, the ith message sent by V when using input x, random coins ω, and receiving messages $\alpha_{[i]}$ from P. Let $\langle P, V \rangle(x)$ denote the verifier's view of an execution of the interactive protocol on an input x. This view includes all messages $\alpha_{[m]}$ sent by the prover, the verifier's random coins ω, and (if V is allowed access to an oracle) the answers to any oracle queries V may have made. We say that $\langle P, V \rangle(x)$ accepts if $V_m(x, \alpha_{[m]}, \omega) = 1$.

We will reserve calligraphic $\mathcal{P}, \mathcal{V}, \mathcal{S}$ to denote the prover, verifier, and simulator in a zero-knowledge protocol, and regular P, V to denote the prover and verifier in a (possibly non-zero-knowledge) interactive protocol.

Definition 4. *A fully black-box construction of a (weak) computational zero-knowledge proof system from one-way permutations for a language L is a tuple of oracle procedures $(\mathcal{P}, \mathcal{V}, \mathcal{S}, M)$ such that there exists a polynomial $T(n)$ satisfying the following properties for every family of permutations $\pi = \{\pi_n\}_{n \geq 1}$:*

Efficiency. *The running times of $\mathcal{V}, \mathcal{S}, M$ are bounded by $T = T(n)$.*

Completeness. *For all $x \in L$: $\Pr[\langle \mathcal{P}^\pi, \mathcal{V}^\pi \rangle(x) \text{ accepts}] \geq 1 - \mathsf{negl}(n)$.*

Soundness. *For all $x \notin L$ and for all (possibly computationally unbounded) $\mathcal{P}^*$,*

$$\Pr[\langle \mathcal{P}^*, \mathcal{V}^\pi \rangle(x) \text{ accepts}] \leq \mathsf{negl}(n).$$

Black-Box Zero-Knowledge. *For all (possibly computationally unbounded) $\mathcal{V}^*, D$ and for all $x \in L$: if*

$$\left| \Pr[D(\langle \mathcal{P}^\pi, \mathcal{V}^* \rangle(x)) = 1] - \Pr[D(\mathcal{S}^{\pi, \mathcal{V}^*}(x)) = 1] \right| > 1/n$$

then M can invert π, namely:

$$\Pr_{y \in \{0,1\}^n} [M^{\pi, \mathcal{V}^*, D}(y) = \pi^{-1}(y)] > 1/T$$

We note that completeness and soundness hold even if the given permutations are not one-way. Also, $\mathcal{V}^*, D$ are quantified after π is fixed and therefore may depend on π.

Comparison with standard definitions of zero-knowledge: The property that makes the above definition *weak* zero knowledge is that we only require the distinguishing advantage to be smaller than $1/n$, rather than negligible (the choice of $1/n$ was arbitrary; any non-negligible function will do). This enables us to consider simulators that run in *strict* polynomial time; it is known that in the standard definition of zero knowledge where the distinguishing advantage is negligible, no strict polynomial-time black-box simulators exist for constant-round protocols [3], although there are examples of non-black-box simulators [2]. It is useful for us to consider strict polynomial-time simulators because defining adaptivity is more straight-forward for such simulators than for expected polynomial-time simulators. This is discussed in the next section.

Nevertheless, we note here that any zero knowledge proof satisfying the standard definition also satisfies the weak definition above: if a simulator S' satisfies the standard definition and runs in expected time T', then a simulator S satisfies the weak definition by running S' for at most $2nT'$ steps, and halting with a failure symbol if S' does not produce an output in that time. By ruling out black-box constructions of weak zero knowledge proofs from one-way permutations, we also rule out proofs satisfying the standard definition. We note that the same discussion applies to the runtime of the reduction algorithm M.

Simplifying assumptions: We assume for simplicity that on inputs of length n, V and S only query π on inputs of length n. We assume that in an honest interaction of the protocol, the last message is from the verifier V to the prover P and contains the verifier's random coins. Clearly this does not affect either zero knowledge or soundness since it occurs after all "meaningful" messages are sent. This assumption allows us to define a transcript to be accepting if the honest verifier would accept that transcript using the coins output in the last message, and this definition remains meaningful even for transcripts generated by cheating verifiers. We assume without loss of generality that the simulator S never asks the same query twice and that it only asks *refinement* queries. Namely, for $i > 1$ and for every query $\alpha_{[i]} = (\alpha_{[i-1]}, \alpha_i)$ that the simulator queries to its cheating verifier black box V^*, it must have previously queried $\alpha_{[i-1]}$ as well. We direct the reader to [14] for a discussion of why this holds without loss of generality.

2.3 Adaptivity

Here we define the *adaptivity* of the simulator, namely how much it uses responses from previous queries to the verifier black-box in order to generate new queries. All of the black-box simulators for constant-round zero knowledge in the literature intuitively work the following way: repeatedly query the cheating verifier with dummy queries enough times until it leaks some secret, then rewind and use this secret to output a simulated transcript [14,5,8,9,35]. The simulator may use the verifier's answers to determine whether to continue with dummy queries or to proceed to the next step of the simulation. If the simulator runs in *expected polynomial time* (rather than strict polynomial time), this procedure lasts indefinitely, making it hard to define the degree of the simulator's adaptivity. This is why we choose to work with *weak* zero knowledge, where the simulation is strict polynomial time; the definition of adaptivity becomes much simpler and more intuitive in this setting. We stress again that this only strengthens our result, as any zero-knowledge proof system satisfying the standard definition also satisfies the weak definition.

Definition 5. *A simulator S running in time T is said to be t-adaptive if it can be decomposed into $t + 1$ oracle machines $S = (S_1, \ldots, S_t, S_{t+1})$ with the following structure. Let x, ω (respectively) be the input and random coins for S. For all permutations π and all cheating verifiers V^*, S^{π, V^*} operates as follows:*

1. *$S_1^{\pi, V^*}(x; \omega)$ generates at most T queries $q_1^{(1)}, \ldots, q_T^{(1)}$ using x, ω. It sends these queries to V^* and gets back answers $\boldsymbol{a}_1 = (a_1^{(1)}, \ldots, a_T^{(1)})$.*

2. *For each phase $j, 1 < j \leq t$, $S_j^{\pi, V^*}(x; \omega, \boldsymbol{a}_{j-1})$ generates at most T queries $q_1^{(j)}, \ldots, q_T^{(j)}$ using x, ω and $\boldsymbol{a}_{j-1}$ which is the concatenation of all oracle answers from phases $1, \ldots, j-1$. S_j^{π, V^*} sets $\boldsymbol{a}_j$ to be the oracle answers $a_1^{(j)}, \ldots, a_T^{(j)}$ for the j'th phase, concatenated with $\boldsymbol{a}_{j-1}$.*
3. *After obtaining $\boldsymbol{a}_t$, $S_{t+1}^{\pi}(x; \omega, \boldsymbol{a}_t)$ computes the final output (notice it does so without calling V^*).*

2.4   The Sam Oracle

Here we provide a description of the Sam oracle as defined in [21]. A more formal description can be found in [21].

Description of Sam_d: Sam_d takes as input a query $q = (i, C_{\mathsf{next}}, C_{\mathsf{prev}}, z)$ and outputs (ω', z'), such that:

1. ω' is chosen uniformly at random from:
   - the domain of C_{next} if $i = 1$.
   - the set $\{\omega \mid C_{\mathsf{prev}}(\omega) = z\}$ if $i > 1$.
2. $z' = C_{\mathsf{next}}(\omega')$.

   The inputs to Sam_d are subject to the following restrictions:

1. The root query in every tree must include a security parameter 1^n such that $d = d(n)$ is the maximum depth query.
2. Queries with $i > d$ receive output $\bot$.
3. If $i > 1$, then the input $(i-1, C_{\mathsf{prev}}, \cdot, \cdot)$ was previously queried and resulted in output (ω, z) for some ω. Note that this restriction imposes a forest structure on the queries.
4. C_{next} is a *refinement* of C_{prev}. Formally: $C_{\mathsf{next}} = (C_{\mathsf{prev}}, \widetilde{C})$ for some circuit $\widetilde{C}$.

For our purposes, it is easier to think of Sam_d as being stateful, in which case the above restrictions can easily be implemented. Technically however Sam_d must be stateless, and so the above restrictions are enforced in [21] by giving Sam_d access to a signature protocol, and having him sign the output to every query, as well as the depth of the query, before returning a response. New queries are required to include a signature on a prior query, demonstrating that the first and third requirements have been met. (The refinement property can be verified by Sam_d independently.) Any query not meeting these restrictions receives output $\bot$. We direct the reader to [21] for the complete details (see also [22] for a precise statement about how to remove state), and we work with a stateful Sam_d for the remainder of this paper.

   We will also consider Sam_d in a relativized world with a random permutation $\pi = \{\pi_n\}_{n \in \mathbb{N}}$, where $\pi_n : \{0,1\}^n \to \{0,1\}^n$ is chosen at random from all permutations mapping $\{0,1\}^n \to \{0,1\}^n$. We let Sam_d^{π} denote Sam_d in this relativized world. Sam_d^{π} is defined exactly as Sam_d, except it accepts circuits $C_{\mathsf{prev}}^{\pi}, C_{\mathsf{next}}^{\pi}$ that can possibly contain π gates.

We will abuse notation and write Sam to denote Sam_d for some $d = O(1)$. Our results will apply to all constant d so this slight abuse does not affect the correctness of our statements.

Using a Prover to Simulate Sam. Let $\mathbf{BPP}^{\mathsf{Sam}[t]}$ denote the class of languages that can be decided efficiently by a machine making at most t adaptive rounds of queries to the oracle Sam. We use the following theorem from [22] which shows that one can simulate this Sam oracle by a constant-round public-coin protocol.

Theorem 1 ([22]). *For any $L \in \mathbf{BPP}^{\mathsf{Sam}[t]}$, it holds that both L and $\overline{L}$ have $\mathbf{AM}[t]$ proofs with an honest prover strategy complexity of $\mathbf{BPP}^{\mathbf{NP}}$.*

3   Proof of Main Theorem

3.1   Overview

As discussed in the Introduction, our proof involves using a particular cheating verifier, $\mathcal{V}^*_{\mathsf{GK}}$ defined in Section 3.2, with the following properties:

- $\mathcal{V}^*_{\mathsf{GK}}$ cannot invert a random permutation π. This implies that the view $\langle \mathcal{P}^\pi, \mathcal{V}^*_{\mathsf{GK}} \rangle(x)$ can be simulated by a simulator $\mathcal{S}^{\pi, \mathcal{V}^*_{\mathsf{GK}}}(x)$ whenever $x \in L$. (Section 3.3)
- The simulator $\mathcal{S}^{\pi, \mathcal{V}^*_{\mathsf{GK}}}(x)$ cannot produce an accepting transcript whenever $x \notin L$. Together with the previous property, this gives a way of deciding L. (Section 3.3)
- One can efficiently generate a transcript according to $\mathcal{S}^{\pi, \mathcal{V}^*_{\mathsf{GK}}}(x)$ in a constant number of rounds with the help of an all-powerful (but possibly cheating) prover. Since, using the output of $\mathcal{S}^{\pi, \mathcal{V}^*_{\mathsf{GK}}}(x)$, one can efficiently decide whether or not $x \in L$, this implies $L \in \mathbf{AM} \cap \mathbf{coAM}$. (Section 3.4)

3.2   Defining $\mathcal{V}^*_{\mathsf{GK}}$

Informally, upon receiving a message, the cheating verifier uniformly chooses a new random tape consistent with the transcript seen so far, and uses this to compute his next message. The formal definition follows, using notation defined in Section 2.1.

Fix any black-box construction of weak zero knowledge from one-way permutations $(\mathcal{P}, \mathcal{V}, \mathcal{S}, M)$. Let $\omega \in \{0,1\}^T$ be a random tape for the honest verifier $\mathcal{V}$ which is divided into next-message functions $\mathcal{V}_1, \ldots, \mathcal{V}_m$. Define

$$R_\omega^{\alpha_{[i]}} = \{\omega' \in \{0,1\}^T \mid \forall j < i, \ \mathcal{V}_j(x, \alpha_{[j]}; \omega) = \mathcal{V}_j(x, \alpha_{[j]}; \omega')\} \qquad (3.1)$$

i.e. the set of random tapes that, given prover messages $\alpha_{[i]}$, produce the same verifier messages as the random tape ω. For the special case where $i = 1$, set $R_\omega^{\alpha_1} = \{0,1\}^T$ for all α_1 and all ω.

Define $\mathcal{V}_{[i]} = (\mathcal{V}_1, \ldots, \mathcal{V}_i)$ to be the circuit that outputs the concatenation of $\mathcal{V}_1, \ldots, \mathcal{V}_i$. Namely, for every $\alpha_{[i]}$ and ω, it holds that

$$\mathcal{V}_{[i]}(\alpha_{[i]}, \omega) = (\mathcal{V}_1(\alpha_1, \omega), \mathcal{V}_2(\alpha_{[2]}, \omega), \ldots, \mathcal{V}_i(\alpha_{[i]}, \omega))$$

For any $\alpha_{[i]}$, let $\mathcal{V}_{[i]}(\alpha_{[i]}, \cdot)$ denote the circuit $\mathcal{V}_{[i]}$ with the input $\alpha_{[i]}$ hard-wired (therefore it takes only input ω.

Definition 6. *The cheating verifier* $\mathcal{V}^*_{\mathsf{GK}} = (\mathcal{V}^*_{\mathsf{GK},1}, \ldots \mathcal{V}^*_{\mathsf{GK},m})$ *is defined using the* Sam^π_m *oracle and a look-up table that associates server queries* $\alpha_{[i]}$ *with* Sam^π_m *oracle responses* (ω, z). *We write* $\mathcal{V}^*_{\mathsf{GK}}$ *with the understanding that the input* x *is hardwired into the verifier and the verifier is allowed oracle access to the permutation* π *and* Sam^π_m.

- $\mathcal{V}^*_{\mathsf{GK},1}(\alpha_1)$: *invoke* $\mathsf{Sam}^\pi_m(1, \mathcal{V}_1(\alpha_1, \cdot), 0, 0)$ *and let* (ω_1, β_1) *be the response. (Here, the 0 inputs are placeholders and can be replaced by anything.) Store* $(\alpha_1, \omega_1, \beta_1)$ *in the look-up table and output* β_1.
- $\mathcal{V}^*_{\mathsf{GK},i}(\alpha_{[i]})$ *for* $i > 1$: *let* $\alpha_{[i]} = (\alpha_{[i-1]}, \alpha_i)$. *Look up the value* $(\alpha_{[i-1]}, \omega_{i-1}, \beta_{[i-1]})$ *stored during a previous query. Query*

$$\mathsf{Sam}^\pi_m(i, \quad \mathcal{V}_{[i]}(\alpha_{[i]}, \cdot), \quad \mathcal{V}_{[i-1]}(\alpha_{[i-1]}, \cdot), \quad \beta_{[i-1]})$$

and let $(\omega_i, \beta_{[i]})$ *be the response. Store* $(\alpha_{[i]}, \omega_i, \beta_{[i]})$ *in the look-up table and output* β_i.

Observe that querying Sam^π_m in the manner described above for the case $i > 1$ returns an ω_i that is distributed uniformly in $R^{\alpha_{[i]}}_{\omega_{i-1}}$.

Recall that we assume the simulator never repeats queries and only makes refinement queries. Therefore, $\mathcal{V}^*_{\mathsf{GK}}$ never tries to store inconsistent entries in the table, and $\mathcal{V}^*_{\mathsf{GK}}$ never queries its table for entries that do not exist. Therefore, $\mathcal{V}^*_{\mathsf{GK}}$'s queries to Sam^π_m always satisfy the restrictions laid out in Section 2.4. Observe that the output of $\langle \mathcal{P}^\pi, \mathcal{V}^*_{\mathsf{GK}} \rangle(x)$ is distributed identically to the honest $\langle \mathcal{P}^\pi, \mathcal{V}^\pi \rangle(x)$.

To complete the description of $\mathcal{V}^*_{\mathsf{GK}}$ we also need to construct a one-way permutation that remains one-way in the presence of a $\mathcal{V}^*_{\mathsf{GK}}$-oracle. To accomplish this, we refer to a result of Haitner et al. [21], which ruled out fully black-box constructions of $o(n/\log n)$-round statistically hiding commitment schemes form one-way permutations (where n is the security parameter). Building on and generalizing the works of [12,36,37], they demonstrated that by choosing π from $\Pi_{k,n}$ for appropriate k, π remains one-way even in the presence of a Sam^π_m-oracle.

Formally, the following lemma follows directly from their results.

Lemma 1 (implicit in [21]). *Suppose* T, k *satisfy* $T^{3m+2} < 2^{k/8}$. *Then, for any oracle machine* A *running in time* T, *it holds that:*

$$\Pr_{\pi \leftarrow_R \Pi_{k,n}, y \leftarrow_R U_n} [A^{\pi, \mathcal{V}^*_{\mathsf{GK}}}(y) = \pi^{-1}(y)] \leq 1/T$$

Proof. This follows from [21, Theorem 5.1], which established the above statement where $\mathcal{V}^*_{\mathsf{GK}}$ is replaced by Sam^π_m. From our definition of $\mathcal{V}^*_{\mathsf{GK}}$, it is clear that one call to $\mathcal{V}^*_{\mathsf{GK}}$ can be implemented using one call to Sam^π_m. Furthermore, as noted above, since we assume $\mathcal{S}$ only makes unique refinement queries, all of the queries that $\mathcal{V}^*_{\mathsf{GK}}$ asks of Sam^π_m satisfy the restrictions in the definition of Sam^π_m.

3.3   Deciding L Using $\mathcal{V}^*_{\mathsf{GK}}$

We prove that $\mathcal{S}^{\pi,\mathcal{V}^*_{\mathsf{GK}}}(x)$ generates an accepting transcript with high probability if and only if $x \in L$.

Lemma 2. *Given any fully black-box construction from one-way functions of a constant-round weak zero knowledge proof $(\mathcal{P}, \mathcal{V}, \mathcal{S}, M)$ for a language L, and any n, k satisfying $T^{3m+2} < 2^{k/16}$, where $2m = O(1)$ is the round complexity of the proof system and $T = poly(n)$ is the strict polynomial bound on the running times of $\mathcal{V}, \mathcal{S}, M$, the following hold:*

1. *If $x \in L$, then $\mathrm{Pr}_{\pi \leftarrow_R \Pi_{k,n}, \mathcal{S}, \mathcal{V}^*_{\mathsf{GK}}}[\mathcal{S}^{\pi,\mathcal{V}^*_{\mathsf{GK}}}$ generates accepting transcript$] \geq 2/3$.*
2. *If $x \notin L$, then $\mathrm{Pr}_{\pi \leftarrow_R \Pi_{k,n}, \mathcal{S}, \mathcal{V}^*_{\mathsf{GK}}}[\mathcal{S}^{\pi,\mathcal{V}^*_{\mathsf{GK}}}$ generates accepting transcript$] \leq 1/3$.*

Proof.
Yes instances: We use the zero-knowledge property of the proof system to prove that for all $x \in L$:

$$\mathrm{Pr}[\mathcal{S}^{\pi,\mathcal{V}^*_{\mathsf{GK}}}(x) \text{ outputs an accepting transcript}] \geq 2/3 \qquad (3.2)$$

The proof proceeds by contradiction, showing that if $\mathcal{S}$ fails to output an accepting transcript with sufficiently high probability then, by the weak zero-knowledge property of $(\mathcal{P}, \mathcal{V}, \mathcal{S}, M)$, M can invert a random permutation $\pi \in \Pi_{k,n}$.

As was noted before, the distributions $\langle \mathcal{P}^\pi, \mathcal{V}^*_{\mathsf{GK}} \rangle(x) = \langle \mathcal{P}^\pi, \mathcal{V}^\pi \rangle(x)$. Therefore, by the completeness of the proof system, for $x \in L$, the transcript $\langle \mathcal{P}^\pi, \mathcal{V}^*_{\mathsf{GK}} \rangle(x)$ is accepted by the honest verifier with probability $1 - \mathsf{negl}(n)$. More formally, $\mathrm{Pr}[\mathcal{V}^\pi_m(x, \langle \mathcal{P}^\pi, \mathcal{V}^*_{\mathsf{GK}} \rangle(x)) = 1] \geq 1 - \mathsf{negl}(n)$.

For the sake of contradiction, assume that $\mathcal{S}^{\pi,\mathcal{V}^*_{\mathsf{GK}}}(x)$ outputs an accepting transcript with probability less than $2/3$. That is, $\mathrm{Pr}[\mathcal{V}^\pi_m(x, \mathcal{S}^{\pi,\mathcal{V}^*_{\mathsf{GK}}}(x)) = 1] < 2/3$. Then we can use the honest verifier $\mathcal{V}$ to distinguish between the prover and simulator output, since $|\mathrm{Pr}[\mathcal{V}^\pi_m(x, \langle \mathcal{P}^\pi, \mathcal{V}^*_{\mathsf{GK}} \rangle) = 1] - \mathrm{Pr}[\mathcal{V}^\pi_m(x, \mathcal{S}^{\pi,\mathcal{V}^*_{\mathsf{GK}}}(x)) = 1]| > 1/3 - \mathsf{negl}(n)$. Therefore, by the weak black-box zero-knowledge property of $(\mathcal{P}, \mathcal{V}, \mathcal{S}, M)$, there exists an oracle machine $M^{\pi,\mathcal{V}^*_{\mathsf{GK}},\mathcal{V}}$ running in time T that can break the one-wayness of π with probability at least $1/T$. We can remove oracle access to $\mathcal{V}$ by having M simulate $\mathcal{V}$ by making at most T oracle calls to π for each call to $\mathcal{V}$. Thus, we get a machine $M^{\pi,\mathcal{V}^*_{\mathsf{GK}}}$ running in time T^2 such that $\mathrm{Pr}_{\pi \leftarrow_R \Pi_{k,n}, y \leftarrow_R U_n}[M^{\pi,\mathcal{V}^*_{\mathsf{GK}}}(y) = \pi^{-1}(y)] \geq 1/T > 1/T^2$. This yields a contradiction to Lemma 1, and Equation (3.2) follows.

No instances: Here, we use statistical soundness (following [23,26,15]) to argue that for all $x \notin L$:

$$\mathrm{Pr}[\mathcal{S}^{\pi,\mathcal{V}^*_{\mathsf{GK}}}(x) \text{ outputs an accepting transcript}] \leq 1/3 \qquad (3.3)$$

The proof proceeds by contradiction, showing that if $\mathcal{S}$ outputs an accepting transcript with high probability, then there exists a cheating prover $\mathcal{P}^*_{\mathsf{GK}}$ that breaks the statistical soundness of the proof system. Let T, the running time of $\mathcal{S}$, be the bound on the total number of $\mathcal{V}^*_{\mathsf{GK}}$ queries made by $\mathcal{S}$, and let m be the round complexity of the zero knowledge proof system. Starting from $\mathcal{V}^*_{\mathsf{GK}}$, we define a new (inefficient) prover strategy $\mathcal{P}^*_{\mathsf{GK}}$ which interacts with an external verifier $\mathcal{V}$ as follows:

1. Choose queries to forward to $\mathcal{V}$: On input x, $\mathcal{P}^*_{\mathsf{GK}}$ picks a random subset of query indices $U = \{j_1, j_2, \ldots, j_m\} \subset [T]$ of size m. The set U represents the queries that $\mathcal{P}^*_{\mathsf{GK}}$ will forward to the verifier $\mathcal{V}$.
2. Simulate $\mathcal{S}^{\pi, \mathcal{V}^*_{\mathsf{GK}}}(x)$: Internally simulate $\mathcal{S}^{\pi, \mathcal{V}^*_{\mathsf{GK}}}(x)$ step by step. We handle the j'th oracle query, q_j, that $\mathcal{S}$ makes to $\mathcal{V}^*_{\mathsf{GK}}$ as follows. Let $q_j = \alpha_{[i]}$ for some $i \leq m$.
   - If $j \notin U$: Simulate $\mathcal{V}^*_{\mathsf{GK}}$ internally to answer q_j. More formally, look up the value $(\alpha_{[i-1]}, \omega)$ stored during a previous $\mathcal{V}^*_{\mathsf{GK}}$ query. (Note that since $\mathcal{S}$ only makes refinement queries, $\mathcal{S}$ must have made such a query.) Choose $\omega' \leftarrow R^{\alpha_{[i]}}_{\omega}$ uniformly at random ($\mathcal{P}^*_{\mathsf{GK}}$ can do this since he is computationally unbounded), store $(\alpha_{[i]}, \omega')$ and output $\mathcal{V}_i(x, \alpha_{[i]}, \omega')$.
   - If $j \in U$: If $q_j = \alpha_{[i]}$ and $i > 1$, forward α_i to the external $\mathcal{V}$. Upon receiving β_i in response, look up the stored value $(\alpha_{[i-1]}, \omega)$ and uniformly sample a random string $\omega'' \leftarrow \{\omega' \in R^{\alpha_{[i]}}_{\omega} \wedge \mathcal{V}_i(x, \alpha_{[i]}, \omega') = \beta_i\}$. Store $(\alpha_{[i]}, \omega'')$ and output β_i.

Note that as long as $\mathcal{S}$ outputs an accepting transcript with noticeable probability when interacting with $\mathcal{V}^*_{\mathsf{GK}}$ on $x \notin L$ then this cheating prover $\mathcal{P}^*_{\mathsf{GK}}$ has a noticeable probability of outputting an accepting transcript when interacting with the honest verifier $\mathcal{V}$. This happens if $\mathcal{P}^*_{\mathsf{GK}}$ chooses U to include exactly the messages that are used by $\mathcal{S}$ in his output. $\mathcal{P}^*_{\mathsf{GK}}$ succeeds in choosing the correct queries with probability at least $1/T^{O(m)}$. Thus, if $\mathcal{S}$ outputs an accepting transcript with probability $> 1/3$ then $\mathcal{P}^*_{\mathsf{GK}}$ outputs an accepting transcript with probability at least $1/3 \cdot 1/T^{O(m)}$ which is non-negligible when $m = O(1)$. This is a contradiction of the fact that the proof has negligible soundness error, thus (3.3) follows.

3.4 Applying Theorem 1 to Remove $\mathcal{V}^*_{\mathsf{GK}}$

We can now combine Lemma 2 and Theorem 1 to prove our main theorem.

Theorem 2. *Suppose there is a black-box construction from a one-way permutation of a constant-round weak zero knowledge proof $(\mathcal{P}, \mathcal{V}, \mathcal{S}, M)$ for a language L, where $\mathcal{S}$ is t-adaptive. Then both L and $\overline{L}$ are in $\mathbf{AM}[t]$ with honest prover complexity $\mathbf{BPP^{NP}}$.*

Proof. From Lemma 2 we already know that $\mathcal{S}^{\pi, \mathcal{V}^*_{\mathsf{GK}}}$ decides L. We will construct an oracle algorithm A based on $\mathcal{S}$, such that A^{Sam} decides L and furthermore the adaptivity of A is the same as the adaptivity of $\mathcal{S}$.

Sampling π Efficiently: By Lemma 1, we know that for π to be one-way in the presence of $\mathcal{V}^*_{\mathsf{GK}}$, it is sufficient to choose $\pi \leftarrow_{\mathrm{R}} \Pi_{k,n}$ with $k = 9(3m+2)\log T = O(\log n)$. Such a permutation can be sampled in polynomial time by sampling a uniform permutation on $k = O(\log n)$ bits. Let $A_1^{\mathcal{V}^*_{\mathsf{GK}}}$ be identical to $\mathcal{S}^{\pi,\mathcal{V}^*_{\mathsf{GK}}}$, except A_1 first samples π itself and then runs $\mathcal{S}^{\pi,\mathcal{V}^*_{\mathsf{GK}}}$.

From Definition 6, it holds that oracle access to $\mathcal{V}^*_{\mathsf{GK}}$ can be implemented using oracle access to Sam and an additional look-up table to associate previous queries with previous oracle responses. Therefore there exists a reduction A^{Sam} that on all inputs behaves identically to $A_1^{\mathcal{V}^*_{\mathsf{GK}}}$, and furthermore the adaptivity of A is identical to the adaptivity of A_1, whose adaptivity in turn is the same as that of $\mathcal{S}$.

Since $\mathcal{S}$ has adaptivity t, this implies that $L \in \mathbf{BPP}^{\mathsf{Sam}[t]}$. We can therefore apply Theorem 1 to conclude the proof.

Acknowledgements

We would like to thank Jonathan Katz for helpful discussions.

References

1. Aiello, W., Hastad, J.: Statistical zero-knowledge languages can be recognized in two rounds. JCSS 42, 327–345 (1991)
2. Barak, B.: How to go beyond the black-box simulation barrier. In: Proc 42nd FOCS, pp. 106–115. IEEE, Los Alamitos (2001)
3. Barak, B., Lindell, Y.: Strict polynomial-time in simulation and extraction. In: STOC, pp. 484–493 (2002)
4. Barak, B., Lindell, Y., Vadhan, S.: Lower bounds for non-black-box zero knowledge. JCSS 72(2), 321–391 (2006)
5. Bellare, M., Jakobsson, M., Yung, M.: Round-optimal zero-knowledge arguments based on any one-way function. In: Fumy, W. (ed.) EUROCRYPT 1997. LNCS, vol. 1233, pp. 280–305. Springer, Heidelberg (1997)
6. Bellare, M., Micali, S., Ostrovsky, R.: Perfect zero-knowledge in constant rounds. In: STOC, pp. 482–493 (1990)
7. Blum, M.: How to prove a theorem so no one else can claim it. In: Proc. ICM (1986)
8. Brassard, G., Crépeau, C., Yung, M.: Everything in NP can be argued in *perfect* zero-knowledge in a *bounded* number of rounds. In: Quisquater, J.-J., Vandewalle, J. (eds.) EUROCRYPT 1989. LNCS, vol. 434, pp. 192–195. Springer, Heidelberg (1990)
9. Feige, U., Shamir, A.: Zero knowledge proofs of knowledge in two rounds. In: Brassard, G. (ed.) CRYPTO 1989. LNCS, vol. 435, pp. 526–544. Springer, Heidelberg (1990)
10. Feige, U., Shamir, A.: Zero knowledge proofs of knowledge in two rounds. In: Brassard, G. (ed.) CRYPTO 1989. LNCS, vol. 435, pp. 526–544. Springer, Heidelberg (1990)
11. Fortnow, L.: The complexity of perfect zero-knowledge. In: STOC '87, pp. 204–209 (1987)

12. Gennaro, R., Gertner, Y., Katz, J., Trevisan, L.: Bounds on the efficiency of generic cryptographic constructions. SIAM J. Comput. 35(1), 217–246 (2005)
13. Goldreich, O.: Foundations of Cryptography: Basic Applications, vol. 2. Cambridge University Press, New York (2004)
14. Goldreich, O., Kahan, A.: How to construct constant-round zero-knowledge proof systems for NP. J. Cryptology 9(3), 167–190 (1996)
15. Goldreich, O., Krawczyk, H.: On the composition of zero-knowledge proof systems. SIAM J. Comput. 25(1), 169–192 (1996)
16. Goldreich, O., Micali, S., Wigderson, A.: Proofs that yield nothing but their validity for all languages in NP have zero-knowledge proof systems. J. ACM 38(3), 691–729 (1991) (prelim. version in FOCS '86)
17. Goldreich, O., Oren, Y.: Definitions and properties of zero-knowledge proof systems 7(1), 1–32 (Winter 1994) (preliminary version in FOCS' 87)
18. Goldwasser, S., Micali, S., Rackoff, C.: The knowledge complexity of interactive proof systems. SIAM J. Comput. 18(1), 186–208 (1989)
19. Goldwasser, S., Sipser, M.: Private coins versus public coins in interactive proof systems. Advances in Computing Research: Randomness and Computation 5, 73–90 (1989)
20. Hada, S., Tanaka, T.: On the existence of 3-round zero-knowledge protocols. In: Krawczyk, H. (ed.) CRYPTO 1998. LNCS, vol. 1462, pp. 408–423. Springer, Heidelberg (1998)
21. Haitner, I., Hoch, J.J., Reingold, O., Segev, G.: Finding collisions in interactive protocols - a tight lower bound on the round complexity of statistically-hiding commitments. In: Proc. FOCS '07, pp. 669–679 (2007)
22. Haitner, I., Mahmoody-Ghidary, M., Xiao, D.: A new sampling protocol and applications to basing cryptography on **NP**-hardnss. In: Proc. CCC, vol. (2010) (to appear. Full version available as ECCC TR-867-09)
23. Haitner, I., Reingold, O., Vadhan, S., Wee, H.: Inaccessible entropy. In: STOC, pp. 611–620 (2009)
24. Håstad, J., Impagliazzo, R., Levin, L.A., Luby, M.: A pseudorandom generator from any one-way function. SIAM J. of Com. 28(4), 1364–1396 (1999) (preliminary versions appeared in STOC' 89 and STOC' 90)
25. Impagliazzo, R., Rudich, S.: Limits on the provable consequences of one-way permutations. In: STOC, pp. 44–61 (1989)
26. Katz, J.: Which languages have 4-round zero-knowledge proofs? In: Canetti, R. (ed.) TCC 2008. LNCS, vol. 4948, pp. 73–88. Springer, Heidelberg (2008)
27. Lund, C., Fortnow, L., Karloff, H.J., Nisan, N.: Algebraic methods for interactive proof systems. In: FOCS, pp. 2–10 (1990)
28. Naor, M.: Bit commitment using pseudorandomness 4(2), 151–158 (1991) (preliminary version in CRYPTO' 89)
29. Ostrovsky, R., Wigderson, A.: One-way functions are essential for non-trivial zero-knowledge. In: ISTCS '93, pp. 3–17 (1993)
30. Pass, R.: Parallel repetition of zero-knowledge proofs and the possibility of basing cryptography on np-hardness. In: IEEE Conference on Computational Complexity, pp. 96–110 (2006)
31. Pass, R., Venkitasubramaniam, M.: Private coins versus public coins in zero-knowledge proof systems. In: Micciancio, D. (ed.) TCC 2010. LNCS, vol. 5978, pp. 588–605. Springer, Heidelberg (2010)
32. Pass, R., Wee, H.: Black-box constructions of two-party protocols from one-way functions. In: Reingold, O. (ed.) TCC 2009. LNCS, vol. 5444, pp. 403–418. Springer, Heidelberg (2009)

33. Pavan, A., Selman, A.L., Sengupta, S., Vinodchandran, N.V.: Polylogarithmic-round interactive proofs for conp collapse the exponential hierarchy. Theor. Comput. Sci. 385(1-3), 167–178 (2007)
34. Reingold, O., Trevisan, L., Vadhan, S.: Notions of reducibility between cryptographic primitives. In: Naor, M. (ed.) TCC 2004. LNCS, vol. 2951, pp. 1–20. Springer, Heidelberg (2004)
35. Rosen, A.: A note on constant-round zero-knowledge proofs for np. In: Naor, M. (ed.) TCC 2004. LNCS, vol. 2951, pp. 191–202. Springer, Heidelberg (2004)
36. Simon, D.R.: Finding collisions on a one-way street: Can secure hash functions be based on general assumptions? In: Nyberg, K. (ed.) EUROCRYPT 1998. LNCS, vol. 1403, pp. 334–345. Springer, Heidelberg (1998)
37. Wee, H.: One-way permutations, interactive hashing and statistically hiding commitments. In: Vadhan, S.P. (ed.) TCC 2007. LNCS, vol. 4392, pp. 419–433. Springer, Heidelberg (2007)

Message Recovery and Pseudo-preimage Attacks on the Compression Function of Hamsi-256

Çağdaş Çalık[1,*] and Meltem Sönmez Turan[2]

[1] Institute of Applied Mathematics, Middle East Technical University, Turkey
ccalik@metu.edu.tr
[2] Computer Security Division, National Institute of Standards and Technology, USA
meltem.turan@nist.gov

Abstract. Hamsi is one of the second round candidates of the SHA-3 competition. In this study, we present non-random differential properties for the compression function of Hamsi-256. Based on these properties, we first demonstrate a distinguishing attack that requires a few evaluations of the compression function. Then, we present a message recovery attack with a complexity of $2^{10.48}$ compression function evaluations. Also, we present a pseudo-preimage attack for the compression function with complexity $2^{254.25}$.

Keywords: Hash functions, SHA-3 competition, pseudo-preimage attacks.

1 Introduction

Hash functions are fundamental components of many cryptographic applications such as digital signatures, random number generation, integrity protection, etc. Due to the recent attacks against commonly used hash functions [10,4,11,3], National Institute of Standards and Technology (NIST) announced the SHA-3 hash function competition to select a new cryptographic hash function to be used as the new standard [7]. In November 2008, NIST received 64 submissions, among these, 51 candidates are considered to meet the minimum submission requirements. In July 2009, NIST announced 14 second round candidates.

Hamsi [6] is one of the second round candidates of the SHA-3 competition, designed by Küçük. Hamsi is based on the Concatenate-Permute-Truncate design strategy and it supports four output sizes; 224, 256, 384 and 512 with two instances Hamsi-256 and Hamsi-512.

According to the first public analysis of Hamsi made by Aumasson [1], the compression function of Hamsi-256 does not behave as a pseudo-random function due to its low algebraic degree. Nikolic [8] found 25-bit pseudo near collisions for the compression function of Hamsi-256 for fixed message blocks. Wang et al. [9] improved this attack and practically showed 23-bit pseudo near collisions for the compression function of Hamsi-256. In a recent study [2], distinguishers

---

* This work was supported in part by TÜBİTAK under grant no. 108T679.

M. Abdalla and P.S.L.M. Barreto (Eds.): LATINCRYPT 2010, LNCS 6212, pp. 205–221, 2010.

and near-collisions for Hamsi-256 compression function and distinguishers for the finalization function are presented.

In this paper, we study the differential properties of Hamsi-256 and observe some non-random differential properties in its compression function. Using these properties, we first present a very efficient distinguisher for the compression function of Hamsi-256, and extend the distinguisher to 5 rounds with complexity 2^{83}. Then, we use the differential properties to recover a message block used in the compression function with a complexity of $2^{10.48}$ compression function evaluations. Also, we present a pseudo-preimage attack for the compression function with complexity $2^{254.25}$ that can trivially be converted to a pseudo second preimage attack to the full hash function with same complexity. The attacks and observations presented in this paper do not affect the security of Hamsi in terms of collision, preimage and second preimage attacks.

The paper is organized as follows. In Sect. 2, we give a brief description of the compression function of Hamsi-256. In Sect. 3, differential properties of the s-box, L transformation and the compression function are given. Sect. 4 includes a distinguisher for the compression function, whereas Sect. 5 gives a message recovery algorithm for the compression function. In Sect. 6 the pseudo-preimage attack for the compression function and its extension as a pseudo second preimage attack to the hash function are described. Finally, we conclude in Sect. 7.

2   Description of the Compression Function of Hamsi-256

In this section, we give a brief overview of the compression function of Hamsi-256. For other versions, the reader may refer to the specification of Hamsi [6]. The notation used in the paper is given below.

Notation	
$\mathbb{F}_4$	Finite Field with 4 elements
$\oplus$	Exclusive Or (XOR)
$\ll$	Left shift
$\lll$	Left rotation
(n, m, d)	Code with length n, dimension m and minimum distance d
C	Compression function
$H^{(i)}$	ith chaining value
h_i	ith bit of the chaining value
$M^{(i)}$	ith message block (32-bit)
M_i	ith bit of the message block
m_i	ith bit of the expanded message
a_x	Hexadecimal representation of the number a

The compression function C of Hamsi-256 accepts a 32-bit message block $M^{(i)}$ and a 256-bit chaining value $H^{(i-1)}$ and outputs a 256-bit chaining value $H^{(i)}$. The function acts on a state of 512 bits, which can be considered as both a 4x4 matrix of 32-bit words and 128 columns each consisting of 4 bits. The compression function is a three round transformation consisting of the following transformations. Addition of Constants, Substitution and Diffusion are considered as a round.

Message Expansion and Initialization of the State. 32-bit message block is expanded to 256 bits using a linear code (128,16,70) over $\mathbb{F}_4$. Then, the expanded message and the chaining value, each of being eight 32-bit words is loaded to the state of Hamsi-256 as given in Fig. 1.

Addition of Constants. The state is XOR'ed with predefined constants and a round counter.

Substitution. Each of the 128 columns of the state goes through a 4x4 s-box.

Diffusion. A linear transformation L, which accepts four 32-bit words, and outputs four 32-bit words is applied to the four independent diagonals of the state.

Truncation and Feed Forward. Second and fourth rows of the state are dropped and the initial CV is feed-forwarded to the truncated state.

$m_0 \ldots m_{31}$	$m_{32} \ldots m_{63}$	$c_0 \ldots c_{31}$	$c_{32} \ldots c_{63}$
$c_{64} \ldots c_{95}$	$c_{96} \ldots c_{127}$	$m_{64} \ldots m_{95}$	$m_{96} \ldots m_{127}$
$m_{128} \ldots m_{159}$	$m_{160} \ldots m_{191}$	$c_{128} \ldots c_{159}$	$c_{160} \ldots c_{191}$
$c_{192} \ldots c_{223}$	$c_{224} \ldots c_{255}$	$m_{192} \ldots m_{223}$	$m_{224} \ldots m_{255}$

Fig. 1. Initial state of the compression function of Hamsi-256

After the initialization of the state from the expanded message and the chaining value, each column of the state holds two bits from the message expansion and two bits from the chaining value. For the first 64 columns, message bits are in first and third position and chaining value bits are in second and fourth position. For the last 64 columns, message bits are in second and fourth position and chaining value bits are in first and third position (See Fig. 1). When we talk about a column we mean a 4-bit value, for example the first column of the state consists of the bits m_0, c_{64}, m_{128} and c_{192}. When we talk about the chaining value bits or message bits in a column we mean a 2-bit value.

3   Differential Properties of Hamsi-256

In this section, we explore the differential properties of the compression function of Hamsi-256. We first analyze Substitution and Diffusion transformations in terms of differences and then present some non-randomness properties of the whole compression function.

3.1 Differential Properties of the Hamsi s-Box

The nonlinearity in Hamsi compression function is obtained by a 4×4 s-box, which is originally used in the block cipher Serpent. The s-box is defined as

$$S = \{8,6,7,9,3,C,A,F,D,1,E,4,0,B,5,2\}.$$

The difference distribution table of the s-box is given in Table 6. Following two properties of the s-box enable us to guess the output difference in the least significant bit which corresponds to the bit in the first row of the state.

Property 1. Let a_x be the input difference. Then, according to Table 6, the output difference can take on the following values $\{2_x, 4_x, 6_x, 8_x, a_x, e_x\}$, in all of which the least significant bit is 0. It means that whenever the second and fourth input bits are complemented simultaneously, the first output bit remains the same with probability 1.

Property 2. Let the input difference be 2_x or 8_x. Then, the output difference can take one of the the following values $\{3_x, 5_x, 7_x, 9_x, d_x, f_x\}$, in all of which the least significant bit is 1, i.e. whenever second or fourth bits of the input are complemented, the first output bit changes with probability 1.

3.2 Differential Properties of L

The diffusion in Hamsi is obtained by the linear transformation $L : \{0,1\}^{128} \to \{0,1\}^{128}$. L accepts four 32-bit words a, b, c, d and outputs four 32-bit words. Following two properties show that the diffusion property of L is limited.

Property 3. Let the Hamming weight of the input difference be 1, then the Hamming weight of the output difference is between 2 and 7. This means that in the Diffusion transformation, each bit in the state affects at most 7 bits.

Property 4. Let the input difference has the form $(0, \delta_b, 0, 0)$, then the output difference is of the form $(?, ?, ?, 0)$. Similarly, $(0, 0, 0, \delta_d) \to (?, 0, ?, ?)$.

3.3 Differential Properties of the Compression Function

In this part, we study the differential properties of the compression function of Hamsi-256. Although the input difference can be given to the message, chaining value or both, for the following property of the message expansion, we consider only the differences in the chaining value.

Due to the (128,16,70) linear code used in the expansion of the message, whenever $\delta \neq 0$ difference is given to the message, at least 70 out of 128 columns change, which means the number of active s-boxes is at least 70. Therefore, it is not easy to control the difference given to the message block.

Controlling the effect of input difference given to the chaining value is easier, since each bit of the chaining value is mapped to a single state bit (See Fig. 1). In the rest of the section, we consider the effect of differences given to the input chaining value on the output chaining value, for fixed messages.

Since each column of the initial state contains two chaining value bits, three different non-zero differences can be given to a column depending on the chaining value bit positions in that column: for the first 64 columns, the difference can be $2_x, 8_x$ or a_x, and for the last 64 columns, the difference can be $1_x, 4_x$ or 5_x. When the message bits in a column are fixed, input is restricted to four possible values, and an input difference divides these four values into two classes of pairs, i.e., for a particular value of message bits and a chaining value difference in a column, we can observe two output differences. Moreover, since we can control the chaining value bits, we have the ability to choose the input values so that a difference of our choice among the two possible differences occurs at the output. The list of output differences for all possible chaining value differences and message bits is given in Table 1. Consider for example the first entry of the table where the message bits in a column are zero and the input difference is 2_x. From the table we see that the output differences can be f_x or 3_x. Actually, when message bits are set to zero, a column may have values $0_x, 2_x, 8_x$ and a_x, and a difference of 2_x induces the input pairs $(0_x, 2_x)$ and $(8_x, a_x)$. The first pair gives the output difference f_x, and the second pair gives the output difference 3_x. We can choose one of the two possible input pairs depending on how we want the difference to propagate.

Table 1. List of possible output differences for each column difference and message value

Message Bits	Difference in Columns 0-63			Difference in Columns 64-127		
	2_x	8_x	a_x	1_x	4_x	5_x
0_x	$f_x,3_x$	$5_x,9_x$	$6_x,a_x$	e_x,f_x	b_x,a_x	$4_x,5_x$
1_x	$f_x,5_x$	$7_x,d_x$	$2_x,8_x$	$e_x,5_x$	$d_x,6_x$	$8_x,3_x$
2_x	$9_x,5_x$	$3_x,f_x$	$6_x,a_x$	c_x,b_x	d_x,a_x	$6_x,1_x$
3_x	$3_x,9_x$	$7_x,d_x$	$e_x,4_x$	$a_x,7_x$	$b_x,6_x$	$c_x,1_x$

We now describe a method to find truncated differetials with probability 1 for the compression function. We do this by marking the state bits that can be affected at any step of the round transformations. After three rounds, if there are any unmarked bits in the state, we will be certain that these bits will not get affected by the initial difference given to the state. However, with the Feed Forward operation some of these unaffected bit positions may coincide with the initial CV difference, hence producing bits which will be complemented certainly. For each of these cases, we know the output difference with probability 1. For simplicity, we will not make a distinction between these two cases and use the term unaffected bits for both of them throughout the paper as the attacks we will describe are independent of this situation.

Clearly, we start with all zero state, set the initial difference and use the following procedures for determining which bits of the state may get affected by the Substitution and Diffusion transformations after three rounds.

Substitution. If any of the bits in a column are affected we mark the whole column as affected, i.e. we set the value of the column to f_x. There is one exception to this rule. In the first Substitution operation we have just one differential path in hand and we know the exact value of the difference, so we can apply the truncated differential property, namely if the difference in a column is a_x, after the Substitution operation the least significant bit of output difference will be zero because of Property 1. So we set the new value of the column as e_x in this case. We cannot apply this rule for the second and third Substitution operations because if a column has the value a_x, this means that the second and fourth bit may be affected with some non-zero probability, but we cannot be sure whether this value is 2_x, 8_x or a_x.

Diffusion. For each bit of the state we precompute a set of state indices which affects this bit of the state. This operation requires negligible amount of computation and memory. For example, the first bit of the state is affected by the state bits $\{18, 19, 28, 166, 329, 335, 492\}$ in the Diffusion operation. (More specifically, since Diffusion is a linear operation the first bit will be set to modulo 2 sum of these bits). If any of these bits were affected we mark the first bit as affected by Diffusion operation. Otherwise, we mark the first state bit as zero, meaning that it is certain that this bit cannot have a difference because none of the bits it depends on is affected at that point. We repeat this operation for all 512 bits of the state.

In Fig. 2, we present an example where $\delta = a_x$ is given to the 7th column of the state, i.e. the 71st and 199th bits of the chaining value are complemented. Then, we examine how δ propagates through the state bits in each step of the round using the technique mentioned above and find out that 228th and 230th bits of the new chaining value will not be affected by this difference.

We have verified the result by randomly selecting 2^{20} chaining values and message blocks. After giving a δ difference to the chaining values, the output differences for each bit is calculated. Fig. 3 shows the number of times the output difference is equal to 1 out of 2^{20} trials. The points lying outside the upper and lower limits show a bias of minimum 0.25. It is clear from the figure that the differences obtained in bits 228 and 230 are equal to zero for all trials.

For a fixed value of message bits in a column, we can use Table 1 in order to trace the effect of a CV difference. As seen from the table, a fixed message value and a CV difference can produce exactly two output differences. We trace each of these output differences (starting from the Diffusion operation) independently to find the unaffected bits for that difference. Combining these two data we can find if there are any output bits which are not affected by any of the initial differences. Putting restriction on message bits allow us to observe more unaffected bits at the output. This is due to the differential propagation in the first Substitution operation. For example, let the difference 5_x be given to a column. If there is no restriction on the

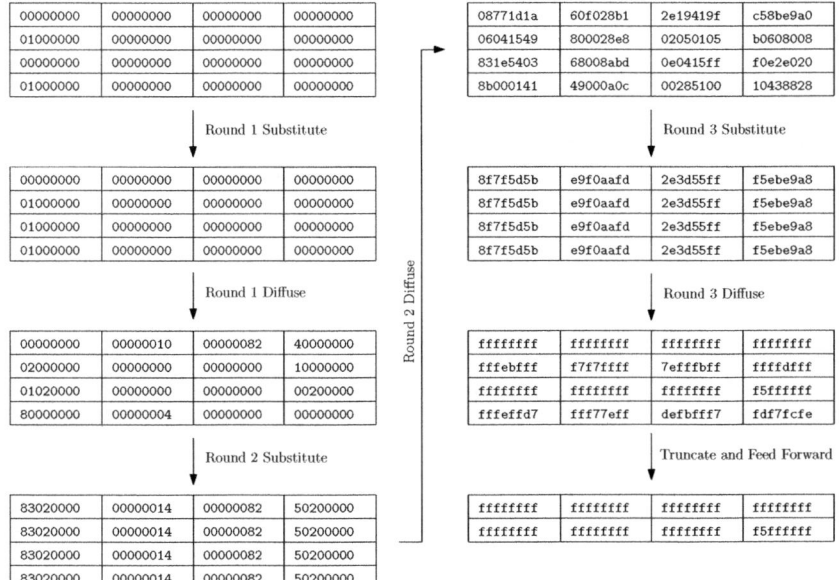

Fig. 2. Propagation of affected bits for the initial difference a_x given to the 7th column

message bits, from Table 1 we can see that seven output differences $\{1_x, 3_x, 4_x, 5_x, 6_x, 8_x, c_x\}$ are possible, affecting all four output bits. However, considering the case where message bits are set to zero for instance, the possible output differences are 4_x and 5_x, affecting only two out of four output bits.

Another factor that affects the number of unaffected bits is the weight of the initial difference in a column. Among the three possible differences that can be given to a column (2 having weight 1 and 1 having weight 2) it turns out that the difference having weight 2 produces a higher number of unaffected bits. This is because of the fact that differences with weight 1 will lead to an output difference of weight at least 2, whereas an input difference of weight 2 can lead to an output difference of weight 1, which causes less diffusion in the second step of the round.

Table 2 gives a list of input differences having weight 1 that do not affect some of the output bits, with the condition that the message bits in the corresponding column are fixed. As an example, whenever 78th bit of the chaining value is complemented, we see that 78th and 150th bits of the output chaining value are not changed, given the message bits in this column are both 1. Each entry in the table requires the message bits of the column to be fixed. The number of messages that satisfy all of these 16 conditions on 8 columns is $2^{32-16} = 2^{16}$.

Table 3 gives a list of the input differences having weight 2 which leads to unaffected output bits. Unlike weight 1 differences, we do not need any conditions on the message bits here. If we also fix the message bits, we can observe up to 62 unaffected output bits.

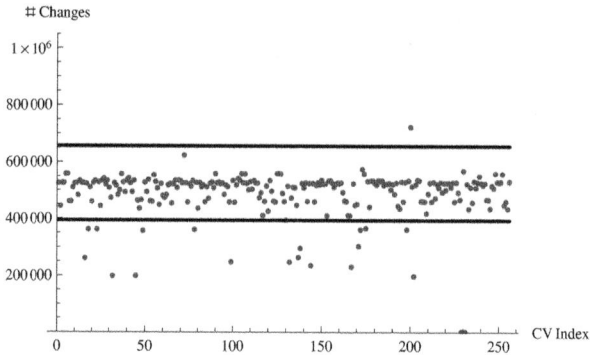

Fig. 3. The number of changes in output chaining value bits after 2-bit difference given to bits 71 and 199

Table 2. List of unaffected output bits for one bit input difference and the condition on message bits

Column	CV bit	Unaffected output bits	Condition
14	78	78,150	$m_{14} = 1, m_{142} = 1$
15	79	79,151	$m_{15} = 1, m_{143} = 1$
46	110	110, 182	$m_{46} = 1, m_{174} = 1$
47	111	111, 183	$m_{47} = 1, m_{175} = 1$
78	130	14, 214	$m_{78} = 0, m_{206} = 0$
79	131	15, 215	$m_{79} = 0, m_{207} = 0$
110	184	46, 246	$m_{110} = 0, m_{138} = 0$
111	185	47, 247	$m_{111} = 0, m_{139} = 0$

4 Distinguishing the Compression Function

Using the differential properties given in Table 3, the compression function of Hamsi-256 can be distinguished from a random function. As an example, consider the difference given to the column 0. Let the message block M be chosen randomly. Then, for any randomly chosen input chaining value H, the 165th and 201st bit of

$$C(H, M) \oplus C(H + \delta_{64} + \delta_{192}, M)$$

will be 0 with probability 1, where δ_i corresponds to the ith bit difference. The experiment can be repeated as many times, say k, to decrease the false alarm probability to 2^{-2k}.

Distinguisher for the Hamsi-256 compression function can also be found for higher number of rounds. A 5-round distinguisher with complexity 2^{83} is given in Appendix B.

5 Message Recovery Using Differential Properties

Based on the observations presented in the previous section, we can mount a message recovery attack on the compression function of Hamsi-256. In this setting, we assume that the message is secret and we can only obtain compression function outputs produced by this secret message and a chaining value of our choice.

Table 3. List of unaffected bits of the output CV given two bit difference to the chaining value in each column

Column	CV bits	Unaffected bits	Column	CV bits	Unaffected bits
0	64,192	165, 201	32	96,224	197, 233
1	65,193	166	33	97,225	198
2	66,194	167	34	98,226	199
3	67,195	168	35	99,227	200
4	68,196	169	36	100,228	201
6	70,198	227	38	102,230	131
7	71,199	228, 230	39	103,231	132, 134
8	72,200	229	40	104,232	133
9	73,201	131, 230	41	105,233	134, 163
10	74,202	132, 231	42	106,234	135, 164
11	75,203	133, 232	43	107,235	136, 165
12	76,204	134, 233	44	108,236	137, 166
13	77,205	135	45	109,237	167
14	78,206	136	46	110,238	168
15	79,207	137	47	111,239	169
26	90,218	195	58	122,250	227
27	91,219	196	59	123,251	228
28	92,220	197	60	124,252	229
29	93,221	198	61	125,253	230
30	94,222	163, 199	62	126,254	195, 231
31	95,223	164, 200	63	127,255	196, 232

The main observation which enables us to make this attack is that the actual values of the message bits in a column of the state affects the differential propagation. Hence, for some particular chaining value difference given to a column of the state, the unaffected bits after the evaluation of the compression function enables us deduce information on the message bits initially contained in the column.

Before explaining the message recovery process, we should decide which columns we have to deal with. Since each column of the state contains two expanded message bits, and message expansion is a linear operation, it is sufficient to recover message bits from any 16 columns of the state with the condition that the equations of the recovered bits are linearly independent so that we have 32 linearly independent linear equations in 32 unknowns, which can be solved easily and will give us the 32-bit message block. However, if we examine the expanded message equations a little carefully, we see that the expanded message bits from 16th to 31th columns of the state are exactly the original message bits. More specifically, 16th column contains M_0 and M_1, 17th column contains M_2 and M_3, and continuing like this the 31st column contains M_{30} and M_{31}. Therefore, we focus on these columns.

Table 4 gives the list of unaffected output bits for all message bit values and two possible chaining value differences that can be given to the 18th column of the state. We emphasize that this list of unaffected bits occur with probability 1. For instance, if the difference in the 18th column is a_x and the message bits in this column are initially zero, then the probability of 26th bit of output chaining value being changed is zero.

If we evaluate two chaining values CV_1 and CV_2 having difference a_x in the 18th column and check whether the 1st bits of the the corresponding output

Table 4. Unaffected output bits given the differences a_x and 2_x to column 18

Column	Difference	Message bits	Unaffected output bits
18	a_x	0_x	26 109 131 140 154 232
18	a_x	1_x	1 3 10 12 26 30 36 39 49 82 84 109 131 133 134 140 148 154 156 169 196 210 212 232 235 239
18	a_x	2_x	26 109 131 140 154 232
18	a_x	3_x	113 169 198 241
18	2_x	0_x	192
18	2_x	$1_x, 2_x, 3_x$	-

chaining values CV_3 and CV_4 match, we can learn whether the message bit values in this column were initially 1_x or not. If the 1st bits of CV_3 and CV_4 do not match then we can be sure that the message bits in the 18th column is not equal to 1_x, because a message value of 1_x in the 18th column guarantees that a difference of a_x will have no effect on the 1st bit of the output chaining value. Of course, there is a probability that the 1st bits of CV_3 and CV_4 being equal even if the message bits were not equal to 1_x. In order to minimize the probability of falsely determining whether an output bit changes with a given difference, we can repeat this process a couple of times and then decide whether it changes or not. If we decide that the message bits in this column were 1_x then we are done. Otherwise we have to do the same experiment but this time checking the 198th bits of the chaining values in order to decide whether the message bits were 3_x. If we also decide that 3_x is not the case then we have two remaining possibilities left, namely 0_x and 2_x, also giving us the information that the least significant bit -the message bit in the first row- is zero. We can decide whether the message bits were 0_x or 2_x by giving this time the difference 2_x to the 18th column and check the 192th bits of the output chaining values.

The same procedure goes for all the columns from 18 to 29, giving us 24 out of 32 message bits. For columns 16,17,30 and 31, if message bits are not 1_x or 3_x, we cannot check whether these message bits are equal to 0_x or 2_x. However, even with this information we obtain the least significant message bits and recover a total number of 28 bits. The remaining 4 message bits can be recovered by repeating this experiment with different columns and substituting the previously found values in the expanded message equations. However, these 4 message bits can be found with less complexity by exhaustive search (checking all 16 possible combinations), since the experiment requires 2^4 pairs of compression function evaluations to recover a single bit. Table 4 gives the list of output chaining values to check in order to recover the message bits of the corresponding columns. A column is firstly checked for the message value of 1_x, and then for 3_x using the indices listed in the first two columns of the table. If it is the case that message bits are not equal to these values, then the final check is done using the indices in the third column of the table in order to decide if the message bits were 0_x or 2_x.

In the best case, the complexity of the attack is $16.k$ where k is the number of trials needed to decide whether an output bit changes or not. We have implemented the attack and observed that $k = 2^4$ is sufficient. In the worst case, we have to make 3 checks per column except for the first and last two columns,

Table 5. List of chaining value bit indices used for message recovery

Column	$m = 1_x$	$m = 3_x$	$m = 2_x$
16	1	196	-
17	0	197	-
18	1	198	192
19	2	199	163
20	0	200	164
21	1	201	165
22	2	243	166
23	3	244	167
24	4	245	168
25	5	147	169
26	6	148	168
27	7	149	169
28	8	150	168
29	9	151	169
30	10	152	-
31	11	153	-

where we can do at most 2 checks, giving us a total of $12 \times 3 + 4 \times 2 = 44$ checks. Hence, adding the possible cost of recovering 4 remaining bits and the fact that checking whether a bit changes requires two evaluations of the compression function, the total complexity is upper bounded by $2 \times 44 \times 2^4 + 2^4 \approx 2^{10.48}$ compression function evaluations.

6 Pseudo-preimages for the Compression Function of Hamsi-256

In this section, we will show that finding preimages for the compression function of Hamsi-256 can be done with less effort than exhaustive search by using the properties mentioned in Sect. 3.

For a random compression function, given any chaining value H^*, it should be 'hard' to compute a previous chaining value H and a message block M such that $C(H, M) = H^*$, which is finding a preimage of the compression function.

A naive method to find a preimage H for a given H^* might be to evaluate all possible H's under a fixed message M and check whether any of them yields H^*. This method cannot be considered as a valid attack because it requires 2^{256} evaluations (for the case of Hamsi-256) in the worst case. Here, we will present a way to reduce this complexity based on the truncated differential properties of the compression function explained in Sect. 3.

According to Table 2, if a bit of the input chaining value with index in

$$I = \{78, 79, 110, 111, 130, 131, 184, 185\}$$

is complemented, then exactly two bits of the output chaining value are not affected. For example, complementing the 78th bit of the input chaining value does not affect the 78th and 150th bits of the output chaining value. For a randomly chosen H and M, if the 78th (resp. 150th) bit of $C(H, M)$ is not equal to the 78th (resp. 150th) bit of H^*, then it is for sure that $C(H + \delta_{78}, M) \neq H^*$.

Therefore, with probability $1/4$, it is not necessary to evaluate $H + \delta_{78}$ (resp. $H + \delta_{150}$). By comparing the values of unaffected output bits of $C(H, M)$ and H^* we can decide whether we need to complement any of the bits in I. If we do not need to complement one of the bits and evaluate the compression function this will be an advantage for us. By eliminating unnecessary evaluations of the compression function in this way, we can reduce the complexity of finding pseudo-preimages for the compression function to $2^{254.25}$. We explain the details of this attack in Appendix C.

6.1   Pseudo Second Preimages for Hamsi-256

The pseudo-preimage attack for the compression function can be extended to a pseudo second preimage attack for the full Hamsi-256. Let $M = M^{(0)} || \ldots || M^{(l)}$ be the padded message and H be the hash of the message using Hamsi-256. First, we calculate $H^{(1)} = C(M^{(0)}, H^{(0)})$, where $H^{(0)}$ is the original initial chaining value. Next, with complexity $2^{254.25}$, we invert $H^{(1)}$ to find another message block M' and $H^{'(1)}$ such that $H^{(1)} = C(M', H^{'(0)})$. Then, we obtain two messages $M^{(0)} || M^{(1)} || \ldots || M^{(l)}$ and $M' || M^{(1)} || \ldots || M^{(l)}$ whose hash value is same starting from the chaining values $H^{(0)}$ and $H^{'(0)}$, respectively.

7   Discussion and Conclusion

In this study, we analyzed the compression function of Hamsi-256. We first evaluated the compression function in terms of its differential properties and presented some non-random differentials with high probabilities. We showed that these differentials can be used to distinguish the compression function of Hamsi from a random function using a few evaluations of the compression function. Then, we extend the distinguisher to 5 rounds with complexity 2^{83}. We also presented a message recovery attack with a complexity of $2^{10.48}$ compression function evaluations. Finally, we presented a pseudo-preimage attack for the compression function with complexity $2^{254.25}$. We showed that the pseudo-preimage attack on the compression function can be converted to a pseudo second-preimage attack on Hamsi-256 with the same complexity. The attacks and observations presented in this paper do not affect the security of Hamsi in terms of collision, preimage and second preimage attacks.

Acknowledgment

The authors would like to thank John Kelsey for his helpful comments and suggestions.

References

1. Aumasson, J.P.: On the Pseudorandomness of Hamsi. NIST mailing list, local link (2009),
   http://ehash.iaik.tugraz.at/uploads/d/db/Hamsi_nonrandomness.txt

2. Aumasson, J.P., Käsper, E., Knudsen, L.R., Matusiewicz, K., Ødegård, R., Peyrin, T., Schläffer, M.: Differential Distinguishers for the Compression Function and Output Transformation of Hamsi-256. Cryptology ePrint Archive, Report 2010/091 (2010), http://eprint.iacr.org/
3. Biham, E., Chen, R., Joux, A., Carribault, P., Lemuet, C., Jalby, W.: Collisions of SHA-0 and Reduced SHA-1. In: Cramer (ed.) [5], pp. 36–57
4. Chabaud, F., Joux, A.: Differential Collisions in SHA-0. In: Krawczyk, H. (ed.) CRYPTO 1998. LNCS, vol. 1462, pp. 56–71. Springer, Heidelberg (1998)
5. Cramer, R. (ed.): EUROCRYPT 2005. LNCS, vol. 3494. Springer, Heidelberg (2005)
6. Küçük, Ö.: The Hash Function Hamsi. Submission to NIST (2008), http://ehash.iaik.tugraz.at/uploads/9/95/Hamsi.pdf
7. National Institute of Standards and Technology: Announcing Request for Candidate Algorithm Nominations for a New Cryptographic Hash Algorithm (SHA-3) Family. Federal Register 27(212), 62212–62220 (2007), http://csrc.nist.gov/groups/ST/hash/documents/FR_Notice_Nov07.pdf
8. Nikolic, I.: Near Collisions for the Compression Function of Hamsi-256. CRYPTO rump session (2009)
9. Wang, M., Wang, X., Jia, K., Wang, W.: New Pseudo-Near-Collision Attack on Reduced-Round of Hamsi-256. Cryptology ePrint Archive, Report 2009/484 (2009)
10. Wang, X., Feng, D., Lai, X., Yu, H.: Collisions for Hash functions MD4, MD5, HAVAL–128 and RIPEMD (2004), http://eprint.iacr.org/2004/199/
11. Wang, X., Yu, H.: How to Break MD5 and Other Hash Functions. In: Cramer (ed.) [5], pp. 19–35

A   Difference Distribution Table of the Hamsi s-Box

Table 6. Difference distribution table of the Hamsi s-box

δ_i/δ_j	0	1	2	3	4	5	6	7	8	9	a	b	c	d	e	f
0	16	0	0	0	0	0	0	0	0	0	0	0	0	0	0	0
1	0	0	0	0	0	2	0	2	0	0	2	2	2	0	4	2
2	0	0	0	4	0	4	0	0	0	4	0	0	0	0	0	4
3	0	4	2	0	0	0	2	0	0	2	0	0	2	0	2	2
4	0	0	0	0	0	0	4	0	0	0	4	4	0	4	0	0
5	0	4	0	2	2	2	2	0	2	0	0	0	2	0	0	0
6	0	0	2	2	2	2	0	0	2	2	0	0	0	0	2	2
7	0	0	0	0	4	2	0	2	0	0	2	2	2	0	0	2
8	0	0	0	2	0	2	0	4	0	2	0	0	0	4	0	2
9	0	0	0	2	0	0	0	2	4	2	2	2	2	0	0	0
a	0	0	2	0	2	0	4	0	2	0	4	0	0	0	2	0
b	0	4	0	0	2	0	2	0	2	2	0	0	2	0	0	2
c	0	0	2	0	2	0	0	0	2	0	0	4	0	4	2	0
d	0	4	2	2	0	2	2	0	0	0	0	0	2	0	2	0
e	0	0	2	0	2	0	0	4	2	0	0	0	0	4	2	0
f	0	0	4	2	0	0	0	2	0	2	2	2	2	0	0	0

B   Differential Characteristic for the 5 Round Distinguisher

We start with a low weight difference in the state and trace this difference in forward and backward direction in order to find a differential characteristic with the highest probability. The best characteristic we have found is shown in Fig. 4. The initial difference leading to this characteristic is a 1-bit difference given to the beginning of the third round. By searching all possible differences in backward direction we could go two rounds and obtained the initial difference for the characteristic. Similarly, we traced the difference in the third round in forward direction for three rounds. In total, we obtained a 5 round characteristic with probability 2^{-126}.

The first substitution layer in the differential characteristic of the distinguisher involves 15 active columns. By choosing an appropriate message block we can guarantee the transition of all the differentials for free. In this case, the complexity of the distinguisher becomes 2^{83}.

C   Calculating the Complexity of Pseudo-preimage Attack for the Compression Function

Although there are eight bit positions in $I = \{78, 79, 110, 111, 130, 131, 184, 185\}$ that lead to unaffected output bits, we will explain the attack for the general case and then pick the best value that gives the lowest attack complexity. Let k be the number of bit positions when complemented results in two unaffected output bits and let $N(\alpha)$ be the set composed of vectors produced by complementing each bit of α, called 1-neighbour vectors of α. We select a subset S of vectors from F_2^k so that the vectors in S together with 1-neighbour vectors of each vector in S covers F_2^k. In other words, each vector in F_2^k is either in S or can be produced by complementing one bit of a vector in S. Let β be an element of F_2^{256-k} so that $\alpha||\beta = H$ will form a chaining value. For a fixed value of β, there are 2^k possible values for α. We will however only evaluate the $C(H, M)$ for the values of $\alpha \in S$. Having evaluated these values we will check whether we need to complement each bit of α and evaluate C or not. The expected number of evaluations we will make is calculated as follows: For all the vectors in F_2^k, we calculate the probability that the vector is going to be evaluated. The vectors in S will definitely be evaluated. The remaining vectors will be evaluated with a probability inversely proportional to the number of vectors they are 1-neighbour to the vectors in S, i.e., if a vector is 1-neighbour of only one vector of S then it is going to be evaluated with a probability of 2^{-2}, which is the probability that the unaffected output bits of $C(H, M)$ and H^* being the same. Generally speaking, if a vector is 1-neighbour of t vectors of S then it will be evaluated with a probability of 2^{-2t}. The expected number of evaluations therefore will be the sum of the probabilities of each vector being evaluated.

Figure 5 demonstrates an example for $k = 4$, where the vectors are shown in binary form. The set $S = \{0000, 0111, 1001, 1110\}$ consists of four elements and

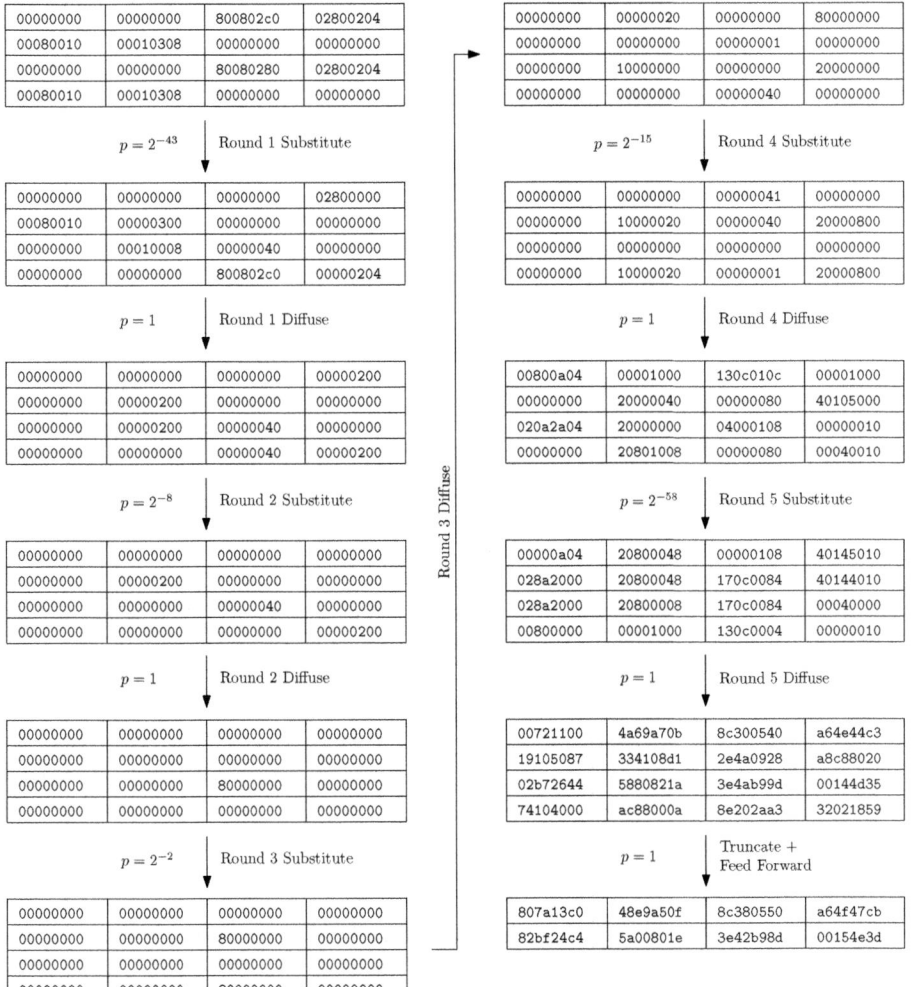

Fig. 4. Differential characteristic for the 5 round distinguisher

1-neighbours of each element of S is also depicted in the figure. It can be easily verified that S and 1-neighbours of S cover F_2^4. Table 7 gives the probabilities of evaluating each vector according to Fig. 5. In the table, *covered by* column indicates the number of vectors in S covering that vector. A dash in the same column means that the vector is in S and will be evaluated certainly. As an example, the vector (0001) is covered by two vectors from S (0000 and 1001), therefore it is going to be evaluated with probability 2^{-4}. The expected number of evaluations for $k = 4$ case is $4 \times 1 + 8 \times 2^{-2} + 4 \times 2^{-4} = 6.25 \approx 2^{2.64}$. This means instead of going through all the 2^4 possible values, we need to evaluate $2^{2.64}$ values.

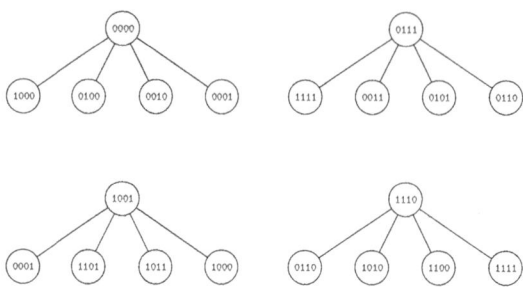

Fig. 5. An example selection of S for $k = 4$

Table 7. The probability of evaluating each vector and the number of times they are covered

Vector	Covered by	Probability	Vector	Covered by	Probability
0000	-	1	1000	2	2^{-4}
0001	2	2^{-4}	1001	-	1
0010	1	2^{-2}	1010	1	2^{-2}
0011	1	2^{-2}	1011	1	2^{-4}
0100	1	2^{-2}	1100	1	2^{-2}
0101	1	2^{-2}	1101	1	2^{-2}
0110	2	2^{-4}	1110	-	1
0111	-	1	1111	2	2^{-4}

We define gain as the ratio of all the vectors to the vectors we expect to evaluate. For $k = 4$, the gain is $\frac{2^4}{2^{2.64}} = 2^{1.36}$. Table 8 lists the number of vectors in S and the gain for all values of k up to 8. The set S for each k in the table is computed by a simple algorithm and seems to be close to optimal. Discussion of how the set S can be formed so that higher gains can be achieved is out of the scope of this study. It can be seen from the table that highest gain is achived for $k = 6$ as $2^{1.75}$. Since we are performing this operation for all values of $\beta \in F_2^{256-k}$, the total complexity of the attack becomes $2^{256-6} 2^{4.25} = 2^{254.25}$. That is, by using the unaffected bits, instead of trying all 2^{256} chaining values, we need to evaluate $2^{254.25}$ chaining values to find a pseudo-preimage. We can choose any 6 bit positions out of 8 to apply the attack, since each of them causes exactly two unaffected bits.

Success Probability. Whenever we fix the value of the message block to M, the compression function $C_M(H^{(i-1)}) = H^{(i)}$ should behave like a random function. The expected size of the range is about $1 - e^{-1} = 0.63$ of the domain size, i.e. on the average $H^{(i)}$ can take 0.63×2^{256} different values. Similarly, let H^* be a 256-bit random value. Then, for any M, there exists a H, such that $C_M(H) = H^*$ with probability 0.63. This is the success rate for one instance of the attack. If the attack does not yield a preimage, it can be repeated using another message block. In this case the complexity increases by a factor of 2 and becomes $2.2^{254.25} = 2^{255.25}$ while the success probability increases to 0.8646. The

Table 8. The effect of size of S on the complexity gain

k	Size of S	Expected number evaluations	Gain
2	2^1	$2^{1.09}$	$2^{0.91}$
3	2^1	$2^{1.81}$	$2^{1.19}$
4	2^2	$2^{2.64}$	$2^{1.36}$
5	2^3	$2^{3.60}$	$2^{1.40}$
6	2^4	$2^{4.25}$	$2^{1.75}$
7	2^4	$2^{5.46}$	$2^{1.54}$
8	2^5	$2^{6.36}$	$2^{1.64}$

attack can be repeated for maximum three times with complexity $2^{255.83}$ and success rate 0.9502. It should be noted that the success rate of the generic attack for this scenario is 63% with complexity of 2^{256}.

D   Extension of the Attacks to Hamsi-512

Hamsi-512 has a similar compression function, consisting of six rounds. The state size of Hamsi-512 is twice the state size of Hamsi-256 (there are 256 4-bit columns), substitution layer and the linear function L is the same. The main difference is the number of times L is applied to the state. In Hamsi-256, L is used 4 times per round, whereas in Hamsi-512 L is used 12 times per round, providing more diffusion.

We analyzed the effect of 1-bit and 2-bit differences on the output chaining values for varying number of rounds just as we did for Hamsi-256. The experiments show that unaffected bits can be observed up to two rounds of the compression function. For three rounds, there are some biased bits. The compression function appears random starting from the fourth round. Although these are preliminary results and can be improved, the properties we have used in mounting attacks to the compression function of Hamsi-256 in this paper does not seem to exist in the compression function of Hamsi-512.

Generic Attacks on Misty Schemes

Valérie Nachef[1], Jacques Patarin[2], and Joana Treger[2]

[1] Department of Mathematics
University of Cergy-Pontoise
CNRS UMR 8088
2 avenue Adolphe Chauvin, 95011 Cergy-Pontoise Cedex, France
[2] Université de Versailles
45 avenue des Etats-Unis, 78035 Versailles Cedex, France
valerie.nachef@u-cergy.fr,
{jacques.patarin,joana.treger}@prism.uvsq.fr

Abstract. Misty schemes are classic cryptographic schemes used to construct pseudo-random permutations from $2n$ bits to $2n$ bits by using d pseudo-random permutations from n bits to n bits. These d permutations will be called the "internal" permutations, and d is the number of rounds of the Misty scheme. Misty schemes are important from a practical point of view since for example, the Kasumi algorithm based on Misty schemes has been adopted as the standard block cipher in the third generation mobile systems. In this paper we describe the best known "generic" attacks on Misty schemes, i.e. attacks when the internal permutations do not have special properties, or are randomly chosen. We describe known plaintext attacks (KPA), non-adaptive chosen plaintext attacks (CPA-1) and adaptive chosen plaintext and ciphertext attacks (CPCA-2) against these schemes. Some of these attacks were previously known, some are new. When $d = 5$ rounds, it is shown in [6] that a CPA-1 exists with complexity 2^n. We will present completely different attacks with $d = 5$ and the same complexity. We will also present new attacks for $d \leq 4$ and $d \geq 6$. For $d \geq 6$ the complexity will be greater than 2^{2n}, so these attacks will be useful only when the number of rounds d is small.

Keywords: Misty permutations, pseudo-random permutations, generic attacks on encryption schemes, Block ciphers.

1 Introduction

A secure block cipher can be seen as a specific implementation of a pseudo-random permutation. They are generally defined by using a recursive construction process. The most studied way to build pseudo-random permutations from previously (and generally smaller) random functions or permutations is the d-round Feistel construction, that we will denote ψ^d: $f = \psi^d(f_1, \ldots, f_d)$, where $f_1, \ldots, f_d$ are functions from n bits to n bits, and f is a permutation from $2n$ bits to $2n$ bits. However, there exist other well known constructions such as for example Massey and Lai's scheme used in IDEA ([7]), unbalanced Feistel schemes with

M. Abdalla and P.S.L.M. Barreto (Eds.): LATINCRYPT 2010, LNCS 6212, pp. 222–240, 2010.

expanding or contracting internal functions ([13,14]), and the Misty construction that we will analyze in this paper. We will denote by M^d, or M_L^d a Misty scheme of d rounds: $f = M^d(f_1, \ldots, f_d)$, where $f_1, \ldots, f_d$ are permutations from n bits to n bits, and f is a permutation from $2n$ bits to $2n$ bits (precise definitions will be given in Section 2). From a practical point of view, it is interesting to study the security of these Misty schemes since this structure is used in real life block ciphers, such as Matsui's Misty block cipher [8], as well as in the Kasumi variant of Misty adopted as standard block cipher for encryption and integrity protection in third generation mobile systems ([2]). In this paper we will study "generic" attacks on Misty schemes, i.e. attacks when the internal permutations $f_1, \ldots, f_d$ do not have special properties, or are randomly chosen. In real block ciphers $f_1, \ldots, f_d$ are never pseudo-random, and there are therefore often better attacks than the generic ones. However, generic attacks are very interesting since they point on general properties of the structure, not on specific problems of the $f_1, \ldots, f_d$. We can consider that they give a minimum number of rounds needed in these schemes for a given wanted security: generally the security with specific $f_1, \ldots, f_d$ is smaller or at best equal compared to that with random $f_1, \ldots, f_d$ since the attacks on random $f_1, \ldots, f_d$ generally also apply to specific $f_1, \ldots, f_d$. (When it is not the case, the security might appear to be based an a very specific and maybe dangerous instantiation). A general presentation of generic attacks on Feistel schemes ([10,19]) and unbalanced Feistel schemes ([13,14]) already exists, but no similar presentation and analysis for Misty schemes was written so far. Some specific results on Misty scheme attacks or security have been already published ([5,15,16,17,18]). Sometimes the previously found attacks are the best known attacks (it is even possible to prove in some cases that they are the best possible attacks). However, as we will see in this paper, sometimes some new and better attacks exist, for example with 4 or more rounds. From a theoretical point of view, analyzing generic attacks on Misty schemes is interesting because Misty schemes have many similarities, but also many differences compared with Feistel schemes ψ^d ([10,19]), unbalanced Feistel schemes with expanding functions F_k^d ([14]) and Butterfly and Benes schemes ([3,12]). For Feistel schemes ψ^d, the best known generic attacks are "2-point attacks", i.e. attacks using correlations on (many) pairs of messages such as differential attacks [10,19]. For unbalanced Feistel schemes with expanding functions the best known generic attacks are "2-point", "4-point", or rectangle attacks with 6, 8, 10,... points (see [14]). For Butterfly schemes, the best known generic attacks are "4-point" attacks ([3,12]). Here for Misty schemes, the best known attacks will sometimes be 2-point attacks, sometimes "4-point" attacks, and they will be based sometimes on the properties of the first n bits of output (S) and sometimes on the Xor of the first n bits of output and the last n bits of output $(S \oplus T)$, combined with the properties of the input $[L, R]$. In fact it was not obvious before making a specific and precise analysis of Misty schemes if these schemes were more or less secure than for example Feistel schemes ψ^d for a given number of rounds. The paper is organized as follows. In Section 2, we give notations, definitions and general properties of Misty schemes. In Section 3, we detail attacks against 1,

2, 3 and 4 rounds. Section 4 is devoted to the study of attacks on 5 rounds. In section 5, we give attacks on 6 rounds. In section 6, we explain how to make a complete study of the 2-point attacks. Our final results are summarized in Section 7.

2   Notations, Definitions and Properties

2.1   Notations

Basic Notations. We use the following notations:

- $I_n = \{0,1\}^n$ is the set of the 2^n strings of length n.
- For $a, b \in I_n$, $[a, b]$ will be the string of length $2n$ which is the concatenation of a and b.
- For $a, b \in I_n$, $a \oplus b$ stands for the bitwise exclusive-or of a and b.
- $\circ$ is the composition of functions.
- The set of all functions from I_n to I_n is F_n. Thus $|F_n| = 2^{n \cdot 2^n}$.
- The set of all permutations from I_n to I_n is B_n. Thus $B_n \subset F_n$ and $|B_n| = (2^n)!$.

L and R Schemes.

- Let f_1 be a permutation of B_n. Let L, R, S and T be elements in I_n. Then by definition: $M_L(f_1)([L, R]) = [S, T] \Leftrightarrow S = R$ and $T = R \oplus f_1(L)$.
  Let $f_1, \ldots, f_d$ be d bijections of B_n. We define:
  $M_L^d(f_1, \ldots, f_d) = M_L(f_d) \circ \ldots \circ M_L(f_2) \circ M_L(f_1)$.
  The permutation $M_L^d(f_1, \ldots, f_d)$ is called a "Misty L scheme with d rounds".

$$L \qquad\qquad\qquad R$$
$$\downarrow \qquad\qquad\qquad \downarrow$$
$$R \qquad\qquad\qquad R \oplus f_1(L)$$

Fig. 1. One round of the Misty L scheme

- Similarly there is a slightly different construction named the Misty R scheme. By definition:
  $M_R(f_1)([L, R]) = [S, T] \Leftrightarrow S = R \oplus f_1(L)$ and $T = f_1(L)$.
  $M_R^d(f_1, \ldots, f_d) = M_R(f_d) \circ \ldots \circ M_R(f_2) \circ M_R(f_1)$.
  The permutation $M_R^d(f_1, \ldots, f_d)$ is called a "Misty R scheme with d rounds".

M_L^d is the "classic" Misty scheme used in cryptography. Therefore when we will call "Misty scheme" we will refer to M_L^d (and not M_R^d). This paper is mainly about M_L^d but we will also rapidly present the (few) security differences between M_R^d and M_L^d.

Fig. 2. One round of the Misty R scheme

Messages and Attacks. In our attacks, we denote by m the number of input/output messages that we use. $\forall i$, $1 \leq i \leq m$, we denote by $[L_i, R_i]$ the cleartext of message i, and by $[S_i, T_i]$ the ciphertext of this message i. Without loss of generality we can always assume that the messages $[L_i, R_i]$ are pairwise distinct ($L_i = L_j$ and $i \neq j \Rightarrow R_i \neq R_j$). In 2-point attacks (respectively 4-point attacks) we use correlations between pairs of messages (respectively 4-tuples of messages).

2.2   Some General Properties of the M_L and M_R Schemes

Inversion. Let $f_1 \in B_n$. Let $\Lambda(f_1)$, or simply Λ, be the permutation of B_{2n} such that

$\forall [L, R] \in I_{2n}$, $\Lambda([L, R]) \overset{def}{=} [f_1(L), R]$. We have $\left(\Lambda(f_1)\right)^{-1} = \Lambda(f_1^{-1})$.

Let μ be the permutation of B_{2n} such that $\forall [L, R] \in I_{2n}$, $\mu([L, R]) \overset{def}{=} [R, L \oplus R]$. We have $\mu^2([L, R]) = [L \oplus R, L]$ and $\mu^3([L, R]) = [L, R]$. Therefore $\mu^3 = Id$, and $\mu^{-1} = \mu^2$.

We see that: $M_L = \mu \circ \Lambda$ and $M_R = \mu^{-1} \circ \Lambda$. Therefore, $M_L^{-1}(f_1) = \Lambda(f_1^{-1}) \circ \mu^{-1} = \mu \circ M_R(f_1^{-1}) \circ \mu^{-1}$. Then for d rounds, we have:
$M_L^{-1}(f_1, \ldots, f_d) = \mu \circ M_R(f_d^{-1}, \ldots, f_1^{-1}) \circ \mu^{-1}$.
This property shows that the inverse of a M_L function is a M_R function, after composing by μ and μ^{-1} on the inputs and outputs. Thus, the security of M_L and M_R will be the same for all attacks where the inputs and outputs have the same possibilities. For example, in KPA (known plaintext attacks), CPCA-1 (non adaptive chosen plaintext and chosen ciphertext attacks) and CPCA-2 (adaptive chosen plaintext and chosen ciphertext attacks) the security of generic M_L and M_R schemes will be the same. In CPA-1 (non adaptive chosen plaintext attacks) and CPA-2 (adaptive chosen plaintext attacks) the security may be different. In this paper we will concentrate the analysis on the classical Misty M_L, and just rapidly give the differences in CPA for M_R.

Formulas for the M_L schemes, definition of the "internal" variable X^i.

1 round. For one round, we have: $\begin{cases} S = R \\ T = R \oplus f_1(L) \end{cases}$. We define $X^1 = R \oplus f_1(L)$.

2 rounds. For 2 rounds, we have: $\begin{cases} S = R \oplus f_1(L) \\ T = R \oplus f_1(L) \oplus f_2(R) \end{cases}$, or alternatively:

$\begin{cases} S = X^1 \\ T \oplus S = f_2(R) \end{cases}$. We write $X^2 = R \oplus f_1(L) \oplus f_2(R) = X^1 \oplus f_2(R)$.

d rounds. More generally, for d rounds, we have: $\begin{cases} S = X^{d-1} \\ T \oplus S = f_d(X^{d-2}) \end{cases}$, where

the X^i variables are defined by induction: $X^{-1} = L$, $X^0 = R$, and $\forall k \in \mathbb{N}$, $k \geq 1$, $X^k = X^{k-1} \oplus f_k(X^{k-2})$.

For message number i, we will denote the value of X^k on this message by $X^k(i)$, or simply X_i^k. For example, $X_i^1 = X^1(i) = R_i \oplus f_1(L_i)$ and $X_i^2 = X^2(i) = R_i \oplus f_1(L_i) \oplus f_2(R_i)$.

Without loss of generality, we can choose messages in the attacks such that $L_i = L_j \Rightarrow R_i \neq R_j$. Then we can notice that:

1. For all $i \neq j$, $L_i = L_j \Rightarrow X_i^1 \neq X_j^1$ (but we can have $L_i = L_j$ and $X_i^2 = X_j^2$).
2. For all $i \neq j$, $R_i = R_j \Rightarrow X_i^1 \neq X_j^1$ and $X_i^2 \neq X_j^2$ (but we can have $R_i = R_j$ and $X_i^3 = X_j^3$).
3. For all $i \neq j$, $X_i^1 = X_j^1 \Rightarrow X_i^2 \neq X_j^2$ and $X_i^3 \neq X_j^3$ (but we can have $X_i^1 = X_j^1$ and $X_i^4 = X_j^4$).
4. etc.

A useful "4-point" property. Let $[L_1, R_1]$, $[L_2, R_2]$, $[L_3, R_3]$, $[L_4, R_4]$ be four messages such that $L_1 \neq L_2$, $R_1 \neq R_2$, $L_3 = L_1$, $R_3 = R_2$, $L_4 = L_2$, $R_1 = R_4$. Therefore we have the 4 messages $[L_1, R_1]$, $[L_2, R_2]$, $[L_1, R_2]$, $[L_2, R_1]$.

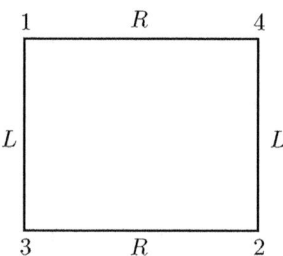

Fig. 3. The equalities in L and R for the "4-point" property

Lemma 1. *For such 4 messages, we always have:*

$$X_1^1 \oplus X_2^1 \oplus X_3^1 \oplus X_4^1 = X_1^2 \oplus X_2^2 \oplus X_3^2 \oplus X_4^2 = 0$$

$$X_1^3 \oplus X_2^3 \oplus X_3^3 \oplus X_4^3 = f_3(X_1^1) \oplus f_3(X_2^1) \oplus f_3(X_3^1) \oplus f_3(X_4^1)$$

(We also have $X_1^4 \oplus X_2^4 \oplus X_3^4 \oplus X_4^4 = X_1^3 \oplus X_2^3 \oplus X_3^3 \oplus X_4^3 \oplus f_4(X_1^2) \oplus f_4(X_2^2) \oplus f_4(X_3^2) \oplus f_4(X_4^2)$)

Proof: These properties are immediately deduced from the definition of the internal variables X^1, X^2, X^3, X^4 and from the fact that $L_3 = L_1$, $R_3 = R_2$, $L_4 = L_2$, $R_4 = R_1$. For all i:

$$X_i^1 \stackrel{def}{=} R_i \oplus f_1(L_i) \quad X_i^3 \stackrel{def}{=} X_i^2 \oplus f_3(X_i^1)$$
$$X_i^2 \stackrel{def}{=} R_i \oplus f_1(L_i) \oplus f_2(R_i) \, ' \quad X_i^4 \stackrel{def}{=} X_i^3 \oplus f_4(X_i^2).$$

$\square$

3   Attacks on M_L^d, $1 \leq d \leq 4$

We will give one attack for each case. Other attacks are performed in the extended version of this paper.

3.1   1 Round

After one round, we have $S = R$. This gives an attack with one message. We just have to check if $S = R$. With a Misty scheme, this happens with probability 1 and with a random permutation with probability $\frac{1}{2^n}$.

3.2   2 Rounds

After 2 rounds we have: $S = R \oplus f_1(L)$ and $T \oplus S = f_2(R)$.

CPA-1 using S. We choose two messages $[L_1, R_1]$ and $[L_2, R_2]$ such that $L_1 = L_2$ and we check if $S_1 \oplus S_2 = R_1 \oplus R_2$. For a Misty scheme this happens with probability 1 and for a random permutation with probability $\frac{1}{2^n}$. This is a CPA-1 with $m = 2$ and $O(1)$ computations.

KPA using S. The CPA-1 can be transformed into a KPA with $m = O(\sqrt{2^n})$ and $O(\sqrt{2^n})$ computations: if $m = O(\sqrt{2^n})$ then by the birthday paradox, we find with a good probability i, j such that $L_i = L_j$ and then we check if $S_i \oplus S_j = R_i \oplus R_j$. There also exists an attack using $S \oplus T$ with the same complexity.

3.3   3 Rounds

For 3 rounds, we have: $S = X^2 = R \oplus f_1(L) \oplus f_2(R)$ and $T \oplus S = f_3(X^1)$.

4-point CPA-1 and KPA using S. There is a CPA-1 with $m = 4$ messages. This attack was already published in [16], but we recall it here for sake of completeness. We choose 4 messages $[L_1, R_1]$, $[L_2, R_2]$, $[L_3, R_3]$, $[L_4, R_4]$ such that $L_3 = L_1$, $R_3 = R_2$, $L_4 = L_2$, $R_1 = R_4$ as in Section 2.2. From lemma 1 of Section 2.2, we have $X_1^2 \oplus X_2^2 \oplus X_3^2 \oplus X_4^2 = 0$, i.e. $S_1 \oplus S_2 \oplus S_3 \oplus S_4 = 0$. With a Misty scheme this happens with probability 1 and with a random permutation with probability $\frac{1}{2^n}$. Thus we have a CPA-1 with $m = 4$ on M_L^3. We can transform this CPA-1 into a KPA. When $m \simeq 2^n$, we can get with a non negligible probability 4 pairwise distinct indices (i, j, k, l) such that $L_i = L_j$, $L_k = L_l$; $R_i = R_k$, $R_j = R_l$ (since $\frac{m^4}{2^{4n}}$ is not negligible if $m \simeq 2^n$) and then we check if $S_i \oplus S_j \oplus S_k \oplus S_l = 0$.

Remark: There are 2-point KPA using $S \oplus T$ or S with the same complexity.

CPCA-2 with $m = 3$. We now give a CPCA-2 with $m = 3$ messages. As far as we know, this attack is new. It is inspired from [10] and [16].

Message 1: we choose $[L_1, R_1]$ randomly and get $[S_1, T_1]$.

Message 2: we choose $[S_2, T_2]$ such that $T_1 \oplus S_1 = T_2 \oplus S_2$ and obtain $[L_2, R_2]$ (inverse query: CPCA-2). Since $T \oplus S = f_3(X^1)$ and f_3 is a bijection we have $T_1 \oplus S_1 = T_2 \oplus S_2 \Leftrightarrow X_1^1 = X_2^1 \Leftrightarrow R_1 \oplus f_1(L_1) = R_2 \oplus f_1(L_2)$.

Message 3: We choose $[L_3, R_3] = [L_1, R_2]$ and we get $[S_3, T_3]$ (direct query). It is easy to check that $S_2 \oplus S_3 = R_1 \oplus R_2 \Leftrightarrow X_1^1 = X_2^1$. Thus for a Misty scheme, $S_2 \oplus S_3 = R_1 \oplus R_2$ appears with probability one and with probability about $\frac{1}{2^n}$ for a random permutation. This gives a CPCA-2 with $m = 3$ and $O(1)$ computations.

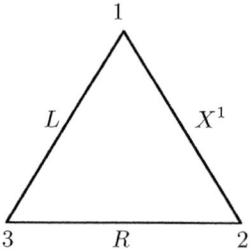

Fig. 4. The equalities in the CPCA-2 attack of M_L^3 with $m = 3$

3.4   4 Rounds

For 4 rounds, we have: $\begin{cases} S = X^2 = R \oplus f_1(L) \oplus f_2(R) \oplus f_3(R \oplus f_1(L)) \\ T \oplus S = f_4(X^2) = f_4(R \oplus f_1(L) \oplus f_2(R)) \end{cases}$.

CPCA-2 with $m = 4$ using $S \oplus T$. Here there is a CPCA-2 with $m = 4$ messages. (This attack was already published in [16], but we recall it here for sake of completeness).

Message 1: we randomly choose $[L_1, R_1]$ and get $[S_1, T_1]$.

Message 2: we choose $[S_2, T_2]$ such that $T_1 \oplus S_1 = T_2 \oplus S_2$. We obtain $[L_2, R_2]$. (Inverse query: this is a CPCA-2). Note that since $T_1 \oplus S_1 = T_2 \oplus S_2$, we have $X_1^2 = X_2^2$ (since $T \oplus S = f_4(X^2)$ and f_4 is a bijection).

Messages 3 and 4: we choose $[L_3, R_3]$ and $[L_4, R_4]$ such that $[L_3, R_3] = [L_1, R_2]$ and $[L_4, R_4] = [L_2, R_1]$. (Direct queries). Then from the "4-point property" (Section 2.2, lemma 1), we have $X_1^2 \oplus X_2^2 \oplus X_3^2 \oplus X_4^2 = 0$. Moreover since here $X_1^2 = X_2^2$, we have: $X_3^2 = X_4^2$, hence this gives $S_3 \oplus T_3 = S_4 \oplus T_4$. This equality will appear with probability 1 on a M_L^4, and with probability $\frac{1}{2^n}$ on a random permutation. This is a CPCA-2 with $m = 4$ and $O(1)$ computations.

This attack can be transformed in CPA-1 and KPA. But there exist better attacks, exposed below.

2-point attack using $S \oplus T$ with $\sqrt{2^n}$ computations in CPA-1 and 2^n in KPA. This attack may be new. However since it is a simple impossible differential attack, it was not difficult to find.

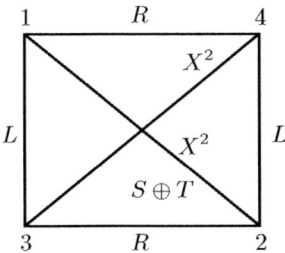

Fig. 5. The equalities in the CPCA-2 attack of M_L^4 with $m = 4$

In CPA-1, we generate m messages such that $\forall i,\ 1 \leq i \leq m,\ R_i = 0$ (or R_i constant). Then we check if there exist $i, j,\ i \neq j$ such that $S_i \oplus T_i = S_j \oplus T_j$. With a random permutation, from the birthday paradox, we will have such collisions when $m \geq O(\sqrt{2^n})$. However on a M_L^4 this is impossible: we have $S \oplus T = f_4(R \oplus f_1(L) \oplus f_2(R))$. Thus, since f_4 and f_1 are permutations, we get

$$\begin{cases} S_i \oplus T_i = S_j \oplus T_j \\ R_i = R_j \end{cases} \Leftrightarrow \begin{cases} R_i = R_j \\ L_i = L_j \end{cases},$$

which is impossible if $i \neq j$.

This CPA-1 can be immediately transformed in a KPA in $O(2^n)$: we look if there are some indices $i \neq j$ such that $T_i \oplus S_i = T_j \oplus S_j$ and $R_i = R_j$. In KPA, for a random permutation this will occur when $m^2 \geq 2^{2n}$, i.e. when $m \geq 2^n$ and with a M_L^4 this will never happen.

4   Attacks on 5 Rounds, with a Complexity Better than 2^{2n}

4.1   4-Point Attacks

For 5 rounds, we have: $\begin{cases} S = X^4 \\ T \oplus S = f_5(X^3) \end{cases}$. There are CPA-1 and KPA on M_L^5 with a complexity $\ll 2^{2n}$. Therefore, to avoid all generic attacks on Misty schemes with a complexity $\ll 2^{2n}$, at least 6 rounds have to be used.

Remark: For Feistel schemes ([10]) the result is similar: we need at least 6 rounds to avoid all attacks with complexity $\ll 2^{2n}$ (there are CPA-1 on ψ^5 in $O(2^n)$, and KPA in $O(2^{\frac{3n}{2}})$). The same holds for Feistel schemes with internal permutations ([19]), with same CPA-1 and KPA complexities (though different attacks). However, the attacks on ψ^5 and M_L^5 are *very* different: on ψ^5 they are 2-point attacks, but on M_L^5, they are 4-point attacks in CPA-1 and in KPA. Moreover, from the computations of Appendix B, we can prove that *all* 2-point attacks on M_L^5 have a complexity greater than 2^{2n}. Therefore it is not possible to find better 2-point attacks since no other 2-point attack exists.

CPA-1 on M_L^5, with complexity $O(2^n)$. The attack works as follows. We choose only 2 values for L: L_1 and L_2. Then, we choose $\simeq 2^n$ values for R_i (i.e. almost all the possible values for R_i). Therefore we have $m \simeq 2 \cdot 2^n$ messages. We count the number $\mathcal{N}$ of (R_i, R_j) values, $R_i \neq R_j$ such that with the 4 following messages:

$$i : [L_1, R_i], \ j : [L_1, R_j], \ i' : [L_2, R_i], \ j' : [L_2, R_j], \text{we have} : \begin{cases} S_i \oplus T_i = S_j \oplus T_j, \\ S_{i'} \oplus T_{i'} = S_{j'} \oplus T_{j'}. \end{cases}$$

Remark: The complexity to compute $\mathcal{N}$ is in $O(2^n)$ since for all R_i value, we compute $[S_i, T_i] = M_L^5([L_1, R_i])$ and $[S_{i'}, T_{i'}] = M_L^5([L_2, R_i])$, store i at the address $[S_i \oplus T_i, S_{i'} \oplus T_{i'}]$ and count the collisions.

We are going to show that for a M_L^5, this number $\mathcal{N}$ is about twice the number we get for a random permutation. Since for a random permutation, we have $\mathcal{N} \simeq \frac{m^2}{2^{2n}}$, we will be able to distinguish when the probability to have $\mathcal{N} \geq 1$ is not negligible, i.e. when $m \geq 2^n$. We can also try another $[L_1, L_2]$; for each $[L_1, L_2]$ the probability of success of this attack is not negligible.

We have $S \oplus T = f_5(X^3)$ and f_5 is a permutation. Therefore:

$$\begin{cases} S_i \oplus T_i = S_j \oplus T_j \\ S_{i'} \oplus T_{i'} = S_{j'} \oplus T_{j'} \end{cases} \Leftrightarrow \begin{cases} X_i^3 = X_j^3 \\ X_{i'}^3 = X_{j'}^3 \end{cases}.$$

Now from the "4-point property" of Section 2.2 (lemma 1), we know that

$$\begin{cases} X_i^1 \oplus X_j^1 \oplus X_{i'}^1 \oplus X_{j'}^1 = 0 \quad (1) \\ X_i^3 \oplus X_j^3 \oplus X_{i'}^3 \oplus X_{j'}^3 = f_3(X_i^1) \oplus f_3(X_j^1) \oplus f_3(X_{i'}^1) \oplus f_3(X_{j'}^1) \quad (2) \end{cases}.$$

Note that $X^1 = f_1(L_1) \oplus R_1$. So $X_i^1 = X_j^1$ is impossible because $L_i = L_j$ and $X_i^1 = X_{i'}^1$ because $R_i = R_{i'}$. However we can have $X_i^1 = X_{j'}^1$ (with probability $\simeq \frac{1}{2^n}$), and if this occurs from (1), then we will also have $X_j^1 = X_{i'}^1$ and if it follows (2), we will have $X_i^3 \oplus X_j^3 \oplus X_{i'}^3 \oplus X_{j'}^3 = 0$ (3).

We now see that for a M_L^5, we have two possibilities to get $\begin{cases} X_i^3 = X_j^3 \\ X_{i'}^3 = X_{j'}^3 \end{cases}$:

1. It can occur for random reasons when $X_i^1 \neq X_{j'}^1$ (probability about $\frac{1}{2^{2n}}$ when R_i and R_j are fixed),
2. It can occur as a consequence of $X_i^1 = X_{j'}^1$ and $X_i^3 = X_j^3$ (probability also about $\frac{1}{2^{2n}}$ when R_i and R_j are fixed).

Thus $\mathcal{N}$ for M_L^5 is about twice $\mathcal{N}$ for a random permutation, as announced. This shows that we can distinguish a random permutation from a M_L^5 in CPA-1 with $m \simeq 2^n$ messages and $O(2^n)$ computations, as claimed.

Transformation into a KPA. The previous attack can be transformed into a KPA with complexity $O(2^{\frac{3n}{2}})$: we count the number $\mathcal{N}$ of (i, j, i', j') such that

$$\begin{cases} L_i = L_j \\ L_{i'} = L_{j'} \neq L_i \end{cases} \text{and} \begin{cases} R_i = R_{i'} \\ R_j = R_{j'} \neq R_i \end{cases} \text{and} \begin{cases} S_i \oplus T_i = S_j \oplus T_j \\ S_{i'} \oplus T_{i'} = S_{j'} \oplus T_{j'} \end{cases}$$

We have $\mathcal{N} \simeq \frac{m^4}{2^{6n}}$ for a random permutation, and $\mathcal{N} \simeq 2\frac{m^4}{2^{6n}}$ for a M_L^5. Therefore this KPA succeeds when $m \geq 2^{\frac{3n}{2}}$.

Remarks:

1. We have implemented these attacks and obtained a confirmation of our results. Details are given in Appendix C.
2. In [5], H. Gilbert and M. Minier proved CPCA-2 security for M_L^5 when $m \leq \sqrt{2^n}$.

4.2 Saturation Attack

This attack was suggested to us by [1] and is related to the attacks published in [6]. For 5 rounds, we have: $S = R \oplus f_1(L) \oplus f_2(R) \oplus f_3(R \oplus f_1(L)) \oplus f_4(R \oplus f_1(L) \oplus f_2(R))$. We choose 2^n messages $[L, R]$ such that $R = 0$ for all messages and L takes all the possible values. Then we compute the Xor of all resulting values S. With a Misty scheme we get 0 with probability 1 since f_1, f_2, f_3 and f_4 are permutations. For a random permutation, we get 0 with probability $\frac{1}{2^n}$. This gives a CPA-1 with complexity $O(2^n)$.

Notice that if among the 2^n inputs and outputs used in this saturation attack, some of them are changed, this attack fails unlike the attacks presented above.

5 Attacks in $O(2^{2n})$ on 6 Rounds

In order to distinguish M_L^d (or M_L^d generators i.e. generators of M_L^d permutations) from random even permutations of B_{2n}, 6 rounds is the maximum number of rounds for which we know attacks in $O(2^{2n})$ computations. (This bound 2^{2n} is important since it is the total number of possible inputs $[L, R]$). The attack will be a *2-point attack* based on $S \oplus T$.

The attack is based on the following theorem.

Theorem 1. *Let $[L_1, R_1]$ and $[L_2, R_2]$ be two messages such that $R_1 = R_2$ and $L_1 \neq L_2$. Let p_1 be the probability that $S_1 \oplus T_1 = S_2 \oplus T_2$ if we have a M_L^6 and p_2 be the probability that $S_1 \oplus T_1 = S_2 \oplus T_2$ if we have a random permutation. Then $p_1 = \frac{2^n - 2}{(2^n - 1)^2}$ and $p_2 = \frac{1}{2^n + 1}$. Therefore p_1 is slightly larger than p_2.*

Proof: For a random permutation, we have $2^{4n} - 2^{2n}$ possibilities for $[S_1, T_1, S_2, T_2]$ (since $S_1 = S_2 \Rightarrow T_1 \neq T_2$), and we have $2^{2n}(2^n - 1)$ of these solutions that satisfy $S_1 \oplus T_1 = S_2 \oplus T_2$ (1) (since we have 2^{2n} possibilities for S_1 and T_1, and then $2^n - 1$ possibilities for $S_2 \neq S_1$). Thus $p_2 = \frac{2^{2n}(2^n - 1)}{2^{4n} - 2^{2n}} = \frac{2^n - 1}{2^{2n} - 1} = \frac{1}{2^n + 1}$. For a M_L^6, we have (since $R_1 = R_2$):

$$S_1 \oplus T_1 = S_2 \oplus T_2 \Leftrightarrow f_6(X_1^4) = f_6(X_2^4)$$
$$\Leftrightarrow X_1^4 = X_2^4$$
$$\Leftrightarrow f_1(L_1) \oplus f_3(R_1 \oplus f_1(L_1)) \oplus f_4(R_1 \oplus f_1(L_1) \oplus f_2(R_1))$$
$$= f_1(L_2) \oplus f_3(R_2 \oplus f_1(L_2)) \oplus f_4(R_2 \oplus f_1(L_2) \oplus f_2(R_2))$$

Let α be the probability that $f_1(L_1) \oplus f_3(R_1 \oplus f_1(L_1)) = f_1(L_2) \oplus f_3(R_1 \oplus f_1(L_2))$ (2). We have $\alpha = \frac{1}{2^n-1}$. Indeed, $L_1 \neq L_2$ and f_1 being a bijection imply $f_1(L_1) \oplus f_1(L_2) \neq 0$. Moreover, f_3 is a bijection and $R_1 = R_2$, thus $f_3(R_1 \oplus f_1(L_2)) \oplus f_3(R_1 \oplus f_1(L_1))$ can take any value but 0 with probability $\frac{1}{2^n-1}$. When (2) occurs, (1) is impossible, since f_1 and f_4 are bijections and $L_1 \neq L_2$. When (2) does not occur, the probability to have (1) is exactly $\frac{1}{2^n-1}$, since f_1 and f_3 are bijections. So we have $p_1 = (1 - \alpha) \cdot \frac{1}{2^n-1}$. This gives $p_1 = \frac{2^n-2}{(2^n-1)^2}$ as claimed. $\square$

Let us now go back to our attack. We count the number $\mathcal{N}$ of messages (i, j), $i < j$ such that $R_i = R_j$ and $S_i \oplus T_i = S_j \oplus T_j$. In KPA, for random permutations, we have $E(\mathcal{N}) = \frac{m(m-1)}{2 \cdot 2^{2n}}$ where m is the number of messages. The standard deviation is[1] $\sigma(\mathcal{N}) = O(\sqrt{E(\mathcal{N})}) = O(\frac{m}{2^n})$. For a M_L^6, we have from theorem 1 above $E(\mathcal{N}) \simeq \frac{m(m-1)}{2 \cdot 2^{2n}}\left(1 + \frac{1}{2^n}\right)$. Therefore, we can distinguish when $\frac{m^2}{2^{3n}} \geq \sigma(\mathcal{N})$, i.e. when $\frac{m^2}{2^{3n}} \geq O(\frac{m}{2^n})$, i.e. $m \geq O(2^{2n})$. The complexity of this KPA is $O(2^{2n})$ (same complexity in CPA-1 and CPCA-2).

Remarks:

1. If we attack a single permutation M_L^6, then $m \leq 2^{2n}$ since 2^{2n} is the total number of possible messages $[L, R] \in I_{2n}$. When the attack needs $m \simeq 2^{2n}$ messages, it has a fixed non-negligible probability of success (not near 0). If we want to have for example a probability of success as near to 1 as wanted, we can assume that we attack M_L^6 generators (with more than one permutation).
2. There exist 4-point KPA on 6 rounds with the same complexity.

6   On the Use of the "h Coefficients" and 2-Point Attacks

In the previous sections, we have studied 2-point attacks or 4-point attacks. As mentioned in Section 4, for 5 rounds, there is no 2-point attack with a complexity similar as the complexity of the 4-point attack. We briefly explain this fact and give an example for 6 rounds. More details are given in Appendix B.

We will systematically analyze all the probability deviation in the M_L^d inputs/outputs compared with truly random permutation of B_{2n}. We only make the analysis for pairs of messages $[L_1, R_1] \rightarrow [S_1, T_1]$ and $[L_2, R_2] \rightarrow [S_2, T_2]$ (with $[L_1, R_1] \neq [L_2, R_2]$ and $[S_1, T_1] \neq [S_2, T_2]$). We find this way the best "2-point attacks", i.e. attacks that use a large number m of messages but that only use correlations on pairs of these messages (such as differential attacks for instance). We will denote by $H(L_1, R_1, L_2, R_2)$, or simply H, the number of internal permutations $(f_1, \ldots, f_d)$ such that:

$$M_L^d(f_1, \ldots, f_d)([L_1, R_1]) = [S_1, T_1] \text{ and } M_L^d(f_1, \ldots, f_d)([L_2, R_2]) = [S_2, T_2].$$

---

[1] This can be proved by using the "covariance formula": $V(\sum_i X_i) = \sum_i V(X_i) + \sum_{i \neq j} Cov(X_i, X_j)$ (#).

The mean value for H is $\frac{|B_n|^d}{2^{2n}(2^{2n}-1)}$ since there are $2^{2n}(2^{2n}-1)$ values for (S_1, T_1, S_2, T_2) such that $[S_1, T_1] \neq [S_2, T_2]$. We will write $h = \frac{H \cdot 2^{4n}}{|B_n|^d}$, and $\overset{\circ}{1}$ stands for the mean value of h: $\overset{\circ}{1} = \frac{1}{1 - \frac{1}{2^{2n}}} = \frac{2^{2n}}{2^{2n}-1}$ and $\epsilon = h - \overset{\circ}{1}$. In the following is explained how to evaluate the different H values, or equivalently the different h or ϵ values. The complete computations are done in Appendix B.

6.1   One Round

For M_L^1, we have: $S = R$ and $T = R \oplus f_1(L)$. Let (C) be the following conditions:
$\begin{cases} S_1 = R_1 \text{ and } S_2 = R_2, \\ L_1 = L_2 \Leftrightarrow T_1 \oplus R_1 = T_2 \oplus R_2. \end{cases}$ When (C) is not satisfied, $H = 0$. When (C) is satisfied, if $L_1 \neq L_2$, $H = \frac{|B_n|}{2^n(2^n-1)}$, and if $L_1 = L_2$, $H = \frac{|B_n|}{2^n}$.

6.2   More Rounds

For two or more rounds, we will distinguish between the following 13 cases (we can check that all possibilities correspond to exactly one of these cases, since $[L_1, R_1] \neq [L_2, R_2]$ and $[S_1, T_1] \neq [S_2, T_2]$).

$1: L_1 \neq L_2, R_1 \neq R_2, S_1 \neq S_2, R_1 \oplus R_2 \neq S_1 \oplus S_2, S_1 \oplus S_2 \neq T_1 \oplus T_2$
$2: L_1 \neq L_2, R_1 = R_2, S_1 \neq S_2, (\text{then } R_1 \oplus R_2 \neq S_1 \oplus S_2), S_1 \oplus S_2 \neq T_1 \oplus T_2$
$3: L_1 = L_2, R_1 \neq R_2, S_1 \neq S_2, R_1 \oplus R_2 \neq S_1 \oplus S_2, S_1 \oplus S_2 \neq T_1 \oplus T_2$
$4: L_1 \neq L_2, R_1 \neq R_2, S_1 \neq S_2, R_1 \oplus R_2 = S_1 \oplus S_2, S_1 \oplus S_2 \neq T_1 \oplus T_2$
$5: L_1 = L_2, R_1 \neq R_2, S_1 \neq S_2, R_1 \oplus R_2 = S_1 \oplus S_2, S_1 \oplus S_2 \neq T_1 \oplus T_2$
$6: L_1 \neq L_2, R_1 \neq R_2, S_1 = S_2, (\text{then } R_1 \oplus R_2 \neq S_1 \oplus S_2) S_1 \oplus S_2 \neq T_1 \oplus T_2$
$7: L_1 \neq L_2, R_1 = R_2, S_1 = S_2, (\text{then } R_1 \oplus R_2 = S_1 \oplus S_2), S_1 \oplus S_2 \neq T_1 \oplus T_2$
$8: L_1 = L_2, R_1 \neq R_2, S_1 = S_2, (\text{then } R_1 \oplus R_2 \neq S_1 \oplus S_2) S_1 \oplus S_2 \neq T_1 \oplus T_2$
$9: L_1 \neq L_2, R_1 \neq R_2, S_1 \neq S_2, R_1 \oplus R_2 \neq S_1 \oplus S_2, S_1 \oplus S_2 = T_1 \oplus T_2$
$10: L_1 \neq L_2, R_1 = R_2, S_1 \neq S_2, R_1 \oplus R_2 \neq S_1 \oplus S_2, S_1 \oplus S_2 = T_1 \oplus T_2$
$11: L_1 = L_2, R_1 \neq R_2, S_1 \neq S_2, R_1 \oplus R_2 \neq S_1 \oplus S_2, S_1 \oplus S_2 = T_1 \oplus T_2$
$12: L_1 \neq L_2, R_1 \neq R_2, S_1 \neq S_2, R_1 \oplus R_2 = S_1 \oplus S_2, S_1 \oplus S_2 = T_1 \oplus T_2$
$13: L_1 = L_2, R_1 \neq R_2, S_1 \neq S_2, R_1 \oplus R_2 = S_1 \oplus S_2, S_1 \oplus S_2 = T_1 \oplus T_2$

We will denote by h_i^d, $1 \leq i \leq 13$, or simply by h_i when d is clearly fixed, the value of h in case i. (Similarly, ϵ_i^d or ϵ_i denotes the value of ϵ in case i). These values are computed by induction (see Appendix B).

6.3   Example of Applications

Let us try to attack M_L^6 with ϵ_{10} (see Appendix B for the notations). First, we have to evaluate ϵ_{10} for 6 rounds. From $(E12)$ we know that $\epsilon_{10}^6 = \epsilon_9^4$. Thus, $\epsilon_{10}^6 = \frac{2^{2n}(2^n-3)}{(2^n-1)^3(2^n+1)} \simeq \frac{1}{2^n}$. Case 10 is when $R_1 = R_2$ and $S_1 \oplus S_2 = T_1 \oplus T_2$.

Table 1. Minimum number A of computations needed to distinguish a Misty generator M_L^d from random even permutations of B_{2n}. For simplicity we denote 2^α for $O(2^\alpha)$.

	KPA	CPA-1	CPCA-2
M_L^1	1	1	1
M_L^2	$\sqrt{2^n}$	2	2
M_L^3	2^n	4	3
M_L^4	2^n	$\sqrt{2^n}$	4
M_L^5	$2^{3n/2}$	2^n	2^n
M_L^6	2^{2n}	2^{2n}	2^{2n}
M_L^7	2^{4n}	2^{4n}	2^{4n}
M_L^8	2^{4n}	2^{4n}	2^{4n}
M_L^9	2^{6n}	2^{6n}	2^{6n}
M_L^{10}	2^{6n}	2^{6n}	2^{6n}
M_L^d, d odd, $d \geq 9$	$2^{(d-3)n}$	$2^{(d-3)n}$	$2^{(d-3)n}$
M_L^d, d even, $d \geq 8$	$2^{(d-4)n}$	$2^{(d-4)n}$	$2^{(d-4)n}$

$\epsilon_{10}^6 \simeq \frac{1}{2^n}$ means that instead of having in KPA about $\frac{m^2}{2^{2n}}$ messages in this case 10, we will have about $\frac{m^2}{2^{2n}}(1 + \frac{1}{2^n})$ such messages. The standard deviation in the case of two point attacks is about the square root of the mean value[2], hence here $\sigma = O(\frac{m}{2^n})$, and we will distinguish when $\frac{m^2}{2^{2n}} \cdot \frac{1}{2^n} \geq \frac{m}{2^n}$, i.e. when $m \geq O(2^{2n})$. This is exactly the two point attacks described in Section 5.

Remarks:

1. From the ϵ_{10}^6 value we can also easily recompute the probabilities p_1 and p_2 of Section 4. $p_2 = \frac{2^{2n}(2^n-1)}{2^{4n}} \overset{\circ}{1}$, since we have $2^{2n}(2^n-1)$ values (S_1, T_1, S_2, T_2) such that $S_1 \oplus S_2 = T_1 \oplus T_2$. This gives $p_2 = \frac{1}{2^n+1}$. Similarly, $p_1 = \frac{2^{2n}(2^n-1)}{2^{4n}}(\overset{\circ}{1} + \epsilon_{10})$, gives $p_1 = \frac{2^n-2}{(2^n-1)^2}$.
2. Theorem 1 of Section 5 can be seen as a property of the h_{10} coefficient, for 6 rounds of Misty.

7   Summary of the Best Known Generic Attacks on Misty Schemes

Our results are summarized in Table 1. In this table, we do not not mention CPA-2 and CPCA-1 since the best known results for these attacks are the same as for CPA-1. We implicitly consider attacks on permutation generators when the complexities are greater than 2^{2n}.

For Misty R schemes, M_R^d, the number of computations is the same, except for 3 rounds in CPA-1, where the best known attack is in $O(\sqrt{2^n})$ computations for M_R^3 (instead of 4 for M_L^3).

---

[2] This can be proved from the covariance formula (#) seen in Section 5.

8   Conclusion

In this paper we presented different kinds of attacks on Misty schemes and our final results are summarized in Section 7. More attacks are given in the extended version of this paper. It is really fascinating to see how many different kind of attacks exist on Misty schemes: there are 2-points attacks on S, 2-points attacks on $S \oplus T$, 4-points attacks on S, 4-points attacks on $S \oplus T$, saturation attacks, brute force attacks, attacks on the signature since Misty schemes are even permutations (see the extended version). This is completely different than for Feistel schemes with internal functions [10], or also Feistel schemes with internal permutations [19]. It is really not obvious to see which attacks give the best complexity before making a systematic and precise analysis.

There are still many open problems on generic Misty schemes. For example, several gaps remain between the proof of security in $O(\sqrt{2^n})$ (birthday bound) obtained in [5,15,17,18] and the best known attacks. For a security less than or equal to 2^n, generalizations of what was done on ψ^k (cf [11,9]) are probably possible.

References

1. Personal Anonymous Communication
2. Specification of the 3GPP Confidentiality and Integrity Algorithm KASUMI, http://www.etsi.org/
3. Aiello, W., Venkatesan, R.: Foiling Birthday Attacks in Length-Doubling Transformations - Benes: A Non-Reversible Alternative to Feistel. In: Maurer, U.M. (ed.) EUROCRYPT 1996. LNCS, vol. 1070, pp. 307–320. Springer, Heidelberg (1996)
4. Coppersmith, D.: Luby-Rackoff: Four Rounds is not enough. Technical report, Technical Report RC20674, IBM Research Report (December 1996)
5. Gilbert, H., Minier, M.: New Results on the Pseudorandomness of Some Blockcipher Constructions. In: Matsui, M. (ed.) FSE 2001. LNCS, vol. 2355, pp. 248–266. Springer, Heidelberg (2002)
6. Knudsen, L., Wagner, D.: Integral Cryptanalysis. In: Daemen, J., Rijmen, V. (eds.) FSE 2002. LNCS, vol. 2365, pp. 112–127. Springer, Heidelberg (2002)
7. Lai, X., Massey, J.L.: A Proposal for a New Block Encryption Standard. In: Damgård, I. (ed.) EUROCRYPT 1990. LNCS, vol. 473, pp. 389–404. Springer, Heidelberg (1991)
8. Matsui, M.: New Block Encryption Algorithm. In: Biham, E. (ed.) FSE 1997. LNCS, vol. 1267, pp. 54–68. Springer, Heidelberg (1997)
9. Maurer, U., Pietrzak, K.: The Security of Many-Round Luby-Rackoff Pseudo-Random Permutations. In: Biham, E. (ed.) EUROCRYPT 2003. LNCS, vol. 2656, pp. 544–561. Springer, Heidelberg (2003)
10. Patarin, J.: Generic Attacks on Feistel Schemes. In: Boyd, C. (ed.) ASIACRYPT 2001. LNCS, vol. 2248, pp. 222–238. Springer, Heidelberg (2001)
11. Patarin, J.: Security of Random Feistel Schemes with 5 or more rounds. In: Franklin, M.K. (ed.) CRYPTO 2004. LNCS, vol. 3152, pp. 106–122. Springer, Heidelberg (2004)
12. Patarin, J.: A Proof of Security in $O(2^n)$ for the Benes Schemes. In: Vaudenay, S. (ed.) AFRICACRYPT 2008. LNCS, vol. 5023, pp. 209–220. Springer, Heidelberg (2008)

13. Patarin, J., Nachef, V., Berbain, C.: Generic Attacks on Unbalanced Feistel Schemes with Contracting Functions. In: Lai, X., Chen, K. (eds.) ASIACRYPT 2006. LNCS, vol. 4284, pp. 396–411. Springer, Heidelberg (2006)
14. Patarin, J., Nachef, V., Berbain, C.: Generic Attacks on Unbalanced Feistel Schemes with Expanding Functions. In: Kurosawa, K. (ed.) ASIACRYPT 2007. LNCS, vol. 4833, pp. 325–341. Springer, Heidelberg (2007)
15. Piret, G., Quisquater, J.-J.: Security of the MISTY structure in the luby-rackoff model: Improved results. In: Handschuh, H., Hasan, A. (eds.) SAC 2004. LNCS, vol. 3357, pp. 100–115. Springer, Heidelberg (2004)
16. Sakurai, K., Zheng, Y.: On Non-Pseudorandomness from Block Ciphers with Provable Immunity Against Linear Cryptanalysis. IEICE Trans. Fundamentals E80-A(1) (January 1997)
17. Sugita, M.: Pseudorandomness of a Block Cipher MISTY. Technical report, Technical Report of IEIECE, ISEC 96-9
18. Sugita, M.: Pseudorandomness of a Block Cipher with Recursive Strictures. Technical report, Technical Report of IEIECE, ISEC 97-9
19. Treger, J., Patarin, J.: Generic Attacks on Feistel Networks with Internal Permutations. In: Preneel, B. (ed.) AFRICACRYPT 2009. LNCS, vol. 5580, pp. 41–59. Springer, Heidelberg (2009)

A   Attacks for 7 Rounds and More than 7 Rounds

The attacks that we have seen for 6 rounds can be extended for $d \geq 7$ rounds in order to distinguish M_L^d generators from random permutations of B_{2n} generators. When $d \geq 7$ the complexity of the best known attacks are strictly greater than 2^{2n} and we will use λ permutations of the generator with $\lambda > 1$.

2-point Attacks when d is even, $d \geq 8$.

Theorem 2. *Let $[L_1, R_1]$ and $[L_2, R_2]$ be two messages such that $R_1 = R_2$ and $L_1 \neq L_2$. Let p_1 be the probability that $S_1 \oplus T_1 = S_2 \oplus T_2$ if we have a M_L^d, d even, $d \geq 6$ and p_2 be the probability that $S_1 \oplus T_1 = S_2 \oplus T_2$ if we have a random permutation. Then $p_1 - p_2 = \frac{(-1)^{\frac{d}{2}+1}}{(2^n)^{\frac{d}{2}-2}} + O\left(\frac{1}{(2^n)^{\frac{d}{2}-1}}\right)$.*

Proof: This can be easily proved directly by induction (it is just a generalization of what we did for Theorem 1), or by using the ϵ_{10} values that we compute in Appendix B.   □

Let us now go back to the attacks. We count the number $\mathcal{N}$ of messages $i, j, i < j$ that belong to the same permutation and such that $R_i = R_j$ and $S_i \oplus T_i = S_j \oplus T_j$.

In KPA, for λ random permutations with m messages per permutation we have: $E(\mathcal{N}) = \lambda \frac{m(m-1)}{2 \cdot 2^{2n}}$ and the standard deviation is $\sigma(\mathcal{N}) = O(\frac{m\sqrt{\lambda}}{2^n})$. (The fact that $\sigma(\mathcal{N}) = \sqrt{E(\mathcal{N})}$ can easily be proved from the "covariance formula" (#) of Section 5). For a M_L^d, d even, $d \geq 6$, we will have $E(\mathcal{N}) \simeq \lambda \frac{m(m-1)}{2 \cdot 2^{2n}}\left(1 + \frac{(-1)^{\frac{d}{2}+1}}{(2^n)^{\frac{d}{2}-2}}\right)$ (cf Theorem 2 above). Therefore we can distinguish when: $\frac{\lambda m^2}{2^{n\frac{d}{2}}} \geq \sigma(\mathcal{N}) = 0(\frac{m\sqrt{\lambda}}{2^n})$, i.e. $\sqrt{\lambda}m \geq 2^{n(\frac{d}{2}-1)}$, or $\lambda m^2 \geq 2^{n(d-2)}$. With $m \simeq 2^{2n}$, this gives $\lambda \geq 2^{n(d-6)}$ and a complexity $\lambda \cdot 2^{2n} = 2^{n(d-4)}$.

Conclusion: when d is even and $d \geq 6$, we can distinguish M_L^d generators from truly random permutation generators of B_{2n} with a complexity in $O(2^{n(d-4)})$.

2-point attack when d is odd, $d \geq 7$. When d increases, the security of M_L^d can only increase, since we have compositions of permutations with independent secret values $f_1, \ldots, f_d$. Since M_L^{d+1} can be attacked in $O(2^{n(d+1-4)}) = O(2^{n(d-3)})$ from the result above, when d is odd the security of M_L^d generators is at maximum in $O(2^{n(d-3)})$. This value $O(2^{n(d-3)})$ can be achieved by computing the number $\mathcal{N}$ of messages i, j, $i < j$ that belong to the same permutation and such that $R_i = R_j$ and $S_i \oplus T_i = S_j \oplus T_j$. (This is the same attack as for d even, but with complexity $O(2^{n(d-3)})$ instead of $O(2^{n(d-4)})$). This 2-point attack using $S \oplus T$ is based on the coefficient ϵ_{10} that is computed in Appendix B. When d is odd, another attack, with the same complexity $O(2^{n(d-3)})$ is obtained by computing the number $\mathcal{N}$ of messages i, j, $i < j$ that belong to the same permutation and such that $L_i = L_j$ and $S_i \oplus T_i = S_j \oplus T_j$. This 2-point attack using $S \oplus T$ is based on the ϵ_{11} coefficient that is computed in Appendix B. The complexity of these attacks ($O(2^{n(d-3)})$) can be easily proved by induction (this is a simple generalization of the 2-point attack given for 6 rounds), or by using the evaluation for the ϵ_{10} and ϵ_{11} coefficients that we compute in Appendix B.

4-point attack when $d \geq 7$. The 4-point attacks given for $d = 6$ can be generalized to attack M_L^d generators for $d \geq 7$. For $d = 6$ and $d = 7$ this will just give the same complexity as the 2-point attacks. For $d \geq 8$ the complexity will be worse. In fact, when $d \geq 6$ the best known 4-point attacks have a complexity of $O(2^{(2d-10)n})$ and this is worse than the complexity $O(2^{(d-4)n})$ for d even or $O(2^{(d-3)n})$ for d odd of the 2-point attacks when $d \geq 8$. (We do not give much details for these 4-point attacks when $d \geq 7$ since the complexities are equal or worse than those of the 2-point attacks).

B   Computation of the "h Coefficients"

In this appendix, we give more details about the computation of the "h coefficients" presented in Section 6.

B.1   2 Rounds

For 2 rounds, we have $S = R \oplus f_1(L)$ and $T \oplus S = f_2(R)$. We can easily compute the h_i values and the $\epsilon_i = h_i - \overset{\circ}{1}$ values. We get for 2 rounds:

$$h_1 = \frac{2^{2n}}{(2^n-1)^2} \; ; \; \epsilon_1 = \frac{2 \cdot 2^{2n}}{(2^n-1)^2(2^n+1)} \simeq \frac{2}{2^n}$$

$$h_2 = 0 \quad\quad ; \; \epsilon_2 = \frac{-2^{2n}}{(2^n-1)(2^n+1)} \simeq -1$$

$$h_3 = 0 \quad\quad ; \quad\quad \epsilon_3 = -\overset{\circ}{1} \simeq -1$$

$$h_4 = 0 \quad\quad ; \quad\quad \epsilon_4 = -\overset{\circ}{1} \simeq -1$$

$$h_5 = \frac{2^{2n}}{2^n-1} \quad ; \; \epsilon_5 = \frac{2^{3n}}{(2^n-1)(2^n+1)} \simeq 2^n$$

$$h_6 = \frac{2^{2n}}{(2^n-1)^2} \; ; \; \epsilon_6 = \frac{2 \cdot 2^{2n}}{(2^n-1)^2(2^n+1)} \simeq \frac{2}{2^n}$$

$$h_7 = 0 \quad\quad ; \quad\quad \epsilon_7 = -\overset{\circ}{1} \simeq -1$$

$$h_8 = 0 \quad\quad ; \quad\quad \epsilon_8 = -\overset{\circ}{1} \simeq -1$$

$$h_9 = 0 \quad\quad ; \quad\quad \epsilon_9 = -\overset{\circ}{1} \simeq -1$$

$$h_{10} = \frac{2^{2n}}{2^n-1} \; ; \; \epsilon_{10} = \frac{2^{3n}}{(2^n-1)(2^n+1)} \simeq 2^n$$

$$h_{11} = 0 \quad\quad ; \quad\quad \epsilon_{11} = -\overset{\circ}{1} \simeq -1$$

$$h_{12} = 0 \quad\quad ; \quad\quad \epsilon_{12} = -\overset{\circ}{1} \simeq -1$$

$$h_{13} = 0 \quad\quad ; \quad\quad \epsilon_{13} = -\overset{\circ}{1} \simeq -1$$

B.2 Induction

Using the fact that M_L^{d+1} is the composition of a M_L^d, and our values of H for M_L^1, we get induction formulas on the h_i coefficients (for $d \geq 2$).

To simplify the notations, we will denote h_i^d by h_i and h_i^{d+1} by h_i'. With these notations, the induction formulas are:

$$(D1) \begin{cases} h_1' = \frac{1}{2^n-1}[(2^n-3)h_1 + h_2 + h_4] \\ h_2' = \frac{1}{2^n-1}[(2^n-2)h_3 + h_5] \\ h_3' = h_1 \\ h_4' = \frac{1}{2^n-1}[(2^n-2)h_1 + h_2] \\ h_5' = h_4 \end{cases}$$

$$(D2) \begin{cases} h_6' = \frac{1}{2^n-1}[(2^n-2)h_6 + h_7] \\ h_7' = h_8 \\ h_8' = h_6 \end{cases} \qquad (D3) \begin{cases} h_9' = \frac{1}{2^n-1}[(2^n-3)h_9 + h_{10} + h_{12}] \\ h_{10}' = \frac{1}{2^n-1}[(2^n-2)h_{11} + h_{13}] \\ h_{11}' = h_9 \\ h_{12}' = \frac{1}{2^n-1}[(2^n-2)h_9 + h_{10}] \\ h_{13}' = h_{12} \end{cases}$$

From these equations we can compute all the h_i^d values, for any $d \geq 2$ by induction from the previous values. We will continue the evaluation in order to see how small the ϵ values are.

We have, for all S_1, T_1, S_2, T_2: $\sum_{L_1,R_1,L_2,R_2} H(L,R,S,T) = |B_n|^d$ $(D4)$ since each output comes from exactly one input. Similarly, for all L_1, R_1, L_2, R_2: $\sum_{S_1,T_1,S_2,T_2} H(L,R,S,T) = |B_n|^d$ $(D5)$ since each input gives exactly one output. With $h = \frac{H \cdot 2^{4n}}{|B_n|^d}$ we obtain: For all S,T: $\sum_{L,R} h(L,R,S,T) = 2^{4n}$ $(D6)$. For all L, R: $\sum_{S,T} h(L,R,S,T) = 2^{4n}$ $(D7)$. When we specify S, T, $(D6)$ gives 3 equations on the h_i values:

- When $S_1 \neq S_2$ and $S_1 \oplus S_2 \neq T_1 \oplus T_2$:
  $(2^n-1)(2^n-2)h_1 + (2^n-1)h_2 + (2^n-2)h_3 + (2^n-1)h_4 + h_5 = 2^{2n}$ $(D8)$
- When $S_1 = S_2$ and $S_1 \oplus S_2 \neq T_1 \oplus T_2$: $(2^n-1)h_6 + h_7 + h_8 = \frac{2^{2n}}{2^n-1}$ $(D9)$.
- When $S_1 \oplus S_2 = T_1 \oplus T_2$ and $S_1 \neq S_2$:
  $(2^n-1)(2^n-2)h_9 + (2^n-1)h_{10} + (2^n-2)h_{11} + (2^n-1)h_{12} + h_{13} = 2^{2n}$ $(D10)$.

Similarly, when we specify values L, R, $(D7)$ gives 3 equations on the h_i values:

- When $L_1 \neq L_2$ and $R_1 \neq R_2$:
  $(2^n-1)(2^n-2)h_1 + (2^n-1)h_4 + (2^n-1)h_6 + (2^n-2)h_9 + h_{12} = 2^{2n}$ $(D11)$.
- When $L_1 = L_2$ and $R_1 \neq R_2$:
  $(2^n-1)(2^n-2)h_3 + (2^n-1)h_5 + (2^n-1)h_8 + (2^n-2)h_{11} + h_{13} = 2^{2n}$ $(D12)$
- When $R_1 = R_2$ and $L_1 \neq L_2$: $(2^n-1)h_2 + h_7 + h_{10} = \frac{2^{2n}}{2^n-1}$ $(D13)$

Indices 1,2,3,4,5. From $(D1)$ and $(D8)$, and by using the ϵ_i variables instead of the h_i variables, $\epsilon_i = h_i - \overset{\circ}{1}$, we get:

$$(E1) \begin{cases} \epsilon_1' = \frac{(2^n-3)\epsilon_1}{2^n-1} + \frac{\epsilon_2}{2^n-1} + \frac{\epsilon_4}{2^n-1} \\ \epsilon_2' = (-2^n+2)\epsilon_1 - \epsilon_2 - \epsilon_4 \\ \epsilon_4' = \frac{(2^n-2)\epsilon_1}{2^n-1} + \frac{\epsilon_2}{2^n-1} \end{cases} \qquad (E2) \begin{cases} \epsilon_3' = \epsilon_1 \\ \epsilon_5' = \epsilon_4 \end{cases}.$$

From these equations, we can compute all the ϵ_i values by induction, but we want more: we want to evaluate how fast the ϵ_i values decrease. We have:
$\epsilon'_1 - \epsilon'_4 = \frac{-(\epsilon_1 - \epsilon_4)}{2^n - 1}$. Thus, by induction: $(\epsilon_1 - \epsilon_4) = \frac{(-1)^k \cdot 2^{2n}}{(2^n - 1)^k}$ $(E3)$. Moreover, if we denote $\epsilon''_i = \epsilon_i^{d+2}$, $\epsilon'_i = \epsilon_i^{d+1}$, $\epsilon_i = \epsilon_i^d$, we have:
$(E4)$ $\epsilon''_1 = \frac{-\epsilon_1 - 2\epsilon'_1 + \epsilon'_4}{2^n - 1}$ $\epsilon''_2 = \epsilon_1 + \epsilon'_1 + \epsilon'_4$; $\epsilon''_4 = \frac{-\epsilon_1 - \epsilon'_1}{2^n - 1}$.
$(E5)$ $\epsilon'_3 = \epsilon_1$ $\epsilon'_5 = \epsilon_4$.

These equations show that the ϵ_i values globally decrease by a factor of about 2^n every 2 rounds (for the indices $1, 2, 3, 4, 5$).

Indices 6,7,8. From $(D2)$ and $(D9)$, and by using the ϵ_i variables instead of the h_i variables, $\epsilon_i = h_i \overset{\circ}{-} 1$,
$(E6)$ $\epsilon'_6 = \frac{-\epsilon_6 - \epsilon_8}{2^n - 1}$, $\epsilon'_8 = \epsilon_6$, and $(E7)$ $\epsilon'_7 = \epsilon_8$.
These equations show that $\epsilon_6, \epsilon_7, \epsilon_8$ will decrease by a factor about 2^n each time we add two rounds.

Indices 9,10,11,12,13. From $(D3)$ and $(D10)$, and by using the ϵ_i variables instead of the h_i variables ($\epsilon_i = h_i \overset{\circ}{-} 1$), we get:

$$(E8) \begin{cases} \epsilon'_9 = \frac{2^n - 3}{2^n - 1}\epsilon_9 + \frac{\epsilon_{10}}{2^n - 1} + \frac{\epsilon_{12}}{2^n - 1} \\ \epsilon'_{10} = (-2^n + 2)\epsilon_9 - \epsilon_{10} - \epsilon_{12} \\ \epsilon'_{12} = \frac{2^n - 2}{2^n - 1}\epsilon_9 + \frac{\epsilon_{10}}{2^n - 1} \end{cases} (E9) \begin{cases} \epsilon'_{11} = \epsilon_9 \\ \epsilon_{13} = \epsilon_{12} \end{cases}$$

Moreover by induction from $(E8)$ and the initial values for 2 rounds, we get $\epsilon_9 = \epsilon_{12}$ (thus $h_9 = h_{12}$). Thus we have:
$(E10)$ $\epsilon'_9 = \frac{2^n - 2}{2^n - 1}\epsilon_9 + \frac{\epsilon_{10}}{2^n - 1}$ $\epsilon'_{10} = (-2^n + 1)\epsilon_9 - \epsilon_{10} = \epsilon_{11}$.
$(E11)$ $\epsilon'_{11} = \epsilon_9$ $\epsilon'_{13} = \epsilon_9$ $\epsilon_{12} = \epsilon_9$.
If we denote $\epsilon''_i = \epsilon_i^{d+2}$, we have: $\epsilon''_{10} = \frac{-\epsilon_{10} - \epsilon'_{10}}{2^n - 1} = \epsilon_9$ $(E12)$
These equations $(E11), (E12)$, show that $\epsilon_9, \epsilon_{10}, \epsilon_{11}, \epsilon_{12}, \epsilon_{13}$ globally decrease by a factor 2^n every two rounds. With the formulas above, we can compute all the values ϵ_i and evaluate ϵ_i for any round.

Expression as power of complex numbers. It is also possible to formulate all the ϵ_i by using these two complex numbers β and λ:
$\lambda = \frac{1}{2(2^n - 1)}(-1 + i\sqrt{4 \cdot 2^n - 5})$ $\beta = \frac{2^{2n}}{(2^n - 1)(2^n + 1)}(2^n + \frac{i(2^n - 2)}{\sqrt{4 \cdot 2^n - 5}})$.
$\lambda, \overline{\lambda}$ and $\frac{-1}{2^n - 1}$ are the 3 eigenvalues that occur in the induction relation among the variables, and we have $|\lambda| = \frac{1}{\sqrt{2^n - 1}}$, and $\lambda^2(2^n - 1) + \lambda + 1 = 0$. Let $Re(z)$ be the real value of a complex number z. Then, after d rounds, we have:

$$\begin{aligned} \epsilon_1^d &= \frac{(-1)^d \cdot 2^{2n}}{(2^n - 1)^{d+1}} + Re(\beta \cdot \lambda^{d+2}) \\ \epsilon_2^d &= Re(\lambda^d \beta) &= \epsilon_9^d \\ \epsilon_3^d &= \frac{(-1)^{d+1} \cdot 2^{2n}}{(2^n - 1)^d} + Re(\beta \cdot \lambda^{d+1}) &= \epsilon_1^{d-1} \end{aligned}$$

Table 2. Average of the number of collisions of type $S_i \oplus T_i = S_j \oplus T_j$ and $S_k \oplus T_k = S_l \oplus T_l$ obtained in the case of a M_L scheme or a random permutation

	Average of the number of collisions $S_i \oplus T_i = S_j \oplus T_j$ and $S_k \oplus T_k = S_l \oplus T_l$ obtained in the case of a M_L scheme	Average of the number of collisions $S_i \oplus T_i = S_j \oplus T_j$ and $S_k \oplus T_k = S_l \oplus T_l$ obtained in the case of a random permutation
$3 \cdot 2^n$ messages $\{[L,R], L=a,b,c,\ R,\in I_n\}$	1	0.23
$4 \cdot 2^n$ messages $\{[L,R], L=a,b,c,\ R \in I_n\}$	1.6	0.84
$5 \cdot 2^n$ messages $\{[L,R], L=a,b,c,d,e,\ R \in I_n\}$	3.15	1.3

$$\epsilon_4^d = \frac{(-1)^{d+1} \cdot 2^{2n}(2^n-2)}{(2^n-1)^{d+1}} + Re(\beta \cdot \lambda^{d+2}) = \epsilon_1^d + \frac{(-1)^{d+1} \cdot 2^{2n}}{(2^n-1)^d}$$
$$\epsilon_5^d = \frac{(-1)^d \cdot 2^{2n}(2^n-2)}{(2^n-1)^d} + Re(\beta \cdot \lambda^{d+1}) = \epsilon_4^{d-1}$$
$$\epsilon_6^d = Re(\lambda^{d+1}\beta) = \epsilon_9^{d+1}$$
$$\epsilon_7^d = Re(\lambda^{d-1}\beta)) = \epsilon_9^{d-1}$$
$$\epsilon_8^d = Re(\lambda^d\beta) = \epsilon_9^d$$
$$\epsilon_9^d = Re(\lambda^d\beta)$$
$$\epsilon_{10}^d = Re(\lambda^{d-2}\beta) = \epsilon_9^{d-2}$$
$$\epsilon_{11}^d = Re(\lambda^{d-1}\beta) = \epsilon_9^{d-1}$$
$$\epsilon_{12}^d = Re(\lambda^d\beta) = \epsilon_9^d$$
$$\epsilon_{13}^d = Re(\lambda^{d-1}\beta) = \epsilon_9^{d-1}$$

C   Experimental Results

We implemented our new 4-point attack on 5-round L schemes described in Section 4. For each test we ran, we generated some messages (i, j, k, l) and then checked the number of collisions $S_i \oplus T_i = S_j \oplus T_j$ and $S_k \oplus T_k = S_l \oplus T_l$ obtained, for all 4-tuples of messages (i, j, k, l) verifying $L_i = L_j$, $L_k = L_l$, $R_i = R_k$, $R_j = R_l$. Note that we considered only one 4-tuple amongst (i, j, k, l), (j, i, l, k), (l, k, j, i) and (k, l, i, j). Table 2 summarizes the results obtained.

The length of the messages considered in this implementation is 32 bits (blocs of length $n = 16$). To simulate random permutations, we used Feistel schemes with a number of rounds between 20 and 50.

As claimed in Section 4, we obtain two times more collisions in the case of a L scheme than in the case of a random permutation. Therefore, we are able to distinguish most of the 5 round L schemes from a random permutation with $O(2^n)$ messages.

Cryptanalysis of the Hidden Matrix Cryptosystem

Jean-Charles Faugère[1], Antoine Joux[2,3], Ludovic Perret[1], and Joana Treger[2]

[1] INRIA, Centre Paris-Rocquencourt, SALSA Project
UPMC, Univ Paris 06, LIP6
CNRS, UMR 7606, LIP6
104, avenue du Président Kennedy
75016 Paris, France
jean-charles.faugere@grobner.org, ludovic.perret@lip6.fr
[2] Université Versailles-Saint Quentin
joana.treger@uvsq.prism.fr
[3] DGA
antoine.joux@m4x.org

Abstract. In this paper, we present an efficient cryptanalysis of the so-called HM cryptosystem which was published at Asiacrypt'1999, and one perturbed version of HM. Until now, this scheme was exempt from cryptanalysis. We first present a distinguisher which uses a differential property of the public key. This distinguisher permits to break one perturbed version of HM. After that, we describe a practical message-recovery attack against HM using Gröbner bases. The attack can be mounted in few hundreds seconds for recommended parameters. It turns out that algebraic systems arising in HM are easier to solve than random systems of the same size. Note that this fact provides another distinguisher for HM. Interestingly enough, we offer an explanation why algebraic systems arising in HM are easy to solve in practice. Briefly, this is due to the apparition of many new linear and quadratic equations during the Gröbner basis computation. More precisely, we provide an upper bound on the maximum degree reached during the Gröbner basis computation (a.k.a. the degree of regularity) of HM systems. For $\mathbb{F}_2$, which is the initial and usual setting of HM, the degree of regularity is upper-bounded by 3. In general, this degree of regularity is upper-bounded by 4. These bounds allow a polynomial-time solving of the system given by the public equations in any case. All in all, we consider that the HM scheme is broken for all practical parameters.

1 Introduction

Multivariate cryptography comprises all the cryptographic schemes that use multivariate polynomials. The use of polynomial systems in cryptography dates back to the mid eighties with the design of C* [16], later followed by many other proposals [19,23,22,14,24,25]. At first glance, many aspects of such systems are

M. Abdalla and P.S.L.M. Barreto (Eds.): LATINCRYPT 2010, LNCS 6212, pp. 241–254, 2010.

tempting for cryptographers. First, basing schemes on the hard problem of solving a system of multivariate equations is very appealing. Indeed, generic algorithms to solve this problem are exponential in the worst case, and solving random system of algebraic equations is also known to be difficult (i.e. exponential) in the average case. Moreover, no quantum algorithm allowing to solve non linear equations exists. Finally, multivariate schemes usually require computations with rather small integers leading to rather efficient smart-card implementations (see for example [5])

Unfortunately, it appears that most multivariate public-key schemes suffer from obvious to less obvious weaknesses ([17,13,9,7] for instance). One reason is that the public-key equations are constructed from a highly structured system of equations. Although the structure is hidden, it can be exploited for instance via differential or Gröbner based techniques. Regarding the intensity of such attacks these last years, it is rather remarkable that the HM cryptosystem [20,21], despite a "special property" pointed out in the original paper, is still standing. In this paper, we use both a property of the differential of the public key and Gröbner basis techniques to attack the HM scheme. The common point between these attacks is that both take advantage on the non-commutativity of the matrices. In particular, we present a message-recovery attack against HM which works on all practical parameters. In addition and in contrast to many cryptanalytic results against multivariate schemes, we are able to theoretically explain why algebraic systems arising in HM are easy to solve in practice.

1.1   Organization of the Paper. Main Results

This paper is organized as follows. In Section 2, we give an introduction on multivariate cryptography and specifically detail the HM construction. In Section 3, we show that the public key equations of HM are distinguishable from a random quadratic system of equations. This property appears by simply considering the differential of the public key. Thanks to this differential, we can mount an attack against a perturbed version of HM [25]. The technique is essentially similar to [10]. Section 4 focuses on the message-recovery. We notice that when applying a Gröbner-based resolution of the system given by the public key, the resolution succeeds for any practical choice of parameters. To illustrate this, we provide experimental results using Gröbner bases, in particular on recommended parameters for HM [20,21]. For instance, our attack can be mounted in few hundreds seconds on previously assumed secure parameters. Besides, we observe that the so-called "degree of regularity", which is the key-parameter for the complexity of Gröbner bases computations, is upper-bounded by 3 when $\mathbb{K} = \mathbb{F}_2$ and 4 otherwise. This allows to obtain a computation in polynomial time in the number of variables. Interestingly enough, we bring elements that help explaining this behavior. Briefly, we show the apparition of many linear and quadratic equations during the Gröbner basis computation. To us, this is very interesting since besides from HFE [18,9,11] multivariate schemes broken by Gröbner based techniques didn't offer such an explanation.

2 Multivariate Cryptology and Hidden Matrix Cryptosystem

A frequently used one-way function in multivariate cryptography is based on the evaluation of a set of algebraic polynomials $\mathbf{p} = (p_1(x_1, \ldots, x_N), \ldots, p_m(x_1, \ldots, x_N)) \in \mathbb{K}[x_1, \ldots, x_N]^m$, namely:

$$\mathbf{m} = (m_1, \ldots, m_N) \in \mathbb{K}^n \longmapsto \mathbf{p}(\mathbf{m}) = (p_1(\mathbf{m}), \ldots, p_m(\mathbf{m})) \in \mathbb{K}^m.$$

The mathematical hard problem underlying this one-way function is :

Polynomial System Solving
INSTANCE : **polynomials** $p_1(x_1, \ldots, x_N), \ldots, p_m(x_1, \ldots, x_N)$ **of** $\mathbb{K}[x_1, \ldots, x_N]$.
QUESTION : **Does there exists** $(z_1, \ldots, z_N) \in \mathbb{K}^n$ **such that**
$$p_1(z_1, \ldots, z_n) = 0, \ldots, p_m(z_1, \ldots, z_n) = 0$$

To introduce a trapdoor in schemes based on such a one-way function, we start from a carefully chosen algebraic system:

$$\mathbf{f} = (f_1(x_1, \ldots, x_N), \ldots, f_m(x_1, \ldots, x_N)),$$

which is *easy* to solve. That is, for all $\mathbf{c} = (c_1, \ldots, c_m) \in \mathbb{K}^m$, there is an efficient method for describing or computing the zeroes of $(f_1(x_1, \ldots, x_N) = c_1, \ldots, f_m(x_1, \ldots, x_N) = c_m)$. Then, in order to hide the specific structure of $\mathbf{f}$, we compose it by two linear (or affine) transformations – represented by invertible matrices – $(S, T) \in GL_N(\mathbb{K}) \times GL_m(\mathbb{K})$, to create a seemingly difficult system of public equations:

$$\mathbf{g}(\mathbf{x}) = (g_1(\mathbf{x}), \ldots, g_m(\mathbf{x})) = T(f_1(S(\mathbf{x})), \ldots, f_m(S(\mathbf{x}))) = T(\mathbf{f}(S(\mathbf{x}))),$$

with $\mathbf{x} = (x_1, \ldots, x_N)$.
The public key of such systems consists of the polynomials of $\mathbf{g}$, and the secret key is made up of the two matrices (S, T) and sometimes also includes $\mathbf{f}$.
To encrypt a message $\mathbf{m} \in \mathbb{K}^N$, we evaluate $\mathbf{g}$ at m, *i.e.*, we compute:

$$\mathbf{c} = (g_1(\mathbf{m}), \ldots, g_m(\mathbf{m})).$$

To recover the correct plaintext from $\mathbf{c}$, the legitimate recipient uses the bijectivity of the linear transformations combined with the particular structure of the polynomials of $\mathbf{f}$. Namely, he computes a value $\mathbf{m}' \in \mathbb{K}^n$ such that $\mathbf{f}(\mathbf{m}') = T^{-1}(\mathbf{c})$. This can be efficiently done due to the particular choice of $\mathbf{f}$. Finally, he recovers the message by evaluating $\mathbf{m} = S^{-1}(\mathbf{m}')$.

Note that this kind of cryptosystem can also be used to compute signatures. To generate the signature $\mathbf{s} \in \mathbb{K}^m$ of a message $\mathbf{m}$, the decryption process is applied to $\mathbf{m}$. To verify a signature $\mathbf{s} \in \mathbb{K}^m$ of a digest $\mathbf{m} \in \mathbb{K}^m$, one checks whether the equality $\mathbf{g}(\mathbf{s}) = \mathbf{m}$ holds.

There are plenty of proposals [19,23,22,14,24] based on this principle which basically differ in the way of constructing the polynomial $\mathbf{f}$. In particular, the so-called Hidden-Matrix (or HM) cryptosystem, which we consider in the present paper, follows this general paradigm. We now detail the construction of $\mathbf{f}$ in this case.

For the record, the HM scheme is based on the former $[C]$ scheme [12]. It was introduced in [20] to thwart an attack presented in this same paper. As pointed in [20], it is possible to construct bi-linear relations relating any pair (plaintext, ciphertext). In HM, the message $\mathbf{m}$ is a vector of length $N = n^2$ over $\mathbb{K}$. Let $\mathcal{M}_n(\mathbb{K})$ be the set of matrices of size $n \times n$ over $\mathbb{K}$. The set of $m = n^2$ polynomials $\mathbf{f}$ corresponds to the application F over $\mathcal{M}_n(\mathbb{K})$ defined as follows:

$$F : X \mapsto X^2 + M \cdot X,$$

where $M \in \mathcal{M}_n(\mathbb{K})$ is a given constant matrix. The public key $\mathbf{g}$ is as "usual" $T \circ F \circ S$, with $S : \mathbb{K}^{n^2} \to \mathcal{M}_n(\mathbb{K})$ and $T : \mathcal{M}_n(\mathbb{K}) \to \mathbb{K}^{n^2}$ two secret invertible affine transformations.

Note that [25] proposes a perturbed [6] version of $[C]$ and HM. The idea is to add randomness in the polynomials of the public key. To do so, we randomly generate a set of m polynomials $\tilde{\mathbf{f}}$ with N variables and a linear transform $\mathbf{R} : \mathbb{K}^N \to \mathbb{K}^r$. The inner polynomial $\tilde{\mathbf{f}}$, constructed as in $[C]$ or HM, is then perturbed by adding $\tilde{\mathbf{f}} \circ \mathbf{R}$ to $\mathbf{f}$, i.e. the inner polynomial is now:

$$\mathbf{f} + \tilde{\mathbf{f}} \circ \mathbf{R}.$$

The rank of r must be small to make the image of $\tilde{\mathbf{f}} \circ \mathbf{R}$ sufficiently small. This is a necessary condition for being able to decrypt [25,6].

3   Differential Property of HM, First Distinguisher

In this part, we present a differential property of the HM cryptosystem. This allows us to efficiently distinguish the equations composing the public key of a HM cryptosystem from a random system of quadratic equations. As previously explained (section 2), the inner function of HM is:

$$F : X \in \mathcal{M}_n(\mathbb{K}) \mapsto X^2 + M \cdot X \in \mathcal{M}_n(\mathbb{K}),$$

with M a secret constant matrix of $\mathcal{M}_n(\mathbb{K})$. The differential of a function f is defined by:

$$\mathrm{D}\,f(x, y) = f(x + y) - f(x) - f(y) + f(0).$$

For a fixed x, this expression also defines the differential of f at the point x in the y variable $\mathrm{D}_x\,f(y)$. Going back to the HM scheme, it follows from this that:

$$\mathrm{D}\,F(X, Y) = X \cdot Y + Y \cdot X. \tag{1}$$

It is interesting to remark that the differential of F is the same as the one of $X \mapsto X^2$ used in $[C]$ ([20,21]). We now arbitrarily fix $X = X_0 \in \mathcal{M}_n(\mathbb{K})$ and consider the following equation in Y:

$$D_{X_0} F(Y) = X_0 \cdot Y + Y \cdot X_0 = 0. \tag{2}$$

This equations yields n^2 linear equations in the n^2 coefficients of Y. For random linear equations, the expected number of solutions is 1. In our case, the solutions of these linear equations correspond to the matrices that commute with X_0 (here, we assume that the characteristic of $\mathbb{K}$ is two). Indeed, thanks to (1), we find that:

$$D_{X_0} F(Y) = 0$$
$$\Leftrightarrow X_0 \cdot Y \quad = Y \cdot X_0.$$

First of all, any polynomial in X_0 commutes with X_0. For a well-chosen X_0, the dimension of the set of all polynomials in X_0 over $\mathbb{K}$ is n. The exact number of linearly independent matrices that commute with a given matrix can be found in [15], chapter VIII. This number is given by the formula $n_1 + 3n_2 + \cdots + (2t - 1)n_t$, where $n_1, \ldots, n_t$ are the degrees of the non constant invariant polynomials. This number is between n and n^2 and about n in most cases. In any case, we can clearly distinguish the set of equations deduced from (2) from a set of random linear equations.

So far, we only considered the inner polynomials of the HM scheme, but the same kind of property propagates throughout the public key $\mathbf{g}$. We consider here, for some fixed vector $\mathbf{x_0}$:

$$D_{\mathbf{x_0}} \mathbf{g}(\mathbf{y}) = c_0, \tag{3}$$

where $c_0 = T_L(S(0))$, with T_L standing for the linear component of T and c_0 obtained as $D\mathbf{g}(0,0)$ over $\mathbb{F}_2$. Equation (3) then yields:

$$D_{\mathbf{x_0}} \mathbf{g}(\mathbf{y}) = c_0 \Leftrightarrow T_L(S(\mathbf{x_0}) \cdot S(\mathbf{y}) + S(\mathbf{y}) \cdot S(\mathbf{x_0})) = 0$$
$$\Leftrightarrow S(\mathbf{x_0}) \cdot S(\mathbf{y}) + S(\mathbf{y}) \cdot S(\mathbf{x_0}) = 0.$$

S being an invertible application, the same reasoning as for F implies that equation (3) has the same number of solutions than equation (2).

This gives an efficient distinguisher between n^2 random quadratic equations in n^2 unknowns and the quadratic equations composing the public key $\mathbf{g}$ of the HM scheme.

In addition, this permits to attack the perturbed version of $[C]$, which correspond to a HM scheme with a zero matrix M ([25]). We have all the tools to adapt the attack described in [10] on a perturbed version of C*. The attack being very similar, we just outline it. The main goal is to recover the linear space $\mathcal{K}$ that cancels the noise. More precisely, $\mathcal{K}$ is defined as the kernel of the affine space $\mathbf{R} \circ S$. As in [10], it is possible to use a differential distinguisher to detect whether a vector $\mathbf{x}$ is in $\mathcal{K}$ or not. Then, a basis of $\mathcal{K}$ can be found. As explained in [10], once in possession of such a basis, one can cancel the noise and mount an attack as against the basic $[C]$ (i.e. find bilinear relations).

4   Message-Recovery Attack

In this part, we first present experimental results when mounting a Gröbner-based message-recovery attack against HM. As already mentioned, this attack works in practice for (previously assumed) secure parameters of HM. This is due to the fact that systems arising in HM are much easier to solve than random algebraic systems of the same size. In particular, the maximum degree reached during the computation of a Gröbner basis is bounded from above by a small constant (3 or 4). This is supported by experimental and theoretical observations.

4.1   Experimental Results and Observations

We take interest in the message-recovery attack, which consists in recovering a message from a given ciphertext. More precisely, let $\mathbf{c} = \mathbf{g}(\mathbf{m})$ be an encryption of a message $\mathbf{m}$. To directly recover $\mathbf{m}$ from $\mathbf{c}$, we have to solve a quadratic system of equations induced by the polynomials of the public key. Namely, we have to solve the following system of n^2 quadratic equations in n^2 variables:

$$\mathbf{g}(\mathbf{x}) - \mathbf{g}(\mathbf{m}) = 0.$$

Here, we assume that the algebraic system is over $\mathbb{F}_2$, as specified in [20] .

In the following table 2 we quote several experimental results obtained when performing a Gröbner-based message-recovery attack on HM, using the F_4 algorithm available in the Magma Computational Algebra System. These results have been obtained with a Xeon 4.2 Ghz 128 Gb of Ram. The attack have been implemented with Magma (v. 15.7). In the table, we include:

- q: the size of the base field $\mathbb{K}$
- n^2: the number of variables of the system
- T: the total time needed for our attack
- Mem: the maximum memory usage
- D_{reg}: the maximal degree reached during the Gröbner basis computation.

In the initial paper [12,20,21], the authors advised to take the parameter n such as $n^2 \geq 64$ (which would correspond to $n^2 \geq 80$ nowadays). Hence, the first major observation is that the attack can be mounted in practice. In fact, the scheme is broken for all practical parameters. A second important remark is that

q	n^2	T	Mem	D_{reg}
2	64	138 s.	1.4 Gb.	3
2	81	685 s.	5.8 Gb.	3
2	100	6249 s.	19 Gb.	3
2	121	6 h.	56 Gb.	3
2	144	26 h.	171 Gb.	3

Fig. 1. Experimental results for the Gröbner-based message-recovery attack over $\mathbb{F}_2$

q	n^2	T	Mem	D_{reg}
65521	25	13 s.	60 Mb.	4
65521	36	790 s.	500 Mb.	4
65521	49	2.7h	3 Gb.	4

Fig. 2. Experimental results for the Gröbner-based message-recovery attack

D_{reg} is always equal to the same value 3. In the next section, we will explain this systematic behavior. Namely, the maximum degree reached during the Gröbner basis computation is upper-bounded by 3 over $\mathbb{F}_2$. In general ($\mathbb{K} \neq \mathbb{F}_2$), it is bounded by 4. This makes our attack polynomial (in the number of variables).

4.2 Explaining the Degree of Regularity

In this part, we explain the experimental behavior observed in Subsection 4.1. Namely, we explain why the maximum degree reached during a Gröbner basis computation is so low for HM (experimentally bounded by 3 or 4), compared with random algebraic equations. This degree, called *degree of regularity*, is the key parameter for understanding the complexity of Gröbner basis computations Indeed, the complexity of computing a Gröbner basis is polynomial in the degree of regularity D_{reg}, namely the complexity is:

$$\mathcal{O}(N^{\omega D_{reg}}),$$

which basically correspond to the complexity of reducing a matrix of size $N^{D_{reg}}$ ($2 < \omega \leq 3$ is the "linear algebra constant", and N the number of variables of the system). The behavior of the degree of regularity D_{reg} is well understood for regular (and semi-regular) systems of equations [1,3,2,4]. On the contrary, as soon as the system has some kind of structure, this degree is much more difficult to predict. In some particular cases, it is however possible to bound the degree of regularity (see the works done on HFE [9,11]). But it is an hard tack in general.

We show here that we can predict the apparition of many quadratic or linear polynomials during the computation of a Gröbner basis of the ideal generated by the public equations of HM. This permits to explain why the degree of regularity is bounded from above by 3 over $\mathbb{F}_2$ and 4 otherwise.

To simplify the analysis, it is sufficient to restrict our attention to the equations generated by the "secret" (or inner) polynomials. Indeed, the degree of regularity of an ideal is generically left invariant by any linear change of the coordinates or generators, that is to say, in our case, we can omit S and T and bound the degree of regularity of the ideal generated by the secret polynomials given by F. Let A be a matrix of $\mathcal{M}_n(\mathbb{K})$. We consider the ideal I generated by the inner equations $F(X) - F(A)$:

$$I = \langle X^2 + M \cdot X - A^2 - M \cdot A \rangle.$$

In the following, we set $B = F(A)$, *i.e.*, $A^2 + M \cdot A = B$. We also define Δ as:

$$\Delta = X^2 + MX - B = 0.$$

The ideal I considered is the ideal generated by all the components of $\Delta_{i,j} = 0$, $1 \leq i, j \leq n$. Our goal is to explain the bound on the degree of regularity of this ideal.

Case $M = 0$. To give an intuition of the phenomena observed regarding this degree of regularity, let us start with the easy case where $M = 0$ (note that this case corresponds in fact to the $[C]$ scheme broken in [20] in a quite similar way). We have $F(X) = X^2$ and $\Delta = X^2 - B = 0$. Let us consider the two following matrix equations:

$$X \cdot \Delta = X^3 - X \cdot B = 0$$
$$\Delta \cdot X = X^3 - B \cdot X = 0.$$

If we subtract them, we obtain the new equation $X \cdot \Delta - \Delta \cdot X = X \cdot B - B \cdot X = 0$, which provides n^2 linear equations in the $X_{i,j}$ unknowns and allow to solve the system.

Going back to Gröbner bases, these equations would appear when using a Gröbner-based algorithm. Such an algorithm applied on I, starts by generating equations of degree one more (namely 3) from the equations given by $\Delta = 0$. In particular, the equations constituting the matrix equation $X \cdot \Delta = 0$ as well as the ones corresponding to $\Delta \cdot X = 0$ appear. Notice that by reductions, the equations given by $X \cdot \Delta - \Delta \cdot X = 0$ also appear during computation. In other words, after just one step of computation, we get the n^2 linear equations which allow to solve the system.

In the previous case $M = 0$, we proved that many linear equations appear when considering equations of degree 3. In the general case $M \neq 0$, something similar is not necessarily likely to happen. However, we will show that also many new quadratic (and sometimes linear) equations appear when considering equations of degree 3 in the general case.

To generalize the previous observation, we need to introduce the following definition:

Definition 1. *We denote by $I_{\leq d}$ the set of all polynomials of I, of degree less or equal to d.*

During the computation, the polynomials generated are obtained by multiplying previously obtained polynomials by monomials and applying possible reductions. Thus, the degree of the polynomials generated during the computation keeps growing until new low-degree polynomials appear, due to reductions of polynomials of higher total degree. In the case of HM, we rapidly (in the sense that we do not need to generate polynomials of high degree) obtain many low-degree polynomials, which explains that the computation ends quickly. This fact is developed in the following parts.

Field of Arbitrary Characteristic. We show here that plenty of new quadratic equations are generated during the computation of a Gröbner basis of I. This result remains valid whatever the characteristic of $\mathbb{K}$ is. Additional properties occur when $\mathbb{K} = \mathbb{F}_2$, that are given later.

Proposition 1 shows that n^2 quadratic equations are obtained at every new step of the Gröbner basis computation. Moreover, the polynomials generated are obtained by multiplying previously obtained matrix equations of degree 2 by X.

Proposition 1. *For all $k \geq 1$, there exist matrices A_k, B_k, C_k and D_k such that:*

$$P_k = X(M^k + A_k)X + B_k \cdot X + X \cdot C_k + D_k \in I_{\leq 3}.$$

This result is obtained by using the same idea as for the case $M = 0$. Proofs of this proposition is given in appendix A.

In this general case, we experimentally observe that the degree of regularity is bounded by 4, *i.e.*, the Gröbner basis algorithm doesn't need to generate polynomials of degree higher than 4 to terminate.

Case $\mathbb{K} = \mathbb{F}_2$. We now focus on the specific case where $\mathbb{K} = \mathbb{F}_2$, which is the classical setting. In this case, not only we get the quadratic equations of the general case, but we also get additional linear equations, described in the propositions below. Here again, all these equations appear while generating polynomials of degree at most 3 in the Gröbner basis computation.

Proposition 2. *Let $Q_0 = tr((M+I)X) - tr(B)$, tr denoting the trace operator. We have that the equations composing Q_0 are in $I_{\leq 3}$.*

Proposition 3. *Let the notations be as in Proposition 1. For all $k \geq 1$, we define $Q_k = (X + B_k \cdot X + X \cdot C_k + D_k)(M^k + A_k)$. For all $k \geq 1$, the linear equation given by the trace of Q_k, $tr(Q_k)$, is in $I_{\leq 3}$:*

$$tr((X + B_k X + X \cdot C_k + D_k)(M^k + A_k)) \in I_{\leq 3}.$$

The Q_k polynomials are deduced from the P_k. Proofs of these propositions can be found in the appendix A.2.

We experimentally observe that the degree of regularity is only 3 in the case where $\mathbb{K} = \mathbb{F}_2$, which means that these low-degree equations even allow to end the computation after generating polynomials of total degree no higher than 3.

Summary. To summarize, the table below gives the number of low-degree equations generated during the Gröbner basis process and their degree, depending on the different cases studied. The index $k_{\max}$ is the number of steps needed in the F_4/F_5 algorithm[1] to compute $I_{\leq d}$. The value of $k_{\max}$ sometimes dictates the number of low-degree polynomials appearing during the computation. For instance, the polynomials indexed by k described in proposition 3 or proposition 1 are obtained at some step k of the establishment of $I_{\leq d}$. Once again, D_{reg} stands for the degree of regularity reached. The validity of the results below have been experimentally verified for up to $n^2 = 144$ for $\mathbb{K} = \mathbb{F}_2$ (and $n = 49$ in other cases).

---

[1] *i.e.*, the F_4 algorithm which uses the F_5 criteria [8].

Case	$M = 0$	$\mathbb{K} = \mathbb{F}_2$	$\mathbb{K} \neq \mathbb{F}_2$
Nb of quadratic eqs	0	$k_{\max} \cdot n^2$	$k_{\max} \cdot n^2$
Nb of linear eqs	n^2	$k_{\max}$	0
Total Nb of quadratic eqs	0	n^3	n^3
Total Nb of linear eqs	n^2	n	0
D_{reg}	3	3	4

Remark 1. Notice that we assume $k_{\max}$ to be equal to n. Indeed, the equations obtained at step k are related to M^k as explained in the propositions above. Hence, after n steps, the equations obtained may then be related to previous ones since M^n reduces to a combinations of powers of M of lower degree[2]. It is then reasonable to set $k_{\max} = n$. In this case, we obtain many new low-degree equations (as quoted in the second part of the table), which allow to understand why the computation ends quickly, and also the difference with $\mathbb{K} \neq \mathbb{F}_2$, and $\mathbb{K} = \mathbb{F}_2$.

Finally, we have computed for several parameters the theoretical degree $D_{\mathrm{reg}}^{\mathrm{Theo}}$ of a semi-regular system [1,3,2,4] having the same number of variables and the same number of equations than an instance of HM (but including the new equations generated).

q	n^2	$D_{\mathrm{reg}}^{\mathrm{Theo}}$
2	64	3
2	81	4
2	100	4
2	121	4
2	144	4
65521	36	4
65521	49	4

This is another indication that the maximum degree reached in HM should be small.

5   Conclusion

In this paper we showed that the Hidden Matrix of [20] is broken. We presented two very efficient distinguishers. The first one is based on solving a system of linear equations deduced from the differential of the public key. The second distinguisher is much stronger since it allows to recover a plaintext from a ciphertext. We observed a very specific behavior during the computation, which we were able to theoretically explain, as for the HFE cryptanalysis [9,11]. Moreover, we derive an attack on the perturbed version of [C] described in [25]. In the original paper [20], the authors did not recommend the use of their scheme, because they suspected not to have noticed some weaknesses; this paper confirms the fears of the authors.

---

[2] This comes from the Cayley-Hamilton theorem.

References

1. Bardet, M.: Étude des systèmes algébriques surdéterminés. Applications aux codes correcteurs et à la cryptographie. PhD thesis, Université de Paris VI (2004)
2. Bardet, M., Faugère, J.-C., Salvy, B.: Complexity study of Gröbner basis computation. Technical report, INRIA (2002), http://www.inria.fr/rrrt/rr-5049.html
3. Bardet, M., Faugère, J.-C., Salvy, B.: On the complexity of Gröbner basis computation of semi-regular overdetermined algebraic equations. In: Proc. International Conference on Polynomial System Solving (ICPSS), pp. 71–75 (2004)
4. Bardet, M., Faugère, J.-C., Salvy, B., Yang, B.-Y.: Asymptotic behaviour of the degree of regularity of semi-regular polynomial systems. In: Proc. of MEGA 2005, Eighth International Symposium on Effective Methods in Algebraic Geometry (2005)
5. Bogdanov, A., Eisenbarth, T., Rupp, A., Wolf, C.: Time-area optimized public-key engines: $\mathcal{MQ}$-cryptosystems as replacement for elliptic curves? In: Oswald, E., Rohatgi, P. (eds.) CHES 2008. LNCS, vol. 5154, pp. 45–61. Springer, Heidelberg (2008)
6. Ding, J.: A new variant of the matsumoto-imai cryptosystem through perturbation. In: Bao, F., Deng, R., Zhou, J. (eds.) PKC 2004. LNCS, vol. 2947, pp. 305–318. Springer, Heidelberg (2004)
7. Dubois, V., Fouque, P.-A., Shamir, A., Stern, J.: Practical cryptanalysis of sflash. In: Menezes, A. (ed.) CRYPTO 2007. LNCS, vol. 4622, pp. 1–12. Springer, Heidelberg (2007)
8. Faugère, J.-C.: A new efficient algorithm for computing Gröbner bases without reduction to zero (F5). In: Mora, T. (ed.) Proceedings of the 2002 International Symposium on Symbolic and Algebraic Computation ISSAC, July 2002, pp. 75–83. ACM Press, New York (2002) ISBN: 1-58113-484-3
9. Faugère, J.-C., Joux, A.: Algebraic cryptanalysis of Hidden Field Equation (HFE) cryptosystems using Gröbner bases. In: Boneh, D. (ed.) CRYPTO 2003. LNCS, vol. 2729, pp. 44–60. Springer, Heidelberg (2003)
10. Fouque, P.-A., Granboulan, L., Stern, J.: Differential cryptanalysis for multivariate schemes. In: Cramer, R. (ed.) EUROCRYPT 2005. LNCS, vol. 3494, pp. 341–353. Springer, Heidelberg (2005)
11. Granboulan, L., Joux, A., Stern, J.: Inverting HFE is quasipolynomial. In: Dwork, C. (ed.) CRYPTO 2006. LNCS, vol. 4117, pp. 345–356. Springer, Heidelberg (2006)
12. Imai, H., Matsumoto, T.: Algebraic Methods for Constructing Asymmetric Cryptosystems. In: Calmet, J. (ed.) AAECC 1985. LNCS, vol. 229, pp. 108–119. Springer, Heidelberg (1986)
13. Kipnis, A., Shamir, A.: Cryptanalysis of the oil and vinegar signature scheme. In: Krawczyk, H. (ed.) CRYPTO 1998. LNCS, vol. 1462, pp. 257–266. Springer, Heidelberg (1998)
14. Koblitz, N.: Algebraic Aspects of Cryptography. Algorithms and Computation in Mathematics, vol. 3. Springer, Heidelberg (1998)
15. Liddl, R., Niederreiter, H.: Introduction to Finite Fields. Longman Higher Education (1983)
16. Matsumoto, T., Imai, H.: Public quadratic polynomial-tuples for efficient signature-verification and message-encryption. In: Günther, C.G. (ed.) EUROCRYPT 1988. LNCS, vol. 330, pp. 419–453. Springer, Heidelberg (1988)
17. Patarin, J.: Cryptanalysis of the matsumoto and imai public key scheme of eurocrypt'88. In: Coppersmith, D. (ed.) CRYPTO 1995. LNCS, vol. 963, pp. 248–261. Springer, Heidelberg (1995)

18. Patarin, J.: Hidden Fields Equations (HFE) and Isomorphisms of Polynomials (IP): two new families of asymmetric algorithms. In: Maurer, U.M. (ed.) EUROCRYPT 1996. LNCS, vol. 1070, pp. 33–48. Springer, Heidelberg (1996)
19. Patarin, J.: The Oil and Vinegar signature scheme. Presented at the Dagstuhl Workshop on Cryptography (1997)
20. Patarin, J., Courtois, N., Goubin, L.: C^*_{-+} and HM: Variations on Two Schemes of T.Matsumoto and H.Imai. In: Ohta, K., Pei, D. (eds.) ASIACRYPT 1998. LNCS, vol. 1514, pp. 35–50. Springer, Heidelberg (1998)
21. Patarin, J., Courtois, N., Goubin, L.: C^*_{-+} and HM: Variations on Two Schemes of T.Matsumoto and H.Imai, Extended Version. Available From the Authors (1998)
22. Patarin, J., Courtois, N., Goubin, L.: Quartz, 128-bit long digital signatures. In: Naccache, D. (ed.) CT-RSA 2001. LNCS, vol. 2020, pp. 282–297. Springer, Heidelberg (2001)
23. Patarin, J., Goubin, L., Courtois, N.: $C^* - +$ and hm: Variations around two schemes of t.matsumoto and h.imai. In: Ohta, K., Pei, D. (eds.) ASIACRYPT 1998. LNCS, vol. 1514, pp. 35–49. Springer, Heidelberg (1998)
24. Wolf, C., Preneel, B.: Taxonomy of Public Key Schemes based on the problem of Multivariate Quadratic equations. Cryptology ePrint Archive, Report 2005/077 (2005), http://eprint.iacr.org/
25. Wu, Z., Ding, J., Gower, J.E., Ye, D.F.: Perturbed hidden matrix cryptosystems. In: Gervasi, O., Gavrilova, M.L., Kumar, V., Laganá, A., Lee, H.P., Mun, Y., Taniar, D., Tan, C.J.K. (eds.) ICCSA 2005. LNCS, vol. 3481, pp. 595–602. Springer, Heidelberg (2005)

A   Proofs of the Propositions

This annex gathers the proofs of the propositions of Section 4.2.

A.1   Proofs of the Propositions in the General Case

Lemma 1. *We have the following n^2 quadratic equations in $I_{\leq 3}$:*

$$P_1 = X \cdot M \cdot X + (B + M^2)X - X \cdot B - M \cdot B \in I_{\leq 3}.$$

Proof. Let Δ be as defined in 4.2. The idea is to write $X^2 = B - M \cdot X$. We then remark that there are two ways to obtain X^3, multiplying the previous equation by X on the left or on the right:

$$X^3 = X \cdot B - X \cdot M \cdot X,$$
$$X^3 = B \cdot X - M \cdot X^2$$
$$= B \cdot X - M \cdot X^2 + M\Delta$$
$$= B \cdot X - M (B - M \cdot X)$$
$$= B \cdot X - M \cdot B + M^2 \cdot X$$

By subtracting the two equations we obtain $\Delta \cdot X - X \cdot \Delta - M \cdot \Delta = X \cdot M \cdot X + (B + M^2) X - X \cdot B - M \cdot B \in I_{\leq 3}$.

It is actually possible to generalize this idea.

Proposition 1. *For all $k \geq 1$ there exist matrices A_k, B_k, C_k and D_k such that:*

$$P_k = X(M^k + A_k)X + B_k \cdot X + X \cdot C_k + D_k \in I_{\leq 3}.$$

Proof. We will proof this result by induction on k. According to lemma 1, the equations induced by P_1 are in $I_{\leq 3}$. Thus, we have:

$$A_1 = 0$$
$$B_1 = B + M^2$$
$$C_1 = -B$$
$$D_1 = -M \cdot B.$$

We suppose that property is true for $P_k, k \geq 1$. It then holds that:

$$-P_k \cdot X = X(M^{k+1} + A_k \cdot M - C_k)X - X(M^k \cdot B + A_k \cdot B)$$
$$+(B_k \cdot M - D_k)X - B_k \cdot B$$
$$= X(M^{k+1} + A_{k+1})X + B_{k+1} \cdot X + X \cdot C_{k+1} + D_{k+1}$$
$$= P_{k+1},$$

with the relations:

$$D_{k+1} = -B_k \cdot B$$
$$A_{k+1} = A_k \cdot M - C_k$$
$$C_{k+1} = -M^k \cdot B - A_k \cdot B$$
$$B_{k+1} = B_k \cdot M - D_k.$$

The equations constituting the components of P_{k+1} are clearly in I_3. This proves the proposition.

A.2 Proofs of the Propositions from the Case $\mathbb{K} = \mathbb{F}_2$

We start by presenting a general lemma on matrices in $\mathcal{M}_n(\mathbb{K})$. Let $D \in \mathcal{M}_n(\mathbb{K})$. In the following, $tr(D)$ stands for the trace of $D \in \mathcal{M}_n(\mathbb{K})$ and C_D for the characteristic polynomial of D. From now on, we always assume that $\mathbb{K} = \mathbb{F}_2$.

Lemma 2. *It holds that $C_D(z) = C_{D^2}(z)$ and $tr(D^2) = tr(D)$.*

Proof. Let $\lambda \in \overline{\mathbb{K}}$ be an eigenvalue of D. That is to say, there exists $u \neq 0$ such that $D \cdot u = \lambda u$. Then we have $D^2 \cdot u = M \cdot \lambda u = \lambda^2 u$. Hence λ^2 is an eigenvalue of D^2. We also denote:

$$C_D(z) = (z - \lambda_1) \cdots (z - \lambda_n)$$
$$= z^n + s_1 z^{n-1} + \ldots + s_n,$$

and

$$C_{D^2}(z) = (z - \lambda_1^2) \ldots (z - \lambda_n^2)$$
$$= z^n + \sigma_1 z^{n-1} + \ldots + \sigma_n,$$

with s_i (resp. σ_i) the i-th elementary symmetric polynomial in λ_i (resp. in λ_i^2). Remark that we have $\sigma_i = s_i^2 = s_i$. Indeed, all these elements are in $\mathbb{F}_2$. This proves the first claim, namely that $C_D(z) = C_{D^2}(z)$.

For the second claim of this lemma, we notice that $tr(D)$ (resp. $tr(D^2)$) is the coefficient of z^{n-1} in $C_D(z)$ (resp. in $C_{D^2}(z)$). As $C_D(z) = C_{D^2}(z)$, the result follows.

From that, we can predict the appearing of new equations during the Gröbner basis computation.

Proposition 2. *Let* $Q_0 = (M+I)X - B$. *The linear equation* $tr(Q_0)$ *is in* $I_{\leq 3}$.

Proof. The application tr being a linear form and since $X^2 + M \cdot X = B$, we have $tr(X^2) + tr(M \cdot X) = tr(B)$. Thanks to lemma 2, we have that $tr(X^2) = tr(X)$; which gives the result announced.

More generally:

Lemma 3. *If* $Q_1 = X \cdot M + (B + M^2)X \cdot M - X \cdot B \cdot M - M \cdot B \cdot M$, *then the linear equation* $tr(Q_1)$ *is in* $I_{\leq 3}$.

Proof. According to Lemma 1, we know that:

$$P_1 = X \cdot M \cdot X + (B + M^2)X - X \cdot B - M \cdot B \in I_{\leq 3}$$

More precisely, the n^2 equations given by the components of P_1 are in $I_{\leq 3}$). Now, multiplying P_1 by M on the right yields:

$$X \cdot M \cdot X \cdot M + (B + M^2)X \cdot M - X \cdot B \cdot M - M \cdot B \cdot M \in I_{\leq 3} \qquad (\star).$$

Thanks to Lemma 2 on the trace, we have that $tr(X \cdot M \cdot X \cdot M) = tr((X \cdot M)^2) = tr(X \cdot M)$. Thus applying the trace to $(\star)$ implies:

$$tr\left(X \cdot M + (B + M^2)X \cdot M - X \cdot B \cdot M - M \cdot B \cdot M\right) \in I_{\leq 3},$$

as announced.

The preceding result was deduced from the existence of P_1 (Lemma 1). However, it is possible to obtain a similar result for all P_k's of Proposition 1.

Proposition 3. *Let the notations be as in Lemma 1 of Section 4.2. For all* $k \geq 1$, *we have that:*

$$Q_k = tr((X + B_k X + X \cdot C_k + D_k)(M^k + A_k)) \in I_{\leq 3}.$$

Proof. From Proposition 1, we deduce that for all $k \geq 1$:

$$P_k = X(M^k + A_k)X + B_k \cdot X + X \cdot C_k + D_k \in I_{\leq 3}.$$

By multiplying on the right by $M^k + A_k$, we have:

$$(X(M^k + A_k))^2 + (B_k \cdot X + X \cdot C_k + D_k)(M^k + A_k) \in I_{\leq 3}.$$

Now $tr((X(M^k + A_k))^2) = tr(X(M^k + A_k))$ by lemma 2. Finally, we obtain:

$$tr((X + B_k \cdot X + X \cdot C_k + D_k)(M^k + A_k)) \in I_{\leq 3}.$$

A Lattice-Based Threshold Ring Signature Scheme*

Pierre-Louis Cayrel[1], Richard Lindner[2],
Markus Rückert[2], and Rosemberg Silva[3]

[1] CASED – Center for Advanced Security Research Darmstadt,
Mornewegstrasse, 32
64293 Darmstadt
Germany
pierre-louis.cayrel@cased.de
[2] Technische Universität Darmstadt
Fachbereich Informatik
Kryptographie und Computeralgebra,
Hochschulstraße 10
64289 Darmstadt
Germany
{rlindner,rueckert}@cdc.informatik.tu-darmstadt.de
[3] State University of Campinas (UNICAMP)
Institute of Computing
P.O. Box 6176
13084-971 Campinas
Brazil
rasilva@ic.unicamp.br

Abstract. In this article, we propose a new lattice-based threshold ring signature scheme, modifying Aguilar's code-based solution to use the short integer solution (SIS) problem as security assumption, instead of the syndrome decoding (SD) problem. By applying the CLRS identification scheme, we are also able to have a performance gain as result of the reduction in the soundness error to $1/2$ per round. Such gain is also maintained through the application of the Fiat-Shamir heuristics to derive signatures from our identification scheme. From security perspective we also have improvements, because our scheme exhibits a worst-case to average-case reduction typical of lattice-based cryptosystems. This gives us confidence that a random choice of parameters results in a system that is hard to break, in average.

Keywords: Identification scheme, lattice-based cryptography, SIS problem, threshold ring signature, zero-knowledge.

1 Introduction

The concept of allowing a member of a group to anonymously sign documents on behalf of the entire group was created by Chaum and van Heyst [13]. In

---

* Supported by The State of São Paulo Research Foundation under grant 2008/07949-8.

M. Abdalla and P.S.L.M. Barreto (Eds.): LATINCRYPT 2010, LNCS 6212, pp. 255–272, 2010.
© Springer-Verlag Berlin Heidelberg 2010

the original scheme, however, there is an entity called group manager that can reveal the identity of the actual signer. A variation of this concept, proposed by Rivest, Shamir and Tauman [27], and called Ring Signature, prevents anonymity from being revoked. It was further extended by Bresson, Stern and Szydlo into a Threshold Ring Signature Scheme, which consists of a protocol that enables a group composed of t people belonging to a larger group of size N to jointly and anonymously sign a given document [9]. The minimum size t of the subgroup required to generate a valid signature is a parameter enforced by the protocol. Aguilar, Cayrel, Gaborit and Laguillaumie [2] made a construction of a TRSS scheme, achieving signature sizes and time complexities that are linear in N and independent of t. Besides, it is existentially unforgeable under chosen message attack in the random oracle model. Let us call their construction TRSS-C (short for Threshold Ring Signature Scheme using Codes).

It is based on error-correcting codes, and is the best known threshold ring signature scheme, from time complexity perspective. Differently from its number-theoretic predecessors, which exhibited a complexity of $\mathcal{O}(t.N)$ (where N is the size the group of users, and t is the size of the sub-group willing to sign a message), TRSS-C has a complexity given by $\mathcal{O}(N)$, clearly independent of the number of users that want to jointly sign a message. However, as seen in [19], signature schemes derived from identification schemes with high soundness error tend to be inefficient in terms of signature size. The same happens to TRSS-C.

1.1   Our Contribution

Our work consists of a lattice-based threshold ring signature scheme, combining Aguilar's [2] and Cayrel's [11] results, and is based on an identification scheme that has lower soundness error. This enables a performance gain due to the smaller number of rounds of execution, as well as an achievement of shorter signatures. The security of our scheme is based on the hardness of the lattice SIS problem. Provided that a suitable set of parameters is used, a reduction from worst-case in Gap-SVP to average-case in SIS is preserved. Such reduction, typical of lattice-based cryptosystems, gives confidence that the construction is safe, even for randomly chosen parameters. Aiming an easier notation, along the text our scheme will be referred to as TRSS-L (Threshold Ring Signature Scheme Based on Lattices).

1.2   Related Work

Code-Based Threshold Ring Signature Schemes
The TRSS-C scheme relies on the hardness of the minimum distance (MD) problem and the existence of collision resistant hash functions as security assumptions [2]. It generalizes the identification scheme designed by Stern [29] and inherits its same limits as far as signature sizes are regarded, when applying the Fiat-Shamir heuristics: a high number of rounds in order to read a specified security level.

The group of signers is composed of t entities out of a group of N. One of the signers is chosen as leader, and executes $t-1$ simultaneous Stern's protocols with the other signers. Such leader applies the Fiat-Shamir heuristic over the generalized Stern's scheme in order to generate signatures. He also generates master commitments, hiding the identity of the signers by means of a product of permutations.

Dallot and Verganaud [15] have also proposed a code-based threshold ring signature scheme. It is not derived from an identification, differently from TRSS-C. Rather, it bears similarly with the CFS signature scheme [14] in the sense of requiring a number of decoding operations that grows with the factorial of the number of errors that its underlying Goppa code can correct. Therefore, though the signatures are short, a considerable computational effort is necessary to generate them. Plus, as opposed to our construction, Dallot's uses trapdoors.

Lattice-Based Signature Schemes
To the best of our knowledge, our threshold ring signature scheme is the first lattice-based. Recently, Brakerski and Kalai [8] presented a generic framework for constructing signature schemes, including ring and identity types, in the standard model. They presented an example based on SIS. Their work does not include threshold constructions, though.

1.3 Organization of the Document

This paper is divided as follows. In Section 2, we give general definitions regarding lattices, identification and ring signature schemes. Then, we describe our lattice-based Threshold Ring Signature Scheme in Section 3. Subsequently, we provide demonstrations of security of our scheme in Section 4. Afterwards, a discussion of performance aspects of the scheme follows in Section 5. Lastly, an appreciation of the scheme and future lines of work are given in Section 6.

This section presented an overview of lattice-based signatures systems and how our proposal relates to them. The next one lists the definitions of some concepts that we use along the text in order to detail the design of our signature scheme. It dedicates special attention to the aspects related to performance and security.

2 Preliminaries

In this part of the article, we give the definition of the hard lattice problem connected with the security of our signature scheme. Furthermore, we detail the code-based construction from which our design derives.

The advent of quantum computers poses a serious threat to Cryptography, due to an algorithm devised by Shor [28] which is able to calculate in polynomial-time prime factorization and discrete logarithms. Post-Quantum Cryptography is a denomination given to the sub-areas that are known to be still resilient to quantum computers. Systems built upon lattice hard problems are included on them.

2.1   Lattices

Besides resilience to known quantum attacks, strong security proofs are an important feature of lattice-based constructions. Here, we show the basic definitions applied in the design of our threshold ring signature scheme.

Definition 1. *A lattice is a discrete subgroup of $\mathbb{R}^m$ with dimension $n \leq m$. In general, for cryptographic applications, it is restricted to $\mathbb{Z}^m$. It can be represented by a basis comprising n linear independent vectors of $\mathbb{R}^m$.*

We define below the hard problems in the lattice domain that serve as security assumptions in the schemes described in this article. The definitions make use of the max-norm or ℓ_∞.

Definition 2. *(Shortest Vector Problem - SVP) Given a lattice basis $\mathbf{B} \in \mathbb{Z}^{m \times n}$, find a non-zero lattice vector $\mathbf{Bx}$ such that $\|\mathbf{Bx}\| \leq \|\mathbf{By}\|$ for any other $\mathbf{y} \in \mathbb{Z}^n \backslash \{0\}$.*

Definition 3. *(Closest Vector Problem - CVP) Given a lattice basis $\mathbf{B} \in \mathbb{Z}^{m \times n}$ and a target vector $\mathbf{t} \in \mathbb{Z}^m$, find $\mathbf{x} \in \mathbb{Z}^n$ such that $\|\mathbf{Bx} - \mathbf{t}\|$ is minimum.*

These two problems also admit approximate formulation, as stated below for a factor γ.

Definition 4. *(Approximate SVP_γ) Given a lattice basis $\mathbf{B} \in \mathbb{Z}^{m \times n}$, find a non-zero lattice vector $\mathbf{Bx}$ such that $\|\mathbf{Bx}\| \leq \gamma \cdot \|\mathbf{By}\|$ for any other $\mathbf{y} \in \mathbb{Z}^n \backslash \{0\}$.*

Definition 5. *(Approximate CVP_γ) Given a lattice basis $\mathbf{B} \in \mathbb{Z}^{m \times n}$ and a target vector $\mathbf{t} \in \mathbb{Z}^m$, find $\mathbf{x} \in \mathbb{Z}^n$ such that $\|\mathbf{Bx} - \mathbf{t}\| \leq \gamma \cdot \|\mathbf{By} - \mathbf{t}\|$ for any other $\mathbf{y} \in \mathbb{Z}^n$.*

In addition to the exact and approximate formulations, one can also state these problems as promises, as outlined below.

Definition 6. *($GapSVP_\gamma$) It is a promise problem for which the YES and NO instances are defined as:*

- *YES: pairs $(\mathbf{B}, r)$ where $\mathbf{B} \in \mathbb{Z}^{m \times n}$ is a lattice basis and $r \in \mathbb{Q}$ is a rational number such that $\|\mathbf{Bz}\| \leq r$ for some $\mathbf{z} \in \mathbb{Z}^n \backslash \{0\}$.*
- *NO: pairs $(\mathbf{B}, r)$ where $\mathbf{B} \in \mathbb{Z}^{m \times n}$ is a lattice basis and $r \in \mathbb{Q}$ is a rational number such that $\|\mathbf{Bz}\| > \gamma \cdot r$ for all $\mathbf{z} \in \mathbb{Z}^n \backslash \{0\}$.*

Definition 7. *($GapCVP_\gamma$) It is a promise problem for which the YES and NO instances are defined as:*

- *YES: triplets $(\mathbf{B}, \mathbf{t}, r)$ where $\mathbf{B} \in \mathbb{Z}^{m \times n}$ is a lattice basis, $\mathbf{t} \in \mathbb{Z}^m$ is a vector, and $r \in \mathbb{Q}$ is a rational number such that $\|\mathbf{Bz} - \mathbf{t}\| \leq r$ for some $\mathbf{z} \in \mathbb{Z}^n$.*
- *NO: triplets $(\mathbf{B}, \mathbf{t}, r)$ where $\mathbf{B} \in \mathbb{Z}^{m \times n}$ is a lattice basis, $\mathbf{t} \in \mathbb{Z}^m$ is a vector, and $r \in \mathbb{Q}$ is a rational number such that $\|\mathbf{Bz} - \mathbf{t}\| > \gamma \cdot r$ for all $\mathbf{z} \in \mathbb{Z}^n$.*

A thorough discussion on the hardness of these problems can be found in [23].

Definition 8. *(Short Integer Solution - SIS) Given* $\mathbf{A} \in \mathbb{Z}^{n \times m}$ *and a prime number* q, *find a vector* $\mathbf{v}$ *in the lattice defined by* $\Lambda_q^\perp = \{\mathbf{x} \in \mathbb{Z}^m \ : \ \mathbf{Ax} = \mathbf{0} \bmod q\}$ *with length limited by* $\|\mathbf{v}\| \leq L$.

From the perspective of cryptography, one of the most interesting results involving lattices consists in showing that breaking a randomly chosen instance in some schemes is at least as hard as finding solutions for worst-case instances of hard lattice problems. In [3] and [4], for example, Ajtai uses computationally intractable approximations of lattice problems as building blocks of cryptosystems.

As far as saving space to represent lattice basis is regarded, Micciancio showed through cyclic lattices that it is possible to reach storage that grows linearly with the lattice dimension [22]. His one-way compression functions also achieved the collision resistance property with the use of ideal lattices, as seen in [20]. Such work also specified the conditions that should be satisfied in order to assure the existence of average-case/worst-case connection.

Lattice applications to identification purposes have also provided good results. For instance, in Lyubashevsky's identification scheme, provably secure against active attacks [18], the hardness assumption is the difficulty in approximating the shortest vector in all lattices to within a factor of $\tilde{O}(n^2)$, where n is a security parameter corresponding to the lattice rank over which the hard problem is defined. The parameters seen there, however, are somewhat big to be considered practical.

By using weaker security assumptions, on the other hand, one can achieve parameters that are small enough to be used in practice, as seen in the identification scheme proposed by Kawachi et al. in [16]. In this later work, the authors suggest to use approximate Gap-SVP or SVP within $\tilde{O}(n)$ factors. Similar approach to improve efficiency was used in CLRS [11], which is one of the pillars of our signature scheme.

2.2   Ideal Lattices

In spite of the good security properties that can be achieved through lattice constructions, one issue has historically been presented as obstacle for their adoption: the huge key sizes. Through ideal lattices, this subject was sucessfully addressed in [20] and [18].

Definition 9. *(Ideal Lattice) Given a lattice* L, *such that* $L \subseteq \mathbb{Z}^n$, *a polynomial* $f(X) = f_0 + \ldots + f_{n-1}X^{n-1} + X^n$ *and a mapping* $\phi_f(v_0, \ldots, v_{n-1}) \longmapsto v_0 + v_1 X + \ldots + v_{n-1}X^{n-1} + f(X)\mathbb{Z}[X]$. L *is considered an ideal lattice, if* $\phi_f(L)$ *is an ideal in* $R_f = \mathbb{Z}[X]/\langle f(X)\rangle$. *Likewise, if* I *is an ideal in* R_f, *then its image* L *under* $\phi_f^{-1}(I)$ *is an ideal sublattice of* $\mathbb{Z}^n$.

Not only does this kind of lattice allow compact basis representation, but also enables efficient use of FFT to carry out operations over its elements. The signature scheme that we propose in this article can profit from these features, when implemented over this kind of lattice.

2.3 Threshold Ring Signatures

We depict here a threshold ring signature scheme, listing its basic operations and main features.

Definition 10. *(Threshold Ring Signature) Given an input security parameter λ, an integer n representing the number of users, and an integer t representing the minimum number of users required to jointly generate a valid signature, threshold ring signature scheme is a set of four algorithms described as below*

- *Setup: generates the public parameters corresponding to the security parameter.*
- *Key Generation: creates pairs of keys (s, p) (one for each user that composes the ring), secret and public respectively, related by a hard problem.*
- *Signature Generation: on input a message m, a set of public keys $\{p_1, \ldots, p_n\}$ and a sub-set of t secret keys, it issues a ring signature σ.*
- *Signature Verification: on input a message m, its ring signature σ and a set of public keys $\{p_1, \ldots, p_n\}$, it outputs 1 in case the signature is valid, and 0 otherwise.*

Definition 11. *(Existentially Unforgeable) A threshold ring signature with parameters (λ, n, t) is considered ϵ-existentially unforgeable, if no probabilistic polynomial time adversary $\mathcal{A}$ can generate a valid signature for any message m with probability higher than ϵ, under the conditions below :*

- *$\mathcal{A}$ knows all n public keys;*
- *$\mathcal{A}$ knows up to $t - 1$ private keys;*
- *$\mathcal{A}$ has access to pairs message-signature (m', σ) with $m \neq m'$.*

Definition 12. *(Unconditionally Source-Hiding) A threshold ring signature with parameters (λ, n, t) is considered to have the anonymity property of unconditionally source-hiding if, for any message m, it is possible to generate the same signature with two different sub-sets of signers having cardinality t.*

The TRSS-C satisfies these two properties, as proved in [2]. So does our scheme, which is built with a very similar structure.

2.4 CLRS Identification Scheme

Our TRSS-L derives its organization from TRSS-C. Both are built on top of identification schemes via standard Fiat-Shamir transformations. We describe here the one used by our scheme. It is called CLRS, and was delineated by Cayrel et al. in [12]. It is lattice-based and aims to deal the soundness error matter that was seen to impact the TRSS-C performance.

As previously mentioned, the TRSS-C employs the code-based predecessor proposed by Stern [29] as one of its pillars. Its security is based on the hardness of the syndrome decoding problem. An improvement over this scheme, exploring dual constructions, was conceived by Véron [30], achieving better communication costs and better efficiency. As the basic Stern's structure, however, its soundness error is still $2/3$.

By modifying the way the commitments are calculated, incorporating a value chosen at random by the verifier, Cayrel and Véron [12] were able to bound the cheating probability within a given round to $1/2$, achieving thus better communication costs. The approach followed is similar to that shown in Figure 2, which corresponds to the CLRS design, that uses the SIS problem as security basis. Both schemes have a soundness error of $1/2$.

The CLRS employs a 5-pass structure, and corresponds to a zero-knowledge interactive proof that an entity, designated by prover $\mathcal{P}$, knows a solution to a hard instance of the inhomogeneous SIS problem. The exact proof for the properties of completeness, soundness and zero-knowledge can be found on [12]. The arguments used in its construction and those used for GCLRS in Subsection 4.1 are alike, regarding the completeness and zero-knowledge properties. The soundness property can be proved by absurd, using the fact that a cheating prover able to correctly answer strictly more than $1/2$ of the possible questions posed by the verifier (in the form of $\alpha \times b$, with $\alpha \in \mathbb{Z}_q^*$ and $b \in \mathbb{F}_2$) will have to answer to, given a fixed pair of commitments c_0 and c_1 occurring in two different rounds, both possible values of b. Provided that the commitment function used is collision resistant, this would imply that the cheating prover is able to solve the SIS, that is known to be hard.

The security (in bits) associated with a given instance of CLRS is, first of all, determined by the parameters that specify the underlying SIS problem. The second aspect to be taken into account is the overall soundness error, which is a function of the number of rounds of execution of the identification scheme. In Table 2 we list the parameters used in an instantiation of our scheme.

2.5   Permutations

The use of permutations, as described below, is of the main tools used in the proposal of Cayrel and Véron [12] to lower the soundness error in a 5-pass construction. It allows the prover to send permutations of q-ary vectors build from private information, without revealing the exact values of the individual coordinates, because they are permuted as well. A similar approach was followed in the CLRS scheme to keep private information concealed when prover and verifier exchange messages over the communication channel, which can be monitored by adversaries.

Definition 13. (Constant n-block permutation) *It is a permutation Σ that acts on N blocks of size n, each of which is considered as a unit.*

Definition 14. (n-block permutation) *Given a vector $v = (V_1, \ldots, V_N)$ of size nN, a family of N permutations $\sigma_i \in S_n$ and a constant n-block permutation Σ, an n-block permutation is defined as the product permutation $\Pi = \Sigma \circ \sigma$ that acts on N blocks of size n as*

$$\Pi(v) = \Sigma(\sigma_1(V_1), \ldots, \sigma_N(V_N)).$$

KEYGEN:

$\mathbf{x} \xleftarrow{\$} \{0,1\}^m$, s.t. $\mathrm{wt}(\mathbf{x}) = m/2$

$\mathbf{A} \xleftarrow{\$} \mathbb{Z}_q^{n \times m}$

$\mathbf{y} \longleftarrow \mathbf{A}\mathbf{x} \bmod q$

COM $\xleftarrow{\$} \mathcal{F}$, suitable family of commitment functions

Output $(\mathrm{sk}, \mathrm{pk}) = (\mathbf{x}, (\mathbf{y}, \mathbf{A}, \mathrm{COM}))$

Fig. 1. Key generation algorithm, parameters n, m, q are public

Prover $\mathcal{P}$	**Verifier** $\mathcal{V}$
$(\mathrm{sk}, \mathrm{pk}) = (\mathbf{x}, (\mathbf{y}, \mathbf{A}, \mathrm{COM}))$	$\mathrm{pk} = \mathbf{y}, \mathbf{A}, \mathrm{COM}$

$\mathbf{u} \xleftarrow{\$} \mathbb{Z}_q^m, \sigma \xleftarrow{\$} S_m$

$\mathbf{r}_0 \xleftarrow{\$} \{0,1\}^n, \mathbf{r}_1 \xleftarrow{\$} \{0,1\}^n$

$c_0 \longleftarrow \mathrm{COM}(\sigma \,||\, \mathbf{A}\mathbf{u}, \mathbf{r}_0)$

$c_1 \longleftarrow \mathrm{COM}(\mathbf{P}_\sigma \mathbf{u} \,||\, \mathbf{P}_\sigma \mathbf{x}, \mathbf{r}_1)$ 　$\xrightarrow{\quad c_0, c_1 \quad}$

$\xleftarrow{\quad \alpha \quad}$ 　$\alpha \xleftarrow{\$} \mathbb{Z}_q^*$

$\beta \longleftarrow \mathbf{P}_\sigma(\mathbf{u} + \alpha \mathbf{x})$ 　$\xrightarrow{\quad \beta \quad}$

$\xleftarrow{\quad b \quad}$ 　$b \xleftarrow{\$} \{0,1\}$

If $b = 0$: 　$\xrightarrow{\quad \sigma, \mathbf{r}_0 \quad}$ 　$c_0 \overset{?}{=} \mathrm{COM}(\sigma \,||\, \mathbf{A}\mathbf{P}_\sigma^{-1}\beta - \alpha \mathbf{y}, \mathbf{r}_0)$

　$\sigma \overset{?}{\in} S_m$

Else: 　$\xrightarrow{\quad \mathbf{P}_\sigma \mathbf{x}, \mathbf{r}_1 \quad}$ 　$c_1 \overset{?}{=} \mathrm{COM}(\beta - \alpha \mathbf{P}_\sigma \mathbf{x} \,||\, \mathbf{P}_\sigma \mathbf{x}, \mathbf{r}_1)$,

　$\mathbf{P}_\sigma \mathbf{x} \overset{?}{\in} \{0,1\}^m$

Fig. 2. CLRS Identification protocol

We have seen in this segment some important concepts from the lattice theory that are necessary to understand the security and performance aspects of our threshold ring signature scheme, and how it compares to its code-based counterpart. In the sequence, we detail our design, by listing and explaining the algorithms that constitute it.

3   Our Lattice-Based Threshold Ring Signature Scheme

We have described and defined the lattice problems and concepts that work as basis for our scheme in the previous section. Now, we detail the algorithms that comprise this scheme.

Taking SIS as security assumption, we modify TRSS-C [2] and obtain a construction that is more efficient than other similar lattice-based solutions, to the best of our knowledge. In order to do so, instead of using Stern's identification scheme as basis, we employ the CLRS scheme [11], which has a lower soundness error (1/2, instead of 2/3) and enables the resulting construct to reach a security goal in fewer rounds of execution.

Some lattice-based identification scheme (see [25], [18] and [17]) have time complexity and public key sizes efficiently given by $\mathcal{O}(n)$. However, they share an inefficiency: for each bit of challenge sent by the verifier, a response with size $\mathcal{O}(n)$ has to be provided by the prover. This implies in huge signature sizes when directly applying the Fiat-Shamir heuristic. The same drawback can be found in TRSS-C. This means that the number of rounds executed by such scheme is given at least by the number of bits of the hash function value (applied to commitments concatenated to the message). Our scheme addresses the first factor by splitting the challenge in two pieces: the messages $\alpha \in \mathbb{Z}_q^*$ and $b \in \mathbb{F}_2$ represented in Figure 2. This bears similarity with the identification scheme described in [19], where the challenge-like bits are assigned to an element of a polynomial ring. Dividing the hash bits over structures that are several bits wide (given by the number of bits to represent α and b, in our case) has as positive effect a fewer number of rounds to generate a signature.

The other factor that impacts the number of rounds of execution is the soundness level required. The higher of the two such values will have to be executed in order to achieve both security goals.

3.1 Adaptations Made to the CLRS Scheme

In the code-based threshold ring signature scheme proposed by Aguilar et al. [2], they replaced the syndrome decoding problem in the underlying Stern's identification scheme by the minimum distance problem in order to preserve anonymity. Instead of having $\mathbf{H}\mathbf{x}^T = y$, with check matrix $\mathbf{H}$ and syndrome y public, and word $\mathbf{x}$ private with a known Hamming weight p, they used $\mathbf{H}\mathbf{x}^T = \mathbf{0}$, what means that the secret keys now correspond to codewords $\mathbf{x}$ with Hamming weight specified by an input parameter. Plus, when the leader is computing the master commitments he can easily satisfy this equation by picking $\mathbf{x} = \mathbf{0}$ for the users that are not signing the message.

For the same reasons, we make an adaptation of the original CLRS construction, so that it can be used in our threshold ring signature scheme. Initially, each user had a key-pair represented by a secret key $\mathbf{x} \in \mathbb{F}_2^m$ and a private key $\mathbf{y} \in \mathbb{Z}^n$ related by the ISIS (Inhomogeneous SIS) problem $\mathbf{A}\mathbf{x} = \mathbf{y} \bmod q$, with $\mathbf{A} \in \mathbb{Z}^{n \times m}$. The secret key can be chosen at random, from a set of binary words of known Hamming weight $m/2$. This can be rewritten as $[\mathbf{A}; -\mathbf{y}][\mathbf{x}; 1]^T = \mathbf{0} \bmod q$. Making $\mathbf{A}' = [\mathbf{A}; -\mathbf{y}]$ and $\mathbf{x}' = [\mathbf{x}; 1]$, we have $\mathbf{A}'\mathbf{x}' = \mathbf{0} \bmod q$. This is analogous to the code-based construction. It works as if every user had the same public key value: the null vector.

In Algorithm 1, the individual matrices $\mathbf{A}_i$ are calculated as described in the paragraph above, so that $\mathbf{A}_i\mathbf{x}_i = 0 \bmod q$. In Section 4, where the security proofs are given, we show that in order to break our system, one must obtain $\mathbf{x}_i$ given $\mathbf{A}_i$, which on its turn implies in being able to solve the SIS problem in the worst case. Given that this latter problem is known to be hard, our system is consequently difficult to break.

The memory size involved in storing the matrices $\mathbf{A}_i$ can be highly optimized by using ideal lattices. As discussed in Section 2, the space required by this kind of lattice grows linearly with the dimension, up to a logarithmic factor.

3.2   Applying Fiat-Shamir Heuristic

From the generalized identification scheme described in Algorithm 1, we obtain a signature scheme by putting a random oracle in the place of the verifier. The source of the random values to be used with α and b is the hash value of the message to be signed concatenated with the commitments of the current round, in order to make difficult to obtain successful forgery .

Using the honest-verifier zero-knowledge nature of our underlying identification scheme and the security results stated by Pointcheval and Stern at [26] and Abdalla et al. [1] regarding the Fiat-Shamir heuristic, we can establish the security of our signature scheme in the random oracle model. In order to do so, we are making the assumption that the security results associated with signature schemes obtained from canonical identification schemes (three passes) via Fiat-Shamir are also valid for our scheme, even though its underlying identification scheme is not canonical (five passes). Their similarity resides in a commitment-challenge-answer structure.

3.3   Description of Our Threshold Ring Signature Scheme

Our TRSS-L is composed of four algorithms: Setup, Key Generation, Signing, Verification. Though its structure is similar to that of the code-based scheme described in [2], the underlying identification scheme and hardness assumptions are considerably different, as emphasized in the discussions regarding security and performance, developed in Sections 4 and 5, respectively.

The **Setup** algorithm, on input a security parameter k, issues the parameters n, m, q that are used by the other three algorithms, and are necessary for the definition of the lattices and their operations.

The **Key Generation** algorithm, on input parameters k, n, m, q, N, generates the N pairs of public and private keys $(\mathbf{x}_i, \mathbf{A}_i)$, with $i \in \{0, \ldots, N-1\}$. All the private keys are binary vectors with Hamming weight $m/2 + 1$ and constitute solutions for the SIS problem $\mathbf{A}_i\mathbf{x}_i = 0 \bmod q$. The public keys are the matrices $\mathbf{A}_i \in \mathbb{Z}_q^{n \times (m+1)}$.

The **Signing** algorithm takes as input a message to be signed, the set of N public keys, t private keys (corresponding to the users willing to sign the message), and a hash function that computes the digest of the message concatenated with the commitments in a given round. This algorithm corresponds to the application of the Fiat-Shamir heuristics to the GCLRS scheme detailed by

Algorithm 1. A group of t users, one of which is the leader L, interact in order to generate a signature. The generalized scheme works as follows: each pair $(signer_i, leader)$ executes the CLRS identification scheme, where $signer_i$ plays as prover and leader L acts as verifier, sharing the same challenges α and b. On its turn, the pair (leader, Verifier) runs an identification scheme as well, where the commitments and answers are compositions involving the values received by the leader from the other signers. As for the non-signing users, the leader generates surrogate private keys comprised of null vectors (which are trivial solutions of the SIS problem). The leader applies block permutations over theses individual values in order to achieve the goal of anonymity. The signature consists of the transcript of the interaction between the leader and the verifier.

The **Verification** algorithm takes as input the public keys of the N users and the signature. Such signature constitutes a communication transcript of a sequence of rounds of the GCLRS scheme. The verification consists in check, depending on the value of the challenges, that the corresponding commitment is correct for every round. The signature is accepted if the check was successful in every round, and rejected otherwise.

The security aspects of the construction corresponding to the algorithms that comprise our scheme will be discussed next. We also give demonstrations that our design is safe, and relate it to the CLRS signature scheme upon which it relies.

4   Security

The previous section described the algorithms that comprise our system. In the sequence, we show them to be secure, with worst-case to average-case reductions that are typical in lattice-based systems.

4.1   Honest-Verifier Zero-Knowledge Proof of Knowledge

We now prove that the Algorithm 1 (GCLRS, short for Generalized CLRS) constitutes a zero-knowledge proof of knowledge of that a group of t-out-of-N users knows t different pairs (secret key, public key). The first element of the pair is a binary vector $\mathbf{x}_i$ of length $m+1$ and Hamming weight $m/2+1$ and the second is a matrix $\mathbf{A}_i \in \mathbb{Z}^{n \times (m+1)}$, such that $\mathbf{A}_i \mathbf{x_i} = 0 \bmod q$, with $i \in \{0, \ldots, N-1\}$. This algorithm can be seen as a composition of t simultaneous executions of the CLRS identification schemes described in Figure 2, which has already been demonstrated to be secure by Cayrel et al. in [11] in the active attack model. We will use this fact and discuss only the security of the composition described in Algorithm 1.

By interacting as verifier with each of the $t-1$ other signers and following the GCLRS protocol, the leader learns nothing about their secret keys, except that they are valid. When playing the role of prover, the leader L, in his interaction with the verifier V, does not leak any private information, either. All that V learns is that t of the users belonging to U have participated to generate a

Algorithm 1. Generalized CLRS Identification Scheme (GCLRS)

---

procedure IDENTIFICATION SCHEME
▷ $U' = \{users\}$ and $S' = \{signers\}$, with $S' \subset U'$, $|S'| = t$ and $|U'| = N$
▷ Prover (pass 1): computes commitments
▷ **Commitment**: performed by signers S', which include the leader L
  for Each signer $i \in S'$ **do**   ▷ Compute commitments
    $\sigma_i \xleftarrow{\$} S_{m+1}$, $\mathbf{u}_i \xleftarrow{\$} \mathbb{Z}_q^{m+1}$, $\mathbf{r}_{0,i} \xleftarrow{\$} \{0,1\}^n$ and $\mathbf{r}_{1,i} \xleftarrow{\$} \{0,1\}^n$
    $c_{0,i} \longleftarrow \text{COM}(\sigma_i \,\|\, \mathbf{A}_i \mathbf{u}_i, \mathbf{r}_{0,i})$ and $c_{1,i} \longleftarrow \text{COM}(\sigma_i(\mathbf{u}_i) \,\|\, \sigma_i(\mathbf{x}_i), \mathbf{r}_{1,i})$
    Send $c_{0,i}$ and $c_{1,i}$ to L
  end for
  For the non-signers $j \in U' \setminus S'$, L performs the same, but with $\mathbf{x}_j \leftarrow 0$
  L chooses a random constant n-block permutation on N blocks Σ .
  L computes the *master commitments* $C_0 = \text{COM}(\Sigma \,\|\, c_{0,1} \,\|\, \dots \,\|\, c_{0,N}, \mathbf{r}_0)$ and
  $C_1 = \text{COM}(\Sigma(c_{1,1}, \dots, c_{0,N}), \mathbf{r}_1)$ and sends them to V
▷ Verifier (pass 2): imposes a value to be used to verify previous commitments
  V sends $\alpha \xleftarrow{\$} \mathbb{Z}_q^*$ to L, which passes it to S'.
▷ Prover (pass 3):
  for Each signer $i \in S'$ **do**
    $\beta_i \leftarrow \sigma_i(\mathbf{u}_i + \alpha \mathbf{x}_i)$
  end for
  For the non-signers $j \in U' \setminus S'$, L performs the same, but with $\mathbf{x}_j \leftarrow 0$
  L sends $\boldsymbol{\beta} = \Sigma(\beta_0, \dots, \beta_{N-1})$ to V.
▷ **Challenge**:
▷ Verifier (pass 4): makes a challenge to leader L
  V sends $b \xleftarrow{\$} \{0,1\}$ to L, which propagates it to S'.
▷ **Answer**:
▷ Prover (pass 5): reveals private information for the current round
  for Each signer $i \in S'$ **do**
    Reveal to L either σ_i or $\sigma_i(\mathbf{x}_i)$, when $b = 0$ or $b = 1$, respectively.
  end for   ▷ For non-signing users, L has chosen default values at the
commitment phase.
  if b is 0 **then**
    Set $\sigma = (\sigma_0, \dots, \sigma_{N-1})$
    L reveals $\Pi = \Sigma \circ \sigma$ and $\Pi(\mathbf{r}_{0,0}, \dots, \mathbf{r}_{0,N-1})$ to V
  else
    Set $\Pi(\mathbf{x}) = \Sigma(\sigma_1(\mathbf{x}_1), \dots, \sigma_{N-1}(\mathbf{x}_{N-1}))$
    L reveals $\Pi(\mathbf{x})$ and $\Pi(\mathbf{r}_{1,0}, \dots, \mathbf{r}_{1,N-1})$ to V
  end if
▷ **Verification**: correctness of *master commitments*, permutations and Hamming
weight.
  if b is 0 **then** ▷ A is matrix whose diagonal corresponds to the public keys A_i
    V checks that $C_0 \stackrel{?}{=} \text{COM}(\Sigma \,\|\, \mathbf{A}\Pi^{-1}(\boldsymbol{\beta}) \,\|\, \mathbf{r}_0)$ and that Π is well formed.
  else
    V checks that $C_1 \stackrel{?}{=} \text{COM}(\boldsymbol{\beta} - \alpha\Pi(\mathbf{x}) \,\|\, \Pi^{-1}(\boldsymbol{\beta}) \,\|\, \mathbf{r}_1)$ and that $\Pi(\mathbf{x})$ has
Hamming weight $t(m/2 + 1)$.
  end if
end procedure

---

binary vector $\mathbf{X}$ of dimension $N(m+1)$ and Hamming weight $t(m/2+1)$ such that $\mathbf{AX} = 0 \bmod q$, where $\mathbf{A}$ is defined as below:

$$\mathbf{A} = \begin{bmatrix} \mathbf{A}_0 & 0 & \cdots & 0 \\ 0 & \mathbf{A}_1 & \cdots & 0 \\ \vdots & \vdots & \ddots & \vdots \\ 0 & 0 & \cdots & \mathbf{A}_{N-1} \end{bmatrix}$$

Lemma 1. *Under the assumption of the hardness of the SIS problem, finding a vector $\mathbf{v}$ with length $N(m+1)$ and Hamming weight $t(m/2+1)$ satisfying $(\mathbf{Av} = 0 \bmod q)$, with $\mathbf{A}$ defined as above, such that the N blocks of length $m+1$ that comprise $\mathbf{v}$ have either 0 or $m/2+1$ as Hamming weight, is also hard.*

Proof: By construction of $\mathbf{A}$ and $\mathbf{v}$, finding a solution of $\mathbf{Av} = 0 \bmod q$ is at least as hard as finding a local solution $\mathbf{v}_i$ to $\mathbf{A}_i\mathbf{v}_i = 0 \bmod q$ with Hamming weight$(\mathbf{v_i}) = m/2+1$, and this latter problem problem is hard under the SIS hardness assumption.   □

Theorem 1. *The GCLRS scheme is an honest verifier zero-knowledge proof of knowledge, with soundness error no greater than 1/2, that a group of t signers knows a vector v of length $N(m+1)$ and Hamming weight $t(m/2+1)$, such that each of the N blocks of size m either weights $m/2+1$ or zero. The scheme is secure in the random oracle model under the SIS problem hardness assumption.*

Proof:

Completeness: An honest set of signers is always able to reveal to the leader the information necessary to compute the individual commitments $c_{0,i}$ or $c_{1,i}$, by revealing σ_i or $\sigma_i(\mathbf{x}_i)$ respectively, depending on the challenge sent by the verifier V. For each component $i \in \{0,\dots,N-1\}$ of the group, we have either weight$(\mathbf{x}_i) = m/2+1$, when the user is signing the message, or weight$(\mathbf{x}_i) = 0$ otherwise. The length of each of those vectors is $m+1$. The leader L, on his turn, is always able to disclose either Π or $\Pi\mathbf{x}$ under the same challenge values. The vector $\mathbf{x}$ is comprised of N components $\mathbf{x}'_i$ that are permutations of $\mathbf{x}_i$, and hence have the same weight. Therefore, $\mathbf{x}$ has overal length $N(m+1)$ and weight $t(m/2+1)$.

Soundness: The soundness error is bounded away from 1, and it cannot be higher than 1/2. The GCLRS scheme is composed of $t-1$ CLRS instances involving $t-1$ distinct pairs (prover, verifier). If GCLRS has a soundness error strictly above 1/2, then a cheating prover can devise a strategy to beat the system with a success probability also above 1/2. Given that CLRS can be reduced to GCLRS (it suffices to make all singing instances equal, and follow the procedure described in Subsection 3.1), we can use the cheating strategy to beat the CLRS scheme also with probability above 1/2. However, this is absurd under the assumption of SIS hardness and the commitment function collision resistance, as seen in [11].

Zero-Knowledge (ZK): Let us build a simulator as described below:

1 $Coin \xleftarrow{\$} \{0,1\}$
2 Prepare to answer a challenge that is equal to $Coin$ as follows:
   - For $Coin = 0$, pick $\mathbf{x}_i$ satisfying $\mathbf{y}_i = \mathbf{A}_i \mathbf{x}_i$, but with high weight, for the t elements of the signing set. According to the way that the parameters were chosen, such solution exists with high probability and is not hard to find. Regarding the other $N - t$ components, just set $\mathbf{x}_i = 0$.
   - For $Coin = 1$, pick $\mathbf{x}_i$ with weight exactly $m/2 + 1$ for the t elements, but without satisfying $\mathbf{y}_i = \mathbf{A}_i \mathbf{x}_i$. The remaining components will be set as null vector.
3 $b \xleftarrow{\$} \{0,1\}$
4 If $Coin$ and b have the same value, register the current round as part of the signature. Otherwise, go back to step 1.
5 Repeat loop until the signature is complete.

The signature generated as above does not involve the actual values of the individual private keys. Besides, the uniformly random choices that are made and registered as signature follow the same distribution of a real one. Hence, looking at the real signature we learn nothing more than what we could have learnt from a simulated one. Therefore, with the simulator constructed as above, we conclude that the zero-knowledge property is observed. □

Theorem 1 implies that the TRSS scheme is existentially unforgeable under chosen message attack in the random oracle model, assuming the hardness of the SIS problem and the existence of a collision resistant commitment function. Given the zero-knowledge property of the scheme, no information is learnt about the private keys, given access to previous signatures of different messages. Besides, even if an adversary is given $t - 1$ private keys, he will not be able to generate a valid signature, unless he is able solve SIS in order to obtain an extra private key, different from those that he already possesses.

Theorem 2. *Our lattice-based threshold ring signature scheme is unconditionally source hiding.*

Proof: Our algorithm is structurally similar to TRSS-C [2]. In both, the entity playing the role of leader creates a secret vector which blockwise corresponds to either permutations of individual private keys or null vectors. Besides, all the individual private keys are binary vectors with exactly the same Hamming weight, and the commitments correspond to one-time pad of the secrets. Hence, the distribution of the commitments associated with a given signer are indistinguishable from a random one, and also from the distribution related to a different user. Therefore, any subset of t users can produce a given signature with equal probability. □

After having discussed security aspects of our threshold ring signature scheme and related it with the hardness of average instances of the SIS problem (to which are proven to exist reductions from worst-case instances of the GapSVP problem), we next show that the design decisions taken allow gains in efficiency as well.

5   Performance

The previous section gave evidences and proofs that our system is safe. We now show that the our design choices result in a construction that is also efficient.

Our scheme can outperform TRSS-C both in terms of signature size and speed of signature generation. These two variables are linked and their reduction represents the combined effect of three different factors discussed below: smaller soundness error, wider challenge values, and use of FFT for performing multiplications.

Let us suppose that TRSS-C has a round communication payload of PL_1, whereas the corresponding value for our scheme is PL_2. The soundness error for the two schemes are $SE_1 = 2/3$ and $SE_2 = 1/2$, respectively. In order to reach a given security level L (representing the probability of successful impersonation or forgery, as specified in ISO/IEC 9798-5, for instance), the two schemes have to be repeated several times, as follows $N_1 = \left\lceil \log_{2/3} L \right\rceil$ and $N_2 = \left\lceil \log_{1/2} L \right\rceil$. Therefore, considering the fist factor (soundness error), the ratio between the two total payloads for reaching the security goal is given by

$$\frac{TPL_1}{TPL_2} = \frac{N_1 \times PL_1}{N_2 \times PL_2} = \log_{\frac{3}{2}} 2 \times \frac{PL_1}{PL_2}$$

As for the second factor represented by wider challenge values, we can have the combined effect of $\alpha \in \mathbb{Z}_q$ and $b \in \mathbb{F}_2$ to play the role of challenges. Provided that the overall soundness requirement is also satisfied (by having a minimum number of rounds executed), this avoids the necessity of executing one round per hash bit. Table 1 shows a numeric comparison between the two schemes. In order to construct this table, the following choices were made. We considered a security level close to 100 bits as constraint. For the hash function, we use the parameters from Table 2, page 90 of [5], which lists the state-of-art values. According to it, a hash length with length 224 bits will provide a level of security of 111, which is close to the value we chose. Regarding the choice of parameters for TRSS-C, we used the results listed in Section 7 of [6], and picked the code length as 2480, with which one can reach a security level of 107 bits.

The third point to consider is the application of ideal lattices in our scheme. This can speed up the most costly operations associated with multiplications between matrices and vectors, and have them executed in time $\mathcal{O}(n \log n)$ instead of $\mathcal{O}(n^2)$.

5.1   Parameters

Similarly as shown in [16], in order to guarantee with overwhelming probability that there are other solutions to $\mathbf{Ax} = \mathbf{0} \bmod q$, besides the private key possessed by each user (which is pivotal in the demonstration of security against concurrent attack), one can make q and m satisfy the relation below

$$q^n \ll card\{\mathbf{x} \in \mathbb{Z}_2^{m+1} : weight(\mathbf{x}) = m/2 + 1\}. \tag{1}$$

Table 1. Comparing TRSS Schemes for N=100, and security=111 bits

Scheme	Signature Size (Mbytes)	Number of Rounds	Hash Length (bits)
TRSS-C	47	190	224
TRSS-L	45	111	224

Table 2. Concrete Parameters

Bit-security	n	m	q	Commitment Length (bits)
111	64	2048	257	224

Besides, q has its value bounded from the following theorem by Micciancio, proved in [24].

Theorem 3. *For any polynomially bounded functions $\beta(n), m(n), q(n) = n^{O(1)}$, with $q(n) \geq 4\sqrt{m(n)}n^{1.5}\beta(n)$ and $\gamma(n) = 14\pi\sqrt{n}\beta(n)$, there is a probabilistic polynomial time reduction from solving $GapCVP_\gamma$ in the worst-case to solving $SIS_{q,m,\gamma}$ on the average with non-negligible probability. In particular, for any $m = \Theta(n \log n)$, there exists $q(n) = O(n^{2.5} \log n)$ and $\gamma = O(n\sqrt{\log n})$, such that solving $SIS_{q,m}$ on the average is at least as hard as solving $GapSVP_\gamma$ in the worst case.*

The parameters that we chose to use with our TRSS, shown in Table 2 are derived from those applied by the SWIFFT lattice-based hash proposed in [21]. The comparison exhibited in Table 1 is based in such choice. The soundness requirement alone makes TRSS-C run 190 rounds. Our scheme, on the other hand, which has lower soundness error, reaches the same goal with 111 rounds.

This section discussed about the efficiency gains that resulted from our design choices, such as the underlying identification scheme with smaller soundness error and the possibility of using ideal lattices. It is important to notice that such choices do not compromise security. In the next section we make an overall appreciation of our construction and present further lines of research associated with it.

6   Conclusions and Further Work

In this work we have shown standard applications of the Fiat-Shamir heuristics to lattice-based identification schemes in order to derive signature schemes with proven security. By means of such construction, we were able to adapt a threshold ring signature scheme from a code-based paradigm, obtaining a construction that is more efficient and has stronger security evidences. Instead of using the syndrome decoding hardness assumption as security basis, we used the SIS problem, with a suitable set of parameters. Such approach enables the application of reductions from worst-case GapSVP to average-case SIS, giving stronger security evidences for the resulting scheme.

In addition, we replaced the Stern's identification construction by the CLRS [11]. Such substitution has two positive effects on the efficiency of the threshold ring signature scheme. It reduces the soundness error from $2/3$ to $1/2$, allowing a specified security level to be reached with a fewer number of interactions. The reduced number of rounds implies in shorter signatures as well.

Our construction can also use ideal lattices. This results in more efficient multiplications of vectors by matrices by means of FFT. Such operations take time $\tilde{\mathcal{O}}(n)$.

As shown in [19], when compared to zero-knowledge constructions, such as Kawachi's [16] or CLRS [11], Lyubashevky's identification scheme provides better results in terms of size, if used in conjunction with Fiat-Shamir heuristics to derive a signature scheme. This is due to its extremely low soundness error. Therefore, a threshold ring signature scheme can make use of this fact to achieve shorter signatures than those shown in the present article. However, some structural changes are necessary in order to obtain the anonymity property possessed by our scheme. It requires a more involved approach than the direct application of TRSS-C construction [2].

References

1. Abdalla, M., An, J.H., Bellare, M., Namprempre, C.: From identification to signatures via the Fiat-Shamir transform: Minimizing assumptions for security and forward-security. In: Knudsen, L.R. (ed.) EUROCRYPT 2002. LNCS, vol. 2332, pp. 418–433. Springer, Heidelberg (2002)
2. Melchor, C.A., Cayrel, P.-L., Gaborit, P.: A new efficient threshold ring signature scheme based on coding theory. In: Buchmann, Ding (eds.) [10], pp. 1–16
3. Ajtai, M.: Generating hard instances of lattice problems. Electronic Colloquium on Computational Complexity (ECCC) 3(7) (1996)
4. Ajtai, M., Dwork, C.: A public-key cryptosystem with worst-case/average-case equivalence. Electronic Colloquium on Computational Complexity (ECCC) 3(65) (1996)
5. Bernstein, D.J., Buchmann, J., Dahmen, E.: Post Quantum Cryptography. Springer Publishing Company, Incorporated, Heidelberg (2008)
6. Bernstein, D.J., Lange, T., Peters, C.: Attacking and defending the mceliece cryptosystem. In: Buchmann, Ding (eds.) [10], pp. 31–46
7. Boyd, C. (ed.): ASIACRYPT 2001. LNCS, vol. 2248. Springer, Heidelberg (2001)
8. Brakerski, Z., Kalai, Y.T.: A framework for efficient signatures, ring signatures and identity based encryption in the standard model. Cryptology ePrint Archive, Report 2010/086 (2010), http://eprint.iacr.org/
9. Bresson, E., Stern, J., Szydlo, M.: Threshold ring signatures and applications to ad-hoc groups. In: Yung, M. (ed.) CRYPTO 2002. LNCS, vol. 2442, pp. 465–480. Springer, Heidelberg (2002)
10. Buchmann, J., Ding, J. (eds.): PQCrypto 2008. LNCS, vol. 5299. Springer, Heidelberg (2008)
11. Cayrel, P.-L., Lindner, R., Rückert, M., Silva, R.: Improved zero-knowledge identification with lattices
12. Cayrel, P.-L., Véron, P.: Improved code-based identification scheme. CoRR, abs/1001.3017 (2010), http://arxiv.org/abs/1001.3017v1

13. Chaum, D., van Heyst, E.: Group signatures. In: Davies, D.W. (ed.) EUROCRYPT 1991. LNCS, vol. 547, pp. 257–265. Springer, Heidelberg (1991)

14. Courtois, N., Finiasz, M., Sendrier, N.: How to achieve a mceliece-based digital signature scheme. In: Boyd (ed.) [7], pp. 157–174

15. Dallot, L., Vergnaud, D.: Provably secure code-based threshold ring signatures. In: Parker, M.G. (ed.) Cryptography and Coding. LNCS, vol. 5921, pp. 222–235. Springer, Heidelberg (2009)

16. Kawachi, A., Tanaka, K., Xagawa, K.: Concurrently secure identification schemes based on the worst-case hardness of lattice problems. In: Pieprzyk, J. (ed.) ASIACRYPT 2008. LNCS, vol. 5350, pp. 372–389. Springer, Heidelberg (2008)

17. Kawachi, A., Tanaka, K., Xagawa, K.: Concurrently secure identification schemes based on the worst-case hardness of lattice problems. In: Pieprzyk, J. (ed.) ASIACRYPT 2008. LNCS, vol. 5350, pp. 372–389. Springer, Heidelberg (2008)

18. Lyubashevsky, V.: Lattice-based identification schemes secure under active attacks. In: Cramer, R. (ed.) PKC 2008. LNCS, vol. 4939, pp. 162–179. Springer, Heidelberg (2008)

19. Lyubashevsky, V.: Fiat-shamir with aborts: Applications to lattice and factoring-based signatures. In: Matsui, M. (ed.) ASIACRYPT 2009. LNCS, vol. 5912, pp. 598–616. Springer, Heidelberg (2009)

20. Lyubashevsky, V., Micciancio, D.: Generalized compact knapsacks are collision resistant. In: Bugliesi, M., Preneel, B., Sassone, V., Wegener, I. (eds.) ICALP 2006. LNCS, vol. 4052, pp. 144–155. Springer, Heidelberg (2006)

21. Lyubashevsky, V., Micciancio, D., Peikert, C., Rosen, A.: Swifft: A modest proposal for fft hashing. In: Nyberg, K. (ed.) FSE 2008. LNCS, vol. 5086, pp. 54–72. Springer, Heidelberg (2008)

22. Micciancio, D.: Generalized compact knapsacks, cyclic lattices, and efficient one-way functions. In: Computational Complexity. Springer, Heidelberg (2007)

23. Micciancio, D., Goldwasser, S.: Complexity of Lattice Problems: a cryptographic perspective, March 2002. The Kluwer International Series in Engineering and Computer Science, vol. 671. Kluwer Academic Publishers, Boston (2002)

24. Micciancio, D., Regev, O.: Worst-case to average-case reductions based on gaussian measures. SIAM J. Comput. 37(1), 267–302 (2007)

25. Micciancio, D., Vadhan, S.P.: Statistical zero-knowledge proofs with efficient provers: Lattice problems and more. In: Boneh, D. (ed.) CRYPTO 2003. LNCS, vol. 2729, pp. 282–298. Springer, Heidelberg (2003)

26. Pointcheval, D., Stern, J.: Security proofs for signature schemes. In: Maurer, U.M. (ed.) EUROCRYPT 1996. LNCS, vol. 1070, pp. 387–398. Springer, Heidelberg (1996)

27. Rivest, R.L., Shamir, A., Tauman, Y.: How to leak a secret. In: Boyd (ed.) [7], pp. 552–565

28. Shor, P.W.: Polynomial-time algorithms for prime factorization and discrete logarithms on a quantum computer. SIAM review 41(2), 303–332 (1999)

29. Stern, J.: A new identification scheme based on syndrome decoding. In: Stinson, D.R. (ed.) CRYPTO 1993. LNCS, vol. 773, pp. 13–21. Springer, Heidelberg (1994)

30. Véron, P.: Improved identification schemes based on error-correcting codes. Appl. Algebra Eng. Commun. Comput. 8(1), 57–69 (1996)

Defeating Any Secret Cryptography with SCARE Attacks

Sylvain Guilley[1], Laurent Sauvage[1], Julien Micolod[2],
Denis Réal[2], and Frédéric Valette[2]

[1] Institut TELECOM, TELECOM ParisTech
CNRS LTCI (UMR 5141)
Département COMELEC, 46 rue Barrault
75 634 PARIS Cedex 13, France
[2] DGA CELAR, La Roche Marguerite, 35 174 Bruz, France

Abstract. This article aims at showing that side-channel analyses constitute powerful tools for reverse-engineering applications. We present two new attacks that only require known plaintext or ciphertext. The first one targets a stream cipher and points out how an attacker can recover unknown linear parts of an algorithm which is in our case the parameters of a Linear Feedback Shift Register. The second technique allows to retrieve an unknown non-linear function such as a substitution box. It can be applied on every kind of symmetric algorithm (typically Feistel or Substitution Permutation Network) and also on stream ciphers.

Twelve years after the first publication about side-channel attacks, we show that the potential of these analyses has been initially seriously under-estimated. Every cryptography, either public or secret, is indeed at risk when implemented in a device accessible by an attacker. This illustrates how vulnerable cryptography is without a trusted tamper-proof hardware support.

1 Introduction

Most cryptanalyses require the knowledge of the attacked algorithm. It is thus tempting for a cryptographic engineer to protect an algorithm by keeping its specifications secret. In this case, the adversary faces the difficulty to attack a blackbox, hardly distinguishable from a random number generator. Only cube attacks succeed in these contexts, provided the cipher can be expressed as a polynomial of low degree.

As early as in the 1880s, Auguste Kerckhoffs [14] pleaded for cryptographic algorithms publication. The traditional approach to discourage algorithms secrecy is the lack of scrutiny, which could mean that original powerful attacks could be devised "out of the box" against the algorithm if it was disclosed. This risk has nowadays almost vanished, since many standardized and thoroughly studied algorithms exist. It is thus easy to mark down a reference algorithm to make it partially customized while maintaining its security level in the meantime. Therefore, the benefit is to dissuade any prospective opponent by adding an effort of

M. Abdalla and P.S.L.M. Barreto (Eds.): LATINCRYPT 2010, LNCS 6212, pp. 273–293, 2010.

algorithm-recovery prior to starting the key-recovery work. The reasoned usage of standard algorithm modification is thus safe from a computational point of view. However, this approach does not provide any improvement in terms of forward secrecy, since once the algorithm-recovery barrier is overcome, the security level is merely that of the underlying standard algorithm.

Another appeal of side-channel analyses (SCA) is their suitability to reverse-engineer an algorithm, a technique known as SCARE. However, although the side-channel attacks database[1] indexes more that 700 bibliographic references about SCA, we have found only 9 (namely [19,21,7,9,27,1,6,22,12], discussed later) that deal with SCARE. This low percentage of SCARE publications is certainly detrimental to the scientific progress on this topic. Most publications so far about SCA reverse-engineering (SCARE) concentrate on block ciphers, where in addition the plaintext can be chosen. In this article, we show that SCARE can be extended to any context where either the plaintext or the ciphertext is only known. We also demonstrate for the first time a SCARE attack on a stream-cipher and on a substitution permutation network (SPN) block cipher. It seems that the potential of SCARE goes much beyond what was previously expected.

Side-channel analyses are attacks that are virtually able to probe any node from a circuit after post-processing of a database of side-channel physical measurements. They make attack strategies such as that of Itai Dinur and Adi Shamir [8] (cryptanalysis using the sole knowledge of one bit amongst the first round state) possible, albeit in a statistical modus operandi. Therefore, we explicit how the techniques known so far, for example that exploit collisions, can be improved and gain generality.

The rest of the paper is organized as follows. Section 2 recalls the public state-of-the-art about SCARE attacks. Sections 3 and 4 describe two new attacks on two representative blocks making up cryptographic algorithms. The first attack shows how the linear part of an unknown stream cipher can be easily recovered using only the knowledge of an initial value. This technique is practically illustrated on a stream cipher similar to those customarily used in RFIDs (called "RFID-like" in the sequel). The second one describes a known plaintext attack on an unknown non-linear function. This method which can be applied either to a Feistel or a SPN block cipher is demonstrated on a DES implementation which is publicly available. Finally, section 5 concludes on the efficiency of our attacks and on further possible improvements. Further considerations about SCARE on stream and block ciphers are given in appendix A and B respectively.

2   SCARE: State-of-the-Art

Physical attacks based on Side Channel Analysis (SCA) or on Fault Analysis (FA) target a secret usually manipulated by a algorithm with public specifications. SCA can also be used for Reverse-Engineering (SCARE) against implementations of a private algorithm.

---

[1] Service hosted by the University of Boston: http://www.sidechannelattacks.com

2.1 State-of-the-Art about Reverse-Engineering of Secret Algorithms Embedded in a Device

Algorithms coded in software are exposed to an illegitimate access of their machine code. Indeed, as the memory is a separate component, it must be readable for its programme to be executed. Therefore, an attack strategy can consist in soldering the memories chips out, which can be done easily without damaging the component, in a view to drive it by a rogue processor that is going to dump the software instead of executing it. As a consequence, it is more secure to conceal the cryptographic algorithm into the cryptographic device. It has been believed for a long time that this was the definitive solution against its retrieval. The smartcards are typical examples of security products that enforce this idea.

2.2 Physical Attacks on Tamper-Proof Hardware

However, attackers became imaginative to read inside the secure chips. As of today, the reverse-engineering of an algorithm embedded in an electronic device can be done by various methods. The most straightforward one is simply to recover the layout by taking pictures of the different technological layers. This is not common practice but some specialized businesses can do so. It was recently illustrated on the example of the NXP MyFare 1k secure memory card, fabricated in an old CMOS technology. In this example, the algorithm was hard-coded, hence its structure was easy to retrieve. However, simple counter-measures can be imagined. For instance, if the structure of interconnected logic gates can be retrieved by microscopy, the content of a non-volatile memory point (such as EEPROM or Flash) is not that easy to read-back optically [2]. Incidentally, it is a natural counter-measure if the algorithm is intended to be customizable.

FPGAs have become a viable alternative to ASICs due to their flexibility and their low cost for small to medium volumes. The functionality of most FPGA (with the remarkable exception of anti-fuse technologies) is stored in volatile memory points. Thus the read-back by invasive methods is also impossible, or at least very difficult. However, the SRAM points value is stored externally in a flash memory. But the high-end FPGA manufacturers (*e.g.* Actel, Altera, Xilinx) encrypt the memory's content. Consequently, bitstream encryption makes reverse-engineering as hard as decryption without the knowledge of the key.

No fault attack against embedded SRAMs (in ASIC or FPGA) aiming at a reverse-engineering is known: it does not seem trivial to deduce any information on a secret architecture by the result of its mutation, even if it is controlled. But another option to retrieve a functionality is to fault the bitstream before it is loaded into the FPGA. Indeed, bitstreams are not well protected against DFA, even if they embed some redundancy, they remain malleable: they can be forged with a high success probability. The idea is not attack the customized parts, but to reduce the number of rounds, for instance, so as to ease the reverse-engineering.

2.3 SCARE Techniques

Physical attacks based on Side Channel Analysis (SCA) or on Fault Analysis (FA) usually target a secret manipulated by a public algorithm. SCA can also be used for Reverse-Engineering (SCARE) against implementations of a private algorithm. We can identify in the publicly available literature three techniques that have been proposed to reverse-engineer an algorithm.

The most natural idea is to use pattern matching techniques. Template Analysis for Reverse-Engineering is mainly used for instructions identification in embedded applications. The feasibility for Java card was shown in [27] and for microcontrollers in [9,12]. The template matching can be optimized by coupling them with instruction sequence statistics.

A second approach is based on classical Correlation Analysis. It has been applied to public key cryptosystems [1] as well as on both hardware or software Feistel scheme implementations. For a software design, one-round intermediate values leak with a high enough signal-to-noise ratio for being guessed by SCA. Indeed, they are computed sequentially and stored in a register. The feasibility of a SCARE for a software DES implementation has been proved in [7]. For a hardware implementation, due to Feistel properties, an accurate side channel analysis permits to guess the output of the Feistel function for any chosen right half plaintext. Then, using interpolation methods, this unknown function can be recovered [22].

The last technique is based on collision analysis and was first applied on the private GSM A3/A8 algorithm where only the overall structure of the algorithm was publicly available. R. Novak proposed a strategy for identifying one confidential substitution table T_2 of this algorithm using collision [19]. Novak generalizes his attack using SDPA (Sign-based DPA) in [21], and summarizes his method in [20]. However, he needs as a prerequisite the knowledge of the secret key and of the confidential substitution sbox (sbox) T_1. This attack was improved in [6]. Combining collisions and CPA principles, both key and sbox T_1 are found back. Then, Novak's attack is applied to discover the remaining confidential information about A3/A8.

3 SCARE on a Stream Cipher

Due to their small size, stream ciphers are often used in smartcard or low power IC. Contrary to block ciphers such as AES, stream ciphers are usually proprietary and dedicated to a specific application. The security of these systems is usually provided by the secrecy of the algorithm. The reverse-engineering of the algorithm is often followed by a cryptanalysis of the system. It has been illustrated by famous examples such as the attacks on the GSM algorithm A5/1 [3] and more recently the cryptanalysis of the MyFare [10] which has followed the recovering of the algorithm CRYPTO1 by [17]. A similar story happened for the DECT Standard Cipher in early 2010 [18]. In this section, we will see how side channel techniques can be efficiently used to reverse-engineer an RFID-like stream cipher. In order to detail our technique, we will simplify our stream cipher by reducing it to a simple Linear Feedback Shift Register (LFSR) followed by some non-linear functions.

3.1 Stream Cipher Presentation

The stream cipher implementation we study in this paper is an LFSR filtered by a non-linear function. The LFSR is an L-bit shift register initialized by a constant seed K that can be considered as the key. Usually, each ciphering j of the stream cipher needs a random initialisation vector noted IV^j used to make each ciphering independent from others ciphering produced by the same key. For each ciphering, at each clock cycle t a bit of IV_t^j XORed with a feedback F_t^j enters into the register. The feedback of the register can be represented as a polynomial P applied on the register. (When there is an XOR connected to a cell i of the register then $P[i] = 1$ else $P[i] = 0$.) The notations are summarized in the figure 1.

- j : The jth experiment.
- t : The tth clock cycle.
- i : The ith bit of the shift register.
- $REG_t^j[i]$: The ith bit of the register at the clock cycle t for the jth experiment.
- IV_t^j : The bit of the IV being input in the register at the clock cycle t for the jth experiment.
- $P[i]$: The ith bit of the LFSR polynomial.
- K : The initialisation seed of the register. It is the same for all the experiments.
- L : The length of the register.
- F_t^j : The feedback at the clock cycle t for the jth experiment.
- FIV_t^j : The feedback depending on IVs at the clock cycle t for the jth experiment.
- FK_t : The feedback depending on the constant seed at the clock cycle t.
- $RADHYP[O]$: The radiation hypothesis on an object O.

Fig. 1. Notations

The feedback F_t^j can be expressed by the following Eq. (1):

$$(F_t^j) = (\bigoplus_{k=0}^{k=L-1} P[k].REG_{t-1}^j[k]) . \tag{1}$$

As the LFSR is linear, its equation can be written as the XOR of two equations, each one represented as an L bit register:

- The first register REG1 is initialized by the seed K. The IV value is null for each experiment. So we can notice that the LFSR has the same state behaviour for each experiment because the feedback only depends on the seed K.

- The second register REG2 is initialized by a seed equal to 0. The value which enters in the register is the IV_t^j so we can compute the state at each time t for each experiment j which depends only on IV.

We can express the feedbacks F_t^j as the XOR of the feedback FK_t and FIV_t^j. And from the Eq. (1), we express FK_t and FIV_t^j in Eq. (2) and (3).

$$(FK_t) = (\bigoplus_{k=0}^{k=L-1} P[k].REG1_{t-1}^j[k]). \tag{2}$$

$$(FIV_t^j) = (\bigoplus_{k=0}^{k=L-1} P[k].REG2_{t-1}^j[k]). \tag{3}$$

Particularly for FIV_t^j we can notice that for $t < L$ the feedback only depends on the t first coefficients of the polynomial. Indeed the initial state of the register is null and is shifted at each clock cycle. We can therefore simplify FIV_t^j by Eq. (4):

$$\forall t < L, (FIV_t^j) = (\bigoplus_{k=0}^{k=t-1} P[k].REG2_k^j[k]). \tag{4}$$

These equations will help us recover the LFSR characteristics L and P by Correlation ElectroMagnetic Analysis (CEMA).

3.2   Target Object for the Side Channel Analysis: Radiation Hypothesis

The first step of a CEMA is to find a relevant radiation hypothesis. In our case, we need to model the behaviour of a register. The current rise during the shifts in a register from '0' to '1' or '1' to '0' is much higher than the static dissipation observed for the holding state. If the low consumption is noted 0 and the high consumption is noted 1 then the consumption of the bit register can be approximate by the XOR between the old and the new value of the register. Table 1 presents this radiation hypothesis for a shift register. A CEMA realized on this object will show when the two bits are manipulated. This classical model is usually known as the Hamming distance model introduced by [4].

For an LFSR, at each clock cycle t, $REG_t^j[i]$ is replaced by $REG_t^j[i-1]$. We can notice that the radiation hypothesis on $REG_t^j[i] \oplus REG_t^j[i-1]$ is equivalent

Table 1. Radiation hypothesis

REG$_t^j$[i]	REG$_t^j$[i-1]	REG$_t^j$[i] xor REG$_t^j$[i-1]	Modelized radiation
0	0	0	0
0	1	1	1
1	0	1	1
1	1	0	0

to the radiation hypothesis on $REG^j_{t-1}[i-1] \oplus REG^j_{t-1}[i-2]$ and step by step to the radiation hypothesis $REG^j_{t-i+1}[1] \oplus REG^j_{t-i+1}[0]$.

In the feedback register, the first state bit corresponding to $REG^j_t[0]$ is replaced by the XOR between $IV^j{}_t$ and the feedback F^j_t.

So the radiation hypothesis on $REG^j_t[i] \oplus REG^j_t[i-1]$ is equivalent to $RADHYP[REG^j_t[0]]$ which can be written according to this expression:

$$RADHYP[REG^j_t[0]] = REG^j_t[0] \oplus IV^j_t \oplus F^j_t . \qquad (5)$$

The problem on $REG^j_t[i]$ therefore boils down to a problem on the first state bit of the register. As done usually, we assume that the effect of a constant can be withdrawn. So we can simplify F^j_t and $RADHYP[REG_t[0]]$ by using Eq. (4).

$$RADHYP[REG^j_t[0]] = REG2^j_t[0] \oplus IV^j_t \oplus (\bigoplus_{k=0}^{k=t-1} P_{t-1}[k].REG2^j_k[k]) . \qquad (6)$$

From Eq. (6) we can announce the Theorem 1, displayed in Fig. 2.

The radiation hypothesis on $REG_t[0]$ only depends on t first bits of the secret P

Fig. 2. Theorem 1

3.3 Recovering LFSR Characteristics

From the radiation hypothesis and j experiments, it is possible to recover the LFSR characteristics (L and P) by CEMA. This recovery is divided in two parts:

1. the search of the register length,
2. the search of the polynomial value.

According to Theorem 1 (figure 2), for $t = 0$ and $i = 0$, the radiation hypothesis $RADHYP[REG^j_0[0]]$ only depends on IV_0. So computing a CEMA on this value let us find the length of the register. Indeed IV_0 is shifted in the register before coming out of it. The number of clock cycles with CEMA peaks indicates the times where IV_0 is shifted and consequently the length L of the shift register.

To find the polynomial P an application of the Theorem 1 (figure 2) by recurrence is done. For each step $0 < t < L$, $P[0, t-1]$ is assumed known. We want to guess $P[t]$. Two CEMAs with $P[t] = 0$ or $P[t] = 1$ permit to check if an XOR is present on $REG[t]$. Step by step it is then possible to find the polynomial by induction. The procedure is illustrated in figure 7 (page 288). For an L bit register, we need to perform L CEMAs to recover the polynomial P. So this attack is linear in the size L of the register.

3.4 Practical Attack

To validate this attack we have implemented a stream cipher in an ALTERA STRATIX FPGA. FPGAs are usually available on the market in thiner technologies than ASICs because the former have the greatest need for improved integration capabilities. Therefore, their elementary logic is consuming and radiating less than ASICs; however, given that they are reconfigurable, any function implemented with user-logic (look-up-tables and commutation/switch matrices) in FPGAs require approximately thirty times more logic than in an hardwired ASIC [15]. Therefore the FPGAs also have an exacerbated side-channel leakage. All in one, the cryptographic designs mapped in FPGAs are often considered more vulnerable to observation attacks than those optimized for ASICs; they however represent a "worst-case" with respect to ASIC, which makes them a good target for security prototyping. The studied stream cipher, represented in Fig. 6, is built with a 32-bit register ($L = 32$) and with 4 non-linear functions called F1, F2, F3 and G. When the stream is on progress, a flag is set in order to synchronise electromagnetic measures. We record 10000 electromagnetic measures ($0 < j \leq 10000$) of 40 clock cycles t with known randomized IVs. The first and the last significant peaks correspond to the flag: stream on progress. The 40 other peaks in the middle correspond to the 40 shifts of the register. The figure 3(a) gives an example of these electromagnetic measures.

From the 10000 electromagnetic measures, CEMAs give the following results figure 3(b). For the true assumption, CEMA peaks appear and for the wrong one we observe noise. On this figure we can observe that the CEMA leaks during 32 clock cycles corresponding to the length L of the register. From these electromagnetic measures we succeed in recovering the LFSR characteristics.

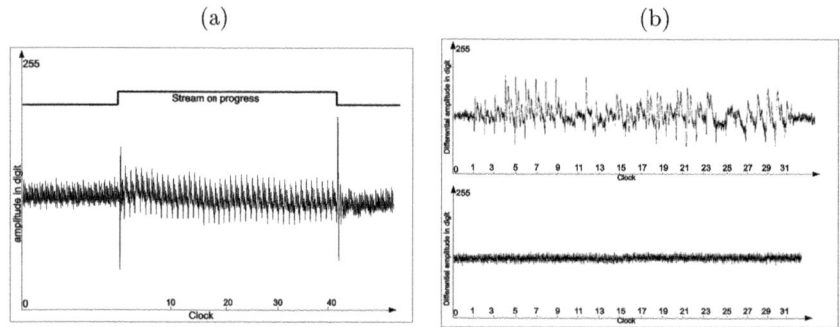

Fig. 3. (a) Electromagnetic measure of the stream cipher and (b) CEMA on the register

3.5   Further Analysis of the SCA Results

We showed earlier how the main characteristics of the LFSR can be easily recovered by SCARE techniques. Looking more precisely at the obtained curves, we can deduce more information leading to a full reverse-engineering of the algorithm. First of all, we can observe as shown in Figure 4(a) that the peaks can be on the top or on the bottom of the curve secondly we can also observe that the peaks are quite different from one clock to another as shown in figure 4(b).

The first difference is a horizontal symmetry due to the feedback constant value. In the previous CEMA, we assume that this constant value has no influence, which was actually not exact. In fact, this value can exchange the two

(a)   (b)

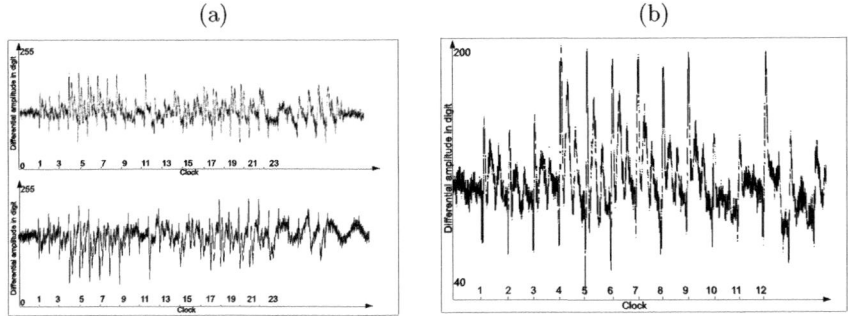

Fig. 4. (a) Key influence on CEMA results and (b) zoom in CEMA traces

considered sets of a CEMA. The obtained curve will be different if this value $FK_t \oplus FK_{t+1}$ is equal to 1 or equal to 0. By observing the curves we can easily deduce whether or not the constant value $FK_t \oplus FK_{t+1}$ is equal to $FK_r \oplus FK_{r+1}$. In the example shown in Figure 4(a), we see that the curves are not identical but symmetrical and we can deduce that $FK_0 \oplus FK_1 = 1 \oplus (FK_1 \oplus FK_2)$ hence $FK_0 = 1 \oplus FK_2$. Doing this observation at each step i from 0 to n will yield n linear equations on FK_t what directly gives linear equations on K_t and allows to retrieve two complementary possibilities for the seed K.

The second difference remains in the size of the peaks at each clock cycle. As we can see on Figure 4(b), the first three peaks are smaller than the next six peaks. Then we observe two small peaks again followed by a larger one and finally two small peaks. To sum up, we obtain small peaks at cycles $\{1, 2, 3, 10, 11, 13, 14\}$ and large peaks at cycles $\{4, 5, 6, 7, 8, 9, 12\}$. The values identified for the large peaks are very closed to the bits that are used in the entry of the non-linear functions. This can be explained by the fact that when the bit changes in the register, it also activates the wires and the logic gates used to compute the non-linear functions. We can note that all the entries of the non-linear functions produce a large peak but we can observe that "ghost peaks" [4] also appeared for example at clock cycle 6. This fact is classically caused by non-modelled biases between the side channel indicator and the implemented objects. Nevertheless, it allows us to reduce the number of possible entries of the non-linear functions.

We now have enough information to perform the full reverse-engineering. Indeed, we know all the information on the LFSR (its initial value and its feedback polynomial) and we also have potential entries for the non-linear functions. To retrieve this function, we can apply the technique presented in the next section.

4   SCARE on Non-linear Functions

All previous publications about SCARE rely on the fact that the message can be chosen. In some of these publications, the key must be known. In others, it shall not be known, however it must remain constant. We will assume that neither the plaintext nor the key is chosen. Additionally, in the proposed methodology, the key can change at every encryption without making the analysis fail.

The specificity of SPN operating at one round per clock period is that the future state cannot be partially known, unlike in Feistel schemes. We illustrate in this section a method to recover the non-linear functions (called sboxes in short) that applies both to SPN and Feistel ciphers. Also, given that confidential algorithms are usually not reconfigurable, it is unlikely to build a precharacterized database of typical SCA signatures. Thus, as no training phase is possible, template [5], stochastic [23] and MIA [11] attacks cannot apply. Under some conditions, called EIS (Equal Images under different Sub-keys), the profiling can be done without changing the secret element. Although this property can be used to characterize devices where the secret element is a key that is injected in a linear way into the algorithm [23], it is of no help to exploit non-linear functions. Therefore, our analysis must rely solely on correlation attacks with an assumed leakage model.

4.1 SCARE Attack Path

This section briefly indicates that an attack path can be defined in SCARE just as in SCA. We assume that the implementation under analysis is in synchronous logic, which means that the hardware resources split into two categories: registers, that evolve all concomitantly at the clock frequency, and combinatorial gates, that evaluate independently at a data-dependent pace. In this context, the easiest resource to identify are the registers. In the mainstream CMOS technology, their leakage is indeed very well captured by the Hamming distance model, already evoked in the Section 3. It means that the number of bits that change in two consecutive values is present in the side-channel emanations. This behavior has been initially underlined for ASICs in [4] and for FPGAs in [24].

The rationale behind our SCARE attack relies on the *identification of transitions* that are predictable and full [24]. The methodology is sketched as follows. We make an architecture hypothesis; if it leads to a significant side-channel signature, it means that the hypothesis is correct. Let us assume for instance that the block encryptor to reverse-engineer is a Feistel scheme. The transition $L_0 \to L_1$ should yield a clear signature in DPA. Now, $L_0 \oplus L_1 = L_0 \oplus R_0$ is independent of the unknown Feistel function. If there is actually one peak, we can validate that:

- The cipher is a Feistel network;
- The Feistel structure is simple (no multiple and/or cross Feistel with quarters of datapath, etc.).

Additionally, we get the following precious information to guide the rest of the analysis:

- What is the side-channel leakage amplitude of 32-bit transitions?
- Where in time is the first round?

The correlation will be $\sqrt{32} \approx 5.66$ times smaller for a mono-bit SCARE attack [25], and the attack can focus on the first clock period: in this example, the peak is maximum at sample 5745. Also, the attacker can take advantage of this signature to tune the empirical parameter ϵ introduced in [16] to make up for the division by abnormally small values.

At the opposite, if no signature is obtained for the $L_0 \rightarrow L_1$ transition, we would conclude that the cipher consumes the whole datapath in one single round. This is typically the case of SPN-type structures.

We do not address in this paper the complete attack path for arbitrary algorithms structures, because exotic features can lead in practice to *ad hoc* attack strategies. Instead, we focus on one blocking point: the reversal of sboxes when only their input or their output is known. In previous attacks, this was done on Feistel schemes, where both inputs and outputs can be controlled individually because the datapath splits into two halves. We do not make this assumption in our attack.

We illustrate the attack on a DES-like cipher, where the sboxes would have been customized. In particular, we use the side-channel measurements of the DPA contest [26], in a view to present results reproducible by our peers. As a matter of fact, the sboxes to retrieve are actually the genuine ones from DES, we pretend not to know. However, we based our attack on the sole knowledge of the right half of the datapath, so as to capture an attacks that could be transposed to SPN ciphers as well.

4.2 Brute-Forcing Sboxes

The attack presented in this section is a brute force retrieval of the sboxes. One vectorial Boolean function $n \rightarrow m$ can be expressed:

- component-wise (*i.e.* as m different Boolean functions sharing the same n inputs),
- using a reduced fanin, thanks to the recursive application of the identity for a Boolean function f: $f(a, b) = \bar{a} \cdot f(0, b) + a \cdot f(1, b)$. At each recursion, the fanin (*i.e.* the number of free variables) is reduced by one.

The attacker has the flexibility to choose the fanin i and the fanout o. In the sequel, we illustrate the case of $i = 2$ and $o = 1$. The complete list for all the $\{0, 1\}^2 \mapsto \{0, 1\}$ functions to retrieve is given in Tab. 2. The terminology is straightforward for most gates; when a gate name ends with A or B, it means that the corresponding input is inversed prior to entering the function. For instance, $\text{AND2B}(A, B) = \text{AND2}(A, \bar{B}) = A \cdot \bar{B}$.

With respect to a canonical attack flow, not all the side-channel traces are processed simultaneously. More precisely, the first step consists in generating a whitelist of traces that keep $6 - i$ bits of the target sbox to a constant value (which is possible since the plaintext is known). Thereafter, a correlation program is called, with 16 weighting functions corresponding to the $2 \rightarrow 1$ sub-tables to guess (Tab. 2) and with the traces restricted to the previously generated

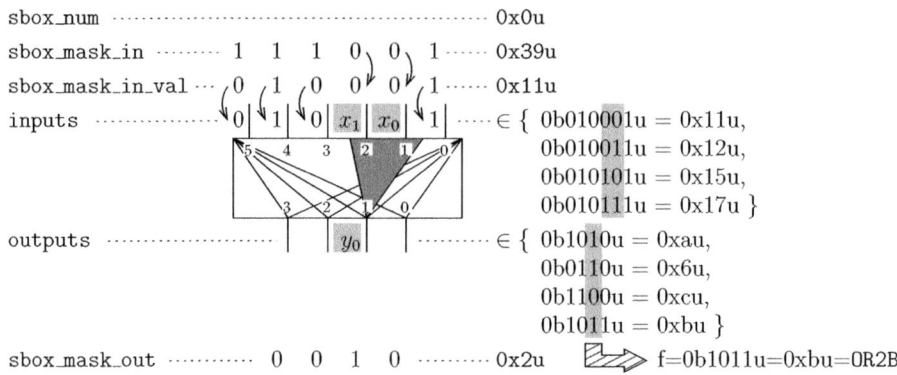

Fig. 5. Parameters `sbox_n`, `sbox_mask_in`, `sbox_mask_in_val` and `sbox_mask_out` that allow for the test of all possible sub-functions of the sboxes array of DES

whitelist. As usual, when few traces are available, it is better to resort to CPA rather than to DPA [4].

The overall process consists in testing all the possible sub-functions of the sboxes, with more or less important restrictions on the inputs (here we keep $i = 2$ free bits) and one or all outputs components (here we illustrate a bit-by-bit component retrieval: $o = 1$). Therefore, to recover one sbox of DES (6 bits $\rightarrow$ 4 bits), $\binom{6}{6-i} \times 2^{6-i} \times \lfloor \frac{4}{o} \rfloor = 960$ CPAs are necessary. The choice for i and o makes it possible for the attacker to explore some trade-offs: the larger i, the more hypotheses to distinguish, but the more traces are suitable for the analysis (because the whitelist contains a ratio of $\frac{1}{2^{6-i}}$ of the available traces); However, the size of the whitelist does not depend on the value of o. Instead, the larger o, the more hypotheses in competition, hence the smaller the noise margin to tell which one is the best.

For the sake of illustration, we take an example depicted in Fig. 5. In this figure, the correct function associated with:

- $sbox\_num = 0x0u$,   (the sbox index, in [0x0u,0x7u])
- $sbox\_mask\_in = 0x39u$,   (the sbox inputs bits that are constant)
- $sbox\_mask\_in\_val = 0x11u$,   (the value of the constant input bits)
- $sbox\_mask\_out = 0x2u$,   (the output bits guessed simultaneously)

is $0b1011u = 0xbu$, hence the OR2B function. By definition, $i \doteq 6 - |sbox\_mask\_in|$ and $o \doteq |sbox\_mask\_out|$. In the figure, x_0 and x_1 are free variables and y_0 is the bit whose activity is predicted in order to retrieve the i-bit $\rightarrow$ o-bit function $DES_0(0, 1, 0, x_1, x_0, 1)$ [2].

One whitelist (screening of traces that keep $6 - i$ bits constant for the targeted sbox) can serve for all the 4 components of the sbox. For instance, the four functions to be found in Fig. 5 are:

1. for sbox_mask_out = 0x1u: 0b1000u = 0x8u, hence AND2,
2. for sbox_mask_out = 0x2u: 0b1011u = 0xbu, hence OR2B,
3. for sbox_mask_out = 0x4u: 0b0110u = 0x6u, hence XOR2,
4. for sbox_mask_out = 0x8u: 0b1101u = 0xdu, hence OR2A.

To be completely accurate, we shall recall that DES has an expansion permutation E before the key mixing. Therefore, the whitelist constrains the two neighbor sboxes in addition to the targeted one. However, the CPA selection function concerns only the o outputs of the sbox. Forcing some bits of the neighbor sboxes or having some of the $6 - i$ active ones shared with them will therefore only affect the structure of the algorithmic noise generated by the $32 - o$ bits of the R register. The impact of E is thus quasi-transparent for the SCARE attacks.

5   Conclusion and Perspectives

Side-channel attacks have been widely studied as a tool to perform key extractions. However, it can be used for other analyses, such as circuits on-line testing or architecture reverse-engineering. We illustrate in this paper that side-channel attacks can be used effectively to reverse-engineer secret algorithms. A practical reverse-engineering of a filtered LFSR is illustrated. In addition, a known-plaintext or known-ciphertext only attack is shown on a SPN or on a Feistel scheme. Those two new attacks demonstrate that SCARE is a technique able to effectively defeat secret cryptography. From the complexity point of view, those SCARE attacks, like the classical side-channel attacks, work whatever the size of the secret to recover. The reason is that they decompose the problem at the bit-level, where an exhaustive search amongst the hypotheses space is possible.

The concrete experiments confirm the efficiency and the practicability of our attacks as we were able to retrieve the full secrets we were looking for. We admit that unexplained correlations were observed, but they have a small impact on the success of our attack. Moreover, it helps us to recover more secret values than we initially though. Indeed, the initial state of the LFSR can be recovered too using our technique. Nevertheless, to precisely understand these observations, we need to model further the radiation of the full algorithm and specific implementation details. We envision this formal model to define precisely the required number of measurements needed for the attack to be successful. Also, we endeavour to apply those attacks on customized version of modern stream ciphers (*e.g.* Grain, Trivium or Mickey).

References

1. Amiel, F., Feix, B., Villegas, K.: Power analysis for secret recovering and reverse engineering of public key algorithms. In: Adams, C., Miri, A., Wiener, M. (eds.) SAC 2007. LNCS, vol. 4876, pp. 110–125. Springer, Heidelberg (2007)
2. Anderson, R.J., Kuhn, M.G.: Low Cost Attacks on Tamper Resistant Devices. In: Christianson, B., Lomas, M. (eds.) Security Protocols 1997. LNCS, vol. 1361, pp. 125–136. Springer, Heidelberg (1998)

3. Biryukov, A., Shamir, A., Wagner, D.: Real Time Cryptanalysis of A5/1 on a PC. In: Schneier, B. (ed.) FSE 2000. LNCS, vol. 1978, pp. 1–18. Springer, Heidelberg (2001)
4. Brier, É., Clavier, C., Olivier, F.: Correlation Power Analysis with a Leakage Model. In: Joye, M., Quisquater, J.-J. (eds.) CHES 2004. LNCS, vol. 3156, pp. 16–29. Springer, Heidelberg (2004)
5. Chari, S., Rao, J.R., Rohatgi, P.: Template Attacks. In: Kaliski Jr., B.S., Koç, Ç.K., Paar, C. (eds.) CHES 2002. LNCS, vol. 2523, pp. 13–28. Springer, Heidelberg (2003)
6. Clavier, C.: An Improved SCARE Cryptanalysis Against a Secret A3/A8 GSM Algorithm. In: McDaniel, P., Gupta, S.K. (eds.) ICISS 2007. LNCS, vol. 4812, pp. 143–155. Springer, Heidelberg (2007)
7. Daudigny, R., Ledig, H., Muller, F., Valette, F.: SCARE of the DES. In: Ioannidis, J., Keromytis, A.D., Yung, M. (eds.) ACNS 2005. LNCS, vol. 3531, pp. 393–406. Springer, Heidelberg (2005)
8. Dinur, I., Shamir, A.: Side Channel Cube Attacks on Block Ciphers. Cryptology ePrint Archive, Report 2009/127 (March 2009), http://eprint.iacr.org/
9. Fournigault, M., Liardet, P.-Y., Teglia, Y., Trémeau, A., Robert-Inacio, F.: Reverse Engineering of Embedded Software Using Syntactic Pattern Recognition. In: Meersman, R., Tari, Z., Herrero, P. (eds.) OTM 2006 Workshops. LNCS, vol. 4277, pp. 527–536. Springer, Heidelberg (2006), doi:10.1007/11915034
10. Garcia, F.D., van Rossum, P., Verdult, R., Schreur, R.W.: Wirelessly Pickpocketing a Mifare Classic Card. In: IEEE Symposium on Security and Privacy — S&P '09, Oakland, California, USA, May 2009. IEEE, Los Alamitos (2009)
11. Gierlichs, B., Batina, L., Tuyls, P., Preneel, B.: Mutual information analysis. In: Oswald, E., Rohatgi, P. (eds.) CHES 2008. LNCS, vol. 5154, pp. 426–442. Springer, Heidelberg (2008)
12. Goldack, M.: Side Channel Based Reverse Engineering for Microcontrollers. Ruhr-Universität-Bochum, Germany (January 2008), http://www.crypto.ruhr-uni-bochum.de/en_theses.html
13. Guilley, S., Hoogvorst, P., Pacalet, R., Schmidt, J.: Improving Side-Channel Attacks by Exploiting Substitution Boxes Properties. In: BFCA, Paris, France, May 02-04, pp. 1–25 (2007), http://www.liafa.jussieu.fr/bfca/, http://www.liafa.jussieu.fr/bfca/books/BFCA07.pdf
14. Kerckhoffs, A.: La cryptographie militaire (1). Journal des sciences militaires 9, 5–38 (1883), http://en.wikipedia.org/wiki/Kerckhoffs_law
15. Kuon, I., Rose, J.: Measuring the Gap Between FPGAs and ASICs. IEEE Transactions on Computer-Aided Design of Integrated Circuits and Systems 26(2), 203–215 (2007)
16. Le, T.-H., Clédière, J., Canovas, C., Robisson, B., Servière, C., Lacoume, J.-L.: A Proposition for Correlation Power Analysis Enhancement. In: Goubin, L., Matsui, M. (eds.) CHES 2006. LNCS, vol. 4249, pp. 174–186. Springer, Heidelberg (2006)
17. Nohl, K., Evans, D., Starbug, Plötz, H.: Reverse-Engineering a Cryptographic RFID Tag. In: van Oorschot, P.C. (ed.) USENIX Security Symposium, San Jose, CA, USA, July 28-August 1, pp. 185–194. USENIX Association
18. Nohl, K., Tews, E., Weinmann, R.-P.: Cryptanalysis of the DECT Standard Cipher. In: Hong, S., Iwata, T. (eds.) FSE 2010. LNCS, vol. 6147, pp. 1–18. Springer, Heidelberg (2010)
19. Novak, R.: Side-channel attack on substitution blocks. In: Zhou, J., Yung, M., Han, Y. (eds.) ACNS 2003. LNCS, vol. 2846, pp. 307–318. Springer, Heidelberg (2003)

20. Novak, R.: Side-channel based reverse engineering of secret algorithms. In: Zajc, B. (ed.) Proceedings of the Twelfth International Electrotechnical and Computer Science Conference (ERK 2003), Ljubljana, Slovenia, September 25-26, pp. 445–448. Slovenska sekcija IEEE (2003)
21. Novak, R.: Sign-based differential power analysis. In: Chae, K.-J., Yung, M. (eds.) WISA 2003. LNCS, vol. 2908, pp. 203–216. Springer, Heidelberg (2004)
22. Réal, D., Dubois, V., Guilloux, A.-M., Valette, F., Drissi, M.: SCARE of an Unknown Hardware Feistel Implementation. In: Grimaud, G., Standaert, F.-X. (eds.) CARDIS 2008. LNCS, vol. 5189, pp. 218–227. Springer, Heidelberg (2008)
23. Schindler, W., Lemke, K., Paar, C.: A Stochastic Model for Differential Side Channel Cryptanalysis. In: Rao, J.R., Sunar, B. (eds.) CHES 2005. LNCS, vol. 3659, pp. 30–46. Springer, Heidelberg (2005)
24. Standaert, F.-X., Örs, S.B., Preneel, B.: Power analysis of an FPGA. In: Joye, M., Quisquater, J.-J. (eds.) CHES 2004. LNCS, vol. 3156, pp. 30–44. Springer, Heidelberg (2004)
25. Standaert, F.-X., Peeters, É., Rouvroy, G., Quisquater, J.-J.: An Overview of Power Analysis Attacks Against Field Programmable Gate Arrays. Proceedings of the IEEE 94(2), 383–394 (2006) (invited Paper)
26. TELECOM ParisTech SEN research group. DPA Contest, 1st edn. (2008/2009) http://www.DPAcontest.org/
27. Vermoen, D., Witteman, M. F., Gaydadjiev, G.: Reverse Engineering Java Card Applets using Power Analysis. In: Sauveron, D., Markantonakis, K., Bilas, A., Quisquater, J.-J. (eds.) WISTP 2007. LNCS, vol. 4462, pp. 138–149. Springer, Heidelberg (2007)

A   Further Considerations about SCARE on a Stream Cipher

The detail of the algorithm used to reverse-engineer the stream cipher presented in Sec. 3.3 and depicted in Fig. 6 is given below.

B   Further Considerations about Brute-Force SCARE on Sboxes

B.1   Comparison of DPA versus SCARE

In this section, we carry out a theoretical comparison between DPA and SCARE for n to 1 Boolean functions. We recall the naming of those functions for $n = 2$ is provided in Tab. 2. This discussion can extend without changes to multi-fanout sub-functions.

The DPA consists in computing the covariance between the curves and a power model. In the ideal case, the curves perfectly contain the power model of the few gates under attack plus a random noise. The attacker thus obtains a collection of: $\mathrm{Cov}(\mathrm{model}_0(k_0), \mathrm{model}_0(k))$; The attacker's goal is to find the correct k_0 amongst the k that are possible. In the usual setup where the key is incorporated into the datapath with a group operation $\oplus$, and where the confusion in implemented by an sbox S, the model_0 is: $x \mapsto S_0(x \oplus k_0)$. The DPA problem consists in finding:

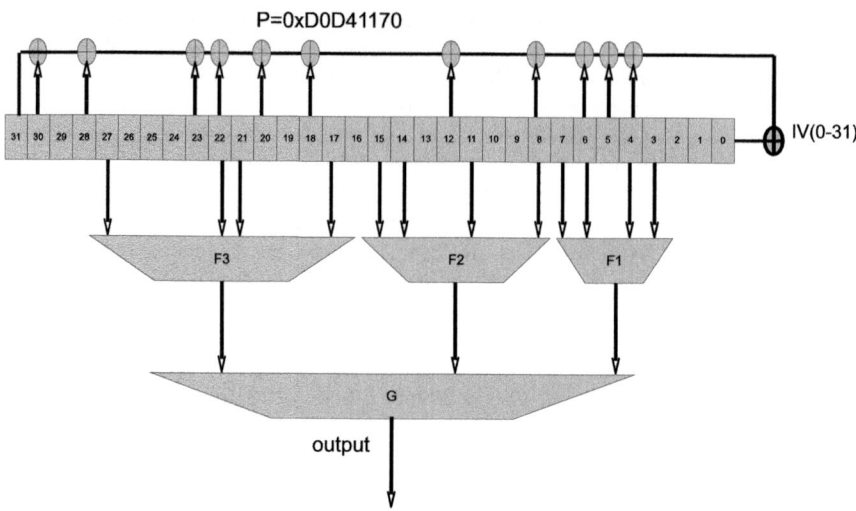

Fig. 6. Stream cipher implementation

- Input
  - IV_t^j with $0 < j \leq 10000$ and the corresponding EM traces
  - L the register length
- Output
  - The feedback polynomial P
- Step 0: is there an XOR on REG[0]?
  - $P \leftarrow 0x00000000$
  - compute CEMA_1 on $REG_1^j[0] \oplus REG_1^j[1] \oplus P[0].REG_0^j[0] = IV_1^j$
  - compute CEMA_2 on $REG_1^j[0] \oplus REG_1^j[1] = IV_0^j \oplus IV_1^j$
  - if CEMA_1 leaks and CEMA_2 doesn't
  - $P \leftarrow P \mid 0x00000001$
  - else if CEMA_2 leaks and CEMA_1 doesn't
  - $P \leftarrow P$
  - else
  - Return Error
  - endif
- Step $t < L$: is there an XOR on REG[t]?
  - $P[0, t-1]$ is already known
  - compute CEMA_1 on $REG_t^j[0] \oplus IV_t^j \bigoplus_{k=0}^{k=t} P[k].REG_{t-1}^j[k] \oplus IV_0$
  - compute CEMA_2 on $REG_t^j[0] \oplus IV_t^j \bigoplus_{k=0}^{k=t} P[k].REG_{t-1}^j[k]$
  - if CEMA_1 leaks and CEMA_2 doesn't
  - $P \leftarrow P \mid (1 << t)$
  - else if CEMA_2 leaks and CEMA_1 doesn't
  - $P \leftarrow P$
  - else
  - Return Error
  - endif
- Return P

Fig. 7. SCARE algorithm to retrieve P

Table 2. Name of the $2 \to 1$ functions

Index of f	$f(\mathbf{B}, \mathbf{A})$				Boolean equation	Name
	$f(1,1)$	$f(1,0)$	$f(0,1)$	$f(0,0)$		
0	0	0	0	0	0	Zero
1	0	0	0	1	$\overline{B+A}$	NOR2
2	0	0	1	0	$\overline{B} \cdot A$	AND2B
3	0	0	1	1	$\overline{B}$	NOTB
4	0	1	0	0	$B \cdot \overline{A}$	AND2A
5	0	1	0	1	$\overline{A}$	NOTA
6	0	1	1	0	$B \oplus A$	XOR2
7	0	1	1	1	$\overline{B \cdot A}$	NAND2
8	1	0	0	0	$B \cdot A$	AND2
9	1	0	0	1	$B \overline{\oplus} A$	XNOR2
10	1	0	1	0	A	A
11	1	0	1	1	$\overline{B} + A$	OR2B
12	1	1	0	0	B	B
13	1	1	0	1	$B + \overline{A}$	OR2A
14	1	1	1	0	$B + A$	OR2
15	1	1	1	1	1	One

$\arg\max_k \sum_{x=0}^{2^n-1} (-1)^{S_0(x \oplus k_0) \oplus S_0(x \oplus k)}$. Of course, the solution is $k = k_0$ (see demonstration in [13]). The difficulty of the problem can be summarized by the noise immunity required to distinguish the auto-correlation from the non-trivial cross-correlations: $\sum_x (-1)^{S_0(x) \oplus S_0(x \oplus \epsilon)}$, $\epsilon \neq 0$.

The SCARE method inspired from the DPA will also use a covariance as an indicator (sometimes called "oracle") to distinguish the correct sboxes guess from the incorrect ones. In this respect, the SCARE attacker will compute similar quantities as for the DPA: $\text{Cov}(\text{model}_0(k_0), \text{model}(k_0))$; In the same setup as described for DPA (group addition of the key and usage of an sbox S_0), SCARE consists in solving: $\arg\max_S \sum_x (-1)^{S_0(x \oplus k_0) \oplus S(x \oplus k_0)}$. Now, an equivalent problem is: $\arg\max_S \sum_x (-1)^{S_0(x) \oplus S(x)}$. Under this form, it appears clearly that **DPA is a particular case of SCARE**, where the set of possible Sboxes to retrieve can be written $S = S_0 \circ \tau_k$ (with τ_k the translation of vector k).

The similarity between DPA and SCARE arises from the fact that:

- the **key mixing** operation just precedes
- the **substitution boxes** layer.

Therefore, the mode of operation of DPA and SCARE target the same transition: $x \to S(x \oplus k)$, where:

- k is the unknown in the case of DPA, whereas
- S is the unknown in the case of SCARE.

Consequently, the attack strategy for SCARE is identical to that of the DPA. For instance, when analyzing a Feistel scheme such as DES, the sensitive transition targeted by both DPA and SCARE will be $R_0 \to R_1$ when attacking the first round, but $L_{15} \to L_{16}$ when attacking the last round.

The space to explore for finding a maximum is of size:

- $\#k = 2^n$, in the case of the DPA, to be contrasted by the
- $\#S = 2^{2^n}$ n-input Boolean functions.

It is thus more likely that DPA key extraction exhibits a larger signal-to-noise ratio than SCARE sbox extraction.

B.2   Specificity of SCARE w.r.t. DPA

Some issues we encountered during the attack are also specific to SCARE. We discuss in this section two of them.

Although a DPA tool can safely decide which sub-key hypothesis is the correct one by selecting the curve with the maximal signal in absolute value, it happens that this selection entails incorrect results in SCARE. Indeed, the correlation with f and with $\overline{f}$ yields exactly opposite results if f is balanced. This noting does not bother either DPA or CPA analyses on sboxes: as the sum of all differential peaks is equal to zero, which means that the second peak after the correct one has a lower amplitude (in absolute value), given that there is only one peak of maximal amplitude. Said differently, SCARE correlation curves for all the hypotheses have a lower contrast than their DPA counterparts. Concretely speaking, this has not been problematic in SCARE for the power measurements we used: power signal is always positive in case of one bit-flip. However, in EMA, this is not true: a bit-flip can be transducted as a negative measurement bias. Now, we assume that an electromagnetic sensor, even if meant to realize near-field side-channel acquisitions, <u>does</u> maintain a constant polarity over the spied sbox. In this case, the complete sbox can be retrieved (up to an unknown bitwise negation), with both a power and an EM analysis. However, the fact the both f and $\overline{f}$ compete as candidate Boolean functions has led to an attack failure, when targeting sbox_num: 0x0, mask_in: 0x0f, mask_in_val: 0x00, mask_out: 0x4. In happens that the highest peak in relative value appears in a secondary bounce, as shown in Fig. 8.

Another peculiarity we came upon is that the automatic sbox recovery on the DPA contest acquisition campaign fails in the two cases:

1. sbox_num = 0x0, mask_in = 0x1e, mask_in_val = 0x02, mask_out = 0x2,
2. sbox_num = 0x0, mask_in = 0x3a, mask_in_val = 0x02, mask_out = 0x2.

Here, we observe 0x0 although the correct function is 0x2. For these attacks, we get only four values of correlation: $\pm 15\,\%$ for 2×2 guesses, and $\pm 5\,\%$ for the 2×6 others. In both cases, we notice that the correlation model $\{-1, -0.5, 0, +0.5, +1\}$ is not satisfied. The singular correlation values are shown in Fig. 9. To contrast this attack with a non-pathological one, we also give the correlations obtained for a complete $2 \to 4$ function recovery in Fig. 10.

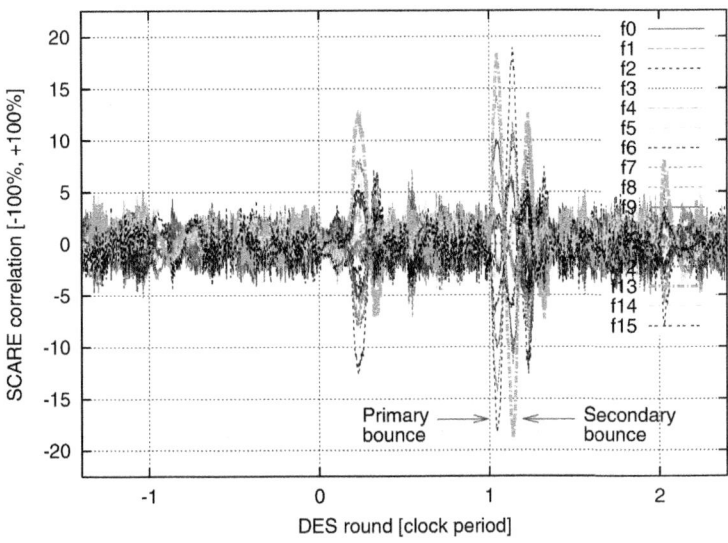

Fig. 8. The correct function is 13, but the complementary 2 is found instead with both guesses in absolute or in relative value

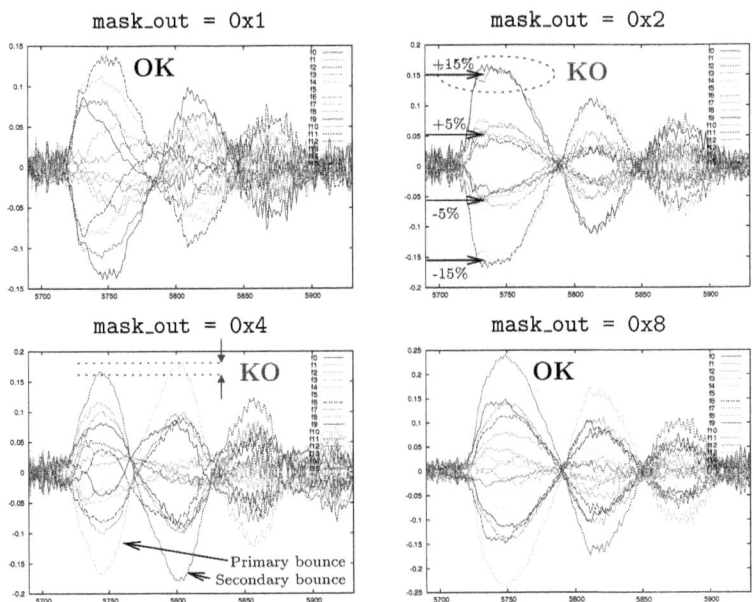

Fig. 9. Correlation traces obtained when retrieving the four Boolean components of the sbox #1, with input mask `0x1e`, and value `0x02`

Finally, in Fig. 9, we observe that the bounces do not have always the same period (for all the hypotheses), especially for mask_out = 0x1 and 0x4. This seems as unphysical as the amplified bounce of mask_out = 0x4. Those artifacts represent SCA second-order effects that make the analyses somehow subtle.

B.3   SCARE on DES Sboxes Results

The figure 11(a) presents the correlation coefficients obtained for the brute-force reverse-engineering of the sbox #7 of DES. We have indicated in green the second largest peaks. It can be seen that sometimes, the first and second largest correlations have about the same value. This is due to the (yet unexplained) degenerescence already observed in Fig. 9 for mask_out = 0x2.

The shape of CPA curve in Fig. 11(a) is in two parts. The explanation for this phenomenon is that, for this acquisition campaign, two bits correlate better than the two others. This is indeed put forward in Fig. 11(b). The reason for the sbox output bits to correlate differently is a priori unknown, since they are treated in a similar way by the permutation layer of DES. The difference might be due to the acquisition conditions.

The two problems mentioned in the previous section are not fatal. By restricting the temporal window for CPA, the secondary negative bounce greater than the actual first one can be trivially filtered out. Indeed, as $(960 - 2)/960 > 99\%$ of the CPAs succeed in $t_0 \approx 5750$, it is easy to infer that there is something fishy

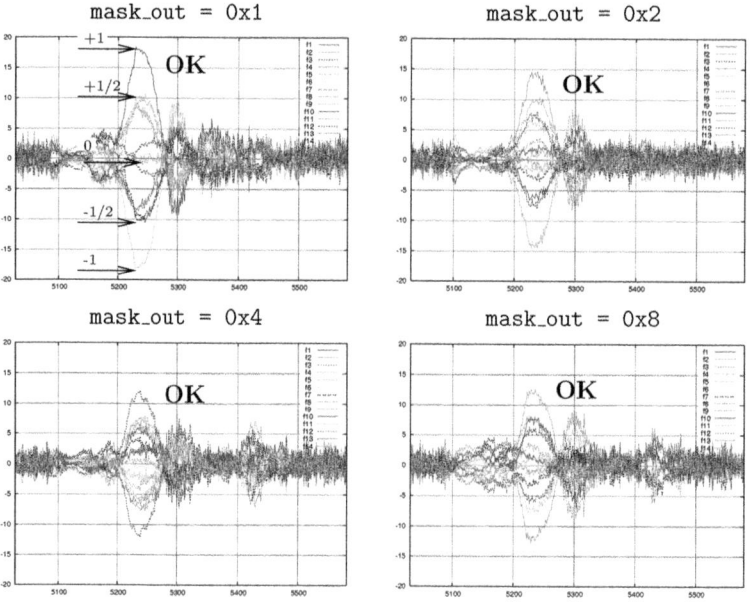

Fig. 10. Correlation traces obtained when retrieving the four Boolean components of the sbox #1, with input mask 0x33, and value 0x00

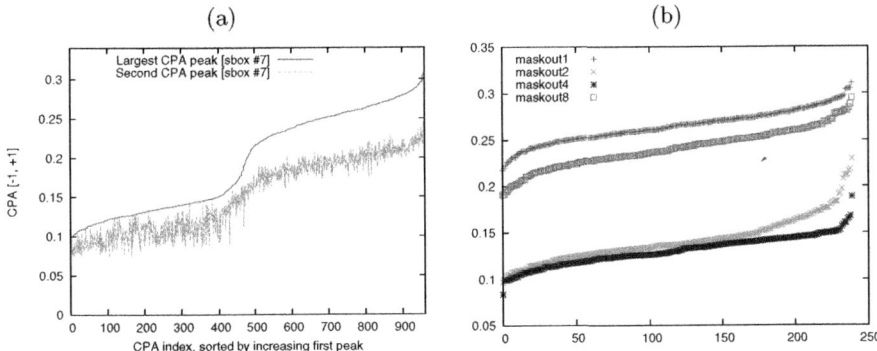

Fig. 11. (a) Correlations obtained for 960 CPAs aiming at retrieving the DES sbox #7; (b) Correlations obtained for each of the 960/4 CPAs aiming at retrieving each fanout bit of the DES sbox #7

about the 2 CPAs with maximum located in $t_1 \approx 5820 \neq t_0$. Regarding the degenerate cases where the correlations are about similar for two key hypotheses, they can be detected by computing the ratio between the first and second best correlations. If it is too close to 1, then both hypotheses can be kept. As these situations happen seldom, very few sboxes candidates will remain after SCARE: a brute force trial of all the candidates will easily discard the wrong hypotheses.

To summarize this section about sboxes retrieval thanks to SCARE, one can say that some adjustments are required for the power analysis to work on one $2 \rightarrow 1$ sub-function, but that subsequent attacks on the $960 - 1$ remaining functions are very reliable. The SCARE oracle is thus a trustworthy tool once tuned.

How Leaky Is an Extractor?

François-Xavier Standaert[*]

Université catholique de Louvain, Crypto Group, Belgium
fstandae@uclouvain.be

Abstract. This paper discusses the security of a leakage-resilient stream cipher presented at FOCS 2008, instantiated in a practical setting. Based on a case study, we put forward implementation weaknesses that can be exploited in a key-recovery attack. We first show that in our experimental context (8-bit device, Hamming weight leakages, Gaussian noise), a successful attack against the investigated stream cipher has lower data complexity than a similar attack against an unprotected AES implementation. We then analyze the origin of the observed weaknesses and relate them with the implementation of extractor that is used in the investigated stream cipher. We finally discuss the implications of these results for the design of leakage-resilient primitives and provide guidelines to improve the construction of FOCS 2008 and its underlying components.

1 Introduction

In a side-channel attack, an adversary attempts to break a cryptographic primitive, by taking advantage of the physical peculiarities of the hardware on which it is running. Typical examples include the power consumption or electromagnetic radiation of small embedded devices. In view of the physical nature of these implementation issues, the first countermeasures to prevent them were mainly designed at the hardware level. But recent results have witnessed a growing interest of the cryptographic community to extend the applicability of provably secure constructions in this new setting. For example, two constructions of leakage-resilient stream ciphers have recently been proposed, at FOCS 2008 and Eurocrypt 2009. The first one is based on the combination of a pseudorandom generator (PRG) and an extractor [4], while the second one only uses a block cipher based PRG as building block. Both constructions are proven leakage-resilient in the standard model, the extractor based construction allowing significantly better security bounds. Both constructions rely on the fact that the amount of information leakage in one iteration of the cipher is bounded in some sense - which has to be guaranteed by hardware designers. This bound is usually referred to as a λ-bit leakage, intuitively meaning that only a part of the internal parameters in the target device is revealed by the physics. Different metrics can be used to quantify this bounded information, *e.g.* [4,7] use the HILL pseudoentropy. In view of the strong nature of these security claims (in particular

---

[*] Research Associate of the Belgian Fund for Scientific Research (FNRS - F.R.S.).

M. Abdalla and P.S.L.M. Barreto (Eds.): LATINCRYPT 2010, LNCS 6212, pp. 294–304, 2010.
© Springer-Verlag Berlin Heidelberg 2010

compared to the limited results provided by hardware-level countermeasures), it is natural to challenge these theoretical constructions, by investigating and quantifying their security properties in actual leaking devices.

In this paper, we consequently study the practical security of the FOCS 2008 stream cipher in an 8-bit device, against standard DPA. In particular, and as a usual scenario for evaluating countermeasures against side-channel attacks, we consider a Hamming weight leakage model with Gaussian noise. We use this case study to discuss some issues left unanswered by theoretical analysis, namely:

- The construction in [4] is based on an extractor, but the actual instance of extractor to use in a practical implementation is left unspecified. Hence, the good selection of an extractor in this context is an open question.
- Given that an extractor is specified, does the addition of this new primitive in the hardware have an impact on the λ-bit leakage assumed in the proofs? And how does this different λ modify the global security of the construction?

Our simulated experiments clearly indicate that if no particular attention is paid, the extractor may be the weak point in this stream cipher construction. More precisely, the success rate of a standard DPA against *one* iteration of the extractor in our target device is (much) higher than the one of a similar standard DPA attack against *several* iterations of an unprotected AES implementation. This is due to the fact that extracting several random bits from weak sources, as required in [4], implies to manipulate the same secret data several times. In other words, the implementation of the extractor has a strong impact on the λ-bit leakage and eventually gives rise to little actual security for the PRG in this case. We then discuss the consequences of these results and provide guidelines, both for improving the selection of the extractors to use in leakage-resilient cryptography and for improving the PRG construction of FOCS 2008.

We note that our results are not in contradiction with [4,7] but emphasize the gap existing between the assumptions of these theoretical works and the specificities of actual implementations. That is, any single gate added in a hardware device, or single line added in a software code, have a potential impact on the information leakages. Hence, it is difficult (if not impossible) to discuss the physical security of a primitive without a precise understanding of the relations between its algorithmic description and its implementation properties. This is especially true when considering primitives such as extractors for which very few experimental attacks have been performed, *e.g.* compared to block ciphers such as the AES Rijndael. That is, as acknowledged by the authors of [4,7], providing means to exploit a bounded leakage per iteration in a stream cipher construction solves only one half of the side-channel issue. It then remains to ensure that a good leakage bound can be guaranteed in practice, using existing hardware. In this paper, we additionally show that the good understanding and evaluation of the low-level characteristics in physical leakages may also motivate better choices for the selection of algorithms to use in order to best face side-channel attacks.

The rest of this paper is structured as follows. Some background information is given in Section 2. The implementation of the FOCS 2008 stream cipher that we target is described in Section 3. Our security analysis and experimental results

are in Section 4. Eventually, Section 5 provides guidelines to improve the design
and analysis of leakage-resilient primitives and Section 6 concludes the paper.

2   Background

The construction. Our analysis focuses on an instantiation of the leakage-
resilient stream cipher of FOCS 2008, represented in Figure 1, in which ext denotes a two-source extractor and PRG a length-tripling Pseudo-Random number
Generator[1]. The components of this construction are as follows.

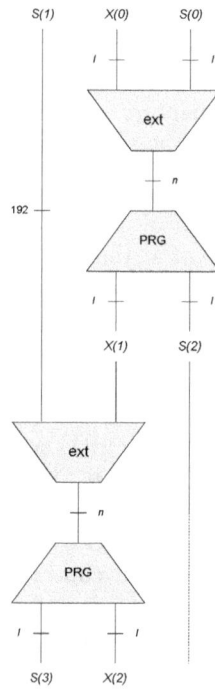

Fig. 1. Leakage-resilient stream cipher from FOCS 2008

Length-tripling PRG. For convenience, and because they are usual targets in
side-channel attacks, we use a length tripling PRG that is based on a block cipher. Let $\mathsf{AES}_k(x)$ denote the encryption of a plaintext x under a key k, we have:

$$\mathsf{PRG} : \{0,1\}^n \mapsto \{0,1\}^{3n} : x \mapsto \Big(\mathsf{AES}_x(c_1), \mathsf{AES}_x(c_2), \mathsf{AES}_x(c_3)\Big),$$

---

[1] This construction does not directly correspond to the one of Dziembowski and
Pietrzak. In [4], Figure 2, the extractor's output is split in two parts: $(K_{i+1}, X_{i+1}) =$
$\mathsf{ext}(K_i, B_i)$, and only one part is sent to the PRG: $B_{i+1} = \mathsf{PRG}'(X_{i+1})$. In our description, the extractor's output is fully transmitted to the PRG. But the instance
in Figure 1 can be seen as a generalization of the FOCS stream cipher by defining
our PRG as $\mathsf{PRG}(K_{i+1}, X_{i+1}) = K_{i+1}\|\mathsf{PRG}'(X_{i+1})$, using notations from [4], which
also makes an easy connection to the Eurocrypt 2009 proposal.

where c_1, c_2, c_3 are three public constant values.

Two-source extractor. We consider the constructions in [3]. They allow extracting many random bits from two weak sources X, Y of the same length l. Let $A_1, A_2, \ldots, A_n$ be $l \times l$ matrixes over $GF[2]$. The proposed extractor is:

$$\text{ext}_A : \{0,1\}^l \times \{0,1\}^l \mapsto \{0,1\}^n : (x,y) \mapsto \left((A_1 x) \cdot y, (A_2 x) \cdot y, \ldots, (A_n x) \cdot y \right),$$

where $\cdot$ is the inner product mod 2 and $A_i x$ is a matrix-vector multiplication over $GF[2]$. In practice, the matrices A_i can be specified in different ways, giving rise to different tradeoffs between the quality of the extraction and the implementation efficiency. For example, [3] mentions cyclic shift matrices, right shift matrices or matrices obtained from error correcting codes.

In the following, and for illustration (no particular constraints are imposed on the extractors in [4]), we will consider cyclic shift matrices [12]. That is, we just define A_i as the linear transformation matrix corresponding to a cyclic shift of $i - 1$ bits, with l a prime having 2 as primitive root, e.g. for $l = 5$:

$$A_1 = \begin{pmatrix} 1\,0\,0\,0\,0 \\ 0\,1\,0\,0\,0 \\ 0\,0\,1\,0\,0 \\ 0\,0\,0\,1\,0 \\ 0\,0\,0\,0\,1 \end{pmatrix}, \quad A_2 = \begin{pmatrix} 0\,1\,0\,0\,0 \\ 0\,0\,1\,0\,0 \\ 0\,0\,0\,1\,0 \\ 0\,0\,0\,0\,1 \\ 1\,0\,0\,0\,0 \end{pmatrix}, \quad \ldots \quad , A_5 = \begin{pmatrix} 0\,0\,0\,0\,1 \\ 1\,0\,0\,0\,0 \\ 0\,1\,0\,0\,0 \\ 0\,0\,1\,0\,0 \\ 0\,0\,0\,1\,0 \end{pmatrix}.$$

3 Implementation

In order to investigate the practical security provided by a stream cipher, it is needed to implement it in a reference device. As a case study (and because they are standard targets in side-channel attacks), we will consider an implementation in a small 8-bit microcontroller. For the AES Rijndael, we can rely on the implementation description provided in [2] for 8-bit processors. In this section, we discuss the implementation of the extractor in a similar device.

First note that, since we use a length tripling PRG based on the AES, the extractor in Figure 1 must generate 128 bits out of two sources of 192 bits. Hence, we will use $l = 193$ and pad one constant bit to the inputs of the extractor[2].

Second, the extractor applies to one public and one secret value. In order to minimize the amount of computations applied to the secret value, we will assume that, when computing $(A_i x) \cdot y$, x is public (hence corresponding to $X(i)$ in Figure 1) and y is private (hence corresponding to $S(i)$ in Figure 1).

Let us denote the cyclic shift of x by $i - 1$ bits as $x_i = \text{rot}(x, i - 1)$. Implementing the extractor essentially corresponds to computing n inner products between 128 public x_i's and the secret y. In an 8-bit device, producing one bit b_i corresponding to one input x_i can be done as follows:

1. Denote the 16 bytes of x_i and y as x_i^j and y^j, respectively, $j \in [1; 16]$.
2. Compute 16 bitwise AND operations: $z_i^j = x_i^j \odot y^j$,

---

[2] This is necessary to meet the constraint that l has to be prime.

3. Compute the bitwise XOR between the 16 z_i^j's: $w_i = \bigoplus_{j=1}^{16} z_i^j$,
4. Compute the XOR between the bits of w_i: $b_i = \bigoplus_{i=1}^{8} w_i(j)$,

where $w_i(j)$ denotes the jth bit of the word w_i. This process then has to be repeated 128 times in order to produce a PRG input (*i.e.* an AES key).

4 Attacking the Leakage-Resilient Stream Cipher

The stream cipher in Figure 1 is composed of a PRG and the previously described extractor. Looking at this construction from an adversarial point of view directly leads to the question: which part of the scheme is better to target? For this purpose, we will consider the resistance of these two parts of the construction against a standard DPA attack, such as formalized in [6]. As far as the PRG implementation is concerned, the situation is quite standard. Following the discussion about practical security in [11], we have a 3-limiting construction, meaning that an adversary is allowed to observe the leakage corresponding to the encryption of three different plaintexts (*i.e.* the constants c_1, c_2, c_3).

Choice of a leakage model and target implementation. In order to compare the security of the PRG to the one of the extractor with respect to side-channel attacks additionally requires to define a leakage model. In the following, we assume the so-called Hamming weight leakage model that is frequently considered to attack CMOS devices. It yields the implementation represented in Figure 2: for each byte of the public x_i and secret y, the adversary recovers the Hamming weight of their bitwise AND (possibly affected by some noise).

It is interesting to note that Figure 2 is very similar to a standard DPA targeting the key addition in the first round of a block cipher. In such a scenario, an adversary would use different plaintexts x_i and obtain the leakages corresponding to $l_i^j = \mathsf{WH}(x_i^j \oplus y^j)$. In the context of our extractor implementation, the only difference is that the bitwise XOR $\oplus$ is replaced by a bitwise AND $\odot$.

Specificities of a DPA against the extractor. The main feature of a DPA against the implementation of Figure 2 is that the leakages do not have symmetry properties (discussed, *e.g.* in [9]), which leads to key dependencies that are rarely observed in side-channel attacks. A simple way to put forward these dependencies is to compute an information theoretic metric such as advocated in [10]. Namely, considering leakages of the form $l_i^j = \mathsf{WH}(x_i^j \odot y^j)$ and removing the i, j indices for clarity, we can compute the following conditional entropy:

$$H[Y|L, X] = - \sum_{y \in \mathcal{Y}} \Pr[y] \sum_{x \in \mathcal{X}} \Pr[x] \int_l \Pr[l|y, x] \log_2 \Pr[y|l, x] \, dl,$$

that is, in our case: $H[Y|\mathsf{WH}(Y \odot X), X]$. This quantity reflects the amount of information that is provided by the leakage (here in a known plaintext scenario).

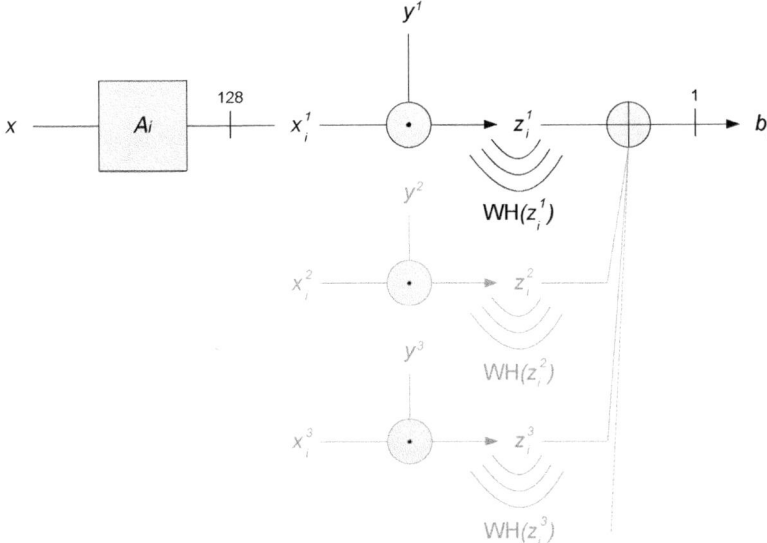

Fig. 2. Leaking implementation of the extractor

Consider a standard DPA where the leakages equal $l_i^j = \mathsf{WH}(x_i^j \oplus y^j)$. Then, because the bitwise XOR is a group operation, we have that:

$$H[Y|L,X] = -\sum_{x \in \mathcal{X}} \Pr[x] \int_l \Pr[l|y,x] \log_2 \Pr[y|l,x] \, dl, \text{ for a given } y, \quad (1)$$

$$= -\sum_{y \in \mathcal{Y}} \Pr[y] \int_l \Pr[l|y,x] \log_2 \Pr[y|l,x] \, dl, \text{ for a given } x. \quad (2)$$

In other words, on average over the public x's, all the secret y's are equally difficult to recover. And on average over the secret y's, all the public x's yield the same amount of information. Quite naturally, the situation becomes different when the bitwise XOR is replaced by a bitwise AND. As a simple example, imagine that one byte j of the public x_i is null. Then, observing the Hamming weight of $0 \odot y^j$ leaks no information at all about y^j. Clearly, the information leakage now depends on both x and y and Equations (1), (2) do not hold anymore.

In fact, one can show that the amount of information leakage in the implementation of Figure 2 depends on the Hamming weights of x and y, by computing:

$$H_x[Y|L,X] = -\sum_{y \in \mathcal{Y}} \Pr[y] \int_l \Pr[l|y,x] \log_2 \Pr[y|l,x] \, dl,$$

$$H_y[Y|L,X] = -\sum_{x \in \mathcal{X}} \Pr[x] \int_l \Pr[l|y,x] \log_2 \Pr[y|l,x] \, dl,$$

that is, the conditional entropies where either the x's or the y's are not uniformly distributed but fixed to an arbitrary value. By computing these quantities for

Hamming weight leakages, we observe that they are equal for all x's and y's having the same Hamming weight. It yields the following vectors:

HW(x)	0	1	2	3	4	5	6	7	8
H$_x[Y\|L, X]$	8.00	7.00	6.50	6.19	5.96	5.80	5.66	5.55	5.45

HW(y)	0	1	2	3	4	5	6	7	8
H$_y[Y\|L, X]$	4.00	5.04	5.75	6.17	6.30	6.17	5.75	5.04	4.00

Intuitively, this means that, on average over the secret y's, the public x's with high Hamming weight yield more information. And on average over the public x's, the secret y's with extreme Hamming weights are easier to recover.

Experimental results. We now compare the security of the extractor with the one of the AES Rijndael. More specifically, the construction in Figure 1 is 3-limiting for the AES and 1-limiting for the extractor. The question we tackle is to know whether it is easier to attack 3 iterations of the AES versus a single iteration of the extractor, in the previously described setting.

Regarding the AES implementation, the typical target operations in a DPA are the first round key addition and S-box layers. Here, we will consider two different attacks. First, a basic (univariate) attack in which only the leakage of the S-box is exploited. Second, an improved (bivariate) attack in which the leakage of both the key addition and the S-box are exploited. In both cases, we use a Bayesian distinguisher (aka template attack) such as described in [1].

Regarding the implementation of the extractor in Figure 2, the key observation is that it re-uses each secret byte n times in order to produce n random bits. Considering the same adversary as for the AES, $i.e.$ a template attack recovering the secret bytes of the extractor one by one, each secret byte can be identified by $n = 128$ bitwise AND computations, even if the construction is 1-limiting.

The success rates of our experiments (each averaged over 1000 independent experiments) evaluated in four different noise scenarios (from low noise: $\sigma_n = 0.5$ to high noise $\sigma_n = 4$), and assuming uniformly random inputs, are represented in Figure 3. For the AES implementation, the X axis represents a number of queries and the bold dots represent the success rates after 1, 2 and 3 queries, as allowed by the construction. For the extractor implementation, the X axis represents the number of elementary operations, that is upper bounded to 128 ($i.e.$ a single execution). It yields the following observations:

- The success rate of a 3-limited adversary against the AES implementation is anyway (much) smaller than the one of a 1-limited adversary against the extractor implementation. This answers the question in the beginning of this section. That is, an adversary who has to attack the PRG in Figure 1 implemented as described in this paper should focus on the extractor (rather than on the AES) in order to recover the secrets $S(i)$.

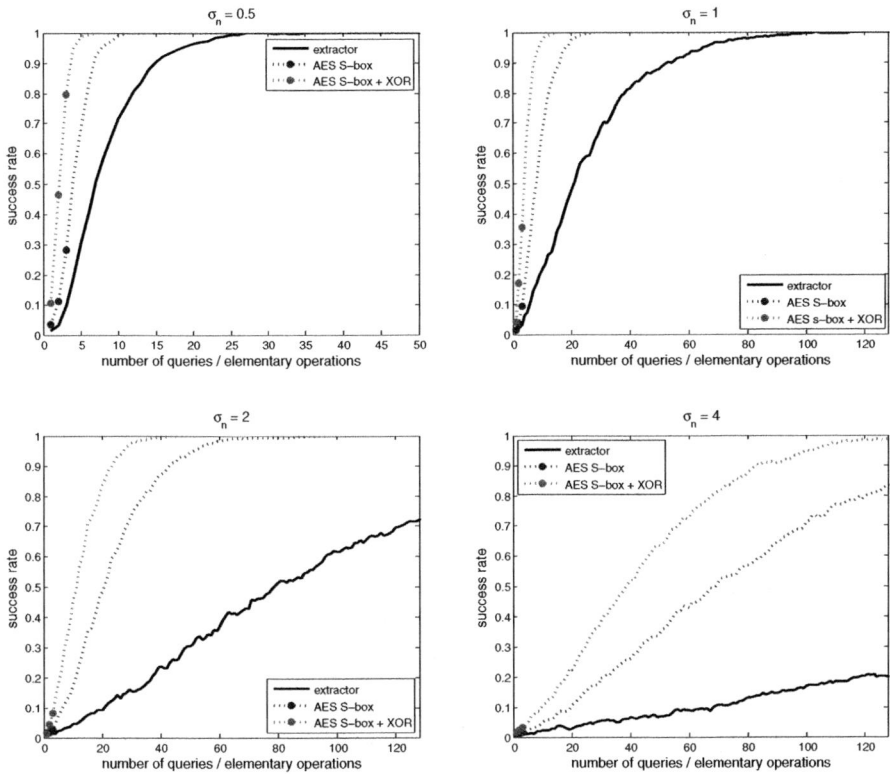

Fig. 3. Success rates of simulated experiments

- Without considering the q-limit, the elementary operations of the extractor are "less informative" than the ones of the AES (as underlined by the previous information theoretic analysis). So, for a similar number of elementary operations observed (*e.g.* considering the AES S-box computations only, meaning one operation per query), the success rate against the AES implementation is higher than the one against the extractor.

5   Consequences

According to the results in the previous section, it is unlikely that any extractor will be able to provide high security levels (specially in small devices) without being combined with other (*e.g.* hardware-level) countermeasures. For example, in view of the implementation in Figure 2, the (time) randomization of the operations to execute could be done quite efficiently, following what has been achieved for the AES Rijndael in [5]. More generally, investigating the applicability of classical countermeasures such as masking and hiding to extractor implementations is an interesting scope for further research, and a necessary step to demonstrate the practical relevance of the FOCS 2008 construction.

Next to these general observations, we now investigate the possibility to propose more specific guidelines for the design of a leakage-resilient stream cipher using underlying principles similar to the ones described in [4].

Improving the extractor. Since it is necessary to protect the extractor implementation with countermeasures in order to guarantee a small enough λ-bit leakage, a natural guideline is to first consider low-complexity extractors. This is motivated both by the intuition that more computation generally give rise to more exploitable information [8] (although this is not a strict statement) and, maybe more importantly, by the need of efficient constructions that can run on a variety of low cost devices. In this respect, it is interesting to note that the majority of previous work in the area of randomness extraction focus on producing outputs as close to uniform as possible, much more than on implementation efficiency. So although constructions such as [3] are already quite efficient, there is probably room for further research in carefully designing extractors that are easy to implement and to protect against side-channel attacks.

Improving the construction. Since the extractor is actually the weak point in the implementation of Figure 2, another possibility is to modify the construction in order to impose a more challenging adversarial context when targeting the extractor with a DPA. For example, in Figure 1, the extractor takes two inputs: one public and one secret. This allows to mount a DPA in a known-plaintext scenario. But by applying the extractor to secret values only (possibly at the cost of some performance loss), the adversary would only be able to mount unknown-plaintext attacks. Interestingly, it is quite easy to quantify the impact of such a modification, in exactly the same setting as in the previous section. That is, we can now compute the following conditional entropy:

$$H_y[Y|L] = - \sum_{x \in \mathcal{X} } \Pr[x] \int_l \Pr[l|y, x] \log_2 \Pr[y|l] \, dl,$$

where the input x is now kept secret. Doing this, the first consequence is that it is impossible to distinguish the secret x values having the same Hamming weight. The second consequence is that the information leakage is reduced as:

HW(y)	0	1	2	3	4	5	6	7	8
$H_y[Y|L, X]$	4.67	6.38	7.29	7.76	7.92	7.84	7.53	7.03	6.33

6   Conclusions

This work first shows that the use of randomness extractors in physically observable cryptography can be paradoxical. On the one hand, they allow recovering (pseudo) entropy losses *if* the implementation of the extractor does not leak too much. On the other hand, the implementation of the extractor can become a better target for a DPA than an AES-based PRG, if no attention is paid. This observation makes a case for always discussing side-channel resistant primitives together with a clear specification of the algorithms they use and the devices on which they run. In particular, the selection of algorithms generally has an impact on both the security level that can be achieved assuming a bounded (so-called λ-bit) leakage per iteration *and* on the very value of the bound λ (as quantified by a success rate in our experiments). Problematically, not considering the overall impact of an algorithm and its implementation features in leakage-resilient cryptography may lead to inconsistencies in the resulting analysis. For example, the stream cipher of FOCS 2008 [4] has better security bounds than the one of Eurocrypt 2009 [7]. But in the practical analysis provided in this paper, the opposite conclusion holds (*i.e.* it is significantly easier to attack the FOCS 2008 construction in our setting). Admittedly, this observation is only based on a single case-study, and it should stimulate further research on the design and implementation of extractors in leakage-resilient cryptography, because of their interesting theoretical properties. However, we believe that our analysis, and the methodological conclusions that it brings, is reflective of a general situation and makes a case for reviewing several recent results in the field in light of a more practical security analysis, *e.g.* using the evaluation tools in [10].

We note again that these observations do not invalidate theoretical analyzes in physically observable cryptography but reduce their practical relevance. They mainly emphasize the need for interaction between formal proofs of physical security and low-level implementation issues. In the end, a useful construction needs to face the full complexity of the attacks, *i.e.* not only to assume small λ-bit leakages but also to find algorithms, and in the end, implementations, for which these small leakages can be obtained. In this respect, a first (and easy to manipulate) design criterion for leakage-resilient constructions would be to minimize the computational complexity of the algorithms that they exploit.

References

1. Chari, S., Rao, J., Rohatgi, P.: Template Attacks. In: Kaliski Jr., B.S., Koç, Ç.K., Paar, C. (eds.) CHES 2002. LNCS, vol. 2523, pp. 13–28. Springer, Heidelberg (2003)
2. Daemen, J., Rijmen, V.: The Design of Rijndael. Springer, Heidelberg (2002)
3. Dodis, Y., Elbaz, A., Oliveira, R., Raz, R.: Improved Randomness Extraction from Two Independent Sources. In: Jansen, K., Khanna, S., Rolim, J.D.P., Ron, D. (eds.) RANDOM 2004 and APPROX 2004. LNCS, vol. 3122, pp. 334–344. Springer, Heidelberg (2004)
4. Dziembowski, S., Pietrzak, K.: Leakage-Resilient Cryptography. In: The proceedings of FOCS 2008, Washington, DC, USA, October 2008, pp. 293–302 (2008)
5. Herbst, C., Oswald, E., Mangard, S.: An AES Smart Card Implementation Resistant to Power Analysis Attacks. In: Zhou, J., Yung, M., Bao, F. (eds.) ACNS 2006. LNCS, vol. 3989, pp. 239–252. Springer, Heidelberg (2006)
6. Mangard, S., Oswald, E., Standaert, F.-X.: One for All - All for One: Unifying Standard DPA Attacks, Cryptology ePrint archive, report 2009/449

7. Pietrzak, K.: A Leakage-Resilient Mode of Operation. In: Joux, A. (ed.) EUROCRYPT 2009. LNCS, vol. 5479, pp. 462–482. Springer, Heidelberg (2010)

8. Renauld, M., Standaert, F.-X., Veyrat-Charvillon, N.: Algebraic Attacks on the AES: Why Time also Matters in DPA. In: Clavier, C., Gaj, K. (eds.) CHES 2009. LNCS, vol. 5747, pp. 97–111. Springer, Heidelberg (2009)

9. Schindler, W., Lemke, K., Paar, C.: A Stochastic Model for Differential Side-Channel Cryptanalysis. In: Rao, J.R., Sunar, B. (eds.) CHES 2005. LNCS, vol. 3659, pp. 30–46. Springer, Heidelberg (2005)

10. Standaert, F.-X., Malkin, T.G., Yung, M.: A Unified Framework for the Analysis of Side-Channel Key Recovery Attacks. In: Joux, A. (ed.) EUROCRYPT 2009. LNCS, vol. 5479, pp. 443–461. Springer, Heidelberg (2010), Extended version available on the Cryptology ePrint Archive, Report 2006/139

11. Standaert, F.-X., Pereira, O., Yu, Y., Quisquater, J.-J., Yung, M., Oswald, E.: Leakage -Resilient Cryptography in Practice. Cryptology ePrint Archive, report 2009/341

12. Vazirani, U.: Efficient Considerations in Using Semi-Random Sources. In: The proceedings of STOC 1987, New York, USA, May 1987, pp. 160–168 (1987)

Combined Implementation Attack Resistant Exponentiation

Jörn-Marc Schmidt[1], Michael Tunstall[2], Roberto Avanzi[3], Ilya Kizhvatov[4], Timo Kasper[3], and David Oswald[3]

[1] Graz University of Technology
Institute for Applied Information Processing and Communications
Inffeldgasse 16a, A–8010 Graz, Austria
joern-marc.schmidt@iaik.tugraz.at
[2] Department of Computer Science, University of Bristol
Merchant Venturers Building, Woodland Road
Bristol BS8 1UB, United Kingdom
tunstall@cs.bris.ac.uk
[3] Ruhr-University Bochum
Horst Görtz Institute for IT Security
Bochum, Germany
{roberto.avanzi,timo.kasper,david.oswald}@rub.de
[4] University of Luxembourg
Computer Science and Communications Research Unit
Luxembourg
ilya.kizhvatov@uni.lu

Abstract. Different types of implementation attacks, like those based on side channel leakage and active fault injection, are often considered as separate threats. Countermeasures are, therefore, often developed and implemented accordingly. However, Amiel et al. showed that an adversary can successfully combine two attack methods to overcome such countermeasures. In this paper, we consider instances of these combined attacks applied to RSA and elliptic curve-based cryptosystems. We show how previously proposed countermeasures may fail to thwart these attacks, and propose a countermeasure that protects the variables in a generic exponentiation algorithm in the same scenario.

Keywords: Combined Implementation Attacks, Countermeasures, Infective Computation, RSA, ECC.

1 Introduction

In order to provide security on an embedded microprocessor, several different threats have to be taken into account. In particular, countermeasures need to be included to prevent implementation attacks, which try to benefit from examining a device and its behavior.

Implementation attacks can be classed as either passive or active. Passive attacks collect information to overcome the security of a device. Such information

M. Abdalla and P.S.L.M. Barreto (Eds.): LATINCRYPT 2010, LNCS 6212, pp. 305–322, 2010.
© Springer-Verlag Berlin Heidelberg 2010

can be the time a computation takes [1], the power consumption [2], or electromagnetic emanations [3]. This information can enable a successful attack, if it correlates with secret data used within computations.

Active attacks try to influence the behavior of a device and determine sensitive information by examining the effects. The active attack we will be considering in this paper is fault analysis, where an attacker attempts to stress a device when it is executing a cryptographic algorithm so that an error is made during the computation [4,5].

The two threat scenarios described above are often considered separately, and many different methods have been considered to protect public key primitives from either side channel or fault analysis. In recent years, some examples of unified countermeasures that protect against both threats at the same time have been proposed for elliptic curve based cryptosystems using ring extensions [6] and for RSA when computed using the Chinese Remainder Theorem [7]. However, in this paper we consider generic exponentiation algorithms.

In 2007, Amiel et al. [8] presented a combined attack on a side channel resistant implementation of the square and multiply algorithm. In this paper, we review and generalize such combined implementation attacks. Furthermore, we propose a method of computing an exponentiation that is resistant to both side channel and fault analysis as well as their combination. The idea is somewhat similar to the idea of *infective computation* [9], where faults in otherwise redundant functions will affect the result of an algorithm.

In this paper, we present a countermeasure that diffuses cryptographic keys and masks intermediate values during computation. As a result, tampering with these values randomizes the computation. Some of the techniques described extend the hardening methods proposed in [10], and demonstrate their applicability when several attack methods are combined.

The remainder of this paper is organized as follows: In Section 2 we lay the background, recalling the necessary facts about exponentiation and scalar multiplication, and describe our attack model. Section 3 is devoted to combined attacks: we described previous attacks, generalize them, and describe a few countermeasures from the literature. Our countermeasure is described in Section 4, for RSA and curve-based cryptosystems. Finally, in Section 5 we conclude.

2   Preliminaries

In this section we define the algorithms that we will be considering as targets and the type of fault an attacker is able to induce.

2.1   Generic Side Channel Resistant Exponentiation

The simplest algorithm for computing an exponentiation is the square and multiply algorithm. This is where an exponent is read left-to-right bit-by-bit, a zero results in a squaring operation being performed, and a one results in a squaring operation followed by a multiplication with the original basis.

Algorithm 1. Left-to-Right Square and Multiply Algorithm

Require: $x \in \mathbb{G}$, $\nu \geq 1$, ℓ the binary length of ν (i.e. $2^{\ell-1} \leq \nu < 2^\ell$)
Ensure: $z = x^\nu$
 1: Construct a random semigroup $\mathbb{H}$, an injective map $\chi : \mathbb{G} \to \mathbb{H}$ satisfying (1).
 2: $R_0 \leftarrow \chi(1)$ // where 1 is the neutral element of $\mathbb{G}$
 3: $R_1 \leftarrow \chi(x)$
 4: $k \leftarrow 0$
 5: $j \leftarrow \ell - 1$
 6: **while** $j \geq 0$ **do**
 7:     $R_0 \leftarrow R_0 \circ R_k$
 8:     $k \leftarrow k \oplus \mathtt{bit}(\nu, j)$
 9:     $j \leftarrow j - \neg k$
10: **end while**
11: $z \leftarrow \chi^{-1}(R_0)$ // the value held in R_0 is mapped back to $\mathbb{G}$
12: **return** z

Algorithm 1 is a square and multiply algorithm where the exponentiation is computed only using one form of the group operation, denoted $\circ$. In other words, an attacker will not be able to distinguish whether the operands are distinct or equal elements by observing a side channel. This is referred to as side channel atomicity [11].

In Algorithm 1 the input is an element x in a (multiplicatively written) group $\mathbb{G}$ and a positive ℓ-bit integer $\nu = (\nu_{\ell-1}, \ldots, \nu_0)$; the output is the element $z = x^\nu$ in $\mathbb{G}$. We also have an injective function $\chi : \mathbb{G} \to \mathbb{H}$ of $\mathbb{G}$ into a semigroup $\mathbb{H}$, where both $\mathbb{H}$ and χ can be constructed at run time in a random manner. We denote the semigroup operation in $\mathbb{H}$ by $\circ$ as well, and we assume that, in practice, it is performed in a very similar way to the operation in $\mathbb{G}$.

It is assumed that the representation of the elements of $\mathbb{H}$ looks "randomized" with respect to the representation of the original elements of $\mathbb{G}$. Being injective, the function χ is, of course, invertible, but we also require that the inverse function be *efficiently* computable and satisfy the property that

$$\chi^{-1}\big(\chi(a) \circ \chi(b)\big) = a \circ b \quad \text{for all } a, b \in \mathbb{G} \ . \tag{1}$$

The neutral element of $\mathbb{G}$ is not necessarily mapped to a neutral element of $\mathbb{H}$ (which we do not even assume to exist—although in many practical examples it will). The input x is, therefore, blinded at the beginning of the algorithm by transferring the computation to $\mathbb{H}$ using χ. From (1) we get that $\chi^{-1}(y^n) = x^n$ with $y = \chi(x)$, i.e. pulling back the result will yield the correct result. We do not assume, *a priori*, that the function χ is deterministic (i.e. two distinct applications of χ to an element $x \in \mathbb{G}$ could yield different elements of $\mathbb{H}$).

The function $\mathtt{bit}(\beta, i)$ returns the i-th bit of β.

RSA: One use of such an algorithm is to implement RSA, where all computations usually take place in the group $\mathbb{Z}_n^*$ (i.e. the set of elements of the ring $\mathbb{Z}_n$ that are invertible with respect to multiplication, where we use the notation $\mathbb{Z}_n$ as a shorthand for $\mathbb{Z}/n\mathbb{Z}$), and the security of the algorithm is based on the problem of factoring the product of two large primes. Let p and q be such primes and $n = pq$ to be their product. The public key e is an integer coprime to $\varphi(n) = (p-1)(q-1)$, where φ is Euler's totient function, and its corresponding secret key d is $d = e^{-1} \bmod \varphi(n)$.

Due to this construction, $m = (m^e)^d \bmod n$ holds for any $m \in \mathbb{Z}_n^*$, which provides the basis for the system. An encrypted message $c = m^e \bmod n$ can be decrypted by computing $m = c^d \bmod n$, a signature $s = m^d \bmod n$ can be verified by checking that $m = s^e \bmod n$ holds.

In computing a modular exponentiation for RSA (using Algorithm 1) $\mathbb{Z}_n$ is extended by multiplying n by some random value r_2, so that the computation takes place modulo some multiple of n (this was first suggested by Shamir [12]). To map R_0 and R_1 we can, for instance, just add some random multiple of n to 1 and x, i.e. in this case $\chi(x) = x + \mathtt{random}() \cdot n \in \mathbb{Z}_{nr_2}$, where $\mathtt{random}()$ returns some random integer.

Thus, the assumption that the representation of R_0 and R_1 will be to randomized with respect to those of 1 and x is fulfilled. Note that the image of $\mathbb{Z}_n^*$ in $\mathbb{Z}_{nr_2}$ will not necessarily be a group, but the value held in R_0 mapped back to $\mathbb{Z}_n^*$ by reducing R_0 modulo n will be correct by (1).

Elliptic Curve Cryptography: An elliptic curve is usually given, for cryptographic purposes, by its equation. The most common form is the *Weierstraß model*, which, for curves defined over prime fields, takes the form $y^2 = x^3 + ax + b$ where a and b are constants. Other models are also possible, notably the *Edwards form* $x^2 + y^2 = c^2 (1 + dx^2 y^2)$ where c and d are constants. In order to apply Algorithm 1 we need to construct a group using the curve: this group $\mathbb{G}$ is just the set of points on the curve (with one additional element, the point at infinity being the neutral element if the curve is given in the Weierstraß model).

The fundamental operation on cryptosystems designed around elliptic curves is the scalar multiplication in a prime order subgroup of the rational point group of an elliptic curve over a finite field: given a point P and an integer (referred to as a scalar) ν, compute $\nu \cdot P = P + P + \cdots + P$ (ν summands). In Algorithm 1 the operation $\circ$ is the addition of two points. The embedding in a larger semigroup will be discussed in detail in §4.2.

Further Countermeasures: In Algorithm 1, and the two specific examples given above, we can note that the exponent ν is not modified by the algorithm. Typically, one would modify the exponent at the beginning of the algorithm such that the bits of the exponent vary from one execution to the next but the correct result is always produced. For example, for RSA we could define

$$\nu' = \nu + w \varphi(n),$$

using the notation above. We define w as a random integer of a suitable bit length that is multiplied by the order of the exponent's group (see [13] for a detailed explanation). An equivalent expression for elliptic curves is $\nu' = \nu + w \#(\mathbb{G})$ where $\#(\mathbb{G})$ is the number of points on the curve.

In this paper we assume that the exponent (or scalar) is blinded, so we do not consider attacks where an attacker is required to derive an exponent through repeated observations of the same exponent, e.g. as it is the case for differential attacks. We consider that an attacker is obliged to derive the exponent from one observation.

2.2   Fault Attack Model

There are several known mechanisms for injecting faults into microprocessors that vary from a glitch in the power supply [4] to using laser light [14]. The following models for the faults that can be created by this method will be used to evaluate the potential for a fault attack to allow a side channel attack to be conducted.

Data randomization: The adversary could change data to a random value. However, the adversary does not control the random value and the new value of the data is unknown to the adversary.

Resetting data: The adversary could force data to the blank state, i.e., reset the bits of a given byte, or bytes, of data back to all zeros or all ones depending on the logical representation.

Modifying opcodes: The adversary could change the instructions executed by the chip's CPU. Additional effects to those given above could include the removal of functions or the breaking of loops.

These three types of attack cover everything that an attacker could hope to do to an implementation of an algorithm. When describing the effectiveness of our countermeasure, we will consider the above models for first-order faults, i.e. an adversary can inject at most one fault during each execution of the algorithm. However, the attacks described in this paper will be based on a fault model derived from the experiments detailed in [8], where it is shown that a fault can be used to affect the bit length of a given variable. In a secure microprocessor the manipulation of a value with a large bit length is typically conducted using a coprocessor. These values will have to be loaded into the coprocessor from a given location of memory over a bus that will only be able to transfer a certain number of bits in one clock cycle. We shall thus consider faults that tamper with this loading process to produce one of the following effects:

1. That a variable is partially or entirely prevented from loading. A smaller amount of data or no data at all is loaded in the coprocessor. The possible effects are that this register is partially or completely zeroed.
2. The memory location from which the data has to be loaded has been tampered with, resulting in the loading of wrong data in the register—this data can be zero in realistic scenarios (for instance, if the location is outside the memory effectively implemented in the embedded device).

Note that there are different ways of achieving these goals (one being the modification of instructions being performed, as noted above). These effects have been shown to be possible experimentally in [8].

3   Combined Attacks

In this section, we present the existing work on combined attacks and generalize the combined attacks. We then describe why many recent countermeasures
designed to thwart side channel and faults attacks do not fully protect an exponentiation algorithm.

3.1   Previous Work

The term *Passive and Active Combined Attacks* (PACA) was introduced by
Amiel et al. [8]. In this work, the authors target a classical side channel resistant
implementation of RSA, such as the algorithm described in Section 2—with the
notation of § 2.1, i.e. the operation is an integer multiplication.

The authors note that fault resistance can be added to the implementation
by placing a classical checking routine that verifies the result at the end of the
computations by raising it to the public exponent e modulo n and comparing
the result to the initial message m. In the following paragraph the combined
implementation attack of [8] is described using Algorithm 1.

Let us consider attacks on RSA, where the operation is a simple multiplication. If a fault is injected to bypass Line 2 of Algorithm 1, which leaves the R_0
uninitialized, which would mean (on many architectures) that R_0 would be set
to 0. After a successful fault, the operation in Line 7 of Algorithm 1 would be
either $R_0 \cdot R_0 = 0 \cdot 0$ or $R_0 \cdot R_1 = 0 \cdot R_1$ ($R_1 \neq 0$). The authors report that these
two patterns can be identified in a power consumption trace. So a classical SPA
attack could be applied, and the knowledge of the sequence of squaring operations and multiplications would lead to the recovery of the private exponent d.
Note that the invocation of a fault checking routine *after* the exponentiation has
taken place will not affect the attack at all.

Along with the combined attack, a countermeasure was proposed in [8] under
the name of Detect and Derive, but it does not prevent combined implementation
attacks, as we will describe below.

3.2   Generalisation to Elliptic Curve Scalar Multiplication

As described above, combined implementation attacks on a side channel resistant
modular exponentiation are based on making operations distinguishable in a side
channel. Faults causing different effects could be used to cause a difference in
a side channel, where the possible range is platform-dependent. For example,
in Algorithm 1 a fault reducing R_0 to some small value (i.e. setting the most
significant bytes of R_0 to 0 an implementation of an side channel attack based
on this is described in [15]) will also suffice on platforms where multiplication of
short operands is distinguishable from that of long operands.

In order to demonstrate that the same attack can be applied to elliptic curve
scalar multiplication, we consider a recent explicit addition formula described
in [16]. The curve is given in Edwards form, its equation is therefore $x^2 + y^2 = c^2 (1 + d\, x^2\, y^2)$ where c and d are constants. One can often take $c = 1$ and d
small for performance reasons. Three coordinates are used, $(X_1 : Y_1 : Z_1)$ with

$X_1, Y_1, Z_1 \neq 0$, to represent the point $(Z_1/X_1, Z_1/Y_1)$ on the Edwards curve. These coordinates are called *inverted Edwards coordinates*.

For any two input points given as $(X_1 : Y_1 : Z_1)$, $(X_2 : Y_2 : Z_2)$, their sum $(X_3 : Y_3 : Z_3)$ is computed by the following sequence of operations:

$$A = Z_1 \cdot Z_2 \; ; \quad B = d \cdot A^2 \; ; \quad C = X_1 \cdot X_2 \; ; \quad D = Y_1 \cdot Y_2 \; ; \quad E = CD \; ;$$
$$H = C - D \; ; \quad I = (X_1 + Y_1) \cdot (X_2 + Y_2) - C - D \; ;$$
$$X_3 = c \cdot (E + B) \cdot H \; ; \quad Y_3 = c \cdot (E - B) \cdot I \; ; \quad Z_3 = A \cdot H \cdot I \; .$$

This is a strongly unified formula for addition of any two points on the curve, i.e., it works if the two inputs are equal. This makes, in theory, the group operations indistinguishable when observed using a side channel.

Now, assume the coordinate of one input is faulted, such that it is, for example, zeroed. Then, one of the multiplications to obtain A, C, or D will be a multiplication by zero. However, if we are doubling a point, i.e. we are adding a point to itself, *both* inputs to this multiplication will be zero and will be visible in a side channel. This would allow an attacker to distinguish between an addition and a doubling operation and derive the scalar used.

All other aspects of the scalar multiplication are essentially the same as in an RSA exponentiation and similar faulting scenarios can be envisioned.

3.3   Countermeasures

Despite the implementation described in [8], recent works on countermeasures for public-key algorithms do not always consider the possibility of a combined attack. As a consequence, many of the recent countermeasures are vulnerable to combined attacks. Here we briefly list some of these countermeasures and discuss their resistance to combined implementation attacks.

We begin with the countermeasure Detect and Derive from [8], which is based on the principle of infective computation introduced in [9]. The basic idea of Detect and Derive is to modify (infect) the secret exponent d with some check value that is dependent on the input variables that should not be modified by a fault (e.g. R_0 in Algorithm 1). The bits of the exponent are then recovered on-the-fly using the value held in R_0. One would expect that, whenever R_0 is modified by a fault, the bits of d would be recovered incorrectly and any information recovered using a side channel would be incorrect. However, the Detect and Derive countermeasure only protects the exponent from being manipulated. This is because the value held in R_0 has to be computed *before* the check value P_1. So, if R_0 is modified by a fault *before* the computation of the check value, d will still be correct and may be visible in a side channel.

Other countermeasures, such as those proposed by Kim et al. [7,17], and the improvements described in [18], are also vulnerable to combined implementation attacks, as they do not change the core exponentiation algorithm. This is because, in our scenario, checking the correct result has been computed at the end of the exponentiation is not sufficient to prevent a combined implementation attack.

Algorithm 2. Atomic double modular exponentiation from [19]

Require: An element $m \in \mathbb{Z}_N$, a chain $\omega(a,b)$ s.t. $a \leq b$, a modulus N
Ensure: The pair of modular powers $(m^a \bmod N, m^b \bmod N)$
1: $R_{(0,0)} \leftarrow 1; R_{(0,1)} \leftarrow m; R_{(1,0)} \leftarrow m$
2: $\gamma \leftarrow 1; \mu \leftarrow 1; i \leftarrow 0$
3: **while** $i < n$ **do**
4: $\quad t \leftarrow \omega_i \wedge \mu; v \leftarrow \omega_{i+1} \wedge \mu$
5: $\quad R_{(0,\gamma \oplus t)} \leftarrow R_{(0,\gamma \oplus t)} \cdot R_{((\mu \oplus 1),\gamma \oplus \mu)} \bmod N$
6: $\quad \mu \leftarrow t \vee (v \oplus 1); \gamma \leftarrow \gamma \oplus t$
7: $\quad i \leftarrow i + \mu + \mu \wedge (t \oplus 1)$
8: **end while**
9: **return** $(R_{\gamma \oplus 1}, R_\gamma)$

The atomic double modular exponentiation of Rivain [19], which is depicted in Algorithm 2, is also potentially vulnerable to a combined implementation attack. We can observe that the value $R_{(1,0)}$ in this algorithm is conditionally used as a multiplier in Line 5. If this value is set to a small value by a fault in Line 1, a side channel trace should reveal the addition chain $\omega(a,b)$ and, therefore, the exponents a and b.

The only countermeasure that we are aware of which will resist a combined implementation attack is described in [20], where an algorithm is presented that is based on the Montgomery Ladder [21]. We can note that this countermeasure provides a method of protecting the intermediate variables of an algorithm. However, it does not protect the exponent from being modified and the integrity of the exponent needs to be verified separately[1]. In the following section we describe a generic countermeasure that also protects the exponent.

4   A Novel Countermeasure against Combined Attacks

In order to protect exponentiation algorithms against combined implementation attacks, we propose a countermeasure, based on *infective computation*, that implicitly checks whether an adversary has tampered with intermediate variables in each loop iteration. If a fault is injected at any point in the algorithm, the remaining bits of the exponent are randomized, so that no exploitable side channel information is leaked.

Our countermeasure involves two ideas. Firstly, all intermediate computations are performed over an extension $\mathbb{H}$ of the group $\mathbb{G}$, as described in Section 2. For the transformation a function like the χ function introduced in § 2.1 is used. The computations take place in a subset of $\mathbb{H}$ and the result is mapped back to $\mathbb{G}$ at the end of the algorithm. The extension $\mathbb{H}$ is based on a random number r_2 that is generated during an initialization phase. In $\mathbb{H}$, we define a checkable property which a "legal" (i.e., correct) value fulfills, but which is violated by a fault with a high probability. An intermediate value is accepted as legal, if it is

---

[1] The same holds for variants [22,23] of Giraud's method [20].

equal to $0 \bmod r_2$. If r_2 is sufficiently large, a tampered value will violate this condition with a very high probability. This checkable property is preserved by multiplications and additions, and thus holds for all cryptographic primitives we consider.

Secondly, a method that checks the validity of the intermediate values and that immediately randomizes the algorithm when it detects a fault is required. We propose to encode the exponent d in an initialization phase and decode it during the computation. The correct decoding depends on the defined property of the intermediate values. Therefore, the exponent is divided into ℓ blocks of W bits: $d \to [d^{(0)}, \ldots, d^{(\ell-1)}]$. A function ψ is applied to each block of d in the initialization phase, yielding ℓ encoded blocks $[\tilde{d}^{(0)}, \ldots, \tilde{d}^{(\ell-1)}]$:

$$[\tilde{d}^{(0)}, \ldots, \tilde{d}^{(\ell-1)}] \leftarrow [\psi_0(d^{(0)}), \ldots, \psi_0(d^{(\ell-1)})] \ .$$

During the exponentiation, the encoding is removed by applying the inverse function ψ^{-1}. This is done iteratively, i.e., one block $\tilde{d}^{(j)}$ is decoded just before its bits are processed during the exponentiation. Naturally, the inversion ψ^{-1} must be efficient and provide sufficient diffusion capabilities in case of a fault. ψ^{-1} delivers the correct decoding, i.e., $\hat{d}$ equals d, if, and only if, a check value α (i.e. the parameter of the function ψ) is equal to zero:

$$[\hat{d}^{(0)}, \ldots, \hat{d}^{(\ell-1)}] \leftarrow [\psi_\alpha^{-1}(\tilde{d}^{(0)}), \ldots, \psi_\alpha^{-1}(\tilde{d}^{(\ell-1)})] \ .$$

The link between the property of legal intermediate values and the correct decoding of the exponent must, therefore, be established by computing α in such a way that it equals zero only if the check condition is fulfilled. The actual realization depends on the ring or group used.

In the following, we describe this property and the corresponding check functions in greater detail for RSA exponentiation in the ring $\mathbb{Z}_n$ and for scalar multiplication in the point group of an elliptic curve. We shall also discuss the security of the protected algorithms and estimate the performance impact of our countermeasures.

4.1   RSA

A possible solution to provide a checkable property is to make the intermediate values a multiple of a random, non-trivial idempotent factor i, i.e., an element for which $i^2 = i$ holds but $i \neq 0$ or 1. The idea of using idempotent elements for constructing a code was first introduced by Proudler [24]. His so-called *AN code* was analyzed and extended for fault detection purposes in [10,25]. In contrast to the previous suggestions, we use the properties of the idempotent not as error detection code for the whole algorithm, but implicitly check intermediates in each step of the algorithm.

In this section, we detail the construction of an idempotent element and its integration into the exponentiation algorithm. Let r_2 be a random value, co-prime to the RSA modulus n. The idempotent element i is an integer modulo

$n r_2$ with the property that $i \equiv 1 \pmod{n}$ and $i \equiv 0 \pmod{r_2}$. Using the Chinese Remainder Theorem (CRT) we can easily find

$$i = (r_2^{-1} \bmod n) \cdot r_2 .$$

However, this expression is only of use if r_2 is invertible modulo n, but since n is assumed to be the product of large primes, and r_2 is chosen to be comparatively small, this is not a problem. According to the defined properties of i and the CRT, $i = i^2 \bmod n r_2$ holds.

In the following, all intermediate values are elements of $\mathbb{Z}_{n r_2}$. We define the embedding of $\mathbb{Z}_n^*$ into $\mathbb{Z}_{n r_2}$ as follows

$$\chi \; : \; \mathbb{Z}_n^* \to \mathbb{Z}_{n r_2} \;, \; x \to i \cdot x \bmod n r_2 .$$

Besides, $\chi(x) \cdot \chi(y) = i \cdot x \cdot i \cdot y = i \cdot x \cdot y = \chi(x \cdot y)$ holds. This is thus an instance of the function χ introduced in §2.1.

For encoding the exponent d, the block length W is chosen to be smaller than the binary length of r_2, i.e., $2^W < r_2$. Then, $\psi \; : \; \mathbb{Z}_{r_2} \times \mathbb{Z}_{r_2} \to \mathbb{Z}_{r_2}$ is defined as:

$$\psi_\alpha(d^{(j)}) = (\alpha + n)^{-1} \cdot d^{(j)} \bmod r_2$$

The inverse $\psi^{-1} \; : \; \mathbb{Z}_{r_2} \times \mathbb{Z}_{r_2} \to \mathbb{Z}_{r_2}$ is given as:

$$\psi_\alpha^{-1}(\tilde{d}^{(l)}) = (\alpha + n) \cdot \tilde{d}^{(l)} \bmod r_2$$

Following the above construction of the idempotent element i, and the χ function, each legal value equals 0 mod r_2, since $i = 0 \bmod r_2$. This also holds for the sum of two intermediate values R_0 and R_1, i.e., $R_0 + R_1 = 0 \bmod r_2$, because of the way we chose our particular χ. Checking the validity of the intermediates can, therefore, be conducted by applying the ψ^{-1} operation to $\alpha = R_0 + R_1$. The computation of n^{-1} can be done together with r_2^{-1} in the initialization phase.

Algorithm 3 shows the whole countermeasure. It comprises exponent blinding, i.e., the addition of a multiple r_1 of the group order $\varphi(n)$. We define the function random$(1, 2^\lambda - 1)$ as returning a random integer $\in \{1, \ldots, 2^\lambda - 1\}$. The blinding is required since an adversary can always recover one bit of information, as shown in the previous section[2].

4.2   Elliptic Curve Exponentiation

In this section we describe a variant of our countermeasure for elliptic curve exponentiation, i.e., scalar multiplication. We want to emphasize the fact that this countermeasure also works for hyperelliptic curves with almost no changes, and can be adapted to any group whose group operations can be described as a sequence of finite field additions, subtractions and multiplications—for example, Trace Zero Varieties [27].

---

[2] The discussion of the bit length governed by λ is beyond the scope of this paper. The interested reader is referred to [26].

Algorithm 3. Resistant Left-to-Right Square and Multiply Algorithm

Require: $d = (d_{t-1}, \ldots, d_0)_2$, $m \in \mathbb{Z}_n$, n, block length W
Ensure: $m^d \bmod n$
1: $r_1 \leftarrow \texttt{random}(1, 2^\lambda - 1)$
2: $r_2 \leftarrow \texttt{random}(1, 2^\lambda - 1)$
3: $i \leftarrow (r_2^{-1} \bmod n) \cdot r_2$
4: $R_0 \leftarrow i \cdot 1 \bmod n\, r_2$ // equals $\chi(1)$
5: $R_1 \leftarrow i \cdot m \bmod n\, r_2$ // equals $\chi(m)$
6: $d \leftarrow d + r_1 \cdot \varphi(n)$
7: $[\tilde{d}^{(0)}, \ldots, \tilde{d}^{(\ell-1)}] \leftarrow [\psi_0(d^{(0)}), \ldots, \psi_0(d^{(\ell-1)})]$ // encode the ℓ blocks of d
8: $k \leftarrow 0$
9: $j \leftarrow \texttt{bit-length}(\tilde{d})\text{-}1$
10: **while** $j \geq 0$ **do**
11:      $R_0 \leftarrow R_0 \cdot R_k \bmod n\, r_2$
12:      **if** $(R_0 = 0)$ or $(R_1 = 0)$ **then**
13:           $[\tilde{d}^{(0)}, \ldots, \tilde{d}^{(\ell-1)}] \leftarrow [1, \ldots, 1]$ // diffuse exponent
14:      **end if**
15:      $\hat{d} \leftarrow \psi^{-1}_{(R_0 + R_1 \bmod r_2)}(\tilde{d}^{(\lfloor j/W \rfloor)})$ // decode the current block
16:      $k \leftarrow k \oplus \texttt{bit}(\hat{d}, j \bmod W)$ // use only the desired bit
17:      $j \leftarrow j - \neg k$
18: **end while**
19: $c \leftarrow R_0 \bmod n$
20: **return** c

Some popular countermeasures against fault attacks on elliptic curve cryptosystems over prime fields work by "enlarging" the group in which computations are performed (for example, see [28]). In these countermeasures one does not work on a curve $E(\mathbb{F}_p)$, one considers a curve $E'(\mathbb{Z}_n)$ with $n = pr$, where r is another prime, such that the coefficients of E', when reduced mod p are just the coefficients of E. This amounts to computing in the group $E(\mathbb{F}_p) \times E''(\mathbb{F}_r)$, where E'' is the elliptic curve over $\mathbb{F}_r$ obtained by reducing the coefficients of E' modulo r. For these countermeasures the group order of $E''(\mathbb{F}_r)$ needs to be known.

One intuitive attempt to adapt the countermeasure of § 4.1 would be to try to work in such a product of elliptic curve groups. There, the role of our idempotent element i would be played by a non-trivial point I on $E'(\mathbb{Z}_{pr})$ that projects to points equal to their doubles on $E(\mathbb{F}_p)$ and $E''(\mathbb{F}_r)$—these must be then the neutral group elements, and thus such a point I does not exist apart from 0 in $\mathbb{Z}_{pr}$.

Instead, we opt for a more straightforward adaptation of the method from § 4.1. As before, given the definition field $\mathbb{F}_p$ of the curve E, we choose a random r_2 (that does not even need to be a prime) and embed the field $\mathbb{F}_p$ into the ring $\mathbb{Z}_{pr_2}$. The idempotent i and the functions χ, ψ are defined as in the RSA case, but with p in place of n.

We assume that we use an inversion-free coordinate system for elliptic curves that can represent the neutral element $\mathcal{O}$ and treat it like any other point. Any point P on the elliptic curve then has a representation with s components $(\pi_1, \ldots, \pi_s)$, where $\pi_1, \ldots, \pi_s \in \mathbb{Z}$.

Algorithm 4. Resistant Left-to-Right Binary Double and Add Algorithm

---

Require: $d = (d_{t-1}, \ldots, d_0)_2$, $P \in E(\mathbb{F}_p)$, block length W, curve-order $\#E(\mathbb{F}_p)$
    Representation of $P = (\pi_1, \ldots, \pi_s)$
    Representation of neutral element $\mathcal{O} = (o_1, \ldots, o_s)$
Ensure: $d \cdot P \in E(\mathbb{F}_p)$
1: $r_1 \leftarrow \mathtt{random}(1, 2^\lambda - 1)$
2: $r_2 \leftarrow \mathtt{random}(1, 2^\lambda - 1)$
3: $i \leftarrow (r_2^{-1} \bmod p) \cdot r_2$
4: $R_0 = (\rho_{0,1}, \ldots, \rho_{0,s}) \leftarrow (i \cdot o_1, \ldots, i \cdot o_s)$
5: $R_1 = (\rho_{1,1}, \ldots, \rho_{1,s}) \leftarrow (i \cdot \pi_1, \ldots, i \cdot \pi_s)$
6: $d \leftarrow d + r_1 \cdot \#E(\mathbb{F}_p)$
7: $[\tilde{d}^{(0)}, \ldots, \tilde{d}^{(\ell-1)}] \leftarrow [\psi_0(d^{(0)}), \ldots, \psi_0(d^{(\ell-1)})]$ // encode the ℓ blocks of d
8: $k \leftarrow 0$
9: $j \leftarrow \mathtt{bit\text{-}length}(\tilde{d})\text{-}1$
10: **while** $j \geq 0$ **do**
11:    $R_0 \leftarrow R_0 + R_k \in E(\mathbb{Z}_{pr_2})$
12:    **if** some selected coordinates of R_0 or R_1 are 0 **then**
13:       $[\tilde{d}_0, \ldots, \tilde{d}_{t-1}] \leftarrow [1, \ldots, 1]$ // diffuse scalar
14:    **end if**
15:    $\hat{d} \leftarrow \psi^{-1}_{\sum_{\nu=1}^s (\rho_{0,\nu} + \rho_{1,\nu})}(\tilde{d}^{(\lfloor j/W \rfloor)})$ // decode the current block
16:    $k \leftarrow k \oplus \mathtt{bit}(\hat{d}, j \bmod W)$ // use only the desired bit
17:    $j \leftarrow j - \neg k$
18: **end while**
19: $C \leftarrow R_0 \bmod p$ // component-wise modular reduction
20: **return** $\mathtt{affine}(C)$ // return the affine representation of C

We observe that $\chi(x) \cdot \chi(y) = i \cdot x \cdot i \cdot y = i \cdot x \cdot y = \chi(x \cdot y)$ and $\chi(x) + \chi(y) = i \cdot x + i \cdot y = i \cdot (x+y) = \chi(x+y)$ holds. In other words, this particular χ is a homomorphism of rings without unit. A group operation on a curve can, therefore, be split into a sequence of field operations, and these are just multiplications, additions and subtractions, but not field inversions[3]. Hence, all computations we need to perform on $\mathbb{Z}_{pr_2}$ are well defined. We can, therefore, transfer (using the map i) the computation to the larger ring and reduce modulo p at the end of the computation. This will return the same result as would be produced if all computations had been done in $\mathbb{F}_p$. The validity check, that is, the computation of $\tilde{\alpha}$, is performed by summing over all components of the two intermediate points $R_0 = (\rho_{0,1}, \ldots, \rho_{0,s})$, $R_1 = (\rho_{1,1}, \ldots, \rho_{1,s})$.

The protected scalar multiplication algorithm is given in Algorithm 4.

4.3   Security Considerations

In this section we discuss the effects of the possible fault attacks described in §2.2, in order to show that our method prevents an adversary from successfully applying a combined implementation attack.

---

[3] Except for a final field inversion to convert the final result to affine coordinates, but this latter operation is done outside the part of the scalar multiplication that needs to be protected.

RSA: The secret exponent in Algorithm 3 is blinded by a random value r_1 and the intermediate variables by r_2. As noted in § 2.1, side channel analysis is not directly possible. A random manipulation of r_1 or r_2 in Lines 1 and 2 does not improve the situation for an adversary, since both values are randomly generated. Erasing r_1 in Line 1 totally, or in parts, or manipulating Line 6 will, at most, remove the exponent blinding. However, the computation is still blinded by r_2. A modification of r_2 cannot remove the blinding, since reducing the size of r_2 will result in a (partial) erasure of the exponent because of the modular reduction in ψ. A partial erasure of r_2 that does not influence its size does not help, since the exponent is still blinded by r_1.

Setting any other value to zero is detected in Line 12, a manipulation in Lines 3-5 or 11 will be detected. If a fault produces a random value it will not be detected with a probability of $\frac{1}{r_2}$. Any detection will result in the exponent being diffused. Manipulating the computation of the initial calculation of ψ (Line 7) is not an option, since it would also destroy the exponent.

The counter value j in Line 9 or in Line 17 of the while loop does not influence the vulnerability of the algorithm to combined attacks, but has to be secured to prevent fault analysis, by having a redundant counter where, for example, we have a counter j and its complement $\bar{j}$. One would then need to verify that the bits of $j \oplus \bar{j}$ consists entirely of ones.

Manipulating k in Line 8 or Line 16 can reveal at most one bit of information in the presence of classical countermeasures that suppress the output. Since we consider that exponent blinding, this does not increase the chances of an adversary recovering the exponent, which also hold for a given exponent (Line 15). The instructions after the while loop do not contain any valuable information that would be of interest to an attacker.

In summary, an adversary has only a chance of $\frac{1}{r_2}$ to retrieve more than one bit information during a computation.

Elliptic Curve Cryptography. Algorithm 4 is mostly an adaption of Algorithm 3 and, in general, similar considerations hold. The probability of success for an adversary is also $\frac{1}{r_2}$, which also holds if a register is only partially zeroed. In fact, all the coordinates of R_0 and R_1 are supposed to be equivalent to 0 (mod r_2) in the case of a non-faulted computation. This also applies to the sum of R_0 and R_1, but, in general, their sum will be a random value if the computation has been faulted. Hence, the scalar will be randomized from that point on with probability $1 - \frac{1}{r_2}$.

Zero Coordinates. Passive attacks that use vanishing coordinates, as first described in [29], are discussed here in the context of combined implementation attacks.

When considering inverted Edwards coordinates there are no points with a zero coordinate. So in Line 12 we can simply verify if a coordinate is equal to zero and then diffuse the scalar.

If we are using a different coordinate system, such as affine, projective, Jacobian, etc. we may have points with zero coordinates. Most of these coordinate systems are based on the Weierstraß form of an elliptic curve and we can, therefore, assume that first two coordinates are typically multiples of the affine coordinates x and y.

Manipulating a point will, in effect, transfer the computation to a different curve [30]. If the attacker erases a coordinate, the corresponding modified point will not be detected at Line 12. Even with unified addition and doubling formulae, the attacker can, therefore, distinguish an addition from a doubling operation, because, in the first case, a multiplication with only one zeroed input will be performed in the formula. In the second case, the two inputs will be the same allowing one bit to be derived.

Blinding the scalar by adding a random multiple of the order of the curve is typically considered a good countermeasure, making the observed bit useless. However, this is not entirely correct if we consider commonly used prime fields where there are lots of consecutive zeros[4].

Also, in this case we may want to ensure that there are no points with zero coordinates on the original curve. Points with a vanishing y-coordinate are not a concern: since they have order two, they cannot appear in the cryptographically relevant group of large prime order. To avoid points with a vanishing x-coordinate it is enough to translate the curve along the x-axis (the explicit formulae may have to be adapted, usually in a straightforward way). In Line 12 it will then suffice to test if any coordinate is zero to prevent this attack scenario. Other, more sophisticated randomization methods for the case of hyperelliptic curves are discussed in [31].

Other Attacks. There are, of course, other types of attacks. For example, sign-change attacks would not be detectable by our form of point blinding by field enlargement. However, these attacks work by reconstructing the scalar from the least significant bit onwards, hence scalar blinding is enough to thwart them, even if the scalar is quite close to a power of two.

4.4   Performance Analysis

The incorporation of the protection mechanisms into the proposed algorithms involves additional computations which naturally affect performance.

RSA: We compare the overhead of our proposal to the implementation of a masked square and multiply algorithm.

For the initialization step, $r_2^{-1} \bmod n$ and $n^{-1} \bmod r_2$ has to be calculated. Both values can be calculated simultaneously in one run of an extended Euclid algorithm (EEA). This would be particularly attractive since one operand is just about one machine word long, so the EEA would begin with a division, and then continue with two single precision operands, leading to several possible optimizations, that can also be combined with a binary approach. But, from a trace of a GCD computation one can in theory reconstruct the original operands "backwards" or at least elicit some information on r_2 – this is even worse if a

---

[4] The impact of the use of these fields is beyond the scope of this paper. Again, the interested reader is referred to [26] for a discussion of this topic.

binary approach is used [32]. In order do avoid possible side-channel leakage of the EEA, Fermat's little theorem can be used for the computation of the inverses. Following this approach, we first raise the (small) value r_2 to the power of $\varphi(n) - 1 = (p-1) \cdot (q-1) - 1$. (Since it is required for the exponent blinding, $\varphi(n)$ is available. We can also compute this power modulo p and q separately and then reconstruct the value using the Chinese Remainder Theorem.) For the result $v = r_2^{-1} \pmod{n}$ holds $v \cdot r_2 = 1 + u \cdot n$ for some integer value u. We can assume $v < n$ and $u < r_2$, and u can be computed by an exact division $u = (v \cdot r_2 - 1)/n$. This exact division requires only multiplications by a (truncated) inverse of n modulo a small power of two (for instance 2^w where w is the bit size of a machine word), that can be quickly precomputed [33]. If this inverse is precomputed and stored, the cost of the second inversion is approximately that of two multiplications of a full operand by a single precision one.

The computation of i and the exponent blinding requires one multiplication each. The initialization of the infective computation requires ℓ multiplications in $\mathbb{Z}_{r_2}$, its computation in the while loop requires a multiplication in $\mathbb{Z}_{r_2}$ per iteration. Furthermore, a conditional branch is required in each run of the loop.

Elliptic Curve Cryptography: Assuming the size of r_2 to be about one machine word, as recommended for the RSA countermeasure, the relative slowdown of the field multiplications is higher than that imposed on a computation of RSA. For example, implementing a 256-bit curve on a 32-bit embedded CPU requires 8 words of storage per operand, masked operands require however 9 words. For primes of general form and interleaved Montgomery multiplication, the complexity of a field operation increases from $2t^2 + t$ to $2(t+1)^2 + (t+1)$ CPU multiplications, which for operands of $t = 8$ words amounts to an increase of 26% in runtime.

An increase in runtime can also be expected from scalar blinding, if a random factor with the size of one machine word is considered. For instance, going from 8-word to 9-word scalars will increase the running time for the scalar multiplication by 12.5%, so a total increase of about 40% can be expected. The cost for setup and scalar diffusion is, in comparison, negligible.

For the computation of inverses, the same considerations as for the RSA case apply (only, in this case $\varphi(n) = n - 1$).

5   Conclusions

In this paper we show that the many countermeasures proposed in the literature do not consider the threat posed by combining different implementation attacks. These algorithms are, therefore, potentially insecure if not implemented carefully.

We present the first countermeasure that protects all the variables of an exponentiation against such combined implementation attacks. Our countermeasure is based on an infective computation strategy that checks the correctness of the intermediate values in each iteration. An adversary cannot learn more than one bit of the exponent during one computation, which does not endanger its security since an exponent will typically be blinded. As we demonstrate, our countermeasure can be applied to algorithms based on RSA or curve-based cryptosystems.

Acknowledgments

The work described in this paper has been supported in part by the European Commission through the ICT programme under contract ICT-2007-216676 ECRYPT II and EPSRC grant EP/F039638/1 "Investigation of Power Analysis Attacks".

The information in this document is provided as is, and no guarantee or warranty is given or implied that the information is fit for any particular purpose. The user thereof uses the information as its sole risk and liability.

References

1. Kocher, P.C.: Timing attacks on implementations of Diffie-Hellman, RSA, DSS, and other systems. In: Koblitz, N. (ed.) CRYPTO 1996. LNCS, vol. 1109, pp. 104–113. Springer, Heidelberg (1996)
2. Kocher, P.C., Jaffe, J., Jun, B.: Differential power analysis. In: Wiener, M. (ed.) CRYPTO 1999. LNCS, vol. 1666, pp. 388–397. Springer, Heidelberg (1999)
3. Gandolfi, K., Mourtel, C., Olivier, F.: Electromagnetic analysis: Concrete results. In: Koç, Ç.K., Naccache, D., Paar, C. (eds.) CHES 2001. LNCS, vol. 2162, pp. 251–261. Springer, Heidelberg (2001)
4. Anderson, R.J., Kuhn, M.G.: Tamper resistance — a cautionary note. In: Adam, N.R., Yesha, Y. (eds.) Electronic Commerce 1994. LNCS, vol. 1028, pp. 1–11. Springer, Heidelberg (1996)
5. Skorobogatov, S.P., Anderson, R.J.: Optical fault induction attacks. In: Kaliski Jr., B.S., Koç, Ç.K., Paar, C. (eds.) CHES 2002. LNCS, vol. 2523, pp. 2–12. Springer, Heidelberg (2003)
6. Baek, Y.J., Vasyltsov, I.: How to prevent DPA and fault attack in a unified way for ECC scalar multiplication — ring extension method. In: Dawson, E., Wong, D.S. (eds.) ISPEC 2007. LNCS, vol. 4464, pp. 225–237. Springer, Heidelberg (2007)
7. Kim, C.H., Quisquater, J.J.: How can we overcome both side channel analysis and fault attacks on RSA-CRT? In: Breveglieri, L., Gueron, S., Koren, I., Naccache, D., Seifert, J.P. (eds.) FDTC 2007, pp. 21–29. IEEE Computer Society, Los Alamitos (2007)
8. Amiel, F., Villegas, K., Feix, B., Marcel, L.: Passive and active combined attacks: Combining fault attacks and side channel analysis. In: Breveglieri, L., Gueron, S., Koren, I., Naccache, D., Seifert, J.P. (eds.) FDTC 2007, pp. 92–102. IEEE Computer Society, Los Alamitos (2007)
9. Yen, S.M., Kim, S., Lim, S., Moon, S.J.: RSA speedup with residue number system immune against hardware fault cryptanalysis. In: Kim, K. (ed.) ICISC 2001. LNCS, vol. 2288, pp. 397–413. Springer, Heidelberg (2002)
10. Gaubatz, G., Sunar, B.: Robust finite field arithmetic for fault-tolerant public-key cryptography. In: Breveglieri, L., Koren, I., Naccache, D., Seifert, J.P. (eds.) FDTC 2006. LNCS, vol. 4236, pp. 196–210. Springer, Heidelberg (2006)

11. Chevallier-Mames, B., Ciet, M., Joye, M.: Low-cost solutions for preventing simple side-channel analysis: Side-channel atomicity. IEEE Transactions on Computers 53(6), 760–768 (2004)
12. Shamir, A.: Improved method and apparatus for protecting public key schemes from timing and fault attacks. US Patent 5991415 (1999)
13. Mangard, S., Oswald, E., Popp, T.: Power Analysis Attacks — Revealing the Secrets of Smart Cards. Springer, Heidelberg (2007)
14. Bar-El, H., Choukri, H., Naccache, D., Tunstall, M., Whelan, C.: The sorcerer's apprentice guide to fault attacks. Proceedings of the IEEE 94(2), 370–382 (2006)
15. Courrége, J.C., Feix, B., Roussellet, M.: Simple power analysis on exponentiation revisited. In: Gollmann, D., Lanet, J.-L., Iguchi-Cartigny, J. (eds.) CARDIS 2010. LNCS, vol. 6035, pp. 65–79. Springer, Heidelberg (2010)
16. Bernstein, D.J., Lange, T.: Inverted Edwards coordinates. In: Boztas, S., Lu, H. (eds.) AAECC 2007. LNCS, vol. 4851, pp. 20–27. Springer, Heidelberg (2007)
17. Kim, C.H., Quisquater, J.J.: Fault attacks for CRT based RSA: New attacks, new results, and new countermeasures. In: Sauveron, D., Markantonakis, K., Bilas, A., Quisquater, J. J. (eds.) WISTP 2007. LNCS, vol. 4462, pp. 215–228. Springer, Heidelberg (2007)
18. Dottax, E., Giraud, C., Rivain, M., Sierra, Y.: On second-order fault analysis resistance for CRT-RSA implementations. In: Markowitch, O., Bilas, A., Hoepman, J.H., Mitchell, C.J., Quisquater, J.J. (eds.) WISTP 2009. LNCS, vol. 5746, pp. 68–83. Springer, Heidelberg (2009)
19. Rivain, M.: Securing RSA against fault analysis by double addition chain exponentiation. In: Fischlin, M. (ed.) CT-RSA 2009. LNCS, vol. 5473, pp. 459–480. Springer, Heidelberg (2009)
20. Giraud, C.: An RSA implementation resistant to fault attacks and to simple power analysis. IEEE Transactions on Computers 12(4), 241–245 (2006)
21. Joye, M., Yen, S.M.: The Montgomery powering ladder. In: Kaliski Jr., B.S., Koç, Ç.K., Paar, C. (eds.) CHES 2002. LNCS, vol. 2523, pp. 291–302. Springer, Heidelberg (2003)
22. Boscher, A., Naciri, R., Prouff, E.: CRT RSA algorithm protected against fault attacks. In: Sauveron, D., Markantonakis, C., Bilas, A., Quisquater, J.J. (eds.) WISTP 2007. LNCS, vol. 4462, pp. 229–243. Springer, Heidelberg (2007)
23. Fumaroli, G., Vigilant, D.: Blinded fault resistant exponentiation. In: Breveglieri, L., Koren, I., Naccache, D., Seifert, J.P. (eds.) FDTC 2006. LNCS, vol. 4236, pp. 62–70. Springer, Heidelberg (2006)
24. Proudler, I.K.: Idempotent AN codes. In: IEE Colloquium on Signal Processing Applications of Finite Field Mathematics, pp. 8/1–8/5. IEEE, Los Alamitos (1989)
25. Medwed, M., Schmidt, J.M.: A generic fault countermeasure providing data and program flow integrity. In: Breveglieri, L., Gueron, S., Koren, I., Naccache, D., Seifert, J.P. (eds.) FDTC 2008, pp. 68–73. IEEE, Los Alamitos (2008)
26. Smart, N., Oswald, E., Page, D.: Randomised representations. In: IET Proceedings on Information Security, vol. 2(2), pp. 19–27 (2008)
27. Lange, T.: Trace zero subvarieties of genus 2 curves for cryptosystems. Journal of the Ramanujan Mathematical Society 19(1), 15–33 (2004)
28. Blömer, J., Otto, M., Seifert, J.P.: Sign change fault attacks on elliptic curve cryptosystems. In: Breveglieri, L., Koren, I., Naccache, D., Seifert, J. P. (eds.) FDTC 2006. LNCS, vol. 4236, pp. 36–52. Springer, Heidelberg (2006)
29. Goubin, L.: A refined power analysis attack on elliptic curve cryptosystems. In: Desmedt, Y. (ed.) PKC 2003. LNCS, vol. 2567, pp. 199–210. Springer, Heidelberg (2002)

30. Biehl, I., Meyer, B., Müller, V.: Differential fault attacks on elliptic curve cryptosystems. In: Bellare, M. (ed.) CRYPTO 2000. LNCS, vol. 1880, pp. 131–146. Springer, Heidelberg (2000)
31. Avanzi, R.M.: Countermeasures against differential power analysis for hyperelliptic curves. In: Walter, C., Koç, Ç.K., Paar, C. (eds.) CHES 2003. LNCS, vol. 2779, pp. 77–88. Springer, Heidelberg (2003)
32. Acimez, O., Gueron, S., Seifert, J.P.: New branch prediction vulnerabilities in OpenSSL and necessary software countermeasures. In: Galbraith, S.D. (ed.) Cryptography and Coding 2007. LNCS, vol. 4887, pp. 185–203. Springer, Heidelberg (2007)
33. Jebelean, T.: An algorithm for exact division. Journal of Symbolic Computation 15(2), 169–180 (1993)

Author Index

GPSR Compliance

The European Union's (EU) General Product Safety Regulation (GPSR)
is a set of rules that requires consumer products to be safe and our
obligations to ensure this.

If you have any concerns about our products, you can contact us on
ProductSafety@springernature.com

In case Publisher is established outside the EU, the EU authorized
representative is:

Springer Nature Customer Service Center GmbH
Europaplatz 3
69115 Heidelberg, Germany

Batch number: 09490872

Printed by Printforce, the Netherlands